FUNDAMENTALS
OF
COUNSELING

Houghton Mifflin Company Boston

Atlanta
Dallas
Geneva, Ill.
Hopewell, N.J.
Palo Alto
London

Second Edition

FUNDAMENTALS OF COUNSELING

BRUCE SHERTZER

SHELLEY C. STONE

Purdue University

To Marcia Gettinger Dye (1934–1966)

Beloved wife of an esteemed colleague

One whose spirit, courage, and sense of humor left a lasting imprint on all who knew her. Her short yet meaningful life made real those enduring and human qualities man responds to in others.

Printed in U.S.A.

Library of Congress Catalog Card Number: 73-9403
ISBN: 0-395-17580-1

CONTENTS

PREFACE

The production of a counseling textbook and its revision is a rich, varied, and protracted experience. It entails frustration, pleasure (perhaps of a masochistic nature), grim persistence, dissonance, insight, but above all, a feeling that closure is lacking. In such undertakings, decision after decision has to be made — decisions concerning level, style, length, inclusion, exclusion, sequence, organization, approach, terminology — even punctuation! We hope some of these decisions were made logically, based upon experience in counseling and a sense of educational strategy.

The second edition of *Fundamentals of Counseling* incorporates several changes. A new chapter on the counselor's work with special clientele subgroups has been added in Part Four. Two chapters in Part One of the first edition were condensed and combined. Part Three — Counseling Approaches — has been expanded by the inclusion of two theories. In addition to these major changes, modifications have been made in each chapter in the book. These changes consist of some deletions and additions that update, expand and clarify the material presented.

Fundamentals of Counseling is designed for use as a textbook in counselor education courses often entitled "Introduction to Counseling," "Techniques of Counseling," "Principles of School Counseling," "Theories of Counseling," "School Counseling Practices," and the like. Such a course is usually taken during the second semester of an academic year of preparation by students with a major area of concentration in counseling and guidance, by student personnel trainees, and by clinical and counseling psychology students (as part of either their major or minor areas of concentration). Other school personnel — teachers, administrators, and social workers — are sometimes "found" in these courses too. The content has been selected with this broad audience in mind. Basically, by choice and design, counseling is treated in educational settings. It should be noted that the book emphasizes counseling rather than the broader range of guidance services and student personnel work, and presupposes some prior preparation in and familiarity with the aforementioned services. It is believed that there are six objectives common to the type of course in which this book will be used:

1. To develop an awareness of how one's self-structure, skills, and competences interact to influence the formation and development of a professional counselor's role.
2. To provide students with a framework that will develop into a perception of what counseling has been, what it is now, and what it may become in the future.
3. To introduce students to representative counseling approaches so that counselee and counselor behavior may be better understood.
4. To promote an understanding of counseling practices, their strengths and their limitations.
5. To provide an orientation to counseling as an emerging profession and to facilitate the individual's development of an identity as a counselor.
6. To help students understand the problems, issues, and concerns confronting counseling practitioners.

This text does not offer a new theory of counseling or introduce any major innovative ideas or practices. Why then has it been written?

First, many existing textbooks present the author's own counseling theory. Often they present counseling "theories" without treating practices, or they discuss techniques without regard to theory. This work incorporates both theory and practice in one volume and takes up a wider range of topics than is usually found in other books.

Second, the book is flexible in organization and comprehensive in treatment so that it can serve the needs of many counselor education institutions offering individualistically oriented introductory counseling courses.

Third, in the fast-growing field of counseling, a great many new developments have occurred during the past five years. These warrant examination by the beginning counselor. No new systematic approach to counseling has arisen recently, but certain approaches — for example, existentialism and behavioral counseling — have increased in popularity. Moreover, knowledge of counselor and counselee behavior has expanded. Our intent has been to consolidate these recent findings meaningfully within the boundaries of existing knowledge.

Fourth, we have attempted to present detailed material of both a factual and interpretive nature, in a style that is easily read and understood and has relevance for students.

We believe that the authors of a counseling textbook should explain and clarify and not urge a particular point of view. For this reason we have attempted to give the student basic facts which will help him draw his own conclusions. Our objective is to develop a coherent framework which includes a good deal of detail and encourages investigation of gaps exposed. By means of this perspective, it is hoped, more workable decisions in the practice of counseling can be made.

The 19 chapters in this book contain an examination in depth of the major findings of those who have studied and presented counseling theory, practices, and processes. We have tried through this revision to keep the material up to date, but perhaps the desire to do so vastly exceeds the accomplishment.

Before the critic who justly complains of incompleteness we bow our heads; but prepotent over the response of *mea culpa* is the one of "Let him try!" We can be certain of two factors. First, we have been conscientious in attempting to be fair and sympathetic to the various theorists and researchers whose views and findings we have dealt with (to the extent that our biases permitted us an objective view). Second, the coverage and its extensive bibliography can serve the student as a bridge to the vast primary literature.

A book of this length is never error free despite great effort to make it so. Publicly we acknowledge responsibility for any such error, although privately each blames the other, our typists, and that mysterious, elusive, and concealed individual, the copyeditor.

Naturally, the assistance of many people in this

endeavor deserves acknowledgment. We are indebted to the authors (and their publishers) who have permitted us to draw upon their works. While footnotes acknowledge permission from Professors Norman Kagan (Michigan State University) and Jane S. O'Hern (Boston University), both have extended the right to use certain experimental materials which they developed. We are grateful for this professional courtesy. A special debt of gratitude is due Professor S. Samuel Shermis of Purdue University's Department of Education for his excellent chapter entitled "Counseling and the Social Sciences."

Finally, two guilty husbands and fathers acknowledge the support and encouragement of two temporarily (20 years!) abandoned families who give meaning to work and life.

Bruce Shertzer
Shelley C. Stone

PART ONE

COUNSELING: PAST AND PRESENT STATUS

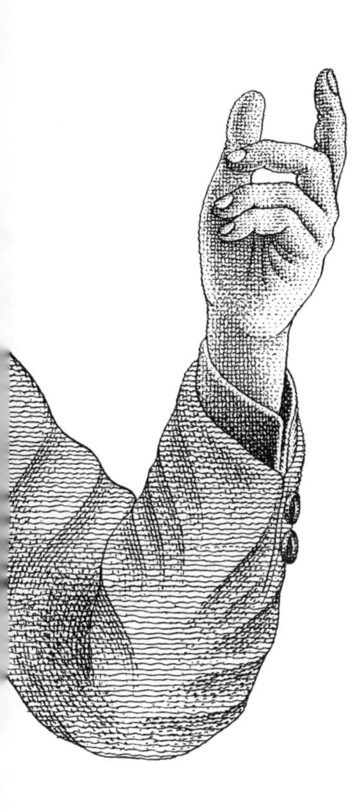

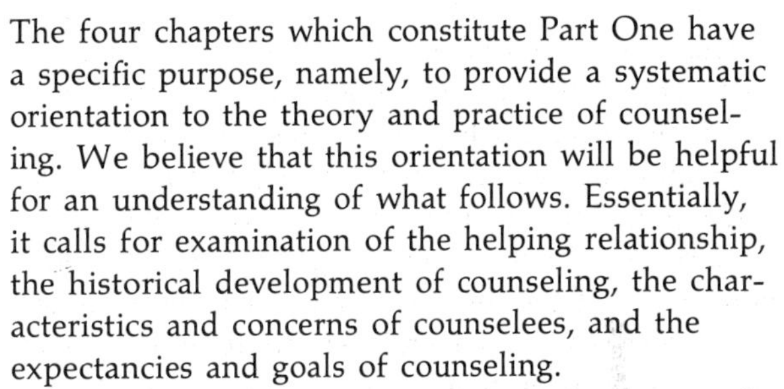

The four chapters which constitute Part One have a specific purpose, namely, to provide a systematic orientation to the theory and practice of counseling. We believe that this orientation will be helpful for an understanding of what follows. Essentially, it calls for examination of the helping relationship, the historical development of counseling, the characteristics and concerns of counselees, and the expectancies and goals of counseling.

Analysis of the four chapters reveals that our direction is from the general (helping relationship) to the more specific (expectancies and goals). This direction seems logically and psychologically sound.

Because counseling is a helping relationship, it seems fitting that Chapter One interpret the helping relationship. Its nature and characteristics are defined and described. Professionals who practice a helping relationship are identified. Similarities and differences between the various helping professions are presented. The chapter returns to counseling per se and terminates with a discussion of definitions of counseling.

The entire development of organized counseling services extends over only six decades. However, its history encompasses the efforts of hundreds of persons, whose activities subdivide into a dozen occupations. Chapter Two traces the origin and development of counseling. Emphasis is placed upon analysis and interpretation of the events, men, and forces instrumental in advancing it to its present state. There is no claim that the chapter gives a comprehensive history of counseling, which would be quite beyond the scope of this book. The intent here is to present as clear a treatment as possible especially of recent developments in the field. These changes are evident in the direction and focus of counseling, its professional organizations and journals, its practitioners, and its critics.

Chapter Three focuses upon the counselee, particularly of school or college age. It examines pertinent views of the developmental characteristics of counselees, some frequently encountered counselee concerns, and selected problems that confront contemporary youth. Such treatment will not, of course, satisfy everyone, and considerable risk attends any generalizing about counselees. Nevertheless, the authors have found the content valuable for encouraging discussion and exploration into why individuals seek counseling.

Chapter Four identifies the expectancies for counseling held by counselees, teachers, parents, administrators, and others. Counseling goals are stated. Finally, counseling expectancies and goals are contrasted.

THE HELPING RELATIONSHIP

1

The words "helping relationship" are used often by counselors, social workers, psychotherapists, and physicians to characterize the services they provide. No doubt the words are meaningful to their users, but are they to others? The phrase "a helping relationship" is deceptively straightforward; most people understand that "helping" means assisting or aiding while "relationship" means some connecting bond or reference. But though many individuals – shoe clerks, soda jerks, bankers, politicians – are engaged in providing services of a helping nature, few of them use the words "helping relationship" to describe their work.

The Nature of the Helping Relationship

Those engaged in helping relationships seem to be markedly out of step with the beat of today's drums. A dozen different revolutions are taking place in industry, education, medicine, and government. They are profoundly affecting every field of human activity: transportation, communication, merchandising, marketing, health, weather control, the substance and structure of work and home life. We live in a time known for its application of scientific knowledge and advanced technology. It is a time aptly characterized decades ago by W. B. Yeats: "The visible world is no longer a reality and the unseen world is no longer a dream."

Electronic data storage and retrieval are commonplace. The focus is upon use of automated equipment in communication, industry, defense, government, and education and has led some to label the era "the computerized age."[1] Certainly the constant and conscious attention to "hardware," as well as the investment of resources devoted to it, *seems* to push to the fringes those whose efforts are directed toward establishing and maintaining helping relationships. The methods used for aiding people to live together amicably on an alarmingly shrinking planet are still rudimentary. This combination of factors confronts society with a fantastic and frightening paradox: We are

[1] Norman Cousins, "The New Computerized Age," *Saturday Review*, July 23, 1966, p. 15.

able to control and improve everything except the one element that may spell the doom of the human race. We have employed talent and unprecedented amounts of money to enable people to live better and longer, to enjoy leisure, and to take full advantage of brilliant technological breakthroughs. But whether people survive and improve depends upon the resolution of man's differences with himself and his fellow man. It is to be hoped that while man's attention is directed to the machine, changes will occur which will fundamentally enrich his relationships with his fellows and permit the genuine betterment of life.

During the past five years, more and more people have become increasingly concerned about improving the "quality of life" in American society. Many aver that those who call for change have in mind a return to some simplistic, bygone notions of an individual's relationship to people and of the environment they share. Others hope that behind the catchwords lies a movement toward establishing meaningful, nonexploitative relationships among men and with the environment.

NEED FOR THE HELPING RELATIONSHIP

Despite technological progress, man's essential and perennial problems remain: Who am I? How did I become the way I am? Am I normal? What is good? What is reality? Of what value is life? How can I be more productive . . . more sensitive . . . more sensible . . . more alive? Man's dreams, drives, concerns, and very humaneness can be observed in a bewildering variety of behavioral situations.

The newborn is equipped with certain basic, biologically determined drives (such as hunger), certain capacities to be stimulated (by touch, light, sound), and certain abilities to respond (gross movements). The human organism moves through a series of developmental stages — infancy, childhood, adolescence, adulthood, maturity, and senility — through maturation and learning. During each stage man accommodates himself in some manner to the tasks, demands, and realities expected of him by others as well as by himself. He learns to walk, to talk, to distinguish right from wrong, to trust, to be independent, to develop a scale of values and an identity as a person, to choose and prepare for an occupation, to live intimately with a spouse, and to perpetuate — to cite but a few tasks. At each stage he orients himself toward goals which give direction and expression to his behavior, actions, feelings, thoughts, and ideals.

From a gross biological point of view, life may be reduced to a simple continuum: birth, maturity, reproduction, death. But even the biologist acknowledges that many other significant events occur along the way. Man himself embroiders upon the fundamental biological pattern. In fulfilling his destiny, every individual experiences these four biological stages. They are often seen as critical periods and approached with varying degrees of apprehension. Some people, acting in response to their culture, habitually treat them in a matter-of-fact manner. Others exhibit much anxiety and uncertainty because their very fate hangs in the balance. Consequently, men are not disposed to leave the outcome supinely to chance. They seek assistance in coping with these crises and the feelings and emotions associated with them.

Significant multiple forces, both external and internal, operate to inhibit as well as facilitate man's definition and perception of his world and himself. Because he often feels distressed, ineffective, bewildered, anxious, disturbed, or uninformed about himself and his world, he turns to others for aid in simplifying reality so that he can effectively cope with it. He seeks help in understanding his and others' behavior, his relationships with others, his decisions, his choices, his situation, his goals — his very being. He seeks help in preventing or remedying stressful situations involving the unpredictability and the inconsistency of existence. In the past man feared realistically the catastrophes of nature, such as plague, drought, famine. Today he fears, perhaps equally realistically, enervation through mechanical equipment. Many have speculated that the complexities and perplexities of the modern world nurture feelings of gnawing uncertainty and powerlessness. A by-product of these feelings is alienation and disaffection. In previous ages, setback, privation, or disease were more readily attributed to divine punishment. With this type of "deified" rationale it seemed reasonably clear when man was to act and when to submit. But in contemporary times few simplistic or clear answers are available.

When things went wrong in our society in the past, political and moral reformers offered solutions. Today, according to the sociologist Halmos,[2] who examined the role of the counselor in contemporary society, confidence in old approaches is lacking, and the search is for help that is more personal and more individual.

The objects of man's apprehensions have changed, but the basic theme remains the same. Adversity and its attendant fear and anxiety have to be managed and mastered. The individual therefore looks for help to overcome unfavorable situations, to establish unity in his life, and to achieve integration of self. He does so because he is capable of learning how to increase his chances for satisfaction and for survival.

When man needs help, he turns to people. Even in those contexts where the nature of the help provided is direct and physical (for example, the administration of medication), the relationship between two people adds much to the experience. To be aware of the importance of personal relationships and to make society less impersonal are the helping person's responsibility, opportunity, and challenge.

HELPING RELATIONSHIP DEFINED

Presumably, when counselors, social workers, and others use the term "helping relationship," they mean the endeavor, by interaction with another person, to contribute in a facilitating, positive way to his improvement. The helping professions engage in activities designed to enable others to understand, to modify, or to enrich their behavior so that growth takes place. They are interested in the behavior of people — living, feeling, knowing people — and in their attitudes, motives, ideas, responses, and needs. The helping person thinks not of individuals as "behavior problems" but as people seeking to discover the substance of life in this cosmos, seeking to feel comfortable about themselves and other people and to meet life's demands productively.

Rogers has defined the helping relationship thus:

> My interest in psychotherapy has brought about in me an interest in every kind of helping relationship. By this term I mean a relationship in which at least one of the parties has the intent of promoting the growth, development, maturity, improved functioning, improved coping with life of the other. The other, in this sense, may be one individual or a group. To put it in another way, a helping relationship might be defined as one in which one of the participants intends that there should come about, in one or both parties, more appreciation of, more expression of, more functional use of the latent inner resources of the individual.[3]

Benjamin defines "helping" as enabling acts, so that those who are helped recognize, feel, know, decide, and choose whether to change. In providing a helping relationship, interviewers give of their time, their capacity to understand and listen, their skill, knowledge, and interest. In short, those who conduct helping relationships draw upon themselves in ways that facilitate and enable others to live more harmoniously and insightfully.[4]

These and other definitions of a helping relationship are sufficiently broad to include many nurturing and uplifting contacts among people. Presumably, bank clerks and politicians do not use the term to describe their work because their occupations, while providing services of an external nature, do not have the primary purpose of facilitating the individual's personal development.

[2] Paul Halmos, *The Faith of the Counsellors* (New York: Schocken Books, Inc., 1966).

[3] Carl R. Rogers. *On Becoming a Person* (Boston: Houghton Mifflin Company, 1961), pp. 39–40. "The Characteristic of a Helping Relationship," *Personnel and Guidance Journal,* Vol. 37 (1958), pp. 6–16. Copyright 1958 American Personnel and Guidance Association. Reprinted with permission.

[4] Alfred Benjamin, *The Helping Interview* (Boston: Houghton Mifflin Company, 1969), pp. ix-x.

However, relationships between teacher and pupil, husband and wife, mother and child, counselor and counselee, psychotherapist and client would normally be called helping relationships.

All too often, "helping relationship" is thought to mean that one person helps one other. In most helping situations this is the case, but the term is also applied to individual-group interactions. Furthermore, some supervisory and administrative relationships are so conducted as to facilitate maximum growth through processes which free individual potentialities.

SOURCES OF HELP

At every stage in life there are sources of help for the individual. Assistance is generally given more freely and systematically to children than to adults, presumably because adults are more nearly in command of their life situations. The home (parent-child relationship) is the principal institution for helping the young child, and the community (through its mental and physical health services) offers assistance and advice to parents. The church is also involved, through its instruction to parents on the rearing of children.

Some people seem to know almost intuitively where to turn for help. By the time a child reaches grade three or four, he knows that the school is a major source of assistance in addition to the home. Indeed, everyone uses several social institutions which have evolved to supplement the family in making life more satisfactory and in making himself a more successful person.

Finally, it should be noted that not all people regard providing help to others as a constructive, positive, function. They view the helping relationship with alarm, contending that it weakens character and is a sign of overindulgence and protectiveness. In this view, the individual who struggles unaided with the inexorable imperatives of life is better equipped for the stresses and strains of survival. But it would seem that a great society and a global civilization, if they are to endure, call for men to serve the interests of all men. The late President Johnson put it simply in these words: "In a land of great wealth, families must not live in poverty. In a land high in harvest, children must not go hungry. In a land of healing miracles, neighbors should not suffer and die unattended."

CHARACTERISTICS OF THE HELPING RELATIONSHIP

The helping relationship is complex and therefore difficult to reduce to its component parts without destroying its meaning. Written descriptions must fractionate its internal, logically consistent pattern. With this limitation noted, 10 characteristics summarizing the nature of the helping relationship will be treated briefly. These elements will, it is hoped, reveal not only that which is essential or typical in the relationship but that which distinguishes it from other relationships. Much research exists to support these descriptive statements. Since the remaining chapters will describe and deal with it, we have chosen not to cite the large number of references from which the characteristics are derived. It should be noted that these descriptions present a general overview of the helping relationship rather than specific qualities established and maintained by a particular professional helping person, such as a school counselor or a psychiatrist. Whitehead's advice should be remembered:

> Should we not distrust that jaunty assurance with which every age prides itself that it at last has hit upon the ultimate concepts in which all that happens can be formulated? The aim of science is to seek the simplest explanations of complex facts. We are apt to fall into the error of thinking that the facts are simple because simplicity is the goal of our quest. The guiding motto in the life of every natural philosopher should be "seek simplicity and distrust it."[5]

1. *The helping relationship is meaningful.* It is valued by the participants, and it is meaningful because it is personal and intimate, because it is relevant, because it is both anxiety-evoking and anxiety-reducing, and because it involves mutual self-commitment.

2. *Affect is evident in a helping relationship.* Affect is

[5] Alfred North Whitehead, *The Concept of Nature* (London: Cambridge University Press, 1920).

present because those in the relationship are self-revealing, self-absorbed, and sensitive to each other. Disclosure of frequently unique and always private perceptions, information, or attitudes produces tension and ambiguity. While both cognitive and affective factors are operative, the emphasis tends to be upon the affective.

3. *Integrity of person is present in the helping relationship.* The participants intend to be intellectually and emotionally honest with each other. Respect is accorded each individual because he is a person of worth. There is a restorative quality to the relationship that excludes sham, pretension, and deceit. The participants relate to each other as authentic, reliable individuals.

4. *The helping relationship takes place by the mutual consent of the individuals involved.* Consent is given either explicitly or implicitly because of choice, tradition, deference, or need. Even in child-parent or teacher-pupil relationships, agreement and/or acquiescence by the participants is needed if the relationship is to be helpful. While individuals can be coerced into certain relationships, the absence of pressure is the hallmark of a helping relationship. The point seems abundantly clear: One cannot be compelled to be helpful or to receive help because the very use of force precludes "helpfulness." Duress tears at the fabric of understanding and creates mistrust rather than bringing about improvement.

5. *The relationship takes place because the individual to be helped needs information, instruction, advice, assistance, understanding, and/or treatment from the other.* The one who seeks help does so because he lacks knowledge or competence, feels distressed, inept, anxious, or ineffective. The one who extends help does so because of greater maturity, the possession of special knowledge or competence, and/or the trust the other places in him. The helper exhibits enough personal power, charm, authority, skill, energy, or perceptiveness to induce and sustain trust so that the individual to be helped believes that he will be prepared, that he will endure, or that somehow he will be better than he was before. The confidence reposed in the helper is a crucial characteristic of the relationship. While helping persons often are viewed as mind readers who have some peculiar capacity for knowing what is going on, in reality they have no completely reliable device for penetrating the thoughts of others. But their experience and training enable them to make more accurate inferences than those who are untutored, and their theories of human behavior permit them to observe more accurately, to infer more precisely, and to organize better the meaning of various kinds of behavior.

6. *The helping relationship is conducted through communication and interaction.* Each participant is affected by the other's verbal and nonverbal communication. The helper and the person helped observe and involve each other's interest and attention. Each talks, reacts, responds to the other verbally as well as nonverbally, and both kinds of behavior have current and residual import. Nonverbal behavior — facial expressions, gestures, body motions — may relate directly to verbal content or to affective experience.

Both parties convey, exchange, transfer, or impart knowledge, information, and/or feelings. Axiomatically, the more lucid and articulate the communication between them, the more meaningful the relationship. The communication and interaction will be both cognitive and affective and will contain both positive and negative experiences — that is, the individual to be helped not only develops new behaviors but may eliminate competing or discordant responses.

7. *Structure is evident in the helping relationship.* The working arrangement for conducting the relationship begins when the helper and the person to be helped come together. Invariably, the latter initially conceives the former as an authority or expert who is to take the lead, while his own role is usually preconceived as that of an "assistant." Both participants introduce their total life experiences into the relationship. Their attitudes stem from these experiences and determine how they relate to each other. The helper is expected to and often does give explanation or definition (sometimes tentatively and ambiguously) as to what may happen in the relationship, and either or both are instrumental in establishing expected outcomes. The clues and

cues each receives from the other determine ways of working together. Although varying amounts of freedom are given to the person who is to be helped, he must have an opportunity to respond and be expansive. Structure varies, depending upon the type of helping relationship, but its essential features — patterns of stimuli and response —are always present. Structure enables the relationship to eventuate in growth and productivity. In reality, responsibility for the structure is reciprocal. Both the helper and the person to be helped have needs — to achieve, to be recognized, to be adequate — that determine structure and set in motion responses which the helping person must be prepared to meet if he is to build a helping relationship.

8. *Collaborative effort marks the helping relationship.* The participants work together toward an acceptable goal. They search for contributions and resources useful in attaining the goal. The one to be helped feels free to reject skills, suggestions, or contributions which seem inappropriate or to accept without resistance those which are appropriate. The helper puts his repertoire of skills and information at the disposal of the other while simultaneously working toward freeing and supporting the individual's selective powers of initiative. He accords dignity to the person to be helped whether the latter accepts or rejects the help. This collaborative effort intensifies the relationship and validates its effectiveness. The helping person's task is to function in such a manner that the other can achieve the emotional strength and security to express his viewpoint, problem, or situation.

9. *The helping person is approachable and secure as a person.* He is accessible in the sense that others feel free to draw close to him. He is accepting of others, their ideas, actions, suggestions. He is free from undue fear, doubt, anxiety. He exhibits steadiness and stability in the relationship.

10. *Change is the object of the helping relationship.* The participants learn from each other, and the experience results in change. The individual to be helped is different from what he was before the relationship. He no longer suffers as much; he is not as disabled; he becomes more aware of himself; he achieves more satisfying ways of behaving; he becomes more of a person. Internal and external change occurs in attitudes, actions, and perceptions of self, others, and world.

Examination of these 10 characteristics reveals that they are to some degree interrelated. For example, the first one (meaningfulness) is certainly either a function or a product of affect (the second one).

Rogers has described the helping relationship with great clarity in the form of searching questions:

Can I *be* in some way which will be perceived by the other person as trustworthy, as dependable or consistent in some deep sense?
Can I be expressive enough as a person that what I am will be communicated unambiguously?
Can I let myself experience positive attitudes toward this other person — attitudes of warmth, caring, liking, interest, respect?
Can I be strong enough as a person to be separate from the other?
Am I secure enough within myself to permit him his separateness?
Can I let myself enter fully into the world of his feelings and personal meanings and see those as he does?
Can I receive him as he is? Can I communicate this attitude?
Can I act with sufficient sensitivity in the relationship that my behavior will not be perceived as a threat?
Can I free him from the threat of external evaluation?
Can I meet this other individual as a person who is in the process of becoming, or will I be bound by his past and by my past? [6]

The Helping Professions

Rogers has noted that the helping person is approachable and secure as a person. Rogers' questions give further insight into the kind of person who can conduct helping relationships. The qualities possessed by counselors will be dealt with at

[6] Rogers, *op. cit.*, condensed from pp. 50–55.

some length in Chapter Five. Treatment here is given to the professions that exist to create and conduct helping relationships. McCully, citing the absence of an authoritative definition of "helping professions," had this to say:

> A helping profession is defined as one which, based upon its specialized knowledge, applies an intellectual technique to the existential affairs of others toward the end of enabling them to cope more effectively with the dilemma and paradoxes that characterize the human condition.[7]

McCully further asserted that the definition did not limit the helping professions to those that practice psychotherapy, that existential problems are those which imply the need for choice or decision, that valuing is central in the relationship, and finally that under this definition counseling psychology and social work would be included as well as two aspiring professions: school psychology and school counseling and, in certain settings, clinical psychology and psychiatry. McCully did not specify which settings ruled out clinical psychology and psychiatry as helping professions. He did identify two characteristics that distinguish helping from other professions:

> The first is that in the application of his intellectual technique to the existential affairs of others, the practitioner cannot do so completely as a scientist. [There are no sure external guides to the resolution of existential problems.]
> The second inference is that in the case of the helping professions the obligation to benefit and not to injure is a much heavier obligation than it is in other professions.[8]

The following view of the helping professions is presented to show (1) the range of individuals engaged in them and (2) the commonalities and differences among them.

[7] C. Harold McCully, "Conceptions of Man and the Helping Professions," *Personnel and Guidance Journal*, Vol. 44 (May, 1966), p. 912.
[8] *Ibid.*

SOCIAL WORK

Social work has frequently been called the "conscience of the community." This description seems to suggest the humanistic philosophical foundation of social work and the community's control over its practice. Improvement of the basic organization of society is a commonly stated purpose of social work. The United Nations characterizes social work as follows: It helps with problems that prevent people from achieving a minimum standard of social and economic well-being; it is a social activity not carried on for personal profit by private practitioners but conducted by governmental or nongovernmental organizations; and it is a liaison activity through which disadvantaged individuals, families, and groups may tap community resources to meet their unsatisfied needs. Initially, correctional work and poverty (administration of poor relief funds) were the major domain of social work. But it now covers unemployment, broken homes, delinquency, family maladjustments, physical and emotional handicaps, racial tension, antisocial behavior, inadequate housing, and community recreation. Most professional social workers provide service directly to individuals, families, or groups.

Social Work Approaches While three basic techniques (casework, group work, and community or social welfare organization) are usually cited as social work approaches, casework is really the core of the professional helping relationship. Casework objectives include remediation of personality defects and maintaining and improving social and personal functioning. Levenstein has noted that

> Social casework moved, in the 1920's, away from the belief that the problems with which it was dealing stemmed mainly from flaws in the social system. The social system was a reality that might require changing, but in any case the individual client's reactions to his environment could be freed from psychological forces that kept him from making the best possible use of himself in the existing situation. With this change in

emphasis came the recognition that the caseworker's assistance to the client required a special relationship between the two of them. The caseworker was no longer just administering distribution of the goods of the agency; the agency was providing a service in the form of a skilled professional with whom the client could interact in such a way as to free his own potentialities for self-help.[9]

While the approach described by Levenstein is still valid, today's caseworker is equally aware that modification and manipulation of the environment of his clients can have tremendous impact in bettering their life conditions.

Caseworkers may arrange financial assistance, facilitate family or institutional care, or plan for health services. Through counseling they seek to modify feelings, attitudes, and behavior detrimental to individual and family development.

Group work, designed to help people benefit from group activities and achieve common goals by working with others, is often employed in youth-serving agencies, settlements, and correctional institutions. Community or social welfare organization is used in planning, organizing, and managing health, welfare, and recreational activities. Organization workers often coordinate community social services and help with fund raising.

Setting In the early 1900's social work was practiced chiefly in correctional institutions and welfare agencies. Since that time there has been a proliferation of practice settings into the medical, school, public assistance, child adoption, legal aid, and other facilities. Its clientele is no longer limited to the economically deprived. Family service and child welfare workers are often employed by government and voluntary agencies; school social workers or "visiting teachers" by school systems; medical social workers by hospitals, health agencies, and public welfare agencies; psychiatric social workers by mental hospitals and community mental health clinics; and rehabilitation social workers by hospitals and governmental agencies.

Psychiatric social workers may be differentiated from other social workers because they deal primarily with emotionally disturbed persons and their families. Their work in mental health clinics and hospitals includes diagnosing psychological, cultural, social, and economic factors which influence the patient's history, health, and general outlook. By counseling, they also help patients to deal with emotional and environmental problems. They assist the members of the patient's family in understanding emotional illness and in determining how they can help. Some psychiatric social workers specialize in children's treatment.

Numbers and Need The *Occupational Outlook Handbook* reports that about 170,000 social workers were employed in 1970.[10] Some 60 per cent were in state, county, and city governmental agencies; about 3 per cent in federal governmental agencies; and the remainder in voluntary or private agencies. Many hold positions in mental health establishments.

Traditionally, women have predominated in the field of social work, but there has been a consistent increase of men. During the 1970's many new social workers will be needed annually to meet expansion and replacement demands. The supply from professional schools of social work is not expected to keep pace with the demand.

Preparation and Professional Organizations Some 70 graduate schools of social work, accredited by the Council of Social Work Education, offered training in 1970. Full professional status requires two years of graduate study. Estimates are that only a fifth of current social workers meet this graduate education criterion. Those who have completed accredited two-year graduate programs of social work are

[9] Sidney Levenstein, *Private Practice in Social Casework* (New York: Columbia University Press, 1964), pp. 23–24.

[10] Department of Labor, *Occupational Outlook Handbook* (Washington: Superintendent of Documents, 1972–1973), p. 268.

eligible for membership in the National Association of Social Workers.

PSYCHIATRY

Psychiatry ("psyche," the mind, plus "iatreia," healing) is a branch of medicine concerned with the study and treatment of disorders of the mind. A psychiatrist is a physician who seeks to prevent, diagnose, and treat mental illness and emotional disorders. Historically, psychiatry dealt with the medical care of the mentally ill, but as its science and art progressed, much of its treatment became nonmedical, for many patients were not ill (in the strict sense of the word), either somatically or mentally. Consequently, the practice of psychiatry is often indistinguishable from other specialties.

Emotional stress, the nation's number one health problem, varies in intensity, severity, and scope, and psychiatrists treat the full range of emotional disorders. Bahn, Conwell, and Hurley, describing a field survey, reported that during a month's sampling of psychiatrists in private practice almost half of the patients were classified as having psychoneurotic disorders and another 26 per cent as having psychotic disorders. Other diagnostic categories included brain syndromes (4 per cent); mental deficiencies (2 per cent); personality disorders (13 per cent); transitional, situational personality disorders (2 per cent); no mental disorder (1 per cent); and others (7 per cent).[11] Psychosis, a severe form of personality disorganization in which the person often cannot distinguish the real from the imaginary, is usually classified as either functional (lacking apparent organic cause) or somatic (organic in nature, such as brain tumor or paresis). "Psychoneurosis" is a term used to designate milder forms of emotional stress. While ill defined, it is often and loosely applied to disorders characterized by anxiety, compulsions, obsessions, fugues, phobias, and motor and sensory manifestations such as tics.

[11] Anita K. Bahn, Margaret Conwell, and Peter Hurley, "Survey of Private Psychiatric Practice," *Archives of General Psychiatry*, Vol. 12 (March, 1965), p. 299.

A psychoanalyst is also a physician and a psychiatrist — there are some exceptions — who treats neuroses primarily but also a great variety of other disorders through use of an approach developed by Sigmund Freud with modifications by his disciples. Psychoanalysis is based upon concepts of unconscious motivation, conflict, and symbolism. Its boundaries are not sharply defined.

Psychiatric Approaches Treatments used by psychiatrists include chemotherapy (administration of antidepressants and sedatives); shock therapy (inducing shock, with or without convulsions, in a patient by means of insulin or electric current through the brain); individual psychotherapy (including hypnosis, suggestion, supportive therapy, re-education, desensitization, and other forms of consultation); group psychotherapy; family therapy; and psychoanalysis. Bahn, Conwell, and Hurley found that of the patients seen by psychiatrists in private practice, 63 per cent were in individual psychotherapy, 25 per cent in chemotherapy, 12 per cent in psychoanalysis, and a small percentage in group, family, and somatic therapy. The percentages reported do not total 100 per cent because one-fourth of the patients were in multiple therapy.[12]

Setting A psychiatrist may concentrate practice on child, adult, or community psychiatry, mental deficiency, alcoholism, geriatrics, military, legal, or industrial psychiatry. As of May, 1972, the American Psychiatry Association reported that some 23,812 psychiatrists were in practice in mainland U.S.A. Of these, 17,846 were members of A.P.A. A 1965 survey reported the type of setting in which they served. Some 54 per cent were in private practice, but only two-fifths were engaged full time in private practice. About 38 per cent served in outpatient clinics, 35 per cent in mental hospitals, 21 per cent in institutions of higher education, 20 per cent in general hospitals, 11 per cent in government administrative agencies; 7 per cent in re-

[12] *Ibid.*

tardation centers and others (3 per cent) in schools, mental health facilities, foundations, and nonhealth settings. The survey also reported 40 per cent in general psychiatry, 25 per cent in adult psychiatry, 9 per cent in psychoanalysis, and 9 per cent in child psychiatry.[13]

Numbers and Need Bahn, Conwell, and Hurley state that "studies in selected areas have indicated that probably as many outpatients are seen by private psychiatrists as by psychiatric clinics which in 1962 served an estimated 750,000 persons in the United States." They also reported that few private patients were nonwhite and that women were overrepresented in the private patient population, as were the single and divorced.[14]

Some 88 per cent of the psychiatrists are men; their median age is 43 (women, 46). Approximately 37 per cent of them have been certified by the American Board of Psychiatry and Neurology.[15] As in other mental health occupations, a great shortage of psychiatrists currently exists. Probably the shortage will grow more critical in the immediate future.

Preparation and Professional Organization Psychiatric practice requires lengthy training. Four years, after college, are spent in medical school followed by one year of hospital internship and three years of residency in an approved hospital or agency concerned with the diagnosis and treatment of mental and emotional disorders. Two additional years of experience are required before examination for certification by the American Board of Psychiatry and Neurology. The American Psychiatric Association includes two major membership types — associate and general. Associate members are physicians who have had one year or more of full time training or experience in psychiatry. A general member is a physician who has been an associate member for at least one year or has had three years' experience in psychiatry.

Musto maintains that American psychiatrists are losing a clear sense of their professional role. In his view, they no longer value psychoanalytically oriented psychotherapy with individual patients. Their concern is with behavior of groups to correct "here and now" feelings and their focus is upon community psychiatry. He charges that the latter places them in administrative roles and removes them from practicing individual psychotherapy.[16]

PSYCHOLOGY

The helping relationship typifies the major activity of clinical, counseling, and school psychologists. Clinical psychology is the largest area of specialization within psychology and is growing relatively larger by the year. While classification of specialties has changed somewhat over the years, the percentage of American Psychological Association members who specialized in clinical psychology increased from 30 per cent in 1948 to 43 per cent in 1951. In 1964, however, 37 per cent of psychologists were in the clinical field, and in 1968 the figure was 29 per cent.[17]

Clinical psychology employs psychological knowledge and practice to help individuals cope with behavioral disorders and secure better adjustment and self-expression. Like his counterpart in psychiatry, the clinical psychologist performs diagnoses, treatment, and prevention of emotional problems, but he does not use chemotherapy, shock therapy, or other medical methods. Historically, the classification and treatment of mental illness was the responsibility of psychiatrists. The need for psychologists arose when it was found that intelligence tests might be helpful in estimating what could be accomplished in psychiatric

[13] Mental Health Manpower, *Occupational and Personal Characteristics of Psychiatrists in the United States — 1965* (Washington: U.S. Department of Health, Education, and Welfare, February, 1966), pp. 1–2.
[14] Bahn, Conwell, and Hurley, *op. cit.*, p. 301.
[15] Mental Health Manpower, *op. cit.*, p. 8.

[16] David F. Musto, "History and Psychiatry's Present State of Transition," *Archives of Psychiatry*, Vol. 23 (November, 1970), p. 385.
[17] Bertita E. Compton, "Psychology's Manpower: The Education and Utilization of Psychologists," *American Psychologist*, Vol. 27 (May, 1972), pp. 355–518.

treatment. With the advent of personality testing, more and more reliance was placed on clinical psychologists for assistance in personality diagnosis. Major functions of the clinical psychologist have evolved from evaluation of behavioral problems to performing psychotherapy, conducting psychological consultation, and carrying on research in treatment procedures and other behavioral concerns.

Counseling psychology is among the more recent psychological specialties. Counseling psychologists are equipped to deal with personal problems not classified as mental illness though they may be sequels or corollaries of either mental or physical illness. Although the boundary between clinical and counseling psychology is not precise, counseling psychologists usually concentrate upon educational-vocational problems and transient situational personal problems and neuroses. Their training internship is spent in settings other than mental hospitals. Chin believes that if counseling and clinical psychology are to remain relevant and viable, a rapprochement is essential, especially in view of contemporary social forces.[18] He foresees more and more similarity between the two disciplines and feels the traditional models are too restrictive to meet current demands on the professions.

School psychologists study school situations to improve learning conditions. In the past, they devoted much time to intellectual evaluation, but their role and function are being redefined. The modern-day school psychologist conducts individual and group psychotherapy with pupils and consults with teachers, parents, counselors, and administrators.

Psychological Approaches Considerable difference exists in theoretical approaches to the helping relationship among psychotherapists. Approaches range from environmental manipulation, supportive therapy, insight therapy, reeducation, persuasion, and attention to intellectual cognitive processes to providing a warm, permissive relationship with a focus upon the affective, emotional processes. Commonalities lie in the establishment of a personal relationship between the participants. Snyder and Snyder cite five differences in approaches to psychotherapy:

> . . . 1) the degree of ambiguity or consistency of therapeutic role, 2) the amount of therapist warmth or coolness, 3) the emphasis upon recall of the past versus dealing with present problems, 4) the degree of activity or passivity of the therapist, and 5) the emphasis on client affect versus cognition.[19]

Setting Clinical and counseling psychologists work in mental and general hospitals, mental health clinics, family service and marriage clinics, Veterans Administration and rehabilitation centers, centers for the aged, courts and prisons, and college and university student counseling centers and psychological clinics. School psychologists serve both elementary and secondary schools.

Numbers and Need Estimates are that in 1972 some 64,000 psychologists were in the nation's manpower pool.[20] There were approximately four male psychologists for each female psychologist. During the 1960's there were more vacancies for psychologists than qualified applicants to fill them. Shortages were severe in state mental hospitals, federal government agencies, and educational institutions (some 56 per cent of psychologists are employed in educational institutions). The early 1970's closed this gap and it was reported that unemployment among psychologists during 1971-72 was one and one-half per cent (experimental psychologists experienced greatest difficulty in finding academic positions). While the 1972-1973 *Occupational Outlook Handbook* reports employment to be "excellent through the 1970's," many involved in the preparation of psychologists believe the 17 per

[18] Arnold H. Chin, "New Perspectives on the Relationship Between Clinical and Counseling Psychology," *Journal of Counseling Psychology*, Vol. 14 (July, 1967), pp. 374–379.

[19] William U. Snyder and B. June Snyder, *The Psychotherapy Relationship* (New York: The Macmillan Company, 1961), p. 10.
[20] Compton, *op. cit.*, p. 469.

cent annual increase in numbers means that the supply will exceed the demand.

Preparation and Professional Organization The Ph.D. degree is needed for most positions in clinical, counseling, and school psychology. In all instances approved preparation includes one year of internship or supervised experience in a setting appropriate to the population the individual will ultimately serve. The American Psychological Association has three types of membership and contains 30 divisions which recognize the specialized interests of its members. Divisional membership frequently requires special qualifications.

The APA was founded in 1892 and incorporated in 1925. By 1972, the APA had grown to over 34,000 members. Its purpose is to advance psychology as a science, a profession, and a way of promoting human welfare. It works toward this goal by holding annual meetings, publishing many psychological journals, and working toward improved training and service. In addition to its three types of membership, APA also examines and approves members for diplomate status in those specialties covered by Boards of Examiners in Professional Psychology and in Psychological Hypnosis.

COUNSELING

Since this book is about counseling, the treatment here of functions, approaches, and setting will be brief. The title "counselor" is used by many individuals to describe what they do. This rather indiscriminate use of the title has been detrimental to attempts at specifying clearly defined functions for those upon whom the title has been conferred (indeed, sometimes self-conferred). The lack of definition by function stems from the fact that counseling (in its modern sense) is relatively new, and confusion and uncertainty are inevitable in any emerging profession. Professional maturation will undoubtedly reduce excessive variation and bring consolidation in function.

Wrenn has summed up the counselor's function, regardless of setting, in a very useful way. He states that it is the function of the counselor

> . . . a) to provide a *relationship* between counselor and counselee, the most prominent quality of which is that of mutual trust of each in the other; b) to provide *alternatives* in self-understanding and in the courses of action open to the client; c) to provide for *some degree of intervention* with the situation in which the client finds himself and with "important others" in the client's immediate life; d) to provide leadership in developing *a healthy psychological environment* for his clients; and, finally, e) to provide for *improvement of the counseling process* through constant individual self-criticism and (for some counselors) extensive attention to improvement of process through research.[21]

Counseling Approaches Many methods are used to create a relationship to assist counselees in self-understanding, select courses of action, intervene in interpersonal situations, and exercise leadership in developing healthy psychological environments. The approaches cited for psychologists — counseling relationships or interviews, use of test and nontest appraisal devices, and consultative endeavors — apply equally well to counselors.

Setting Estimates are that during 1972 some 75,000 counselors (recognized as such by competent authority) were employed in various settings in the United States. The settings in which they worked illustrate in some measure the degree of public support for such services in our society. The predominant setting is the school. While historically the secondary school level has been the major locus, today counselors in substantial numbers work in elementary schools, junior colleges, technical institutes, colleges, and universities. The United States Employment Service, rehabilitation centers, churches, Veterans Administration installations, the Peace Corps, city welfare agencies, Economic Opportunity Act programs, community action programs, private practice — all these make use of counselors.

[21] C. Gilbert Wrenn, "Crisis in Counseling: A Commentary and a Contribution," in John F. McGowan (ed.), *Counselor Development in American Society* (Washington: U.S. Department of Labor, 1965), p. 237.

Numbers and Need The number of individuals who bear the title "counselor" is extremely difficult to secure, but, as already mentioned, it is estimated (by state certification, by being employed and assigned the title, etc.) at 75,000. Some work part time. Approximately 54,000 are employed in educational institutions. Based on desirable counselor-client ratios, strong arguments can be made for increases in the number of counselors. The need for counselors is unprecedented and will continue over the next several years. Expansion of counseling services within the many available settings makes it impossible to meet the demand, let alone provide replacements due to retirement, acceptance of administrative assignments, etc. Replacement demands alone amount to approximately 10 per cent each year. This imbalance is expected to persist for the next few years. The "need" for counselors should not be confused with actual "demand." Demands are contingent upon the degree to which our society values such services and is willing to support them financially.

Preparation and Professional Organization Most states require counselors employed in public schools to be certified by state departments of education. Educational requirements for work in rehabilitation, employment, and the like vary. A master's degree in counseling is more and more being accepted as the *minimal* preparation. Counselor education programs at the graduate level are available in approximately 378 colleges and universities, most frequently in the departments of education and/or psychology.[22]

Two professional organizations claim the loyalty of most professional counselors: the American Personnel and Guidance Association and, to a somewhat lesser degree, the American Psychological Association. A discussion of these organizations is presented in Chapter Two.

[22] Joseph W. Hollis and Richard A. Wantz, *Counselor Education Directory: Personnel and Programs* (Muncie, Indiana: Ball State Book Store, January, 1971), p. 5.

SUMMARY

The demand for a helping relationship in our society has resulted in the establishment of several types of professionals. Boundaries, focus, goals, and significance of their service are transitory, uncertain, and often the subject of dispute. More important are the following three observations: (1) A core of common elements exists among the multiplicity of individuals who conduct a helping relationship, regardless of title or setting. (2) These emerging professional helping specialists have the opportunity to achieve role and function definition by experimentation, discussion, and interaction with each other and their publics. (3) There are good opportunities for responsible work in these professional specialties.

The Helping Professions – Commonalities and Differences

COMMONALITIES

More qualities are shared than separate the helping professions. Of the many qualities held in common, five will be commented on here.

1. The concept that behavior is caused and can be modified is shared by all helping professions. It is agreed that every act is an attempt to satisfy some need, that a behavioral pattern is the result of many causes, and that any single cause may lead to many different sorts of adaptation. While the latitude for change may vary considerably among individuals, it is widely assumed that almost all have the potentiality for changing behavioral liabilities and deficits. For some the psychological barriers to change are immense, and modification is extremely difficult to achieve.
2. The ultimate goal of all helping professions is to help individuals become more fully functioning persons and achieve integration, personal identity, and self-actualization.
3. The primary means of extending assistance is through a helping relationship, the major characteristics of which have already been presented. It is

through a personal, interacting relationship that helping skills and attitudes are productively released to enable the person needing assistance to cope with his "difficulties and concerns."

4. All helping professions emphasize prevention. Each one knows that care and treatment are not enough, that causes must be uncovered. Individual treatment alone is inadequate because of the magnitude of mental problems among the public. Substantial attention has to be given to prophylaxis. While preventive efforts have been slow and often uncertain, education of the public about interpersonal behavior has been a long-term crusade for the National Association for Mental Health. Preventive efforts have been designed to inform the public on (a) the care provided patients in state hospitals and community centers, (b) the magnitude and nature of mental disorder, (c) the characteristics of good mental health, (d) misconceptions about mental disorder and interpersonal relationships, and (e) ways to enable individuals, particularly teachers and parents, to make discriminations and judgments concerning behavior and personal development.

Helping specialists give a preventive focus to their work when they foster a client's interest in improving his relationship with others. When clients become aware that their needs are reflected in how they relate to others, their flexibility may increase — and hence their acceptance of others' behavior. Certainly, achieving insight into one's values, expectations, and goals often brings realization and modification of the demands one makes upon others.

5. Practitioners in all helping professions undergo a period of preparation and training. The length of preparation varies, but the goal is understanding behavior and creating helping relationships.

DIFFERENCES

Attempts to differentiate social work, psychiatry, psychotherapy, and counseling have not had much success. Many helping specialists believe that differences are artificial, contrived, and theoretical rather than qualitative and practical. Others insist that the distinctions are there and should be known if for no other reason than the fact that the specialties exist.

1. Professional preparation and training varies. As noted above, the length of professional preparation differs substantially. Two years of graduate work is the established standard in social work; psychiatry is a specialty attained in a two- to four-year program after receiving the medical degree while psychoanalysis as a specialty requires an additional two to four years of preparation. Counseling and clinical psychology call for the doctor of philosophy degree. Two years of graduate study is now the established standard for school counseling personnel.

Perhaps more important than length of preparation is the stress given certain content areas. Certainly social workers, prepared in graduate schools of social work, are more intimately grounded in societal and environmental bases of behavior. Study of individual development as affected by social environment, groups as a context for human interaction, family organization, forces producing social organization and disorganization, and the influence of the presence, beliefs, actions, and symbols of other men on behavior provides a backdrop for a social worker's interpretation and understanding of human behavior and his establishing of a helping relationship.

The focus of psychiatric education is upon study of the total personality. Psychoneuroses and allied conditions, functional psychoses, and psychopathic conditions, deviations, and addictions are extensively studied. Personality development, unconscious motivation, and dynamic consideration of clinical cases are emphasized. Among the trends in psychiatric education is the fact that psychiatry is taught more and more during all four years of medical education rather than as a postmedical specialty. Raskin reports training programs are moving toward an integrated theory of psychiatry in an attempt to coordinate neurobiological, physiological, and sociological data.[23]

[23] David Raskin, "Psychiatric Training in the 70's—Toward a Shift in Emphasis," *The American Journal of Psychiatry*, Vol. 128 (March, 1972), p. 1130.

Preparation in clinical psychology emphasizes behavioral pathology, personality evaluation — especially diagnosis of emotional disorders — and, increasingly, psychotherapeutic involvement. On the other hand, preparation in counseling psychology stresses total development of the "normal" personality. In fact, preparation programs for counseling and clinical psychologists are rather similar. The clinician's preparation does tend to contain a greater emphasis upon the more seriously disabling psychological disturbances. Preparation in counseling and guidance pays major attention to developmental behavior and seeks to improve the quality of the helping relationship.

2. Recipients of the helping service extended by social workers, psychiatrists, psychotherapists, and counselors differ somewhat. Psychiatrists and clinical psychologists usually treat individuals with psychological disorders ranging from transient personal problems and neuroses to chronic psychoses which are disabling, incapacitating, or disintegrating. Counseling psychologists, social workers, and counselors help essentially "normal" people remove frustrations and obstacles — ranging from situational temporary concerns, educational and vocational decisions, transient moderate-to-severe personal problems to neuroses — which impair their development. The term "patient" is more often applied to the recipient of psychiatric and psychotherapeutic services while "counselee" and "client" are generally preferred by counseling psychologists, social workers, and counselors.

3. Depth of involvement and length of treatment may vary. Psychiatry and psychotherapy usually entail a deeper involvement with the individual's personality since they are more often concerned with the amelioration of serious behavioral conditions. The counseling relationship is likely to be characterized by less intensity of emotional expression than is found in the psychiatric relationship. Psychotherapy usually takes a longer period of time with its focus upon personality reorganization whereas counseling is conducted in shorter, more limited contacts.

4. The typical setting in which social work, psychiatry, counseling, and clinical psychology and counseling are performed varies somewhat. The usual locale for psychiatrists and clinical psychologists is a hospital. Counseling psychologists and social workers frequently practice in community clinics. Counselors are found predominantly in educational settings. It should be noted (see pp. 9–15) that variety characterizes the setting for all helping professions.

Buchheimer and Balogh have identified some distinctions between and among social conversation, advisement, counseling, and psychotherapy. "Status quo" denotes the purpose of social conversation since those involved maintain any distortion or play any role that they consciously or unconsciously desire. "A priori" refers to the object of advisement conversation since the person being advised is related to predetermined conditions and confronted with his capacity to meet these conditions, and with the possibility and probability of meeting them. Some facet of the advisee — some sample of his behavior — is abstracted from him, considered representative of him, and related to a set of general conditions. "Ad hoc" is applicable to the counseling conversation since the counselee expresses his point of view toward the world. The assumption is that this point of view is distorted and that through counseling he will revise it and alter his behavior. Finally, "a posteriori" characterizes the therapeutic conversation since the approach is historic and symbolic and relies upon reactivation and consideration of unconscious material to achieve personality reorganization.[24]

What Is Counseling?

The foregoing material described counseling as a helping profession. Since this book is about counseling and those who practice it, some definition of counseling seems imperative if its boundaries are to be known.

Although "counseling" is a word used by many to describe what they do, dictionary definitions

[24] Arnold Buchheimer and Sara Carter Balogh, *The Counseling Relationship* (Chicago: Science Research Associates, Inc., 1961), p. x.

stress advice and mental exchange of ideas. The Latin *consilium* meant "with" or "together" plus "take" or "grasp" whereas in Anglo-Saxon *sellan* meant "to sell" or "deliver to." *Webster's New World Dictionary* (1962) identifies a legal adviser at an embassy, a lawyer, and a person in charge of a group of children at a camp as "counselors." The historical use of advice to define "counsel" still is prevalent and is the cause of much conflict and confusion when counselors in educational and non-educational settings insist that they do not parcel out advice. Nor is the situation helped when automobile salesmen and representatives from brokers' firms, loan agencies, and mortuaries distribute cards bearing such titles as "Automotive Counselor," "Investment Counselor," "Financial Counselor," and "Grief Counselor!" Perhaps there is one saving grace — they usually spell the word "counsellor!"

"Counseling" has been used to denote a wide range of procedures including advice giving, encouragement, information giving, test interpretation, and psychoanalysis. H. B. and A. C. English define counseling as "a relationship in which one person endeavors to help another to understand and to solve his adjustment problems."[25] They point out (1) that areas of adjustment are often indicated (e.g., educational counseling, vocational counseling, personal-social counseling), (2) that reference is usually to helping "normal counselees" but creeps imperceptibly into the field of psychotherapy, and (3) that while everyone occasionally undertakes counseling the word is preferably retricted to professionally trained persons.

A few of the definitions of counseling contained in the literature are given here. They reflect some of the subtle differences that have been emphasized or have evolved over the years.

> . . . a process in which the counselor assists the counselee to make interpretations of facts relating to a choice, plan, or adjustments which he needs to make.[26]

> . . . a process which takes place in a one-to-one relationship between an individual troubled by problems with which he cannot cope alone, and a professional worker whose training and experience have qualified him to help others reach solutions to various types of personal difficulties.[27]

> . . . the process by which the structure of the self is relaxed in the safety of the relationship with the therapist, and previously denied experiences are perceived and then integrated into an altered self.[28]

> . . . that interaction which a) occurs between two individuals called a counselor and client; b) takes place in a professional setting, and c) is initiated and maintained as a means of facilitating changes in the behavior of a client.[29]

> . . . the process involving interpersonal relationships between a therapist and one or more clients by which the former employs psychological methods based on systematic knowledge of the human personality in attempting to improve the mental health of the latter.[30]

> . . . helping an individual become aware of himself and the ways in which he is reacting to the behavioral influences of his environment. It further helps him to establish some personal meaning for this behavior and to develop and clarify a set of goals and values for future behavior.[31]

> . . . a process by which a troubled person (the client) is helped to feel and behave in a more personally satisfying manner through interaction with an uninvolved person (the counselor) who provides information and reactions which stimulate the client to develop behaviors which enable him to deal more effectively with himself and his environment.[32]

These definitions presented chronologically are representative of several dozen that are available and can profitably be examined for chronological

[25] H. B. and A. C. English, *A Comprehensive Dictionary of Psychological and Psychoanalytical Terms* (New York: David McKay Co., Inc., 1958), p. 127.
[26] Glenn E. Smith, *Counseling in the Secondary School* (New York: The Macmillan Company, 1955), p. 156.
[27] Milton E. Hahn and Malcolm S. MacLean, *Counseling Psychology* (New York: McGraw-Hill Book Co., Inc., 1955), p. 6.
[28] Carl R. Rogers, " 'Client-Centered' Psychotherapy," *Scientific American*, Vol. 187 (November, 1952), p. 70.
[29] Harold Pepinsky and Pauline Pepinsky, *Counseling Theory and Practice* (New York: The Ronald Press Company, 1954), p. 3.
[30] C. Patterson, *Counseling and Psychotherapy: Theory and Practice* (New York: Harper & Brothers, 1959), p. 13.
[31] Donald H. Blocher, *Developmental Counseling* (New York: The Ronald Press Company, 1966), p. 5.
[32] Edwin C. Lewis, *The Psychology of Counseling* (New York: Holt, Rinehart and Winston, Inc., 1970), p. 10.

changes and meanings. Some of the more obvious differences are presented here.

1. The early emphasis was upon cognitive concerns ("make interpretations of facts") while more current definitions stress affective experiences ("establish some personal meaning for this behavior") as well as cognitive dimensions.
2. Earlier definitions identified counseling as a dyadic (one-to-one) relationship, whereas current definitions usually refer to more than one counselee.
3. All definitions state or imply that counseling is a process. Process (any phenomenon which shows continuous change in time) implies that counseling is not a single event but involves sequential actions and practices progressing toward a goal.
4. The definitions usually specify that a relationship is involved and that it is characterized by warmth, permissiveness, understanding, acceptance, etc.
5. Some definitions describe the participants: the counselor as a professional or as older or as more mature or as possessing special knowledge; the client as troubled, anxious, upset, or frustrated.
6. Most definitions indicate that the effect of counseling is improvement or change in client behavior.

Patterson has noted that it is sometimes useful to approach a definition by exclusion or designating what a thing is *not*.[33] By exclusion, many of the misconceptions surrounding counseling can be identified. Among Patterson's exclusions (paraphrased here) are that counseling

1. is not the giving of information, though information may be given in counseling.
2. is not the giving of advice, suggestions and recommendations (advice should be recognized as such and not camouflaged as counseling).
3. is not influencing attitudes, beliefs, or behavior by means of persuading, leading, or convincing, no matter how indirectly, subtly, or painlessly.
4. is not the influencing of behavior by admonishing, warning, threatening, or compelling without the use of physical force or coercion (counseling is not discipline).
5. is not the selection and assignment of individuals for various jobs or activities (counseling is not personnel work even though the same tests may be used in both).
6. is not interviewing (while interviewing is involved, it is not synonymous).

The nature of counseling, according to Patterson, is to be found in the following characteristics:

1. Counseling is concerned with influencing voluntary behavior change on the part of the client (client wants to change and seeks counselor's help to change).
2. The purpose of counseling is to provide conditions which facilitate voluntary change (conditions such as the individual's right to make choices, to be independent and autonomous).
3. As in all relationships, limits are imposed upon the counselee (limits are determined by counseling goals which in turn are influenced by the counselor's values and philosophy).
4. Conditions facilitating behavioral change are provided through interviews (not all counseling is interviewing, but counseling always involves interviewing).
5. Listening is present in counseling but not all counseling is listening.
6. The counselor understands his client (the distinction between the way others understand and counselors understand is qualitative rather than quantitative and understanding alone does not differentiate counseling from other situations).
7. Counseling is conducted in privacy and the discussion is confidential.

A final crucial characteristic Patterson cites is that counseling involves an interview conducted in private in which the counselor listens and attempts to understand the client, and in which it is expected that there will be a change in the client's behavior in some ways which he himself chooses or decides. Finally, two other characteristics necessary

[33] C. H. Patterson, Ed., *The Counselor in the School* (New York: McGraw-Hill Book Company, 1967), pp. 219–227.

for a relationship to be labeled counseling are: that the client have a psychological problem, and that the counselor be someone skilled in working with clients with psychological problems.

We have no new definition of counseling. An adaptation of Blocher's definition seems most adequate and is used throughout this book: *Counseling is an interaction process which facilitates meaningful understanding of self and environment and results in the establishment and/or clarification of goals and values for future behavior.*

Annotated References

Benjamin, Alfred. *The Helping Interview.* Boston: Houghton Mifflin Company, 1969. 171 pp.

Benjamin describes the conditions influencing helping interviews, the philosophy behind them, and communications within them. His book amply illustrates helping relationships.

Cook, David R. (ed.). *Guidance for Education in Revolution.* Boston: Allyn and Bacon, 1971. 567 pp.

Part one (pp. 1–64) presents the historical and philosophical context of helping relationships and a statement about humanness. The chapter on humanness seeks to come to grips with what it means to be a human being and to make sense out of existence.

Halmos, Paul. *The Faith of the Counsellors.* New York: Schocken Books, Inc., 1966. 220 pp.

Halmos, a sociology professor at the University of Wales in Cardiff, examines the beliefs underlying the counselor's role in our social matrix. He believes that the counselor's functions emerged from the demands of present-day society, demands for certainty and simplicity. Because old approaches are suspect, they tend to be discarded, and man turns to counselors, who provide personal and individual assistance. This book has much that is provocative and much to stimulate counselor self-appraisal.

Rogers, Carl. *On Becoming a Person.* Boston: Houghton Mifflin Company, 1961. 421 pp.

Chapter 2, "Some Hypotheses Regarding the Facilitation of Personal Growth," and Chapter 3, "The Characteristics of a Helping Relationship," are especially useful. Rogers discusses the dimensions of the helping relationship, client motivation for change, research findings, and creation of a helping relationship.

Further References

Astor, Martin H. "Transpersonal Approaches to Counseling." *Personnel and Guidance Journal,* Vol. 50 (June, 1972). pp. 801–808.

Atkin, Jerry. "Counseling in an Age of Crisis." *Personnel and Guidance Journal,* Vol. 50 (May, 1972). pp. 719–724.

Cheiken, Martin. "Counseling: Activist or Reactivist?" *The School Counselor,* Vol. 19 (November, 1971). pp. 68–71.

Ciavarella, Michael A. "Toward an Integrated Theory of Educational and Vocational Choice." *Vocational Guidance Quarterly,* Vol. 20 (June, 1972). pp. 251–258.

Dilley, Joseph S. "Anti-shrinkthink." *Personnel and Guidance Journal,* Vol. 50 (March, 1972). pp. 567–572.

Eckerson, Louise O. "The White House Conference: Tips or Taps for Counselors?" *Personnel and Guidance Journal,* Vol. 50 (November, 1971). pp. 167–174.

Gamboa, Anthony M. Jr., Kelly, William F. and Kolveit, Thomas H. "The Humanistic Counselor in a Technocratic Society." *The School Counselor,* Vol. 19 (January, 1972). pp. 160–166.

Schmidt, Lyle D. and Strong, Stanley R. "Attractiveness and Influence in Counseling." *Journal of Counseling Psychology,* Vol. 18 (July, 1971). pp. 348–351.

Sprinthall, Norman A. "Humanism: A New Bag of Virtues for Guidance?" *Personnel and Guidance Journal,* Vol. 50 (January, 1972). pp. 349–356.

Van Riper, B. W. "Toward a Separate Professional Identity." *Journal of Counseling Psychology,* Vol. 19 (March, 1972). pp. 117–120.

Williamson, E. G. "The Future Lies Open." *Personnel and Guidance Journal,* Vol. 50 (February, 1972). pp. 426–433.

Winborn, Bob S. and Rowe, Warren. "Self-Actualization and the Communication of Facilitative Conditions — A Replication." *Journal of Counseling Psychology,* Vol. 19 (January, 1972). pp. 26–29.

COUNSELING: ORIGIN AND DEVELOPMENT

2

Remembering past events is often a favored activity of those who are bored or driven to despair by the world about them. Perhaps their contemplation of times gone by brings relief from current anxieties and difficult decisions. But it has another meaning to those who not only observe but also participate in the challenge of today and help create the promise of tomorrow. Careful examination of the past illuminates the present and suggests the pattern of the future. That which *is now* was shaped by the experiences of a *then* that extends back in an unbroken sequence.

This chapter is designed to show where counseling has been and how it arrived at its present state. Reflection will suggest, however, that the past is in reality intelligible only across spans of time much longer than that in which we have had organized counseling services. The chapter deals with five major subjects: the historical development of counseling, its current status, its professional organizations and journals, counselor supply and demand, and the criticisms leveled at it and its practitioners.

Historical Development

As is true of all histories, that of counseling reflects continuous change and progressive development. This does not mean that there have not been crises or that development has necessarily been smooth or uniform. Counseling has been and continues to be a dynamic movement. It is important for every counselor to be acquainted with the broad dimensions of its evolutionary process, since, as Santayana has said, "Those who cannot remember the past are condemned to repeat it."

Landmarks or "firsts" in the history of counseling, such as who the first counselor was, are hard to establish with any degree of certainty. Resolving the issue of "first" depends upon how counseling is defined. If its traditional definition — giving of advice — is accepted, then the point at which man first sought and received verbal aid or instruction from another marked the advent of counseling.

Some would point out that certain counseling concepts can be traced back to the Greek philosophers, to parts of the Old Testament, or to other early sources. In this sense, the social philosophers of ancient Greece (e.g. Plato [427–347 B.C.] and Aristotle [384–322 B.C.]), the hedonists, the philosophers of the British associationist school (such as Locke [1632–1704], Berkeley [1685–1753], Hume [1711–1776], and James Mill [1773–1836]), and others were influential because they sought to define the nature of man, the nature of society, and the relationship between the individual and society.

AN AMERICAN PRODUCT

Counseling emerged and developed as an American product. In no other country has it flowered as it has here. Why it emerged in America has never been satisfactorily explained. Some claim that the American social environment, strongly influenced by the belief in the importance of the individual, was especially congenial to its development.

The pervasive concept of individualism, the lack of rigid class lines, the incentive to exercise one's talents to the best of one's ability may have provided a philosophical base, or perhaps counseling originated in America because our economic system was affluent enough to afford it. It may have appeared here because our society has long been child centered (some say child ridden). Undoubtedly all these factors were instrumental in its emergence in America.

HISTORICAL EVENTS

But restricted to its modern and technical definition, counseling has a much more contemporary history and therefore a much shorter one. Its highly significant events have been capsuled and presented chronologically by Borow.[1] Some of them, abstracted from his work, are discussed here.

[1] Henry Borow (ed.), *Man in a World of Work* (Boston: Houghton Mifflin Company, 1964), pp. 48–62.

Formative Period Counseling may have begun in 1898 when Jesse B. Davis began work as a counselor at Central High School in Detroit, Michigan. For 10 years he helped students with educational and vocational problems. William R. Harper, first president of the University of Chicago, in an 1899 address entitled "Scientific Study of the Student" urged individualized instruction and prophesied the advent of college personnel specialists. In 1906 Eli Weaver published the booklet *Choosing a Career*. The Vocational Bureau of Boston opened in 1908 with Frank Parsons as its director and counselor. His report (1909) to its Executive Committee described guidance procedures employed with some 80 young people who made use of its services. Simultaneously, William Healy was conducting meetings in Chicago, to plan the Juvenile Psychopathic Institute he started the following year. This was the first systematic effort to provide psychiatric examination for juvenile offenders — actually the first child guidance clinic. In 1909 Parsons' book *Choosing a Vocation* was published posthumously. The first national guidance conference took place in Boston in 1910. A year later Harvard University offered the first university-level course in vocational guidance, with Meyer Bloomfield as instructor. In 1912 Grand Rapids, Michigan, established a citywide guidance department in its school system. The year 1913 marked the founding of the National Vocational Guidance Association at Grand Rapids.

Later Developments We pick up the narrative again years after this pioneering period. The Occupational Information and Guidance Service was organized in 1938 in the U.S. Office of Education with Harry A. Jager as chief. In 1939 the first edition of the *Dictionary of Occupational Titles* was published. The year 1942 marks the publication of the *History of Vocational Guidance*, written by John M. Brewer. The use of federal funds for vocational guidance was authorized under the George-Deen Act in 1938 and later in the George-Barden Act of 1946. Five years later (1951) the American Personnel and Guidance Association was formed. After

Sputnik I was launched by the Russians in October, 1957, the National Defense Education Act of 1958 was passed by Congress and provided funds (Title 5) for strengthening school guidance programs and for preparing school counselors. The Commission on Guidance in American Schools (administered by the APGA) reported (1962) its examination of the current status and future prospects of counseling and its far-reaching recommendations. The report, *The Counselor in a Changing World*, was written by C. Gilbert Wrenn. In 1964, Title 5 was amended by Congress to include the preparation of elementary school counselors in institute programs, and financial support was given to elementary school guidance programs at the local level. This amendment also provided for the preparation of counselors for higher education settings.

Current Developments The 1960–1970 period was a time during which impressive gains were made in numbers of counselors prepared and employed. During these years attention was focused upon clarifying counselor role and function, upon accountability in counseling, upon the use of group approaches, upon computer applications to career information, and upon the use of behavior modification techniques. During the early 1970's, many school counselors were involved in recasting their efforts to provide vocational or career counseling.

HISTORICAL FACTORS AND FORCES

While these events outline chronologically the historical development of counseling, they only mark the high tides of certain prevailing forces that facilitated counseling's development. This is to say that the evolution of modern concepts and techniques of counseling is best seen as a movement influenced by social, psychological, and environmental factors. The climate provided by the interaction of these factors enabled counseling to emerge and maintain itself.

At first glance the factors appear to be so numerous that any attempt to analyze their cause-and-effect relationships seems hopeless. No one, in fact, has been able to suggest any acceptable single factor that gives *the* key to understanding the historical process. This does not mean, however, that the history of counseling must be confined to description or that it is impossible to show that some forces had relatively greater influence on the character of counseling than others.

The Influence of Social Reform Generations of Americans have been stirred by the exposure of social problems. The growth in the 1800's of cities, great fortunes, and new ways of living brought economic and social inequities. From 1890 to 1920 the entire fabric of American life was subjected to careful analysis and severe criticism. Aroused by the horror of poverty, injustice, and corruption, individuals and groups sought reform. Jacob Riis published his epoch-making book, *How the Other Half Lives;* Ida Tarbell contributed her *History of the Standard Oil Company* and David Graham Phillips his history of corruption in politics entitled *The Treason of the Senate;* Upton Sinclair published his story of the Chicago stockyards, *The Jungle,* and John Spargo his shocking chronicle of child labor, *The Bitter Cry of the Children.* Although some of these and other accounts were exaggerated, for the most part the criticisms were just and reforms long overdue. Public opinion forced thoroughgoing reforms. For every evil a remedy was sought. The poverty, misery, and unemployment which came as a result of the transformation of America into an industrialized and urbanized society led to the establishment of organized charities, settlement houses, philanthropic associations, and government bureaus for corrective and custodial services.

Reformers attempted to remove the fundamental causes of poverty, crime, and ignorance. Especially notable was the twentieth-century concern for the welfare of children. Creation of playgrounds and parks, more understanding treatment of children who came into conflict with the law, and correction of child labor abuses were brought about. That society was in part responsible for the wretched situation was recognized by reformers. Better conditions of living, continuous employment, and general education — conditions which strike at the causes of poverty and crime — were themes mounted and enlarged upon by numerous social reformers. Their belief that society could be improved led them to view the schools as an important place to initiate preventive efforts. Perhaps even more important, the climate which demanded the elimination of prevailing inequities established by the reform movement permitted and facilitated the beginning of counseling.

Vocational Guidance Most authorities[2] identify the emergence of *vocational* guidance as the beginning of modern-day counseling. The work of Jesse B. Davis in Detroit, the publications of Eli Weaver, and the activities of Frank Parsons in Boston have been cited. Parsons, often called the "father of vocational guidance," began his work at the Vocational Bureau to improve the postschool placement of individuals. Philanthropic contributions enabled the Vocational Bureau to open its doors in January, 1908. In his report to the Vocational Bureau's Executive Committee Parsons coined the term "vocational guidance" to describe the methods he used with young people and urged that vocational guidance become part of the public school program with experts to conduct it.

Parsons' observations of young people led him to the conclusion that they needed careful and systematic help in choosing a vocation. His idea was to match the characteristics of the individual to the requirements of the occupation. He reasoned that three major steps were necessary in selecting a vocation and that they suggested how an experienced counselor could assist the young person. These steps may be summarized as *man analysis* — careful study of the counselee's capabilities, interests, and temperaments; *job analysis* — counselee study of occupational opportunities, requirements, and employment prospects in various lines of work; and *true reasoning* on the relationships between these two sets of data.

While man-job congruence had been expressed at intervals by others prior to Parsons, he was able to institutionalize and implement it. Further, the concept remained viable for a long period of time and vestiges of it are still encountered in much counseling offered in today's schools, community clinics, and employment and rehabilitation counseling centers. Parsons was inventive in calling for the use of psychological techniques to diagnose the individual's characteristics. From his initial effort and that of others, vocational guidance spread to schools in Cincinnati, Philadelphia, Omaha, Salt Lake City, Seattle, San Francisco, and other cities.

The Child Study Movement The child study movement contributed to the development of counseling. G. Stanley Hall of Clark University aroused popular interest in child study. Through his influence the child came to be looked upon as an individual person, and studies were made of his physical and mental characteristics. During the 1920's and 1930's child study centers in some states (California, Iowa, Minnesota) and scientific journals and organizations designed to promote the well-being of children came into existence. The questionnaire method of inquiry, popularized by Hall, resulted in the rapid accumulation of data relating to different phases of the mental life of all ages. Hall is also credited with introducing Freudian concepts of child development into American education and psychology.

The effect of the child study movement in America was fourfold: (1) It emphasized the individual as the focal point of study; (2) it stressed the importance of the formative years as the foundation for mature personality development; (3) it pointed up the need for reliable factual knowledge about children; and (4) it led to better controlled, more analytical and accurate methods of child study.

[2] See Donald E. Super, "Transition: From Vocational Guidance to Counseling Psychology," *Journal of Counseling Psychology*, Vol. 2 (Spring, 1955), pp. 3-9; Committee on Definition, Division of Counseling Psychology, "Counseling Psychology as a Specialty," *American Psychologist*, Vol. 11 (June, 1956), pp. 282-285; Borow (ed.), *op. cit.*, pp. 45-47; and Carroll H. Miller, *Foundations of Guidance* (New York: Harper & Brothers, 1961), pp. 144-173.

Psychometrics Another factor instrumental in the development of counseling was the testing movement. The first psychological laboratory was established in 1879 by Wilhelm Wundt in Leipzig, Germany. Based upon the assumption that human behavior conforms to natural law and can be investigated by the scientific approach, experimental psychological laboratories mushroomed. Research was undertaken in several of these laboratories to assess intelligence. A standardized scale for measuring general intelligence was devised by Albert Binet and Théophile Simon in Paris in 1905, subsequently revised in 1908 and 1911, and there appeared a long series of modifications of the scale here in America by Goddard, Kuhlmann, Terman, Yerkes, Pintner, and many others. With the entry of the United States into World War I, testing procedures were initiated for screening out military draftees with mental handicaps and for identifying intellectually superior candidates for officer training. The Army Alpha and the Army Beta test and other group tests of verbal and nonverbal ability were the products of these efforts. Then came the development of personality, interest, and special aptitude tests. The prototype of personality tests was the Personal Data Sheet devised by Robert Woodworth during World War I as a rough screen to identify seriously neurotic men who would be unfit for military service.

Thorndike and Hagen suggest that the development of psychometrics may be divided into four stages.[3] The first, the pioneering phase, from 1900 to 1915, included the first Binet scales and the American revisions, the appearance of group intelligence tests, and the administration of the first standardized achievement tests. The second stage, from 1915 to 1930, the "boom stage," saw the advent of the Army Alpha and Beta tests and the widespread development of group intelligence and achievement tests for schools and other uses. Interest inventories, such as the Strong Vocational Interest Blank, emerged. Testing of special aptitudes in music (1919), mechanics (1926), and art (1929) was initiated and refined. The third stage, from 1930 to 1945, was cited by Thorndike and Hagen as denoting a shift in emphasis from the construction of more instruments to a critical evaluation of existing tests. While all types of tests were subjected to criticism, personality and interest measures were censured most severely since they were most vulnerable.

The fourth period, from 1945 to 1960, was a time when test "batteries" and large-scale testing programs emerged. It was, in effect, a second boom period, this time in the administration and use of testing batteries. Since 1960 many have been highly critical of using tests for educational and job selection. They believe that current tests penalize minority group individuals who have not had equal educational opportunities.

Discontent with standardized paper and pencil tests has led to experimental attempts to assess intelligence by physiological and other means. One such effort is the neural efficiency analyzer, developed by John Ertl, which measures the efficiency and the speed with which impulses are transmitted from one neuron to another in the brain. Reports describing his work as a breakthrough[4] are probably premature, for much remains to be done before such a claim can be validated. Those knowledgeable of the history of ability testing will recall that intelligence assessment originated in efforts based upon physiological measures, e.g., reaction time, which proved nonproductive.

The testing movement influenced counseling in that it (1) led to the objective study of individual differences, such as sex, race, and social status differences; (2) served as a base for development of the trait and factor concept of personality; (3) enabled scientific investigations to be made of problems like the rate of growth of intelligence and the constancy of intelligence quotient over a period of

[3] R. L. Thorndike and Elizabeth Hagen, *Measurement and Evaluation in Psychology and Education,* 3rd ed. (New York: John Wiley & Sons, Inc., 1969), pp. 5–7.

[4] "Goodbye I.Q., Hello EI (Ertl Index)," *Phi Delta Kappan,* Vol. 54 (October, 1972), pp. 89–94.

time; (4) focused attention upon the diagnosis and evaluation of maladjustment; (5) facilitated prediction, classification, and placement of individuals; and (6) resulted in the formulation and publication of a code of ethics to be used as a guide for responsible testing practices.

Influence of the Mental Health Movement Sparked by Clifford Beers' book *A Mind That Found Itself* (the story of his experiences, observations, and recovery during three years in mental hospitals), a group of people led by Beers organized the Connecticut Society for Mental Hygiene (1908). This marked the beginning of the organized mental health movement in America. Beers also supplied the leadership for the formation (1909) of the National Committee for Mental Hygiene (now the National Association for Mental Health). This association has been responsible for or contributed to significant innovations in legislative reform, aftercare, and free clinics for the mentally ill. Most assuredly, it has reduced public apathy and resistance to the discussion of mental illness and mental health. Beginning as a humanitarian program designed to ameliorate the living conditions of those who had succumbed to serious mental disorders, the Association endeavored to insure humane treatment, adequate living quarters, and intelligent commitment laws. Later, the Association focused upon the study, treatment, and rehabilitation of individuals suffering from less serious mental disorders. Its work and influence have been broad in scope and far-reaching in effect. By calling attention to the need for prevention and early identification and treatment, it has encouraged educators and parents to become more sensitive to the deep insecurities and loss of identity among youth and has thus fostered the initiation of counseling programs in schools and community clinics.

The Psychoanalytic Movement Modern psychotherapy may be said to have had its beginning in the pioneering work of Sigmund Freud toward the close of the last century and at the beginning of the present one. It eventually reached into and affected virtually every area of contemporary life. Freud's psychoanalytic methods and his elaborate theory of the structure of personality and of the causes of mental illness aroused a flurry of interest when he delivered, at the invitation of G. Stanley Hall, a series of five lectures at Clark University from Monday, September 6, 1909, through Friday, September 10, 1909. This was the first official recognition of a young science.

Although Freudian ideas exerted scant influence on the initial emergence of counseling, since educators received little training in psychology, its later influence may be seen in methods of individual diagnosis, evaluation, and treatment. Freud was the first to assert that the sexual development of the individual follows a pattern as definite and predictable as that of other aspects of the individual's life. Psychoanalysis contributed to the growth of counseling in that it offered a formulation of personality which had heuristic value and stressed the motivated character of all behavior. Psychoanalytic concepts permeate the whole of psychology, which is the basis of counselor education.

Compulsory Education After 1880, when the legal status of the high school as a free public institution became established, school enrollments increased substantially. As the number of students increased, the curriculum was changed to meet the needs, interests, and abilities of a heterogeneous population. The effect was reciprocal, for the enriched and broadened curriculum was not only a result of increased enrollment, but also a cause of retaining still more pupils.

Compulsory school attendance, improved child labor laws, and expanded curricula brought thousands of young people into school who sometimes had no desire to be there and few clear ideas of why they were there or what they wanted. School administrators soon saw that individual, personal attention was needed to help each individual marshal his assets to find his way through the school and the complex environment outside it.

Client-Centered Therapy In its early history clinical psychology was deeply committed to mental testing and personality evaluation. It showed little interest in psychotherapy until the 1930's. Carl Rogers' book *Counseling and Psychotherapy* (1942) marked an ideological turning point from psychometrics to therapy. Client-centered counseling placed little stress on diagnosis and testing but emphasized the quality of the interpersonal relationship. Through the leadership, research, and publications of Carl Rogers and others the highly directive, paternalistic methods and authoritarian attitudes characterizing early counseling efforts were modified. Super sums up the influence of client-centered therapy in these words:

> It has made vocational counselors, whether psychologists or otherwise, more aware of the unity of personality, of the fact that one counsels people rather than problems, of the fact that problems of adjustment in one aspect of living have effects on other aspects of life, and of the complexity of the processes of counseling concerning any type of individual adjustment, whether in the field of occupation, of group living, or of personal values. It has, perhaps even more importantly, provided counselors of all types with a better understanding of counseling processes and techniques.[5]

Depression and War The spectacular stock market crash of 1929 was followed by a rapid deterioration of virtually every branch of economic activity. Large-scale unemployment (resulting in deterioration of morale, loss of trade skills, etc.) led to the establishment (Wagner-Peyser Act, 1933) of the United States Employment Service to provide testing, counseling, and placement services to workers. When the United States entered the Second World War, military and civilian manpower problems became acute. Selection, training, and placement procedures were refined as a result of military and civilian research efforts. Products of these efforts were the Army General Classification Test (1941) and the U.S. Employment Service General Aptitude Test Battery (1945). Counseling centers were established in the Veterans Administration to render service to disabled veterans (Public Law 16) and later to all veterans (Public Laws 346, 895, 550, and 89-358). The civil service position of Counseling Psychologist was established in 1952, and in 1954 the Office of Vocational Rehabilitation was created and began administration of training contracts to prepare vocational rehabilitation counselors. In short, depression and war influenced the development of counseling by highlighting the critical need for counselors and, through the urgency it generated, the need to refine and improve psychometric instruments, counseling, and placement methods.

[5] Super, *op. cit.*, p. 4.

Federal Government Support The federal government, principally through the Departments of Labor and of Health, Education, and Welfare, has been influential in the development of counseling. The George-Reed (1929), George-Ellzy (1934), George-Deen (1936), and George-Barden (1946) acts, all dealing with vocational education, paved the way for establishing guidance divisions within state departments of education. In 1938 the U.S. Office of Education created the Occupational Information and Guidance Services Bureau with Harry Jager as director. Its publications and research efforts consistently stressed the need for school counselors and the kinds of services they provide.

Counseling, in settings ranging through rehabilitation centers, community agencies, veterans agencies, mental health centers, schools, and colleges, has received support from at least 17 federal acts. Substantial financial assistance was given for preparing counselors and employing them through the National Defense Education Act of 1958 and its subsequent extensions. This was the source of much stimulation to school counseling.

Summary Various social, economic, educational, and psychological forces have encouraged and facilitated the growth of counseling although the exact influence of each of these factors is not easy to determine. Certainly its present status, the expectations held for it, the criticisms made of it, its purpose, and many other characteristics may be traced back to the ideas, ideals, and patterns inherent in these forces.

INFLUENTIAL INDIVIDUALS

The entire history of modern-day counseling in the United States extends over about six decades. The field includes workers whose orientations and efforts subdivide into a dozen different occupations. Often questions are raised in graduate counseling courses as to which individuals have spurred counseling the most. Material previously cited in this chapter clearly shows that many have contributed. Any attempt to identify those who were most influential necessarily requires personal judgment. Nevertheless, the authors have selected some men whose contributions have current impact because of their research, writings, or personal persuasiveness. It is to be hoped that this presentation will be helpful in updating and balancing the historical perspective of a dynamic and rapidly growing field of endeavor.

Some of those named have worked on the periphery of the counseling movement; that is, they are not or have not been counselors or psychologists as such. In the authors' judgment, however, all of the following individuals have been highly influential in the development of counseling.

Frank Parsons (1854–1908) Parsons is cited for his originating and pioneering work in vocational guidance and for his formulation of man-job congruence. E. G. Williamson credits Frank Parsons, William Rainey Harper, and Lightner Witmer as innovators in the use of modern techniques and concepts of counseling. He selects Harper as the one who originated a concept of counseling recognizable to current practitioners.[6]

Sigmund Freud (1856–1939) Freudian psychoanalysis constituted a revolutionary movement in treating emotional illness. It led to scientific investigation of unresolved, unconscious conflicts. Freud's many contributions to present-day counseling practices include the case history approach, free association, defense mechanisms, transference, and interpretation. Clinical psychology in the 1930's and 1940's was particularly affected by Freud, as was indeed the entire field of psychology, psychiatry, and social work.

E. G. Williamson (1900 –) Williamson's *How to Counsel Students* (1939) and *Counseling Adolescents* (1950) were particularly influential in describing counseling based upon a trait and factor approach to the study and understanding of personality. The work of early counselors, especially school counselors, was predicated upon the concepts and practices described by Williamson.

Carl Rogers (1902 –) Reference has already been made to Rogers' contributions. Through his writings — particularly *Counseling and Psychotherapy* (1942), *Client-Centered Therapy* (1951), and *On Becoming a Person* (1961) — research literature, and persuasive presentations, Rogers has had a profound impact upon counseling. He stimulated an examination of counseling assumptions and processes. His self-theory-based approach to personality and counseling provided an enduring focus. He has conducted and encouraged much research in counseling processes, practices, and outcomes and has heavily emphasized the importance of the counselor as a person, particularly with respect to the influence of the counselor's attitudes upon the counselee. He has extended man's basic knowledge of how to deal with interpersonal conflict and has identified and stressed the skills and attitudes necessary to advance human relationships. More recently, he has conducted and described intensive group experiences in ways that many find acceptable and useful.

Donald G. Paterson (1892–1961) Paterson is recognized for his work in student appraisal, diagnosis, and conceptualization of personnel services. He

[6] E. G. Williamson, *Vocational Counseling* (New York: McGraw-Hill Book Co., Inc., 1965), pp. 72–89.

was instrumental in initiating tests of mechanical aptitudes, developing diagnostic services based upon adaptations of social casework methods, initiating occupational ability profiles, predicting scholastic success, and identifying the services contained in a comprehensive personnel program. Paterson was particularly instrumental in advancing vocational counseling.

C. Gilbert Wrenn (1902–) Wrenn's contributions to the field of counseling have been made in numerous ways: provocative journal articles and books, elective and appointed offices and committee assignments in the American Personnel and Guidance Association and the American Psychological Association, consultant activities with the Department of Labor and the Office of Education, to cite but a few. In our judgement, his major influence has been in effectively articulating a centralist position in counseling. He has been able to bring unity and order to the many diversities in counseling theory and practice. By identifying common threads among unlike positions and by abstracting pertinent, usable ideas and practices, Wrenn has created a model which has much meaning for many counseling practitioners. His imaginatively crafted *Counselor in a Changing World* made meaningful the facts that the counselor's world is changing and that counselors need to understand change, the counseling process, and themselves. Further, through the book he has advanced the general public's understanding of counseling and counselors.

Donald E. Super (1910–) Super's multiple contributions include his perceptive evaluation of current developments in the field and his monumental work in vocational testing and appraisal. Perhaps most important, in our judgment, are his constructive efforts to formulate career choice theory which have had an enduring impact upon the ways counselors think about vocational decision-making situations. In addition, his research efforts in vocational choice development have stimulated research by others as well as providing a modern scientific approach to applying theoretical formulations.

John W. M. Rothney (1906 –) Rothney has long served the field as an able, provocative, yet constructive critic of tests and testing practices. His numerous, comprehensive studies of superior students were a major undertaking. Most notable, however, has been his longitudinal study of differences among counseled and uncounseled high school students.

James B. Conant (1893 –) It is our opinion that Conant's recommendations[7] on counselor-student ratio and the employment of counselors in schools strongly affected school superintendents and board of education members. Conant's books on the schools have been widely read and have provoked much public discussion. Assuredly, his recommendations helped many school counselors to make gains in staffing programs.

Harold McCully (1906–1965) and Ralph Bedell (1904 –) These two men directed the NDEA Counseling and Guidance Institutes for the U.S. Office of Education and were instrumental in advancing the education of counselors. In our view the emphasis (starting in the early 1960's) upon self-examination in counselor education was facilitated by their leadership efforts. Their insistence upon supervised counseling practice in counselor education programs advanced the quality of preparation.

Recent contributors During the past five years several individuals have emerged who have made promising contributions to counseling through research:

1. *John D. Krumboltz* and *Carl E. Thoresen.* These two individuals (independently and collectively) have conducted research in the efficacy of behavioral counseling and written extensively about its application.
2. *Robert R. Carkhuff* and *Charles B. Truax.* Based upon counseling components identified as essential

[7] James B. Conant, *The American High School Today* (New York: McGraw-Hill Book Co., Inc., 1959).

by Carl Rogers, Carkhuff and Truax (collectively and independently) have investigated unconditional positive regard, empathy, warmth, and concreteness as facilitating conditions in counseling. They have developed approaches to measure the extent to which these facilitating conditions are provided in counseling and have designed training programs to teach these conditions not only to counselors but also to paraprofessionals.

3. *Norman Kagan.* Kagan inventively used video taping in his research on counseling behaviors. The Interpersonal Recall studies represented important contributions to research on counseling and the training of counselors.

4. *Jules Zimmer.* Zimmer has devoted his research efforts to the detailed study of the communication process in counseling. His work gives promise of improved rigor and has stimulated others to examine counselor-client communications, styles, and effect.

5. *George Gazda* and *Merle Ohlsen.* Individually, each has contributed through his extensive writings about group procedures in counseling.

Others The individuals cited above are only a sample of those who have influenced the development of counseling. There are many others: Dugald Arbuckle, Nicholas Hobbs, Robert Hoppock, Abraham Maslow, C. H. Patterson, H. J. Peters, Edward Roeber, Leona Tyler, to cite but a few. The list would be long and space inadequate to do justice to them.

Current Status of Counseling

The rate of counseling development has not followed a steady upward curve. Counseling at present justifies being termed *emergent,* and is marked by both continuity and discontinuity. It spurts ahead, then settles down to a slow steady pace. New imbalances induce a new burst of growth. At this time little is really known about why development is sometimes so vigorous and dynamic and sometimes so sluggish.

The years since 1958 have been a period of rapid advancement for counseling. The 1960's were particularly years of rapid growth. However, the early 1970's were a time of some retrenchment, particularly in numbers of school counselors employed. The following points convey some ideas about the current status of counseling and counseling personnel.

1. *Professional associations.* It should be noted that professional associations have attracted and held an unprecedented number of members. Simultaneously, many members of the major association for counselors — the American Personnel and Guidance Association — questioned whether the Association was delivering the kind of services needed and desired by its membership. Other members urged that APGA take a more activist position on some of the current social, political, and professional problems that confront counselors as professionals and as citizens. Still others believed that the governance of APGA should be restructured to provide better representation to members and to establish some measure of continuity among elected officers. In summary, change marks the current status of professional associations for counselors. While membership continues to increase, changes have taken place in what members expect of their association in respect to governance, conventions, and delivery of services.

2. *Professional journals and publications.* A more complete account of this topic is given in the next section. It is sufficient to say here that professional journals designed for counselors are thriving. Not only has the number of journals increased but their size has expanded. Moreover, publications other than journals — monographs, digests, newsletters — have increased rapidly. Finally, other media such as films, filmstrips, audio and video tape, records and cassettes are being slowly but increasingly utilized to transmit information about counseling and counselors to the public and to the student.

3. *Public's belief about counselors.* The evidence on the public's belief about counseling is scanty. Dur-

ing the years 1970–1972 some school districts, particularly large city districts such as Chicago and Gary, Indiana, reduced the number of school counselors they employed. In these school districts, financial revenues did not keep pace with rising costs and brought about curtailments among many sectors of the school. On the other hand, the Gallup Poll published in October, 1970 queried a national sample about their attitudes toward counselors. One of the questions asked was "How do you feel about having guidance counselors in the public schools? Do you think they are worth the added cost?" The reaction is described in Table 2.1.

Table 2.1 Public attitudes toward counselors

	National Totals	*No children in school*	*Public school parents*	*High school juniors and seniors*
Yes, worth it	73%	69%	79%	83%
No, not worth it	16	17	14	16
No opinion	1	14	7	1

SOURCE: George Gallup, "The Public's Attitude Toward the Public Schools," *Phi Delta Kappan*, Vol. LII (October, 1970). By permission of George Gallup and *Phi Delta Kappan*

Parochial school parents had attitudes similar to public school parents: 79 per cent reported that counselors were worth the extra cost; 12 per cent believed they were not and nine per cent had no opinion. Many would interpret this poll data as suggesting that the public is highly interested in counseling services.

4. *Prestige of counselors.* The prestige attached to an occupation presumably has an impact, not only upon whether individuals enter and continue in it, but also upon how well they function within the institution that employs them. Granger's study of the prestige rankings of individuals in psychological professions placed school counselors near the bottom (among 20 specialties) of the psychologist's hierarchy.[8] More recently, Granger's questionnaire was modified by Kondrasuk[9] and given to 292 graduate students in the Department of Psychology, University of Minnesota. High school counselors were ranked above psychometrists and employment interviewers but below the other 16 job titles including vocational rehabilitation counselor, school psychologist, social psychologist, clinical psychologist, etc. Kondrasuk points out that research on occupational prestige of jobs is viewed as repugnant by many psychologists who believe it to be a deterrent to building a profession and especially harmful to low-ranking areas such as school counselors.

When school counselors are compared to educational professionals other than psychologists, their prestige rankings differ dramatically. Moses and Delaney, studying the hierarchy of common school occupations, reported counselors ranked sixth among 18 relatively distinct positions.[10] They were placed below teachers, but above school psychologists. Scott and Cherlin asked students in graduate courses in guidance, school administration, and supervision of instruction to rank 14 school occupations. High school counselors ranked eighth (below superintendents, principals, school psychologists, supervisors of instruction, directors of guidance, and departmental chairmen) among the 14 occupations, but above teachers, social workers, librarians, nurses, and head custodians. Scott and Cherlin believe that school counselors are placed consistently near teachers in prestige because of the similarity of salaries and the fact that teaching experience has been required of counselors.[11]

These data indicate that currently the prestige or occupational status of counselors varies according to with whom they are compared and who does the ratings. Counselors rank low on the psycho-

[8] S. G. Granger, "Psychologists' Prestige Rankings of Twenty Psychological Occupations," *Journal of Counseling Psychology*, Vol. 6 (Fall, 1959), pp. 183–188.

[9] John N. Kondrasuk, "Graduate Students' Rankings of Prestige Among Occupations in Psychology," *Journal of Counseling Psychology*, Vol. 18 (March, 1971), pp. 142–146.

[10] H. Moses and D. J. Delaney, "Status of School Personnel," *Journal of the Student Personnel Association for Teacher Education*, Vol. 9 (December, 1971), pp. 41–46.

[11] C. Winfield Scott and Mary M. Cherlin, "Occupational Status of the High School Counselor," *Vocational Guidance Quarterly*, Vol. 20 (September, 1971), pp. 31–38.

logical hierarchy but among school personnel they fare much better. No doubt, the attractiveness of the occupation will improve as the counselor's identity is clarified and his preparation becomes more rigorous.

5. *Counselor practices.* The dyadic relationship is still the most common mode of operation among counselors. The last few years have brought increasingly to the front counselor practices that facilitate career development. During 1972 the U.S. Office of Education sought to implement "career education" so that whenever a student left school he would have requisite employment skills. Counselors have begun to dust off old practices and develop new ones to assist students in vocational development. The current status of counselor practices includes increasing use of group counseling and intensive group experiences to facilitate personal development. Slowly but surely, the use of behavior modification techniques is permeating counselor practices.

6. *Counselor role and function.* This perennial problem is still unresolved. More and more counselors have invested time and effort in defining their role and function. Agreement seems to be increasing that the counselor functions as a counselor to individuals and small groups and as a consultant to others in the institution or agency in which he is employed as well as to others significant in the life of his client.

7. *Numbers and need.* The force of counselors in the United States, Great Britain, and France grows ever larger. While the growth in the United States during 1970–1972 seems to have slowed somewhat, the number of counselors continues to increase. The need as represented in desirable counselor-client ratios continues to be urgent.

8. *Counselor preparation.* As pointed out in Chapter One, some 378 colleges and universities are preparing counselors. Counselor preparation is changing. Today's programs give high priority to supervised counseling practice with individuals and groups, to counseling skill-building laboratories, to the use of simulated materials in classroom activities, and to more intensive treatment of a broader range of counseling theories. Problems persist in the selection of students for programs. Despite the oversupply of school and college teachers and in part because of it, ever-increasing numbers of students are applying for admission to graduate programs in counselor education. The authors' experience is that these candidates are younger, brighter, and better prepared in social sciences than their predecessors of five or ten years ago.

9. *Federal government support.* Since 1967, the amount of financial support categorically earmarked for counselor preparation and employment has declined. While sizeable amounts are available from the Education Professions Development Act, Elementary and Secondary Education Act, and the Vocational Education Act and its later amendments, these funds have shrunk from those provided during the years of the National Defense Education Act of 1958 and its amendments.

The current status of counseling, then, is one of fluidity. Though the years 1970–1972 may be viewed in retrospect as a period when counseling reached a plateau, there is little evidence to justify pessimism about its future. The changes that have taken place do not mean that the future will be settled and inactive. Struggles for power and prestige seem ever-present among counseling practitioners. Differences in opinion exist and will persist among counselors themselves as well as between counselors and other groups. It is highly probable that the process of defining these differences will permit new functions and new specialties to emerge.

The need to communicate more effectively to the public and to other professionals what the counselor is and what he does will require resourceful and able practitioners. Counselors with enthusiasm, confidence, and sensitivity can build upon their calling's fine foundation.

Professional Organizations and Journals

THE APGA

The first national conference on vocational guidance was conducted in Boston in 1910. This was followed in 1912 by a second conference in New

York and in 1913 by the founding of the National Vocational Guidance Association in Grand Rapids, Michigan. Frank M. Leavitt of the University of Chicago served as first president of the Association. In 1924 the National Association of Appointment Secretaries, forerunner of the current American College Personnel Association, was formed.

Several professional organizations (National Vocational Guidance Association, American College Personnel Association, National Association of Guidance Supervisors and Counselor Trainers) merged in 1951 to form the American Personnel and Guidance Association (APGA). Its purposes are stated in its 1973 by-laws:

> The purposes of the American Personnel and Guidance Association are to enhance individual human development by: seeking to advance the scientific discipline of guidance, counseling and personnel work; by conducting and fostering programs of education in the field of guidance, counseling and personnel; by promoting sound guidance, counseling and personnel practices in the interests of society and the individual; by stimulating, promoting and conducting programs of scientific research and of education in the field of guidance, counseling, and personnel work; by publishing scientific, educational, and professional literature; by advancing high standards of professional conduct; by conducting scientific educational and professional meetings and conferences; by informing and educating the general public about the human development profession; by establishing contacts with various organizations for scientific and educational pursuits; and by examining conditions which create barriers to individual development and working to remove them.

Currently, the organization has ten divisions:

American College Personnel Association (ACPA) is the division uniting student personnel workers employed in colleges and universities. The division publishes a journal, *Journal of College Student Personnel,* which concentrates upon student personnel practices and research. An APCA monograph series is also available. Two types of membership are available, general and student.

Association for Counselor Education and Supervision (ACES) is the division for those who are engaged in either the professional preparation or the local and state supervision of counselors. Regional meetings are conducted in addition to the national convention. Its journal, *Counselor Education and Supervision,* is currently published on a quarterly basis. Membership is of two types, regular and associate. Associate membership is available to graduate students.

National Vocational Guidance Association (NVGA) is the division which focuses attention upon work, career development, and vocational guidance practices and procedures. Its journal, *Vocational Guidance Quarterly,* presents current developments and applications of new techniques and procedures. Three types of membership are available. General (nonvoting) membership is for those interested in but not employed in guidance. Associate membership is for those who have a bachelor's degree plus one year of experience in guidance and personnel work. Professional membership is available for those with a bachelor's degree, 30 graduate semester hours in specific areas of training, four years of appropriate experience, and current employment (half-time or more) in guidance and personnel work.

Student Personnel Association for Teacher Education (SPATE) is the division for those engaged primarily in student personnel work in teacher education institutions. A quarterly, *SPATE Journal,* is published.

American School Counselor Association (ASCA) is the division serving school counselors. ASCA publishes the *School Counselor* five times each year, a newsletter, and other publications. Three types of membership are available: *active* for those who are elementary or secondary school counselors, *associate* for those employed in institutions other than elementary or secondary schools with primary responsibility for rendering or supervising elementary or secondary school guidance services, *student* for certified graduate students enrolled half-time or more.

American Rehabilitation Counseling Association (ARCA) is the division for those employed or interested in rehabilitation counseling. Professional and associate memberships are available. It publishes the *Rehabilitation Counseling Bulletin.*

Association for Measurement and Evaluation (AME) is the division available for those who participate or are interested in guidance measurement and evaluation. It publishes the journal *Measurement and Evaluation in Guidance* which appears four times per year.

National Employment Counselors Association (NECA) was formed in 1966. Its purpose is to foster employment counseling, and its membership is composed of people who counsel in the employment setting or who have a related interest in education or research. It publishes the *Journal of Employment Counseling*. Four categories of membership are available. Two of these, student and associate, are nonvoting. The regular and professional members have full organizational privileges.

Association for Non-White Concerns (ANWC) was chartered in April, 1972. Its first president, Samuel Johnson, and his fellow officers have established a newsletter and a journal. The major purpose of this new division, according to its petition for membership, is "to give particular emphasis in the area of charitable and educational activities designed to assist and further the interests of nonwhites by seeking to eliminate prejudice and discrimination, defending human and civil rights secured by law, presenting opinion on controversial issues, and otherwise attempting to lessen the burdens of the United States government, so as to secure equality regarding treatment, advancement, qualification and status of non-white individuals in personnel and guidance work." Three categories of membership are available: regular, associate, and student.

The National Catholic Guidance Conference (NCGC) petition for divisional membership was accepted by the APGA Board of Directors in July, 1973. As this book goes to press the new division is developing mechanisms to serve its members.

The American School Counselors Association contains the largest membership of the APGA divisions. Analysis of the ten divisions shows that some represent professional interests while others reflect functions and settings. An individual holds general membership in the APGA and may belong to one or more divisions depending upon his interests and qualifications. In addition to divisional membership, state branches have been chartered by APGA in most of the 50 states. A state branch in turn charters chapters (regional organizations) and divisions (ACPA, ACES, ASCA, etc.) within the state.

The present APGA governmental structure consists of a Senate, elected from the various divisions and state branches; a Board of Directors, composed of divisional presidents and eight branch representatives plus the APGA president, president-elect, past president, and the APGA executive director and treasurer (ex officio); and an Executive Committee composed of the APGA president, past president, president-elect, two members of the Board of Directors and treasurer and executive director (ex officio). APGA government is complex, unwieldy, and overburdensome. Each division has a somewhat parallel governmental structure and the inevitable overlap between the divisions and the APGA's central government, coupled with a network of standing and ad hoc committees appointed to investigate basic professional issues or to accomplish certain goals, hinders the organization's functioning.

The APGA conducts a placement service at its national convention and publishes a *Placement Service Bulletin* seven times a year, listing positions open in the field of guidance and personnel work and publicizing APGA members' availability for employment. The International Association of Counseling Services, an affiliate of APGA, publishes a list of counseling agencies which meet the professional standards established by the Association. A directory gives address, office hours, fees, clientele served, and professional staff of each agency.

The APGA has long been involved in securing federal legislation to provide financial support for the preparation and employment of counselors. It has actively sought to interpret counseling, guidance, and student personnel work to the public and to other professional organizations.

THE APA DIVISION OF COUNSELING PSYCHOLOGY

The Division of Counseling Psychology (Division 17) of the American Psychological Association is part of another association which claims the professional loyalty of counselors. Division 17 exists to give recognition to the specialized interests of psychologists concerned with counseling. After becoming an APA member, and if he meets additional specialized requirements, an individual may join the Division of Counseling Psychology, originally called the Division of Counseling and Guidance but renamed in 1953. Throughout the years, the Division has issued policy studies of its specialty and conducted research on the expectations, characteristics, and attitudes of its members. It also sponsors symposia at conventions as well as local and regional discussions. By the early 1970's, Division 17, with over 2,000 fellows, members, and associates on its membership roles, was one of the larger divisions of the American Psychological Association.

JOURNALS

Today's counselor must examine a veritable outpouring of professional literature. In addition to the journals generic to counseling, he must be conversant with literature from related, sometimes external, areas. A few of the journals designed specifically for counselors which students will find helpful in their years of preparation are described here:

1. The *Personnel and Guidance Journal* is published 10 times a year by the APGA. Its current editor is Leo Goldman, Professor of Education, City College of New York, who changed its format when he became editor. Its highly readable issues contain discursive statements on issues, theories, and practices. Each issue usually contains a book review section, letters to the editor, an editorial page, a section on practices entitled "In the Field," and seven or eight articles.

2. The *Journal of Counseling Psychology* appears six times a year. Published for its first 13 years by the group of psychologists who initiated it, it came under the sponsorship of the American Psychological Association in January, 1967. The *Journal* was started in 1954 by a corporation composed of 26 members (including Hugh Bell, Irwin Berg, Arthur Brayfield, Milton Hahn, Carl Rogers, Francis Robinson, Harold Seashore, Donald Super, and Gilbert Wrenn – the latter its editor for the first 10 years). The current editor is Ralph Berdie, Professor of Psychology, University of Minnesota. It is a publication designed to present research on counseling theory and practices. Each issue usually contains 18 to 20 articles, a test review section, and a book review section. An interesting history of the *Journal* has recently been written by its first editor.[12]

3. The *Vocational Guidance Quarterly* is published by the National Vocational Guidance Association, a division of the APGA. Its present editor is Daniel Sinick, Professor of Education, George Washington University. Its articles interpret the role of work in American society as well as describe vocational guidance developments, ideas, and applications of new techniques and procedures. Each issue contains 12 to 15 articles, a "Briefing the Journals" section, and a book review section.

4. *The School Counselor* is a publication issued five times a year by the American School Counselor Association. Its editor is Barbara G. Peterson, University of Santa Clara. It includes articles on school counseling practices and research, book reviews, and a letters to the editor section.

5. The *Journal of College Student Personnel* is published six times a year by the American College Personnel Association and is edited by Albert B. Hood, University of Iowa. It focuses primarily upon administration, services, and research in the relatively broad area of college student personnel work.

6. *Educational and Psychological Measurement* is a privately published journal under the editorship of G. Frederick Kuder that appears four times a year. It contains articles on measurement problems and

[12] C. Gilbert Wrenn, "Birth and Early Childhood of a Journal," *Journal of Counseling Psychology*, Vol. 13 (Winter, 1966), pp. 485–488.

individual differences, research reports on the development and use of tests in education, industry, and government, descriptions of testing programs, miscellaneous notes on measurement, and a book review section.

Other important professional journals include the *Journal of Consulting and Clinical Psychology, Counselor Education and Supervision,* the *Journal of Educational Psychology,* the *American Psychologist,* the *Journal of Abnormal Psychology,* and the *Review of Educational Research.*

Counselors: Numbers, Need, and Supply

NUMBERS

A precise census of counselors practicing in the United States is almost impossible to obtain. First, the problem of who is to be counted as a "counselor" again arises since the conditions under which a person is classified as a counselor have yet to be determined. Second, some individuals who serve as counselors also serve in other capacities for varying amounts of their time. Translation of the actual allotted share of counseling time into full-time equivalents produces marginal data at best. Third, no single authority exists to recognize counselors. In some settings, e.g., private practice, no legal or administrative authority may exist for recognizing counselors. The authority to confer the title "counselor" is held by many persons, agencies, and organizations. Seemingly, the employer exercises this right. Undoubtedly, the employer's judgment is guided by legislative, regulatory, and policy stipulations imposed upon institutional settings. But the title is often abused: people are called "counselors" who have not been prepared as such. Indeed, the title may at times be self-conferred.

Periodically, individuals, professional organizations, and federal government agencies have estimated the number of counselors working in the United States. Van Hoose, for example, has conducted three surveys of the number of counselors employed in elementary schools. He and his associate reported that during 1970–1971, some 7,982 counselors were employed in the 50 states, the District of Columbia and the Virgin Islands. Of this number, 78 per cent were employed full-time.[13] Based upon previous surveys of elementary school counselors, Van Hoose and Carlson concluded that counselors increased by approximately 1,000 per year in elementary schools.

It was observed in Chapter One that approximately 80,000 counselors are at work in America. The numbers of counselors believed employed, classified by various settings, are presented in Table 2.2. For many reasons these numbers represent only best estimates made by many people in the profession. Previously, the Guidance and Personnel Services Branch of the U.S. Office of Education was a reliable source of information about the supply of counselors, particularly school counselors. However, the branch was discontinued in 1970 and this source no longer exists to provide such data. However, Metz and his associates of the National Center for Educational Statistics, Department of Health, Education, and Welfare reported

Table 2.2 Number of counselors by setting, 1970

Setting	*Estimated number (full-time equivalent)*
Adult centers, pastoral, community and private practice	2,000
Veterans Administration services	1,000
State employment services	6,000
Rehabilitation counselors	13,000
Colleges and universities	5,000
Junior and community colleges	1,500
Technical institutes, vocational schools	1,000
High schools	43,200
Elementary schools	9,000

SOURCE: Based on data in the 1972–1973 *Occupational Outlook Handbook* and estimates by central office staff in the American Personnel and Guidance Association.

[13] William H. Van Hoose and Jon Carlson, "Counselors in the Elementary School: 1970–1971," *Personnel and Guidance Journal,* Vol. 50 (April, 1972), pp. 679–682.

66,000 public school counselors employed in the spring of 1970.[14]

Secondary school counselors made dramatic gains in numbers during the 1960's. Table 2.3 shows the rapid increase in their numbers and the corollary decrease in counselor-pupil ratios. In Table 2.3, "guidance personnel" includes school counselors and directors or supervisors of guidance. Since 1960, there has been approximately a 10 per cent annual increase in public secondary school counselors.

NEED

The critical shortage of counselors during the 1960's came at a time when demands for them were exceptionally high. Several reasons can be advanced for the high demand during that time: (1) Educational enrollment rose at all levels and brought with it a commitment for additional personnel to insure quality education. (2) The public called for more and more counseling services because it has realized it lives in a progressively more complex society. (3) Federal government financial support stimulated counselor employment in a variety of educational and noneducational agencies. (4) Increased school consolidation generally provided better school budgets enabling schools to employ counselors. (5) More and more parents sent their children to college, with school counselors inevitably seen as assisting in the attainment of that objective. (6) Educators and professional organizations supported and publicized the need for an adequate ratio of counselors to counselees. (7) Counseling services were extended to elementary schools, junior colleges, and higher educational institutions, and more intensive attention was given to staffing community counseling centers.

Table 2.3 Number of secondary school guidance personnel employed and counselor-pupil ratio, 1958–1970

Year	*Total full-time equivalents*	*Counselor-pupil ratios*
1958–59	12,000	1–960
1962–63	27,180	1–530
1966-67	36,200	1–470
1970–71	43,200	1–460

SOURCE: Based on data from U.S. Office of Education, personal communications from Dr. Frank Sievers and from central office staff members, American Personnel and Guidance Association.

Estimates of the number of counselors needed now and in the future (1) are based upon attaining some ratio of counselors to counselees deemed necessary or desirable to provide adequate counseling service, (2) normally reflect only the supply needed for traditional or existing settings, and (3) often fail to take into account attrition rates. Many projections are based upon one full-time counselor for 600 pupils in elementary schools, one full-time counselor for 300 pupils in secondary schools, and one full-time counselor for 750 or 1,000 students in junior colleges, four-year colleges, and universities.

Many counseling practitioners take issue with the ratios used in estimating the need for counselors. They question, for example, the adequacy of a ratio of one full-time counselor to 600 elementary school pupils or to 1,000 college students. Many believe that while some fixed ratio of clients to a full-time counselor is desirable and useful, other factors have to be taken into account such as the characteristics of the setting and the community being served. To replace a counselor-pupil ratio, Hitchcock recommended one full-time counselor for not more than seven full-time teachers in elementary and secondary schools, junior colleges, colleges, and universities. He proposed that in noneducational settings the number of counselors be based upon the population to be served. For example, to provide counseling services for the labor force he suggested (upon recommendation by John F. McGowan) that 50 per cent of the individuals 22 years of age and younger need counseling, 10 per cent of those from 22 to 44, and 25 per cent of

[14] A. Stafford Metz, Leslie J. Silverman, Dyckman W. Vermilye, and P. J. McDonough, *Counselors in Public Schools Spring 1970* (Washington, D.C.: U.S. Government Printing Office, 1973), p. 1.

Table 2.4 Earned degrees in counseling

Year	COUNSELING AND GUIDANCE				REHABILITATION COUNSELOR TRAINING			
	Master's		*Doctorate*		*Master's*		*Doctorate*	
	Men	*Women*	*Men*	*Women*	*Men*	*Women*	*Men*	*Women*
1970–71	6,614	6,800	440	116	—	—	—	—
1969–70	5,434	5,549	411	121	342	261	33	3
1968–69	4,760	4,651	330	71	319	275	24	1
1967–68	4,376	4,049	290	70	220	164	30	9
1966–67	3,725	3,276	227	73	159	91	7	1
1965–66	3,125	2,756	232	54	91	50	1	0
1964–65	2,718	2,258	201	36	81	34	4	3
1963–64	2,501	2,078	189	41	—	—	—	—

SOURCE: *Earned Degrees Conferred.* Washington, D.C.: U.S. Department of Health, Education and Welfare (annual publication).

those aged 45 years and older. Dropouts and the handicapped will need even more help.[15]

An important factor to be borne in mind is that estimates of the need for counselors are based upon attaining a ratio desired by the profession of counselors to students. Whether schools and communities, individually and collectively, agree with the profession's judgment and try to attain that ratio is seriously open to question. Actual demands (i.e., actual job openings) for counselors are often markedly different from demands based upon desirable ratios established by professional groups.

The Bureau of Labor Statistics estimated that 71,000 counselors were employed in 1968 and projected that 107,000 counselors would be required in 1980. Despite the fact that this represents a 49.8 per cent change in some 12 years, the supply is estimated to be below requirements.[16] The manpower requirements for school counselors are projected to increase 40 per cent between 1968 and 1980. This represents a slower annual rate of growth, 3.2 per cent, than the 1961 to 1968 period when employed school counselors increased annually by about 6 per cent.

[15] Arthur A. Hitchcock, "Counselors: Supply, Demand and Need," in John F. McGowan (ed.), *Counselor Development in American Society* (Washington: U.S. Department of Labor and U.S. Office of Education, June, 1965), p. 87.

[16] Bureau of Labor Statistics, *Bulletin 1676,* Washington, D.C.: Department of Labor, 1970, p. 1.

SUPPLY

The supply of counselors is dependent upon graduate degree production. This production has increased by about 1,000 per year. Table 2.4 presents data on master's and doctorate degrees awarded in "counseling and guidance" and in "rehabilitation counselor training". Not included in this table are the numbers of master's and doctorate degrees awarded in rehabilitation counseling in psychology or the doctorates awarded in counseling psychology.

Factors Affecting Counselor Supply and Demand

The fact that many variables interact to influence the supply and demand for counselors makes it difficult if not impossible to gauge the impact of each separately. These factors are identified and discussed in this section.

COUNSELOR PREPARATION

The supply of counselors available obviously depends upon how many complete preparation. Approximately 11,000 counselors currently (1972–1973) are prepared annually at the master's degree level. It should be recognized that present professional standards for secondary school counselors specify two years of graduate education. While some 378 institutions offer counselor preparation, most of them do not at present provide two graduate years of counselor education.

Hilsinger reported that a direct relationship exists between the number of counselors who enter the field and the number of counselor educators available to prepare them. Based upon an examination of 50 counselor education programs, the ratio of new counselors to counselor educators was seven to one. Some 1,011 counselor educators were available (not all of them full-time) in 1964. Hilsinger suggests that having more counselor educators would increase the number of new counselors available.[17]

Some counselor educators have proposed that financial support available from the U.S. Office of Education and other federal sources be used to strengthen some of the less productive counselor education institutions. Of the 378 institutions offering such preparation, probably only 75 to 100 have programs adequate to meet the minimally acceptable professional standards of content, staff, and resources. Consequently, if "weaker" institutions could be reinforced in quality and quantity (including students and counselor educators), the supply of counselors would be increased.

ATTRITION

Loss of counselors occurs in three major ways: (1) After preparation some do not enter the field. (2) Experienced counselors leave the field because they accept administrative assignments or return to teaching, etc. (3) Retirements and deaths remove some. Reliable data are not available to document the exact loss for any one of these reasons. The U.S. Office of Education reported a 5 per cent attrition rate among individuals who completed academic year NDEA Counseling and Guidance Institutes. But data from institute program participants are probably misleading since nationwide there is a higher loss of counselors who, after completing preparation, do not enter the field. Many counselors report that in their school systems there are individuals who have a master's degree with major concentration in counseling but who have no desire to leave teaching assignments.

Annual attrition among teachers exceeds 20 per cent. Estimates of annual attrition among counselors vary from 15 per cent for employment service counselors to 9 per cent among rehabilitation counselors. The Bureau of Labor Statistics estimates attrition among school counselors at 8–10 per cent and that, during the period 1968 to 1980, some 23,000 school counselors will be needed to replace those who die, retire, or leave the field for some reason.

SALARIES

The authors believe that many male counselors are forced out of counseling and into administrative positions by economic necessity. Some alert school administrators have attempted to remedy this situation by paying counselors increments (from $300 to $900) above teacher salary schedules. Others give extended contracts (11 or 12 months) rather than the usual academic year contracts (9 or 10 months).

Even where salary schedules exist, salaries are affected by supply and demand. When demands for counselors are high, salary is often used to attract competent counselors. While salary is only one of many factors which bear upon recruiting and retaining able people, it is an extremely important one. The prestige attached to a position is also partially a function of salary. According to the American School Counselors Association, $9,000 was the average annual salary of school counselors in 1970–1971.

WORKING CONDITIONS

In far too many situations, counselors are expected to practice in inadequate physical facilities. Moreover, most counseling staffs (equally true of other school staffs) are not given adequate secretarial and clerical assistance. Finally, counseling – the function for which counselors are presumably em-

[17] Roderick A. Hilsinger, "Projections of Counselor Supply and Demand in Elementary, Secondary and Higher Education," paper presented at the meeting of NDEA Counseling and Guidance Institute Directors, Chicago, Illinois, April 7–10, 1965.

ployed — is often usurped by quasi-administrative tasks and demands. The net effect of these poor working conditions is to discourage some competent counselors and cause them to seek employment elsewhere.

Current Criticisms

This chapter has, it is hoped, enabled the reader to gain a historical perspective of counseling, but it is incomplete without an understanding of the persistent and pervasive criticisms leveled against counseling and its practitioners. Locating the criticisms in a particular time period is extremely difficult, simply because most of them represent issues that cannot be satisfactorily resolved or that, if laid to rest at one time, tend to reemerge at another. Some charges have their roots in fundamental attitudes about the nature of man. Others appear to be related to difficulties involved in altering the status quo or introducing innovations. Still others derive from scientifically based thinking or expert judgment within the field of counseling and related disciplines.

The criticisms considered in this section are highly interrelated. They can be separated only for discussion purposes. The knowledgeable critic uses them all, directly or implicitly, in either their outright or disguised forms. The knowledgeable practitioner should be prepared to cope with these charges as well as others in a manner which honors the critic's position yet clearly defends viable alternatives.

First, it can be said that the utility of counseling cannot be demonstrated. It must be recognized at the outset that questioning the efficacy of counseling and other helping relationships is always legitimate. It is a challenge that should be raised not only by critics but equally often by counseling practitioners.

This particular criticism appears to stem from three major sources. One source is that group which is predisposed philosophically to regard the helping of others as inappropriate. Their beliefs require them to view the need for or the provision of personal help as a sign of weakness and character deficiency.

A second source is those who have tried counseling in some form and emerged disgruntled and unsatisfied. The causes of such experience-based beliefs are undoubtedly complex. Certainly contributing to this attitude would be such factors as unrealistic initial expectations, counselor incompetence, and anxiety and defensiveness found among clients who have attempted to modify their life situations and were unable to do so.

A third source, and in some ways the most damning, is the findings of practitioners themselves. In this instance, the question of the utility of counseling is posed by the professional about his own activities in a systematic attempt to evaluate his and others' results. If the relatively limited number of studies of the outcomes of counseling and psychotherapy are taken at face value, the results are discouraging to the practitioner and tend to support the critics. This criticism, the evidence supporting it, and the problems inherent in outcome research will be discussed in greater detail in Chapter Seventeen.

A second criticism is that counseling fosters in its recipients a "play it safe" approach to life. Vocational counselors, particularly, are sometimes charged with encouraging their clients to enter safe, secure occupations. Often this criticism is coupled with another: that counseling leads to conformity despite its avowed concern with the uniqueness of the individual and that it tends to discourage high-risk ventures. It is sometimes true that activities which involve a gamble, whether economic or personal, may be abandoned when a person examines them carefully. A rational, studied approach often does encourage caution. In addition, the very evidence used by counselors which may dissuade the individual from risking himself often rests on shaky grounds (e.g., test results from instruments of doubtful utility). However, the alternative seems to be action by impulse, which may pay high dividends but which may also result in personal disaster.

The position of counseling in regard to this criticism is obvious. Decision making is required and since man strives to be rational, choices are best made thoughtfully and with full awareness of all factors involved. In the area of choice making in particular, counselors must realize how their personal values may influence client change. More specifically, the counselor's own needs for safety and security should not be the basis for discouraging his clients' undertakings.

The third criticism, closely related to the second, is that counselors deceive themselves and others by talking about freedom of choice but actually practice a deterministic psychology. Prior experience, early life influences by others, and available opportunities all help determine the current life of the individual. For example, it would seem obvious that a decision to enter a specific school curriculum at a relatively early age automatically limits the choices and opportunities available later on. Life itself is in many ways deterministic, each step affecting the direction of the next one. If, through counseling, an individual is better able to perceive the alternative routes ahead, at least he participates actively in the determinism. The counselor's function is to provide the information about opportunities and to assist the client to gain self-knowledge which permits him to choose appropriately among alternatives. Obviously, the counselor must accept the fact that whether he wishes it or not he occupies an influential position in decisions made by those he serves.

A fourth criticism is that counseling does not represent a discipline in and of itself. This charge seems a straw man, and it is applicable to many if not all fields which attempt to assist others. Outside the rarefied atmosphere of academic life, few if any "disciplines" exist, especially if the term is used to indicate a specific body of knowledge. In most fields practitioners draw heavily upon bits and pieces of many disciplines. The counselor's subject matter is man himself and, beyond this, man in relation to other men and the environment they share. Hence, virtually any knowledge is of value in helping another in his struggle to cope with life's problems. Although some kinds of knowledge are undoubtedly more valuable than others, the intent here is to underscore the difficulty of confining counselor preparation to a narrow field which is then labeled a "discipline." The general area of knowledge encompassed by the behavioral and life sciences represents the base for the preparation of counselors. It includes psychology, sociology, biology, anthropology, economics, and political science.

A fifth criticism, directly related to the previous one, is that counselors are inadequately prepared to perform the tasks assigned them. If, as pointed out above, the domain of counselors is man, preparation will always be inadequate. Certainly it must continue beyond the formal preparation period. The whole issue becomes confounded when one considers the variety of personnel and situational demands in the field. As described in Chapter One, many of the helping professions overlap considerably while at the same time varying in the specificity of tasks from setting to setting. There is little argument about the tasks of the school physician because his activities within the school are clearly defined and limited to his professional competences. At present the school counselor remains many things to many people and sometimes nothing to some. To level the charge of inadequate preparation without adequate agreement regarding job expectancies seems the height of presumption. If a counselor is one who counsels (as indicated in the first chapter of this volume), the required preparation for his task seems relatively clear. Unfortunately today's school counselor, somewhat like the school's all-purpose room, has a multiplicity of functions but simultaneously is inadequate for any specific activity. One solution to this paradox lies in a specific definition of role and function within the setting accompanied by increased specialization of personnel where the setting requires diverse kinds of activities.

A sixth criticism is that counseling is extended only to selected subpopulations rather than provided for all. Counselors have been charged with giving preferential attention to such groups as the college bound, disruptive students, etc. In theory at least, counseling is available to all students; undoubtedly in practice it is available to all in only some situations. However, in certain settings it may be quite legitimate to focus attention upon specific subgroups. For example, potential dropouts may become a focal point if the need is great and if the individuals responsible have the integrity to admit and defend a restricted practice. It should be kept in mind that restricting services to a specific group must be based upon a thorough demonstration of need and should be subject to continuous review.

A seventh criticism is that counseling practitioners pamper their clients. The counselor who exhibits warmth and understanding is sometimes called "soft" and overindulgent. His acceptance of the individual is interpreted as sanctioning any form of behavior. This criticism usually comes from people who find it difficult to separate the individual from his actions. Most counselors not only are predisposed to believe, but during training are thoroughly steeped in, the credo that the individual's worth is independent of his actions and behavior. To label this basic attitude toward human beings mollycoddling is to question the integrity of a group whose ultimate goal is to assist the individual to cope constructively rather than destructively with his problems. Unquestionably the counselor is less concerned with a specific behavioral act than with the motivation behind it and its potentially harmful consequences to the individual and ultimately to society. No counselor need feel constrained to apologize for his acceptance of the worth of an individual.

An eighth criticism is that counseling is an unwarranted invasion of privacy. The right to privacy — exemption of one's intimate affairs, characteristics, books, papers from the scrutiny of others — is fundamental. This kind of criticism assumes that individuals can have counseling imposed upon them, an extremely unlikely circumstance. It is questionable that any counselor can successfully exceed the limitations set by the counselee himself in the relationship. Even if the counselee does not seek assistance voluntarily, in reality he controls the content of and places restraints on the interaction. Even in the most extreme example, where the client is very young, naïve, or psychologically highly vulnerable, built-in safeguards exist in codes of ethics and institutional checks which make it difficult for a counselor to engage in a "seduction of the innocent." Every counselor has a primary obligation to respect the integrity of those with whom he works.

Finally, counseling practitioners are criticized for overreliance on professional jargon in their communications with others. The implication here is that a jingoistic double-talk based upon pseudo-psychometric, pseudo-Freudian terminology serves as a smoke screen which counselors use to confuse and control others. To some degree every profession creates its own technical language. However, the use (or misuse) of such terminology with those who are unfamiliar with it fosters misunderstanding and negative reactions. By its very nature, technical language is intended as a shorthand permitting economical communication among those conversant with it. The very fact that it is a professional "shorthand" makes it unsuitable and confusing for use with "outsiders." The true professional seeks to communicate in precise, understandable terms. For counselors to do otherwise creates misunderstanding, and because of misunderstanding they risk the brand "charlatan" in its clearest sense — "one who pretends to knowledge."

These criticisms frequently have a devastating effect upon counselors in preparation, particularly if in discussing them one admits that they have some validity. Recognition of such problems is essential in preparing for many fields of endeavor. The idealized image of an occupation is seldom accurate. No occupation can discharge all of its obligations to the satisfaction of everyone. Without doubt to some degree all occupational groups perform on faith tempered with the hope of resolving glaring deficiencies.

Criticism is useful in encouraging examination of what is known and what is not known in the field. Too many counselors cannot bring themselves to believe that any criticism is honestly motivated. Correction of shoddy practices and shallow thinking is an ever-present responsibility of the professional counselor. It is to be hoped that criticism, both from within and without the field, leads to an examined professional life and eventually stimulates improvement in counseling practices.

Annotated References

Borow, Henry. *Man in a World at Work.* Boston: Houghton Mifflin Company, 1964. 606 pp.

Chapter 1, by Carroll H. Miller, presents the changes that have occurred in vocational guidance. Chapter 3, by Henry Borow, identifies by date certain notable events in the history of vocational guidance.

Hansen, Donald A. (ed.). *Explorations in Sociology and Counseling.* Boston: Houghton Mifflin Company, 1968. 456 pp.

This book presents an interesting view of counseling by professionals outside the field. A series of 15 essays by sociologists is provided that examines counseling within its social context.

Robinson, Francis P. "Counseling Psychology Since the Northwestern Conference," in Albert S. Thompson and Donald E. Super (eds.), *The Professional Preparation of Counseling Psychologists.* New York: Bureau of Publications, Teachers College, Columbia University, 1964. 165 pp.

Robinson reports the developments that have taken place in counseling psychology since 1951. He presents changes that have occurred in Division 17 membership, professional journals, counselor education, and national legislation.

Tyler, Leona E. *The Work of the Counselor,* 3rd ed. New York: Appleton-Century-Crofts, Inc., 1969. 274 pp.

Chapter 1 (pp. 1–20) briefly treats the historical origins of counseling. Tyler cites vocational guidance and the mental health movement as producing counseling as it is known today.

Van Hoose, William H. and Pietrofesa, John J. (eds.). *Counseling and Guidance in the Twentieth Century.* Boston: Houghton Mifflin Company, 1970. 346 pp.

The book provides a sampling of leaders active in the counseling field. The 22 individuals provide an autobiographical sketch, some ideas about counseling, its past and present, and a list of their publications.

Williamson, E. G. *Vocational Counseling.* New York: McGraw-Hill Book Co., Inc., 1965. 229 pp.

Part II (pp. 47–149) discusses the discovery of the individual student, the originators of systems of counseling, and the developments in vocational and industrial psychology. Williamson identifies three individuals as originators of counseling.

Further References

Anthony, John and Lister, James. "Secondary School Counseling: A Preliminary Investigation." *The School Counselor,* Vol. 19 (May, 1972). pp. 378–381.

Arbuckle, Dugald S. "Educating Who for What?" *Counselor Education and Supervision,* Vol. 2 (September, 1971). pp. 41–48.

Biggs, Donald A., Foxley, Cecelia, and Solberg, S. Jane. "Attractive and Expert Student Personnel Workers of the 1970's." *Journal of College Student Personnel,* Vol. 13 (July, 1972). pp. 297–300.

Bloland, Paul A. "Ecumenicalism in College Student Personnel." *Journal of College Student Personnel,* Vol. 13 (March, 1972). pp. 102–111.

Carkhuff, Robert R. "Principles of Social Action in Training for New Careers in Human Services." *Journal of Counseling Psychology,* Vol. 18 (March, 1971). pp. 147–151.

Eckerson, Louise O. "The White House Conference: Tips or Taps for Counselors?" *Personnel and Guidance Journal,* Vol. 50 (November, 1971). pp. 167–174.

Hoyt, Donald P. "AGPA: Cherish or Perish?" *Personnel and Guidance Journal,* Vol. 49 (February, 1971). pp. 431–438.

Kondrasuk, John N. "Graduate Students' Rankings of Prestige Among Occupations in Psychology." *Journal of Counseling Psychology,* Vol. 18 (March, 1971). pp. 142–146.

Panther, Edward E. "Counselors and Legislators: A Case History." *Personnel and Guidance Journal,* Vol. 50 (April, 1972). pp. 667–672.

Scott, C. Winfield and Cherlin, Mary Monroe. "Occupational Status of the High School Counselor."

Vocational Guidance Quarterly. Vol. 20 (September, 1971). pp. 31–38.

Sinick, Daniel and Miller, Leonard. "A Reminiscence: Half a Hundred Years in Guidance." *Personnel and Guidance Journal*, Vol. 50 (February, 1972). pp. 434–443.

Van Riper, B. W. "Toward a Separate Professional Identity." *Journal of Counseling Psychology*, Vol. 19 (March, 1972). pp. 117–120.

Whiteley, John M. and Sprandel, Hazel Z. "APGA as a Political Organization." *Personnel and Guidance Journal*, Vol. 50 (February, 1972). pp. 475–481.

Williamson, E. G. "The Future Lies Open." *Personnel and Guidance Journal*, Vol. 50 (February, 1972). pp. 426–433.

Zytowski, Donald. "Four Hundred Years Before Parsons." *Personnel and Guidance Journal*, Vol. 50 (February, 1972). pp. 443–450.

THE COUNSELEE: DEVELOPMENTAL CHARACTERISTICS AND CONCERNS

3

Counseling requires that two individuals attempt to verbalize intellectually that which for both lies at an emotional and existential level. Acceptance of this view of counseling presents a dilemma to the participants and complicates description by those who seek to write about it. As noted at the outset of this book, the counselor approaches the situation committed to providing a helping relationship. The counselee approaches the situation, usually in a highly vulnerable state, seeking assistance. Yet he does so in a way that will permit him to salvage his own self-esteem and personal integrity.

Each participant seeks to communicate with the other. The counselor's efforts are directed primarily toward providing acceptance, understanding, and freedom in order to facilitate communication. The client, while he may not use the same labels, is looking for these conditions because they are necessary to the clarification, understanding, and solution of his own concerns. The client presents himself as he perceives himself to be or as he would like to be perceived. Although it is sometimes difficult to maintain, this is the only productive view of the situation the counselor can permit himself.

Regardless of what the client initially submits, he is trying to tell the counselor what troubles him. Often he attempts to do this through what appear to the counselor as disconnected examples. In fact, however, they typify a recurring concern or a core problem which manifests itself in diverse, seemingly unrelated areas. In his eagerness to secure help, he may assault the counselor with a multitude of facts and descriptions which for him clearly illustrate a basic concern but which often confuse and sometimes exasperate the counselor. The counselee would like to do simultaneously all the things individuals do in interpersonal situations: present himself favorably, respond intelligently, stay in control of himself and the situation, etc. Yet he must also say "I need help" in a way that will "purchase" assistance while maintaining his self-respect.

All of this, and more, the counselor must accept as part of the human condition the counselee brings to the setting. Once having done so, he may for his own convenience apply to the counseling interaction some "objective" criteria in order to make sense of what is happening. It is essential that an understanding of the basic human condition precede the application of intellectual efforts to describe and understand the individual who seeks help.

The social sciences, especially psychology and sociology, provide the counseling practitioner with a variety of ways of thinking about clients. Some, if not most, of the tools from the social sciences are descriptive rather than explanatory. Definitive answers are not always available, but normative data and cultural expectancies can often be graphically illustrated.

Developmental Characteristics of Counselees

Two approaches to viewing the developmental characteristics of the rather broad age group upon which this book focuses (6 to 22) have been presented by Havighurst[1] and Erikson.[2] Despite the fact that these two attempts to explain human development derive from different sources and treat their subject matter at different depths, they are complementary. Havighurst presents development within a sociopsychological framework which is particularly attractive in an educational setting. Erikson's developmental theories, on the other hand, have a psychoanalytic origin and set forth the psychodynamics of human behavior at various stages.

DEVELOPMENTAL TASKS

Havighurst explains that developmental tasks are the learnings an individual must acquire if he is to be judged and to judge himself a reasonably happy, successful person. He defines a developmental task as "a task which arises at or about a certain period in the life of the individual, successful achievement of which leads to his happiness and to success with later tasks, while failure leads to unhappiness in the individual, disapproval by the society, and difficulty with later tasks."[3] Essentially, Havighurst is pointing out that developmental tasks, like biological growth, follow a pattern and build upon each other. They are partly biologically, partly culturally, and partly psychologically determined. For instance, an infant must follow the sequence of learning to creep-stand-walk, then advance to talking before he progresses to reading and the games of childhood. Accomplishment of these tasks at appropriate ages permits and fosters movement to adolescence and subsequently to adulthood.

The age at which a specific developmental task is learned varies among cultures and among social classes within cultures. For example, cultures differ in their timing and methods of toilet training. Toilet training in American culture, compared to others, tends to be early and severe. Middle-class parents handle it differently from the way lower-class parents do. Some tasks, such as dating, are found only within certain cultures.

At every stage of life sources of help exist for the individual in achieving developmental tasks. Assistance is more readily and systematically available to children than to adults since the latter are presumably more able to control their life situations. The family is a fundamental source of aid, followed by the school, church, community agencies, etc. Each individual draws upon the assistance of several social institutions to cope with and accomplish developmental tasks.

Havighurst points out that development is continuous and that there is no abrupt or marked change at a given period in time. Further, developmental tasks change within a culture from time to time; for example, marriage now occurs earlier than it did two decades ago. Finally, each developmental task can be broken down into units or smaller tasks.

Below is presented an outline of Havighurst's

[1] Robert J. Havighurst, *Human Development and Education* (New York: David McKay Co., Inc., 1953).
[2] Erik H. Erikson, *Childhood and Society*, 2nd ed. (New York: W. W. Norton & Company, Inc., 1963).

[3] Havighurst, *op. cit.*, p. 2.

developmental tasks at successive stages, from middle childhood through early adulthood.

Middle Childhood: Age 6–11

1. Learning physical skills necessary for ordinary games
2. Building wholesome attitudes toward oneself as a growing organism
3. Learning to get along with age-mates
4. Learning an appropriate masculine or feminine social role
5. Developing fundamental skills in reading, writing, and calculating
6. Developing concepts necessary for everyday living
7. Developing conscience, morality, and a scale of values
8. Achieving personal independence
9. Developing attitudes toward social groups and institutions

Adolescence: Age 12–18

1. Achieving new and more mature relations with age-mates of both sexes
2. Achieving a masculine or feminine social role
3. Accepting one's physique and using the body effectively
4. Achieving emotional independence of parents and other adults
5. Achieving assurance of economic independence
6. Selecting and preparing for an occupation
7. Preparing for marriage and family life
8. Developing intellectual skills and concepts necessary for civic competence
9. Desiring and achieving socially responsible behavior
10. Acquiring a set of values and an ethical system as a guide to behavior

Early Adulthood: Age 19–30

1. Selecting a mate
2. Learning to live with a marriage partner
3. Starting a family
4. Rearing children
5. Managing a home
6. Getting started in an occupation
7. Taking on civic responsibility
8. Finding a congenial social group

These achievements, expected of its members by the culture at particular ages, have been analyzed and sorted by Havighurst according to their biological, psychological, and cultural bases. The tasks fit together in a pattern, with growth being continuous. Experience and successful accomplishment of one task pave the way for achievement of later tasks. Cronbach has summarized in tabular form some of the major tasks and some of the conditions affecting their development.[4] His tabular description is presented here as Table 3.1.

Evidently tasks are related to certain fundamental psychological and social needs and involve ways of discovering means for satisfying them. Cronbach's placement of the tasks within a need theory context is a convenient way of analyzing behavior and personality. Whenever an individual acts, he is presumably trying to satisfy some psychological or physiological need. If the counselor can recognize the need, he can help find appropriate ways of meeting it.

STAGES OF IDENTITY CRISES

Erikson has outlined a sequence of psychosocial development. The individual solution of tasks within each phase of development is prepared in previous phases, worked on, and then further refined in subsequent ones. While each phase is described in terms of the extremes of successful and unsuccessful solutions which can be arrived at within it, generally the outcome is a balance between these polarities.

Erikson has elaborated upon his ideas of how the healthy individual emerges from his inner and outer conflicts with an increased sense of inner unity, good judgment, and capacity to do well.[5] A fundamental premise underlying his description of growth is the *epigenetic principle*. Basically, this states

[4] Lee J. Cronbach, *Educational Psychology*, 2nd ed. (New York: Harcourt, Brace & World, Inc., 1963), pp. 110–111.
[5] Erik H. Erikson, *Identity, Youth, and Crisis* (New York: W. W. Norton and Company, Inc., 1968), 336 pp.

Table 3.1 *Some developmental tasks of American children*

Age	*Physical landmarks*	*Characterization*	*Need for affection*	*Need for approval by authority figures*	*Need for approval by peers*	*Need for independence*	*Need for competence and self-respect*
0–1½	Creep by age 1	Dependent; Learn to interpret sensory impressions	Establish feeding schedule, weaning; Develop confidence in adult care				Master objects within reach; Gain eye-hand coordination
2–4 Early childhood	Walk and talk by age 2	Energetic play; Social regulation imposed with or without understanding	Accept newborn brother or sister; Form secure identification with like-sex parent	Accept rules, schedules, denial of wishes; Begin to understand principles behind regulations	Develop social skills: share, take turns, inhibit aggression; Learn property rights	Accept separation from parent; Express own desires via requests; Successfully make demands on others	Accept and meet parental performance standards; Successfully make demands on environment
5–9 Early schooling		Adapt to organization; Develop tool skills		Accept rules and procedures; Control emotions; Understand rights of others; Accept teacher as model and guide	Care for own appearance; Win acceptance in school group; Develop play skills		Master schoolwork; Master physical skills for games; Accept own physical characteristics, aptitude for school
10–11 Middle childhood	Growth spurts	Stable group activities; Projects extending over longer periods		Make effort toward school achievement	Conform to sex role; Accept group code; Learn to compete within the code	Carry on tasks without supervision; Enjoy own industriousness; Accept some conflict with authority	Develop interests; Find means of earning pocket money
12–16 Early adolescence	Puberty: Girls 10–15 Boys 12–17	Dating begins; Increased sense of unique personality, planning for future		Accept more impersonal direction in departmentalized school	Gain acceptance from opposite sex; Acquire new sex roles	Find satisfaction in nonfamily recreations	Accept own body, role of own sex; Accept own abilities and talents; Find vocational direction
17–20 Later adolescence	Growth tapers off	Car gives freedom from supervision; Serious preparation for work; Courtship	Form close comradeship with member(s) of opposite sex	Hold selves to schedule, complete tasks defined in general terms		Make serious decisions without reliance on adults; Take responsibility for car, job	Choose specific vocational goal and develop vocational skill; Find part-time job
21–26 Transition		Mating; Establishment of own home, start of career	Attain sex adjustment in marriage; Devote selves to infant (girls)	Apply standards set by authority to one's own work with minimal supervision		Make decisions despite parental opposition; Plans with spouse	Establish selves in "respectable" job

SOURCE: From *Educational Psychology*, Second Edition, by Lee J. Cronbach, copyright, 1954, © 1962, 1963, by Harcourt Brace Jovanovich, Inc., and reproduced with their permission.

that "anything that grows has a *ground plan*, and that out of this ground plan the *parts* arise, each part having its *time* of special ascendancy until all parts have arisen to form a *functioning whole*."[6] Personality develops according to steps predetermined in the individual's readiness; each item of personality is systematically related to all others, and all depend upon the proper development in the proper sequence.

The individual's encounter with his environment conveys to him particular ideas and concepts which contribute to his character, efficiency, and health. Erikson describes each encounter with its resulting crisis for each stage of development. A *crisis* exists "because incipient growth and awareness in a new part function together with a shift in instinctual energy and yet also cause specific vulnerability in that part."[7] Successive steps constitute

[6] *Ibid.*, p. 92.

[7] *Ibid.*, p. 95.

potential crises because of changes in the individual's perspective.

It should be noted that his use of the word "crisis" is not in the sense of impending catastrophe. Rather, it designates "a necessary turning point, a crucial moment, when development must move one way or another, marshaling resources of growth, recovery, and further differentiation."[8]

Erikson's concept of *mutuality* specifies that the crucial coordination is between the individual and his social environment and that this coordination is mutually determined. Care-taking persons (e.g., mother) are coordinated to the developing individual by their specific responsiveness to his needs and, in turn, by phase needs of their own.

Individuals who are significant to the person communicate hospitality for him which, in turn, makes him hospitable to them. This mutual affirmation activates the individual. When significant others *deny* the individual, this *reciprocal negation* arouses hate or, at the very least, ambivalence. The individual is uncertain where he stands in relation to others.

Erikson uses the concept *identity* to refer to "a persistent sameness within oneself (selfsameness) and a persistent sharing of some kind of essential character with others."[9] He further explains that identity has a number of connotations:

> At one time, then, it will appear to refer to a conscious sense of *individual identity;* at another to an unconscious striving for a *continuity* of *personal character;* at a third, as a criterion for the silent doings of *ego synthesis;* and, finally, as a maintenance of an inner *solidarity* with a group's ideals and identity.[10]

A sense of identity — that this is the real me — is described by Erikson as a process "located" in the core of each person and in the core of his communal culture. A person's identity is formed by a

> . . . process of simultaneous reflection and observation, a process taking place on all levels of mental functioning, by which the individual judges himself in the light of what he perceives to be the way in which others judge him in comparison to themselves and to a typology significant to them; while he judges their way of judging him in the light of how he perceives himself in comparison to them and to types that have become relevant to him. This process is, luckily, and necessarily, for the most part unconscious except where inner conditions and outer circumstances combine to aggravate a painful, or elated, "identity consciousness."
>
> Furthermore, the process described is always changing and developing; at its best it is a process of increasing differentiation, and it becomes ever more inclusive as the individual grows aware of a widening circle of others significant to him, from the maternal person to "mankind." The process "begins" somewhere in the first true "meeting" of mother and baby as two persons who can touch and recognize each other, and it does not "end" until a man's power of mutual affirmation wanes. As pointed out, however, the process has its normative crisis in adolescence, and is in many ways determined by what went before and determines much that follows.[11]

Erikson identifies and describes the ego qualities which emerge during critical periods of development. These are briefly sketched here from his portrayal of the eight stages of man.[12]

Basic Trust Versus Basic Mistrust The first component is an attitude toward oneself and the world derived principally from the experiences of the first year of life. "Basic" means that it is not especially conscious, but a "sense" of it pervades the individual. "Trust" implies that one learns to rely on sameness and continuity of others and simultaneously learns to trust oneself. Mothers create a sense of trust or confidence by their sensitive ministrations to their infants' needs. Trust forms the basis for a sense of identity, of feeling "all right," of being oneself, of becoming what other people trust one will become. Trust derives from maternal care, but it depends less upon the receiving of food or demonstrations of love than upon the

[8] *Ibid.*, p. 16.
[9] Erik H. Erikson, "Identity and the Life Cycle," *Psychological Issues*, Vol. 1, Monograph 1 (1959), p. 102.
[10] *Ibid.*, p. 102.
[11] Erikson, *Identity, Youth and Crisis*, pp. 22–23.
[12] *Ibid.*, pp. 91–141.

quality of the relationship. In short, during the first year the child develops a belief in the goodness of the world, taught to him by familiar and predictable and affectionate qualities in his relations with people. Otherwise, he develops a sense of mistrust and anticipates unpleasantness in the world.

Autonomy Versus Shame and Doubt Muscular maturation sets the stage for the individual's experimentation with "holding on" and "letting go," e.g., bladder and bowel elimination. Conflict within these modalities leads to either hostile or benign expectations and attitudes. "To hold" can mean to become destructive, cruel, and restraining or it can become a pattern of care — "to have and to hold." "To let go" can turn into a loosening of destructive forces or a relaxed "let pass." Outer controls on the infant should be firmly reassuring during this stage. His environment must be such as to encourage him to "stand on his own" yet protect him from meaningless experiences of shame and early doubt. Too much shaming leads to a secret determination to try to get away from things and to doubt.

This stage of development — decisive for the eventual ratio of love and hate, cooperation and willingness, freedom of self-expression and its suppression — is a reflection of the parents' dignity as individuals. The sense of autonomy is fostered from a sense of self-control without loss of self-esteem. In short, during his second and third years the healthy individual acquires a sense of his own individual existence and the power of decision.

Initiative Versus Guilt The child of four or five is faced with the next step and next crisis: finding out what kind of person he is going to be. Erikson cites three strong developments which help at this stage: (1) The child learns to move around more freely and therefore establishes a wider radius of goals. (2) The child's sense of language becomes perfected to the point where he understands and can ask about many things. (3) Language and locomotion permit him to expand his imagination over so many things that he cannot avoid frightening himself with what he has dreamed.[13] The individual emerges from this stage with a sense of initiative (or motion into the future) or a sense of guilt.

The child is now developing the prerequisites for masculine and feminine initiative, i.e., the selection of social goals and perseverance in approaching them. However, secret fantasies may result in a deep sense of guilt. He may feel guilty for mere thoughts and for deeds which no one has seen or knows about. Conscience, the governor of initiative, becomes established. The child who is developing well establishes a set of inner controls over his initiative lest it carry him too far and he hurt himself or other people. Early prevention and alleviation of hatred and guilt, by caretaking people who feel equal in worth although different in kind, function, or age, permit peaceful cultivation of initiative and a free sense of enterprise.

Industry Versus Inferiority Erikson has characterized this stage as "I am what I learn." The individual develops a sense of industry by adjusting himself to the inorganic laws of the tool world. His aim is to bring a productive situation to completion. Through some form of systematic instruction he learns the fundamentals of technology. Danger lies in outer and inner hindrances to the use of new capacities which lead to despair, discouragement, and feelings of inadequacy and inferiority. This is a decisive stage because industry involves doing things beside and with others. The child experiences his first sense of division of labor and of equality of opportunity.

Identity Versus Role Confusion Puberty brings a questioning of the sameness and continuities relied on at earlier stages. Faced with a physiological revolution within themselves, youth are concerned with what they appear to be in the eyes of others as compared to what they feel they are. *Role confusion,* or the inability to fix upon the kind of person one wants to be, is the danger of this stage. It

[13] *Ibid.,* p. 115.

may derive from previous doubt as to sexual identity or it may be based upon the inability to settle on an occupational identity. "Falling in love" may be an attempt to arrive at a definition of identity by projecting one's diffused ego image on another and seeing it reflected and gradually clarified.

Intimacy Versus Isolation The successful search for identity leads to a willingness to fuse with others. The individual is ready for intimacy, ready to commit himself to affiliations and partnerships. Close affiliations, friendships, sexual union – all call for commitments, sacrifices, and compromises. Avoidance of such experiences because of fear of ego loss may lead to a sense of isolation and self-absorption. The counterpart of intimacy, according to Erikson, is distantiation or the repudiation or isolation of forces and people believed to be inimical to oneself.

Generativity Versus Stagnation The concern in this stage is in establishing and guiding the next generation. Generativity incorporates productivity and creativity and may be applied not just to offspring but to altruistic concerns. Regression from generativity may lead to pseudo-intimacy with a pervading sense of stagnation and interpersonal impoverishment.

Integrity Versus Despair The final stage is characterized by belief in oneself and one's particular life cycle. Integrity is the belief in the value or goodness of one's contributions to humankind. Loss of integrity is signified by despair, by fear of death, by displeasure with particular institutions and people (allied with the individual's contempt of himself).

Erikson's diagram of the life cycle is presented here as Figure 3.1. The diagonal represents the normative sequence of psychosocial gains. The squares of the diagonal signify progression through time of a differentiation of parts and indicates that each item is systematically related to all others. Each item exists in some form before its crucial time normally arrives.

SOME FUNDAMENTAL SIMILARITIES

Zaccaria analyzed the work of Havighurst and Erikson as well as Super,[14] and reported that a cluster of common elements could be identified in their literature and research. He identifies 15 statements with which Havighurst, Erikson, and Super appear to be in agreement. They are reproduced here in his words.

1. Individual growth and development are continuous.
2. Individual growth can be divided into periods or life stages for descriptive purposes.
3. Individuals in each life stage can be characterized by certain general characteristics that they have in common.
4. Most individuals in a given culture pass through similar developmental stages.
5. The society makes certain demands upon individuals.
6. These demands are relatively uniform for all members of the society.
7. The demands differ from stage to stage as the individual goes through the developmental process.
8. Developmental crises occur when the individual perceives the demand to alter his present behavior and master new learnings.
9. In meeting and mastering developmental crises, the individual moves from one developmental stage of maturity to another developmental stage of maturity.
10. The task appears in its purest form at one stage.
11. Preparation for meeting the developmental crises or developmental tasks occurs in the life stage prior to the stage in which it must be mastered.
12. The developmental task or crisis may arise again during a later phase in somewhat different form.
13. The crisis or task must be mastered before the individual can successfully move on to a subsequent developmental stage.
14. Meeting the crisis successfully by learning the required task leads to societal approval, happiness, and success with later crises and their correlative tasks.
15. Failing in meeting a task or crisis leads to disapproval by society.[15]

[14] Donald E. Super, *Career Development: Self Concept Theory* (New York: College Entrance Examination Board, 1963).
[15] Joseph S. Zaccaria, "Developmental Tasks: Implications for the Goals of Guidance," *Personnel and Guidance Journal,* Vol. 44 (December, 1965), p. 373.

Figure 3.1 Erikson's stages of man

	1.	2.	3.	4.	5.	6.	7.	8.
1. INFANCY	*Trust vs. Mistrust*				*Mutual recognition vs. Autistic isolation*			
2. EARLY CHILDHOOD		*Autonomy vs. Shame, Doubt*			*Will to be oneself vs. Self-doubt*			
3. PLAY AGE			*Initiative vs. Guilt*		*Anticipation of roles vs. Role inhibition*			
4. SCHOOL AGE				*Industry vs. Inferiority*	*Task identification vs. Sense of futility*			
5. ADOLESCENCE	*Time perspective vs. Time confusion*	*Self-certainty vs. Self-consciousness*	*Role experimentation vs. Role fixation*	*Apprenticeship vs. Work paralysis*	*Identity vs. Identity confusion*	*Sexual polarization vs. Bisexual confusion*	*Leader commitment vs. Authority confusion*	*Ideological commitment vs. Confusion of values*
6. YOUNG ADULT					*Solidarity vs. Social isolation*	*Intimacy vs. Isolation*		
7. ADULTHOOD							*Generativity vs. Stagnation*	
8. MATURE AGE								*Integrity vs. Despair*

CONCEPT OF NORMALITY

School counselors usually distinguish themselves from clinical psychologists or psychiatrists, who work predominantly with abnormal or disturbed individuals, by asserting that their clients are normal. But how is normality to be defined? Thompson, for example, reported that the "typical" high school student is either in the college preparatory (43 per cent) or the general curriculum (24 per cent); makes grades of C (49 per cent) or B (31 per cent); attends church once a week (44 per cent) or "seldom attends church" (31 per cent); and is interested in a wide range of occupations.[16] Is this the school counselor's clientele?

Abnormal behavior is usually regarded as a departure from the normal, differing from it in kind. Others view it as an extension of the habitual range, distinctive only in degree. For example, Sigmund Freud pointed out that neurotic conflict is not very different in content from the normative conflicts which every individual experiences in childhood, the residues of which every adult carries with him in the recesses of his personality. He believed that man, in order to remain psychologically alive, constantly resolves these conflicts just as his body unceasingly combats the encroachment of physical deterioration.

Much literature exists dealing with the characteristics of the behavioral deviant, the disturbed and the anxious, but much less is known about the nature of psychological normality. Basically, two approaches to defining "normality" have been used. First, normality has been related to the statistical facts of "average" or "typical." By this approach, the average individual and those near him (conventionally, those in a distribution obtained from any measure who are one standard deviation above and below the mean) are considered normal. Individuals above and below this central area in a distribution would be labeled abnormal. The second approach is to consider "normality" a relative thing. Normality means acceptance by reference to some group. Groups or cultures vary in what is considered acceptable. This approach raises the issue of whether normality is not basically conforming behavior. In respect to both conceptions of normality Shoben has pointed out that

> The terms "usual" or "most frequent" or "average" are meaningless without reference to some group, and this state of affairs poses two problems. First, conformity in itself, as history abundantly demonstrates, is a dubious guide to conduct. Innovation is as necessary to a culture's survival as are tradition and conservation, and conformity has frequently meant acquiescence in conditions undermining the maturity and positive development of human beings rather than their enhancement . . . Second, relativistic conceptions of normality pose serious questions as to the reference group against which any individual is to be assessed.[17]

Normality has been variously described as natural, efficient, adaptive, balanced, conscious, or managed behavior. After summarizing different views of the concept of normality held by psychologists, psychiatrists, educators, and others, Mowrer defined it this way:

> Every human society is organized and conducted on the basis of certain principles – which are best described as social ethics. These principles have been worked out over a long period of time, with many mistakes and much suffering. Each individual born into a human society is under pressure to adopt the approved ways of that society, and each individual experiences in the course of his development some of the struggles, difficulties, and dilemmas which were involved in the evolution of his society. To the extent that an individual is able in his lifetime to assimilate the historically hard-won wisdom of society and to experience the fruits thereof, he may be said to be normal; to the extent that he fails, he is abnormal.[18]

[16] O. E. Thompson, "What Is the High School Student of Today Like?" *Journal of Secondary Education,* Vol. 36 (April, 1961), pp. 210–219.

[17] Edward Joseph Shoben, Jr., "Toward a Concept of the Normal Personality," *The American Psychologist,* Vol. 12 (April, 1957), pp. 183–189.

[18] O. H. Mowrer, "What Is Normal Behavior?" in L. A. Pennington and Irwin A. Berg (eds.), *An Introduction to Clinical Psychology* (New York: The Ronald Press Company, 1954), p. 86.

Perhaps what school counselors really mean when they say that their clientele is made up of normal individuals is that their services are available to all students. Further, counseling is not restricted to a narrow segment of the population characterized by deficit. Although those with severe deficits of one kind or another are likely to be referred to more specialized personnel, it seems fairly obvious that those at the positive pole of any description (e.g., the gifted) which purports to describe normality are not referred because positive behavior is rarely seen as abnormal. Clearly, the service demands upon school counselors are made mainly by psychologically intact individuals confronted with the usual developmental stresses of human existence.

Several general descriptions of the mentally healthy individual have been advanced. Jahoda calls a person psychologically healthy who actively masters his environment, shows a considerable unity of personality, and is able to perceive himself and his world realistically.[19] Such an individual is independent and able to function effectively without making undue demands upon others. Shoben's definition goes beyond self-sufficiency.[20] He proposes that the healthy person exhibits self-control, personal responsibility, social responsibility, social interest, and ideals. Shoben believes that his tentative formulation of integrative adjustment avoids the notion that the normal person is always happy and free from conflict, or without problems, but acknowledges that he is one who may fall short of his ideals because of ignorance, the limitations under which he lives, or immediate pressures. Further, he may at times behave in ways that prove shortsighted or self-defeating.

Hountras describes the psychologically healthy individual in these words:

1. He has self-respect, and respect and confidence in others, the essence of a wholesome attitude toward life.
2. He assumes responsibility for his behavior and experiences satisfaction in work and play activities.
3. He demonstrates a sensitivity to the needs of others.
4. He sets realistic goals which are capable of attainment.
5. He has goals, interests, and sources of gratification which are within the limits of social approval.
6. He employs a problem-solving approach when confronted by obstacles and uncertainties.
7. He has insight into his own needs as they influence his interaction with others.
8. He develops a philosophy of life which incorporates the values, beliefs, ideals and expectancies that guide his behavior and integrate the various facets of his personality.[21]

Yamamoto[22] presents, in tabular form (see Table 3.2), some characteristics of the emotionally healthy person set forth by various authors. His own concept of such a person describes one who lives fully at that point of his or her development and is constantly "becoming" or actively changing himself and his environment to attain the next stage.

Many protest the use of terminology such as "mental illness" and insist that decisions regarding maladaptive behavior rest primarily upon judgments involving conventionality and social norms. The concept of mental illness is not analogous to that of physical illness, in which deviation from optimal organic functioning serves as a base for decisions.

Common Counselee Concerns

Sociologists study the young, politicians profess to worry about them, and parents, teachers, and counselors try to understand them. Few diagnoses as to what they are really like are accurate. Too often, the complaint is that they are insolent, unkempt, and unprepossessing. But war between the

[19] Marie Jahoda, "Toward a Social Psychology of Mental Health," in M. F. E. Senn (ed.), *Symposium on the Healthy Personality* (New York: Josiah Macy, Jr. Foundation, 1950).
[20] Shoben, *op. cit.*, p. 189.
[21] Peter T. Hountras (ed.), *Mental Hygiene* (Columbus, Ohio: Charles E. Merrill Books, Inc., 1961), p. 11.
[22] Kaoru Yamomoto, "The 'Healthy Person': A Review," *Personnel and Guidance Journal,* Vol. 44 (Feb., 1966), pp. 596–603.

Table 3.2 Models of a healthy person postulated by several authors

Shoben (1957)	*Jahoda (1958)*	*Allport (1960)*	*Rogers (1962)*	*Combs (1962)*
			Openness to experience	Openness to experience and acceptance
Self-control	Accepting attitudes toward self	Self-objectification	Trust in one's organism	Positive view of self
Personal responsibility	Growth and self-actualization	Ego-extension		
Social responsibility		Warm and deep relation to others		
Democratic social interest		Compassionate regard for all	(Trustworthiness of human nature)*	Identification with others
Values and standards	Integration	Unifying philosophy of life	Living as a process (existential living)	
	Autonomy			
	Perception of reality	Realistic perceptions		Rich and available perceptual field
	Environmental mastery	Realistic coping skills and abilities		
			(Creativity)	(Well-informed) (Imaginative and creative)

*Characteristics in parentheses are implied or deduced corollaries of the respective models.

SOURCE: Kaoru Yamamoto, "The 'Healthy Person': A Review," *Personnel and Guidance Journal,* Vol. 44 (February, 1966), p. 600. Copyright © 1966 American Personnel and Guidance Association. Reprinted with permission.

generations is nothing new. Socrates bitterly attacked youth's "bad manners, contempt for authority, disrespect for their elders. Children nowadays are tyrants." All through history, denouncing the young has been a tonic for tired blood. Conversely, defying elders is hygienic for the young. A child's task is self-definition (see Havighurst and Erikson); unless the child can distinguish himself from his culture, though on the culture's terms, the child never quite becomes an adult. Growing up is a process that requires forces and people against whom one can push in order to become stronger.

Growth requires limited war against worthy opponents because a child matures by testing himself against limits set by "caring" adults. Study after study shows that two factors are vital to a child's later independence: first, warmly firm parents who admire each other and on whom he can model himself while breaking away; second, opportunities to prove his competence in work and love. Youth often reveal in what they say their special awareness of the faults and virtues of the adult world; they hold up a mirror to society. They expect much from this world and are ready to give much; for example, many have made sincere commitments to civil rights, the Peace Corps, Vista, and the like.

CAUSES OF YOUTH PROBLEMS

That we live in a time of widening uncertainty and chronic stress has been observed by many chroniclers. Tuchman has stated,

> Man in the twentieth century is not a creature to be envied. Formerly he believed himself created by the divine spark. Now, bereft of that proud confidence, and contemplating his recent record and present problems, he can no longer, like the Psalmist, respect himself as "a little lower than the angels." He cannot picture himself today, as Michelangelo did on the Sistine ceiling, in the calm and noble image of Adam receiving the spark from the finger of God. Overtaken by doubt of human purpose and divine purpose, he doubts his capacity to be good or even to survive. He has lost certainty, including moral and ethical certainty, and is left with a sense of footloose purposelessness and self-disgust. . . .[23]

Numerous other statements alluding to the problems and complexity of today's world could be cited. While their validity probably cannot be seriously questioned and while their ready acceptance frequently stems from their persuasive nature, in our opinion they frequently appear to underrate the very segment of humanity with which they are concerned. The contemporary world may be more complex or more anxiety provoking, less safe and secure in the eyes of adults who were born and reared at an earlier point in time. What seems to be missing in such views is the obvious fact that man adapts, copes with, and masters that which has historically confronted him.

The child born into the atomic age may not suffer and be as incapacitated by events as his elders fear. Although the same threat is there for the adult and the youth, it is a fact of the latter's existence and has not been suddenly thrust upon him. For this reason it may not affect him to the degree that adults think that it would. It could probably be demonstrated that many anxiety-producing factors either no longer exist or have diminished impact in contemporary society. Perhaps physical health is a good example. Many major diseases which constantly threatened society 50 years ago are relatively rare in modern America. Each man is a product of *his own* times. He deals with that which confronts him regardless of the dire predictions of those of an earlier age group.

A final point relates to the fact that anxiety may be provoked by adults in youth, who would otherwise actively seek to master those things which confront them. Adults who are uneasy about increasing traffic on highways may detrimentally transmit their concern to youth, who might otherwise naturally adapt their driving habits to the conditions facing them.

Often ignored is the stunning fact that most American youngsters now work harder, think deeper, love more, and even look better than any previous generation. But admittedly, something is obviously wrong among some segments of the youth culture. Quite a few youngsters are clearly discontented. Even more disturbing, too many youngsters are withdrawing rather than warring. Alienation drives both high school and college students into private exile. At the heart of this anomie lie vast technological changes in Western culture that have steadily lengthened childhood and sharply diminished communication between generations. In primitive cultures, boys became men immediately upon surviving harsh rites of passage. In agrarian societies, a hard-working farmer's son rap-

[23] Barbara W. Tuchman, "The Historian's Opportunity," *Saturday Review,* February 25, 1967, p. 28.

idly became a certified adult. Until recently, puberty occurred at about 14 or 15, marriage two or three years later. The label "teen-ager" would have been inconceivable for such 17-year-old adults as Joan of Arc or surveyor George Washington.

Today, the pressure is to stay in school to be better prepared for life in a complex society. Ironically, better nutrition has meanwhile quickened puberty. Youth are now biological adults at 12 or 13, but they usually cannot legally work full time at even the few remaining unskilled jobs until they are at least 16; until recently they were draftable at 18, they could not vote until 21, and are often economically dependent on their parents until 24 or 25. In effect, they may stay children for more than a decade after becoming adults.

Numerous factors have been ascribed as the root of youth's problems. Those identified by Goodman, who for 30 years has lectured (Institute for Policy Studies) and written on social problems, are here summarized:

1. Modern societies have failed to provide a world *for* the young to take part in as they grow up. Youth are excluded as partners in society, are unnecessarily unproductive, and therefore create problems in order to make their presence known.

2. Youth are processed, restricted, and trained for other people's purposes and goals.

3. Youth increasingly distrust grownup purposes and goals. They are suspicious of adults because of our hypocrisy, role playing, profit motivation, and face-saving behavior.

4. Adult leaders are incompetent and their ideas are inadequate and often irrelevant to the conditions of modern life.

5. While the physical sciences have advanced geometrically, the social sciences have lagged. Youth believe and have responded to the barrage of social criticism by becoming beat, hep, conformist, delinquent, apathetic, and dissenting.

6. The methods and tradition of American schooling work to *arrest* maturation. Compulsory, and compulsive, schooling which extends into college age and a "schoolmarm" attitude which pervades the entire system cause many to revolt.

7. Youth revolt is not an attempt to repossess their rights as young people, whether adolescents, workmen, or students. "Rather they regard themselves as an isolated class, as the *only* people. They have turned us out and turned us off."[24]

Surveys have described the problems and concerns of the elementary, secondary, and college age groups. Their chief value is in alerting counselors to areas of sensitivity among their clientele.

CONCERNS OF ELEMENTARY SCHOOL CHILDREN

"Wanted: Someone to care for a child outside of the home, six hours a day. Must teach him to read and write and to respond and be responsive to others." This fictitious want ad appears every fall when millions of youngsters swarm into the nation's public and private elementary schools. Elementary public schools enrolled some 32.4 million in 1971. The elementary nonpublic sector of the educational system enrolled an additional 4.2 million in 1971. Perhaps these numbers convey some idea of the problems confronting the schools as they attempt to provide an educationally meaningful experience for youngsters. But all too often, numbers obscure the wide range of behavior, the different bases of motivation and aspiration, the differential in experiences which exist among the millions who attend school.

Elementary school pupils are in the process of becoming — physically, socially, emotionally, and as total personalities. Their experiences in coping with normal developmental tasks vary widely. These developmental differences create adjustment problems both in the tasks of school and in social life.

No matter how exacting or ingenious an educational program may be, it cannot reach children who are beset with psychological and emotional disturbances. Recent estimates are that up to 10 per cent of school children have emotional distur-

[24] Paul Goodman, "Moral Youth in an Immoral Society," *The Young Americans* (New York: Time, Inc., 1966), pp. 18–19.

bances that require professional treatment. Furthermore, in the nation's 15 largest city schools, roughly a third of their 3.7 million children need special education help. Besides being ineffectual learners themselves, such children often hamper classroom activities and need an inordinate amount of teacher time.

Taken at face value, the term "emotional disorder" would appear to be almost self-defining. The simplistic view of this condition is that a disproportionate emotional reaction attends a reality situation. "Maladjustment" and "behavior disorder" frequently are used interchangeably with the term "emotional disturbance." A useful example of a description of the emotionally disturbed student is to be found in the Administrative Manual of the Bureau of Educationally Handicapped and used with Title VI of the Elementary and Secondary Education Act. This source says the disturbed child is characterized by: (1) an inability to learn which cannot be explained by intellectual, sensory, or health factors; (2) an inability to establish or maintain satisfactory interpersonal relationships with peers and teachers; (3) inappropriate types of behavior or feelings under normal circumstances; (4) a generally pervasive mood of unhappiness or depression; and (5) a tendency to develop physical symptoms, pains, or fears associated with personal or school problems. It is within this type of working definition or description that most school personnel, including counselors, operate in making day-to-day judgments about the presence, degree, and effects of emotional disturbance on pupils.

Stennet reported that between five and 10 per cent of a total sample of 1500 children between the ages of nine and 11 had "adjustive difficulties" of sufficient severity to warrant professional attention. Further, 22 per cent could be labeled "emotionally handicapped children," in either moderate or severe form. Some 78 per cent of the emotionally handicapped boys and 66 per cent of the emotionally handicapped girls had learning disabilities and were frequently absent from school, did not do well in their school work, and were either older or younger than their class group.[25]

However, estimates of the number of school children encountered each year who exhibit some emotional, behavior, or psychosomatic problem vary widely. This variation is due to the lack of a common definition and to differences in the cutoff points used in categorizing a student as disturbed. Interwoven with these factors are the criteria employed in making judgments which stem from definition and which affect the precision of decisions. Without detailing the literature, estimates can be found which vary from four to 20 per cent. Even though precision in rates is not possible, if one applies either extreme of this range to the total U.S. school enrollment, one is faced with a tremendous number of elementary school children who need help.

Certain other problems must be pointed out regarding estimates of emotional disturbance among school children. Estimates do not necessarily apply in all settings since the incidence of disturbance varies, depending on the type of school setting measured, e.g., inner city or suburban school, and the student population within the setting. Estimates within two apparently similar settings may also vary according to the level of awareness of the staff and the services available within the school or community. A sensitive, child-centered, and alert staff with many special services available may identify a far larger number of children needing specialized assistance than a less sensitive staff. In short, estimates of nationwide scope are of little value in a specific locality. An illustration of this fact can be found in recent statistics on dropouts. Many Americans were shocked to hear that tremendous percentages of children leave school early. Incidences were quoted as high as 50 or 60 per cent, with little clarification of the fact that some suburban schools have very low dropout

[25] R. G. Stennet, "Emotional Handicap in the Elementary Years: Phase or Disease," *American Journal of Orthopsychiatry*, Vol. 36 (March, 1966), pp. 444–449.

rates while some inner city schools have extremely high rates.

Lastly, it must be added that the very seriously disturbed children are not often found in public schools. Such children are either institutionalized or placed in special private school settings because they cannot cope with a regular school environment. Those emotionally disturbed children who are in public schools would usually be judged as having mild, minor, or transitory problems stemming from developmental or situational causes.

A not uncommon, serious concern for some elementary school children is a feeling of panic about attending school. Traditional concepts of school phobia have been primarily psychoanalytical in nature, stressing the parent-child separation or sexual aspects of the disorder. Long states that the phobic child views school as a "preaversive stimulus" in that he regards separation from a parent (usually the mother) as a loss of positive reinforcement. Excessive dependency creates fear of separation. Long suggests that counselors employ behavior modification treatment procedures, primarily desensitization, for elementary school phobia cases.[26]

[26] James D. Long, "School Phobia and the Elementary Counselor," *Elementary School Guidance and Counseling,* Vol. 5 (May, 1971), pp. 289–294.

A child seldom recognizes the source of a problem which limits his school performance. One who is uninterested in reading is usually not aware that the lack of interest is related to emotional stress incurred at home or at school. He cannot tell why his work falls below teachers' and parents' expectations and may have little conception of what these expectations are. But beginning with the first day in kindergarten a child may demonstrate that something is wrong. He may present evidence of inner disturbance, he may act aggressively, he may fail to function properly as part of a group. That teachers perceive these problems can be amply demonstrated, but how well do children recognize them?

Mangan and Shafer secured children's opinions (fifth through eighth grades) as to the seriousness of certain behaviors.[27] Using the types of behavior listed by Wickman (and by other researchers), the two authors interviewed 101 children, grades five through eight, in public, private and parochial schools. Table 3.3 reports their comparative findings.

[27] Thomas Mangan and David Shafer, "Behavior Problems of Children as Viewed by Children in the Fifth through Eighth Grades," *Journal of Educational Research,* Vol. 56 (October, 1962), pp. 104–106.

Table 3.3 Behavior problems viewed by children — grades 5–8: results of interviews

Ranking by the various groups	R_1	R_2	R_3	R_4	R_5	R_6
1. Stealing	1	1	1	8	0	1
2. Skipping school	2	4	3	17	6	17
3. Cheating	3	7	15	24	1	3
4. Destroying school material	4	8	6	21	0	2
5. Temper tantrum	5	11	11	15	9	12
6. Lying	6	3	8	19	3	4
7. Obscene materials	7	2	13	32	4	7
8. Swearing	8.5	13	37	45	2.5	15
9. Smoking	8.5	16	34	46	24.5	32
10. Disobedience	10	9	9	38	10	9
11. Defiance	11	5	5	29	6	5
12. Lack of interest	12	12	19	23	2	19
13. Impoliteness	13	14	20	40	4	13

(continued on p. 60)

Table 3.3 *(continued)*

Ranking by the various groups	R_1	R_2	R_3	R_4	R_5	R_6
14. Thoughtlessness	14.5	35	42	36	29.5	42
15. Bullying	14.5	6	2	5	9.5	6
16. Imaginative lying	16.5	39	46	37	10.5	35
17. Resentful	16.5	26	10	7	9.5	20
18. Unreliable	18	10	7	20	11	10
19. Slovenly in appearance	19	31	39	30	9	37
20. Easily discouraged	20	20	21	14	1	11
21. Selfishness	21	21	16	25	8	18
22. Inattention	22.5	23	25	28	14.5	36
23. Quarrelsomeness	22.5	24	17	26	1.5	14
24. Domineering	24	30	18	16	8	22
25. Inquisitiveness	25.5	41	44	41	13.5	44
26. Silliness	25.5	36	27	35	3.5	40
27. Suspiciousness	27	34	32	4	14	28
28. Careless in work	28	22	31	39	14	33
29. Overcritical	29	42	29	13	8	21
30. Stubbornness	30	29	35	34	10	39
31. Disorderliness	32.5	18	26	42	9.5	23
32. Interrupting	32.5	40	45	44	1.5	45
33. Sullenness	32.5	32	27	22	2.5	29
34. Laziness	32.5	15	29	33	17.5	26
35. Suggestible	35	25	22	12	13	27
36. Tardiness	36	27	41	43	6	43
37. Tattling	37	43	43	31	12	30
38. Physical coward	38	28	28	18	0	31
39. Dreaminess	39	38	36	10	4	38
40. Unsocial	40.5	37	12	1	8.5	16
41. Unhappy	40.5	19	4	2	22.5	8
42. Whispering, note writing	42	44	47	47	4	46
43. Sensitiveness	43	45	30	9	1	41
44. Fearfulness	44	33	23	3	13	24
45. Nervousness	45	17	14	11	9	25
46. Restlessness	46	46	40	27	1	47
47. Shyness	47	47	32	6	0	34

Legend
R_1 — The authors' (sample, N = 101)
R_2 — Wickman's Traditional Teachers
R_3 — Wickman's Modern Teachers
R_4 — Wickman's Mental Hygienists
R_5 — Porter's High School Seniors
R_6 — Porter's College Seniors

Using Spearman's formula, we obtained the following correlations:
With the Wickman traditional teachers, +.746
With the Wickman modern teachers, +.457
With the Wickman mental hygienists, —.196
With the Porter high school seniors, +.712
With the Porter college seniors, +.610

SOURCE: Thomas Mangan and David Shafer, "Behavior Problems of Children as Viewed by Children in the Fifth through Eighth Grades," *Journal of Educational Research*, Vol. 56 (October, 1962), pp. 104–106.

These 101 children believed that stealing, skipping school, cheating, destroying school material, and temper tantrums were the most serious of 47 listed behaviors. Mangan and Shafer concluded that children tend to acquire the attitudes of their teachers toward certain behavioral types and retain these attitudes through high school and even college.

Rice examined the types of concerns referred to a central guidance agency at different grade levels.[28] Those mentioned consistently by teachers in referring pupils were categorized as (1) emotional problems such as anxiety, hyperactivity, immaturity, impulsivity, moodiness, and withdrawal; (2) intellectual disabilities such as short attention span, low ability, defective memory, perceptual malfunctioning, poor study habits, underachieving, and inability to understand; (3) motivational inadequacies including lack of ambition, poor or negative attitudes, frustrations, lack of interests, and low levels of aspiration; (4) moral defects such as lying, obscenity, psychosexual indiscretions, stealing, and undeveloped values; (5) physical ailments including chronic illness, poor health habits, orthopedic handicaps, and psychosomatic manifestations; (6) social maladjustment including aggressive antisocial behavior, family conflicts, isolation, and uncouth behavior. Table 3.4 shows these referrals.

Rice noted that primary pupils were referred largely for intellectual problems, particularly those involving low ability. Other problem categories were mentioned, but not as repeatedly or as consistently as at higher grade levels. Intermediate pupils were also referred primarily for intellectual problems, but more perceptual difficulties complicated by underachieving were included. Teachers increasingly referred intermediate pupils because of social problems.

Radin categorized the behavioral concerns of elementary pupils as viewed by teachers and others in the following way: (1) academic problems, which include underachievement, overachievement, erratic or uneven performance; (2) social problems with peers and siblings, including aggressive or submissive behavior; (3) conflicts with authority figures, including teachers and parents, such as defiant or submissive behavior; (4) overt behavioral manifestations, such as tics, nail biting, thumb sucking, toilet problems, exhibitionism, phobias, fire setting, speech peculiarities, and other bizarre behaviors.[29]

[28] Joseph P. Rice, Jr., "Types of Problems Referred to a Central Guidance Agency at Different Grade Levels," *Personnel and Guidance Journal*, Vol. 42 (September, 1963), pp. 52–55.

[29] Sherwin S. Radin, "Mental Health Problems of School Children," *Journal of School Health*, Vol. 33 (June, 1963), p. 252.

Table 3.4 Types of problems referred to a central guidance agency at various grade levels by per cent (N = 283)

	PRIMARY (1–3) N = 70		INTERMEDIATE (4–6) N = 88		JUNIOR HIGH (7–9) N = 80		HIGH (10–12) N = 45		
Problem Categories	*Reason*	*Mention*	*Reason*	*Mention*	*Reason*	*Mention*	*Reason*	*Mention*	X^2
Emotional reactions	12.9	31.4	13.6	30.7	10.0	38.8	13.3	35.6	0.60
Intellectual disabilities	55.7	37.1	47.7	31.8	18.8	42.5	35.6	33.3	24.90[a]
Motivational inadequacy	5.7	21.4	8.0	13.6	10.0	15.0	17.8	20.0	5.37
Moral defect	2.9	11.4	3.4	15.9	22.5	47.5	13.3	40.0	22.45[a]
Physical ailments	8.6	28.6	2.3	17.0	5.0	12.5	4.4	11.1	3.43
Social maladjustment	14.3	44.3	25.0	45.4	33.8	48.8	15.6	33.3	9.59[b]

[a] Significant at the 1 per cent level with three degrees of freedom.
[b] Significant at the 5 per cent level with three degrees of freedom.

SOURCE: Joseph P. Rice, Jr., "Types of Problems Referred to a Central Guidance Agency at Different Grade Levels," *Personnel and Guidance Journal*, Vol. 42 (September, 1963), pp. 52–55.

In the classroom the quiet youngster is often perceived by teachers as less of a problem than the aggressive youngster. Wickman, in an extensive investigation four decades ago of teachers' attitudes toward children's behavior, reported that the more extrovertive reactions such as whispering, defiance, profanity, moving about, lack of courtesy to members of the opposite sex, destroying school property, lying, and the like were believed by the majority of classroom teachers to be symptomatic of maladjustment. On the other hand, the types of pupil behavior often associated by clinicians with maladjustment, such as unsociability, suspicion, depression, sensitiveness, and fearfulness, were rated by teachers as harmless and even desirable forms of adjustment to school life.[30]

In the years since Wickman's study was made, greater emphasis has been placed upon an understanding not only of the child's emotional needs but also of his way of defending himself or dealing with his environment. Recognition of the teacher's interactions with pupils has been related increasingly to the teacher's drives or motivations and to the reciprocal interaction of both teacher and pupil in the dynamic field of classroom processes.

That teachers and mental hygienists have moved closer together in their judgments of the serious behavior problems of children than they were at the time of the Wickman report (1928) is illustrated by the research findings of Hunter.[31] His comparative data are presented in Table 3.5. However, teachers still consider politeness and obedience to be criteria of good adjustment, while clinicians place less emphasis upon these traits and regard them as being equivocal as indices of satisfactory mental health. Illustrations of the differences may be seen in the 10 most frequently cited behaviors (see Table 3.5).

Table 3.5 Rank order comparison of ratings by teachers in 1955 and by teachers and mental hygienists in 1926 of the relative seriousness of 10 behavior problems

308 TEACHERS (1955) *Hunter*	511 TEACHERS (1926) *Wickman*	30 MENTAL HYGIENISTS (1926) *Wickman*
1. Stealing	Heterosexual activity	Unsocial, withdrawn
2. Destroying school materials	Stealing	Suspiciousness
3. Truancy	Masturbation	Unhappy, depressed
4. Cruelty, bullying	Obscene notes, talk	Resentfulness
5. Unhappy, depressed	Untruthfulness	Fearfulness
6. Impertinence, defiance	Truancy	Cruelty, bullying
7. Untruthfulness	Impertinence	Easily discouraged
8. Unreliableness	Cruelty, bullying	Overcritical of others
9. Disobedience	Cheating	Sensitiveness
10. Heterosexual activity	Destroying school materials	Domineering

SOURCE: E. C. Hunter, "Changes in Teachers' Attitude Toward Children's Behavior Over the Last Thirty Years," *Mental Hygiene*, Vol. 41 (January, 1957), pp. 3–11.

Studies abound which give information about children's behavior as seen from the position of the outsider. Much less is known about how it looks from the point of view of the child himself. Yet modern psychological theory assigns a crucial role to the child's perception of self and the world about him as a causative agent of behavior. Combs and Soper designed research which sought to shed light on the relationships between how children perceive themselves and the world in which they live, on the one hand, and how they behave in

[30] E. K. Wickman, *Children's Behavior and Teachers' Attitudes* (New York: Commonwealth Fund, 1928), Chaps. 5–9.
[31] E. C. Hunter, "Changes in Teachers' Attitude Toward Children's Behavior Over the Last Thirty Years," *Mental Hygiene*, Vol. 41 (January, 1957), pp. 3–11.

school, on the other.[32] Perceptual data (trained observers' inferences as a result of five contacts under two different conditions) and behavioral data (general behavior, skills, and vital statistics) were obtained from 61 children in kindergarten and first grade. The general conclusions drawn by these two authors are cited here:

1. The child's feeling of personal adequacy has a pervasive importance in his perceptual organization. This finding lends support to the centrality assigned by perceptual psychological theory to the feeling of adequacy as a basic human motivation. It has implications also for educational planning and underscores the importance of success in the child's school experiences.

2. The values held by teachers are revealed in the judgments they make about child behavior. Teacher values are so sharply revealed by factor analyses of their behavioral ratings of children as to provide an effective projective test of the teacher's own value structure.

3. Correlation between children's perceptions of themselves and their world, on the one hand, with their behavior as described by teachers, on the other, is positive but low. The private world of the child has important differences from the judgments made about him by observers.

4. Important changes occur in children's perceptions and behavior with progression from kindergarten through first grade. Most significant is a reduced feeling of adequacy.

5. Significant predictions about behavior can be made a year in advance from a knowledge of the child's perceptual orientation. Such predictions, furthermore, can be made from comparatively small samples of behavior and suggest a valuable new dimension for diagnosis.

6. The observer himself can be used as an instrument to provide stable and reliable data for research. When used with proper safeguards it appears such data can provide valuable additions to traditional tools of research.

Like many institutions, the school tends to be a world unto itself. All too often the school attempts to deal with seriously disturbed pupils in educational terms, using discipline and exhortation. By the time patience is exhausted, serious damage may be done. Skillful referral to community mental health agencies is too frequently overlooked or pursued too late.

The problems of children of low-income families have been highlighted by testimony on the Elementary and Secondary Education Act of 1965 given to the Senate Subcommittee on Education. Ten million children in elementary and secondary schools whose families earn less than $3,000 annually are handicapped by cultural experiences, parental indifference, and a multiplicity of unmet needs. Frederick Bertolaet, in his testimony, cited several characteristics of the culturally disadvantaged child.[33] They are reproduced here.

The teacher may note these characteristics:
- Lack of response to conventional classroom approaches
- Inadequate performance in communication skills
- Socially unacceptable behavior
- Indifference to responsibility
- Nonpurposeful activity
- Physical defects and poor health habits
- Exaggerated importance of status symbols

Study of the culturally disadvantaged child's home and family is likely to reveal:
- Low formal educational level
- Limited vocational and economic competence
- Low social and economic expectancy
- Vulnerability to exploitation
- Conflicting social mores
- Disoriented and disrupted family patterns
- Indifference to health needs

[32] Arthur W. Combs and Daniel W. Soper, *The Relationships of Child Perceptions to Achievement and Behavior in the Early School Years* (Moravia, N.Y.: Chronicle Guidance Publications, 1965–1966).

[33] Elementary and Secondary Education Act of 1965, *Hearings Before the Subcommittee on Education,* Eighty-Ninth Congress, First Session, on S. 370, Part 2, pp. 1193–1196.

High level tension and emotional response
Lack of cultural resources
Lack of privacy for family members
Apathy toward school and community responsibilities

These characteristics and conditions cause children to gain less from schooling than they might and less than they need to function as competent citizens. The typical school has not been prepared to compensate for the various deprivations which exist in the lives of such children. Further, the reinforcements the children need are often intangible: an acceptable self-image, an implicit sense of identification with a stable family, security and freedom from emotional want, self-confidence and motivation to achieve. These positive factors are essential to the healthy development of the child. They are the firm ground beneath the learning process.

CONCERNS OF THE HIGH SCHOOL STUDENT

The concerns of high school students evolve from developmental tasks and from living within the social system represented by the school. The employment of a counselor in a school is usually based upon the premise that students have certain unmet needs that necessitate a counseling relationship. Some of these needs are rooted in the modifications that have been made in some schools. Greater use is being made of educational technology, teacher aides, team teaching, and small instructional groups. Subject matter, particularly mathematics, science, and foreign languages, continues to be emphasized along with attention to the career education of students. During the next few years it is believed that (1) the traditional role of the teacher will undergo change, (2) newly inducted teachers may know more about content and less about the educative process, (3) newly inducted teachers may be less knowledgeable about students, about individual differences, and about student motivation and (4) the quantity of work required of students will increase. It is to be hoped that these changes will in fact result in a new intellectual rigor and a new qualitative excellence in education. We know no one in favor of soft education. But there are clouds on the horizon. Writing in *Saturday Review*, Benizet observed that "excellence" has become a true sentence stopper in education, but says that unfortunately "some have used excellence as a call for a series of counter marches in education; others are using it to back their own opinions about whom, what, and how to teach."[34] He asks whether our drive toward excellence is in fact aggravating the "College Board Neurosis" in which parents believe the SAT score is "the knell that summons to heaven or hell." Should excellence, he writes, be equated with quantity of study? Will the "heavy assignment binge" cause a tired boy to become twice as smart by studying four hours a night instead of two?

Mallery responds to Benizet's questions with some foreboding findings. Mallery visited eight selected high schools in an attempt to determine the impact the high school had on the student's life and his thinking.[35] This, Mallery believed, has been overlooked in the current concern with standards and "excellence." In seven of the schools Mallery found a remarkably consistent pattern. Students voiced a pervasively negative reaction to the curriculum and to "subjects" because they seemed dead, inert, unreal, and unrelated to life and to the community. Over and over students referred to the curriculum as "theirs," meaning the teachers'. This attitude is caught in the following direct quotes from students:

> We just seem to do the homework, memorize, take tests, and get the marks. It's all just to get into college. I'd like some chance to think some in a course. Where is this big deal about education widening the horizons and challenging the mind about life, and all that?

> Everything's all known and worked out. Even the teacher's course is all finished. There's nothing for us to do but learn the answers and agree.

[34] Louis T. Benizet, "The Trouble with Excellence," *Saturday Review*, October 21, 1962.
[35] David Mallery, *The High School Student Speaks Out* (New York: Harper & Row, Publishers, 1962).

I haven't had a chance in any course to really think.

The school is not supposed to influence you. It's where you do the assignment.

What these students were seeking and generally not finding, according to Mallery, were (1) the opportunity to bear genuine responsibility within the school and outside (students wanted to go beyond doing assignments and keeping out of trouble), (2) purpose; striving for high marks and test scores was not enough, and (3) the challenge to think, to explore, and to come to grips with their work in each subject in some kind of personal, meaningful way.

While space does not permit describing the one comprehensive high school that Mallery visited that stands in sharp contrast to the other seven, his report is recommended reading. One point, however, should be emphasized. In the face of the pervasive attitude which Mallery found in seven of the eight high schools visited, there is grave doubt that a professional counselor could, through the individual counseling of students and performance of the other peripheral activities that have traditionally been included in a "guidance program," exercise more than a marginal influence. The prevailing learning environment and resultant student attitudes would likely frustrate and probably defeat him.

Today, there is danger that too many individuals confuse education with the "programming" of students for information storage and retrieval as though they were machines. These are the dangers of compulsive attention to content in the absence of attention to process. Tiedeman has recently declared that "If the student is to become responsible and hence 'to outlive his teachings' . . . he must consider the *process* of education simultaneously with its content."[36] Heathers has defined the process of education as (1) acquiring the power to assimilate through the framing and solving of problems, (2) exercising initiative for, and during the course of, problem solving, and (3) evaluating one's efforts at problem solving using mastery as a criterion.[37] This process stands in bold relief to information storage and retrieval. Process is something that takes place within the individual learner. Process implies motivation, action, initiative, value judgments, and responsibility on the part of the student.

Some youth report difficulty with and concern about developmental tasks. Based upon some 17,600 high school pupils drawn from all sections of the United States, the Purdue Opinion Panel[38] reported that high school students worry most about (1) family life in the future (finding a suitable mate, deciding "whether I'm in love"), (2) having their own money and (3) jobs. Little concern was expressed by these students about (1) their behavior or (2) their skills and abilities. Table 3.6 summarized the proportions of responses by these youth. As can be seen by examining the data reported in Table 3.6 (See p. 66), considerable concern about developmental tasks is expressed by girls, especially about physique, friendships, family life, values, and self.

Gibson and Mitchell surveyed educators in Great Britain and the United States to compare the educational and vocational problems that affect secondary school students in these two countries. These educators' ranking of the seriousness of 22 problems is reported in Table 3.7 (See p. 67).

As the data in Table 3.7 reveal, the problem of pupils failing to work to capacity or achieve near capacity was viewed as most serious by the school administrators, teachers and counseling-psychological personnel in both countries. These two researchers interviewed a small sampling of pupils in both countries. Their interviews indicated that American pupils were most concerned with, in order, (1) lack of appropriate curricular offerings, (2) lack of post-high school vocational and techni-

[36] David V. Tiedeman. *Status and Prospect in Counseling Psychology.* Cambridge, Massachusetts: Graduate School of Education, Harvard University, (mimeo).

[37] Glen L. Heathers, *Notes on the Strategy of Educational Reform,* (New York: Experimental Teaching Center, School of Education, New York University), (mimeo).

[38] The Purdue Opinion Panel, *Counseling and Educational Needs of Adolescents,* Report of Poll 93 (Lafayette, Indiana: Measurement and Research Center, Purdue University, January, 1973), p. 10.

Table 3.6 Purdue opinion panel report on high school students' concerns about developmental tasks

	VERY MUCH		SOME		LITTLE OR NOT MUCH	
Developmental Concerns	*Boys*	*Girls*	*Boys*	*Girls*	*Boys*	*Girls*
My physique	26%	44%	29%	28%	44%	28%
Friendships	33	32	26	26	41	42
Relationship with parents/adults	25	34	26	25	48	41
Having own money	40	42	22	24	34	31
Job or occupation	37	39	27	27	32	31
Skills and abilities	20	18	28	28	50	52
My behavior	17	17	20	21	61	60
Family life in future	37	53	25	23	37	23
Values	25	33	26	25	46	41
Myself (who I am, what I can do)	29	38	25	23	42	36

SOURCE: Based on The Purdue Opinion Panel, Report of Poll 93, *Counseling and Educational Needs of Adolescents*, Lafayette, Indiana: Purdue University, Measurement and Research Center, January, 1973.

cal educational opportunities and (3) inadequate guidance programs. Their British counterparts were most concerned about (1) lack of job opportunities, (2) lack of post-high school vocational and technical educational opportunities and (3) inadequate guidance programs.[39]

Mezzano administered a questionnaire (based on the Mooney Problem Check List) to some 1,495 students enrolled in grades seven through 12 in three Wisconsin public school communities. The rankings given to certain problem areas are reported in Table 3.8 (See p. 68). These data reveal that high among students' concerns are those that involve educational and vocational opportunities, followed by school life. Mezzano also asked these students to indicate their preference for talking to a male or female counselor, given these problem areas. Most students (both boys and girls) chose to discuss most of these concerns with male counselors.[40]

Diederich and Jackson have identified two forms of student failure in the classroom. The unsuccessful attempt to master required material is the most well known. Equally important, but less widely discussed, is the second form, the student who fails to accept as his own the goals and values of the school. Numerous surveys report that between 25 to 30 per cent of high school students are "dissatisfied" with school. Boys are generally more dissatisfied than girls. The two forms of failure – the academic and the attitudinal – are commonly thought to be closely related. The usual premise is that the student who does well in school likes or is satisfied with school. But the findings of many studies indicate that this premise does not hold true. Teenagers' dissatisfaction or discontent with their school experiences appear to be a reflection of their total psychological *elan* rather than a specific reaction to their academic progress or lack of it. Diederich and Jackson surveyed 258 high school juniors and reported that there was no significant relationship between the students' evaluation of school experiences and their achievement, as measured by standardized tests and teachers' grades. Teachers rated satisfied students as less impulsive and more responsible than average students.[41]

[39] Robert L. Gibson and Marianne H. Mitchell, "Theirs and Ours: Educational-Vocational Problems in Britain and the United States," *Vocational Guidance Quarterly*, Vol. 19 (December, 1970), pp. 108–112.

[40] Joseph Mezzano, "Concerns of Students and Preference for Male and Female Counselors," *Vocational Guidance Quarterly*, Vol. 20 (September, 1971), pp. 42–47.

[41] Richard C. Diederich and Philip W. Jackson, "Satisfied and Dissatisfied Students," *Personnel and Guidance Journal*, Vol. 47 (March 1969), pp. 641–649.

Table 3.7 Rankings of seriousness of 22 problems by British and American educators

Problem	RANKING United States	British Isles
Failing to work to capacity	1	1
Home environment	2	2
Failure to acquire basic reading, writing, and reasoning skills	3	18
Behavior out of school	4	6
Lack of interest in the academic program	5	3
Lack of appropriate curriculum	6.5	7
Lack of parental cooperation	6.5	8
No post high school-vocational-technical educational opportunities	8	21
Outdated or inadequate vocational-technical facilities	9	16
Lack of public understanding and cooperation	10	15
No jobs for graduates	11.5	4
Inadequate guidance programs	11.5	17
Neighborhood environment	13	14
Lack of financial resources	14	19
Excessive employment	15	10
Outdated or inadequate physical facilities in general	16.5	20
Inability to hold science or technical faculty	16.5	11.5
Lack of interest in school activities	18	5
Dropping out of school	19	22
Behavior in school	20	9
Inability to hold a quality faculty	21	13
Failure to aspire to appropriate careers	22	11.5

SOURCE: Robert L. Gibson and Marianne H. Mitchell, "Theirs and Ours: Educational-Vocational Problems in Britain and the United States," *Vocational Guidance Quarterly*, Vol. 19 (December, 1970), p. 110. Copyright © 1970 American Personnel and Guidance Association. Reprinted with permission.

Zytowski and his associates sought to validate James B. Conant's proposition that problems in the city slum are the reverse of those in the suburbs.[42] Guidance personnel from schools typical of each category were asked to report the frequency with which clients presented certain types of problems. In both city and suburbs the preponderant need was in the area of educational and vocational choice and relationships with teachers. Significant differences (.05 and .01 levels) were found in other distributions. City counselors report more problems of relationships with authorities, racial differences, health and nutrition problems. Suburban counselors report problems involving moral and ethical conduct, feelings of inferiority, sibling and peer relationships, and religious behavior. The authors conclude that, while supporting Conant's proposition of differences between the two types of school, the data could not demonstrate that one situation was the reverse of the other.

The observation that more and more high school students devote more and more of their time to study is validated by student self-reports. Comparative data in Table 3.9 (See p. 68), reporting the time spent on homework outside of school each day, are drawn from Purdue Opinion Polls.

High school youth's plans for the future are reported in Table 3.10 (See p. 68). Especially noteworthy is the changing proportion who plan to attend college or other institutions to obtain special training. The adolescent's uncertainty about future plans is reported in Table 3.11 (See p. 69). The attitude of high school graduates as to how school had helped them in preparation for life activities is reported in Figure 3.2 (See p. 69).

A government publication discloses that young people are sick fewer days than older people or children.[43] They average 6.3 days in bed because of illness per person per year, compared with 7.8 days for the 5 to 14 age group and 8.5 days for people 25 and older. Days of restricted activity (13.5 per person per year) were also lower, 16.4 days for children 5 to 14 and 24.1 days for people 25 and over. Injuries to youth cause the greater proportion (13 per cent) of their short-term illnesses. The highest proportion of illnesses (61 per

[42] Donald G. Zytowski, Mary Mason, William Roche, and Alfred Weissman, "Client Needs in Cities and Suburbs," *Personnel and Guidance Journal*, Vol. 43 (September, 1969), pp. 41–44.

[43] *Problems of Youth* (Washington: Government Printing Office, 1964).

Table 3.8 Ranking of areas of concern by boys and girls

	GRADE	7TH		8TH		9TH		10TH		11TH		12TH	
Area of concern	*N=*	*boys* 132	*girls* 117	*boys* 119	*girls* 120	*boys* 244	*girls* 247	*boys* 74	*girls* 92	*boys* 105	*girls* 77	*boys* 71	*girls* 97
Health/physical development		4	1	4	1	3	3	6	3	7	5	6	6
School		3	2	1	3	2	1.5	2	5	2	3	2	3
Home and family		1	3	3	2	5	4	4	3	4	7	5	5
Boy-girl relationships		5	6	5	4	4	5	3	6	3	4	4	2
Future—educational/ vocational		2	4	2	5	1	1.5	1	1	1	1	1	1
Moral and religious		7	7	6	6	7	7	7	7	6	6	7	7
Self-centered		6	5	7	7	6	6	5	3	5	2	3	4

SOURCE: Joseph Mezzano, "Concerns of Students and Preference for Male and Female Counselors," *Vocational Guidance Quarterly*, Vol. 20 (September, 1971), p. 45. Copyright © 1971 American Personnel and Guidance Association. Reprinted with permission.

cent) was caused by respiratory diseases – sore throats, colds, influenza, tonsilitis, etc. Orthopedic impairments, including paralysis and amputations, are by far the greatest cripplers of youth aged 15-24, causing six out of 10 disabilities. Over 90,000 youth nationwide were in institutions for long-term care in 1960. The mentally retarded and mentally ill comprise almost three-fourths of this group.

The previous requirement that young men be given a military service qualifying examination has produced data which reflect the problems of adolescents. A total of 49.8 per cent failed the mental and/or physical tests at their preinduction examination in 1962; some 21.5 per cent failed their mental tests, 3 per cent failed both medical and mental tests, and 22.7 per cent were disqualified for duty by failure to meet the special physical requirements of the military services. Figure 3.3 presents the reasons why these men were found unqualified for military service.

The problems of the adult world as viewed by adolescents comprise a subject rarely studied.

Table 3.9 Time spent on homework outside of school each day

Amount of time	*Poll 18 1948*	*Poll 65 1962*	*Poll 79 1967*
No time	14%	4%	1%
Less than one hour	45	28	32
1 to 2 hours	33	42	47
More than 2 hours	8	22	20
No response	0	4	0

SOURCE: Purdue Opinion Panel, *High School Students' Leisure Time Activities and Attitudes Toward Network Television*, Poll 79 and other Polls (Lafayette, Indiana: Measurement and Research Center, Purdue University, February, 1967), p. 5a.

Table 3.10 Students' plans for the future

Post-high school plans	*Poll 29 1951*	*Poll 41 1955*	*Poll 63 1961*	*Poll 85 1968*	*Poll 95 1972*
Go to college	35%	37%	45%	53%	47%
Special training	12	12	13	17	13
Go to work	26	23	17	10	20
Military service	11	12	12	7	5
Other plans or don't know	16	16	9	12	15

SOURCE: Purdue Opinion Panel, *Evaluation of Educational Attitudes*, Polls 93 and 95 (Lafayette, Indiana: Measurement and Research Center, Purdue University, August, 1972), p. 1a.

Table 3.11 Degree of certainty of students' post-high school plans

Degree of certainty	*College* %	*Training other than college* %	*Work* %	*Military service* %	*Other plans* %
Definitely know what I will do	28	26	12	18	10
Family sure of my plans	57	56	55	57	33
Have a plan, but will probably change it	11	14	20	16	31
Have no idea of what I will do	3	4	11	7	26

SOURCE: Purdue Opinion Panel, *Youth's Vocational Plans and Attitudes Toward School,* Poll 78 (Lafayette, Indiana: Measurement and Research Center, Purdue University, November, 1966), pp. 3a–4a.

Adams (reporting in 1963) asked 4,000 boys and girls, ranging in age from 10 to 19, what they considered the major problems of their country. About two-thirds cited international problems (war with Russia) and one-fourth domestic problems (civil rights). Adams found that concern with international problems tended to decrease with age but interest in domestic issues increased with age.[44]

More high school students today are seeing the counselor than in previous years. During the past five years, the proportion of high school students who have not talked to a counselor declined from 34 to 15 per cent. Table 3.12 (See p. 71) reports students' contacts with counselors, 1966 to 1971.

During the past few years, the Purdue Opinion Panel has assessed the degree of concern students have about their vocational choices or decisions. Table 3.13 (See p. 71) reports the most current data collected on this matter. Students who plan to attend college express "very much" concern about making vocational decisions. They report that they need information and help to choose a vocation, to

[44] James F. Adams, "Adolescent Opinion on National Problems," *Personnel and Guidance Journal,* Vol. 42 (December, 1963), pp. 397–400.

Figure 3.2 Attitude of high school graduates as to how school had helped them in preparation for life activities

PERCENT OF FORMER STUDENTS WHO FELT SCHOOL HELPED

	A GREAT DEAL	SOME	LITTLE OR NONE
Getting along with people	56%	35%	6%
Using good English	52%	33%	12%
Using mathematical skills	43%	34%	18%
Reading efficiently	41%	35%	18%
Preparing for college	41%	35%	19%
Understanding oneself	32%	42%	22%
Solving personal problems	31%	36%	29%
Care of health	29%	46%	21%
Business problems	28%	36%	29%
Getting a job	24%	37%	33%
Community affairs	24%	37%	29%
Leisure activities	20%	45%	28%
Marriage	15%	29%	46%
Handling money	15%	34%	42%

NOTE: "Uncertain" responses ranging from 3 to 10 per cent in the various categories are not shown.

SOURCE: California State Department of Education, *Now Hear Youth,* Vol. 22, No. 9, p. 21.

Figure 3.3 Young men found unqualified for military service, 1962: reasons for medical disqualifications, medical diagnosis, and frequency of defect per 10,000 medically disqualified youth

SOURCE: "One-Third of a Nation," a report of young men found unqualified for military service of the President's Task Force on Manpower Conservation, January, 1964, p. 26.

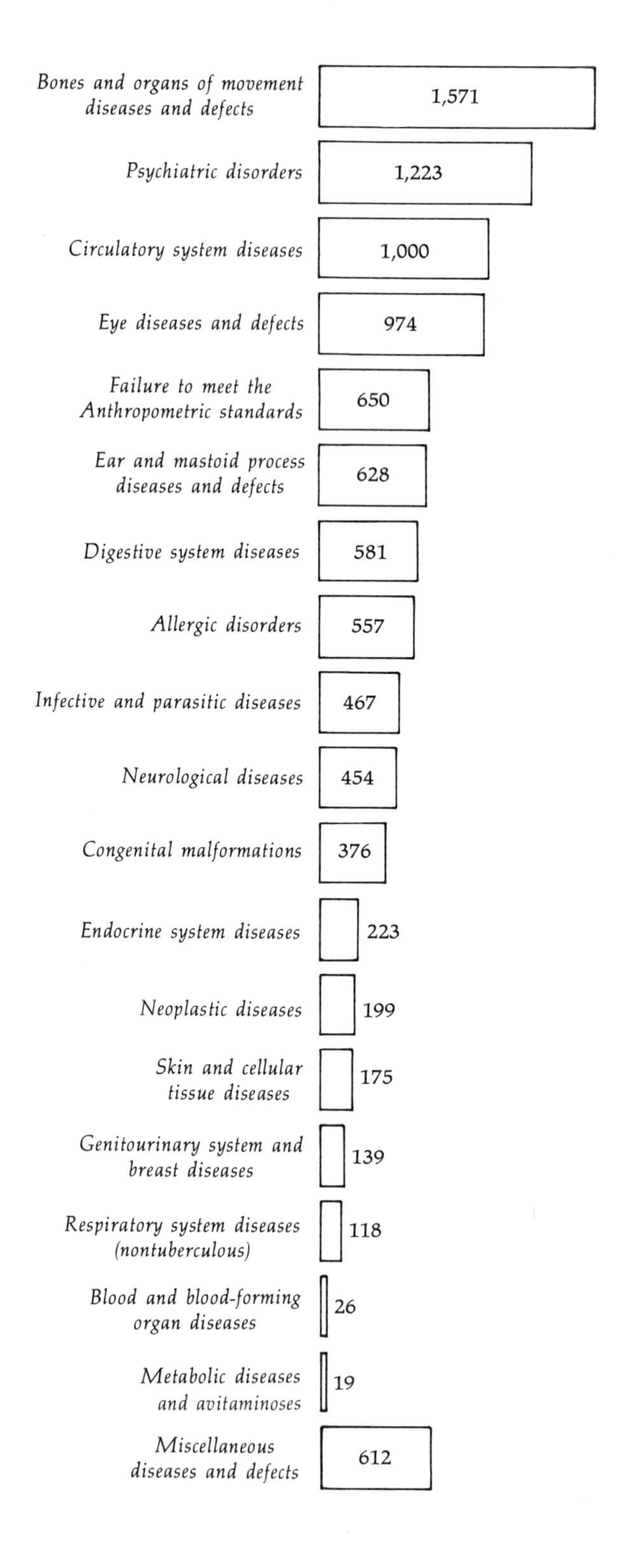

understand themselves, their interests, skills, and values. The counselor and parents are viewed as the best sources of assistance with vocational planning and choice making.

CONCERNS OF COLLEGE STUDENTS

Houston[45] reviewed the research on the sources and effects of psychological problems of college students. As expected, the general academic area is consistently identified as most stressful for students. Other prevalent problems include dating, making and breaking friendships, becoming independent of parents and making vocational plans. Houston reports that freshmen experience more problems than students during the other three years of college. A greater proportion of freshmen seek psychological assistance than upperclassmen. Peak periods of help seeking occur at mid-term and final examination times. Anxiety, depression, character traits, or emotional sensitivity were reported as hampering some 12 to 35 per cent of students across various campuses. Concern over studies, unusual physical complaints and difficulties with interpersonal relationships often led to successful or attempted suicide. In summary, both psychological and academic adjustment are influenced by college students' problems. Houston believes college students' anxiety states may be related in some complex, as yet unclear, fashion to their current or anticipated academic performance.

The functions frequently performed in a college

[45] B. Kent Houston, "Sources, Effects and Individual Vulnerability of Psychological Problems for College Students," *Journal of Counseling Psychology*, Vol. 18 (March, 1971), pp. 157–161.

Table 3.12 Students' contacts with counselors 1966 to 1971

Talked to counselor last year	*Poll 78 1966*	*Poll 85 1968*	*Poll 88 1970*	*Poll 93 1971*
Never	34%	22%	21%	15%
Once or twice	40	45	41	44
Three or four times	16	22	22	23
Five times or more	9	9	15	15

SOURCE: Purdue Opinion Panel, *Counseling and Educational Needs of Adolescents*, Poll 92 (Lafayette, Indiana: Measurement and Research Center, Purdue University, January, 1972), p. 9.

Table 3.13 Degree of student concern about making vocational decisions

Degree of concern	*Grade 10*	*Grade 11*	*Grade 12*
Very much	19%	27%	39%
Quite a bit	26	28	28
Somewhat	25	23	17
A little	16	10	7
Not very much	13	12	9

SOURCE: Purdue Opinion Panel, *Vocational Plans and Preferences of Adolescents*, Poll 94 (Lafayette, Indiana: Measurement and Research Center, Purdue University, May, 1972), p. 5a.

counseling center are educational counseling for choice of major, vocational counseling for choice of a career, and personal counseling for self-understanding and interpersonal relationships. Sharp and Marra[46] point out that different college counseling centers vary considerably in the students they attract. Variation may be due to the staff, campus climate, and range of services available. They inspected eight years of client problems classified by members of the Counseling Division, University of Wyoming. The distribution by diagnostic classification is presented in Table 3.14. As can be seen in Table 3.14, more and more students with emo-

[46] W. Harry Sharp and Herbert A. Marra, "Factors Related to Classification of Client Problems, Number of Counseling Sessions and Trends of Client Problems," *Journal of Counseling Psychology*, Vol. 18 (March, 1971), pp. 117–122.

Table 3.14 Percentage distribution of college students' problems by diagnostic classification 1960 - 1967

Year	*Vocational*	*Emotional*	*Educational*
1960–61	43.3	10.0	46.6
1961–62	39.2	17.7	43.0
1962–63	42.0	14.8	43.2
1963–64	41.1	27.0	31.9
1964–65	38.5	20.5	41.0
1965–66	51.4	35.3	13.4
1966–67	43.9	38.7	17.4
1967–68	42.7	45.0	12.3

SOURCE: W. Harry Sharp and Herbert A. Marra, "Factors Related to Classification of Client Problem, Number of Counseling Sessions and Trends of Client Problems," *Journal of Counseling Psychology*, Vol. 18 (March, 1971), p. 120. Copyright © 1971 American Psychological Association. Reprinted with permission.

tional problems are using college counseling services. However, in a review of studies of the emotional health of college students, Segal[47] stated that the degree of college students' emotional health reported by various investigators varied according to the classification scheme used. Nevertheless, he believed that the emotional status of roughly one-third of college students was sufficiently disturbed to "give pause to a psychiatric evaluator."

Hecklinger[48] investigated whether students who were undecided about their vocational plans were less satisfied with college than students who were decided. His subjects — 125 men and 231 women — were members of the junior class at Trenton State College, New Jersey. His qualified conclusion (only two of eight analyses were significant) was that undecided students were less satisfied with the college environment, as measured by Part II, College Student Questionnaire.

Hoffman, calling for a wider and more intensive counseling effort in colleges, cites the following statistics:

[47] B. E. Segal, "Epidemiology of Emotional Disturbance Among College Undergraduates: A Review and Analysis," *Journal of Nervous and Mental Disease*, Vol. 143 (October, 1966), pp. 348–362.

[48] Fred J. Hecklinger, "The Undecided Student — Is He Less Satisfied with College?" *Journal of College Student Personnel*, Vol. 13 (May, 1972), pp. 247–251.

(1) About 10 per cent of all college students have serious emotional problems that require the services of a psychiatrist if one is available.
(2) Among college students the suicide rate is about 1.5 out of every 10,000 or higher by 50 per cent than that of the population at large.
(3) Psychotic breaks which require hospitalization or other restraints occur at the rate of two for each 1,000 students.
(4) More than 50 per cent of students who start college in any given year fail to graduate.[49]

Hoffman suggests that collegiate institutions of all sizes will need to increase and improve their counseling services, from student contact with the faculty up through psychiatric treatment.

Special Problems of Youth

The impact of international and national events upon American life during the last three decades has produced a number of problems with which the schools and colleges must cope. To treat each one carefully and fully is beyond the scope of this chapter, but six major problems will be briefly discussed. Most assuredly, they are not entirely school problems. Their origin lies in the complex social discontinuities that exist in America, and their solution lies in a multi-institutional approach.

SCHOOL AND COLLEGE DROPOUT

As of 1972, most teenagers, 15 to 19, were in school but most young adults, 20 to 24, were not. Seven out of 10 teenage youth but only 1.5 of every 100 of the young adult group were in school. The proportion in the teenage category was slightly higher in urban areas (70.9 per cent) than in rural areas (67.8 per cent) and considerably higher for the young adult group, which has 17.2 per cent urban young people in school compared with 8 per cent for rural areas. Although more young people are getting a high school education today (1970, 72 per cent; 1930, 57 per cent; 1910, 45 percent) than ever before and the percentage of college-age people actually in college is expected to grow markedly by 1985 (1970, 25 per cent of those 18 to 24 years old compared to a projected 40 per cent in 1985), dropouts pose a major problem to school and college personnel. The point of greatest danger for high school dropouts has moved from the eighth to the tenth grade in three decades.

Study after study has probed for the reasons why students leave school. These studies have, with remarkable consistency, arrived at similar conclusions. Typical reasons for dropping out of school are work, early marriage, grade failures, inability to get along with teachers, dislike of social relationships in the school, and a belief that school course work is unrelated to individual needs. An Indiana study of some 9,257 dropouts during the 1964–1965 school year reported that (1) over half were in the average range or above in mental ability, (2) three-fourths had no record of delinquency, (3) three-fourths had never been retained in secondary school, (4) almost half had never had a conference with a counselor, (5) almost half had fathers who were employed in semiskilled and unskilled occupations, (6) two-thirds were not gainfully employed while in school and did not own a car, (7) nearly 69 per cent reported that their natural parents had never been divorced, and (8) over half of the parents had attitudes that were passive or in favor of the student's dropping out of school.[50] The four major reasons for leaving *cited by the dropouts* were to earn money (14 per cent), to get married (14 per cent), dislike of subjects (13 per cent), and constant failure (12 per cent). The four major reasons given by school officials were failure (29 per cent), need to work (18 per cent), marriage and pregnancy (17 per cent), and incorrigibility (13 per cent).

Leubling summarizes counselor descriptions of dropouts.[51] He reported that dropouts (1) distrust-

[49] Randell W. Hoffman, "Counseling and the College," *Improving College and University Teaching*, Vol. 13 (Winter, 1965), pp. 16–18.

[50] Rolla F. Pruett, Bruce Shertzer, and Fay A. Clardy, *Survey Report of Indiana School Dropouts for the Year 1964–65*, Bulletin 254 (Indianapolis: Indiana State Department of Public Instruction, January, 1967).

[51] Harry E. Leubling, "Counseling with Dropouts: A Three-Year Study," *Vocational Guidance Quarterly*, Vol. 15 (March, 1967), pp. 173–180.

ed and suspected authority, (2) had unrealistic aspirations and work attitudes, (3) were hypersensitive to criticism or rejection, (4) had a facade of "toughness," (5) evidenced dependency needs, (6) possessed impaired and confused self-concepts, and (7) rejected social values. Their presenting problems to counselors included (1) employment, (2) family relationships, (3) health concerns, (4) school-related difficulties, (5) anxiety, and (6) responsibility for raising children.

Increasingly the college dropout is becoming the focus of widespread concern. A dropout rate of approximately 60 per cent nationally over the four-year period has been reported by Iffert,[52] whose data were based upon a sample of 13,700 students carefully followed up over four years. However, it is to be noted that the rate varies greatly with the type of institution. Public institutions, according to Iffert, show an average rate of 67 per cent while private institutions show only 52 per cent. Summerskill, in a survey covering the rates of attrition from 1913 to the present, found that attrition varied from 12 to 82 per cent, with a median loss of 50 per cent.[53]

Many descriptive studies indicate that the most crucial college dropout period is the freshman year, with the chances for survival increasing to 65 per cent or better by the junior year. The most commonly stated reasons for leaving college include (1) lack of finances, (2) academic difficulty, (3) dissatisfaction with program and college, (4) marriage, (5) military service, and (6) illness. Goetz and Leach sent 359 randomly selected freshmen (1962) at the University of New Mexico a questionnaire related to attrition.[54] A 60 per cent return was obtained – from 102 who continued, 65 who withdrew, and 25 who were suspended. The attitudes of those who withdrew and those who continued were compared regarding teachers, counselors, facilities, and various personal experiences and conditions that might lead to withdrawal. The results did not substantiate commonly cited reasons for withdrawing from college. In fact, continuers were more negative toward college environment than those who withdrew.

Demos investigated the reasons for withdrawal from college given by students and the reasons assigned by counselors who interviewed the students. The most popular reason given by students is that they need a job, yet counselors were of the opinion that this was a secondary or tertiary reason and that the primary cause was more likely to be lack of motivation or poor academic performance.[55]

Williams persuasively argues that consideration of the college environment would help to resolve some of the apparent contradictions among the various characteristics attributed to the college dropout.[56] He offers the hypothesis that a student is more likely to leave college when behavior reinforced by the college environment is incompatible with behavior previously reinforced. Therefore, interpersonal relationships with peers, instructors, and significant others are conceptualized as the processes mediating reinforcement for college students. Further, parents, teachers, and others view the act of dropping out of school as a social ill to be eradicated. Consequently this viewpoint reinforces the negative values comprising the self-concepts of students who leave school. Potential dropouts cannot make the changes in self-perception requisite to changes in overt behavior.

Associated with the above concept is the view that some students seem almost predestined to leave college because they are pulled in opposite directions by the reinforcement of opposing modes of behavior. Williams points out that the potential dropout may well perform some actions oriented toward achieving the goal of a college degree and

[52] R. E. Iffert, *Retention and Withdrawal of College Students*, Bulletin 1958, No. 1, U.S. Office of Education (Washington: U.S. Government Printing Office, 1958).

[53] J. Summerskill, "Dropouts from College," in N. Sanford (ed.), *The American College* (New York: John Wiley & Sons, Inc., 1962), pp. 627–658.

[54] Walter Goetz and Donald Leach, "The Disappearing Student," *Personnel and Guidance Journal*, Vol. 45 (May, 1967), pp. 883–887.

[55] George D. Demos, "Analysis of College Dropouts – Some Manifest and Covert Reasons," *Personnel and Guidance Journal*, Vol. 46 (March, 1968), pp. 681–684.

[56] Vernon Williams, "The College Dropout: Qualities of His Environment," *Personnel and Guidance Journal*, Vol. 45 (May, 1967), pp. 878–882.

engage in other actions directed away from that goal. Further, the avoidance component in such a conflict appears to be stronger than the approach component. Student personnel workers at all levels, Williams suggests, should begin to question with students and their parents the assumption that higher education is necessary for attaining the good life. He doubts that recommending counseling and psychotherapy for all students in conflict is realistic because of (1) lack of demonstrable gains and (2) strain on available resources.

Smith's critical and painful examination of why she dropped out of college offers some corroboration of Williams' hypotheses.[57] She relates her view of the pressures on students from society's "Great Plan" for the young and critically evaluates some of the implicit assumptions of higher education. The "Great Plan" is that students traverse from elementary school to high school to college and perhaps to graduate school so that they will be educated, responsible, useful citizens of whom their parents and educators can be proud. College pressures, nameless but pervasive, determine that certain students will drop out and others continue until graduation.

> Schools are geared to the future and to achievement. Consequently, every stage in the educational process becomes to the student a transition or a means to something else. You are in continual process of preparing or being measured for something – regents, college boards, graduate study, career, "responsibility," etc. Elementary school is a means to high school, high school to college, college to a good job and respectable place in society. Reading a book is a step toward passing a course, which is a step toward getting a diploma, which is a step toward college, a good job, etc. You are strongly urged at each step to do the best you can. Unfortunately, your "best" is compared with everyone else's "best" in the multitudes of percentiles that populate our schools.[58]

The future of the school dropout is bleak. Marginal employment, proneness to delinquency, anxiety, humiliation, and the inability to live life as a fully developed person are usually in store. Because contemporary America lacks any provisions for living in decent poverty, many dropouts rapidly retreat to hopelessness and apathy and become another generation of the community dependent, living on welfare, in the clinics, and in jail.

[57] Louise Smith, "A Statistic Strikes Back," *Personnel and Guidance Journal*, Vol. 45 (May, 1967), pp. 872–877.
[58] Ibid., p. 873.

PREGNANCIES, YOUTHFUL MARRIAGES, AND DIVORCE

According to a recent *Time* article,[59] teenage girls are greatly misinformed about the times they are most likely to become pregnant, and most teenagers do not use contraceptives. *Time* reported that Melvin Zelnik and John Kantner, two demographers who prepared a study for the President's Commission on Population Growth and the American Future, interviewed 4,611 unmarried white and black women, aged 15 to 19. While error-free statistics about sexual habits are difficult to come by, these demographers project from their sample that at age 15, 13.8 per cent of unmarried girls have experienced sexual intercourse. For age 16, the figure was 21.2 per cent; age 17, 26.6 per cent; age 18, 37.1 per cent; and age 19, 46.1 per cent. Even so, Zelnik and Kantner conclude that "the picture is not one of rampant sexuality among the sexually inexperienced." Nevertheless, youth's sexual revolution is not just franker talk and greater openness; more teenagers, especially younger ones, are having at least occasional sexual intercourse.

The pregnancy rate among unmarried girls continues to spiral. The number of illegitimate births per thousand teenagers has risen from 8.3 in 1940 to 19.8 in 1972. Of an estimated 1.5 million abortions performed in the U.S. in 1971, it is believed that close to one third were performed on teenagers. Nationwide, the pregnancy rate from college to college varies from six to 15 per cent.

Though the number of very youthful marriages seems to be declining, one-fourth of all 18- and 19-year-olds are married. The number of teenage brides who are pregnant when they walk down the aisle is impossible to compute. However, some es-

[59] Melvin Zelnik and John Kantner, *Time*, August 21, 1972, pp. 34–40.

timates exist which indicate that the pregnancy rate among teenage brides at the time of marriage may be as high as 33 per cent. While clearly not all youthful marriages occur because of pregnancy, it is reasonable to conclude that pregnancy is an influential factor in many youthful marriages. Otherwise, the couples would wait a few years to marry.

Currently there are 350 divorces for every 1,000 marriages. The divorce rate among teenagers is about two to four times higher than for those who marry later. This means that a teenage marriage has no better than a 50-50 chance of survival.

An overwhelming percentage of youth who marry in high school leave school and only a few reenter. Burchinal reveals that teenage marriage interferes with educational attainment.[60] He reported that 9 out of 10 teenagers who married were girls, and that 80 per cent of the high school girls dropped out of school. From many studies of teenage marriages Burchinal concluded that these youth (1) had known each other less than a year, (2) had had very short engagements, if any, (3) had low incomes and accepted help from their parents, and (4) had babies before they built a sound husband-wife relationship.

Although the curtailment of education is serious in itself, the personal, social, and legal aspects of early marriage are even more disturbing. Annulment and divorce rates are highest among those who marry in their teens.

CRIME AND DELINQUENCY

Delinquency is now recognized as a pervasive social problem, although little is known empirically about its origin. By any standard of measurement, the statistics are staggering, and their impact can be felt at every level of American life. One boy in every six will turn up in a juvenile court for a nontraffic offense before he is 18. Over one-fourth of all persons arrested by police in 1970 were in the age group 16 to 24, easily the most lawless group in America. Delinquency cases handled by the juvenile courts increased 10 per cent in 1962 over the previous year, at a time when the total child population in this age group (10 to 17) increased by only 3½ per cent. Six out of 10 delinquents are 16 or under.

Charges brought against boys are generally more serious than those against girls. More than half of the offenses committed by girls were for conduct not ordinarily considered a crime, such as "runaway," "truancy," "curfew," and the like, but only one-fifth of the boys were charged with these minor offenses. About half of the offenses committed by boys were against property — "larceny," "auto theft," "vandalism," "robbery," and "burglary."

Available evidence suggests that delinquent behavior is higher in economically depressed sectors of urban areas. But delinquent behavior patterns can be found in all parts of American society. The number of concealed delinquent acts is probably also large. By some estimates, undetected delinquency is as much as triple that which is discovered. Further, undetected as well as unrecorded delinquency is more common among middle and higher income groups.

The most frequent disposition of delinquency cases is "warning" or "adjusted." The publication *Problems of Youth* states that, while the complaint was not substantiated in approximately 7 per cent of the cases, a delinquent act was usually identified. However, the stability of the child's family and his potential for receiving proper parental supervision brought about dispositions of "warning" or "adjusted."

Juvenile courts in the United States have long made their own rules and regulations and generally answer to no higher authority. The first juvenile court, created in 1899 in Illinois, was established not to punish children but to treat them. Presiding judges were given great latitude in disposition of cases. But, however high the motive or enlightened the practice that led to the development of the juvenile court system, inequities and impingements upon individual rights developed. In May, 1967, the Supreme Court *In the Matter of Gault* ruled that an accused juvenile is entitled to timely notice of the charges against him. He must be given the

[60] Lee G. Burchinal, "Can Teenagers Make a Go of Marriage?" *PTA*, Vol. 55 (February, 1961), pp. 4–7.

right to confront and cross-examine witnesses against him. He must be told of his right to counsel and counsel must be provided if he is indigent. He must be told of his right to remain silent. The majority opinion delivered by Justice Fortas noted that it was still acceptable for the courts to keep a juvenile's record secret to protect him. The juvenile can still be classified as a delinquent instead of a criminal, and a record of delinquency need not operate as a civil disability or disqualify him for civil service appointment.

A publication of Mobilization for Youth cites the following causes of delinquent behavior in youth living in disadvantaged areas:

1. Discrepancies between social and economic aspirations and opportunities to achieve these aspirations by legitimate means.
2. Emphasis on upward mobility causes dissatisfaction and discontent with present positions.
3. Traditional channels to higher positions, such as through education, are restricted for large categories of people.
4. Self-defeating attitudes and behavior adaptations that become "functionally autonomous" – that is, once they come into existence, they tend to persist quite independent of the forces to which they were originally a response.
5. A feeling of alienation from the social order, conventional rules, and ideologies.[61]

The cost of combating juvenile delinquency—detection, study, diagnosis, treatment—is high. But the real tragedy lies in the human suffering, misery, and waste of human lives.

YOUTH UNEMPLOYMENT

The importance of work is self-evident. Gainful employment is the accepted means of attaining monetary rewards in our money-oriented culture. Since 1947, the unemployment rate for teenagers (16 to 19) has been higher—sometimes three times higher—than for the total labor force. Estimates are that during the 1970's the problems of youthful unemployment will be aggravated by the entry of 26 million new workers into the labor market, or an increase of 40 per cent over the entries during the preceding decade.

Job opportunities fluctuate with the economy and vary by geographic region. Labor force participation for young people tends to be somewhat higher than the national average for those in the mid-western, mountain, and Pacific states. The greatest single concentration of employed teenagers (14 to 19) is in wholesale and retail trade, followed by manufacturing. Approximately one-third of young workers are school dropouts. Unemployment among dropouts tends to be twice as high as that for high school graduates.

The traditional first jobs for young men which generally require little or no skill are diminishing in number. These entry jobs—as laborers, operatives, farm workers—which provided for about 60 per cent of employed young men entering the labor force are rapidly disappearing because of mechanization.

The creation of new jobs and employment opportunities for young people is a responsibility shared by local, state, and national agencies. But school personnel can publicize existing opportunities and the routes to taking advantage of them. Sensitive vocational counseling can aid youth in trial work experiences, developing career plans, and clarifying what preparation is needed for careers.

ALCOHOL AND DRUGS

Counselors are increasingly dealing with alcohol and drug problems among secondary school students. Riester and Zucker point out that pressures to conform to certain drinking norms exist in every society that makes use of beverage alcohol. These two investigators examined teenage drinking customs in the context of the informal social structure of the high school. Their subjects were the entire junior and senior classes (754) of a public high school in a Middle Atlantic state. Some of their principal findings were that (1) the frequency of

[61] *A Proposal for the Prevention and Control of Delinquency by Expanding Opportunities* (New York: Mobilization for Youth, December 9, 1961), pp. 46–66.

drinking and the amount consumed are related to informal social status group membership (college-bound, "leathers," [described by the investigators as young persons not involved in school activities, who were often discipline problems, and who spent their nonschool time working or hanging around town], average or quiet students, intellectuals, true individuals or hippies, students who go steady); identification with either the collegiate or "leather" subgroups is associated with high use of alcohol; (2) religious affiliations are not related to teenagers' use or nonuse of alcohol; (3) students' whose parents are semiprofessional drink more frequently than students whose parents are in other social positions; (4) high use of alcohol is not related to lower social class background; (5) nonwhites were characterized as low users (nondrinkers and moderates) of alcohol; (6) teenagers are more likely to be high users if both parents are users of alcohol; and (7) the most frequent situation for using alcohol is a social one involving groups of people, rather than solitude or the company of one friend of the opposite sex. Riester and Zucker reported that 91 per cent of the juniors and seniors have consumed alcohol.[62]

Hard data about teenage drug use are limited; estimates vary widely, ranging from as low as 5 to as high as 70 per cent among some groups in some schools. Hager, Vener, and Stewart[63] investigated drug use among 4,220 white, middle-American adolescents in grades eight through 12 in three communities selected deliberately to ascertain socioeconomic influences on drug use. One community was predominantly upper-middle, lower-upper class, the second was mainly lower-middle and upper-lower class, and the third was primarily a working class semirural area. Table 3.15 (See p. 78) presents their report on the use of various drugs by age of students. As shown by Table 3.15, the youth of this middle-American sample were not deeply involved in drug use.

These authors reported that greater drug use was associated with higher socioeconomic communities (hard drugs excepted). Marijuana consumption, for example, increased from about six per cent in the working-class community to a high of almost 21 per cent in the professional-managerial community. Hager and his associates suggest that

> . . . drug users may comprise a subculture in which the use of one drug greatly increases one's chances of using other drugs. Hard drugs do not seem to be as integral a part of this drug subculture.[64]

VENEREAL DISEASE

Next to the common cold, syphilis and gonorrhea are the most common infectious diseases among young people, outranking hepatitis, measles, mumps, scarlet fever, strep throat, and tuberculosis combined. The incidence of syphilis is much lower than gonorrhea; however, syphilis is a much more serious disease.

In 1970 there were at least 3,000 cases of syphilis among the 27 million U.S. teenagers and 150,000 cases of gonorrhea, more than in any other country except Sweden and Denmark. From 1960 to 1970 the number of reported VD cases among girls, age 15 to 19, increased 144 per cent. The percentage known does not begin to tell the story, for it is estimated that at least three out of four cases go unreported.

Penicillin and the antibiotics brought into mass production during World War II came close to eliminating venereal diseases in America. But since 1970 more and more people, particularly teenagers, have become infected. There is, in fact, a largely unnoticed epidemic of venereal disease among teenagers — an epidemic infecting youngsters from all social strata.

One of the problems involved is the sexual ignorance of teenagers. Girls with gonorrhea often do not know they have it. Boys may have a vague

[62] Albert E. Riester and Robert A. Zucker, "Adolescent Social Structure and Drinking Behavior," *Personnel and Guidance Journal*, Vol. 47 (December, 1968), pp. 304–312.

[63] David L. Hager, Arthur M. Vener, and Cyrus S. Stewart, "Patterns of Adolescent Drug Use in Middle America," *Journal of Counseling Psychology*, Vol. 18 (July, 1971), pp. 292–297.

[64] *Ibid.*, p. 296.

Table 3.15 Drug use by age (In per cents)

Age	*N*	*Never used*	*Once*	*2–4 times*	*5–7 times*	*8 or more times*
13 years and younger	816					
Marijuana		95.0	2.3	1.1	.6	1.0
Hallucinogens		97.0	1.2	.9	.5	.4
Amphetamines		96.7	1.7	.6	.1	.9
Hard		97.4	1.0	1.0	.2	.4
14 years	907					
Marijuana		93.5	2.6	1.3	.6	2.0
Hallucinogens		95.0	2.3	.9	.5	1.3
Amphetamines		95.2	2.0	1.5	.3	1.0
Hard		97.2	1.5	.1	.2	1.0
15 years	823					
Marijuana		89.7	3.0	2.3	1.0	4.0
Hallucinogens		94.0	3.2	.8	1.5	.5
Amphetamines		94.2	2.0	1.6	.6	1.6
Hard		97.0	1.2	.9	.5	.4
16 years	867					
Marijuana		81.8	5.7	3.8	1.7	7.0
Hallucinogens		90.4	3.5	2.6	.7	2.8
Amphetamines		90.7	3.0	3.5	.6	2.2
Hard		97.0	1.0	.7	.5	.8
17 years and older	807					
Marijuana		77.9	4.2	5.2	2.5	10.2
Hallucinogens		90.5	2.6	2.9	2.0	2.0
Amphetamines		88.9	3.3	3.3	1.4	3.1
Hard		97.3	1.3	.4	.4	.6

SOURCE: David L. Hager, Arthur M. Vener, and Cyrus S. Stewart, "Patterns of Adolescent Drug Use in Middle America," *Journal of Counseling Psychology*, Vol. 18 (July, 1971), p. 294. Copyright © 1971 American Psychological Association. Reprinted with permission.

idea that penicillin will cure it, then take ineffective tablets to cure themselves. Since the initial symptoms normally disappear in a few weeks, they often believe they are cured — usually they are not.

Boys are more readily aware of the symptoms of gonorrhea — a discharge, difficulty or strain in urinating. That the discharge goes away without treatment does not mean the disease is cured. Actually, the infection begins to go further up the urinary tract and beyond, sometimes involving other organs. For the girl, a discharge as a symptom of gonorrhea is more complicated, since some discharge is normal in females. It may go unnoticed until the fallopian tubes become infected and pain sets in. Before the infection reaches this point, changes in color and odor of the discharge will develop as early symptoms. However, there are 10 or more causes for such discharges, therefore a discharge does not always signify gonorrhea. Symptoms of syphilis are more difficult to spot than are those of gonorrhea. They include fever, rash, loss of hair, and even a sore that is not painful.

Through ignorance, promiscuity, and a changing morality, this hidden epidemic spreads its gray plague.

SUMMARY

In our society the above problem areas are natural occurrences during the developmental processes. The selection cited is not complete but does represent areas in which various age groups are frequently involved. For this reason most if not all counselors in the school setting will come into contact with these problems at some time during their careers. While in some instances the percentages reported are small, the absolute numbers they represent are not. They are of major concern to adults because each is potentially tremendously damaging to the individual. It is when such severe problems occur that the individual is most in need of assistance of many kinds. Among these is the helping relationship provided by the counselor in avoiding such problems, coping with them if present, or dealing with their aftereffects.

Annotated References

Erikson, Erik H. *Identity, Youth and Crisis.* New York: W. W. Norton and Company, Inc., 1968, 336 pp.

Chapter 3 (pp. 91–141) describes the eight stages of man and chapter 4 (pp. 141–207) presents autobiographical material from Bernard Shaw to illustrate creative confusion associated with the age of identity. Additionally, clinical case material is used to illustrate severe identity confusion.

Havighurst, Robert J. *Human Development and Education.* New York: David McKay Co., Inc., 1953. 338 pp.

The book is organized into five parts paralleling stages of human development. The developmental tasks of each stage are identified, discussed, and illustrated. Studies of developmental tasks in middle childhood and adolescence are presented.

Joint Commission on Mental Health of Children. *Crisis in Child Mental Health: Challenge for the 1970's.* New York: Harper and Row, 1970. 578 pp.

Chapter 2 (pp. 137–163) presents the impact of contemporary American society on children's mental health. Some of the major problems faced by large numbers of youth are described along with the special problems of various subgroups, such as the poor.

Sherif, Muzafer, and Sherif, Carolyn W. (eds.). *Problems of Youth: Transition to Adulthood in a Changing World.* Chicago: Aldine Publishing Company, 1965.

Many of the chapters were based on papers delivered (May, 1964) to the Fifth Social Psychology Symposium (University of Oklahoma). The contributions include adolescent attitudes and goals (John E. Horrocks), youth subculture (David Gottlieb), youth in lower-class settings (Arthur Pearl), and gang delinquency (James F. Short, Jr.).

Further References

Adkins, Walter R. "Life Skills: Structured Counseling for the Disadvantaged." *Personnel and Guidance Journal,* Vol. 49 (October, 1970). pp. 108–116.

Allen, Dean A. "Underachievement is Many-Sided." *Personnel and Guidance Journal,* Vol. 49 (March, 1971). pp. 529–532.

Aubrey, Roger. "School-Community Drug Prevention Programs." *Personnel and Guidance Journal,* Vol. 50 (September, 1971). pp. 17–24.

Berdie, Ralph F. "The Study of University Students: Analyses and Recommendations." *Journal of College Student Personnel,* Vol. 13 (January, 1972). pp. 4–11.

Bickford, John. "The Search for Identity." *The School Counselor,* Vol. 19 (January, 1972). pp. 191–194.

Crabbe, Julie L. and Scott, William A. "Academic and Personal Adjustment." *Journal of Counseling Psychology,* Vol. 19 (January, 1972). pp. 58–64.

Fischer, Ronald W. "Mental Institutions and Similar Phenomena Called Schools." *Personnel and Guidance Journal,* Vol. 50 (September, 1971). pp. 45–51.

Hecklinger, Fred J. "The Undecided Student — Is He Less Satisfied with College?" *Journal of College Student Personnel,* Vol. 13 (May, 1972). pp. 247–251.

Huberty, David J. "Drug Abuse: A Frame of Reference." *The School Counselor,* Vol. 19 (March, 1972). pp. 284–287.

Jackson, Barry and Van Zoost, Brenda. "Changing Study Behaviors Through Reinforcement Contingencies." *Journal of Counseling Psychology,* Vol. 19 (May, 1972). pp. 192–195.

Kelly, Gary F. "Group Guidance on Sex Education." *Personnel and Guidance Journal,* Vol. 49 (June, 1971). pp. 809–814.

Losak, John. "Do Remedial Programs Really Work?" *Personnel and Guidance Journal,* Vol. 50 (January, 1972). pp. 383–387.

Stanford, Gene. "Psychological Education in the Classroom." *Personnel and Guidance Journal,* Vol. 50 (March, 1972). pp. 585–592.

COUNSELING: EXPECTATIONS AND GOALS

4

Since the intent of Part One is to provide an orientation to counseling, it would seem imperative that consideration be given to the expectancies and goals of counseling. The term "expectancies" refers to the anticipations held, or the inferences made, about counseling. "Goal" is the end result sought through counseling. This chapter will analyze what certain groups and individuals expect or want from counseling compared to the goals that have been stated for counseling.

Expectancies for Counseling

The expectancies for counseling are diverse, often contradictory, and sometimes impossible. They are derived from experience, stem from need, and are nurtured by hope among those who seek assistance and those who provide it.

EXPECTANCIES OF COUNSELEES

The majority of counselees expect counseling to produce personal solutions for them. Those in stressful situations anticipate that counseling will bring relief. Those who are vacillating over a decision expect counseling to result in a choice. Those who perceive themselves as personally unpopular expect counseling to lead to their becoming popular. Those who are lonely expect solace and the discovery of ways to interact meaningfully with others. Those who want to go to college view counseling as guaranteeing them admission, scholarship, or financial aid. Those who are about to fail, either in school or in other ventures, expect failure to turn to success as a result of counseling. Those who seek employment counseling expect quick placement, job satisfaction, and easy promotion.

All too often, it is presumed that counseling will be of short duration. The counselee usually expects to be tested, "analyzed," and above all, directed or told how and what to do to obtain whatever it was that led him to seek counseling. These remarks demand consideration of the form counseling takes rather than the product of counseling and will be taken up in Chapter Seventeen.

Little research has been directed specifically toward determining what counselees expect. However, examination of the studies now to be discussed, grouped by type of population studied, amplifies the inferences relating to expectancies stated above.

High School Students The following are representative of studies conducted with high school age groups. The expectations of 181 secondary school students were obtained by Gladstein before and after counseling.[1] His subjects were clients who came to the University of Rochester Practicum Counseling Center from nine different schools representing various ethnic, socioeconomic, and religious backgrounds. Some 17 different statements were used to classify what these students expected to accomplish in counseling before experiencing it. For example, they expected to do general career planning; obtain help in choosing a vocation; discover their abilities, interests, capabilities; come to understand themselves better; to pick the right college; improve their study habits, etc. Contrary to many reports, their expectations were not restricted to educational-vocational matters, either before or after counseling.

Van Riper examined junior high school students' perceptions of the counselor's role, how helpful the assistance given by counselors was to students, and to what extent counselors were utilized by students.[2] He reported that students expect counselors to help them with educational planning and, to a lesser extent, with other school problems. His subjects did not regard highly the assistance given by counselors, but they reported that counselors were more often helpful to them than teachers or principals but were rated as less helpful than other students.

Perrone, Weiking, and Nagel asked junior high school students and their parents and teachers to express their views of the counseling function.[3] These authors sought to determine (1) the student types requiring counseling and the degree required as seen by junior high school students, parents and teachers, (2) whether the three groups differed in the degree of counseling they recommended for the 14 student types, (3) whether students who indicated (via the Mooney Problem Checklist) many problems differed from those who indicated few problems in the degree of counseling they recommended for the 14 student types, and (4) whether parents of students who indicated many problems differed from parents of students who indicated few problems in the degree of counseling recommended. Significant differences were reported between parents and students and parents and teachers, but no significant difference was obtained between students and teachers. Parents, the authors suggested, were more in favor of intensive counseling than either teachers or students. In respect to the degree of counseling recommended for the 14 student types, the analysis did not yield any significant difference among the three groups although teachers valued counseling least. Comparison of students who indicated more problems ($\bar{X}$ = 53.1 on the Mooney) with students who indicated few problems ($\bar{X}$ = 5.5 on the Mooney) showed some significant differences in the amount of counseling recommended. Those with fewer problems recommended more counseling for the "Queer" student type whereas those with more problems recommended greater counseling for the "Homely" student type. There was no significant difference between parents of the two student groups.

Kerr studied counseling and college decision making by surveying 1,350 seniors in 33 school systems in Iowa.[4] Some 83 per cent of the sample

[1] Gerald A. Gladstein, "Client Expectations, Counseling Experience and Satisfaction," *Journal of Counseling Psychology*, Vol. 16 (November, 1969), pp. 476–481.

[2] B. W. Van Riper, "Student Perception: The Counselor is What He Does," *The School Counselor*, Vol. 19 (September, 1971), pp. 53–56.

[3] Philip A. Perrone, Mary L. Weiking, and Elwyn H. Nagel, "The Counseling Function as Seen by Students, Parents and Teachers," *Journal of Counseling Psychology*, Vol. 12 (Summer, 1965), pp. 148–152.

[4] William D. Kerr, "Student Perceptions of Counselor Role in the College Decision," *Personnel and Guidance Journal*, Vol. 41 (December, 1962), pp. 337–342.

said that counseling helped them make college decisions and was a source of information for them.

While not directly related to expectations, Thompson sought to ascertain the characteristics of the secondary school counselor's ideal client.[5] He noted that previous research had indicated that many therapists' descriptions of their preferred clients indicated that they wanted them to be youthful, attractive, verbal, sensitive, and intelligent. Thompson reported that high school counselors' "ideal" client achieved highly in school and had aspirations for the future. The "nonpreferred" client experienced emotional problems and conflicts with others such as parents, school authorities, and peers.

College Students Perceptions of how various campus groups view counseling were evaluated by Warman.[6] A 100-item questionnaire was administered to 250 college students. The results were factor-analyzed, yielding one general and three specific factors. The questionnaires were then scored on the specific factors (college routine, vocational choice, and adjustment to self), and comparisons were made among the subjects. Help in vocational choice was rated as most appropriate for discussion in college counseling centers, followed by college routine problems. Adjustment to self and others was rated as least appropriate. Warman suggested that if counselors are to provide the full range of appropriate counseling services, they must better orient and educate others as to what counseling is and can do. Form administered a counseling attitude scale to 604 Michigan State University students.[7] He reported that students generally held favorable attitudes toward counseling. The more contacts they had with counselors, the more favorable the attitude. His findings confirm the proposition that student attitudes toward counseling are affected by prior contact and experience.

Wilcove and Sharp followed up Warman's investigations and surveyed parents of students, student services personnel, faculty, counselors, and the student body at the University of Wyoming to gain an understanding of how they viewed the counseling center. All groups except counselors endorsed (in order) vocational choice, college routine, and adjustment to self and others as being appropriate for discussion at the college counseling center. Counselors thought that students' "adjustment problems" were more appropriate for their services than did the other groups.[8] Resnick and Gelso also replicated and extended Warman's study. They reported that all groups viewed problems of "adjustment to self and others" as more appropriate for counseling attention now than a decade ago. However, their data did not suggest that counselors had succeeded in reducing the communications gap between themselves and such other relevant groups as faculty, students, and parents.[9]

Strong and his associates[10] compared 67 female college students' views of counselors, advisers, and psychiatrists. Counselors and advisers were viewed as more warm and friendly than psychiatrists. Psychiatrists were considered appropriate sources of help for specific personal problems but students regarded counselors as likely to help them achieve personal development and gain knowledge of their strengths and weaknesses.

Why some students fail to make use of university counseling facilities was investigated by Snyder,

[5] Charles L. Thompson, "The Secondary School Counselor's Ideal Client," *Journal of Counseling Psychology,* Vol. 16 (January, 1969), pp. 69–74.

[6] Roy E. Warman, "Differential Perceptions of Counseling Role," *Journal of Counseling Psychology,* Vol. 7 (Winter, 1960), pp. 269–274.

[7] Arnold Form, "Measurement of Student Attitudes Toward Counseling Services," *Personnel and Guidance Journal,* Vol. 32 (October, 1953), pp. 84–87.

[8] Gerry Wilcove and W. Harry Sharp, "Differential Perceptions of a College Counseling Center," *Journal of Counseling Psychology,* Vol. 18 (January, 1971), pp. 60–63.

[9] Harvey Resnick and Charles J. Gelso, "Differential Perceptions of Counseling Role: A Reexamination," *Journal of Counseling Psychology,* Vol. 18 (November, 1971), pp. 549–553.

[10] Stanley R. Strong, Darwin D. Handel and Joseph C. Bratton, "College Students' Views of Campus Help-Givers: Counselors, Advisors, and Psychiatrists," *Journal of Counseling Psychology,* Vol. 18 (May, 1971), pp. 234–238.

Hill, and Derksen.[11] They hypothesized that stigma, seriousness of problems, student attitudes, counseling experience, and information (or lack of it) would effect students' use of counseling services. Their findings were that students were favorable to counseling; stigma was of little concern; students generally possessed little information about counseling; and friends were the first choice of help with personal and social problems (close relatives were the second choice and faculty and psychological services the last choice).

Grosz investigated the effect of positive and negative client expectations for counseling upon the initial interview.[12] Thirty subjects (college students) were randomly assigned to a positive expectation group, a negative expectation group, or a control group. The positive group was exposed to prerecorded tapes presenting positive aspects of counseling while the negative group was exposed to tapes presenting negative aspects. The 30 subjects were given a pretreatment semantic differential scale which revealed that the positive and control group members held more favorable attitudes than negative group members. Following a 30-minute counseling session, however, no significant difference was found in the relationships established despite precounseling differences. This suggests that diversity in client expectations need not interfere with the counseling relationship if counselors handle them skillfully.

PARENT EXPECTATIONS

Dunlop surveyed the attitudes of counselor educators, counselors, high school administrators, parents, and high school seniors to determine their perceptions of the appropriateness of counselor performance of various defined tasks.[13] Tasks were representative of several areas commonly associated with counseling, including educational, vocational, and personal counseling and testing and diagnosis. All groups reacted favorably to counseling associated with educational and vocational planning. Dunlop comments that "The expectation by students and parents that counselors should serve as advice-givers leads to speculation that their experiences with counselors have led to this kind of expectation."[14]

One parent, Janet Worthington, believes that counselors are extensions of parents and facilitators of learning. An important dimension in their work, according to her, is that counselors accept each student as he is.[15]

According to many surveys, parents expect counseling to improve student selection of high school subjects and to help students formulate plans for future education or work. They do *not* expect it to be as powerful or useful in resolving personal-emotional social problems as it is in educational-vocational situations. Thus from the parents' point of view counseling (1) exists primarily for generating programs of study for students, (2) has a persuasive function in the individual's educational and vocational development, and (3) remedies child-rearing errors. Most counselors would regard the first expectation as outmoded and/or naive and the second and third expectations as unrealistic or ill conceived. Counseling cannot provide children with "instant aspiration" or persuade them to make "right" choices and decisions especially if "right" is defined as synonymous with agreement or submission to parental demands and desires.

TEACHER EXPECTATIONS

Gibson's 1965 survey revealed that 208 seconary school teachers in 18 schools in a four-state area recognized counseling as the primary responsibility of school counselors.[16] However, their

[11] John F. Snyder, Clara E. Hill, and Timothy P. Derksen, "Why Some Students Do Not Use University Counseling Facilities," *Journal of Counseling Psychology*, Vol. 18 (July, 1972), pp. 263–268.
[12] Richard D. Grosz, "Effect of Client Expectations on the Counseling Relationship," *Personnel and Guidance Journal*, Vol. 46 (April, 1968), pp. 797–800.
[13] Richard S. Dunlop, "Professional Educators, Parents, and Students Assess the Counselor's Role," *Personnel and Guidance Journal*, Vol. 43 (June, 1965), pp. 1024–1028.

[14] *Ibid.*, p. 1028.
[15] Janet Worthington, "A Parent's View of School Counselors," *The School Counselor*, Vol. 19 (May, 1972), pp. 339–340.
[16] Robert F. Gibson, "Teacher Opinions of High School Guidance Program," *Personnel and Guidance Journal*, Vol. 44 (December, 1965), pp. 416–422.

responses to the questionnaire and to individual interviews led Gibson to conclude that they did not understand counseling and that "Many seemed to feel that it was a 'telling' or 'directing' process. . . ."[17] It should be noted that these teachers were employed in high schools where guidance services had been in existence for at least four years.

Many school counselors believe that teachers have little understanding of counseling. But some current research reports evidence to the contrary. For example, Kandor and his associates[18] reported that practicing teachers, practicing counselors, student teachers, and student counselors agreed more than they disagreed about functions counselors were to perform. These four groups differed on nine of 26 statements about counselor behavior. The greatest discrepancy occurred in areas of discipline, students' freedom of choice, and use of class time for counseling activities. Maser also presented a counselor function inventory to counselors, administrators, and teachers employed in a Seattle school district, and reported high agreement ($r = .80$ and $.90$) among these three groups about appropriate counselor functions.[19]

While little direct evidence exists to substantiate it, the major impression is that teachers expect counseling to reduce or eliminate pupil behavior that causes classroom friction and disturbance; that is, it is intended for students who either directly disturb the teacher or disrupt the teaching of other students. In short, teachers expect counselors to engage in activities that make teaching easier and more effective.

EXPECTATIONS OF SCHOOL ADMINISTRATORS

School principals' views of six counselor role dimensions were compared by Hart and Prince[20] with "ideal" counselor roles set forth by counselor educators. The school principals ($n = 164$) were those in Utah who had three or more years of administrative experience. The principals disagreed with counselor educators about counselors being involved in clerical tasks, maintaining confidentiality of client communications, providing personal-emotional counseling, and some non-counseling functions. However, those principals with some counselor training or experience were closer to counselor educators in expectations concerning discipline, confidentiality, and clerical tasks than those principals without such training or experience. But the views of all these principals contrasted markedly with the ideal counselor role defined by counselor educators. These findings led Hart and Prince to conclude that "The conflict is real; school counselors are taught many role philosophies and behaviors which are in conflict with the expectations of principals."

The authors have four impressions of school administrators' expectations for counseling. First, they assume that it will result in an efficient school organization. Filbeck's comparison of the views of high school counselors and principals reflected that the latter wanted counseling to be supportive of school policies and to reinforce student conformity and acceptance of the status quo.[21] Chenault and Seegars report that principals frequently complain of counselors' not accepting "the responsibility necessary for their place in the administrative pattern."[22] In short, counseling ought to produce fewer organizational disruptions, reduce conflict and friction among personnel, and smooth educational production. Far too many administrators expect counselors to ferret out information on students' misbehaviors and pass it on to them so that they can take action. Obviously forgotten or ignored is the notion that the school as an institution should also liberate individual diversity, originality,

[17] *Ibid.*, p. 421.
[18] Joseph Kandor, Charles Pulvino, and Richard R. Stevic, "Counselor-Role Perception: A Method for Determining Agreement and Disagreement," *The School Counselor*, Vol. 18 (May, 1971), pp. 373–382.
[19] Arthur L. Maser, "Counselor Functions in Secondary Schools," *The School Counselor*, Vol. 18 (May, 1971), pp. 367–372.
[20] Darrell H. Hart and Donald J. Prince, "Role Conflict for School Counselors: Training Versus Job Demands," *Personnel and Guidance Journal*, Vol. 48 (January, 1970), pp. 374–380.

[21] Robert W. Filbeck, "Perceptions of Appropriateness of Counselor Behavior: A Comparison of Counselors and Principals," *Personnel and Guidance Journal*, Vol. 43 (May, 1965), pp. 891–896.
[22] Joann Chenault and James E. Seegars, Jr., "The Interpersonal Diagnosis of Principals and Counselors," *Personnel and Guidance Journal*, Vol. 41 (October, 1962), p. 121.

and inventiveness despite the sometimes disruptive and unconventional directions these latter pursuits take.

The second impression is that school administrators view counseling primarily as educational and vocational advising. They expect students to be told what academic subjects they should take, what colleges to enter, and what jobs they should seek.

The third impression is that school administrators expect little or nothing from counseling. Some tolerate it and its practitioners, because a group of their articulate patrons demand it, because other schools have it, or because accrediting associations require it as a criterion for membership. They do not understand counseling; they never have, and make no effort to comprehend what it has to offer. Study after study could be cited to show that counselors frequently serve as attendance clerks, quasi administrators, substitute teachers, and the like. Certainly under such conditions administrators must not expect much of counseling per se.

The fourth impression is that administrators expect counseling to solve every educational difficulty and to remedy every real and imagined community ill. Some administrators, in fending off criticisms that the school has failed to cope with school dropouts or to provide for disadvantaged children, or in responding to demands that the school develop compensatory programs for these and other situations, have cited the existence of counseling in their schools as a solution. Their easy answer that counseling is the magic cure for these diverse troubles is absurd. Such social symptoms stem from pervasive sociological, economic, and psychological disharmonies in our culture. To see them as isolated problems to be solved or even ameliorated by counseling is inappropriate. Although counseling may be *one* useful agent in their prevention and alleviation, it is obviously inadequate as a cure-all. It cannot materially alter or eradicate a host of social defects.

Samler points out that administrative attitudes toward counseling are often skeptical and inimical to its practice. While he does not believe these attitudes are pervasive, he states that:

> Such personnel [administrators] seem to feel that counseling may not really be necessary and when pressed see it as a kind of coddling. Since nevertheless, the work has to be done, they feel short cuts could be used and the entire process rationalized. They feel that with the passage of time counselors should become sufficiently competent to do the work faster, so that production can be stepped up. They are convinced that counseling means something going on with a client; when the counselor doesn't have a person at his desk, he is goofing off.[23]

EXPECTATIONS OF GOVERNMENTAL AGENCIES

Expectations for counseling by governmental agencies are difficult to pin down since they shift with variations in policy across time. Despite this, several recent trends are discernible. Government personnel seem to expect one of two things of counseling. The first is that counseling will identify and nurture human talent. Indeed, Title V was included in the National Defense Education Act of 1958 for that very purpose. One has only to read the employment advertisements in current newspapers to become aware of the demand for highly trained persons in almost every field of endeavor. The advent of Sputnik in October, 1957, brought with it the notion that education was the nation's defense. Schools were to engage in an unprecedented search for talent. Counseling was supposed to ferret out more of our brighter youngsters and encourage them to obtain advanced education that would enable them to employ their preidentified and labeled talents at the highest levels of production.

The second is that counseling is to be used to put youngsters into careers where manpower shortages exist. Counseling is seen as a means of persuading or directing individuals into critical occupations. Provisions for counseling services have been written into legislation dealing with manpower, development training programs, school dropouts, migratory workers, and the like.

The key issue here is whether counseling is to

[23] Joseph Samler, "The Counseling Service in the Administrative Setting: Problems and Possible Solutions," *Personnel and Guidance Journal,* Vol. 44 (March, 1966), p. 716.

serve as a manipulative experience to satisfy manpower needs for the nation. If so, the mental health and welfare of the individual are relegated to a lesser position. Mathewson has warned,

> Philosophically, the right and freedom of the individual to shape his own life pattern — including the kind of occupation he will pursue — is fundamental; it cannot be nibbled away at, or infringed upon, without destroying one of the basic precepts of our social philosophy. This flag of faith must be nailed to the mast because such words as "persuade" and "direct" have already been used to designate what counselors should be doing to meet manpower needs in the Cold War. Go farther in that direction and we could come to the word "compel."[24]

SUMMARY

The overwhelming lay expectation for counseling is that it direct or manage the affairs of those who seek it. Many do not know and are puzzled over what counseling is and can do. Failure to understand its true purposes has led to countless mistaken and unrealistic assumptions. Everyone would like to find specific remedies in counseling for an almost infinite array of problems. An important objective for every counselor is enlightening our society as to the legitimate goals and realistic limitations of counseling.

Goals of Counseling

Are the public's counseling expectancies and the practitioner's statements of counseling goals congruent, or can they become so?

Questions about counseling goals and/or expected outcomes are rightfully raised by individuals preparing to become counselors, by those who seek counseling, by other helping specialists, by public officials in various organizations and agencies, and by the public. The queries take many forms and reflect several levels of sophistication. The following questions are examples:

What do you try to do in counseling?
What is the purpose of counseling?
What is the aim of counseling?
What are the objectives of counseling?
What results are expected from counseling?

Essentially, the words "try to do," "purpose," "aim," "objective," are loosely used as synonyms for "goal," which is generally preferred by professional counselors. More precisely, "purpose" refers to that which makes a goal attractive. "Goal" is defined as the end result sought or, in this case, the objective which counseling strives to accomplish.

Statements of counseling goals are often general, vague, and rife with implications. In examining them, an additional problem may be noted: To what degree is the goal dependent upon the counselee or upon the counselor?

BEHAVIORAL CHANGE

Almost all statements indicate that the goal of counseling is to effect change in behavior which will enable the counselee to live a more productive, satisfying life as he defines it within society's limitations. Areas often mentioned where change may be desirable are relations with others, family situations, academic achievement, job experiences, and the like. Rogers points out that one outcome of counseling is that experiences are not as threatening, the individual has less anxiety, and his goals are more nearly in harmony with his perceived self and appear more achievable. "Thus therapy produces a change in personality organization and structure, and a change in behavior, both of which are relatively permanent,"[25] and the "essential outcome is a more broadly based structure of self, an inclusion of a greater proportion of experience as a part of self, and a more comfortable and realistic adjustment to life."[26] Change as a goal may be more simply defined as redirection of typical responses to frustrations or different attitudes toward other people or to self.

[24] Robert H. Mathewson, "Manpower of Persons: A Critical Issue," *Personnel and Guidance Journal*, Vol. 43 (December, 1964), p. 339.

[25] Carl R. Rogers, *Client-Centered Therapy* (Boston: Houghton Mifflin Company, 1951), p. 195.
[26] *Ibid.*

Boy and Pine describe their client-centered counseling goal in these words:

> . . . to help the student become more mature and more self-actuated, to help the student move forward in a more positive and constructive way, to help the student grow toward socialization by utilizing his own resources and potential. . . . The counselee's perceptions change, and as the result of newly acquired insights there is a positive reorientation of personality and living for the counselee.[27]

POSITIVE MENTAL HEALTH

Some have identified the preservation or attainment of positive mental health as the goal of counseling. If it is reached, the individual achieves integration, adjustment, and positive identification with others. He learns to accept responsibility, to be independent, and to gain behavioral integration. More than 20 years ago Thorne said the major objective of personality counseling was to protect and secure mental health by preventing or modifying pathogenic etiologic factors productive of maladjustment or mental disorder.[28] More recently, Patterson has stated that "Since the goal of counseling is the preservation, or restoration, of good mental health, or self-esteem, then it follows that the counseling situation must be characterized by an absence of threat."[29]

Some see the goal of counseling as prevention of certain kinds of problems. Identification and treatment of persons who have a high probability of developing pathology or who show signs of developing pathology could only be labeled "prevention" in a relative way since the symptoms indicate an already existent problem. In this case, counseling is prophylactic only in the sense of preventing a small problem from getting worse.

Kell and Mueller, in their examination of impact and change in counseling relationships, suggest that what is failure to one counselor may be success to another. They indicate that counselors may wish to help clients learn that all human beings share likenesses. To them, "Promotion and development of feelings of being like, sharing with, and getting and giving interactive rewards from other human beings is a legitimate counseling objective."[30]

PROBLEM RESOLUTION

The goal of counseling is sometimes thought to be the resolution of whatever problems were brought to the counseling relationship. Krumboltz, in presenting the rationale and research of behavioral counseling, reasoned,

> The central reason for the existence of counseling is based on the fact that people have problems that they are unable to resolve by themselves. They come to counselors because they have been led to believe that the counselor will be of some assistance to them in resolving their problems. The central purpose of counseling, then, is to help each client resolve those problems for which he seeks help.[31]

In an earlier statement comparing the goals of client-centered counseling with those of behavioral counseling, Krumboltz stated,

> While not relinquishing his ethical responsibility for helping the client define worthwhile goals, the behavioral counselor is primarily interested in helping the client change whichever behavior the client wishes to change. If the client wishes to overcome an overpowering fear of taking tests, then the counselor endeavors to structure a situation where his fear can become extinguished. He makes no pretense of working toward high-sounding and elaborate goals which involve a whole restructuring of the client's personality. He is only interested in helping the client make the particular change that the client himself desires. Therefore, the behavioral counselor

[27] Angelo V. Boy and Gerald J. Pine, *Client-Centered Counseling in the Secondary School* (Boston: Houghton Mifflin Company, 1963), p. 43.
[28] Frederick C. Thorne, *Principles of Personality Counseling* (Brandon, Vt.: Journal of Clinical Psychology, 1950), p. 89.
[29] C. H. Patterson, *Counseling and Guidance in Schools: A First Course* (New York: Appleton-Century-Crofts, Inc., 1966), p. 142.
[30] Bill L. Kell and William J. Mueller, *Impact and Change* (New York: Appleton-Century-Crofts, Inc., 1966), p. 142.
[31] John D. Krumboltz, "Behavioral Counseling: Rationale and Research." *Personnel and Guidance Journal,* Vol. 44 (December, 1965), pp. 383–384.

would actually play a smaller part in determining the goals of counseling than would the client-centered counselor.[32]

In commenting upon the article, Patterson, responded,

Do such counselors accept all the goals of all clients? I don't believe this. Are the immediate, professed goals of the client his ultimate or real goals? I doubt this. Acceptance by the counselor of such limited, immediate goals may prevent his recognizing and accepting different, more long-term goals. Clients, when given the opportunity, appear to desire and accept the goals of the client-centered counselor; indeed, many of the expressed goals of the client (*e.g.*, "All I want is to get rid of my fear of giving speeches in class") cannot be adequately achieved without, or except by working toward, broader goals of self-understanding, self-acceptance, etc.[33]

And in a further comment Patterson pointed out that

It is thus not a matter of who selects goals, but what are the goals of counseling or psychotherapy. The counselor who "makes no pretense of working toward high-sounding and elaborate goals" is thereby not necessarily free of such goals. He is imposing ultimate goals whether he knows it or not — such goals as dependence, short-term gratification, or accomplishment or removal of symptoms.[34]

In a later analysis of behavioral goals for counseling, Krumboltz argues against putting counseling goals in terms of subjective states such as "self-understanding" and "self-acceptance."[35] He believes that goal statements such as these lack precision and are incapable of being assessed. He urges that counseling goals be couched in terms of objective behavior changes. His three criteria for judging counseling goals are as follows:

1. The goals of counseling should be capable of being stated differently for each individual client.
2. The goals of counseling for each client should be compatible with, though not necessarily identical to, the values of his counselor.
3. The degree to which the goals of counseling are attained by each client should be observable.[36]

Krumboltz constructs three categories of behavioral goals: altering maladaptive behavior, learning the decision-making process, and preventing problems. Examples of the first type include "increasing socially assertive responses" and "learning to respond calmly to hostile remarks." Examples of the second category are "generating a list of all possible courses of action" and "generalizing the decision making process to future problems." In the third category are such examples as "planning an educational program in child rearing techniques for parents" and "evaluating the effectiveness of preventive and remedial programs."

Wolpe and his associates see the goal of counseling as relieving suffering and disability. "It is both inevitable and reasonable that the patient will ultimately appraise his therapy in terms of the relief that he will experience — just as he would if his suffering were due to an organic disease." [37]

PERSONAL EFFECTIVENESS

Closely related to preservation of good mental health and behavioral change is the goal of improving personal effectiveness. Blocher defines the effective person in this way:

. . . the effective person is seen as being able to *commit* himself to projects, investing time and energy and being willing to take appropriate economic, psychological, and physical risks. He is seen as having the competence to recognize, define and solve problems. He is seen as reasonably *consistent* across and within his typical role situation. He is seen as being able to *think* in different and original, i.e., *creative*, ways. Finally, he is able to *control*

[32] John D. Krumboltz, "Parable of the Good Counselor," *Personnel and Guidance Journal*, Vol. 43 (October, 1964), p. 121.
[33] C. H. Patterson, "Comment," *Personnel and Guidance Journal*, Vol. 43 (October, 1964), p. 125.
[34] *Ibid.*, p. 125.
[35] John D. Krumboltz, "Behavioral Goals of Counseling," *Journal of Counseling Psychology*, Vol. 13 (Summer, 1966), pp. 153–159.

[36] *Ibid.*, pp. 154–155.
[37] Joseph Wolpe, Andrew Salter, and L. J. Reyna (eds.), *The Conditioning Therapies* (New York: Holt, Rinehart & Winston, Inc., 1964), p. 5.

impulses and produce appropriate responses to frustration, hostility, and ambiguity.[38]

In a later work, Blocher identified two counseling goals.[39] First, counseling seeks to maximize an individual's possible freedom within the limitations supplied by himself and his environment, and second, counseling seeks to maximize the individual's effectiveness by giving him control over his environment and the responses within him that are evoked by the environment.

Shoben also sees personal development as the goal of counseling. He defines counseling as a developmental experience in which problem solution or decision making foster personal growth.[40] Tiedeman has stated that

> The goal of guidance is not the specific place that a person occupies in a social order; rather its goal is both the placing with children of responsibility for *being* and the development of their confidence in *becoming.* It is a focus on this *change mechanism* which has been absent in programs of guidance.[41]

DECISION MAKING

To some the goal of counseling is to enable the individual to make decisions that are of critical importance to him. It is not the counselor's job to decide what decisions the counselee should make or to choose alternate courses of action for him. Decisions are the counselee's own, and he must know why and how he made them. He learns to estimate probable consequences in terms of personal sacrifice, time, energy, money, risk, and the like. He learns to take cognizance of the range of values and to bring his own choice of values into full consciousness in the decision making. Representative of this view of counseling is the writing of Katz, who sees the beginning and terminating of high school as two critical decision-making points.[42] Over two decades ago Williamson defined the objectives of counseling as follows: "... the counselor assists the student to choose goals which will yield maximum satisfaction within the limits of those compromises necessitated by uncontrolled and uncontrollable factors in the individual and in society itself."[43]

Counseling helps individuals obtain information and to clarify and sort out personal characteristics and emotional concerns which may interfere with or be related to making decisions. It helps them acquire understanding, not only of abilities, interests, and opportunities, but also of emotions and attitudes which can influence choice and decision.

Tyler has defined the goal of counseling primarily as decision making:

> ... The purpose of counseling is to facilitate wise choices of the sort on which the person's later development depends. Counseling should not be *just* for persons who are anxious, unhappy, or unable to cope with the circumstances of their lives.[44]

Reaves and Reaves have stated that "The primary objective in counseling is that of stimulating the individual to evaluate, make, accept and act upon his choice."[45] Counseling, then, helps the individual learn what is needed to choose and subsequently to make choices. In this way he becomes independently able to cope with future decisions.

[38] Donald H. Blocher, "Wanted: A Science of Human Effectiveness," *Personnel and Guidance Journal,* Vol. 44 (March, 1966), p. 731.

[39] Donald H. Blocher, *Developmental Counseling* (New York: The Ronald Press Company, 1966), pp. 5–6.

[40] Edward S. Shoben, Jr., "The Counseling Experience as Personal Development," *Personnel and Guidance Journal,* Vol. 44 (November, 1965), p. 230.

[41] David Tiedeman, "Purposing Through Education: The Further Delineation of Goal and Program for Guidance," in Edward Landy and Paul A. Perry (eds.), *Guidance in American Education: Backgrounds and Prospects* (Cambridge, Mass.: Harvard University Press, 1964), p. 172.

[42] Martin Katz, *Decisions and Values: A Rationale for Secondary School Guidance* (New York: College Entrance Examination Board, 1963).

[43] E. G. Williamson, *Counseling Adolescents* (New York: McGraw-Hill Book Co., Inc., 1950), p. 221.

[44] Leona E. Tyler, *The Work of the Counselor,* 3rd. ed. (New York: Appleton-Century-Crofts, Inc., 1969), p. 13.

[45] Gayle Clark Reaves and Leonard E. Reaves, III, "The Counselor and Preventive Psychiatry," *Personnel and Guidance Journal,* Vol. 43 (March, 1965), p. 663.

UNACCEPTABLE GOALS

Arbuckle considers the following counseling goals unacceptable or questionable: (1) counselor solution of counselee's problems, (2) counselee happiness or satisfaction (Arbuckle views this as a by-product rather than a primary objective), (3) making society happy and satisfied with the counselee, (4) persuading the counselee to make decisions and choices that are "right." Further, Arbuckle believes there is consensus among counselors on the following statements: (1) Objectives are affected by the humanistic feeling that man is capable of self-determination. (2) Counselors help counselees move toward self-acceptance and self-understanding. (3) Counseling helps individuals develop a higher level of honesty, particularly honesty toward self. (4) Objectives should be based on counselee need rather than counselor need.[46]

Arbuckle's listing of questionable counseling goals amplifies the treatment given to the topic by Walker and Peiffer.[47] The latter doubt the feasibility of stating counseling goals in terms of counselee self-adjustment since a psychotic might well have reached an acceptable level of adjustment on a purely private basis. Client contentment similarly cannot be defended, say Walker and Peiffer, because for example schizophrenics are not necessarily unhappy.

CLASSIFICATION OF GOALS

Byrne has usefully separated counseling goals into three categories: ultimate, intermediate, and immediate.[48] Ultimate goals take their substance from views of universal man and of the nature of life. They are philosophical goals. Intermediate goals relate to the reasons why individuals seek counseling. Immediate goals are the moment-by-moment intentions in counseling. "To help the individual maintain an adequate level of development," "to help the individual become and remain a constructive, well-adjusted, happy, mentally healthy person," "to help the individual develop his potentialities" — all these are classified by Byrne as intermediate goals. He defines an ultimate counseling goal in these words:

> The counselor's goal, firmly based on the human worth of the individual, regardless of education, intelligence, color or background, is to use his technical skills (a) to help each counselee attain and maintain an awareness of self so that he can be responsible for himself, (b) to help each counselee confront threats to his being, and thus to open further the way for the counselee to increase his concern for others' well-being, (c) to help each counselee bring into full operation his unique potential in compatibility with his own life style and within the ethical limits of society.[49]

Byrne adds that each counselor has to hold to a goal which includes values, encompasses a comprehensive psychological view of behavior, and applies to all counselees.

Dolliver classifies counselor goals as expressive or instrumental.[50] The expressive goal spurs the counselee to be more expressive and is usually stated in self terms (such as Freud's — to live, to love, and to work — or personal happiness, etc.). The instrumental goal is usually more specific; it refers to a reduction in certain kinds of behavior, for example. Dolliver believes that the expressive and instrumental approaches may, at times, be complementary but generally are not.

Frey subjected statements of goals and processes set forth by various counseling theorists to analysis of variance techniques to determine their similarities and differences. He employed C. H. Patterson's[51] linear arrangement of classifying counseling

[46] Dugald S. Arbuckle, *Counseling: Philosophy, Theory and Practice* (Boston: Allyn and Bacon, Inc., 1965), pp. 56–63.
[47] Donald E. Walker and Herbert E. Peiffer, Jr., "The Goals of Counseling," *Journal of Counseling Psychology*, Vol. 4 (Fall, 1957), pp. 204–209.
[48] Richard Hill Byrne, *The School Counselor* (Boston: Houghton Mifflin Company, 1963), pp. 6–25.
[49] *Ibid.*, pp. 19–20.
[50] Robert H. Dolliver, " 'Expressive' and 'Instrumental' Conceptualizations of Counseling," *Journal of Counseling Psychology*, Vol. 12 (Winter, 1965), pp. 414–417.
[51] C. H. Patterson, *Theories of Counseling and Psychotherapy* (New York: Harper and Row, 1966), p. 6.

theories, going from highly rational approaches at one end of the continuum to strongly affective approaches at the other. Counseling goals were classified by the action-insight dichotomy formulated by London.[52] The theorists selected include Alexander (Psychoanalytic therapy), Dreikurs (Adlerian therapy), Dollard and Miller (Reinforcement therapy), Ellis (Rational-Emotive therapy), Frankl (Logotherapy), Krumboltz (Behavioral therapy), Rogers (Client-Centered therapy), Thorne (Eclectic therapy), Williamson (Trait and factor counseling), and Wolpe (Therapy by reciprocal inhibition). Some 37 counseling students rated 671 process statements and 318 goal statements. Mean ratings and standard deviations were computed across the theorists' statements on both process and goal dimensions. Figure 4.1 depicts the results. Analysis

Figure 4.1 The London-Patterson model

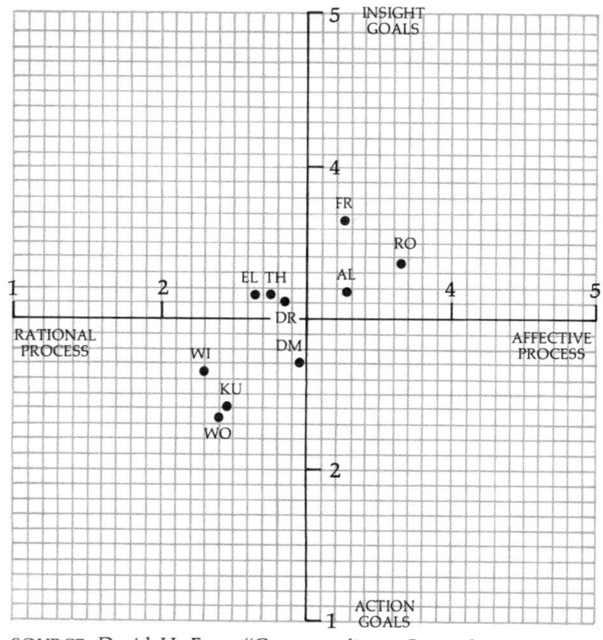

SOURCE: David H. Frey, "Conceptualizing Counseling Theories: A Content Analysis of Process and Goal Statements," *Counselor Education and Supervision,* Vol. 11 (January, 1972), p. 245. Copyright 1972 American Personnel and Guidance Association. Reprinted with permission.

[52] Perry London, *The Modes and Morals of Psychotherapy* (New York: Holt, Rinehart and Winston, 1964), p. 34.

of variance techniques, followed where appropriate by Newman-Keuls procedures for making post hoc comparisons, revealed the following similarities and differences in these theorists' goal statements:

<u>*WO KU*</u>   <u>*WI DM*</u>   <u>*DR TH EL AL*</u>   <u>*RO*</u>   <u>*FR*</u>

Wolpe and Krumboltz do not differ from each other and are more action oriented than all other theorists. At the other end of the continuum, Frankl is the most insight-directed and differs from Rogers, the second most insight-oriented theorist. A midrange insight group is composed of Dreikurs, Thorne, Ellis, and Alexander while Williamson and Dollard and Miller are together near the action end of the goal axis. Frey points out that these results could be influenced by item selection procedures and rater reliability.[53]

CLARIFICATION OF GOAL STATEMENTS

The reader who attempts to chop his way out of the semantic jungle of descriptions of counseling goals and outcomes is frequently lost. Three points may help him. First, the goals expressed by these and other individuals may reflect their own needs rather than those of the clients. In this case they are indicative of their authors' professional background, experience, and philosophy.

For example, Thompson and Zimmerman[54] administered a goal checklist to 315 clients and their 27 counselors at several points during the counseling process. Clients were asked to check the goals they thought appropriate for themselves, while counselors were asked to check goals they considered appropriate for their clients. Correlation coefficients between counselors and clients in the same time period, and between counselors with themselves and clients with themselves at different time periods were not high. These authors conclude that

[53] David H. Frey, "Conceptualizing Counseling Theories: A Content Analysis of Process and Goal Statements," *Counselor Education and Supervision,* Vol. 11 (June, 1972), pp. 243–250.
[54] Andrew Thompson and Robert Zimmerman, "Goals of Counseling: Whose? When?", *Journal of Counseling Psychology,* Vol. 16 (March, 1969), pp. 121–125.

there is little correlation between counselor goals and client goals, regardless of time period.

Further, both sets of goals show much instability. The major problem, according to Thompson and Zimmerman, is that many clients have feelings of general confusion or discomfort which they find difficult to translate into specific goals. If they could do so, doubtless they would not need or seek counseling.

Second, perhaps there are more likenesses than differences among the statements of counseling goals. Patterson, viewing goals against a backdrop of various counseling orientations, says,

> It may be more difficult to find commonalities among goals than among concepts and techniques. However, the differences may not be as great as they at first appear. The behavior therapists, though they emphasize the removal of symptoms as an objective goal, also seem to recognize a broader goal. They apparently expect the client to feel better, to function better in life and its various aspects, to achieve at a higher level – in short to live up to his potential. . . . There also seems to be general acceptance of the desirability of responsibility and independence as outcomes of counseling or psychotherapy.[55]

Stefflre agrees that there are many common elements among the various systems of counseling:

> All seek a free, informed, responsible person conscious of himself – his strength and weaknesses, his sickness and health – and capable of viewing the world unblinking and unafraid; capable, too, of making decisions for himself in harmony with his unique nature and at least minimal societal requirements. It is not true, as their enemies may contend, that the client-centered counselor seeks anarchy, that the psychoanalytic counselor seeks an orgy of impulse gratification, or that the trait-and-behavioral-theoretical counselors seek a brave new world of controlled robots.[56]

[55] C. H. Patterson, *Theories of Counseling and Psychotherapy* (New York: Harper & Row, Publishers, 1967), p. 498.
[56] Buford Stefflre, "A Summing Up," in Buford Stefflre and W. Harold Grant (eds.), *Theories of Counseling*, 2nd ed. (New York: McGraw Hill Book Co., Inc., 1972), p. 302.

Third, the focus of all counseling goals is the achievement of personal effectiveness that is both satisfactory to the individual and within society's limitations. In this framework it must be recognized that satisfaction can be achieved in diverse ways and that social limitations have been clearly documented as differing markedly from culture to culture and even from subsociety to subsociety within a culture. If one accepts this view, many of the quibbles over goals shrink to differences among the criteria used to judge and document counseling's efficacy. Behaviorally oriented counselors may speak of symptom reduction or symptom removal as indexes of movement toward personal effectiveness. More existentially oriented counselors use terms more commonly found in discussions of philosophies of life – self-enhancement, personal fulfillment, achievement of personal needs at a highly abstract level – but the terms are all suggestive of achieving personal effectiveness.

Needless to say, a whole spectrum of counseling goal statements exists, but whether they serve any purpose other than convincing the counselor of his own personal effectiveness within a socially approved context is questionable. The counselor must use words – verbal criteria of progress which make sense of his activities – in an effort to make rational to himself what he does and to convey the meaning of his activities to others. The degree to which he is successful in this pursuit justifies his existence to himself and the value of his service to others. Undoubtedly his choice of words is crucial, but their importance lies in their acceptance by the consumer. Nevertheless, one must recognize that the consumer is not always the only judge of the effectiveness of counseling. His perception and definition of the help he receives – indeed, the very meaning he assigns to it – may bear no relationship to what the counselor is trying to do.

Expectancies and Goals Compared

What various individuals and groups expect of counseling often differs from the goals expressed by its practitioners. Counseling is usually thought to be something *done to* or for the counselee while goal statements generally specify that it is the recipient who acts, decides, changes, becomes, etc. Seemingly the assignment and acceptance of responsibility for what takes place in counseling differs substantially between the two. Perhaps this distinction is too subtle to be communicated to and understood by the public.

Furthermore, expectations indicate that counseling is most appropriate for the individual who is in a crisis situation whereas counseling goals tend to portray counseling as most appropriate for the person who seeks self-understanding and growth rather than a solution for an immediate, pressing concern. Perhaps the real difference lies in whether counseling is to be viewed as remedial or generative. Expectancies are likely to stress remediation and repair; goal statements imply that counseling should be preventive or generative in nature.

One quality reflected by both expectancies and goals, almost without exception, is that there is little or no limitation upon what counseling can do. It is almost as though counseling is the answer to all manner of societal and personal difficulties. One wonders sometimes whether either the public or the practitioners of counseling are concerned about clearly defining situations where counseling may be most appropriate. The problem of setting appropriate boundaries for counseling takes on an ever increasing urgency with the continued expansion of this service into more and more settings.

Annotated References

Arbuckle, Dugald S. *Counseling: Philosophy, Theory and Practice.* Boston: Allyn and Bacon, Inc., 1965. 415 pp.
The first part (pp. 49–63) of Chapter 2, "The Counseling Process," concentrates upon the objectives of counseling. Arbuckle points out that the counselor in preparation must come to some understanding of the basic purpose of the profession he plans to enter.

Berenson, Bernard G. and Carkhuff, Robert R. (eds.). *Sources of Gain in Counseling and Psychotherapy.* New York: Holt, Rinehart and Winston, Inc., 1967. 449 pp.
Part I (pp. 21–56) presents Hans J. Eysenck's report on the inefficacy of therapy with adults, Eugene Levitt's evaluative findings of therapy with children and Allen Bergin's review and critique of their two reports.

Byrne, Richard Hill. *The School Counselor.* Boston: Houghton Mifflin Company, 1963. 295 pp.
Chapter 1 (pp. 3–25) discusses counseling goals by first describing differences in two counselors at work. Counseling goals are defined and goal statements are evaluated. An ultimate counseling goal is stated and clarified.

Krumboltz, John D. (ed.). *Revolution in Counseling.* Boston: Houghton Mifflin Company, 1966. 121 pp.
Chapter 1 (pp. 3–26), by Krumboltz, discusses counselor conceptualization and definition of client problems. Methods to accomplish counselor goals and to evaluate counseling success are presented.

Annotated References

Arbuckle, Dugald S. "The Counselor: Who? What?" *Personnel and Guidance Journal,* Vol. 50 (June, 1972). pp. 785–791.

Atkin, Jerry. "Counseling in an Age of Crisis." *Personnel and Guidance Journal,* Vol. 50 (May, 1972). pp. 719–724.

Carmical, LaVerne and Calvin, Leland, Jr. "Functions Selected by School Counselors." *The School Counselor,* Vol. 17 (March, 1970). pp. 280–285.

Clarke, Joanna and Waters, Henrietta. "Counseling the Culturally Deprived: A Survey of High School Counselor's Opinions and Attitudes." *The School Counselor,* Vol. 19 (January, 1972). pp. 201–209.

Frey, David H. "Conceptualizing Counseling Theories: A Content Analysis of Process and Goal Statements." *Counselor Education and Supervision,* Vol. 11 (June, 1972). pp. 243–250.

Graf, Robert W., Danish, Steven, and Austin, Brian. "Reactions to Three Kinds of Vocational Educational Counseling." *Journal of Counseling Psychology,* Vol. 19 (May, 1972). pp. 224–228.

Hays, Donald G. "Counselor – What Are You Worth?" *The School Counselor,* Vol. 19 (May, 1972). pp. 309–312.

Krumboltz, John D. "Parable of the Good Counselor." *Personnel and Guidance Journal,* Vol. 43 (October, 1964). pp. 118–124.

Krumboltz, John D. "Behavioral Counseling: Rationale and Research." *Personnel and Guidance Journal,* Vol. 44 (December, 1965). pp. 383–387.

Krumboltz, John D. "Behavioral Goals for Counseling." *Journal of Counseling Psychology,* Vol. 13 (Summer, 1966). pp. 153–159.

Kushel, Gerald. "The Counselor's Image and the Chameleon." *The School Counselor,* Vol. 17 (March, 1970). pp. 286–291.

Maser, Arthur L. "Counselor Function in Secondary Schools." *The School Counselor,* Vol. 18 (May, 1971). pp. 367–372.

Perrone, Philip A., Weiking, Mary L., and Nagel, Elwyn H. "The Counseling Function as Seen by Students, Parents and Teachers." *Journal of Counseling Psychology,* Vol. 12 (Summer, 1965). pp. 148–152.

Samler, Joseph. "The Counseling Service in the Administrative Setting: Problems and Possible Solutions." *Personnel and Guidance Journal,* Vol. 44 (March, 1966). pp. 715–722.

Shoben, Edward J. "The Counseling Experience as Personal Development." *Personnel and Guidance Journal,* Vol. 44 (November, 1965). pp. 224–230.

Snyder, John F., Hill, Clara E., and Derkson, Timothy P. "Why Some Students Do Not Use University Counseling Facilities." *Journal of Counseling Psychology,* Vol. 19 (July, 1972). pp. 262–267.

Thompson, Andrew and Zimmerman, Robert. "Goals of Counseling: Whose? When?" *Journal of Counseling Psychology,* Vol. 16 (March, 1969). pp. 121–125.

Van Riper, B. W. "Student Perception: The Counselor Is What He Does." *The School Counselor,* Vol. 19 (September, 1971). pp. 53–57.

PART TWO

THE COUNSELOR

Part Two focuses upon counselor characteristics and role and function.

Chapter Five is based upon an extensive literature on the subject of the characteristics of counselors. There are many reasons why this scholarly literature exists and why it continues to expand. Personal experience and contact with many counselors indicate that most of them engage in self-examination to try to ascertain why they entered or continued in the field and why they were successful with one person or in one situation but not with others in different situations. But identifying the characteristics of counselors and counselees is difficult, and understanding the effects and interaction of personal and other characteristics in the counseling process is an extremely complex endeavor. More, of course, is known than was the case a decade ago. Much remains to be done.

In Chapter Six attention is given to the meanings of role, function, and role conflict. Role theory and the role of the counselor are treated. Some of the forces and factors which cause role variability are identified and discussed. Finally, descriptions are presented of current counselor role behavior.

COUNSELOR AND COUNSELEE CHARACTERISTICS

5

The importance of the counselor's characteristics to counseling outcome has long been recognized. It is he who by training and professional obligation is charged with creating the climate of the counseling relationship. But the counselee's personality structure too has been demonstrated to have a direct effect upon the counseling relationship and its outcome. In reality, both personalities interact. Each brings to the relationship his preferred method of interacting with others and his needs, conflicts, and unique life style.

This chapter reviews the major research efforts which have been directed toward identifying counselor and counselee characteristics. The content is divided among seven areas: (1) approaches, techniques, and criteria utilized in studying counselor characteristics, (2) characteristics of counselors, (3) characteristics which distinguish effective from ineffective counselors, (4) characteristics of counselees, (5) similarities of counselor and counselee characteristics, (6) complementary counselor and counselee characteristics, and (7) summary comments.The reader may notice that many of the studies cited employ noncounseling terminology. Such studies are often conducted in clinical settings where terminology often differs, but where the activities engaged in are highly similar to counseling as it is broadly defined.

Approaches, Techniques, and Criteria for Studying Counselor Characteristics

APPROACHES UTILIZED

Usually, investigations of counselor characteristics have been approached in four ways. Each of these will be identified and a brief description given of selected literature which illustrates it.

Speculation Many have speculated about the characteristics considered essential in an effective counselor. In 1949 the National Vocational Guidance Association issued a statement that counselors, ideally, were interested in people, patient, sensitive to others, emotionally stable, objective, respectful of facts, and trusted by others.[1] Hamrin and Paulsen reported a study in which 91 counselors listed traits which, in their judgment, facilitated counseling.[2] In order of frequency these included (1) understanding, (2) sympathetic attitude, (3) friendliness, (4) sense of humor, (5) stability, (6) patience, (7) objectivity, (8) sincerity, (9) tact, (10) fairness, (11) tolerance, (12) neatness, (13) calmness, (14) broad-mindedness, (15) kindliness, (16) pleasantness, (17) social intelligence, and (18) poise. In Mowrer's judgment, personal maturity is the most important characteristic for counselors, but he noted that there is no valid way to assess it.[3]

The Association for Counselor Education and Supervision has indicated that a counselor should have six basic qualities: belief in each individual, commitment to individual human values, alertness to the world, open-mindedness, understanding of self, and professional commitment.[4] Parker has asserted that the counselor should possess a sensitivity to others, the ability to analyze objectively another's strengths and weaknesses, an awareness of the nature and extent of individual differences, and the ability to identify (diagnose) learning difficulties.[5]

All these lists of counselor traits reveal considerable agreement. All want the counselor to be a psychologically healthy person. They tend to reflect an idealized personality. It should be noted that essentially the same qualities apply equally well to ideal teachers, physicians, astronauts, etc. Cottle pointed out that, while these listings were helpful, they were unsatisfactory because (1) they represented merely the opinions of the people who made them, (2) they failed to distinguish the counselor from other school personnel, (3) the traits of successful counselors vary so widely that it is difficult to select one list as being satisfactory, and (4) it is the interrelations or pattern of characteristics that is important.[6]

Serious study of counselor characteristics has moved from such "armchair" listings to investigating what distinguishes counselors from noncounselors and what the relationship is between counselor characteristics and counselor effectiveness. Both the nature and the complexity of the research have changed as investigators moved from mere speculation to formalized research efforts.

Identifying Effective and Ineffective Groups The second approach to identifying counselor characteristics involves designating effective and ineffective counselors and ascertaining what distinguishes the two groups. A study by Stefflre, King, and Leafgren is typical of this approach.[7]

Stefflre, King, and Leafgren used Q-sort judgments by peers as their criterion for designating the nine most effective and nine least effective counselor trainees. The two groups were compared on four dimensions: (1) academic aptitude and performance as measured by the Miller Analogies Test, pre- and post-Tests of Knowledge of Guidance, grade-point average on undergraduate and graduate pre-NDEA Counseling Institute work, and Institute field and class work; (2) interests and values as measured by the Educational Interest Inventory and the Social Welfare and Business Contact scales of the Strong Vocational Interest Blank (SVIB); (3) personality characteristics as measured by the Taylor Manifest Anxiety Scale (TMAS), the Rokeach Dogmatism Scale, and the Edwards Personal Preference Schedule (EPPS); (4) self-concept as measured by the Bills Index of Adjustment and Values and a Discrepancy score obtained from the dif-

[1] National Vocational Guidance Association, *Counselor Preparation* (Washington: The Association, 1949).
[2] S. A. Hamrin and Blanche P. Paulsen, *Counseling Adolescents* (Chicago: Science Research Associates, Inc., 1950), p. 323.
[3] O. H. Mowrer, "Training in Psychotherapy," *Journal of Consulting Psychology,* Vol. 15 (August, 1951), pp. 274–277.
[4] Association for Counselor Education and Supervision, "The Counselor: Professional Preparation and Role," *Personnel and Guidance Journal,* Vol. 42 (December, 1964), pp. 536–541.
[5] Clyde Parker, "The Place of Counseling in the Preparation of Student Personnel Workers," *Personnel and Guidance Journal,* Vol. 45 (November, 1966), pp. 259–260.
[6] William C. Cottle, "Personal Characteristics of Counselors: I," *Personnel and Guidance Journal,* Vol. 31 (April, 1953), pp. 445–450.
[7] Buford Stefflre, Paul King, and F. Leafgren, "Characteristics of Counselors Judged by Their Peers," *Journal of Counseling Psychology,* Vol. 9 (Winter, 1962), pp. 335–340.

ference between the position each trainee thought the average group would give him and the position he was actually assigned. The authors reported significant differences between the effective and ineffective counselor samples on the four dimensions considered in the study. The effective group earned higher scores on the instruments measuring academic aptitude and performance. They had significantly higher scores on the SVIB Social Welfare scales and significantly higher Deference and Order scores (EPPS) than the ineffective group. Significant differences in the groups' Discrepancy scores suggested that in terms of self-concept the effective counselors underestimated themselves and the ineffective ones overestimated themselves.

Hypothesized Characteristics The third approach consists in ascertaining whether certain characteristics which have been hypothesized as necessary for counseling are in fact present and operative. Typically selected for investigation are those personality characteristics which previous research demonstrates or which counseling theory suggests may be associated with counselor effectiveness. Bandura's research into the relationship between counselor personality and counselor effectiveness is representative of many studies using this approach.[8]

In investigating the relationship between counselor anxiety and counselor effectiveness, Bandura tested the hypotheses that competent psychotherapists (1) are less anxious than those judged to be less competent and (2) possess greater insight into the nature of their own anxieties than do less competent therapists. Forty-two therapists from four clinical settings were the subjects of the study. Each subject rated himself and all other subjects as to degree of anxiety with respect to dependency, hostility, and sex. The average rating assigned to each subject constituted the anxiety measure. The insight measure was defined in terms of the relative discrepancy between the subject's self-rating and the average group rating for the subject. Supervisor ratings were used as the criterion measure of therapeutic competence. Bandura found support for his first hypothesis, but his second was not confirmed. Anxious therapists were rated less competent than were those low in anxiety, but neither therapist degree of insight into the nature of his anxiety nor therapist self-rating of anxiety was significantly related to supervisor ratings of competence. The author concluded that "the presence of anxiety in the therapist, whether recognized or not, affects his ability to do successful psychotherapy and insight into his anxieties alone is not sufficient."[9]

Correlational Analysis The fourth approach to the study of counselor characteristics involves exploring the relationship between certain counselor variables and some criterion measure of effectiveness derived from correlational analysis. A study by Johnson *et al.* is representative of this highly empirical approach.[10] Johnson and her associates used multiple regression analysis to find the relationship between five predictor measures of counselor nonintellective characteristics and five criterion measures of counselor effectiveness. The California Personality Inventory (CPI), the Edwards Personal Preference Schedule, the Guilford-Zimmerman Temperament Survey (GZTS), the Minnesota Multiphasic Personality Inventory (MMPI), and the Strong Vocational Interest Blank – Male (SVIB) were used to measure the nonintellective characteristics of 99 counselors. The five criterion measures of counselor effectiveness included (1) the Purdue Q-sort, used to ascertain counselor perception of the client and counselee self-perception; (2) the Counselor Rating Scale (CRS), a 5-point, 23-item, 3-factor rating scale wherein counselees evaluated their counseling experience; (3) peer ratings,

[8] A. Bandura, "Psychotherapists' Anxiety Level, Self Insight, and Psychotherapeutic Competence," *Journal of Abnormal Social Psychology,* Vol. 52 (May, 1956), pp. 333–337.

[9] *Ibid.,* p. 337.

[10] D. J. Johnson, B. Shertzer, J. D. Linden, and S. C. Stone, "The Relationship of Counselor Candidate Characteristics and Counseling Effectiveness," *Counselor Education and Supervision,* Vol. 6 (Summer, 1967), pp. 297–304.

a Q-technique with which counselor trainees judged each other in terms of (a) academic effectiveness, (b) counseling effectiveness, and (c) social effectiveness; (4) supervisor grades for performance in the counseling practicum course; and (5) the Graduate Cumulative Index, an average of grades in both didactic and practicum courses in the counselor education program. Multiple regression analysis was used to determine the relative weights of the 10 measures.

The analysis suggested that among the combination of predictors, practicum grade appeared to be most useful, and a prediction equation for counseling effectiveness was derived. The prediction equation consisted of a weighted combination of Factor A from the CRS and peer ratings for academic effectiveness. Exploratory correlational analysis was used to identify the nonintellective variables that were related to practicum grade and the criterion predictor. The criterion predictor and practicum grade correlated .68 for males and .70 for females. Practicum grade alone was used as the criterion of counselor effectiveness in subsequent analysis.

Five predictor variables were found by Johnson and her associates to be associated with counselor effectiveness in practicum. The Architect (SVIB) and Well-Being (CPI) scales were identified as male predictors; Schizophrenia (MMPI), Friendliness (GZTS), and Dentist (SVIB) scales were found to be negatively associated with effectiveness for females. Prediction equations using these variables were computed, and counselor trainees were grouped by sex into high (effective), medium, and low (ineffective) groups. The three predictors for females and the Well-Being scale for males were verified by cross-validation using analysis of variance and Newman-Keuls procedures. The authors concluded,

> Effective male counselor trainees may be characterized as confident, friendly, affable, accepting and liking. They appeared to be generally satisfied with themselves and their surroundings.
>
> Effective female counselor candidates . . . presented themselves as outgoing and efficient, giving an appearance of confidence. They appeared to be assertive and person- rather than object-oriented.
>
> Effective male and female counselor candidates tended to be more like each other than like members of the less effective group of their own sex or stereotypes of their own sex or both.[11]

TECHNIQUES USED IN ASSESSING COUNSELOR CHARACTERISTICS

Self-Report Techniques The self-report technique consists of administering selected, usually standardized self-report personality and interest inventories to the counselor sample. Virtually all of the objective personality and interest inventories have been used. However, dissatisfaction with the available instruments and a desire to gather data which supplements objective personality test data have led to the development of new self-report techniques: Q-sorts designed to measure counselor self-concept (see Lesser,[12] and Johnson *et al.*[13]), specially designed counselor self-rating scales (see Streitfeld[14]), and counselor-written human relations incidents (see Combs and Soper[15]).

Rating Techniques Rating techniques have been used to assess counselor personality in two ways: (1) to identify the personal characteristics which counselors themselves and/or the recipients of counseling believe are related to counselor effectiveness and (2) to assess counselor personality characteristics, usually by means of counselor and/or supervisors' ratings. Each approach will be briefly described.

Studies by Arbuckle[16] and Pohlman and Robin-

[11] *Ibid.*, pp. 301–302.
[12] W. M. Lesser, "The Relationship Between Counseling Progress and Empathic Understanding," *Journal of Counseling Psychology*, Vol. 8 (Winter, 1961), pp. 330–336.
[13] *Op. cit.*
[14] J. W. Streitfeld, "Expressed Acceptance of Self and Others by Psychotherapists," *Journal of Consulting Psychology*, Vol. 23 (October, 1959), pp. 435–441.
[15] A. W. Combs and D. W. Soper, "The Perceptual Organization of Effective Counselors," *Journal of Counseling Psychology*, Vol. 10 (Fall, 1963), pp. 222–226.
[16] D. S. Arbuckle, "Client Perception of Counselor Personality," *Journal of Counseling Psychology*, Vol. 3 (Summer, 1956), pp. 93–96.

son[17] illustrate the use of rating scales devised from suggestions by counselors and/or counselees. Arbuckle asked counselor trainees to list in order of preference the three traits they would most and least prefer in counselors. Tolerance, warmth, and interest were traits most preferred. Lack of understanding, disinterest, and aggressiveness were traits least preferred. Pohlman and Robinson, operating on the premise that the counseling situation has its annoying as well as pleasant features for the client and that knowledge about the client's reaction to these features will be helpful to the counselor, attempted to determine the degree to which certain types of counselor behavior and certain aspects of the counseling situation were annoying or pleasing to clients. A 92-item questionnaire describing counselor behaviors and other aspects of the counseling situation was presented to freshmen enrolled in a "How to Study" course, who rated the items on a five-point scale. Students reported as displeasing those counselor behaviors which indicated a lack of respect — aloofness, insincerity, interrupting, yawning, lacking warmth, etc. Ratings of various speech or hearing handicaps ranged from mild dislike to neutrality.

A study by McDougall and Reitan illustrates the utilization of peer and supervisory ratings.[18] Peer ratings, supervisory ratings, and counselor trainees' self-ratings were compared on four factors: (1) academic understanding, (2) class contribution, (3) self-insight or the degree to which individual self-concept was congruent with the rater's view, and (4) counseling potential. The authors reported that peer ratings of academic understanding, class contribution, and counseling potential showed a close correspondence with supervisors' ratings on the same factors. There was a high degree of association between peer ratings of academic understanding and class contribution and between peer ratings of self-insight and counseling potential.

CRITERION MEASURES OF EFFECTIVENESS

Four types of criteria are most common: supervisor ratings, counselor's peer ratings, client ratings, and Q-techniques. These may also be viewed as representing measures of counselor effectiveness which are external and internal to the counseling activity itself. Under this classification scheme, supervisor and peer ratings are considered external observer measures of counselor effectiveness and client ratings and Q-techniques performed by clients and/or counselors as internal measures.

Supervisor Ratings The most widely used criterion of counselor effectiveness appears to be the supervisor rating. Researchers have employed supervisor ratings of observed or taped interview (Brown[19]); supervisor global ratings of counselors based upon knowledge of a given counselor's work with several counselees and/or long-term counseling with a single client (Streitfeld, 1959; Kazienko and Neidt[20]; and Combs and Soper, 1963); and supervisor ratings in the form of practicum grades (Johnson *et al.*, 1967).

Peer Ratings Sociometric techniques hold promise as evaluative measures, since group members presumably have the opportunity to observe each other under more varied circumstances than do supervisors or other individuals who come in contact with members of a counseling group for a limited time. Furthermore, group pressure and interaction among the members influence the individual's behavior. One's peers know the limit to which he can be pushed and they sometimes test it. Frequently they see him in the unguarded

[17] E. Pohlman and F. P. Robinson, "Client Reactions to Some Aspects of the Counseling Situation," *Personnel and Guidance Journal,* Vol. 38 (March, 1960), pp. 546–551.

[18] W. P. McDougall and H. M. Reitan, "The Use of a Peer Rating Technique in Appraising Selected Attributes of Counselor Trainees," *Counselor Education and Supervision,* Vol. 1 (Winter, 1961), pp. 72–76.

[19] D. J. Brown, "An Investigation of the Relationship Between Certain Characteristics of Guidance Counselors and Performance in Supervised Counseling Interviews," unpublished doctoral dissertation, The Ohio State University, 1960.

[20] L. W. Kazienko and C. O. Neidt, "Self Descriptions of Good and Poor Counselor Trainees," *Counselor Education and Supervision,* Vol. 1 (Spring, 1962), pp. 106–123.

moment and hear the chance remark. Sociometric techniques have been used to identify counselors who were considered effective by Arbuckle (1956), Brown (1960), Stefflre *et al.* (1962), McDougall and Reitan (1961), and Johnson *et al.* (1967).

Client Ratings Client judgments of counselor effectiveness have not been used as frequently as supervisor or peer ratings, for professional counselors are divided over their importance and validity. Studies using client judgment as a criterion have typically been based on specially developed rating scales. Correll[21] used the Anderson and Anderson[22] rating scale to measure the quality of communication in the counseling interview. Grigg used a Client Observation Report (COR) to ascertain: (1) the client's perceptions of the counselor's reactions to him, (2) the client's reaction to the counseling experience, (3) the techniques employed most often by the counselor to begin the counseling interview, (4) the client's appraisal of the counselor; and also to obtain (5) a comparison of the counselor during the first interview with the counselor during the last interview on the first four variables, (6) a rating of how the client felt during the typical counseling hour, and (7) an appraisal of whether counseling had been useful.[23]

Linden, Stone, and Shertzer developed a Counselor Evaluation Inventory (CEI) to measure clients' reactions to their counseling experiences.[24] The CEI yielded scores on three factors: Counseling Climate (Factor X), Counselor Comfort (Factor Y), and Client Satisfaction (Factor Z). In addition, a total score was demonstrated to be parsimonious in respect to assessing counselor effectiveness. Kelz also has devised and evaluated an eight-category instrument for rating counseling conducted by counselor trainees.[25]

[21] P. T. Correll, "Factors Influencing Communication in Counseling," unpublished doctoral dissertation, University of Missouri, 1955.
[22] R. P. Anderson and G. V. Anderson, "The Development of an Instrument for Measuring Rapport," *Personnel and Guidance Journal,* Vol. 41 (September, 1962), pp. 18–24.
[23] A. E. Grigg, "Client Response to Counselors at Different Levels of Experience," *Journal of Counseling Psychology,* Vol. 8 (Fall, 1961), pp. 217–222.
[24] J. D. Linden, S. C. Stone, and Bruce Shertzer, "Development and Evaluation of an Inventory for Rating Counselors," *Personnel and Guidance Journal,* Vol. 44 (November, 1965), pp. 267–276.

Characteristics of Counselors

The search for characteristics basic to counseling effectiveness led to the realization that their identification could not be studied independently of the counseling process. Yet in this extraordinarily complex interpersonal process the counselor's personality traits are only one set of variables which interact with other sets of variables. The ideal approach would be the simultaneous investigation of the network of variables manifested in the actual counseling process. However, counseling's fundamental service orientation places severe constraints on "live" data collection. The ethical concern for the individual legitimately limits research efforts. Finally, studies of the counselor's personality *assume* that it is relevant to counselor effectiveness. Sprinthall, Whiteley, and Mosher question the advisability of continuing along this line of inquiry.[26] They believe that research focused on counselor behavior would be more fruitful.

The material in this section is organized around some rather arbitrarily established headings selected to convey the essence of research relating to the topic.

ATTITUDES

After analyzing three dilemmas faced by counselors, C. Gilbert Wrenn concludes that "To become involved with one's clients and one's profession must not mean neglect of the most potent single element in the counseling relationship. This is the *person* of the counselor, his sense of reality,

[25] James W. Kelz, "The Development and Evaluation of a Measure of Counselor Effectiveness," *Personnel and Guidance Journal,* Vol. 44 (January, 1966), pp. 511–516.
[26] Norman A. Sprinthall, John M. Whiteley, and Ralph L. Mosher, "Cognitive Flexibility: A Focus for Research on Counselor Effectiveness," *Counselor Education and Supervision,* Vol. 5 (Summer, 1966), pp. 188–197.

his self trust, his increasing awareness of beauty and the joy of living, and his open regard for others." [27]

Studying the degree of annoyance or pleasure clients feel when presented with descriptions of counseling situations, Pohlman and Robinson (1960) concluded that certain mannerisms were regarded as annoying but *not* as much as was the counselor's attitude. Waskow tested the hypothesis that the degree of counselor acceptance, interest, refusal to be judgmental, and expressiveness is directly related to how much the client both discusses and expresses his feelings.[28] Ratings of counselor attitudes and client discussion and expression of feeling were based on interview material received in three ways: reading transcripts, listening to tape recordings, and listening to filtered tape recordings. Waskow reported significant relationships under all three rating conditions between the counselor's judgmental attitude and the client's discussion of feeling. No other significant relationship was found. As this finding was the opposite of that predicted, Waskow postulated that (1) judgmental counselors directly reinforce the client's talking about feelings and (2) the more judgmental counselor is seen as being more "forceful" and hence may be responsible for the client's increased discussion of his feelings. However, subsequent analysis of the data offered no support for the proposed explanations. Waskow returned to the definition of the judgmental attitude and decided that it included not only the dimension of evaluation on the counselor's part but also an element of assurance that the counselor knows what he's talking about and is the authority in the situation. (A judgmental counselor was defined as one who seems evaluative, sets himself up as the judge, seems to push his own views as correct, and acts as if he knows the answers.) Waskow suggested that the assurance conveyed by the counselor provided some security for the client and made it easier for him to discuss his feelings because the counselor acted as if he were able to deal with them and offer some solution.

A counselor's beliefs about the nature of man is thought to influence the way he responds to and deals with clients. Dole and his colleagues[29] studied 166 graduate students in counseling psychology, clinical psychology, and vocational rehabilitation programs to determine their philosophies of human nature. The students tended to have a neutral or slightly favorable attitude toward other persons and to endorse the belief that human behavior was complex and variable. These graduate students did not differ by subspecialty in their responses to the Philosophies of Human Nature scales.

Gendlin reported modifications in client-centered therapy as a result of working with psychotics.[30] The modifications involved attitudes rather than client-centered behavior. He stated that (1) therapeutic attitudes manifest themselves in interactive behavior through genuine therapist self-expression, (2) open interaction affects the nature of the client's present experiencing process, and therefore, in spite of threat and withdrawal, he may find himself experiencing more optimally. Mahan and Wicas, in their study of several dimensions of counselor personality, consistently found a high degree of counselor reliance on the "rational" in man.[31] When such a counselor is confronted with a client's emotional behavior, they suggested, he is likely to have difficulty communicating with the client, become threatened and defensive, or become irrationally identified with the client. Demos and Zuwaylif reported that effective counselors

[27] C. Gilbert Wrenn, "The Three Worlds of the Counselor," *Personnel and Guidance Journal,* Vol. 49 (October, 1970), pp. 91–96.

[28] I. E. Waskow, "Counselor Attitudes and Client Behavior," *Journal of Consulting Psychology,* Vol. 27 (October, 1963), pp. 405–412.

[29] Arthur A. Dole, Jack Nottingham, and Lawrence S. Wrightsman, Jr., "Beliefs about Human Nature Held by Counseling, Clinical and Rehabilitation Students," *Journal of Counseling Psychology,* Vol. 16 (May, 1969), pp. 197–202.

[30] E. T. Gendlin, "Client-Centered Development and Work with Schizophrenics," *Journal of Counseling Psychology,* Vol. 9 (Fall, 1962), pp. 205–211.

[31] T. Mahan and E. Wicas, "Counselor Personality Characteristics: A Preliminary Exploration," *Counselor Education and Supervision,* Vol. 3 (Winter, 1964), pp. 78–83.

possessed more nurturance and affiliation while less effective counselors exhibited more autonomy, abasement, and aggression.[32]

Strupp also emphasized that the therapist's attitudes and perceptions can be communicated to the patient and structure the therapeutic relationship.[33] From his study of 134 therapists he broadly defined two groups: (1) more person oriented, showing deep understanding and respect and seeing the person behind the neurotic aspects of his personality; and (2) more symptom oriented, making more judgments, labeling and reacting to the neurotic defenses and character structure rather than the person. Strupp, therefore, identifies the counselor's dual contribution to the treatment process as personal and technical. The former facilitates the establishment of an interpersonal relationship in which constructive personality change can take place. Technical knowledge may then be applied. Both are necessary.

Truax studied the conditions of empathic understanding of the client, unconditional positive regard for the client, and therapist self-congruence.[34] His data suggest that the therapist who provides these conditions facilitates constructive personality change. His sample included a most difficult patient population, hospitalized schizophrenics.

In a somewhat similar study Barrett-Leonard related clients' constructive personality change to the following five variables: therapist's level of regard for his client, extent to which his regard is unconditional, degree of empathic understanding, therapist's congruence, and his willingness to be known.[35] Data collected after five interviews indicated that the first four variables were positively correlated with change. The association between the measured relationship and change was generally stronger when the client's rather than the therapist's perception of the relationship was used. But at termination, the change-relationship associations were stronger when the therapist's judgments were used. However, therapist and client joint perception of the relationship provided a more precise and discriminating prediction of assessed change than did their separate perceptions. The investigator then suggested that there are "good" therapists and "good" clients with respect to the ability to respond well to the four variables. The combination of the two would imply an excellent prognosis for therapy. A poor therapist paired with a poor client would be unlikely to produce good therapy. Also a good client paired with a poor therapist may perceive the response positively and have a productive therapeutic experience, while a good therapist with a poor client may ultimately succeed in communicating the qualities of the four variables and thus help the client. This study provides a desirable model for future research.

Similar results were found by Ashby, Ford, Guerney, and Guerney.[36] Therapists differed in the amount of guardedness or defensiveness they engendered in clients whose views of the therapeutic relationship depended on the interaction of their own dynamics, the kind of therapy administered, and the individual characteristics of the therapists.

Lesser (1961), investigating the relationship between counseling progress and counselor empathic understanding, hypothesized that (1) counseling progress is positively related to the counselor's empathic understanding of his client and (2) counseling progress and empathic understanding are positively related to the degree of similarity between client's and counselor's self-concept.[37] The Empathic Understanding Scale completed by counselors and their clients, the Felt Similarity Scale com-

[32] George D. Demos and Fadel H. Zuwaylif, "Characteristics of Effective Counselors," *Counselor Education and Supervision,* Vol. 5 (Spring, 1966), pp. 163–165.

[33] H. H. Strupp, "The Psychotherapist's Contribution to the Treatment Process," *Behavioral Science,* Vol. 3 (January, 1958), pp. 34–67.

[34] C. B. Truax, "Effective Ingredients in Psychotherapy: An Approach to Unraveling the Patient-Therapist Interaction," *Journal of Counseling Psychology,* Vol. 10 (Fall, 1963), pp. 256–263.

[35] G. T. Barrett-Leonard, "Dimensions of Therapist Response as Causal Factors in Therapeutic Change," *Psychological Monographs,* Vol. 76 (whole No. 562, 1962), No. 43.

[36] J. D. Ashby, D. H. Ford, B. G. Guerney, Jr., and L. F. Guerney, "Effects of a Reflective and a Leading Type of Psychotherapy," *Psychological Monographs,* Vol. 71 (March, 1957), No. 24.

[37] Lesser, *op. cit.*

pleted by counselors, and a 100-item Q-sort completed by counselors and their clients furnished the basic data for the study. Clients completed two sets of Q-sorts. The client initially sorted the cards as he saw himself and as he would most like to be; after 12 hours of counseling, he again sorted the cards as he then saw himself and as he would most like to be. Counseling progress was determined by comparing the client's pre- and post-sorts with 12 hours of counseling intervening. The degree of similarity between client and counselor self-concepts was measured by comparing the counselors' and clients' Q-sorts. Lesser reported that the counselor's empathic understanding as measured was unrelated to counseling progress or to similarity. Similarity between client and counselor self-perception was negatively related to counseling progress, but correct awareness by the counselor of similarity between himself and client was positively related to counseling progress.

Streitfeld (1959) tested the hypothesis that better psychotherapists (as judged by their supervisors) are more accepting of others and more self-accepting than are poorer psychotherapists.[38] Two expressed acceptance ratings of therapeutic ability were obtained from the therapist sample. Correlational analysis was used to determine the relationships between (1) the subjects' expressed acceptance ratings and the criterion — supervisors' rating of therapeutic ability — and (2) self-ratings of therapeutic ability and the criterion. Streitfeld reported no significant relationship between supervisors' ratings of therapeutic ability and subjects' acceptance of self and others. However, subjects' self-ratings of their therapeutic ability were positively related to their expressed acceptance of others.

Donnan and Harlan administered the Sixteen Personality Factor Questionnaire to 41 student counselors and 41 student administrators enrolled in graduate courses. School counselors differed significantly from school administrators in five traits. First, counselors seemed mature and calm, while administrators were emotional. Second, counselors tended to be casual and undependable; administrators were conscientious and persistent. Third, counselors were tender-minded, administrators tough-minded. Fourth, counselors scored as trusting and adaptable while administrators scored as suspicious. Fifth, counselors were forthright and natural, while administrators were shrewd and calculating.[39]

RACE, SEX, AGE

Vontress, in a series of articles, has called attention to the impact of racial differences upon counseling.[40] He believes that it is difficult for white counselors to establish and maintain relationships with black clients. Similarly, the black counselor may find it difficult to relate to the black client unless the counselor projects himself as "black." Vontress suggests (1) that it is easier for any counselor to establish a working relationship with a "colored" client than it is with either a "Negro" or a "black"; (2) that working relationships with black, Negro, or colored females can be established more easily than with males and (3) that rapport can be achieved more quickly with individuals of African descent who live in the South than with those who live in other parts of the country.

Some years ago Farson concluded that "The counselor is a woman."[41] His thesis was that counselor behaviors were fundamentally those society attributed to women: tenderness, gentleness, receptiveness, passiveness. McClain, investigating "Is the Counselor a Woman?", reported that both men and women counselors in his study appeared to possess in acceptable degrees the femininity and requisite ego-strength that Farson deemed appropriate for the successful counselor.[42] Pointing out that recent research portrays the counselor not only as tender, gentle, and loving but also active,

[38] Streitfeld, *op. cit.*

[39] Hugh H. Donnan and Grady Harland, "Personality of Counselors and Administrators," *Personnel and Guidance Journal,* Vol. 47 (November, 1968), pp. 228–232.

[40] Clement E. Vontress, "Racial Differences: Impediments of Rapport," *Journal of Counseling Psychology,* Vol. 18 (January, 1971), pp. 7–13.

[41] Robert E. Farson, "The Counselor Is a Woman," *Journal of Counseling Psychology,* Vol. 1 (Winter, 1954), pp. 221–223.

[42] E. W. McClain, "Is the Counselor a Woman?" *Personnel and Guidance Journal,* Vol. 46 (January, 1968), pp. 444–448.

assertive, and able to confront and interpret immediate interactions when they occur, Carkhuff and Berenson[43] suggest that "The counselor is a man and a woman." They believe that, depending upon the interaction of counselor, client, contextual and environmental variables, the counselor usually initiates the relationship with "nurturant responsiveness," but that later in the relationship the counselor shifts to more active, assertive, confronting behaviors to enable the client to act upon his own perceptions.

Hopke and Rochester reported that effective counselors were younger and had fewer years of teaching experience than their less effective counterparts.[44] In a later study, Rochester[45] held sex and age variables constant in an investigation of attitude changes (based upon Porter's Test of Counselor Attitudes) of some 229 counselor students at the beginning and end of a year-long preparation program. Female students differed from male students in that they were more accepting of "probing" attitudes at the onset of their program. Pre-post comparisons of age classifications revealed that (1) students age 23–27 became more accepting of "probing" attitudes and less accepting of "interpretative" attitudes, (2) the age group 28–35 found the "interpretative" attitude less acceptable, and (3) the 36–56 age group became more accepting of "understanding" attitudes, more accepting of "probing" attitudes, and less accepting of "evaluative" attitudes.

PREVIOUS EXPERIENCES

Kehas and Morris[46] investigated the way in which counselors who had taught were influenced by their earlier experience, and concluded that having been a teacher (1) was useful to the counselor in understanding and working with counselees and teachers on student-teacher problems and (2) was dysfunctional to the extent that it (a) gave rise to ambivalent feelings about the teaching and counseling role, (b) demanded change in perspective toward the student, the school system, and teachers and (c) caused conflict by the necessity of changing the appeals, rewards, and punishments used with students. In a second article[47] these investigators reported on their 12 subjects' intra-role conflict about, and motivation for, changing from teaching to counseling. They pointed out that the expectations of the counselor held by others are bewildering, diverse, and contradictory. In such intra-role conflicts, previous teaching experience can be a help or hindrance depending on whether the counselor views the expectations as legitimate. These 12 subjects' motivations for becoming counselors stemmed primarily from their dissatisfaction with the total educational process and their desire for personal growth. In becoming counselors, some sought to become expressive leaders.

TRANSPARENCY

Successful counseling facilitates counselee self-disclosure and self-exploration. It is successful because the individual verbalizes and comes to know his beliefs, motives, fears, relationships to others and life's decisions. Truax and Carkhuff have presented research supporting a significant relationship between counselor transparency and counselee self-disclosure.[48] They reported that the greater the self-exploration, the greater the constructive personality change. An exception to this finding was the delinquent adolescent involved in group psychotherapy; for him the less self-exploration, the greater the positive personality change.

[43] Robert R. Carkhuff and Bernard G. Berenson, "The Counselor Is a Man and a Woman," *Personnel and Guidance Journal,* Vol. 48 (September, 1969), pp. 24–28.
[44] William E. Hopke and Dean E. Rochester, "Characteristics of Effective and Use of Effective Counselors," *Illinois Guidance and Personnel Quarterly,* Vol. 33 (Fall, 1969), pp. 24–28.
[45] Dean E. Rochester, "Sex and Age as Factors Relating to Attitude Changes," *Counselor Education and Supervision,* Vol. 11 (March, 1972), pp. 214–218.
[46] Chris D. Kehas and Jane L. Morris, "Perceptions in Role Change from Teacher to Counselor," *Counselor Education and Supervision,* Vol. 9 (Summer, 1970), pp. 248–258.
[47] Chris D. Kehas and Jane L. Morris, "Perceptions in Role Change from Teacher to Counselor: Intra-Role Conflict and Motivation for Change," *Counselor Education and Supervision,* Vol. 10 (Spring, 1971), pp. 200–208.
[48] Charles B. Truax and Robert R. Carkhuff, "Client and Therapist Transparency in the Psychotherapeutic Encounter," *Journal of Counseling Psychology,* Vol. 12 (Spring, 1965), pp. 3–9.

Branan[49] varied the rates of counselors' self-disclosure to groups of graduate students, but reported that this did not bring about more student self-disclosure, nor did it affect the students' ratings of their counselors' genuineness, empathy, or self-disclosure. However, Strong and Schmidt[50] report positive student reactions to interviewer self-disclosures. Jourard and Jaffee[51] sought to determine whether subjects would follow the leader and emulate the disclosing behaviors of an experimenter, not only in terms of variety of content but also in direction of self-revealing remarks. The experimenter openly and honestly discussed her thoughts and feelings regarding each of 20 topics, and elicited the reactions of 40 female subjects. The treatment of the four groups of subjects varied only in the length of attention to different topics. Jourard and Jaffee reported that when the experimenter spoke briefly, the subjects spoke briefly; when the experimenter spoke at length, the subjects spoke significantly longer. Contrary to expectation, the subjects tended to talk longer on highly intimate topics.

Schmidt and Strong[52] and Strong and Dixon[53] instructed interviewers to reveal experiences and feelings either similar or dissimilar to those expressed by subjects. Similar disclosures resulted in warmly positive reactions while the outcome of dissimilar disclosures was negative reactions. Murphy and Strong[54] reported that 64 college males were interviewed individually for 20 minutes about how college had altered their friendships, values, and plans. The interviewers disclosed experiences and feelings similar to those revealed by the students zero, two, four, and eight times during the interviews. The interviewers' self-disclosures impressed the students with the interviewers' willingness to be known as persons, and increased the students' feelings of warmth, friendliness, and of being understood. These investigators suggest that the timing of self-disclosure is as important as their frequency in the interview.

COUNSELOR ACTIVITY

Grigg and Goodstein followed up 288 former counselees at the University of Iowa Counseling Service.[55] They reported that those individuals who saw their counselors as taking an active role were more likely to report a favorable outcome for counseling than those who saw their counselors as passive listeners. Counselees who had been more comfortable and relaxed during counseling tended to feel they had more favorable results from the experience. Those who had had personal counseling reported more favorable outcomes when they felt that their counselors were working closely with them toward solution of the problems and fewer favorable outcomes when they felt that the counselor was merely listening to them or was too concerned with test results. Bohn sought to clarify relationships of counselor dominance, experience, and client type with directiveness.[56] Experienced counselors were significantly less directive than inexperienced counselors. The dependent counselee elicited the most directiveness.

Smith and Martinson[57] investigated the effects of

[49] John M. Branan, "Client Reaction to Counselor's Use of Self Experience," *Personnel and Guidance Journal*, Vol. 45 (February, 1967), pp. 568–572.
[50] Stanley R. Strong and Lyle D. Schmidt, "Trustworthiness and Influence in Counseling," *Journal of Counseling Psychology*, Vol. 17 (May, 1970), pp. 197–200.
[51] Sidney M. Jourard and Peggy L. Jaffe, "Influence of an Interviewer's Disclosure on the Self-Disclosing Behavior of Interviewees," *Journal of Counseling Psychology*, Vol. 17 (May, 1970), pp. 252–257.
[52] Lyle D. Schmidt and Stanley R. Strong, "Attractiveness and Influence in Counseling," *Journal of Counseling Psychology*, Vol. 18 (July, 1971), pp. 348–351.
[53] Stanley R. Strong and David R. Dixon, "Expertness, Attractiveness and Influence in Counseling," *Journal of Counseling*, Vol. 18 (November, 1971), pp. 562–570.
[54] Kevin C. Murphy and Stanley R. Strong, "Some Effects of Similarity Self-Disclosure," *Journal of Counseling Psychology*, Vol. 19 (March, 1972), pp. 121–124.
[55] A. E. Grigg and L. D. Goodstein, "The Use of Clients as Judges of the Counselor's Performance," *Journal of Counseling Psychology*, Vol. 4 (Spring, 1957), pp. 31–36.
[56] Martin J. Bohn, Jr., "Counselor Behavior as a Function of Counselor Dominance, Counselor Experience and Client Type," *Journal of Counseling Psychology*, Vol. 12 (Winter, 1965), pp. 346–352.
[57] William D. Smith and William D. Martinson, "Counselors' and Counselees' Learning Style on Interview Behavior," *Journal of Counseling Psychology*, Vol. 18 (March, 1971), pp. 138–141.

counselors' and counselees' learning styles on interview interaction behavior. Various combinations of counselors and clients were used whose learning styles suggested preferences for unstructured learning (called "impulsive learners" because they were friendly, changeable, quick thinking, and quick acting) and counselors and clients whose learning styles suggested preference for structured learning (called "constricted learners" because they were reserved, conscientious, and conservative). Their findings were that "impulsive" counselors differed from "constricted" counselors only in "directive" behavior when both interviewed "impulsive" clients. The two types did not differ in respect to nondirective behaviors, leading behaviors, clients' following behaviors, or clients' positive or negative feelings about the interviews.

Presumably, the counselor's gestures and body movements have an impact upon the client's reactions to him and his verbal communications. Such gestures and body shifts are believed to either accentuate or deny the counselor's verbal expression. Strong and his associates[58] explored the extent to which exposure to counselors' verbal and nonverbal behavior prompted different descriptions of counselors by clients than exposure to counselors' verbal behavior alone. Their thesis was that if the counselor's verbal and nonverbal expressions are congruent, then counselors need not be concerned about nonverbal behavior. If, however, nonverbal cues alter the significance of verbal cues, then counselors must control their nonverbal behavior to avoid a contradictory impact on clients. Their findings were that subjects who saw and heard counselors described them more negatively than subjects who only heard them. Presumably, some visual cues disrupted the subjects' positive image of "counselor." The counselor who moved frequently, changed body position, smiled, frowned, gestured, etc., provoked more positive descriptions than the counselor who remained as "still" as possible.

[58] Stanley R. Strong, Ronald G. Taylor, Joseph C. Bratton and Rodney G. Loper, "Nonverbal Behavior and Perceived Counselor Characteristics," *Journal of Counseling Psychology*, Vol. 18 (November, 1971), pp. 554–561.

MOTIVATION AND EXPECTANCIES FOR CHANGE

Wallach and Strupp hypothesized that (1) the more highly motivated patient will engender in the therapist a warmer attitude and (2) a warmer therapist attitude is associated with more favorable perceptions of the patient, including clinical judgments, prognostic estimates, and treatment plans.[59] Their data, drawn from a sample of 82 experienced therapists, supported the hypotheses. In other words, the personality of the counselor is an integral part of his clinical judgments and counseling practices. Heller and Goldstein reported partial support for their hypothesis that favorable therapist expectancies function in the therapeutic relationship.[60] Goldstein further investigated the relationship between client's and therapist's expectancies of personality change and client-perceived personality change due to therapy.[61] He used a sample of 30 clients randomly assigned to therapy and control groups, and his data strongly suggest that the expectancies held by the therapist are considerably more important than those held by the client. He raised the question as to how expectancies are communicated to the client. Duration of therapy was significantly related to both therapist and combined client and therapist expectations of client personality change.

SIMILARITY TO COUNSELEE

Whitehorn and Betz reported that therapists who had high success rates with schizophrenic patients (A therapists) were different from therapists who had low success rates with schizophrenics (B thera-

[59] M. S. Wallach and H. H. Strupp, "Psychotherapists, Clinical Judgments and Attitudes Toward Patients," *Journal of Consulting Psychology*, Vol. 24 (August, 1960), pp. 316–323.
[60] K. Heller and A. P. Goldstein, "Client Dependency and Therapist Expectancy as Relationship-Maintaining Variables in Psychotherapy," *Journal of Consulting Psychology*, Vol. 25 (October, 1961), pp. 371–375.
[61] A. P. Goldstein, "Therapist and Client Expectation of Personality Changes in Psychotherapy," *Journal of Counseling Psychology*, Vol. 7 (Fall, 1960), pp. 180–184.

pists).[62] Since success with one kind of patient did not correlate very highly with success with another type of patient, they assumed that the difference was the result of the interaction between a certain type of patient and a certain type of therapist. The A therapists approached patients' problems in a personal way, gained a trusted confidential relationship, and participated more actively with the patient. The B therapists were more interested in the psychopathology, were passively permissive, and attempted to develop insight by interpretation. In a later report (1960) the same researchers investigated the distinguishing personality characteristics of the A and B therapists,[63] using the Strong Vocational Interest Blank. Interest patterns of A and B therapists were validated on another group of therapists. The basic difference was an attitude of expecting and respecting spontaneity rather than restricting it. Also the A therapists emphasized solving of individual problems for achieving goals with broadly interpreted social mores and expectations. This facilitated the patient's discovering and solving his problems and participating in life. The authors suggest that "compatibilities and incompatibilities between physicians and patients become a relevant framework of reference for studying the intrinsic nature of the recovery process."[64]

An attempt was made by McNair, Callahan, and Lorr to validate the Whitehorn and Betz findings on a group of nonschizophrenic outpatients.[65] They identified A and B therapists by their responses to the 23 SVIB items reported by Whitehorn and Betz. Using therapists' and patients' reports, they found that patients treated by B therapists improved significantly more than patients of A therapists — just the opposite of the Whitehorn and Betz results. The authors explain that the 23-item A-B scale could be unreliable. Also an internal consistency analysis of the scale indicated that B therapists had more interests in common with the patients and more similar life backgrounds and experiences. Despite the disagreement of the results, both studies indicate that different counselors achieve different results with different counselees, and that similarity of interests, life background, and experiences appear to be significant factors in the counseling relationship and interaction.

Boyd[66] reported that while A and B counselors' interviews contained the same type of verbal content, B's clients produced interviews containing more speculative, confrontive, challenging, and thought-provoking statements than A's clients. He suggests that counselor behavior is to some extent under the control of the client.

Kunce and Anderson[67] studied the assignment of clients to counselors. Some 63 graduate students were given summaries of seven client cases. Each counselor was ranked by his colleagues according to his competence to handle each of the cases. Counselors were then classified into two groups: those given clients who were "agitated" (anxious, tense), and those given clients who were "constrained" (cool, pessimistic). Clinical interpretations of the Minnesota Multiphasic Personality Inventory scores of counselors to whom agitated clients were referred revealed them to be often academically or esthetically oriented, tending to be self-sufficient and interested in other people.

Edwards and Edgerly[68] hypothesized that the counselor and client who are cognitively similar in the meaning they attach to relevant concepts

[62] J. C. Whitehorn and B. Betz, "A Study of Psychotherapeutic Relationships Between Physician and Schizophrenic Patients," *American Journal of Psychiatry,* Vol. 111 (November, 1954), pp. 321–331.
[63] J. C. Whitehorn and B. Betz, "Further Studies of the Data as a Crucial Variable in the Outcome of Treatment with Schizophrenic Patients," *American Journal of Psychiatry,* Vol. 117 (September, 1960), pp. 215–223.
[64] *Ibid.,* p. 218.
[65] D. M. McNair, D. M. Callahan, and M. Lorr, "Therapist 'Type' and Patient Response to Psychotherapy," *Journal of Consulting Psychology,* Vol. 26 (October, 1962), pp. 425–429.

[66] Robert E. Boyd, "Whitehorn-Betz A-B Score as an Effector of Client-Counselor Interaction," *Journal of Counseling Psychology,* Vol. 17 (May, 1970), pp. 279–283.
[67] Joseph Kunce and Wayne Anderson, "Counselor-Client Similarity and Referral Bias," *Journal of Counseling Psychology,* Vol. 17 (March, 1970), pp. 102–106.
[68] Billy C. Edwards and John W. Edgerly, "Effects of Counselor-Client Cognitive Congruence on Counseling Outcome in Brief Counseling," *Journal of Counseling Psychology,* Vol. 17 (July, 1970), pp. 313–318.

would make more progress. Accordingly, they matched clients to counselors and assessed outcomes. But the clients who were different from their counselors changed significantly and more consistently than those who were similar to their counselors. Accordingly, they suggest that certain types of counselors are more effective with some types of clients than others.

PERCEPTIONS

Parloff investigated the degree to which the quality of the therapeutic relationship established by two equally "expert" therapists varied according to the therapist's personality and his perceptions of his patients.[69] Both therapists alternately treated the same patient. The therapist who was judged as integrating the better social relationship with the client was rated as establishing the better therapeutic relationship. The quality of the therapeutic relationship varied positively with the degree to which the therapist perceived the client as approximating his ideal patient. In a later study, also involving group therapy, Parloff found that patients who established better relationships with their therapists tended to show greater improvement and to continue in therapy.[70]

Combs and Soper (1963) studied 12 variables concerning counselors' characteristic ways of perceiving, which they inferred from "blind analysis" of descriptions of four "human relations incidents," and compared them to rank in counselor training.[71] All but two rank order correlations were significant at the .01 level. With respect to general perceptual orientation, the highly ranked counselors perceived from an internal rather than external frame of reference, and in terms of people rather than things.

Strong[72] conceptualized counseling as an interpersonal influence process. It is fundamental to this view that the counselor present himself in such a way that clients see him as attractive, trustworthy, and expert. According to Strong, these characteristics influence the client, and those counselors so perceived by their clients are more influential than those counselors who are not. Support for this conclusion about perceived expertness has been reported by Strong and Schmidt,[73] previously cited.

PRESENCE OF ANXIETY

Bandura (1965) had 42 therapists rate each other on three central conflict areas: dependency, hostility, and sexuality.[74] Anxious therapists were rated less competent than those who were low in anxiety; no relationship existed between therapist's degree of insight into the nature of his anxiety and competence, and no relationship existed between therapist's self-rating of anxiety and competence. Therefore, presence of anxiety in the counselor, whether recognized or not, affects his ability to do successful counseling. Insight into anxiety alone is not enough.

Russell and Snyder studied the relationship of counselor experience, hostile or friendly demeanor of the client, and counselor anxiety.[75] They hypothesized that (1) counselors, regardless of experience, would display greater anxiety in interviews with hostile clients and (2) the more experienced counselors would display less anxiety than inexperienced counselors in interviews with both hostile and friendly clients. Ten experienced and 10 inexperienced counselors conducted two inter-

[69] M. B. Parloff, "Some Factors Affecting the Quality of Therapeutic Relationships," *Journal of Abnormal Social Psychology,* Vol. 52 (January, 1956), pp. 5–10.
[70] M. B. Parloff, "Therapist-Patient Relationships and Outcome of Psychotherapy," *Journal of Counseling Psychology,* Vol. 25 (February, 1961), pp. 29–38.
[71] Combs and Soper, *op. cit.*

[72] Stanley R. Strong, "Counseling: An Interpersonal Influence Process," *Journal of Counseling Psychology,* Vol. 15 (May, 1968), pp. 215–224.
[73] Stanley R. Strong and Lyle D. Schmidt, "Expertness and Influence in Counseling," *Journal of Counseling Psychology,* Vol. 17 (January, 1970), pp. 81–87.
[74] Bandura, *op. cit.*
[75] P. D. Russell and W. U. Snyder, "Counselor Anxiety in Relation to Amount of Clinical Experience and Quality of Affect Demonstrated by Clients," *Journal of Consulting Psychology,* Vol. 27 (August, 1963), pp. 358–363.

views, in one of which a client actor reacted in a hostile manner. (There were two client actors, both of whom assumed friendly and hostile client roles with different counselors.) Counselor anxiety was measured by palm sweating, eye-blink rate, client actor estimate, and judgments of verbal anxiety made by independent judges.The authors found support for the first hypothesis but no conclusive support for the second. They concluded that modifying some of the anxiety measures, extending the interview beyond 30 minutes, and redefining the experienced and inexperienced groups might increase support for the second hypothesis.

COMMUNICATION

Parloff, Iflund, and Goldstein investigated the communication of values in psychotherapy with paranoid schizophrenic patients.[76] Two findings concerning congruence between counselor and counselee are relevant here. First, congruence varied systematically. Patient anxiety mounted over the weekend with disruption of the relationship. Relief and increase in efficiency came with resumption of the relationship on Monday. Second, an individual who later improved shifted his values toward the therapist's significantly more than the patient who did not improve. Rosenthal reported that patients who improved tended to revise certain moral values in the direction of their therapists' while the moral values of patients who did not improve tended to become less like their therapists'.[77]

Brams studied the relationship between counselor trainees' personality characteristics and their ability to communicate effectively with their clients in counseling interviews.[78] The study used correlational techniques to investigate the relationship between 27 counselor trainees' (22 males and 5 females) scores on the MMPI, the Taylor MAS, the Index of Adjustment and Values (IAV), the Berkley Public Opinion Questionnaire, and a 50-item scale developed by Anderson and Anderson (1962), which served as the criterion measure of effectiveness. Correlations between judges' ratings and scores on the MMPI, the Taylor MAS, and the IAV were not significant, but a significant negative correlation was found between judges' ratings of communication effectiveness and scores on the Berkley POQ. Brams concluded that the negative relationship between the criterion and Berkley POQ scores offered tentative support for the hypothesis that counselors who create successful counseling relationships are more tolerant of ambiguous material than are less successful counselors.

Wallach reported that a majority of undergraduate college students preferred therapists who were critical thinkers, phrased things well, were thoughtful, saw things in proper perspective, were aware of alternatives, and allowed clients to make their own decisions.[79] Therapists labeled "nurturant" or "model" were not as highly preferred as the "critic" just described. Pallone and Grande analyzed 80 secondary school counselee interviews to determine effects of four modes of counselor verbal behavior upon relevant communication of the counselee's problem.[80] They concluded that (1) counselor verbal mode significantly affects client problem-relevant communication ratio, (2) interaction between verbal mode and client problem focus significantly affects problem-relevant communication, (3) client experience of rapport is not significantly affected by problem focus, verbal mode, or focus-mode interaction, and (4) a mild negative relationship exists between problem-relevant ratio and rapport.

[76] M. B. P. Parloff, B. Iflund, and N. Goldstein, "Communication of 'Therapy Values' Between Therapist and Schizophrenic Patients," *Journal of Nervous and Mental Diseases,* Vol. 130 (March, 1960), pp. 193–199.

[77] D. Rosenthal, "Changes in Some Moral Values Following Psychotherapy," *Journal of Consulting Psychology,* Vol. 19 (December, 1955), pp. 431–436.

[78] J. Brams, "Counselor Characteristics and Effective Communication in Counseling," *Journal of Counseling Psychology,* Vol. 8 (Spring, 1961), pp. 25–30.

[79] M. S. Wallach, "Authoritarianism and Therapist Preference," *Journal of Clinical Psychology,* Vol. 18 (July, 1962), pp. 325–327.

[80] N. J. Pallone and P. P. Grande, "Counselor Verbal Mode, Problem-Relevant Communication and Client Rapport," *Journal of Counseling Psychology,* Vol. 12 (Winter, 1965), pp. 359–365.

Mickelson and Stevic[81] hypothesized that behavioral counselors who were facilitative, i.e., high in warmth, empathy, and genuineness, would be more effective than nonfacilitative counselors. Both types of counselors received equal amounts of training in verbal reinforcement procedures. The criterion was the frequency of the clients' information-seeking, and their hypothesis was duly confirmed.

SELF-CONCEPT

Kazienko and Neidt (1962) studied the personality characteristics of male counselor trainees enrolled in 25 summer NDEA Counseling and Guidance Institutes who were identified by the professional staffs as being in the top and bottom 25 per cent of their Institute groups.[82] Using the Bennett Polydiagnostic Index, subjects described themselves in terms of self-concept, motivating forces, values, and feelings about others. The "good" and "poor" counselor trainee groups' descriptions of themselves were compared. In terms of self-concept, the good counselors perceived themselves as serious, earnest, patient, soft spoken; aware of personal self-centeredness; more domestic than social; and not of mechanical or industrial inclination. The poor counselors did not recognize qualities of seriousness or patience in self, tended toward loudness of voice, were not aware of any personal self-centeredness, and saw self as normally domestic and social and as of mechanical and industrial inclination. Descriptions of motivation suggested that the good counselor was concerned about possessing a measure of security but inclined to reject need for wealth, while the poor counselor was neither moved nor unmoved by prospects of security and riches. In the area of values, the good counselor group was found to reject cunningness and shrewdness, to feel that people should have the right to be different, and to place little value on severity and strictness. The poor counselor group was found to emphasize conformity and tended toward strict adherence to rules. With respect to feelings about others, the good group viewed people as possessing an adequate measure of intellectual ability though self-centered, while the poor group gave others no particular credit for intellectual assets.

NEEDS AND VALUES

Tollefson investigated the relationship between counselor need orientation, counselor effectiveness, and counselor personality.[83] Effectiveness was assessed by two internal criterion measures (CEI ratings and Q-sort data) and two external criterion measures (supervisor-completed CEI ratings and course grades). Personality was assessed by 10 instruments including the Fundamental Interpersonal Relations Organization Scale (FIRO-B), the Rorschach, and the Thematic Apperception Test. Sixteen counselor trainees were selected on the basis of the Edwards Personal Preference Schedule factor scores for two factors: "Nurturant Orientation" and "Administrative Orientation." Four groups of counselors were studied: High Nurturant (three males and two females), Low Nurturant (three males), High Administrative (three males and two females), and Low Administrative (three males). Nurturant need orientation was assumed to be most directly related to counseling effectiveness.

There was indeed a relationship between counselor need orientation, counselor effectiveness, and counselor personality. Need orientation was related to motivation for entering counselor preparation and approach to counseling. High school counselees rated High Nurturant and Low Administrative groups as most effective while practicum supervisors rated High Nurturant and High Administrative groups as most effective. Personality differences among the groups were such that it was suggested that High Nurturant and Low Adminis-

[81] Douglas J. Mickelson and Richard Stevic, "Differential Effects of Facilitative and Non-facilitative Behavioral Counselors," *Journal of Counseling Psychology,* Vol. 18 (July, 1971), pp. 314–319.
[82] Kazienko and Neidt, *op. cit.*

[83] N. F. Tollefson, "Relationship of Counselor Need Orientation to Counselor Effectiveness and Counselor Personality," unpublished doctoral dissertation, Purdue University, 1965.

trative were intrapunitive, sensitive to and accepting of feelings of self and others, and perceptive of self in relationship to others.

Mills, Chestnut, and Hartzell computed an obverse component analysis for the EPPS scores of 37 counselors of varying degrees of experience.[84] Five nonrandom components were determined and scores on each were correlated with EPPS need scores. Judges agreed on characteristics of counselors on four of five factors. The Social Service Component accounted for 46 percent of total variance; component two, related to counselor's sex, accounted for 10 per cent; component three, nondirective, accounted for 7 per cent; and component four, false aggression, accounted for 6 per cent. Finally, an unnamed component accounted for 5 per cent of total variance. Nejedlo and Farwell explored the amount of agreement among counselors and their administrators with regard to value orientations held by each and their role expectations for the counselor.[85] No significant relationship existed.

Characteristics Distinguishing Effective from Ineffective Counselors

Much work has recently been directed to identifying the characteristics of effective counselors. The literature suggests that effective counselors can be separated somewhat from their less effective counterparts on three dimensions: experience, type of relationship established, and nonintellective factors. However, nonintellective measures have not consistently discriminated between the two groups. Distinctions seem due to differences in the intensity rather than to the presence or absence of given characteristics.

[84] David H. Mills, William J. Chestnut, and John P. Hartzell, "The Needs of Counselors: A Component Analysis," *Journal of Counseling Psychology*, Vol. 13 (Spring, 1966), pp. 82–84.
[85] Robert J. Nejedlo and Gail F. Farwell, "Value Orientations and School Counselor Role Expectations," *Counselor Education and Supervision*, Vol. 5 (Winter, 1966), pp. 61–67.

EXPERIENCE

There is substantial evidence that experience is an important variable in counselor effectiveness. Fiedler's investigations indicated that (1) better trained therapists of varying therapy orientations agreed more highly with each other in their concept of an ideal therapeutic relationship than they agreed with less well trained therapists within their own school,[86] and (2) the therapeutic relationship created by experts of one school resembled more closely that created by experts of other schools than it resembled relationships created by nonexperts in the same school.[87]

Rogers demonstrated that more experienced counselors offered more congruence, empathy, and unconditional positive regard than did their less experienced counterparts and were more successful in communicating these conditions to their clients.[88] Experienced counselors were perceived by their clients to offer a higher level of those conditions, and their clients showed more change over the course of counseling.

TYPE OF COUNSELING RELATIONSHIP

Studies by Fiedler (December, 1950, 1951), Seeman,[89] Parloff,[90] and Rogers (1962) suggest that effective counseling is related to the type of relation-

[86] F. E. Fiedler, "The Concept of an Ideal Therapeutic Relationship," *Journal of Consulting Psychology*, Vol. 14 (August, 1950), pp. 239–245.
[87] F. E. Fiedler, "A Comparison of Therapeutic Relationships in Psychoanalytical, Nondirective and Adlerian Therapy," *Journal of Consulting Psychology*, Vol. 14 (December, 1950), pp. 436–445; F. E. Fiedler, "Factor Analysis of Psychoanalytic, Nondirective, and Adlerian Therapeutic Relationships," *Journal of Consulting Psychology*, Vol. 15 (February, 1951), pp. 32–38.
[88] C. R. Rogers, "The Interpersonal Relationship: The Core of Guidance," *Harvard Educational Review*, Vol. 32 (Fall, 1962), pp. 416–429.
[89] J. Seeman, "Counselor Judgments of Therapeutic Process and Outcome," reported in C. R. Rogers and R. F. Dymond (eds.), *Psychotherapy and Personality Change* (Chicago: University of Chicago Press, 1954), pp. 99–108.
[90] M. B. Parloff, "Therapist-Patient Relationships and Outcome of Psychotherapy," *Journal of Consulting Psychology*, Vol. 25 (February, 1961), pp. 29–38.

ship a counselor establishes with his client. Fiedler's now classic studies indicate that there are common characteristics in the counseling relationships achieved by experienced counselors regardless of the theoretical orientation of the counselors. Experts, he reported, differ from nonexperts in their ability to (1) communicate with and understand their clients, (2) maintain an appropriate emotional distance, and (3) divest themselves of status concerns in regard to their clients. Seeman (1954) demonstrated that success in psychotherapy is closely associated with the emotional quality of the relationship. Parloff's study of group therapeutic relationships and outcomes of treatment indicated that clients who establish better relationships with their therapists tend to show greater improvement than those whose relationships with the same therapists are not as good. Rogers, in a series of investigations referred to earlier, reported, "The major finding from all of the studies is that those clients in relationships marked by a high level of counselor congruence, empathy, and unconditional positive regard show constructive personality change and development."[91]

Foulds sought to pinpoint the correlation between dogmatism (as measured by the Rokeach Dogmatism Scale) and ability to communicate facilitative counseling conditions (as measured by the Carkhuff Scales) of 30 graduate students in an initial counseling practicum.[92] Trained judges observed the degree of empathic understanding, positive regard, and facilitative genuineness extended to clients by the 30 students. Since no significant correlation emerged from the study, Foulds suggested that more than one type of dogmatism may exist; i.e., a "benevolent" dogmatism may not interfere with a person's ability to communicate facilitative conditions, while a "nonbenevolent" type would destroy such conditions. In an earlier investigation[93] Foulds reported that certain personality characteristics believed associated with self-actualization were related significantly to the ability of the counselor to communicate empathic understanding and facilitative genuineness. Logically, those counselors who are psychologically healthy should be able to extend high levels of facilitative conditions to clients. However, Winborn and Rowe[94] replicated the Foulds study but could not confirm his findings.

NONINTELLECTIVE FACTORS

Studies of the relationship between counselor effectiveness and personality show that effective counselors can be distinguished from less effective counselors in regard to (1) self-concept, motivation, values, feelings about others, and perceptual organization and (2) performance on certain standardized personality and interest inventories (Arbuckle, 1956; Brown, 1960; Stefflre *et al.*, 1962; Brams, 1961; and Johnson *et al.*, 1967). Further, counselor effectiveness is associated with tolerance for ambiguity, understanding of the client, maturity, ability to maintain an appropriate emotional distance from the client, and ability to establish good social relationships with nonclients.

According to Wicas and Mahan, "high rated" counselors were anxious, sensitive to the expectations of others and society, patient and nonaggressive in interpersonal relationships, and concerned about social progress but always with appropriate self-control.[95] While many of their findings indicated a pleasant, stable, dedicated person, they also reported undesirable traits such as low originality,

[91] Rogers, *op. cit.*, p. 425.

[92] Melvin L. Foulds, "Dogmatism and Ability to Communicate Facilitative Conditions During Counseling," *Counselor Education and Supervision*, Vol. 11 (December, 1971), pp. 110–114.

[93] Melvin L. Foulds, "Self-Actualization and the Communication of Facilitative Conditions During Counseling," *Journal of Counseling Psychology*, Vol. 16 (March, 1969), pp. 132-136.

[94] Bob B. Winborn and Wayne Rowe, "Self-Actualization and the Communication of Facilitative Conditions – A Replication," *Journal of Counseling Psychology*, Vol. 19 (January, 1972), pp. 26–29.

[95] Edward A. Wicas and Thomas W. Mahan, Jr., "Characteristics of Counselors Rated Effective by Supervisors and Peers," *Counselor Education and Supervision*, Vol. 6 (Fall, 1966), pp. 50–56.

rejection of contemplation, lack of persistence, and a conservative orientation to social problems.

Brams (1961) found that effective communication in the counseling interview was related to the counselor's tolerance for ambiguity. Fiedler (December, 1950) reported that expert therapists differed from nonexperts in their ability to understand and communicate with their clients. Heine[96] and Cartwright and Lerner[97] demonstrated that empathic understanding of the client was positively associated with client improvement. However, Lesser suggested (1961) that empathic understanding as measured was unrelated to counseling progress.

Rogers feels that the optimal helping relationship is created by a person who is psychologically mature.[98] Luborsky reported that supervisors rated psychiatric residents in the top 13 per cent of their class as more mature, emotionally controlled, and normal than residents in the bottom 13 per cent.[99]

Carson and Heine found a curvilinear relationship between client and counselor similarity and counseling success and concluded that either extreme similarity or dissimilarity impedes effective counseling.[100] Wallach and Strupp, in a factor-analytic study of two samples of psychotherapists' practices, identified four factors, but maintenance of personal distance accounted for the largest percentage of the total variance.[101] McNair, Callahan, and Lorr (1962) identified impersonal versus personal approaches effective with clients as one of three therapeutic technique factors or dimensions.[102]

Luborsky, Holt, and Morrow reported that psychiatrists in training who were rated as the better therapists established better relationships with the ward staff and the research project staff, and that ratings of personal liking for the therapist by the research staff were a better predictor of therapist competence than the other methods used.[103] Fiedler stated that therapists and laymen described their concept of the "ideal therapeutic relationships" in similar terms. He concluded that "a good therapeutic relationship is very much like any good relationship."[104] Parloff's study of counselor social attitudes indicated that therapists who had better social relationships with nonclients established better counseling relationships with their clients.[105]

Rickenbaugh, Heaps, and Finley[106] examined 67 college students on academic probation to determine their perception of the counselor's comfort, the counseling climate, and their own satisfaction (as measured by the Counselor Evaluation Inventory). The counselors' effectiveness rating was based on degree of positive change in their clients' academic performance. Of the three factors described above, only the client's perception of the counselor's comfort was found to be significantly related to counselor effectiveness. The investigators concluded that counselor effectiveness varies as a function of counselor comfort and that counselors tend to become more comfortable with experience.

[96] R. W. Heine, "An Investigation of the Relationship Between Changes and Responsible Factors as Seen by Clients Following Treatment by Psychotherapists of the Psychoanalytical, Adlerian, and Non-Directive Schools," unpublished doctoral dissertation, University of Chicago, 1950.

[97] R. D. Cartwright and B. Lerner, "Empathy, Need to Change, and Improvement with Psychotherapy," *Journal of Consulting Psychology*, Vol. 27 (February, 1963), pp. 138–144.

[98] C. R. Rogers, "The Characteristics of a Helping Relationship," *Personnel and Guidance Journal*, Vol. 37 (September, 1958), pp. 5–15.

[99] L. B. Luborsky, "The Personality of the Psychotherapist," *Menninger Quarterly*, Vol. 6 (December, 1952), pp. 1–6.

[100] R. C. Carson and R. W. Heine, "Similarity and Success in Therapeutic Dyads," *Journal of Consulting Psychology*, Vol. 26 (February, 1962), pp. 38–43.

[101] M. S. Wallach and H. H. Strupp, "Dimensions of Psychotherapists' Activity," *Journal of Consulting Psychology*, Vol. 28 (April, 1964), pp. 120–125.

[102] McNair, Callahan, and Lorr, *op. cit.*

[103] L. B. Luborsky, R. R. Holt, and W. R. Morrow, "Interim Report of the Research Project on the Selection of Medical Men for Psychiatric Training," *Bulletin of the Menninger Clinic*, Vol. 14 (January, 1950), pp. 92–101.

[104] Fiedler, "The Concept of an Ideal Therapeutic Relationship," p. 244.

[105] Parloff, "Some Factors Affecting the Quality of Therapeutic Relationships," pp. 5–10.

[106] Karl Rickabaugh, Richard A. Heaps, and Robert E. Finley, "Counselor Comfort, Counseling Climate and Client Satisfaction; Client Ratings and Academic Improvement," *Counselor Education and Supervision*, Vol. 11 (March, 1972), pp. 219–223.

Characteristics of Counselees

The counselee's personality is becoming of more and more concern to researchers. Goldstein concluded that in the absence of formal psychotherapy a significant relationship exists between the degree of patient's expectation for improvement and the degree of "non-specific therapy remission."[107] His data for a sample of 15 no-therapy control patients supported his contention that spontaneous recovery is not really spontaneous but a function of identifiable causative factors. The amount of attention and contact – in the form of intake, periodic interviewing, and testing – that a patient experiences before formal therapy has a "placebo" effect. Improvement is therefore due to the favorable expectation of improvement from therapy and the placebo effect.

Kirtner and Cartwright classified 26 patients in client-centered therapy as to length of therapy and outcome.[108] They found that therapy length-by-outcome is related to the personality structure of the clients at the beginning of therapy. The "short-success" group showed a generally higher level of personality integration, were rather open in their impulse life, and were a good deal less confused about their sex role than the other groups. The "short-failure" group showed a generally low level of personality integration and an extreme underlying sense of incapacity to deal with their life situation.

SIMILARITY TO COUNSELOR

Heller and Goldstein (1961) studied 30 clients randomly assigned to therapy (10 therapists) and to a control group.[109] They found a strong positive relationship between client pretherapy attraction to the therapist and (1) client self-descriptive and behavioral dependency before therapy and (2) client self-descriptive but not behavioral movement toward independence over the course of therapy.

In a somewhat similar study, Goldstein and Shipman reported a significant relationship between the therapist's and the patient's characteristics.[110] A patient's expectations of symptom reduction due to therapy were positively and curvilinearly related to perceived initial interview symptom reduction, and positively and linearly related to degree of patient pretherapy symptom intensity. How favorable the therapist was toward psychiatry and psychotherapy related positively to how much symptom reduction occurred.

EXPECTATIONS

Goldstein investigated the relationship between client expectations of personality change and client perceived personality change due to psychotherapy.[111] No significant correlation was found between client, therapist, or combined client and therapist expectancies and perceived personality change. However, duration of psychotherapy was significantly related to both therapist and combined client and therapist expectancies of client personality change. Severinsen, studying client expectation and perception of counseling and their relationship to satisfaction with counseling, reported that dissatisfaction seemed to be related to dissimilarity of expected counselor behavior and perceived counselor behavior, regardless of direction of dissimilarity.[112] According to McNair, Lorr, and Callahan, motivation for psychotherapy is one significant predictor of continuation in therapy.[113]

[107] A. P. Goldstein, "Patient's Expectancies and Non-specific Therapy as a Basis for (un) Spontaneous Remission," *Journal of Clinical Psychology,* Vol. 16 (October, 1960), pp. 399–403.
[108] W. L. Kirtner and D. S. Cartwright, "Success and Failure in Client-Centered Therapy as a Function of Client Personality Variables," *Journal of Consulting Psychology,* Vol. 22 (August, 1963), pp. 259–264.
[109] Heller and Goldstein, *op. cit.*

[110] A. P. Goldstein and W. G. Shipman, "Patient Expectancies, Symptom Reduction and Aspects of the Initial Psychotherapeutic Interview," *Journal of Clinical Psychology,* Vol. 17 (April, 1961), pp. 129–133.
[111] A. P. Goldstein, "Therapist and Client Expectation of Personality Changes in Psychotherapy," *Journal of Counseling Psychology,* Vol. 7 (Fall, 1960), pp. 180–184.
[112] K. Norman Severinsen, "Client Expectation and Perception of the Counselor's Role and Their Relationship to Client Satisfaction," *Journal of Counseling Psychology,* Vol. 13 (Spring, 1966), pp. 109–112.
[113] D. M. McNair, M. Lorr, and D. M. Callahan, "Patient and Therapist Influences on Quitting Psychotherapy," *Journal of Consulting Psychology,* Vol. 27 (February, 1963), pp. 10–17.

Further, those who remain in therapy and those who terminate early are two distinct populations which elicit different interaction patterns from different groups of therapists. Projective techniques have also been found by Libo to be valid predictors of motivation and continuation in therapy.[114]

Heine and Trosman reported that neither presenting complaint nor degree of conviction that treatment would help was related to continuation in therapy.[115] The significant variable was mutuality of expectation between patient and therapist. Those who continued conceptualized the experience in a manner more congruous with the therapist's role image. The modal expectations of the therapist were that the patient (1) desire a relationship in which he had the opportunity to talk freely about himself and his discomforts, (2) see the relationship as instrumental to discomfort relief rather than as an impersonal manipulation by the therapist, and (3) perceive himself as having some responsibility for the outcome.

Raskin attempted to clarify the meaning of motivation to enter therapy by identifying the variables therapists associate with it.[116] Of 15 variables examined, several were significantly correlated with the therapist's ratings of the patient's motivation—patient's education, occupational level, awareness of psychological difficulties, and type of treatment expected. One therapist variable, liking for the patient, was significantly correlated with the motivation ratings. The only factor consistently associated with low ratings on the motivation scale was the patient's expectation for medical treatment, including drugs. In the opinion of Grant and Grant, their rankings of therapy readiness suggest that the attitudinal set of the clients can be readily observed by trained people.[117] They propose the use of observed estimates of verbal facility, expression of feelings, ability to express and deal with real problems, aims in therapy, concept of responsibility in therapy, and amount of existing anxiety.

Kaul and Parker[118] point out that (a) the expectations of the client are potential therapeutic agents, (b) expectations are learned and can be modified, (c) one index of successful counseling is the client's acquisition of a new conceptual scheme for understanding his behavior, (d) the similarity of the client's new conceptual scheme to that of the counselor will affect the judged degree of counseling success, and (e) the client's faith in the counselor is more important than the "validity" of the counselor's techniques. They evaluated the effects of suggestibility and expectancy in a counseling analogue. Suggestibility was assessed both objectively and subjectively by the Barker Suggestibility Scale. Some 126 upper division and graduate students were classified as highly suggestible, middle in suggestibility and low in suggestibility within each method (objective and subjective). Two levels of expectancy were established. Subjects were paired into homogeneous objective suggestibility and expectancy dyads. The dyads completed the 10 programs of the general relationship program which served as the counseling analogue. Three criterion measures (semantic differential scales, content test, and client satisfaction rating scales) were employed. Kaul and Parker reported that subjectively experienced suggestibility was more closely related to attitude change than objective suggestibility, and that the generalized expectancy treatments were ineffective in influencing criterion scores.

The client's trust in a counselor was investigated

[114] L. M. Libo, "The Projective Expression of Patient-Therapist Attraction," *Journal of Clinical Psychology,* Vol. 13 (January, 1957), pp. 33–36.

[115] R. W. Heine and H. Trosman, "Initial Expectations of the Doctor-Patient Interaction as a Factor in Continuation in Psychotherapy," *Psychiatry,* Vol. 23 (August, 1960), pp. 275–278.

[116] A. Raskin, "Factors Therapists Associate with Motivation to Enter Therapy," *Journal of Clinical Psychology,* Vol. 17 (January, 1961), pp. 62–65.

[117] J. D. Grant and M. Q. Grant, " 'Therapy Readiness' as a Research Variable," *Journal of Consulting Psychology,* Vol. 14 (April, 1950), pp. 156–157.

[118] Theodore J. Kaul and Clyde A. Parker, "Suggestibility and Expectancy in a Counseling Analogue," *Journal of Counseling Psychology,* Vol. 18 (November, 1971), pp. 536–541.

by Kaul and Schmidt.[119] Some 32 senior and graduate students viewed 24 short videotaped scenes of interviewers who exhibited combinations of trustworthy and untrustworthy content and manner, then rated the interviewer's trustworthiness. Analysis of the ratings indicated that the interviewer's manner influenced trust ratings more than the content of his remarks. Kaul and Schmidt suggest that the training of counselors should include attention to manner as well as content of communication with the client.

Hypothesizing that counseling effectiveness is a result of the client's confidence in the ability of the system used to help him deal with his problems, Bednar and Parker[120] investigated whether two different counseling methods were equally effective in helping similar clients. They reported that (1) different counseling-treatment procedures were equally successful in effecting change of equivalent magnitude, but in divergent directions, (2) there was no difference between the two counseling treatments in client satisfaction despite the opposite directions of change; (3) susceptibility to persuasion and heightened expectations did not significantly influence the magnitude of change, and (4) subjects who were classified as highly persuasible viewed the counseling treatments as more valuable to themselves and others, and expressed greater interest both in continuing treatment and attempting new behaviors.

Doubtless an important component in the client's expectations of counseling is his trust in the counselor. Clients who trust counselors presumably believe that they are expert. Expertness is often communicated by such factors as status introductions, prestige symbols, degrees, etc. Schmidt and Strong[121] explain that "The client's perception of the counselor's expertness is one of the factors which moderates the degree to which the client will change his views to those of the counselor rather than discredit the counselor." They reported that counselors identified as expert (actually the inexperienced counselors) were viewed as relaxed, interested, friendly, attentive, and confident. Conversely, the nonexpert counselors (actually the experienced ones) were viewed as awkward, tense, uneasy, and nonconfident.

Guttman and Haase[122] investigated the effects of an experimentally-induced set of "expertness" on 31 male college freshmen clients' evaluations of brief vocational counseling. They reported that these clients responded more favorably to relationship aspects of the interview with a counselor who was introduced as an nonexpert, that informational recall was greater for clients interviewed by expert counselors, and that global ratings did not differentiate between expert and nonexpert counselors. Guttman and Haase contend that "expertness" as an enhancing quality in counselors has been overemphasized.

NEED TO CHANGE

Cartwright and Lerner (1963) found that the patient's initial need to change and the therapist's final level of empathic understanding were directly related to improvement.[123] If these two variables were considered jointly, they proposed, a predictive model for therapy length and success could be derived.

Taulbee compared MMPI and Rorschach responses of 85 psychoneurotic veterans who were classified as "continuers" and "attriters" in therapy.[124] The groups were matched with respect to mean age and education. The "attriters" were char-

[119] Theodore J. Kaul and Lyle D. Schmidt, "Dimensions of Interviewer Trustworthiness," *Journal of Counseling Psychology,* Vol. 18 (November, 1971) pp. 542–548.

[120] Richard L. Bedner and Clyde A. Parker, "Client Susceptibility to Persuasion and Counseling Outcome," *Journal of Counseling Psychology,* Vol. 16 (September, 1969), pp. 415–420.

[121] Lyle D. Schmidt and Stanley R. Strong, " 'Expert' and 'Nonexpert' Counselors," *Journal of Counseling Psychology,* Vol. 17 (March, 1970), pp. 115–118.

[122] Mary A. Julius Guttman and Richard F. Haase, "Effect of Experimentally Induced Sets of High and Low 'Expertness' During Brief Vocational Counseling," *Counselor Education and Supervision,* Vol. 11. (March, 1972), pp. 171–177.

[123] Cartwright and Lerner, *op. cit.*

[124] E. Taulbee, "Relationships Between Certain Personality Variables and Continuation in Psychotherapy," *Journal of Consulting Psychology,* Vol. 22 (April, 1958), pp. 83–89.

acterized as impersonal, matter of fact, intellectualizing, and responding only to a limited range of emotional stimulations. The "continuers" were less defensive and more persistent, anxious, sensitive, and dependent than the "attriters." They were more conscious of feelings of inadequacy, inferiority, and depression, and had better potential for self-appraisal, emotional responsiveness, and a more introspective attitude. Some of the evidence suggested that these personality variables were associated with therapeutic improvement as well. Rosenberg, also working with neurotic veterans, identified the following personality characteristics with therapeutic improvement: superior intelligence, ability to produce associations easily, flexibility, wide range of interests, ability to feel deeply, sensitivity to environment, high energy level, and relative freedom from concerns about health.[125]

SEX DIFFERENCES

Heilbrun investigated personality differences between male and female counseling subjects who discontinued therapy relatively early versus those who continued.[126] For most of the personality variables he found a "sex by stay" category interaction. One of his inferences was that the non-stay client, male or female, conformed most closely to the cultural and personal stereotype appropriate to his or her sex. Non-stay clients as compared to females who stayed were less achieving, autonomous, and dominant and more deferent and abasing. Heilbrun's explanation was that the more masculine, independent male finds it difficult to accept the subordinate status of a client, whereas the more feminine male has less difficulty in playing such a role. Further, in the case of the effeminate male client there is an increased likelihood of early identification and a greater bond with the male counselor.

Cartwright and Lerner (1963) also found a difference in interaction related to sex.[127] Two success groups were identified: same-sex patients of experienced therapists whose psychological distance from the therapist was initially reduced, and opposite-sex patients of inexperienced therapists whose psychological distance from the therapist initially increased.

Fuller reported that clients with precounseling preference for a female counselor were more likely to change preference after counseling than were those who had preferred male counselors.[128] No relationship was established between initial preferences and counseling variables.

LIKABILITY

"Client likability" was studied by Stoler, who presented taped segments of interviews to 10 raters.[129] His data suggest that client likability may be related to success in therapy.

Mullen and Abeles investigated the relationship of liking, empathy, and therapist experience to positive change in therapy.[130] They reported that "high liking" and "high empathy" together did not necessarily produce a successful outcome, though a post hoc analysis of their data showed a positive relationship between "high empathy" alone and successful outcome. Inexperienced therapists were generally less empathic. Empathy and liking were not related to successful outcome for experienced therapists, but were for inexperienced therapists.

[125] S. Rosenberg, "The Relationship of Certain Personality Factors to Prognosis in Therapy," *Journal of Clinical Psychology,* Vol. 10 (October, 1954), pp. 341–345.
[126] A. B. Heilbrun, Jr., "Male and Female Personality Correlates of Early Termination in Counseling," *Journal of Counseling Psychology,* Vol. 8 (Spring, 1961), pp. 31–36.
[127] Cartwright and Lerner, *op. cit.*
[128] E. F. Fuller, "Preferences for Male or Female Counselors," *Personnel and Guidance Journal,* Vol. 42 (January, 1964), pp. 463–467.
[129] N. Stoler, "Client Likability: A Variable in the Study of Psychotherapy," *Journal of Consulting Psychology,* Vol. 27 (April, 1963), pp. 175–178.
[130] John Mullen and Norman Abeles, "Relationships of Liking, Empathy and Therapists Experience to Outcome of Therapy," *Journal of Counseling Psychology,* Vol. 18 (January, 1971), pp. 39–43.

MENTAL HEALTH

With a sample of 100 male veterans Conrad associated judgments by a therapist at the initial interview with length of patient's stay in therapy.[131] Using his own mental health checklist, which described individual functioning in terms of positive mental health, social conformity, and behavior pathology, he discovered, on the basis of first ratings, that (1) psychopathology noted at first interview does not offer grounds for predicting length of stay in therapy, (2) high scores on social conformity combined with low scores on positive mental health will be associated with immediate rejection of therapy, (3) low scores on social conformity will be associated with a tentative testing out of therapy and inattendance, and (4) high scores on positive mental health will be associated with long-term continuation of therapy. The combined sequences of ratings at various stages of therapy suggest that (1) persistence in therapy will be associated with increasing scores in positive mental health; (2) when positive mental health and social conformity increase together, the patient is likely to discontinue therapy; and (3) when positive mental health is high, social conformity low, and pathology increasing, the patient tends to stay in therapy. However, Hunt, Ewing, LaForge, and Gilbert, in a preliminary report on therapeutic research at the University of Illinois, advise caution in making clinical predictions on the basis of client characteristics judged by interviewers.[132]

INTROVERSION

Mendelsohn and Kirk, using the Briggs-Myers Type Indicator, reported that freshmen at the University of California who seek counseling score less toward the judging side and more toward the introversion side of the respective dimensions.[133] Customary attention to subjective experiences (characteristic of the intuitive type) and greater tolerance for ambiguity (characteristic of the perceptive type) seem to predispose such individuals to make use of counseling.

DEPENDENCY

Schuldt assessed changes in clients' expression of dependency as a function of approach-avoidance of therapists.[134] His results suggest, among other things, that clients in all stages of therapy tend to continue expressions of dependency when such responses are approached by therapists and to discontinue them when they are avoided by therapists; also that clients initiate significantly more dependency responses during the initial rather than the final stage of therapy. Gamsky and Farwell investigated counselor verbal behavior as a function of the focus of client hostility.[135] Client hostility toward the counselor evoked greater negative reactions than hostility directed toward others. Caracena hypothesized that the approach and avoidance of dependency by counselors elicited and reinforced clients' statements about dependency and that termination of or remaining in treatment was associated with such counselor behavior.[136] Content analysis of 72 interviews reflected that approach elicits and avoidance discourages further discussion. However, length of stay in treatment was not demonstrated.

[131] D. C. Conrad, "The Duration of the Therapeutic Relationship and Therapists' Successive Judgments of Patients' Mental Health," *Journal of Clinical Psychology*, Vol. 10 (July, 1954), pp. 229–233.

[132] J. Hunt, T. Ewing, R. LaForge, and W. Gilbert, "An Integrated Approach to Research on Therapeutic Counseling with Samples of Results," *Journal of Counseling Psychology*, Vol. 6 (Spring, 1959), pp. 46–54.

[133] G. A. Mendelsohn and B. A. Kirk, "Personality Differences Between Students Who Do and Do Not Use a Counseling Facility," *Journal of Counseling Psychology*, Vol. 9 (Winter, 1962), pp. 341–346.

[134] W. J. Schuldt, "Psychotherapists' Approach-Avoidance Responses and Clients' Expressions of Dependency," *Journal of Counseling Psychology*, Vol. 13 (Summer, 1966), pp. 178–183.

[135] N. R. Gamsky and G. F. Farwell, "Counselor Verbal Behavior as a Function of Client Hostility," *Journal of Counseling Psychology*, Vol. 13 (Summer, 1966), pp. 184–190.

[136] Philip F. Caracena, "Elicitation of Dependency Expressions in the Initial Stage of Psychotherapy," *Journal of Counseling Psychology*, Vol. 12 (Fall, 1965), pp. 268–274.

At a VA mental hygiene clinic Hiler investigated whether different types of therapists tend to lose or hold in treatment different kinds of patients.[137] Patients were classified as "remainers" and "terminators" and were also characterized by productivity on the Rorschach Test. Results showed that (1) therapists in general differed in regard to the type of patients who continued or discontinued treatment with them; (2) professional specialization seemed unrelated to the type of patients who continued or discontinued; (3) sex of therapists made a difference – females tended to keep in treatment more of the unproductive patients but to lose more of the productive patients than did the males; (4) therapists rated as most warm and friendly were able to keep in treatment a larger percentage of unproductive patients than therapists rated as least warm and friendly; (5) therapists rated as most competent at analytically oriented therapy were likely to lose fewer productive patients than therapists rated as least competent; and (6) rated passivity of therapist seemed unrelated to the productivity of patients remaining in therapy.

Similarity of Counselor and Counselee Characteristics

Mendelsohn and Geller matched counselor and client for similarity on judgment-perception, thinking-feeling, sensation-intuition, and extroversion-introversion.[138] Similarity was linearly associated with greater length of counseling; that is, the greater the client-counselor difference score for each dimension, the fewer the sessions. Mendelsohn replicated the study and reported that while client personality affects the decision to seek counseling, client-counselor matching is a more important determinant of its outcome.[139] In a different study the same authors investigated the relationship between client-counselor similarity and counseling outcome.[140] Criterion variables were Evaluation, Comfort-Rapport, and Judged Competence. Client-counselor dyads were classified as high, middle, and low similarity and as same or opposite sex. The effects of similarity on outcome varied with the criterion used. More specifically, (1) Evaluation is curvilinearly related to similarity, middle similarity producing the highest scores; (2) Comfort-Rapport scores are related to high similarity for freshmen but to middle similarity for nonfreshmen; (3) on both dimensions low similarity leads to more favorable ratings by nonfreshmen but to less favorable ratings by freshmen; (4) in general, the effects of similarity are more pronounced in opposite than same-sex matchings, particularly for nonfreshmen; and (5) high ratings of Judged Competence seem to be associated with the extroversion-introversion and thinking-feeling dimensions of client personality rather than with client-counselor similarity.

CONGRUENCE

Carson and Heine hypothesized that as patient-therapist personality dissimilarity increases through a range from maximum to minimum congruence there will be a corresponding increase in therapeutic success up to a certain point, beyond which further increases in dissimilarity will be associated with decreasing success.[141] Their rationale was that if he is very much like the client, the therapist may be unable to maintain objectivity and if he is very much unlike the client, he may be unable to empathically understand him. Clients and thera-

[137] E. W. Hiler, "An Analysis of Patient-Therapist Compatibility," *Journal of Consulting Psychology,* Vol. 22 (October, 1958), pp. 341–347.
[138] G. A. Mendelsohn and M. H. Geller, "Effects of Counselor-Client Similarity on the Outcome of Counseling," *Journal of Counseling Psychology,* Vol. 10 (Spring, 1963), pp. 71–77.
[139] Gerald A. Mendelsohn, "Effects of Client Personality and Client-Counselor Similarity on the Duration of Counseling: A Replication and Extension," *Journal of Counseling Psychology,* Vol. 13 (Summer, 1966), pp. 228–234.
[140] G. A. Mendelsohn and M. H. Geller, "Structure of Client Attitudes Toward Counseling and Their Relation to Client-Counselor Similarity," *Journal of Consulting Psychology,* Vol. 29 (February, 1965), pp. 63–72.
[141] Carson and Heine, *op. cit.*

pists (fourth-year medical students in psychiatry) were matched on MMPI profiles. Supervisor ratings were the criterion measures. The hypothesis was supported.

Gerler found partial support for the curvilinear relationship between client and therapist similarity in rated personality traits and favorable outcome of therapy.[142] When the dyads were matched on the basis of conflict areas (measured by means of self and ideal sorts), his data again suggested curvilinearity but were not statistically significant.

LIFE SITUATIONS

Holsman matched therapists and patients for similarity in life situations — age, education, occupation, intelligence, religion, and race — and found it significantly related to the outpatient's social adaptation.[143] The hypotheses with respect to the inpatient sample were not confirmed, but the tendency was in the hypothesized direction.

Axelrod matched clients and therapists for similarity on the basis of flexibility, breadth of interest, and intelligence.[144] The sample included 40 psychoneurotic VA patients and 10 psychiatrists. Psychiatrists who were orderly, controlled, precise, self-critical, and prone to intellectualizing were successful with patients of like characteristics. To Axelrod the prominence of intellective factors in the positive results also suggests that similarity of thought processes is conducive to successful therapy.

COUNSELING PROGRESS

Lesser (1961) related counseling progress to similarity, felt or perceived similarity, and empathic understanding.[145] His data indicated that counseling progress was not related to his measure of empathic understanding. Similarity between counselor and client self-concepts was significantly but negatively related to counseling progress. However, accurate awareness of similarity was positively related to counseling progress. Lesser concluded that the counselor's accurate perception of similarity facilitates communication both of words and of feelings and thus hinders overestimation of similarity. The counselor, in other words, is able to overcome the negative aspects of similarity in the counseling process when he correctly perceives the similarity.

COMPATIBILITY

Sapolsky investigated the effect of patient-doctor compatibility upon the outcome of hospital treatment and upon perceptions of each other developed in the dyadic relationship.[146] The FIRO-B was used to measure the degree of compatibility between the three psychiatric residents and their respective patients. Osgood's Semantic Differential Technique was used to measure the effect of the compatibility variable on the way the patient perceived his doctor and felt perceived by him. The criterion measure was the supervisor's rating of improvement. He reported a positive correlation of .45 (significant at the .05 level) between compatibility scores and outcome and concluded that "this effect on outcome of treatment appeared to have occurred through the differential effect the compatibility variable had on the way the therapist was perceived by the patient."

Persons and Pepinsky reported that 30 of 41 incarcerated delinquents were judged to have been successfully treated following 20 weeks of individual and group psychotherapy.[147] The delinquents

[142] W. Gerler, "Outcome of Psychotherapy as a Function of Client-Counselor Similarity," *Dissertation Abstracts*, Vol. 18, #1864 (May, 1958).
[143] M. S. Holsman, "The Significance of the Value Systems of Patient and Therapist for the Outcome of Psychotherapy," *Dissertation Abstracts*, Vol. 22, #4073 (May, 1962).
[144] J. Axelrod, "An Evaluation of the Effects on Progress in Therapy of Similarities and Differences Between the Personalities of Patients and Their Therapists," Pub. #3604, New York University, July, 1952.

[145] Lesser, *op. cit.*
[146] A. Sapolsky, "Relationship Between Patient-Doctor Compatibility, Mutual Perception, and Outcome of Treatment," *Journal of Abnormal Psychology*, Vol. 70 (February, 1965), pp. 70–76.
[147] Roy W. Persons and Harold B. Pepinsky, "Convergence in Psychotherapy with Delinquent Boys," *Journal of Counseling Psychology*, Vol. 13 (Fall, 1966), pp. 329–334.

tended to become more similar (converge) to their therapists than to nominal leaders in therapy groups. Shifts were toward counselors' personality traits, value patterns, and behavioral routines.

SOCIAL PRESENCE

With a sample of 58 counselees and three counselors, Tuma and Gustad found that close resemblance between counselee and counselor on measures of dominance, social presence, and social participation was positively related to the client's self-learning in counseling.[148] Counselors with essentially the same methods with similar clients produced different effects in self-learning.

Deane and Ansbacher report that because of commonality of background and language, the attendant has the best opportunities of any member of the state hospital staff for communicating and relating with the patient.[149] His lay approach has been found more effective than the "deeper" interpretations of the professional.

VALUES

Cook compared high, medium, and low groups (based upon degree of similarity in values between client and counselor) in respect to change in evaluative meanings of "me", the "ideal student," "my future occupation," and "education."[150] Significant differences occurred for "education" and "my future occupation" and suggested a curvilinear relationship, with the medium similarity group showing a more positive change in meaning than the high or low group.

[148] A. H. Tuma and J. W. Gustad, "The Effects of Client and Counselor Personality Characteristics on Client Learning in Counseling," *Journal of Counseling Psychology,* Vol. 4 (Summer, 1957), pp. 136–141.
[149] W. M. Deane and H. L. Ansbacher, "Attendant-Patient Commonality as a Psychotherapeutic Factor," *Journal of Individual Psychology,* Vol. 18 (November, 1962), pp. 157–167.
[150] Thomas E. Cook, "The Influence of Client-Counselor Value Similarity on Change in Meaning During Brief Counseling," *Journal of Counseling Psychology,* Vol. 13 (Spring, 1966), pp. 77–81.

Complementary Characteristics

Research focusing upon the interaction of clients and counselors matched on complementary personality characteristics is a relatively recent development.

Similarity, as used in the preceding section, means resemblance or being nearly alike, while *complementary,* discussed here, refers to counselor-counselee characteristics which mutually make up what is lacking in the other.

Snyder's research extended over four years, with 20 therapy cases.[151] The clients were a homogeneous group, 19 graduate students in psychology and one instructor in an allied department. Snyder was the only therapist involved in the study. The average number of interviews, each tape-recorded, was 25.5. After every interview each client completed a 200-item questionnaire reporting his attitudes toward the therapy and/or the therapist. In addition, on a 196-item questionnaire the therapist gave his estimate of the client's feelings toward him, of the client's progress in therapy, and of postinterview need structure. These questionnaires, the Therapist Affect Scale and the Client Affect Scale, were used to secure the therapist's and client's overall interaction and also their interview-by-interview change in affect. Factor analysis revealed two factors on each scale. Those on the client scale were labeled "active resistance or hostility" and "passive resistance or withdrawal." Those on the therapist scale were labeled "impatience with the client" and "anger or irritation with him." Clients were followed up one to three years after therapy terminated. Snyder classified and analyzed his data on the three continua of affect, control, and disclosure. Through the course of therapy, clients seemed to fall into two groups — "better" and "poorer." For the therapist, the therapeutic relationship and interaction appeared to be better when the client and therapist complemented

[151] W. U. Snyder, *The Psychotherapy Relationship* (New York: The Macmillan Company, 1961).

each other on these three personality characteristics.

In two studies (Bandura, Lipsher, and Miller,[152] and Winder, Farrukh, Bandura, and Rau[153]) some evidence was given that the therapist's interpersonal behavior influenced the client's interview behavior and continuation in therapy. Heller, Myers, and Kline attempted to see whether the behavior of the therapist is influenced in any way by the interview behavior of the client.[154] Their "clients" were four student actors who were interviewed by 34 counselors in training. The dimensions of behavior studied were control and affect. The hypotheses were as follows: (1) Dominant client behavior will evoke dependent interviewer behavior; (2) dependent client behavior will evoke dominant interviewer behavior; (3) hostile client behavior will evoke hostile interviewer behavior; (4) friendly client behavior will evoke friendly interviewer behavior; and (5) hostile client behavior will evoke interviewer anxiety. All hypotheses were tenable except the fifth, implying complementarity on the control dimension and similarity on the affect dimension.

Russell and Snyder (1963) also investigated the effect of hostile or friendly client behavior on counselor anxiety.[155] They used two client actors and 20 counselors. Independent variables were client behavior and amount of counseling experience. The four measures of the dependent variable of counselor anxiety were palm sweating, eye-blink rate, client actor estimates of counselor anxiety, and independent judgment of verbal anxiety in counselors' protocols. The data indicated that hostile client behavior led to significantly greater anxiety than friendly client behavior and that the amount of experience had little effect on the degree of counselor anxiety in either hostile or friendly interviews.

Paravonian hypothesized that clients whose reported interpersonal needs were (1) similar or (2) complementary to those of their counselors would evaluate their counseling as more effective than clients whose interpersonal needs were (1) dissimilar or (2) uncomplementary to those of their counselors.[156] Interpersonal need areas of control and affection were considered. Self-report estimates of the needs to express control, to want control, to express affection, and to want affection were measured by means of FIRO-B. Subjects included 56 counselor trainees enrolled in counseling practicum and 310 high school student counselees. Support for the hypotheses could not be demonstrated.

Summary Comments

Long, complex chapters deserve short summaries. Review of the material presented in this chapter leads to the following concluding remarks about the characteristics of counselors and counselees.

1. Tolerance for ambiguity, maturity, understanding, ability to maintain an appropriate emotional distance from the counselee, and ability to maintain good social relationships with noncounselees are characteristics demonstrated to be *associated* with counselor effectiveness. While psychometric data reflect that, as a group, counselors exhibit greater needs on variables such as intraception, exhibition, affiliation, and the like, nonintellective measures have not consistently discriminated between so-called effective and ineffective counselors.

[152] A. Bandura, H. Lipsher, and B. Miller, "The Psychotherapist's Approach-Avoidance Reactions to Patient's Expression of Hostility," *Journal of Consulting Psychology*, Vol. 24 (February, 1960), pp. 1–8.

[153] C. Winder, A. Z. Farrukh, A. Bandura, and L. C. Rau, "Dependency of Patient's Psychotherapists' Responses and Aspects of Psychotherapy," *Journal of Consulting Psychology*, Vol. 26 (April, 1962), pp. 129–134.

[154] K. Heller, R. A. Myers, and L. V. Kline, "Interviewer Behavior as a Function of Standardized Client Roles," *Journal of Consulting Psychology*, Vol. 27 (April, 1963), pp. 117–122.

[155] Russell and Snyder, *op. cit.*

[156] S. D. Paravonian, "The Effects of Counselor-Client Compatibility on the Client's Evaluation of the Effectiveness of the Counseling Relationship," unpublished doctoral dissertation, Purdue University, 1966.

Distinctions between the two groups seem due to differences in the intensity of characteristics rather than to the presence or absence of a given characteristic in an individual counselor. Further, the discriminating traits found are not independent of the particular design, analysis procedure, and effectiveness measures employed in the study.

2. Counselee personality variables — expectancies concerning counseling, motivation, need to change, potential for self-appraisal, emotional responsiveness, introspective attitude, intelligence, flexibility, range of interests, level of personality integration, and social conformity — influence the direction, length, and outcome of the counseling relationship.

3. Experienced counselors are more effective than inexperienced ones.

4. Researchers have measured the personality characteristics of counselors and counselees by a great variety of techniques. Standardized self-report personality and interest inventories have been used frequently but have been harshly criticized, chiefly because of their unsuitability for testing psychologically knowledgeable trainees and clients and because of their lack of sensitivity. The diversity of the methods employed in published studies of counselor and counselee characteristics and effectiveness attests to a lack of satisfaction with the results obtained. Intimately related to this dissatisfaction is the problem of the definition and measurement of adequate effectiveness criteria for assessing counseling activity. Despite these crucial factors, some criteria do appear to be more promising than others. Those who use sociometrics and the Q-techniques have expressed the belief that they are fruitful methods worthy of continued investigation. Ratings by expert judges, supervisors, and peers typify other useful though limited criteria.

5. Attempts to surmount measurement and criterion problems are suggested by certain trends in the study of counselor and counselee characteristics. One is toward the use of multiple measures of personality. Another is toward author-developed methods for assessing personality variables and counselor effectiveness. Finally, internal and external multiple criteria in assessing counselor effectiveness are being used.

6. Investigations of the connection between counselor personality and effectiveness need to be directed not only toward identifying distinguishing characteristics but toward providing empirical and/or theoretical bases for explaining how differences in characteristics are related to differences in effectiveness. There is also a need for identifying personality characteristics associated with effectiveness rather than with lack of effectiveness. The latter type of descriptions provides criteria for judging ineffectiveness rather than effectiveness. The existing data imply that absence of undesired characteristics rather than possession of desired accounts for effectiveness.

7. An untapped reservoir for studying practicing counselor characteristics, rather than those of counselor trainees, lies in elementary and secondary schools. Study of the relationship between counselor characteristics and effectiveness utilizing counselors in these settings should examine methods of assigning students to counselors.

8. At the present time, the counseling profession is unable to demonstrate consistently that a single trait or pattern of traits distinguishes an individual who is or will be a "good" counselor. Good counseling, like good teaching, is a highly complex activity which is situationally dependent upon the counselor, the counselee, the setting, the topic, and the conditions under which it is conducted.

Annotated References

Arbuckle, Dugald S. *Counseling, Theory and Practice.* Boston: Allyn and Bacon, Inc., 1965. 415 pp.

Chapter 3 (pp. 85–117) examines the personality of the counselor. Arbuckle provides a synthesis of the literature on the topic in a very readable form. He also presents a brief statement about the counselor's job.

Patterson, C. H. "The Selection of Counselors," in John M. Whiteley (ed.), *Research in Counseling.* Columbus, Ohio: Charles E. Merrill, Inc., 1967. pp. 69–101.

Patterson evaluates the research on the characteristics of counselors and the selection of candidates for research programs. He then presents the implications for research in terms of selection and theory and practice.

Tyler, Leona E. *The Work of the Counselor,* 3rd ed. New York: Appleton-Century-Crofts, 1969. 274 pp.
The problems of selecting candidates for counselors are set forth by Tyler. Research on the characteristics of counselors is explained and certain implications drawn about current research.

Further References

Bednar, Richard L. "Therapeutic Relationship of A-B Therapists as Perceived by Client and Therapist." *Journal of Counseling Psychology,* Vol. 17 (March, 1970). pp. 119–122.

Bednar, Richard L. and Parker, Clyde A. "Client Susceptibility to Persuasion and Counseling Outcome." *Journal of Counseling Psychology,* Vol. 16 (September, 1969). pp. 415–420.

Boyd, Robert E. "Whitehorn-Betz A-B Score as an Effector of Client-Counselor Interaction." *Journal of Counseling Psychology,* Vol. 17 (May, 1970). pp. 279–283.

Carkhuff, Robert R. and Banks, George. "Training as a Preferred Mode of Facilitating Relations Between Races and Generations." *Journal of Counseling Psychology,* Vol. 17 (September, 1970). pp. 413–418.

Carkhuff, Robert R. and Berenson, Bernard G. "The Counselor Is a Man and a Woman." *Personnel and Guidance Journal,* Vol. 48 (September, 1969). pp. 24–28.

Dole, Arthur A., Nottingham, Jack, and Wrightsman, Lawrence S. Jr., "Beliefs about Human Nature Held by Counseling, Clinical, and Rehabilitation Students." *Journal of Counseling Psychology,* Vol. 16 (May, 1969). pp. 197–202.

Donnan, Hugh H. and Harlan, Grady. "Personality of Counselors and Administrators." *Personnel and Guidance Journal,* Vol. 47 (November, 1968). pp. 228–232.

Edwards, Billy C. and Edgerly, John W. "Effects of Counselor-Client Cognitive Congruence on Counseling Outcome in Brief Counseling." *Journal of Counseling Psychology,* Vol. 17 (July, 1970). pp. 313–318.

Foulds, Melvin L. "Dogmatism and Ability to Communicate Facilitative Conditions During Counseling." *Counselor Education and Supervision,* Vol. 11 (December, 1971). pp. 110–114.

Greenberg, Bradley S., Kagan, Norman, and Bowes, John. "Dimensions of Empathic Judgment of Clients by Counselors." *Journal of Counseling Psychology,* Vol. 16 (July, 1969). pp. 303–308.

Hackney, Harold L., Ivey, Allen E., and Oetting, Eugene R. "Attending, Island, and Hiatus Behavior: A Process Conception of Counselor and Client Interaction." *Journal of Counseling Psychology,* Vol. 17 (July, 1970). pp. 342–346.

Howard, Kenneth I., Orlinsky, David E., and Trattner, James H. "Therapist Orientation and Patient Experience in Psychotherapy." *Journal of Counseling Psychology,* Vol. 17 (May, 1970). pp. 263–270.

Johnson, David W. "Effects of the Order of Expressing Warmth and Anger on the Actor and the Listener." *Journal of Counseling Psychology,* Vol. 18 (November, 1971). pp. 571–578.

Jourard, Sidney M., and Jaffe, Peggy E. "Influence of an Interviewer's Disclosure on the Self-Disclosing Behavior of Interviewees." *Journal of Counseling Psychology,* Vol. 17 (May, 1970). pp. 252–257.

Kaul, Theodore J. and Parker, Clyde A. "Suggestibility and Expectancy in a Counseling Analogue." *Journal of Counseling Psychology,* Vol. 18 (November, 1971). pp. 536–541.

Kaul, Theodore J. and Schmidt, Lyle D. "Dimensions of Interviewer Trustworthiness." *Journal of Counseling Psychology,* Vol. 18 (November, 1971). pp. 542–548.

Kunce, Joseph and Anderson, Wayne. "Counselor-Client Similarity and Referral Bias." *Journal of Counseling Psychology,* Vol. 17 (March, 1970). pp. 102–106.

Mickelson, Douglas J., and Stevic, Richard R. "Differential Effects of Facilitative and Nonfacilitative Behavioral Counselors." *Journal of Counseling Psychology,* Vol. 18 (July, 1971). pp. 314–319.

Mullen, John and Abeles, Norman. "Relationship of Liking, Empathy, and Therapist's Experience to Outcome of Therapy." *Journal of Counseling Psychology,* Vol. 18 (January, 1971). pp. 39–43.

Murphy, Kevin C. and Strong, Stanley R. "Some Effects of Similarity Self-Disclosure." *Journal of Counseling Psychology,* Vol. 19 (March, 1972). pp. 121–124.

Namenek, Andre A. and Schultdt, W. John. "Differential Effects of Experimenters' Personality and Instructional Sets on Verbal Conditioning." *Journal of Counseling Psychology,* Vol. 18 (March, 1971). pp. 170–172.

Passons, William R. and Olsen, LeRoy C. "Relationship of Counselor Characteristics and Empathic Sensitivity." *Journal of Counseling Psychology,* Vol. 16 (September, 1969). pp. 440–445.

Reagles, Kenneth W., Wright, George N., and Butler, Alfred J. "Rehabilitation Gain: Relationship with Client Characteristics and Counselor Intervention." *Journal of Counseling Psychology,* Vol. 18 (September, 1971). pp. 490–495.

Rickabaugh, Karl, Heaps, Richard A., and Finley, Robert. "Counselor Comfort, Counseling Climate, and Client Satisfaction: Client Ratings and Academic Improvement." *Counselor Education and Supervision,* Vol. 11 (March, 1972). pp. 219–223.

Rochester, Dean E. "Sex and Age as Factors Relating to Counselor Attitude Change." *Counselor Education and Supervision,* Vol. 11 (March, 1972). pp. 214–218.

Schmidt, Lyle D. and Strong, Stanley R. " 'Expert' and 'Inexpert' Counselors." *Journal of Counseling Psychology,* Vol. 17 (March, 1970). pp. 115–118.

Schmidt, Lyle D. and Strong, Stanley R. "Attractiveness and Influence in Counseling." *Journal of Counseling Psychology,* Vol. 18 (July, 1971). pp. 348–351.

Smith, William D. and Martinson, William D. "Counselors' and Counselees' Learning Style on Interview Behavior." *Journal of Counseling Psychology,* Vol. 18 (March, 1971). pp. 138–141.

Strong, Stanley R. and Dixon, David N. "Expertness, Attractiveness, and Influence in Counseling." *Journal of Counseling Psychology,* Vol. 18 (November, 1971). pp. 562–570.

Strong, Stanley R. and Gray, Bonnie L. "Social Comparison, Self-Evaluation, and Influence in Counseling." *Journal of Counseling Psychology,* Vol. 19 (May, 1972). pp. 178–183.

Strong, Stanley R. and Schmidt, Lyle D. "Trustworthiness and Influence in Counseling." *Journal of Counseling Psychology,* Vol. 17 (May, 1970). pp. 197–204.

Strong, Stanley R., Taylor, Ronald G., Bratton, Joseph C., and Loper, Rodney G. "Nonverbal Behavior and Perceived Counselor Characteristics." *Journal of Counseling Psychology,* Vol. 18 (November, 1971). pp. 554–561.

Vontress, Clemmont E. "Racial Differences: Impediments to Rapport." *Journal of Counseling Psychology,* Vol. 18 (January, 1971). pp. 7–13.

Vontress, Clemmont E. "The Black Militant as a Counselor." *Personnel and Guidance Journal,* Vol. 50 (March, 1972). pp. 574, 576–580.

Widgery, Robin and Stackpole, Cecil. "Desk Position, Interviewee Anxiety, and Interviewer Credibility: An Example of Cognitive-Balance in a Dyad." *Journal of Counseling Psychology,* Vol. 19 (May, 1972). pp. 173–177.

Winborn, Bob S. and Rowe, Wayne. "Self-Actualization and the Communication of Facilitative Conditions — A Replication." *Journal of Counseling Psychology,* Vol. 19 (January, 1972). pp. 26–29.

Wrenn, C. Gilbert. "The Three Worlds of the Counselor." *Personnel and Guidance Journal,* Vol. 49 (October, 1970). pp. 91–97.

Zimmer, Jules M. and Pepyne, Edward W. "A Descriptive and Comparative Study of Dimensions of Counselor Response." *Journal of Counseling Psychology,* Vol. 18 (September, 1971). pp. 441–447.

COUNSELOR ROLE AND FUNCTION

6

During the 1960's the topic of counselor role and function increasingly engaged the attention of counselors, counselor educators, and educational administrators. This interest led to a proliferation of articles in the counseling literature. For some counseling practitioners, analysis of counselor role is threatening and anxiety provoking because all too often a gap is revealed between an ideal and the reality of their position. For others, analysis of counselor role is viewed as an authentic search for professional identity. Still others wonder why counselors are so concerned about role and function since effective professionals do not search for identity but live it.

This final chapter in Part Two defines certain basic concepts of role and function, explores role theory and counselor role, identifies the major reasons for counselor role variability, and presents some current descriptive statements of counselor role and function.

The Concepts of Role and Function

For the most part, the words "role and function" have been used, perhaps erroneously, almost as one term in the literature and in informal discussion by counselors. The word "role" has been adopted by social psychologists and sociologists to designate the customary complex of behavior associated with a particular status or position. Perhaps it will be meaningful at this time to identify and clarify certain terms used in discussing counselor role and function. Clarifying terms is one of the oldest duties of the methodologist and, unfortunately, one which never ends.

DEFINITION OF ROLE

The position of counselor should be viewed as an inherent part of a social system. "Social system" does not refer to society or to a state or even necessarily to a large aggregate of people; it means any group of individuals who live and interact with one another, such as a community, a school, or even a classroom within a school. The interactional network of relationships between and among offices, positions, or statuses is referred to as the structure of the society. It is the means of interrelating and regulating individuals and groups. Position is defined as a location or a unit of the social structure. Positions denote the statuses of an individual with reference to other members and are attained in various ways. If they are sought and attained through striving and competitive mastery of the rights and obligations linked to them, they may be termed *achieved* positions or statuses. Other positions, called *ascribed,* devolve upon the individual by virtue of certain biological attributes: race, sex, age, or preexisting social affinities such as parents' status. One position is distinguished from another by the functions performed for the group and carries with it special rights and obligations. In a high position or status the rights and obligations command prestige, which when translated into action means power or the capacity to influence and direct the behavior of others.

Bentley has noted that

> . . . successful performance in a position depends upon (1) his [the member's] awareness and understanding of the rights and obligations, and (2) his willingness to abide by the patterned nature of such rights and obligations. Some positions are rigidly structured and little leeway is allowed the occupant. . . . In other positions, less rigidly defined, the individual is quite free to introduce variation in the performance of his duties and in his interpretation of his rights.[1]

There can be no position without a role and no role without a position. Role is often defined by the individual's behavior in performing the rights and obligations of his position. Because in his life situation every individual has multiple positions, he plays many different roles. In one sense, each of us is to some degree an actor or a poser, for living in society may be viewed as a playing of roles. At different times, therefore, different roles become prominent. Several roles may be operative simultaneously, but the intensity of their demands for effective fulfillment varies.

Social psychologists have drawn an important distinction between position and role. Role is expected behavior that is approved for the occupant of a defined position. A position is a unit of society or a location in a social structure. Yinger defines role in these words: "*Role* is a unit of culture; it refers to the rights and duties, the normatively approved patterns of behavior for the occupants of a given position."[2]

When the counselor puts into effect the obligations and responsibilities of his position, he is said to be performing his role. A role is a prescription for behavior "inferred from how various persons behave in particular positions, how others behave toward them, and how they all describe the rights and duties in verbal behavior."[3] Parsons and Shils have defined role in this way:

> The role is that organized sector of an actor's orientation which constitutes and defines his participation in an interactive process. It involves a set of complementary expectations concerning his own actions and those of others with whom he interacts. Both the actor and those with whom he interacts possess these expectations.[4]

Bentley, in criticizing the present authors for their loose usage of the term "role," has urged that it be defined as the way an individual actually performs in a given position as distinct from how he is supposed to perform. He has sought to restrict usage of the term to denote "what a person actually does."[5] But Ivey and Robin have pointed out that role is a normative concept: "Roles are the sets of norms or expectations of behavior that are assigned by significant others to a specific position. Another way of understanding this concept and its

[1] Joseph C. Bentley, "Role Theory in Counseling: A Problem in Definition," *Personnel and Guidance Journal,* Vol. 45 (September, 1965), p. 13.

[2] J. Milton Yinger, *Toward a Field Theory of Behavior* (New York: McGraw-Hill Book Co., Inc., 1965), p. 99.

[3] *Ibid.,* p. 100.

[4] Talcott Parsons and Edward A. Shils (eds.), *Toward a General Theory of Action* (New York: Harper & Row, Publishers, 1962), p. 23.

[5] Bentley, *op. cit.,* p. 13.

function is to note that roles provide a method of organizing expectations by reference to a social structure."[6] And Yinger points out that "we can say that a role is the list of what most members of a social group believe a position occupant should and should not, may and may not, do. It is not a list of what most occupants of a position in fact do."[7] Yinger adds that role requirements range from those that are mandatory (the absence of which would indicate that the role was not performed at all) to those that are optional (ways of behaving that are permissible). It would seem that what Bentley defined as role, Yinger defined as internalized role while Ivey and Robin, in turn, regard what an individual taking a position actually does as "role behavior." Perhaps all that these differences indicate is that the concept "role" is frequently used in different ways and that consensus as to what it means is lacking. The role of the counselor is most simply defined as the expectations and directives for behavior connected with his position. As such, it is the counselor's blueprint for action.

ROLE EXPECTATIONS

The occupant of any given role is not a passive agent. He performs in interactive situations with other individuals who perceive and react to him. These individuals have certain expectations based upon needs or conditions of existence that must be secured and maintained if they and the social unit are to function. Their expectations form the "normatively approved patterns of behavior" referred to in Yinger's definition of role. The normative aspects involved led Ivey and Robin to define expectation as a "norm."

> A norm is defined as an expectation of behavior, stemming from a general social agreement or from those whose judgments are psychologically significant to the actor or group of actors. Psychologically, norms are expectations for behavior held by those whose reactions are emotionally meaningful to the actor — friends and certain professional colleagues, for example. Sociologically, norms are expectations for behavior by those who, by common agreement, have legitimate concern with and/or authority over the actor's behavior — in the case of the school counselor, examples would be teachers and the principal.[8]

Other individuals in the social structure interact with and desire certain behavior from the role occupant. They anticipate that he will act in ways considered appropriate to his role. Role expectations constitute a definition of behavior that is proper for the role. Both the individual who enacts the role and others with whom he interacts expect that he will act in particular ways. Sarbin and Jones believe that role expectations arise in this way:

> A role expectation is a cognitive structure inferred, on the stimulus side, from the person's previous commerce with regularities in others' behaviors, and, on the response side, from the person's tendency to group a number of descriptions of actions and qualities together with the name of a specific social position.[9]

Their comment indicates that expectations spring from previous contact with others who held the position as well as from notions of what the individual occupying the position should do.

Role expectancies sometimes conflict. Differences may occur (1) between what the individual expects to be able to do and what others expect of him and (2) between the expectations he holds for the role and the demands of the role.

ROLE PERCEPTIONS

Roles are complementary or interdependent in that each role derives its meaning from other relat-

[6] Allen E. Ivey and Stanley S. Robin, "Role Theory, Role Conflict and Counseling," *Journal of Counseling Psychology,* Vol. 13 (Spring, 1966), p. 30.
[7] Yinger, *op. cit.,* p. 100.

[8] Ivey and Robin, *op. cit.,* p. 30. Copyright 1966 by the American Psychological Association, and reproduced by permission.
[9] Theodore R. Sarbin and Donald S. Jones, "An Experimental Analysis of Role Behavior," in Eleanor E. Maccoby, Theodore M. Newcomb, and Eugene L. Hartley (eds.), *Readings in Social Psychology* (New York: Holt, Rinehart & Winston, Inc., 1958), p. 465.

ed roles within a social setting. No role is performed in exactly the same way by any two individuals. Performance depends upon how each person perceives, interprets, and acts upon the obligations and rights of a position. It also depends upon his perceptions of others' expectations for his behavior in the role. Normally, enactment of a role can only approximate the performance of previous role incumbents.

The occupant's idiosyncratic personality is brought to the role. His personal expectations, needs, goals, attitudes, achievements, and skills shape his responses to role demands and subsequently influence performance. The role is stamped by his unique pattern of behavior. Yinger uses the term "internalized role" to refer to

> . . . a given individual's tendencies to perform a role in a given way. This is clearly different from the role itself, which is a cultural construct. Internalized role has a particular person's mark or style imprinted on it, for it is affected by all the positions he occupies, by the ways in which he learned the role, and by the total personality system in which it is embedded.[10]

Internalized role results from *role perceptions* — ways the occupant personally views and defines the rights and obligations of the position.

An individual's perceptions may lead him to emphasize certain dimensions of the role and deemphasize others. Variation in role performance may result from how the incumbent internalizes the role or may occur because his other roles intrude upon it.

Much speculation has gone into how personality variables influence role behavior. Yinger identifies four self-related variables that affect it:

1. Differences in internalized role. We are unlikely to be successful in predicting role performance until we know, among other things, how the individuals involved define the rights and duties.
2. The significance of the position to the individual's self-identification. This affects his readiness to accept the role definition of others. If the position is relatively unimportant, few other personality forces are drawn into the performance; if the position is at the center of the individual's identity, however, other personality tendencies, not related to the role, will influence the performance.
3. Other positions being occupied. If the selection process draws persons into position A who have highly dissimilar position constellations (one occupying B, C, and D; another occupying E, F, and G, etc.), role performance is likely to vary more widely than if all those in position A share positions B, C, and D as well.
4. The degree of similarity in personality tendencies not related to the role. Individuals who vary in authoritarianism, intelligence, level of energy, and values, for example, are likely to perform the same role in different ways.[11]

ROLE CONFLICT

Conflict may occur whenever expectations cannot be harmonized. Gross, Mason and McEachern, have defined role conflict as "Any situation in which the incumbent of a position perceives that he is confronted with incompatible expectations. . . ."[12] They also present the various meanings ascribed to role conflict by different social scientists, summarized here as (1) any incompatible expectation to which an individual is exposed, whether he is aware of the conflict or not, (2) situations in which the actor perceives incompatible expectations, (3) exposure to conflicting expectations because the individual occupies two or more positions simultaneously, and (4) contradictory expectations derived from an actor's occupancy of a single position.

Ivey and Robin believe that role conflict occurs in a situation "in which there is systematic difficulty involved in assuming, maintaining a role, or functioning in a role situation."[13] These authors pose four types of role conflict for the school counselor:

1. Role conflict stemming from role definers: There are situations in which legitimate role definers disagree

[10] Yinger, *op. cit.*, p. 99.

[11] *Ibid.*, p. 112.

[12] N. C. Gross, W. S. Mason, and A. W. McEachern, *Explorations in Role Analysis: Studies of the School Superintendency Role* (New York: Wiley, 1958), p. 448.

[13] Ivey and Robin, *op. cit.*, p. 30.

about the normative content of a role; e.g., the principal thinks the counselor should supervise study hall, the counselor or the teachers do not see this as one of his duties. Another example would be differences in specifications of the role of the school counselor held by counselor trainers and practicing counselors.

2. Role conflict internal to the role: The definers of a role may be in agreement and their role specifications congruent, yet the various expectations confronting the role taker are such that the individual cannot fulfill all of the obligations in the role. An example of this is the counselor who may be expected to be a confidant of his client and an administrator enforcing rules at the same time. The conflict here is within the individual counselor while assuming his role even though he and all other role definers may have agreed to the above role definition. He now faces mutually exclusive and contradictory role expectations and cannot behave in a manner as to fulfill simultaneously all the expectations and obligations of the counselor role.

3. Role conflict stemming from the role in interaction with the social system: (a) A type of "functional" role conflict occurs when the normative prescriptions of a role are not sufficient to allow the role taker to perform the functions expected of his role in the larger social system in which it is situated. An example of this type of role conflict would be the professionally trained counselor working in an institutional setting where the definition of his role confines him to brief contact with each client, thereby making impossible the results of counseling which all expect of his efforts. (b) Role conflict also arises because of the multiplicity of roles an individual assumes. Some elements in separate roles are incompatible. For example, in some school systems an individual is expected to be a teacher or a clerk in addition to being a counselor. Situations arise in which the individual cannot behave in such a manner as to meet the expectations associated with the several roles.

4. Role conflict stemming from the interaction of the individual and his role: This is the situation where the role definers' demands exceed the limits of the role taker's capacity. Resisting forces may arise out of the counselor's needs to safeguard his well-being or psychological integrity. In effect, the individual is unable to maintain his role competently.[14]

[14] *Ibid.*, pp. 30–31. Copyright 1966 by the American Psychological Association, and reproduced by permission.

Yinger differentiates between internal and external role conflict.[15] Internal role conflict takes place when a person has internalized a role that incorporates contradictory expectations or when he holds two or more positions that carry incompatible role expectations, whether recognized or not. External role conflict occurs when one is faced with incompatible expectations from two or more individuals. Yinger's definition is broader than that of Gross, McEachern, and Mason, who refer only to perceived incompatibilities. Yinger notes that when role conflict is limited to only perceived incompatibilities, important aspects of conflict are excluded since unperceived conflicts in others' expectations affect *their* behavior.

Role conflict can spring from expectations that are legitimate or illegitimate. Gross, McEachern, and Mason differentiate a legitimate from an illegitimate expectation on the basis of whether the incumbent of a position believes others have or do not have a right to hold the expectation.[16] Legitimate expectations are called perceived obligations while illegitimate expectations are called perceived pressures.

ROLE VERSUS FUNCTIONS

It was previously noted that in the counseling literature "role" and "function" are often used synonymously. Distinctions between the two terms are not easy or clear-cut. Role has been defined as the expectations and directives for behavior connected with a position whereas function is usually defined as the activities assigned to a role. Wrenn has stated that the distinction between the two may be conceptualized as one of purpose (role) and process (function) or as one of ends (role) and means (function).[17] He noted too that many individuals and groups may be concerned with defining the role of the counselor in whatever setting he

[15] Yinger, *op. cit.*, p. 115.

[16] Gross, McEachern, and Mason, *op. cit.*, p. 448.

[17] C. Gilbert Wrenn,"Crises in Counseling: A Commentary and a Contribution," in John F. McGowan (ed.), *Counselor Development in American Society* (Washington: U.S. Department of Labor and U.S. Office of Education, June, 1965), p. 235.

works but that functions are the exclusive domain of the professional counselor.

Role Theory and Counselor Role

The previous section has indicated that (1) role is a complex of behavior resulting from multiple expectations and institutional directives and (2) many forces and factors influence role enactment. An adequate treatment of role theory is much beyond the scope of this volume. For those who are interested, an extensive formulation of role theory is provided by Parsons and Shils and their associates.[18]

Getzels' schematic model of role theory is presented here as Figure 6.1 to help the reader visualize in their entirety the interrelationships among the various facets.[19] The important aspect of the figure is that it utilizes three dimensions — anthropological, sociological, and psychological — in seeking to understand and present human behavior. Any behavioral act is conceived of as deriving simultaneously from all three dimensions. Behavioral interaction between one individual and another results from their attempts to cope with an environment consisting of patterns of expectations for both which are consistent with their own independent value orientations. Values interact with expectations and need-dispositions. Institutions and individuals are surrounded by cultural mores and values. The character of both the institution and the individual is to some extent determined by the ethos of the social group. Each institution has expectations for the individuals who occupy certain positions and enact certain roles, and each individual has a particular set of need-dispositions. Role expectations and need-dispositions are derived from the values of the culture.

Figure 6.1 Behavior as a function of social system

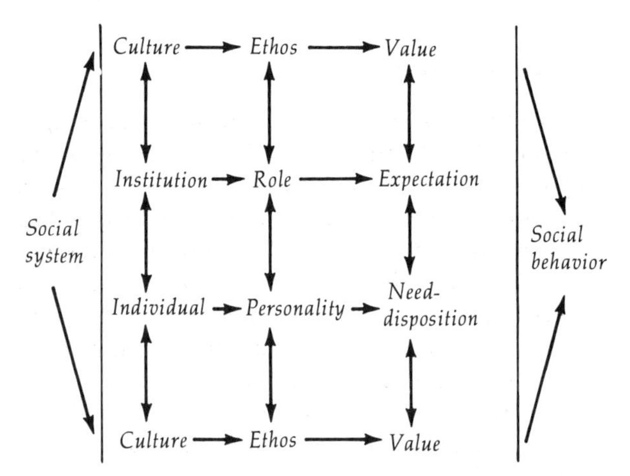

SOURCE: Jacob W. Getzels, "Conflict and Role Behavior in the Educational Setting," in W. W. Charters, Jr., and N. L. Gage (eds.), *Readings in the Social Psychology of Education* (Boston: Allyn and Bacon, Inc., 1963). Reprinted by permission.

For purposes of discussion only, the anthropological and sociological dimensions (upper two in Figure 6.1) taken alone define acceptable institutional behavior. They are useful in understanding the role of the counselor or any other role within an institution, such as the school. As a social institution the school exists for a purpose. Although the purpose may vary somewhat from school to school, it is derived from the culture. But by using only the upper two dimensions we get a dehumanized, oversimplified, and somewhat mechanical picture of the total situation. The psychological or idiographic dimension (third level in Figure 6.1) introduces the flesh-and-blood aspect. True, the upper two dimensions may in large part prescribe the functions performed by the role incumbent, but it is the individual who gives life and meaning to these activities. It is his unique, personalized interpretation and perception of role expectancies that culminate in manifest behavior.

UNDERSTANDING THE COUNSELOR ROLE

Figure 6.2 portrays the major factors involved in understanding individual behavior in the counseling role. The role of the counselor is determined

[18] Parsons and Shils (eds.), *op. cit.*
[19] Jacob W. Getzels, "Conflict and Role Behavior in the Educational Setting," in W. W. Charters, Jr., and N. L. Gage (eds.), *Readings in the Social Psychology of Education* (Boston: Allyn and Bacon, Inc., 1963), pp. 309–318.

not only by institutional prescriptions and proscriptions but also by the expectations which "external determining others" in his institutional environment hold for him. These significant others translate self and institutional requirements into expectations and evaluate counselor behavior according to them. Thus the individual who occupies the position of counselor does so by virtue of certain internal determining factors which contribute to his personal makeup and subsequently to the enactment of his role. It should be clearly understood that each of the external determining others listed in Figure 6.2 is influenced by the same internal determining factors as is the counselor.

COUNSELOR'S PERCEPTION OF ROLE

The reader would do well to remember that perceptions of counselor role — and ultimately behavior — are influenced by the internal determining factors cited in Figure 6.2. The elements contributing to the helping relationship (see Chapter One) and the research relating to counselor characteristics and effectiveness (see Chapter Five) testify to the variety of factors impinging upon the individual in his efforts to define and enact his role. Appell has commented upon the effect of the counselor's personality on his counseling behavior:

> The most significant resource a counselor brings to a helping relationship is himself. It is difficult to understand how a counselor unaware of his own emotional needs, of his expectations of himself as well as others, of his rights and privileges in relationships, can be sensitive enough to such factors in his counselee. More than that, it would seem that he needs to experience himself as a person of worth and of individuality before he can afford another such privileges. Indeed, in a most profound sense, the greater his congruence, the freer he can be in assisting others to actualize themselves.[20]

Figure 6.2 Determinants of counselor role

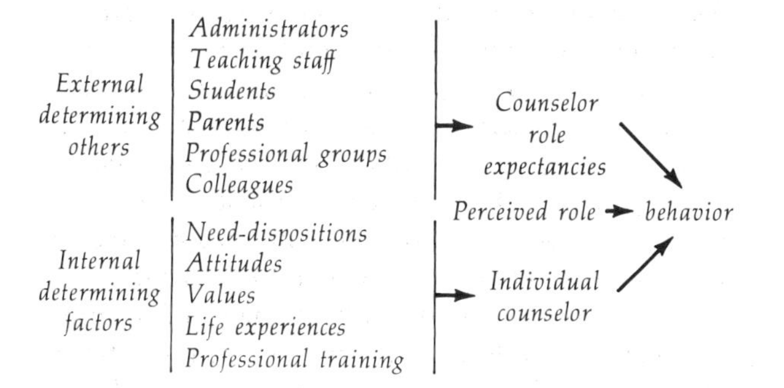

Williamson too indicates that the counselor's philosophy shows through his behavior, that his efforts in relating with counselees stem from his own acceptance of himself as he is, and that his behavior should reveal that he carries on his own "independent intellectual life," both in his specialty and in the broad literature of human cultures.[21] Certainly many of the differences among counseling practitioners could be understood on the basis of these factors alone. However, since such factors interact with the other variables presented in the upper section of Figure 6.2, we must look further for full understanding.

OTHERS' PERCEPTIONS

Many sources document the commonalities and differences existing among influential persons who perceive and affect the counselor's role. Most of this literature indicates a long history of conflict and misunderstanding as well as positive views of counselor role. Each of the "others" listed in the upper portion of Figure 6.2 holds expectations based upon what he thinks the counselor is, makes demands upon the counselor in an effort to have his own personal needs met, and evaluates the counselor's success as a counselor through his own perceptual screen.

Understandably, conflict occurs when the counselor behaves in a way that is inconsistent with what is anticipated. It is equally obvious that counselors who behave successfully must work toward

[20] Moray L. Appell, "Self Understanding for the Guidance Counselor," *Personnel and Guidance Journal*, Vol. 42 (October, 1963), p. 148.

[21] E. G. Williamson, "The Counselor as Technique," *Personnel and Guidance Journal*, Vol. 41 (October, 1962), pp. 108–111.

resolution of potential conflicts. Resolution comes through a mixture of acknowledging and meeting the demands of others, educating others and creating accurate and legitimate expectations in them, and adequately coping with personal views regarding his role.

A RESEARCH PARADIGM FOR COUNSELOR ROLE

Ivey and Robin have presented a paradigm for researching the role of the high school counselor.[22] It aids in analyzing counselor role and functions and identifies possible sources of role conflict. These authors point out that determiners of the high school counselor's role are school boards, administrators, teachers, students, counselors, parents, community pressure groups, and the counseling profession, all interacting and influencing one another in their definitions of the counselor's role while simultaneously being influenced by interaction with the counselor. Ivey and Robin have schematically patterned these interactions, as shown in Figure 6.3. Three key concepts should be noted. First, since students, teachers, and administrators are more involved than others in the high school social system, they constitute primary reference groups in defining the counselor's role. Second, the arrows between "other social systems" and "high school social system" through the dotted line separating the two represent the constant flow of people and ideas between the school and the world at large. Third, the arrows from the school counselors to the service groups represent patterns of mutual interaction. These groups have the same type of interaction with one another.

Figure 6.3 School counselor role definers

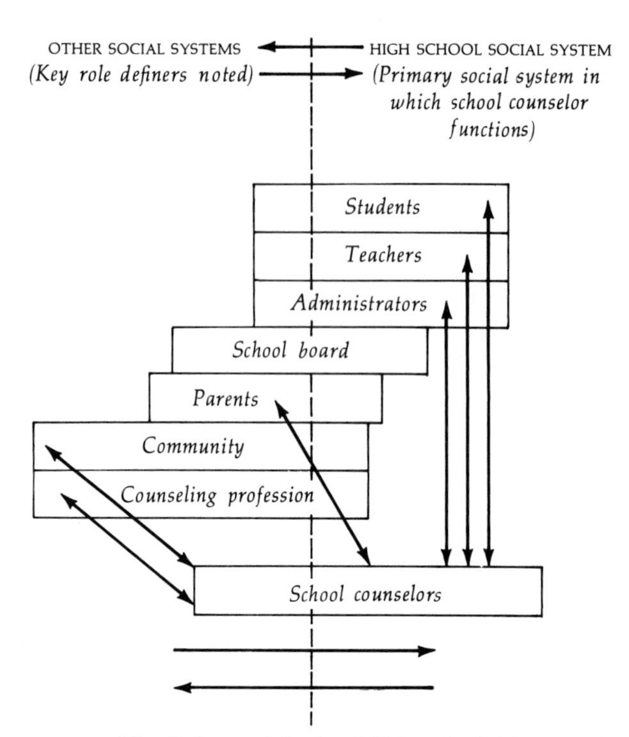

SOURCE: Allen E. Ivey and Stanley S. Robin, "Role Theory, Role Conflict, and Counseling," *Journal of Counseling Psychology*, Vol. 13 (Spring, 1966), p. 31. Copyright 1966 by the American Psychological Association, and reproduced by permission.

Ivey and Robin's schematic presentation of the specific role of the counselor is shown in Figure 6.4. Here is the counselor's inner world. In essence it is what underlies role conflicts, decisions, and resolutions of school counselors in general. The authors make a number of relevant comments about this graphic representation. First, each counselor operates both within the high school social system and in other social systems; these systems interact and affect the counselor, who in turn affects the systems. Second, many factors influence the counselor's role behavior — his personality, for example, and the role expectations of others. Third, the counselor's internalization of the expectations constitutes his perceptions for role behavior.

Ivey and Robin suggest that their research paradigm would be useful in (1) assessments of attitudes and expectations that significant others have for counselor role, (2) examining the counselor's personal characteristics, his perceptions of his role, and his perceptions of others' expectations, and (3) the application of role theory, particularly the concept of role behavior, to counseling process and interpersonal interview interaction. In their view, moreover, counselor role will not be clarified until dimensions of role conflict are identified and taken into account. They recommend that research be

[22] Ivey and Robin, *op. cit.*, pp. 31–35.

Figure 6.4 The school counselor(s) role

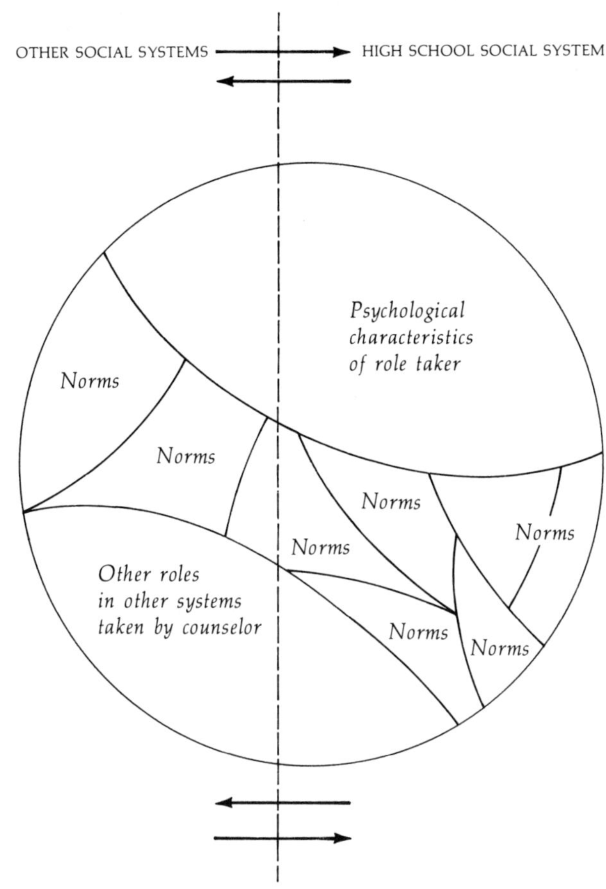

SOURCE: Allen E. Ivey and Stanley S. Robin, "Role Theory, Role Conflict, and Counseling," *Journal of Counseling Psychology*, Vol. 13 (Spring, 1966), p. 31. Copyright 1966 by the American Psychological Association, and reproduced by permission.

conducted into (1) conflict stemming from role definers, (2) conflict internal to the role, (3) conflict stemming from role interaction with the social system, and (4) conflict stemming from the interaction of the individual and his role.

Forces and Factors Causing Counselor Role Variability

The two preceding sections of this chapter have made it clear, that (1) a precise definition of counselor role has not yet been achieved and (2) many individual forces and factors are involved in counselor role definition. We shall now inquire into the forces and factors that are related to or affect role variability.

STRIVINGS FOR PROFESSIONALIZATION AND CAREER COMMITMENT

Entry into a profession demands specific behaviors from the aspirant. An occupation, such as counseling, which is striving for professional status, appears to demand certain characteristics. Criteria by which to judge professional status have resulted from endeavors to analyze the difference between occupations classified as professions and those not so classified. Uppermost among these criteria are: (1) that an occupational group possess some unique skill or service, and (2) that it establish a priority or monopoly in the meeting of a social need. Ethical codes, training standards, entry requirements and the indoctrination of new members soon follow these criteria. As this process becomes formalized, the individual worker is increasingly tied more closely to the group and tends to identify with those who epitomize the established worker. The willingness of the aspiring counselor to identify with the role projected as the professional image appears to be a source of some role variability. Growth toward professional status by individuals who enter the counseling occupation constitutes a process of socialization and identification. Through these interactions, career commitment is fostered. Responsibility and commitment are discussed by McCully, who states that "whether the occupation (counseling) moves on to become a profession will depend upon how serious qualified members of the occupation are in the quest, upon the price they are willing to pay in terms of effort and clear thinking, and upon the degree to which they are willing to accept responsibility."[23] The identification process and its corollary commitment appear to be related to the degree to which the worker perceives an occupation as capable of meeting his needs. Seeking vocation-

[23] C. H. McCully, "Professionalization: Symbol or Substance?" *Counselor Education and Supervision*, Vol. 2 (Spring, 1963), pp. 106–112.

al goals involves awareness of the perceived need satisfaction offered by the occupation. Norris[24] collected biographical and other data to assess the characteristics of those who entered the counselor training program at Michigan State University between the years 1945 and 1957. Ranked entry motives of those seeking counselor training were:

1. A desire to work with people (65 per cent)
2. Influence of a particular person (41 per cent)
3. The courses sounded interesting (31 per cent)
4. Liked the first course in guidance (25 per cent)
5. Hope to become a better teacher (23 per cent)
6. Increased salary potential (11 per cent)
7. Self understanding (6 per cent)
8. Need the classes to accept job (6 per cent)

Munger, Brown and Needham,[25] surveying the graduates of an NDEA Counseling and Guidance Institute (N = 20), sought information related to post institute occupational and educational status, career aspirations and present job role. They reported that 75 per cent hoped to leave their present position of school counselor to become college counselors, school administrators, or school psychologists. Factor analytic procedures were applied to the occupational choice motives of counselors by Schutz and Mazer.[26] A sample of 153 graduate students in counseling completed 60 Likert-type items which yielded 18 rotated factors. Factors reflecting adient aspects of the profession as well as socially acceptable motives were obtained. Aversive factors, by which the candidate wished to avoid some occupational situations, were also revealed. The adient factors involved entering counseling because it represents (1) a search for personal status, (2) helping others, (3) opportunities for research, (4) a ladder of success, (5) an opportunity to listen to others and thereby learn about oneself, (6) a means to extend personal influence, (7) an opportunity for creativity, and (8) a means to maintain school relationships. The avoidance factors, on the other hand, involved (1) the fear of personal threat, (2) avoidance of the business world, (3) dislike of physical labor, (4) avoidance of competition, and (5) maintenance of present health. This study suggests great heterogeneity in entry motives as well as variation in the characteristics of those receiving training.

Stevic,[27] in his doctoral research, studied counselor role, commitment, and marginality. Two instruments were developed to assess commitment preferences and actual commitment as evidenced by the subjects' present counseling function. Rankings of counseling activities and the correlation between preparation and commitment, as well as the effect of environmental press on counselor preferences, were investigated. The subjects believed that the counselor's main functions were to provide services to individual students and to foster and maintain staff relationships. However, the acceptance of professional responsibility was seen as being least important for the practitioner. The amount of graduate training was demonstrated to correlate with commitment. Likewise, the number of years of counseling experience was an effective predictor of commitment. Stevic noted that certain situational pressures affect the degree of counselor investment and goal striving behavior toward his ideal role. He concluded that these pressures might be altered if the counselor was militant. Stevic recommended additional graduate training to increase commitment and an analysis of personal ideals and goals. Currently, then, school counselors appear to have no clear role commitment and therefore respond to situational pressures by reacting to each incident without a consistent personal counseling philosophy or accepted professional policies to guide them.

[24] Willa Norris, "More Than a Decade of Training Guidance and Personnel Workers," *Personnel and Guidance Journal,* Vol. 39 (December, 1960), pp. 287–291.

[25] Paul F. Munger, D. F. Brown, and J. T. Needham, "NDEA Institute Participants Two Years Later," *Personnel and Guidance Journal,* Vol. 42 (June, 1964), pp. 987–990.

[26] R. E. Schutz and G. E. Mazer, "A Factor Analysis of Occupational Choice Motives of Counselors," *Journal of Counseling Psychology,* Vol. 11 (Fall, 1964), pp. 267–271.

[27] Stevic, R. R. The School Counselor's Role: Commitment and Marginality. Unpublished doctoral dissertation, The Ohio State University, 1963.

MARGINAL STATUS

Many school counselors hold other positions along with their counseling position. Some are counselor-teachers, counselor-coaches, counselor-principals. This dual status led Arbuckle to comment,

> It is interesting to note that of all these groups [teachers, administrators, and special service administrators], it is only the school counselor who is willing to accept the part-time, dual-role status. Other professional workers may spend only part of their time in the services of the school, but they are not part-time doctors, or part-time nurses, or part-time psychiatrists. They are medical doctors, or nurses, or psychologists or psychiatrists. Like pregnancy, "they are or they ain't," and there is no in-between status. We have no doctor-teacher, or nurse-principal, or psychologist-janitor, but we have thousands of teacher-counselors, or even more absurd, principal-counselors, and even, horror added upon horror, superintendent-counselors. Even worse, this schizophrenic fellow doesn't seem to mind this dual or triple status, and goes blithely walking off in several directions, at the same time, quite unaware that one set of feet is falling over the other.[28]

Surely if counseling is not seen as a lifetime career, only marginal commitment can be made to the role. While today the pattern shows some signs of breaking up, an all too obvious career pattern for male counselors is that they become counselors on their way to becoming administrators. Excluding the increased financial rewards realized by traveling this route, it should be noted that certain subtle motivations contribute to this pattern, which culminate in specific undesirable outcomes. Stefflre has charged that such a career line represents "waste" recruitment for the profession:

> Many counselors remain counselors only a few years while they gather their strength for the climb to the next plateau. Former counselors who are now administrators, supervisors, or college instructors are all evidence of "waste" recruitment in the sense that they did not have a lasting and firm identification with the occupation of the school counselor. It seems clear that at the present time most of the school counselors in America do not identify with this occupation. Less than a third of them, for example, are members of the national organization devoted to their special emphasis — the American School Counselor Association. They think of themselves as teachers who are temporary refugees from the classroom or as potential administrators waiting in the wings for their cues.
>
> One of the causes of this lack of identification is illuminated by the concept of the marginal man. In education, the most recognized, valued, and consensually accepted roles are those of the classroom teacher and the administrator. The counselor role is not as clear, nor as well validated by educational history, and the other workers in schools may have some difficulty in clarifying this marginal position. Is this marginal man — the school counselor — simply a teacher who has a new assignment; is he a psychologist who has strayed temporarily from his clinic; is he a sub-administrator who has managed to place himself on the administrative salary schedule; or is he a kind of office worker who is giving prestige and dignity to what are essentially clerical tasks? [29]

Wrenn, summarizing what the school counselor was like in 1962, presented data drawn from a national sample from Project Talent's population.[30] Only 20 per cent of the nationwide secondary school counselor sample were full time and only 55 per cent half time or more. The national average was one counselor per school. Perhaps even more damning, the average counselor devoted only three periods per day to working directly with pupils.

In part-time, dual-role assignments the counselor is neither fish nor fowl and cannot identify professionally with either role. Many of the some 50,000

[28] Dugald S. Arbuckle, "The Conflicting Functions of the School Counselor," *Counselor Education and Supervision,* Vol. 1 (Winter, 1961), p. 56.

[29] Buford Stefflre, "What Price Professionalization?" *Personnel and Guidance Journal,* Vol. 42 (March, 1964), p. 654. Copyright © 1964 American Personnel and Guidance Association. Reprinted with permission.

[30] C. Gilbert Wrenn, *The Counselor in a Changing World* (Washington: American Personnel and Guidance Association, 1962), pp. 113–118.

present-day school counselors are teacher-counselors because administrative officers of the school want it that way. Why? The present authors have speculated that

> . . . one hidden reason administrators retain part-time, dual role teacher-counselors is that they are afraid the full-time counselor may become too popular with teachers and too frequently sought after by pupils. Counselors in full-time positions dim the shining spotlight traditionally accorded administrators in the school. By dividing the counselor's functions, by draining away his time in a multiplicity of activities, the administrator makes the counselor a marginal man and renders him ineffective and less of a threat. This kind of misutilization of staff, while resulting in the removal of a competitor, negatively affects the school's guidance services by forcing the counselor to be ineffective as a counselor. It could be speculated that many counselors who find themselves in such a dilemma often do precisely what the administrator hopes they will not do. They leave their marginal position for the more clearly defined, more influential role of principal.[31]

SOCIAL FORCES

Hill points out that role clarification will not be easy because of five conditions.[32] (1) Because the counselor is a member of a new profession, he experiences what all new professionals do: lack of understanding of his functions, lack of professional acceptance among his publics, and discouraging confusion, even among his colleagues. (2) Because school counseling is a public service profession, the counselor is under the general direction of a lay board of education; many people, therefore, are involved in defining his functions. (3) The school counselor's work, however defined, is complicated and demanding. (4) The counselor's position requires that he help young people predict both their futures and the general future of society; clarification is complicated by the immature character of his tools and by the rapidity of social and economic change. (5) Since counseling is built upon a comparatively new ideal – the dignity, worth, and independence of each person – this ideal is not tenaciously rooted or immune from attack and the counselor has not only to practice but to defend it.

To Hill's five conditions others could be added: (1) The tremendous expansion of counseling services has brought with it diverse responsibilities and demands, (2) there is an increase in counseling specialties, and (3) there is diversity in state counselor certification patterns.

Many significant social forces – legislative acts, manpower demands, family adjustments, judicial decrees – influence counselor role. Brown identifies (1) tendencies toward the group and away from the individual, (2) the search for understanding among youth who have never known a world at peace, (3) changes in schools which place greater emphasis upon the individual for his own learning, (4) increasing involvement of the student with a greater number of teachers, and (5) the spread of inanimate aids to learning, such as television, programmed instruction, overhead projectors, and language laboratories.[33] Because of these social changes, Brown believes counselor role will change in the following ways: (1) The counselor will have to know more about each child – his aspirations, hopes, dreams, his fears; his motivation; how he learns and under what conditions, at what pace, and for what purpose. (2) The counselor will have increasingly to help teachers understand and know better each student. (3) The counselor's knowledge and sensitivity will be used to find better ways of evaluating students' work and the related problem of motivation for learning. (4) More of the burden of "caring" for the child will fall to the counselor as teachers become more specialized and academically oriented. (5) The counselor will be involved in assessing the impact upon students of the changes that take place in schools.

[31] Bruce Shertzer and Shelley C. Stone, "Challenges Confronting School Counselors," *The School Counselor,* Vol. 12 (May, 1965), p. 237. Copyright © 1965 American Personnel and Guidance Association. Reprinted with permission.

[32] George E. Hill, "How to Define the Functions of the School Counselor," *Counselor Education and Supervision,* Vol. 3 (Winter, 1964), pp. 56–61.

[33] Charles E. Brown, "The Counselor in a Changing School," *The School Counselor,* Vol. 11 (December, 1963), pp. 86–93.

Moore and Gaier also point to certain social forces that affect the counselor's role: (1) belief in equal opportunities and social mobility for all, (2) pressures from national manpower demands, and (3) pressures to seek out and encourage members of minority groups to achieve.[34] They suggest that mobility, either upward or downward, often increases prejudice because of prestige insecurity; that manpower demands may be viewed as a way of entering upper social strata; and that the counselor has to consider the needs of youth.

RELUCTANCE TO CHANGE

One deterrent to clarifying counselor role is the resistance to change among counseling practitioners. Some cling inexorably to the crust of custom, tradition, and inertia. Their interest is best served by lack of role clarification. This type of resistance is an old story and can likewise be seen in other professions, such as medicine and law. The sense of consistency and security experienced by the individual who is habituated to a particular role concept makes it difficult for him to accommodate a new conception. When he is subjected to the demands of a different role definition, the potential of failure to achieve a personal accommodation to it looms large. Transition from the old to the new has its perils, for when men give up the assurance of old certitudes, frequently they fear they may never attain such assurance in the new.

Roskens has commented that self-imposed encumbrances, myopic vision, and sterile imagination hinder the development of a rigorous and vital counseling discipline.[35] He calls for a "marked propensity for change" within counseling ranks. He cites four factors — the confusion attached to the terms "guidance" and "counseling," the inability of counselors to establish and communicate a theoretical frame of reference, the maintenance of a "dependency complex" among some counselees seen by counselors, and the segmenting of counseling into personal, vocational, and educational — as limiting clarification of counseling role.

PROFESSIONAL ISOLATION

There is no doubt that the counselor's work setting is associated with counselor role definition. The work setting of one counselor may be shared by other counselors, while that of another counselor may include teachers and administrators but no other counselor.

Wasson and Strowig noted that "a rapidly growing body of research and theory regarding social conformity, reference group processes, and cognitive dissonance appears to offer plausible support to certain differentiations between professionally isolated and unisolated counselors."[36] They sought to determine (1) whether the isolated counselor (no other counselor in the school) was distinguished from the nonisolated counselor, (2) whether isolated counselors were more satisfied with their jobs than nonisolates, (3) whether isolated counselors believed that teachers and administrators were more supportive of guidance, and (4) whether isolated counselors were less active in professional organizations than their nonisolated counterparts. Their subjects were counselors in 40 Wisconsin secondary schools (20 with more than one counselor and 20 with but a single counselor). Isolates rated their positions as more satisfying than did nonisolated counselors ($P < .05$). Isolated counselors perceived their administrators and faculties as more supportive of guidance than did nonisolates ($P < .01$). Nonisolated counselors used the counseling profession as a source of leadership in their work and reported more professional reading than did isolated counselors ($P < .01$). However, no significant difference was found between the two groups' participation in professional organizations.

[34] Gilbert D. Moore and Eugene L. Gaier, "Social Forces and Counselor Role," *Counselor Education and Supervision,* Vol. 3 (Fall, 1963), pp. 29–36.

[35] Ronald W. Roskens, "Memorandum to Counselors: 'Pry Loose Old Walls,' " *The School Counselor,* Vol. 11 (December, 1963), pp. 79–84.

[36] Robert M. Wasson and R. Wray Strowig, "Professional Isolation and Counselor Role," *Personnel and Guidance Journal,* Vol. 43 (January, 1965), pp. 457–460.

Wasson and Strowig report that professionally isolated counselors tend to use teachers and administrators as reference groups more than do those who work in schools with other counselors.

Kaplan has also stated that "New counselors who work 'alone' as the only counselor on the staff in a school system report a greater number of problems in performing their duties than do other new counselors."[37]

DETERMINING OTHERS

It has been said many times in this book and elsewhere that the expectations of others in the counselor's work situation bear upon role definition. While these determining others do not all share equally in role definition, their conflicting expectations are another reason why consensus has yet to be reached in defining counselor role. The most frequently mentioned groups include counselor educators, state guidance supervisors, state license certifiers, school administrators, professional organizations, students, parents, teachers, school board members, and community laymen.

The expectations these groups hold for the counselor have been the subject of much research inquiry. Since summaries of the latter have been reported previously by these authors,[38] no attempt will be made to cover it here. However, some comments are in order: Counselor educators are much involved in defining counselor role through the preparation program. State directors of guidance and those who certify school counselors significantly influence counselors. Every state requires certification of school counselors. State directors of guidance are instrumental in determining the criteria by which counselors and their schools will be supported by state and federal funds. The administrator who nominates, selects, and recommends to his school board the appointment of school counselors is influential; all too often, he is the one who directs their day-to-day efforts and thus does more to define who and what counselors are than any other single individual. Teachers and other school workers hold expectations for counselors that often conflict with the counselor's own role perceptions. Students and parents have definite ideas about the counselor which must be taken into account; the effect of their expectations upon actual counselor functioning has yet to be established, but more and more attention is being paid to the matter. Professional guidance organizations have long appointed committees and task forces to formulate statements of counselor role.

Using two previous studies which examined the perceptions of counselor educators and of school counselors relative to role determinants as a basis, Herr and Cramer examined the degree of congruity in rank order determinants between these two groups.[39] The earlier studies were those of Cramer,[40] who polled 131 counselor educators of wide geographic dispersion, and Mayer,[41] who used a similar questionnaire with 400 New York State public school counselors. Table 6.1 reproduces Herr and Cramer's rank order of role determinants as perceived by selected counselor educators compared to counselors working in New York State public schools.

The similarities and differences between the two groups in their perceptions of counselor role determinants seem self-evident. More fundamental is why disparities exist. Herr and Cramer speculate that counselor educators lack objectivity in their

[37] Bernard A. Kaplan, "The New Counselor and His Professional Problems," *Personnel and Guidance Journal,* Vol. 42 (January, 1964), pp. 473–478.

[38] See Bruce Shertzer and Shelley C. Stone, *Fundamentals of Guidance,* 2nd ed. (Boston: Houghton Mifflin Company, 1971), pp. 158–164.

[39] Edwin L. Herr and Stanley H. Cramer, "Counselor Role Determinants as Perceived by Counselor Educators and School Counselors," *Counselor Education and Supervision,* Vol. 5 (Fall, 1965), pp. 3–8.

[40] Stanley H. Cramer, "A Collation of the Roles of the Secondary School Counselor and the School Psychologist as Perceived by Educators of Counselors and Educators of School Psychologists," unpublished doctor of education dissertation, Teachers College, Columbia University, 1964.

[41] Frank C. Mayer, "An Investigation of Role Perception of Secondary School Guidance Counselors in New York State," unpublished doctor of education dissertation, Teachers College, Columbia University, 1963.

Table 6.1 Perceptions of counselor role determinants by selected counselor educators as compared to New York State school counselors

Rank	Counselor educators Determinant (Cramer) (N = 131)	Rank	New York State school counselors Determinant (Mayer) (N = 400)
1.5	Counselor educators	1	Principal
1.5	Abilities of counselor	2	Abilities of counselor
3	Principal	3	Guidance supervisor
4	Superintendent	4	Students
5	Guidance supervisor	5	Superintendent
6	Community	6	Teachers
7	Board of education	7	Parents
8	Students	8	Board of education
9	Teachers	9	Community
10	Professional organizations	10	Counselor educators
11	Parents	11	State education department
12	State education department	12	Professional organizations

SOURCE: Edwin L. Herr and Stanley H. Cramer, "Counselor Role Determinants as Perceived by Counselor Educators and School Counselors," *Counselor Education and Supervision*, Vol. 5 (Fall, 1965), p. 4. Copyright © 1965 American Personnel and Guidance Association. Reprinted with permission.

perception of training as a prime determinant because they are threatened and seek to justify their importance in the subsequent life of practicing school counselors. It may be, they also add, that counselor educators lack sufficient experience in secondary schools and maintain little contact with counselors after they complete training; hence they are unfamiliar with issues and pressures existing in the school situation. Haettenschwiller points out that while counselor educators are responsible for communicating the professional attributes of the counselor's role, they lack the sanctions to make sure that counselors enact role behaviors in accordance with the profession's views. Rather, it is the principal who is able to apply positive sanctions (such as praise, providing secretarial help, salary increases) or negative sanctions (criticism, termination of contract, etc.)[42] The low ranking given to professional organizations and state education departments as role determinants was seen by Herr and Cramer as stemming from the lack of consensus on what school counselors should be doing. The low ranking of students as role determinants by counselor educators raises questions as to whether student needs so often cited in the literature are realities or illusions to the group.

Present Conceptions of Counselor Role and Function

Answering the ubiquitous questions "Who am I?" (role) and "What do I do?" (function) is a provocative, urgent, and continuing challenge to every individual in the counseling profession. The role of the counselor as an adequately educated, professionally competent, functioning person reacting and relating to the needs of those he serves is but in the formative stage in most work settings. Clarification of the role will lead to commitment to the tasks of the occupation. It will enable the school counselor, for instance, to differentiate his services to students from the services provided by others — psychologists, teachers, etc. Counselors, individually and collectively, retain the responsibility for functionally differentiating their services from those provided by others.

This is not to say that all counselors will work in identical fashion. One counselor's functions will differ from those of others in terms of the setting in which he works, his personality, and his training and experience. But despite diversity of individual activities, commonalities do exist among counselors and make possible a generalized definition of function. If counselors themselves do not take primary responsibility for this definition, others, by default, will do so. The definition must be firm enough to provide counselors a basis for

[42] Dunstan L. Haettenschwiller, "Control of the Counselor's Role," *Journal of Counseling Psychology*, Vol. 17 (September, 1970), pp. 437–442.

professional identity but at the same time sufficiently flexible to encourage growth and change within the profession.

When school counselors belonging to the American School Counselor Association were asked what they expected the basic activities in 1980 would be, 57 per cent of the suggestions involved counseling with students.[43] One wonders why counseling is for the future. Why not now? Surely the need is as great now as it will be in another 5 years.

The counselors' commitment to provide counseling is far too often conspicuous by its absence in actual performance. Many counselors describe their work in terms of child accounting, ranging from attendance to the granting of excuses, administering discipline, substitute teaching, sponsoring group activities, and *some* counseling. In study after study counselors have indicated that their actual role behavior fell short of an idealized role definition. Stevic has commented upon this gap:

> This suggests that the counselor has learned to identify certain activities as representing an idealized, other established role although he may not have learned how to go about making this role operative. The counselor needs to spend time thinking what his commitment should and can be and then, more importantly, how he can perform in accordance with that commitment.[44]

Martinson and Winborn believe that the counselor's inability to define his role may be due to his (1) too willing assumption of any task to gain school acceptance, (2) undue striving to please, and (3) conflicts stemming from past experience as a teacher.[45]

A GRAPHIC VIEW OF COUNSELOR ROLE

Farrah believes that the distinction between counselor role and function is clarified by Figure 6.5. Her graphic representation of the role of the counselor shows the interrelationship of the various areas in which the counselor is involved and the functions derived from the role.[46] Formulation of role enables the counselor to define various goals toward which he will be working. Counselor functions, then, are those activities in which he engages to reach his goals or fulfill his role.

THE COUNSELOR AS A QUASI ADMINISTRATOR

Traditionally, the role enacted by many counselors was that of a quasi administrator or an administrative handyman. The counselor often served as administrator when the principal was out of the building, took disciplinary action, was responsible for extracurricular activities, sponsored the student council, assigned teachers and students to classes, administered schoolwide achievement and ability tests, and enrolled new students; when he interviewed students individually, it was usually only for program planning purposes. Presumably, few counselor education programs prepared the individual for this burden but the situation demanded that he shoulder it. Counselors often were given or assumed the title "dean of boys" or "dean of girls."

Until 1960 this role description was the most frequently encountered one in American secondary schools. It stressed little counseling contact with students, leaning rather toward efficient administrative management of the student body. Hidden beneath tiers of officialdom, bureaucracy, and formality, the student was often forgotten. Apparently there was neither time, opportunity, nor interest to provide the individual contact necessary to implement counseling services as such in the school. Because the counselor lacked the requisite skills and educational experiences, the comfortable role of administrative student body management was both attractive and fitting as he entered the field. Although vestiges of this outmoded concept remain,

[43] Reported in Wrenn, *The Counselor in a Changing World,* pp. 113–118.
[44] Richard Stevic, "A New Strategy for Assessing Counselor Role," *The School Counselor,* Vol. 14 (November, 1966), p. 95.
[45] William D. Martinson and Bob Winborn, "Are We Our Worst Enemies?" *The School Counselor,* Vol. 12 (December, 1964), pp. 86–87.
[46] Ann Farrah, "Counselor Role: A Graphic View," *The School Counselor,* Vol. 13 (May, 1966), pp. 223–224.

Figure 6.5 Counselor role and functions

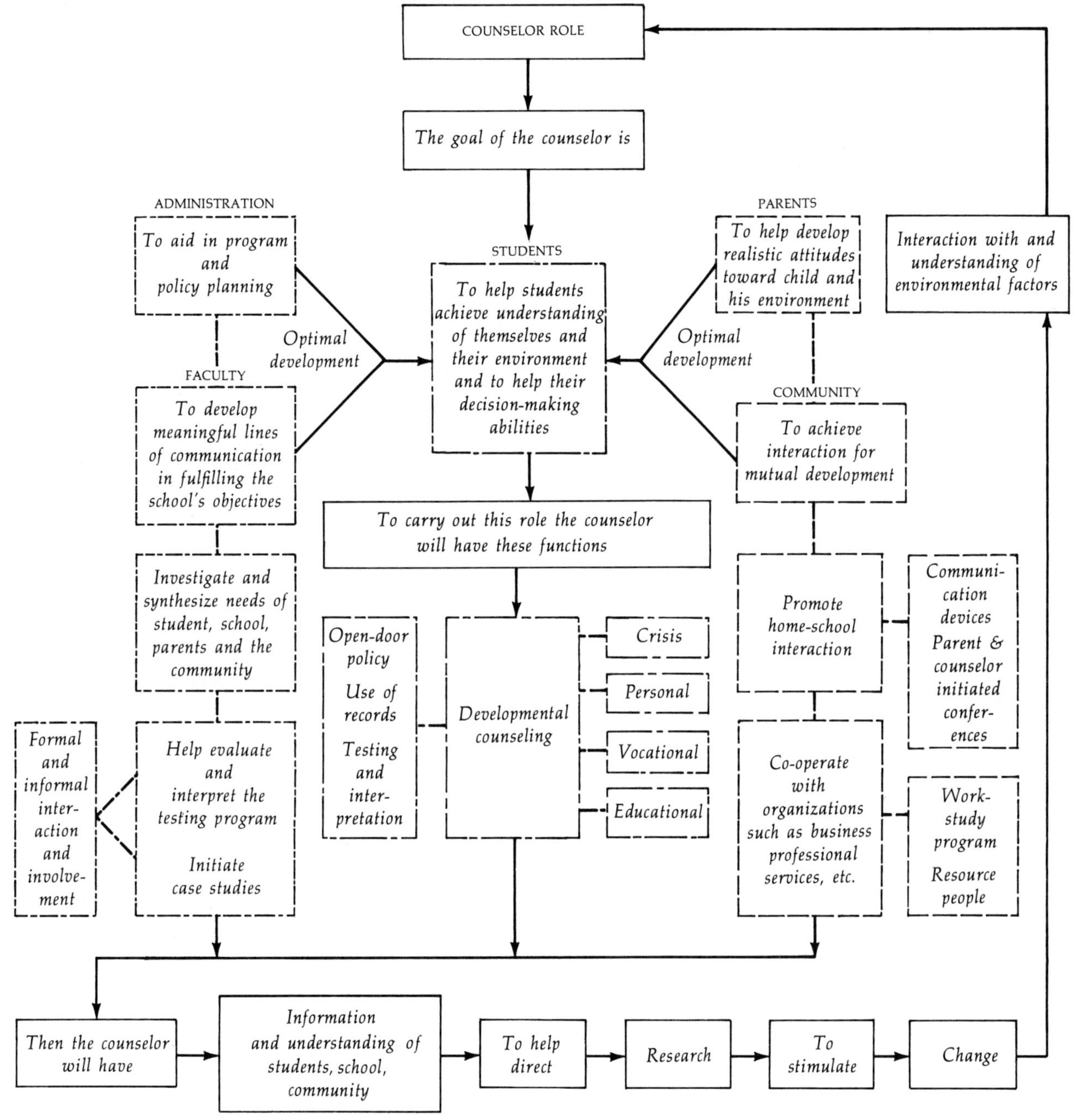

SOURCE: Ann Farrah, "Counselor Role: a Graphic View," *The School Counselor,* Vol. 13 (May, 1966), pp. 224–225. Copyright © 1966 American Personnel and Guidance Association. Reprinted with permission.

marked change began with the entry (1959) of counselors prepared under the NDEA Counseling and Guidance Institutes. The change was due to many factors, but a most instrumental one was the requirement of a counseling practicum in the entry-level preparation of counselors. The institute program certainly helped foster full-time counselor study and generally upgraded counselor education.

COUNSELOR DEFINED AS A GENERALIST

One definition of the counselor is that he is a generalist. Dugan defined the generalist as the counselor who gives priority to orientation, group guidance, registration, class scheduling, course changes, cumulative record development, testing and other appraisal, special class placement, scholarship and college application information and procedures, etc., in addition to some counseling.[47] Those who view the counselor as a specialist contend that his task is to counteract the harmful effects of specialization and impersonality. His objective is to facilitate individual learning, personal planning, and decision making and to be the prime advocate urging attention to individual differences. Essentially, those who view the counselor as a generalist believe that he coordinates and administers services and resources. He gives less time to counseling and more time to improving the relationships among teachers, administrators, parents and community resource personnel, and students. Advocates of a generalist's role for the counselor believe that his preparation lacks sufficient depth to enable him to perform in any other than a preventive, developmental way.

Effective discharge of the responsibilities frequently attributed to the generalist would demand a social scientist possessing uncommon background and preparation. In effect his role would overlap with the roles of even more of the school personnel than at present. He would, by definition, not only preempt responsibilities of teachers and mental hygiene workers but duplicate the efforts of curriculum specialists, principals, and perhaps even superintendents. Many believe that a more restricted role would be more suitable.

COUNSELOR DEFINED AS A SPECIALIST

Dugan's definition of the counselor as a specialist was that he would give counseling priority over all other activities and ideally would counsel exclusively.[48] Those who advance this counselor role claim that the generalist role spreads the counselor so thinly that he has little or no impact upon students. Further, teachers and others with preparation different from the counselor's could conduct many of the services performed by a generalist. Finally, the need is great for intensive, therapeutic counseling to foster individual development.

Knowles and Shertzer devised an attitude scale containing 80 items which reflected the specialist and generalist viewpoints.[49] It was submitted to a random sample of 500 members of the Association for Counselor Education and Supervision, 500 members of the American Association of School Administrators, and 500 members of the American School Counselor Association. Usable returns were received from 291 (58 per cent) ACES members, 289 (58 per cent) ASCA members, and 287 (57 per cent) AASA members. Factor analysis was used to arrive at an empirical grouping of the 80 items which provided a further basis of comparison among the different professional groups. While ACES, ASCA, and AASA members clustered around the middle of the scale, significant differences were found among the groups in their attitudes toward the secondary school counselor's role. These differences may be explained in terms of experience and training; that is, those who have had many courses in guidance, counseling, and psychology tend toward the specialist position

[47] Willis E. Dugan, "Guidance in the 1970's," *The School Counselor,* Vol. 10 (March, 1963), pp. 96–100.

[48] *Ibid.*

[49] Richard T. Knowles and Bruce Shertzer, "Attitudes Toward the School Counselor's Role," *Counselor Education and Supervision,* Vol. 5 (Fall, 1965), pp. 9–20.

whereas those with more secondary school experience and less course work tend toward the generalist position.

> These results indicate that a counselor is probably trained to be a specialist in a counseling setting and hired to be a generalist in the total school setting. The counselor himself takes a middle-of-the-road position, although his attitudes toward his role more closely resemble the individual who trains him than the person who hires him. It would seem imperative that these three groups discuss their differences and come to a close agreement concerning the role of the secondary school counselor. This agreement might lead to less tension because each group, including counselors, would have more similar expectations concerning counselor role. But, more importantly, it would lead to more effective service to students.[50]

Later, these two authors administered the scale to a random sample of 123 members of Division 16 of the American Psychological Association.[51] Usable returns were received from 74 (60 per cent). School psychologists perceived counselors as being generalists more than did ACES members ($P < .001$) and even ASCA ($P < .05$). However, they did not see the counselor as a generalist as much as did school administrators ($P < .001$). The question arises as to why school psychologists did not follow the pattern expected on the basis of training and experience since these two variables had earlier been shown to be significant. Knowles and Shertzer speculated,

> Our explanation for the pattern of school psychologists' scores may be found in the area of role perception. An individual is apt to see the roles of others from a perceptual framework in which his own role is the center. When another person's role overlaps with one's own, the tendency is to emphasize role differences in order to maintain a consistent role perception. The result is a clear, formal perceptual differentiation of roles despite the fact that in reality they may not be so clearly distinct.[52]

COUNSELOR DEFINED AS AN AGENT FOR CHANGE

Among recent role formulations is that of the counselor as an agent for change. In this view the counselor not only is an expert in learning theory — he knows the barriers that prevent and the conditions that facilitate learning — but he is able to communicate his knowledge meaningfully to others. He is sophisticated in the features and consequences of social change and can make innovations in the institution in which he is employed.

The late C. Harold McCully, Specialist in Guidance, U.S. Office of Education, was one who regarded the counselor as an agent for change. He cited four shortcomings in American social processes and two in the schools which he believed provided mandates for defining the school counselor as an agent of change.[53] The social needs or shortcomings included (1) loss of effective methods for inducting youth into full participating membership in adult society, (2) work instability which results from the accelerated change of a rapidly advancing technology, (3) an "overdeveloped" society which needs increasingly more trained manpower at the highest levels of intellectual ability and constantly decreasing manpower at the lowest reaches of mental ability, and (4) an increasingly corporate society which depresses individualism. The shortcomings of the school included (1) its failure to deal with individual differences and (2) its failure to expect and obtain excellence among all pupils.

McCully believed that these forces threaten individuality and self-definition and cause an increasing sense of meaninglessness and alienation. It is the counselor's job to intervene in the lives of individuals to combat and arrest these trends, to en-

[50] *Ibid.*, p. 17.
[51] Richard Knowles and Bruce Shertzer, "Attitudes of School Psychologists Toward the Role of the School Counselor," *Journal of School Psychology*, Vol. 4 (Summer, 1966), pp. 30–36.

[52] *Ibid.*, p. 34.
[53] C. Harold McCully, "The Counselor — Instrument of Change," *Teachers College Record*, Vol. 66 (February, 1965), pp. 405–412.

able individuals to experience the meaning of freedom and responsibility.

Blocher's approach to counseling is centered around facilitating human development, which is an interaction process between the individual and his environment.[54] "Unless the developing individual can exist in a milieu within family, within school, and within community where some rather high degree of understanding of developing needs and processes can be found, much of the work of the counselor will be hopelessly difficult."[55] Blocher seems dubious that the counselor can serve as a change agent for three reasons: (1) Present counselors lack the training, background and experience (that of a behavioral scientist), (2) the role of the counselor does not permit him to operate as an effective agent of change (the boat rocker often is not seen as a helping person), and (3) his position in the school is not such that he can become an effective agent of change (present-day counselors are neither administrators nor teachers but rather operate in a "no man's land").

Shoben is another who seeks to have counselors think of themselves as change agents.[56] In his view the counselor should serve (1) as a human feedback mechanism for assessing the impact of the school and informing its personnel thereof and (2) as a catalyst for clarifying the character of the school as a community and as a source of appropriate models for developing youngsters.

> Willy-nilly, the school represents a society-in-little. The challenge before it is whether it can transform itself into a developmentally productive one on an articulate and informed basis and, by a regular and planful process of self-appraisal, maintain itself as a true growth enhancing community. In such an effort to sharpen the impact of the school and to give it greater cogency for individual students, guidance workers can play a key role, forging, in the course of it, a genuine new profession for themselves.[57]

Baker and Cramer[58] view the counselor-as-change-agent as one who moves against the status quo when he believes it hurts those he is trying to help. However, they also believe that today's counselor cannot be active as a change agent because there is no power base to support him, either in the school or the profession, and because the status quo forces would retaliate and inundate counselors who actively promoted change. These authors believe that the most that can be presently expected is for counselors to help clients choose some course of action which the clients themselves initiate. In so doing, change may be achieved without the counselor risking direct confrontation with status quo oriented people in his institution and profession.

COUNSELOR DEFINED AS A SPECIALIST IN PSYCHOLOGICAL EDUCATION

Counselors who assume this role would be responsible for developing and implementing systematic curriculum activities and programs designed to facilitate self-development. Many have noted that educational institutions offer courses designed to develop the intellect but few provide systematic ways to facilitate emotional development. Ivey and Weinstein[59] described the content of two programs they constructed separately to refocus what counselors do. According to their view, the counselor would be involved in developing a psychological curriculum offered in group settings ranging from year-long elective courses to short, experimental minicourses in self-understanding and human relations. Such curricular activities would help individuals exhibit personal openness, spontaneity, emotional expressiveness and relaxation.

[54] Donald Blocher, "Can the Counselor Function as an Effective Agent of Change?" *The School Counselor,* Vol. 13 (May, 1966), pp. 202–205.
[55] *Ibid.*, p. 203.
[56] E. Shoben, Jr., "Guidance: Remedial Function or Social Reconstruction?" *Harvard Educational Review,* Vol. 32 (Fall, 1962), pp. 431–443.
[57] *Ibid.*, p. 442.
[58] Stanley B. Baker and Stanley H. Cramer, "Counselor or Change Agent: Support From the Profession," *Personnel and Guidance Journal,* Vol. 50 (April, 1972), pp. 661–665.
[59] Allen E. Ivey and Gerald Weinstein, "The Counselor as Specialist in Psychological Education," *Personnel and Guidance Journal,* Vol. 49 (October 1970), pp. 98–107.

Sprinthall[60] asked whether those who urge humanistic guidance do not beg the question of goals and objectives as much as those who stress decision making, adjustment, individualization of learning, etc. He pointed out that while openness, spontaneity, etc., are topical and current, they are still arbitrary, time-limited, and situational goals. A suggested alternative, presented by Mosher and Sprinthall[61] is lodged in developmental psychology where interventions promote personal, moral, or attitudinal growth and development in a sequence of stages.

COUNSELOR DEFINED AS AN APPLIED BEHAVIORAL SCIENTIST

Counselors are increasingly portrayed as applied behavioral scientists. Berdie's description of the 1980 counselor outlines an educational program to prepare such practitioners.[62] According to Berdie, the counselor's job will be to apply theory and research derived from the various behavioral sciences to help individuals and institutions achieve their purposes. He predicts that counselors will provide "... experiences that will facilitate individual development most efficiently."

The image of the counselor as an applied behavioral scientist suggests that he arranges experiences so that his clients learn to act upon their environment. Matheny[63] urges counselors to make better use of school and community environments to provide concrete experiences so that students can more fully identify their interests, aptitudes, and values. The counselor as a behavioral scientist would be engaged in formulating and providing his clients with real and simulated work as well as social experiences that correct and extend their decision making and interpersonal relationships.

COUNSELOR DEFINED AS A CONTINGENCY MANAGER

The emerging and fast-growing use of technology and behavior modification techniques in counseling has led many to describe the school counselor as one who serves as a contingency manager and consultant to teachers who apply behavior modification in their classrooms. A contingency manager is defined by Toews[64] as a person who arranges consequences for behavior, i.e., he *pays off* for behavior. Toews presents several case studies which illustrate how counselors perform these two principal functions.

THE COUNSELOR-CONSULTANT ROLE

Current descriptions of counselor role (published as well as verbal) most commonly define the counselor as one who (1) counsels individuals and small groups and (2) consults with teachers, administrators, parents, and others. While this definition has yet to achieve universal acceptance, it has become increasingly prominent. More and more counselors agree that facilitating the personal development of individuals in these two ways is indeed the essence of their work.

COUNSELOR AS A HELPING PROFESSIONAL

In a very provocative article on professionalization Stefflre discussed the process of identifying with an occupation.[65] The elements are four-fold: (1) acceptance of the name of the occupation as a part of the self-concept of the worker, (2) commitment to the task of the occupation, (3) commitment to the goals of the institution, and (4) recognition of the significance of the

[60] Norman A. Sprinthall, "Humanism: A New Bag of Virtues for Guidance?" *Personnel and Guidance Journal,* Vol. 50 (January 1972), pp. 349–356.
[61] Ralph L. Mosher and Norman A. Sprinthall, "Psychological Education in Secondary Schools: A Program to Promote Individual and Human Development," *American Psychologist,* Vol. 25 (October, 1970), pp. 911–924.
[62] Ralph F. Berdie, "The 1980 Counselor: Applied Behavioral Scientist," *Personnel and Guidance Journal,* Vol. 50 (February 1972), p. 451.
[63] Kenneth Matheny, "Counselors as Environmental Engineers," *Personnel and Guidance Journal,* Vol. 49 (February 1971), pp. 439–444.

[64] Jay M. Toews, "The Counselor as a Contingency Manager," *Personnel and Guidance Journal,* Vol. 48 (October, 1969), pp. 127–134.
[65] Stefflre, *op. cit.*

occupation to society. Stefflre was dubious that present-day counselors met these criteria to any great extent.

> As an occupation becomes a profession its members select an appropriate "hidden audience" for which their role will be played. What is the hidden audience for school counselors? Some seem to be doing their job so as to merit the attention and the applause of psychologists. They identify with psychologists, they think of themselves as psychological counselors, they have little feeling for education, and may wince at being called educators (or worse – "educationists"). Other counselors may select as their hidden audience the school administrator and behave in a way to attract his admiration. Still others may select as their hidden audience teachers or students or the community. However, the number of school counselors who select other school counselors as their hidden audience would seem to be few. Our professional identification is so diffused that we cannot select a model for ourselves from among ourselves but rather must look elsewhere for significant professional others.[66]

Since the task of establishing and integrating a professional identity is difficult, unsatisfactory completion is not uncommon. Verbalizing "this is what I am as a counselor" involves public self-definition and consequently immobilizes some counselors when they are faced with declaring themselves. But more and more are painfully aware of the demand to do so. Commitment to a role model is often avoided because the individual is aware of internal confusion and does not wish to come to terms with his uncertainties, ambivalence, and incompatibilities. For some counselors the lure of an external answer is great indeed. They find it easier to believe that the problem of counselor role lies not with themselves but outside; it is something that exists for others and may perhaps be clutched and made their own.

Some authoritative statements of professional leaders and associations define the counselor as a helping person who counsels and consults. Roeber has studied roles and functions of counselors in various settings.[67] For the employment service counselor he says,

> This array of statements rather clearly defines a counselor's role(s) as one of helping clients (of any age, sex, occupational history) to higher levels of vocational adjustment . . . a counselor in the employment service "is more concerned with the tangible or *product* aspects of counseling outcome than with reconstructing the emotive or process of a counselee's personality." His immediate task is helping a client become optimally employed as quickly as feasible, relying upon other agency or community resources when employability depends upon fundamental, long-term changes in attitudes, values, needs, and other personality dimensions. As stated earlier, an employment counselor's role is rather clear-cut and unequivocal, a condition that is unique to this group of counselors as contrasted with subsequent groups.[68]

Roeber defined the roles of counselors who work in state rehabilitation settings and in the Veterans Administration Department of Medicine and Surgery and the Department of Veterans Benefits:

> . . . a rehabilitation counselor, like an employment counselor, is concerned with optimum vocational adjustment of his clients. However, a rehabilitation counselor is constantly working within medical limits, those associated with his client's disabilities as well as those imposed by the nature of different work, and educational settings. These are four roles which are more explicitly stated in the case of rehabilitation counselors than are apparent from statements about the roles of employment counselors: (a) rehabilitation counselors are much more active in coordinating all services, medical and community agencies, for their clients; (b) rehabilitation counselors are much more active in arranging for employment of clients; (c) rehabilitation counselors are permitted more freedom in providing assistance until vocational adjustment is or seems assured; and (d) rehabilitation counselors are given more latitude in providing assistance in cases where personal or emotional problems are affecting rehabilitation efforts.[69]

[66] *Ibid.*, pp. 656–657.

[67] Edward C. Roeber, "Roles and Functions of Professionally Trained Counselors," in McGowan (ed.), *op. cit.*, pp. 193–210.

[68] *Ibid.*, p. 195.

[69] *Ibid.*, pp. 196–197.

Roeber's statement with respect to counselors employed in educational settings is as follows:

> . . . a school counselor is concerned with developmental needs and problems of pupils. As immediate roles are examined, a school counselor seems to be concerned with helping pupils understand themselves and accept themselves and the world in which they live. In addition the counselor helps pupils develop a sense of responsibility for and a competency in decision-making.[70]

Roeber goes on to enumerate the functions of counselors in each of these settings.

Wrenn, noting the distinction between performing a function directly and seeing that it is done, proposed that the school counselor is responsible directly for

> a. *Counseling with students* on matters of self-understanding, decision-making, and planning, using both the interview and group situations;
> b. *consulting with staff and parents* on questions of student understanding and management;
> c. *studying changes in the character of the student population* and making a continuing interpretation of this information to the school administration and to curriculum-development committees;
> d. *performing a liaison function* between other school and community counseling resources and facilitating their use by teachers and students.[71]

In his second look at counselor role — some three years later — Wrenn pointed out that he would build certain emphases but not replace his 1962 statement. These emphases were four in number: (1) The school counselor is a team worker always — with teacher, parent, and principal — and he must help them achieve some of their goals. (2) The school counselor is a member of the educational staff of the school and system and therefore not immune to the weary plague of housekeeping duties. (3) The counselor assists the student in better self-understanding, in gaining a sense of self-identity — but as a means to an end rather than as an end in itself. (4) Vocational counseling should be given added emphasis and an attempt made to have counselors see an occupation as part of one's vocation, one's purpose in or commitment to life.[72]

Still later Wrenn proposed a statement of the functions of counselors, regardless of setting. Though it was cited in Chapter One of this book, we repeat it here:

> The function of the counselor in any setting is (a) to provide a *relationship* between counselor and counselee, the most prominent quality of which is that of mutual trust of each in the other; (b) to provide *alternatives* in self-understanding and in the courses of action open to the client; (c) to provide for *some degree of intervention* with the situation in which the client finds himself and with "important others" in the client's immediate life; (d) to provide leadership in developing *a healthy psychological environment* for his clients, and, finally, (e) to provide for *improvement of the counseling process* through constant individual self-criticism and (for some counselors) extensive attention to improvement of process through research.[73]

The American School Counselor Association has published a statement of counselor role and function. Formally started in August, 1962, and submitted to the membership for approval in February, 1964, the statement was completed in March, 1964, and approved by over 90 per cent of the members. The following quotation is drawn from the "professional rationale" of the statement.

> The counselor is dedicated to the idea that most pupils will enhance and enrich their personal development and self-fulfillment by means of making more intelligent decisions if given the opportunity to experience an accepting, non-evaluating relationship in which one is helped to better understand himself, the environment he perceives, and the relationship between these. Counseling is essentially such a relationship. The school counselor

[70] *Ibid.*, p. 195.
[71] Wrenn, *The Counselor in a Changing World*, p. 141.
[72] C. Gilbert Wrenn, "A Second Look," in John F. Loughary, Robert O. Stripling, and Paul W. Fitzgerald (eds.), *Counseling: A Growing Profession* (Washington : American Personnel and Guidance Association, 1965), pp. 59–61.
[73] Wrenn, "Crisis in Counseling: A Commentary and a Contribution," in McGowan (ed.), *op. cit.*, p. 237.

views himself as a person on the school staff with the professional competencies, behavioral science understandings, philosophical orientation and position within the school necessary to provide such help to pupils.[74]

Annotated References

Bentley, Joseph C. (ed.). *The Counselor's Role.* Boston: Houghton Mifflin Company, 1968. 399 pp.

Bentley has selected some 50 journal articles and portions of books that examine various aspects of counselor role and functions. Attention is given to role theory, role expectations, role performance, role conflict, and the future counselor's role. These well-chosen selections highlight the diversity that attend this subject.

Johnson, Dorothy E. and Vestermark, Mary J. *Barriers and Hazards in Counseling.* Boston: Houghton Mifflin Company, 1970. 244 pp.

Part One (pp. 7–86) presents some of the blocks that prevent the counselor from being effective. Treatment is given to the counselor's self-image and professional role, the effects of time and physical setting on the counselor and the many commitments involved. These two authors have presented some very vivid barriers and hazards that face a counselor.

Loughary, John W., *et al.* (eds.). *Counseling: A Growing Profession.* Washington: American Personnel and Guidance Association, 1965. 106 pp.

The book is concerned with the professionalization of counseling. Each of the five chapters is written by someone with nationally recognized competence in counseling. A good understanding of the processes involved in an association's drive to secure preparation standards and a role definition for its members is provided. The chapters by Loughary on new challenges for counselors and by Wrenn on a second look at his previous recommendations for counseling are particularly timely, informative, well written.

Further References

Arbuckle, Dugald S. "Does the School Really Need Counselors?" *The School Counselor,* Vol. 17 (May, 1970). pp. 325–330.

[74] American School Counselor Association, *Statement of Policy for Secondary School Counselors* (Washington: American Personnel and Guidance Association, 1964).

Arbuckle, Dugald S. "The Counselor: Who? What?" *The Personnel and Guidance Journal,* Vol. 50 (June, 1972). pp. 785–791.

Aspy, David N. "The Helper's Tools: Chicken Soup or Rifles." *The Personnel and Guidance Journal,* Vol. 49 (October, 1970). pp. 117–118.

Baker, Stanley B. and Cramer, Stanley H. "Counselor or Change Agent: Support from the Profession." *The Personnel and Guidance Journal,* Vol. 50 (April, 1972). pp. 661–666.

Berdie, Ralph E. "The 1980 Counselor: Applied Behavioral Scientist." *The Personnel and Guidance Journal,* Vol. 50 (February, 1972). pp. 451–456.

Boller, Jon D. "Counselor Certification: Who Still Needs Teaching Experience?" *The Personnel and Guidance Journal,* Vol. 50 (January, 1972). pp. 388–391.

Boy, Angelo V. "The Elementary School Counselor's Role Dilemma." *The School Counselor,* Vol. 19 (January, 1972). pp. 167–172.

Carey, Albert R. and Garris, Donald. "Counselor-Role Differentiation: A New Tack?" *The School Counselor,* Vol. 18 (May, 1971). pp. 349–352.

Cheikin, Martin. "Counseling: Activist or Reactivist." *The School Counselor,* Vol. 19 (November, 1971). pp. 68–70.

Chenault, Joann. "Help-Giving and Morality." *The Personnel and Guidance Journal,* Vol. 48 (October, 1969). pp. 89–96.

Ciavarella, Michael A. and Doolittle, Lawrence W. "The Ombudsman: Relevant Role Model for the Counselor." *The School Counselor,* Vol. 17 (May, 1970). pp. 331–336.

Donigian, Jeremiah and Giglio, Alice. "The Comprehensive Family Counselor: An Innovative Approach to School Counseling." *The School Counselor,* Vol. 19 (November, 1971). pp. 97–101.

Dworkin, Edward P. and Dworkin, Anita L. "The Activist Counselor." *The Personnel and Guidance Journal,* Vol. 49 (May, 1971). pp. 748–753.

Gamboa, Anthony M., Jr. "The Humanistic Counselor in a Technocratic Society." *The School Counselor,* Vol. 19 (January, 1972). pp. 160–166.

Haettenschwiller, Dunstan L. "Control of the Counselor's Role." *Journal of Counseling Psychology,* Vol. 17 (September, 1970). pp. 437–442.

Ivey, Allen E. and Weinstein, Gerald. "The Counselor as Specialist in Psychological Education." *The Personnel and Guidance Journal,* Vol. 49 (October, 1970). pp. 98–107.

Lindberg, Robert E. and Wrenn, C. Gilbert. "Minority Teachers Become Minority Counselors." *The Personnel and Guidance Journal,* Vol. 50 (January, 1972). pp. 371–378.

Lundquist, Gerald W. and Chamley, John C. "Counselor-Consultant: A Move Toward Effectiveness." *The School Counselor,* Vol. 18 (May, 1971). pp. 362–366.

Maser, Arthur L. "Counselor Function in Secondary Schools." *The School Counselor,* Vol. 18 (May, 1971). pp. 367–372.

Matheny, Kenneth. "Counselors as Environmental Engineers." *The Personnel and Guidance Journal,* Vol. 49 (February, 1971). pp. 439–444.

Pancrazio, James J. "The School Counselor as a Human Relations Consultant." *The School Counselor,* Vol. 19 (November, 1971). pp. 81–87.

Sprinthall, Norman A. "A Curriculum for Secondary Schools: Counselors as Teachers for Psychological Growth." *The School Counselor,* Vol. 20 (May, 1973). pp. 361–369.

Toews, Jay M. "The Counselor as Contingency Manager." *The Personnel and Guidance Journal,* Vol. 48 (October, 1969). pp. 127–133.

Trotter, Ann B., Gozali, Joav, and Cunningham, Lila Jane. "Family Participation in the Treatment of Alcoholism." *The Personnel and Guidance Journal,* Vol. 48 (October, 1969). pp. 140–143.

Trotzer, James P. "Do Counselors Do What They Are Taught?" *The School Counselor,* Vol. 18 (May, 1971). pp. 335–342.

Van Hoose, William H. and Kurtz, Sister Marie. "Status of Guidance in the Elementary School: 1968–69." *The Personnel and Guidance Journal,* Vol. 48 (January, 1970). pp. 374–380.

Vassos, Sonya T. and Taylor, Vaughn K. "Militancy and Counselor Relationships Within School and Community." *The School Counselor,* Vol. 17 (May, 1970). pp. 350–356.

PART THREE

COUNSELING APPROACHES

In the substantive body of knowledge which counselors are expected to be able to use are insights about man drawn from the social sciences and explanations of what takes place in counseling provided by counseling theorists. The four chapters in Part Three are directed to them.

Increasing recognition has been given to the fact that counselor skills should be based upon theory and research in the social and behavioral sciences. The intent in Chapter Seven is to identify and describe the contributions that related disciplines — religion, philosophy, political science, anthropology, psychology, economics, sociology — have made to counseling. There is no pretense that each is comprehensively treated. While these disciplines are presented in separate sections for clarity and emphasis, the unity and interrelationships of their contributions are of paramount importance.

Chapters Eight and Nine deal with nine counseling viewpoints. To report even briefly all counseling approaches is beyond the scope of this book. Nor is it possible to treat comprehensively the nine selected for discussion here. Rather, these two chapters have three primary aims: (1) to introduce the fundamental aspects of what nine theoretical viewpoints believe occurs in a counseling relationship, (2) to encourage counselors in preparation to examine the differences and similarities that exist among these theories, and (3) to encourage counselors to sift through theories to ascertain their own stands vis à vis various theoretical positions. While experience is always much richer than the language of science can make allowance for, counseling theories are attempts to organize what occurs in counseling into a coherent pattern. The assumptions or postulates in counseling theory are approximate generalizations usually based upon empirical observations. Some incompleteness is always present but is accepted for the sake of greater simplicity. The point is that although counseling theories are incomplete, the counselor cannot wait until perfection is attained. He must operate on the evidence available to him. Examining conflicting theories is sometimes a traumatizing experience. Closer reflection may reveal, in some cases, that theories complement rather than contradict each other.

Chapter Ten shows how the understandings drawn from the social sciences and counseling theories are utilized by the counselor to develop a personalized philosophy of counseling. Building such a philosophy is a continuous process for those who remain in counseling. The theory and philosophy evolved by the counselor will depend upon his understanding of himself, his views of man, and his experiences.

COUNSELING AND THE SOCIAL SCIENCES

by S. Samuel Shermis

7

The theory and practice of counseling has been expanded and refined both by practitioners within the field and through the use of insights from that group of disciplines known as the social sciences. Psychology, sociology, economics, anthropology, and political science have, particularly during this century, provided both data and comprehensive hypotheses which have been used by counselors. It is the author's belief that a nontechnical discussion of the social sciences, some of their salient characteristics, and their relationship to counseling will assist the future counselor.

What Are the "Social Sciences"?

The social sciences arose in the last two centuries as thinkers applied the method of the physical and natural sciences to understanding human behavior. Since about the 16th century scientists had made astounding progress in explaining the behavior of chemicals, planets, machines, and animals. It appeared to some that if the basic mode of inquiry employed by chemists, astronomers, physicists, and biologists could be used to study human behavior, perhaps a body of information could be built up that was just as accurate and dependable. For most of recorded history, observations of human behavior had been made by discerning and intelligent persons. But such observation, made almost exclusively by poets, novelists, and philosophers, seemed unsystematic, often inaccurate, and sometimes distorted by biases. If the *method* of hypothesis construction, detailed and recorded observation, experimentation, and mathematical analysis could be applied to human social interactions, society could perhaps gain useful insights into why and how people behaved the way they did.

From the perspective of the second half of the 20th century it now appears that social scientists cannot provide the dependability or accuracy of chemists and physicists. Nor, it is now felt by

S. Samuel Shermis is Associate Professor, Department of Education, Purdue University. The authors are pleased to present his treatment of this topic.

many, are the insights of artists completely irrelevant. With the humility forced by a century of experience, social scientists can claim to offer only modest and limited generalizations about human behavior. These are, nevertheless, exceedingly useful. For example, thanks to economists, we know enough to prevent the kind of depression that forced our economy to grind almost to a standstill in 1929. The sociologist's observations required a rather drastic change in our way of looking at the constitutional provision for equal protection: the *Brown vs. Topeka Board of Education* Supreme Court decision of 1954 was based on psychological and sociological data about the effects of segregation. It was, in part, the information of anthropologists who advised General MacArthur in 1945 that enabled the occupation of Japan to proceed as smoothly as it did. It may be asserted that the systematic and tested knowledge of social scientists — although clearly lacking the precision of physical scientists — has allowed societies to operate with fewer crises and dislocations and less friction than in any previous century. What, then, are the characteristics of that mode of inquiry which has provided this limited but useful knowledge?

The social sciences are a loose collection of disciplines which have in common, first, a concern for the study of collective human behavior, and second, a self-conscious use of the scientific method. By "collective" we mean that social scientists study human behavior not as it is exhibited by individual human beings but as it takes place in groups. The groups may range in size from a handful of subjects to an entire culture.[1] The emphasis is on *patterns* of behavior. The social sciences are also scientific in the sense that they use the scientific method of knowing; that is, they make use of hypotheses, perform experiments, collect empirical data, utilize mathematics in the analysis of the data, make predictions, formulate theories, and modify them in the light of more and better data. The social sciences are scientific in another sense. Their procedures are usually characterized by openness, flexibility, precision, willingness to change interpretations, disinclination to generalize recklessly, and a desire to follow data to conclusions which may not be particularly pleasant.

Which disciplines are clearly social sciences is arguable, although most would agree that economics, anthropology, sociology, political science, and psychology are social sciences.[2] Before we deal with these, the discussion will first turn to philosophy and religion, for certain philosophical and theological tenets have seeped into the method and assumptions of the social sciences. That is, from several thousand years of philosophical and theological thought there has emerged a body of *assumptions* — often unspoken and not consciously realized beliefs — that have formed the *Weltanschauung* in which social scientists work. *Weltanschauung* is a German word which means something like "the given intellectual atmosphere of a particular century and culture." Most are not able to identify their intellectual atmosphere and their philosophical assumptions. But there *is* a system of unarticulated beliefs, positions, attitudes, and values which influence thinking, and it is to theology and philosophy that we must turn to see what some of them are and how they have functioned.

Religion and Philosophy

This section is entitled "Religion and Philosophy" even though many will object to coupling the two concepts. To some, religion has to do with the worship of a supernatural deity whereas philosophy is concerned with cool and rational analysis of problems of knowledge and value. Such an oversimplification — rather widespread even among those who should know better — ignores the fact that until fairly recently there was no clear dif-

[1] See, for example, Clyde Kluckhohn, *Mirror for Man* (New York: McGraw-Hill Book Co., Inc., 1944).

[2] Whether history is or ought to be a social science or a member of the humanities is likely to depend upon the outlook of a given historian.

ference between the two activities. Historically, the sharpened distinction between them is a 19th-century phenomenon.

The development of Western philosophy did not take place apart from the Judeo-Christian religious tradition. Concern for "individualism," problems of knowing, value issues, and theories of human nature are not simply "philosophical"; they were also of interest to those who considered themselves basically religious. The best illustration is the history of the concern for individualism in our own society. Some of the most articulate spokesmen for the inherent importance of the individual were Thomas Jefferson, Henry Thoreau, and John Dewey. Although not usually identified with a formal religion, all three derived their inspiration from religious sources: Jefferson was a Deist, Thoreau was part of New England religious transcendentalism, and Dewey was strongly influenced by his parents' Congregationalism and by the religious reformers of his time.

The point is that positions of interest to counselors have long historical roots in a Western tradition which was at the same time both a religious and a philosophical one. With this explanation, let us consider the concept "individualism."

INDIVIDUAL IMPORTANCE

From religion and philosophy in Western civilization have emerged a number of beliefs which are more correctly described as attitudes than positions. First is the importance accorded the individual. Slowly, over several thousand years, the idea has evolved that individuals matter, not for what they can accomplish, not for their services to the state, but because they have value in and of themselves. This attitude, usually designated individualism, has several implications. A person may develop his uniqueness and emphasize his individuality — provided this does not conflict with other values.[3] Individuals ought to be encouraged by significant persons to develop their uniqueness and, under certain circumstances, should be given positive assistance.

Although this may seem an obvious position, it should be pointed out that in another culture a person with problems may be told that his troubles lie in his antisocial attitudes, that if he were to obey the elders, stop rebelling against authority, or observe the regulations more closely, his troubles would cease. In our culture a counselor may take the position that what an individual needs is encouragement to make a more independent, autonomous decision. To encourage an individual to make an autonomous decision implies that one has the right to be unique, to make decisions independently, and to be respected in so doing. Such a view reflects one important strand of religious and philosophical belief in Western civilization.

RATIONALISM

Another important assumption is that rationality provides a more adequate solution to personal problems than irrationality. Again, such an attitude is not universally held. For instance, anthropologists indicate that in some cultures a person with a serious psychiatric or physical disability will consult a witch doctor, who may offer incantations, perform dances, or encourage the afflicted to say special prayers on his own behalf.[4] Social scientists who have taken a new look at these irrational methods concede that they may be quite effective.[5] However, counseling in our dominant culture is based on the assumption that rationality offers the most reliable means of solving problems.

Rationality here refers to the belief that there is a cause-and-effect relationship in the world, that by ordinary deductive and inductive procedures, and by thinking consecutively, one may make accurate diagnoses and formulate desirable solutions. Consecutive, logical, rational thought has been regarded by most philosophers from Aristotle to the

[3] In many societies, particularly preliterate ones, group cohesiveness is so important that what we would call harmless individualism is seen as dangerous, group-threatening, aberrant behavior.

[4] See Ari Kiev, *Magic, Faith, and Healing* (New York: Free Press of Glencoe, Inc., 1964).
[5] *Ibid.*

present as the preferred mode of problem solving. To attribute problems to bad luck, the intervention of hostile spirits or fate, or to substitute wishful thinking or magic for logical analysis of events is — from the standpoint of Western rationalistic philosophy — not a fruitful way of dealing with human problems.

TWO APPROACHES

From philosophy has developed an awareness that man can look at himself in two different ways. Employing *introspection* he can search within himself. He can ask himself what he has seen and experienced and, by reflection, decide what his experiences mean. Or he can *observe the behavior of others* and, by classifying different or similar kinds of behavior, attempt to arrive at reliable generalizations.

These approaches have had a long and somewhat conflicting history. The tendency has been to choose one or the other as exclusive modes of inquiry. Socrates, for instance, felt that objective observation was so inherently unreliable that it could yield only deception, or at best second-order truths. In the late 19th and early 20th centuries social scientists, particularly psychologists, turned away from introspection and began to think not only that it was possible to observe objectively and make completely accurate reports of observed behavior but that this was the sole scientific avenue to truth. The feeling seemed to be that introspection, perhaps appropriate for poets or dramatists, was completely irrelevant to science.[6]

With the recent emphasis on creativity and the rise of existentialism or neophenomenalism,[7] many counseling theoreticians are showing a renewed interest in introspection — although the term "introspection" is not usually employed. At any rate, it seems clear that the reports of how an individual perceives his world or the way he feels about himself constitutes an important source of valid evidence about that individual. This does not, of course, deny that data about a person secured by objective tests may also be another source of evidence. At present, counselors make use of both kinds of evidence — objective information and reports of personal feelings — although it may be hard to know when to employ each kind of evidence.

VALUE THEORY

Even though social scientists have often rejected — and even ridiculed — philosophy,[8] many of them have come to see that philosophical analysis, of at least two kinds, is quite useful and perhaps necessary. These two types of analysis, called technically ontology and axiology, are concerned, respectively, with perceptions of *reality* and with *value theory.* Both entire cultures and individuals within cultures seem to have distinctive ways of looking at reality. For instance, if we compare the medieval world, with its belief in the literal existence of supernatural powers (ghosts, spirits, imps, devils, succubi, incubi, angels), and the 20th century, which tends to deny supernatural manifestations and leans heavily on experimental science, we see a contrast in modes of perceiving reality. To the medieval world imps sent by the devil to plague God-fearing men were as real as molecules are to us.[9] Perhaps because of an awareness of theories of reality and of differing perceptions social scientists have largely abandoned the search for absolutes — that is, never-changing and completely permanent truth — and have been content to settle for more modest and limited generalizations.

Awareness of value theory has also influenced both the method and the content of the social sciences. Social psychologists and sociologists have

[6] See the section on natural law in S. Samuel Shermis, *Philosophic Foundations of Education* (New York: American Book Company, 1967).

[7] "Phenomenalism" is a late 19th and early 20th century school of both philosophy and psychology in which the emphasis is on human experience as the starting point in the search for truth.

[8] It has been held that philosophy was simply speculation and had little to do with observation, data gathering, testing, and mathematical analysis. Probably the more recently trained and more sophisticated social scientists realize that their philosophical assumptions influence not only the way they perceive the world but also the conclusions they reach.

[9] See Rossell H. Robbins, *Encyclopedia of Witchcraft and Demonology* (New York: Crown Publishers, Inc., 1959).

recently been studying values, primarily by looking closely at the wants, preferences, and desires of individuals, cultures, subcultures, and even civilizations. For instance, although Americans are prone to perceive the suppression of individual freedom in Communist or Socialist countries as a very bad thing, they often fail to realize that free expression is simply not seen by them as a dominant value. Soviet observers of the American scene are equally shocked at what they look on as our obsession with private property and profit, which they are likely to consider harmful and corrupting.[10] In other words, Soviet and American value structures are different. Although stating it this way may appear to be a platitude, the inability of members of each culture to perceive the other's value structure has engendered considerable suspicion and perhaps endangered world peace.[11]

Counselors can make direct use of a number of philosophical constructs in the area of values. Some philosophers have categorized two kinds of values: *conceived* and *operative.* A conceived value is one which an individual verbalizes. An operative value is what he is observed to desire. For instance, one may express health as a conceived value; he says that he believes it is important to stay healthy. This same person may smoke two packs of cigarettes a day, even though he "knows" that he is probably injuring his health. The counselor will frequently note that his client is suffering from a personal problem which upon analysis may be diagnosed as a conflict between a conceived and an operative value. One may simultaneously say that it is a good thing to obey authority yet in fact experience constant friction with parents because he feels they are unreasonable.

In this instance we can perhaps appreciate the growing awareness of philosophy by counselors. The boy or girl who has strife-ridden relationships with parents or other authorities provides a problem that counselors tend to analyze in psychological terms; and of course it is a psychological problem. But the problem may also be approached with the philosopher's insights, and to see the distinction between an operative and a conceived value may enhance both the counselor's understanding of the problem and his treatment of it.

PHILOSOPHICAL AND PSYCHOLOGICAL INTEGRATION

Another illustration of the bearing of philosophy on counselors is shown in the similarity between an integrated personality and an integrated philosophical system. There seems to be some agreement that in a healthy personality the different elements are integrated. The individual's perception of himself is in harmony with reality; his desires match his moral code; his value structure is so arranged that he knows not only what he wants but how much he wants it. In philosophical terms, he has an integrated axiological position — a harmonious relationship between all parts of his wants, wishes, and desires.

From philosophy — particularly some recent schools of philosophy — we have come to see that it is possible to put together either a piecemeal, haphazard, eclectic patchwork of philosophical positions or a unified, harmonious, consistent position. Realization of this fact by counselors suggests that the goal of counseling may be phrased in philosophical terms: To assist an individual to reach the maximum use of his potential requires that he develop a consistent philosophical outlook.

PHILOSOPHY AS A PLAN FOR LIVING

The last point suggests that the definition of philosophy — or rather, one definition of philosophy[12] — is of potential interest to counselors. Phil-

[10] We are indebted to social psychologist Urie Bronfenbrenner for his detailed studies of Soviet life and value structure. See his "Soviet Methods of Character Education: Some Implications for Research," *American Psychologist,* Vol. 17 (August, 1962), pp. 550–564.

[11] C. E. Osgood, *An Alternative to War or Surrender* (Urbana: University of Illinois Press, 1962).

[12] One sure way of engaging a philosopher in a dispute is to quote a definition of philosophy. Beyond a belief that philosophy is systematic and that it deals with basic assumptions we make about the world, there is little agreement as to definition.

osophy has been defined as a plan for living.[13] Behind this very short and simple definition lie some fairly profound meanings. Philosophy is in part an analysis of what people do. It is an analysis not of a given action at one particular time and place but rather of the generalized *meaning* of that action. To analyze human behavior in philosophical terms is to ask serious questions about what a person values, whether he *should* value it, whether this value fits in with a pattern of values, whether the valuing of something hampers or assists other important values. Further, philosophy asks questions about existence and reality; e.g., What do I take to be real, and what is the meaning of this reality? This last question suggests another philosophical category, theories of knowledge. Theories of knowledge have to do with types and validity of knowledge. Important questions are, How do I know what is true? How can I be certain? Is it possible to arrive at certain knowledge, or is all knowledge uncertain and shifting?[14]

These questions are precisely the ones an individual asks when he faces a problem and begins to think about some of its deeper meanings and implications. A student who comes to talk to a counselor about a possible vocational choice will, if he wishes to think in a considered, reflective fashion, ask questions about reality, values, and knowledge. Why? Because he must ask, What vocation should I choose that will satisfy my values and meet my needs? If this vocation requires x number of years of training, do I want it badly enough to expend the time, energy, and money? How do I *know* that I have the necessary abilities and personality for this job? And in the asking of these questions, he will possibly come to see that his answer depends upon what he *takes* to be real.

As people make vocational choices — and meet many other important problems — they begin to work out a pattern of beliefs, which may prove adequate or inadequate in helping them live their lives. That is, a pattern of beliefs may be self-defeating (it may result in unwise choices which in due time create frustration and failure) or it may help a person make the kind of choices that result in a rich and meaningful life, one that is lived with a maximum of zest. This is the kind of existence about which laymen say, "His life has a good deal of meaning."

[13] See Ernest E. Bayles, *Democratic Educational Theory* (New York: Harper & Brothers, 1961).

[14] See "The Language of Epistemology," in Shermis, *op. cit.*

Sociology and Anthropology

Sociology and anthropology arose in the 19th century as certain investigators began systematically to study the social interactions of cultures both present and past.[15] Cultural (or social) anthropologists tend to look at what they call cultural universals — behavior which may be found in all known cultures — such as religion, technology, the family, music, art, written or folk literature, and others. Although anthropologists differ somewhat at the theoretical level, there seems to be some agreement that their function is to investigate cultural patterns in order to see how the collective behavior forms a unity. Sociologists have many of the same concerns and use the same procedures as anthropologists, but they are likely to emphasize particular institutions within a culture. In our society sociologists have studied the Hollywood movie industry, socioeconomic class, foreman-worker relations, Puerto Rican slum dwellers, the function of dance studios, the John Birch society, and the current interest in flying saucers.

RELATIVISM

From the methods of investigation of these two disciplines — assisted perhaps by philosophers — has developed the notion of relativism. In

[15] It will help readers relatively unfamiliar with the social sciences if they will think of anthropology and sociology — and all other social sciences — as a circus tent containing a number of big shows and numerous sideshows. Anthropologists, for instance, may engage in the same activities as biologists, geneticists, chemists, archeologists, statisticians, and philosophers. That is, the interests and methods of inquiry of investigators in the field of anthropology owe much to other disciplines.

previous centuries social thinkers tended to assert that there were indeed good and true values and whatever varied from these values was undesirable, dangerous, or evil. In the last century it was discovered that the supposedly eternally true and good absolute was, in fact, the particular preference of a particular group at a particular time. Values, it was seen, not only varied from place to place but changed slowly even within a certain geographical location. The inability to see one's own values in relation to others' or to perceive that values within a given place do change had resulted in equating the values of one's own culture with absolutes.

The theory that values were related to culture, historical time, and geographical location flowed from the sociologists' and anthropologists' study of behavior *among* and *within* cultures. Not only does behavior vary considerably, but even a particular kind of behavior is perceived differently by different persons. For instance, sexual patterns are far from uniform. All cultures, say anthropologists, have rules and regulations about sexual behavior, but what is believed good in a Polynesian culture may be thought reprehensible in another culture. Premarital sexual intercourse, for example, is usually proscribed in our culture, but Margaret Mead discovered that Polynesian culture had no such prohibition.[16]

Sociologists have uncovered often disturbing differences within our culture. It is widely believed that economic self-interest is an absolutely dependable motivation; people work because they wish to accumulate money in order to buy possessions, gain status, etc.; to motivate someone, we offer him money as a reward. However, the hill folk in the Appalachians do not hold money in the same esteem as the dominant culture does. A man may find a job but work for only a few weeks, just long enough to earn the money to visit his cousin in the next county. He values a certain kind of personal relationship much more than he values money. His perception of money is different from that of the dominant culture and his value structure is different. He is not motivated by what is thought to be a powerful incentive.

By the same token, there are differences in perceptions of education. Education is held by the dominant culture to be an unqualifiedly good thing; it not only liberates one, expands his horizons, but is also the means of "rising" in the world. However, many lower-class persons believe that education is actually detrimental: it makes one less warmly human; it turns children away from their parents; it fills minds with weird ideas and — among some religious fundamentalists — is felt to make people ungodly and irreligious.

The differences in the perception of values have important implications for psychologists, sociologists, social workers, teachers, and counselors. Counselors no longer find it effective to express indignation toward their lower-class students and deliver lectures on the students' faulty attitudes. Despite the seeming inappropriateness or self-defeating results of such attitudes the student has learned them in much the same way that the counselor has learned his. Another implication, developed by Carl R. Rogers, is that the counselor will be ineffective unless he can somehow enter the frame of reference, the value structure, of his client.[17] Looking at attitudes, values, beliefs, and behavior from an external, foreign vantage does not seem to assist the counselor very much in dealing with the client's problems.

To understand that values differ and that counselors need to view the perceptions of clients in a more sensitive and sympathetic light does not, of course, eliminate the problem of deciding which values are to be preferred. It is useful to understand that the Mexican child views work differently from the way a middle-class child in the United States does, and it is valuable to realize that a

[16] Margaret Mead, *Growing Up in New Guinea* (New York: Mentor Books, New American Library, 1953) and *Coming of Age in Samoa* (New York: Mentor Books, New American Library, 1949).

[17] Carl R. Rogers, *Client-Centered Therapy* (Boston: Houghton Mifflin Company, 1951) and *On Becoming a Person. A Therapist's View of Psychotherapy* (Boston: Houghton Mifflin Company, 1961).

lower-class child may not have the repugnance for physical conflict of a middle-class youth, but the value issue is not thereby settled. However, when the counselor is aware that clients do have a value structure and do not see parts of the world the same way he does, he is in a better position to establish a closer working relationship with them. When values and behavior no longer seem perverse, outlandish, or immoral, some of the barriers which prevent effective interaction have been removed.

Another implication of the method and findings of anthropologists, sociologists, and biological scientists is that human behavior is not determined in advance by heredity, nor is an individual a passive object to be shaped by his environment. Neither environmental determinism nor its opposite, hereditarianism, is seen as a particularly fruitful way of explaining behavior. Human beings are the product of an interaction between their biological inheritance and their social and physical environment.[18] To gain a relatively adequate description of what a person is and does requires that we examine him both as an individual and as a member of a group. Studying a unique individual yields data that are different from, but not necessarily contradictory to, the kind of data derived from looking at him as a group member.

The significance of this position can be seen only if we contrast it with the 19th-century view of man and his behavior. The tendency then was to insist either that man was "formed" by his environment or that his destiny was irrevocably sealed by heredity. Those who took the former stand suggested that all one needed to do was change the conditions of his environment and man could be changed in any desired direction. Those who believed the latter felt that no amount of environmental change could affect man, for he would be precisely whatever he would be. There seemed no other course, therefore, but to ignore either inherited influences or environment.

With the shift to an interactive position it became possible for social and biological scientists to study man in his totality. Anthropologists could investigate cultural patterns, sociologists began to look at class structure, both of them could concentrate on value structure and on the ways values are altered. Another significant change flowing from this new view of human nature was that social scientists from different disciplines merged their knowledge and methods in a combined approach known as the "interdisciplinary" method. What have been some of the findings of this approach, and how can they be utilized by counselors?

CLASS AND STATUS

In the 1920's, sociologists such as the Lynds and W. Lloyd Warner became interested in the phenomenon of social class.[19] Their findings are, by now, a standard part of every introductory sociology course. But the implications of their findings have yet to be widely understood. Despite the official democratic dogma that the United States was a one-class society, it was demonstrated that there was a large lower socioeconomic and a small but powerful upper class. The lower class, although not comparable to a peasantry, was seen to be impoverished, politically powerless, and very much at a disadvantage in terms of education, housing, and the law. The young people of the lower class tend to disvalue education, to drop out early, to exhibit hostility to teachers and other school officials, to mate somewhat freely, to settle disputes with physical violence, to be indifferent to cleanliness, and to be in constant trouble with the law. We have recently discovered that they constitute an enormous liability in a changing, automated, and technologically sophisticated society. In short, we discovered precisely what was not supposed to be there: A large part of society did not share in the

[18] Although — and this is frustrating — precisely what is an inherited characteristic and what is clearly the function of environment becomes increasingly less and not more clear! See Morris Bigge and Maurice P. Hunt, *Psychological Foundations of Education* (New York: Harper & Row, Publishers, 1962).

[19] W. Lloyd Warner, *Yankee City* (New Haven, Conn.: Yale University Press, 1963), and Robert and Helen Merrell Lynd, *Middletown* (New York: Harcourt, Brace & Co., 1929).

dominant American values (often called the "American dream") and, despite official dogma, faced barriers to vertical mobility.

As sociologists began to look at the behavior of this class with some objectivity, they also focused on the response of schools to lower-class youth — who frequently are also members of racial and ethnic minorities. They discovered that teachers, either middle class themselves or inclined to identify with middle-class values, were often indifferent or hostile to their lower-class students. Counselors in particular were somewhat puzzled by these children. A counselor could cope with misbehaving middle-class students by the usual means, but threats to fail or expel children who were indifferent to grades and who actively disliked school did not avail. Nor was it altogether clear to counselors that they *should* threaten or punish them, for such behavior was frowned upon by most counseling theorists. Even more recently, investigators have been asking whether counselors who are themselves racially prejudiced can relate effectively to minority group members.[20]

At the other end of the class spectrum, sociologists began to illuminate motives that proved to be embarrassing. The exertion of effort to gain status or prestige is widely regarded as stemming from less pure motivation. Thus, if a scientist works long hours in a laboratory, his efforts will be approved as beneficial for humanity — the discovery of a new drug, say, or a new inoculation process. He is not likely to say that he is working for recognition, fame, or status; if he does, he will be regarded as improperly motivated. Similarly, it may be seen but denied that a very powerful motivant for students is status: the status that accrues when one makes A grades, is a member of the football squad, or is accepted by one of the "better" colleges.

Counselors are often pressured to see that Junior takes a college prep curriculum or to pull wires so that Junior looks good to Princeton. They may succumb to such pressures, although reluctantly, because they know that Junior cannot handle a college prep curriculum and has no business applying to Princeton. To refuse to knuckle under to the pressures is perhaps to invite the criticism that one is not doing all he can for the students. Heretofore it has been unthinkable for the harassed school counselor to discuss the issue of status frankly with parents for this would be considered both bad taste and poor public relations. The point is that, while one may talk of getting a "quality" education for his child, the real motivation may be to acquire status. The real motive, the acquisition of status, is concealed from oneself.

BEHAVIORAL CHANGE AND CONTINUITY

Social scientists have revealed that behavior is likely to persist over a long period of time. Although individuals are relatively plastic — in the sense that behavioral change *does* take place — the patterns of a given culture, subculture, or other group tend to resist change. It is the failure to realize this that has defeated so many well-intentioned attempts by counselors and teachers.

Influenced by the prevailing norms of his environment, an individual does not shuck them off when he enters a different environment with different norms. Having learned a code of behavior in his home for the first six years, he does not typically make a radical change to accommodate the new environment. For many a lower-class child the school is a new environment, and much in it is at variance with what he has learned is proper and desirable. Thus the school's attempt to change his behavior fails. He grows up to become the kind of adult his parents are — and raises his own children in much the same way. That is, the behavior patterns of the lower-class poor[21] endure from decade to decade. If counselors and teachers wish to have some effect on behavior, they seemingly must understand more about the mechanics of behavioral persistence and change.

[20] See Robert L. Milliken and John Patterson, "Relationship of Dogmatism and Prejudice to Counseling," *Counselor Education and Supervision*, Vol. 6 (Winter, 1967), pp. 125–129.

[21] Such blunt terminology as "lower-class poor" is currently unfashionable. We now talk of the "disadvantaged," the "culturally backward," or the "culturally different."

Another kind of problem, resulting from behavior rigidity, is essentially the middle-class dilemma of confused sexual role. The behavior expected of a boy or girl is not, as anthropologists have pointed out, unvarying. Sexual roles are defined by each culture: This particular activity, this manner of dress, this kind of behavior are deemed masculine or feminine, and the definition of masculinity or femininity is by no means as universal as is usually believed. In past years the woman in our culture was supposed to be a subservient wife, a demure helpmate who bore and raised children and submitted patiently to her husband. The husband was expected to be the chief breadwinner and the head of the household. This description sounds quaint now, for much has happened to alter the traditional roles of husband and wife — including more education for girls. Girls are encouraged to take an academic major, to go to college and graduate school, to choose "exciting" careers, and, in general, to carve out an existence for themselves wholly independent of motherhood.

Unfortunately, as women are emancipated from the older roles and trained for new ones, individual girls or women are not able to make a clear identification with either. Thus, while a young girl may be encouraged to develop her talent by going to college, she is also pushed toward "going steady," engagement, marriage. Whichever choice she makes, judged by one set of values, is wrong. Too, the proper role of the well-educated wife and mother is by no means plain. She is told to find "fulfillment" in marriage, but the usual child raising, conventional community affairs, and entertainment often seem most unfulfilling.[22]

The counselor who cannot convince the mathematically talented girl to take trigonometry because, in the girl's eyes, math and science are not "girls' subjects" is a victim of cultural conflict. At one time math and science were *not* "girls' subjects" because girls were not thought to have sufficient brains to profit by intellectually demanding studies. That they can is a matter of psychological fact; that the *perception* of their inadequacy, born of a time when women were regarded as morally and intellectually inferior, has changed but little is also a matter of fact. What is at fault is described as the *social* or *cultural lag*: Technological conditions have changed, but habits and beliefs from previous times persist — and conflict with the cultural patterns engendered by the new technology.

[22] See Betty Friedan, *The Feminine Mystique* (New York: W. W. Norton & Company, Inc., 1963).

THE SCIENTIFIC METHOD

Counselors, as we have seen, have learned a great deal from the content of anthropology and sociology. Information about social class, cultural patterns, the hidden motivation of status, and the cultural lag has much bearing on what counselors do. However, equally important is the method by which knowledge is acquired. Although the scientific method of knowing has been built up by all of the social, physical, and natural sciences, we are particularly indebted to sociology and anthropology. The last 50 years have seen the replacement of absolutistic, one-sided (e.g., hereditarian *or* environmentalist), and sentimental views of man and society by much more dependable and fruitful outlooks.

Just as it is no longer acceptable for a teacher or counselor to say, "Well, of course Joe flunked all of his subjects; what else could one expect of Mexicans?", it is no longer reasonable to assert, "We'd better install a vocational curriculum and counsel these kids into it because they are not going to be helped by anything else." The patent absurdity of these two quotations is essentially a testimony to the method and content of the social sciences and to the effect they have had in forcing us to substitute empirical data in place of wishful thinking, romanticism, and tradition.

Political Science

Political science concerns itself with the examination of political power. This oversimplified statement conceals both the complexity of political power and the variety of methods employed by political scientists to investigate the subject. Political scientists' interests include Congressional behavior, the collection of financial contributions to political parties by industry, the voting patterns of upstate New York Catholics, the oratory of southern "redneck" politicians, the distribution of power in General Motors, and the public school as a political institution. A good many political scientists do not gather empirical data or observe particular institutions but interpret and analyze the mass of material collected by others. They are called political theorists, and their mode of inquiry is almost indistinguishable from that of philosophers.

Political science assumed its present shape with the writings of Niccolò Machiavelli, the Italian Renaissance diplomat and writer. Machiavelli was perhaps the first thinker to base his analysis of political power on the observed behavior of diplomats, princes, church officials, military leaders, and the like.[23] His advice to Cosimo de' Medici, to whom he dedicated his book, *The Prince*, is simply the acute perceptions of an experienced observer of the most effective techniques of gaining and holding political power. Since his time political scientists have expanded their investigation to include the uses of political power in a vast number of circumstances. What theories have political scientists devised, and how could they assist counselors?

POWER – WHAT IS IT?

Investigators of industry and government early in this century became aware of the difference between the symbol of power and the actual reality. Those who were supposed to command, those who had the appearance of power, were not always the ones who actually exercised power. The prime minister, king, or school superintendent, it was discovered, frequently did not make decisions, nor was he able to insist that others comply with his decisions. This observation led to a definition of power which, in simplified terms, is the actual and effective use of authority in such a way that when one gives a command, it will, in fact, be obeyed. The *nominal* holder of power – the mayor, senator, principal, or chamber of commerce leader – may or may not be the real wielder of power. The latter may be unknown to the public, may consist of a small oligarchy, may deny that he has any power, or may be identical with the nominal holder of power.[24]

THE POWER STRUCTURE

The political scientist's concentration on power and those who control it has led to a construct known as "power structure." The remarkable thing about a power structure is that it is not supposed to exist. According to the democratic mythology, the people always hold power; only leaders elected by them may exercise power and then in but a limited way. To talk about a power structure – a power "elite," in the words of the late C. Wright Mills – seems a flat contradiction in a democracy. However, a power structure apparently exists, is clearly operative in any community, and has much relevance to public schools.

Counselors frequently complain because they are relegated to quasi-administrative jobs or purely clerical ones. Although they have been told that their job is to counsel with boys and girls, they spend more and more time in checking attendance, seeking scholarships, sponsoring student government, or doing other jobs distantly related to counseling. Yet they are reluctant to tell administrators that they are counselors and that they cannot or will not be an arm of the administration. They seem to feel that the administrator is "in charge" of the school, that he has authority, and that they have no choice but to accede to his wishes. This

[23] Most of the political theorizing previously was an attempt to justify clerical power. The rationale was essentially theological. See Chester C. Maxey, *Political Philosophies* (New York: The Macmillan Company, 1950).

[24] A friend of the author's was attempting to gather data for a dissertation in political science. He visited selected members of the community, told them of his research, and asked them to cooperate in a study of the local power structure. In each case he was rapidly and nervously escorted to the door. Then he changed his tactics and informed them that he was studying "community leaders." He was courteously welcomed and given all the information he needed.

attitude ignores two questions: Where, exactly, does an administrator's authority stop? Does he have the authority to assign a counselor jobs which simply do not fit within the latter's professionally defined responsibilities? If these questions are asked, it may be seen that the administrator does not have anything like unlimited power.

Another problem is raised by the counselors' relationships to the children of those families who function as the power structure in a community. The verbalized belief is that the school is a place for all the children of all the people, that no special privileges ought to be extended to any group, and that the children are to be treated alike. In fact, the children of "community leaders" are given preferential treatment in scheduling, in grading, in cocurricular affairs, and in reduced punishments for infraction of rules. Rather than tangle with the Joneses, who are known to swing much weight, the new counselor or teacher is told to "ease off," to avoid coming into conflict, to compromise or not do anything to endanger next month's school bond election.

Of crucial concern to counselors, teachers, and all school people is the relationship of the school, the community, and the power structure. Those within education have expressed approximately the same grievances and the same beliefs for a century.[25] Changes in schools, when they do arrive, come so slowly that they are almost invariably too little or too late. One analysis of the relatively slow improvements holds that real power does not lie in the hands of professional educators.[26] Quite typically it lies in the hands of the power structure *outside* education, at both the local and the state level. Thus, local boards of education, consisting almost always of upper-middle-class or upper-class laymen, make decisions as to curriculum, salary, personnel, standards, and so on that are often contrary to the desires of professional school people. At the state level, certification commissions — which grant licenses or certificates to administrators, counselors, school psychologists, teachers, and others — are staffed entirely by laymen. Indeed, a number of state constitutions specifically prohibit professional persons from serving on certification commissions. To be blunt, the raising of professional standards for a number of school positions (e.g., psychologists) is hampered in several states. On the face of it, no one could conceivably advance a rational argument for supporting low standards. Yet a moment's reflection will disclose that the higher the licensing standards, the higher the salary; the higher the salary, the more money required to support education. It is the property tax — which falls most heavily on large property owners who are most likely to be the power structure — that largely finances education. The power structure, therefore, often acts against schools whenever the schools wish to engage in activities that are perceived to be against its interests.[27]

The point is not that the power structure behaves in an unethical or illegal manner — although it may at times. The point is that there is a power structure, which is not supposed to exist and the operations of which tend to be ignored, particularly by school people. For this reason Professor Myron Lieberman, in dealing with political power and the education profession, suggests that teachers have the responsibility of understanding and using political power.[28] Unless they do, school people will continue to be in the position of making demands which will never be met.

[25] On the unlikely assumption that the reader is not aware of them, we list: low salaries, unstable tenure, inadequate facilities, too little opportunity to introduce innovations, lack of academic freedom, lack of support for the teacher in enforcing discipline, too much time spent on clerical details, and a plethora of rules and regulations that have little to do with teaching or learning.

[26] See Myron Lieberman, *Education as a Profession* (Englewood Cliffs, N. J.: Prentice-Hall, Inc., 1956) and *The Future of Public Education* (Chicago: University of Chicago Press, 1960).

[27] In a town in which the author lived the power structure threw its weight behind an enrichment program and a stronger college prep curriculum. It defeated a program to strengthen remedial reading, vocational training, and the counseling program. The latter improvement would have benefited lower-class, minority students, who were in the numerical majority.

[28] He makes the suggestion in both *Education as a Profession* and *The Future of Public Education.*

DEMOCRACY

Democracy was not invented by political scientists, but political scientists and historians have devoted much time to describing it and theorizing about it. A good deal of what has been written and said in an attempt to relate democracy with education is a mixture of hollow verbalisms and clichés. The tendency is to confuse democracy with freedom or liberty — it is associated with freedom but is not the equivalent of it — or else to state that democracy *requires* social equality, economic opportunity, education, or a vast number of other values.

Democracy is simply a sociopolitical form of organization in which the people make basic decisions and elect those who govern them. In addition, there is an implication that whatever decision is made, unless it is rescinded or modified, all will abide by it equally.[29]

Strictly speaking, a democracy does not require any specific amount of any particular kind of education. In some democracies public education has been undeveloped; in others it is widespread. It does not seem to be particularly defensible to state that because we have a democracy everyone must go to school.

However, one does seem justified in saying that, given the complexity of the decision-making process in this country, decision-making skills are required. They can be learned in classrooms as teachers show students how to use information, formulate hypotheses, spot logical fallacies, and learn the values of compromise and adjustment. It is precisely the emphasis on decision making that should distinguish schools in a democracy from those in a nondemocratic or a totalitarian country — although American teachers are often hard put to explain just why this is so.[30]

[29] Bayles, *op. cit.*

[30] Do not for a moment believe that any system of education will necessarily be dedicated to producing an electorate trained to make decisions. An educational system may be devised to indoctrinate the young in unquestioning obedience to higher authority. Or it may be created to turn out highly skilled technicians who function quite well as technicians.

Viewed from this framework, the counselor in a democracy has an analogous function. In our democracy, which is characterized by a considerable degree of freedom and openness, emphasis is also placed on independent decision making in other than political contexts. Persons are generally called upon to make choices about vocation, future education and training, mate, number of children, location, size, and cost of a dwelling, and an almost infinite variety of other matters.[31] Counselors, therefore, are seemingly required to help the young who are their clientele to be more thoughtful and reflective — i.e., to be more skillful in decision making.

The counselor functions not to help an individual to become more competent at this or that decision, although he may be called upon for advice or help on a particular problem. The counselor, theoreticians generally feel, is supposed to help individuals be more autonomous, more independent, more intelligent as individuals. The assumption is that as a result of counseling a person does not become more effective in simply one area, say about vocational goals, but becomes more effective in all areas of his life.

Definitions of counseling and the many theoretical systems that are used to describe the role of counselors are discussed elsewhere in this book. Suffice it to say here that, by any definition of counseling, the end result is an individual who is able to think about his problems in a more competent or effective way than he did before. It is the focus on decision making or problem solving and its relation to democracy and counseling which appears to be most important.

In sum, the political scientist's notion of democracy as a political decision-making method has been extended into other areas. One is not only free to make a wide variety of decisions but expected to do so. Schools therefore have the unique

[31] In other societies one's vocation may be inherited or chosen for him by the government. The children may be raised by the state in nursery schools. One's parents may arrange one's marriage. Or children are raised in a particular predetermined, prescribed manner.

responsibility of helping future adults become more proficient at decision making. From this point of view, counselors are persons who, working in a one-to-one relationship, assist in the improvement of decision making.

Economics

Economics is that social science which studies the pattern of human production, consumption, and distribution. As may be inferred from the preceding examination of sociology, anthropology, and political science, it is a discipline whose members pursue many different specialties. Some economists, called econometricians, specialize in the compilation and analysis of economic statistics. Others study the economic history of a particular country or even of a particular industry. Some economists specialize in a particular part of the world, as, for instance, Soviet Russia or Latin America. Some study one institution, such as money and banking. Some share the same interests as political scientists or sociologists,[32] and others work closely with anthropologists. The father of modern-day economics, Adam Smith, thought of himself as philosopher, and a number of economists today are essentially philosophers.

MAN AS AN ECONOMIC BEING

Men everywhere are economic beings. They produce things, have systems for distributing them, and consume them. Some economic systems are extremely complex — our own, for example, or Soviet Russia's or that of any highly industrialized society. Others are comparatively simple, such as that of the Australian Bushman, who has very little in the way of technology and is a nomadic hunter and food gatherer. In the process of producing, distributing, and consuming, different cultures devise rather elaborate systems and procedures, which have implications for much more than economic activities. For instance, the accumulation of economic power in our society — and many others — almost always generates political power, and this, as we have seen, creates political problems. Or, in the process of devising a monetary and banking system to finance complex factories, there are ramifications extending to much more than factories.[33] Likewise, the system of longterm financing of industry and agriculture, called the stock market, has raised a host of ethical problems relating to the honest sale of stocks and bonds.

Nobody, apparently, is able to stand aloof from economic activities. By the very existence of the need to satisfy their wants for food, shelter, clothing, and other things all individuals are enmeshed in an economy. But, what is important from our standpoint, the way people theorize about economic activities also constitutes a set of influences, and it is the influence of economic theorizing that we propose to examine.[34]

ECONOMIC THEORY

Economist John Kenneth Galbraith, Harvard professor, former ambassador to India, and popular writer and lecturer, has advanced an explanation of economic theory as it affects production and consumption.[35] The classical economists who wrote in the late 18th century and in the 19th operated under the assumption that production would always be unable to satisfy consumption. That is,

[32] For instance, economist Peter Drucker's *The Concept of a Corporation* (New York: Mentor Books, New American Library, 1964) is a study of General Motors which includes an analysis of administration, a discussion of the values involved in the organization, and an examination of the relationship of both of these to economic goals. This one book, therefore, ranges from political science through sociology to philosophy, but the context is an economic institution.

[33] As these words are written, the interest rates on loans are extremely high. It is currently too expensive for some to borrow money to expand factories — and schools.

[34] For a good summary of economic theory see Robert Heilbronner's *The Worldly Philosophers* (New York: Simon and Schuster, Inc., 1953).

[35] Economics has been called "the dismal science," possibly because the prose of economists is depressingly difficult to read. Galbraith is one of the few exceptions. Readers unfamiliar with economics who wish to inquire further into Galbraith's theories should consult his *American Capitalism: The Concept of Countervailing Power* (Boston: Houghton Mifflin Company, 1962).

human wants would always outstrip the capacity of factories and farms to meet them. An economy of scarcity was implied, in which most men would be in need, famines would always threaten, and poverty would be the norm. Were we to examine the world with the eyes of Adam Smith, Thomas Malthus, David Ricardo, and others, we would probably agree: Both the official Report of the Children's Employment Commission of 1842 and the writer Charles Dickens described the pervasive poverty and social instability of 19th-century England.[36]

However, in this country in particular, a happy combination of abundant natural resources, a useful system of waterways, the presence of a large labor force which became increasingly better trained, a steady supply of fertile inventors,[37] and an absence of destructive and costly wars has made possible what was unimaginable 100 or more years ago: an economy of abundance. Our factories and farms have been able to produce more than we can consume. (The author is aware that this hypothesis does not account for the fact that we, too, have a large number of people without sufficient purchasing power to buy what they want or need. Nevertheless, we have enormously increased the capacity of factories and farms to produce.)

Thus, we have something of a paradox: We are operating on the economic theory of a century ago, which held that human wants would never be met adequately by the means of production; but, in fact, our technology has enabled us to produce goods in numbers larger than most of us can consume. One would imagine, if the basic tenet of capitalism[38] were entirely true, that factory owners would simply produce fewer products, just enough to meet consumer need. However, says Galbraith, this is not the case. Given the capacity of factories to produce more than can be consumed, we have *increased* our productive capacity and trained the populace to consume ever more and more. Advertising, for instance, is designed to whet our appetites for things which, in all probability, we could easily exist without. Designing products deliberately to malfunction after a certain period of time, or changing styles on expensive commodities such as refrigerators, ranges, and automobiles (quaintly called "planned obsolescence") is a device, apparently, to get consumers to chuck their products away and buy new ones. Another such economic technique includes long-term installment buying: Many have sadly observed that the 36-month automobile contract is paid up about the time the manufacturer introduces a new style — or about the time the automobile falls apart.

With such extremely effective production, the result is a materialistic philosophy and large numbers of people who perpetually generate desires for material objects and status. Both are of direct concern to counselors, who must work with student value conflicts. The materialistic philosophy may be seen in the pervasive, continual, and seemingly irrational desire to own things. Some recent studies have noted a close correlation between high school student possession of automobiles and poor academic grades. In view of the many millions of dollars automobile manufacturers spend to create a desire for their product,[39] it is scarcely a mystery that students look for after-hours jobs in order to buy and maintain cars. The problem is of course compounded by the fact that, once the cars are bought, students apparently drive them in preference to studying.

A materialistic philosophy would not be inappropriate if there were no other contending philosophies. However, there is also the philosophy emphasizing the importance of the intangibles — good

[36] The rereading of any short story or novel of Dickens is recommended. However, instead of reading it as a sentimental and romanticized story, approach his *Christmas Carol, Oliver Twist,* or *David Copperfield* as a commentary on urban poverty, exploitation, selfishness, crime, and social injustice.

[37] This needs qualification. We have, to be sure, ingenious inventors, but we have rarely produced originators in the sense of scientists who discovered basic scientific principles. These, for the most part, originated in Europe, and Americans such as Ford and Edison *adapted* principles in order to make machines or industries that could produce products.

[38] By the law of supply and demand the amount produced by a manufacturer is governed by the existing and effective demand for that product.

[39] For a popular treatment see Vance Packard, *The Waste Makers* (New York: David McKay Co., Inc., 1966), and Ralph Nader, *Unsafe at Any Speed* (New York: Grossman Publishers, Inc., 1965).

character, cooperation, self-denial, studying for its own sake. A young person growing up in our culture is faced by a very basic value conflict in that he simply does not know what is good. Should he exhibit expensive and stylish clothing or is it better to study for its purely intellectual values? The counselor, in one sense, actually contributes to this value conflict, for at the same time that the administrator, the teacher, and the counselor talk about the values inherent in knowledge for its own sake they display charts comparing the lifetime salaries of those who do and do not go to college.

Much attention has been paid recently to the hostility, uncooperativeness, and antiauthoritarian attitudes of lower-class students. Many studies have been made of minority and lower-class behavior, and a wide variety of causes have been adduced to explain it. However, a relatively ignored factor is frustration — the frustration of having one's appetite for goods and status whetted and then being unable to gratify it. Other cultures have large masses of poor people, larger and poorer than our own. But ours are told from infancy that one must own possessions, that possessions lend status, yet for a number of reasons they are unable to purchase what is held up as supremely desirable. It does not seem far-fetched to conjecture that some of the rebelliousness and aggressiveness of minorities, often directed at teachers and school property, is simply displaced aggression against a society that expertly and systematically frustrates them.

Many other instances could be cited wherein our economy predisposes to value conflicts. One more fairly simple one will suffice. Cigarette smoking is uniformly denounced by schools, and sufficient scientific evidence has been gathered to show causal relationship between cigarette smoking and diseases ranging from cancer to emphysema. Notwithstanding this and the propaganda barrage directed against cigarettes in social studies, biology, and health classes, students continue to find themselves in trouble with the vice-principal for smoking illegally on school grounds. Again, the millions of dollars spent on advertising by tobacco manufacturers have paid off by convincing young people that smoking is sophisticated and chic. If one asks a basic question: Why does our society tolerate and even encourage the tobacco industry by means of agricultural subsidies? the answer is not difficult to find. The growing, manufacture, and distribution of tobacco is a billion-dollar industry, and harming the tobacco industry would, it is held, wreak havoc with our economy. The point is that the decision to perpetuate the tobacco industry is one in which the value of health is weighed against an economic value, and the economic value, at least up until now, has clearly prevailed. Given the extremely high cultural value placed upon the alleged economic desirability of selling cars and cigarettes, it behooves counselors to think more seriously about the importance of economic values in our way of life.

ECONOMIC MOTIVATION

The discussion above leads us naturally into a consideration of the meaning of economic motivation. To say that all of us respond to economic motivation is too simple. The history of Western civilization has seen a rather ambiguous attitude toward it. During the early Christian and medieval periods, the official belief was that the good man was one who spent his time contemplating God and withdrawing from the world, for love of money, status, wealth, and possessions was at the root of all evil.[40] A desire either to realize a profit from one's investment in time or money or to own possessions was considered incompatible with a good life. With the rise of capitalism, however, grew the belief that not only was economic motivation legitimate but the good man was one who finished his life as the successful entrepreneur, owner of a large fortune, and possessor of many goods. Today, both traditions exist side by side: We are told that it is desirable to live in tranquillity and to be happy with our lot, and we are also told that it is better to be ambitious, work hard, make more money, and increase our supply of

[40] This point is developed by R. H. Tawney in *Religion and the Rise of Capitalism* (New York: Mentor Books, New American Library, 1942).

goods. Counselors would do well to understand this cultural contradiction because it is often internalized by students and appears to be a factor in pre-disposing toward intrapersonal conflict.

The same thing is a factor in the life of counselors and teachers. One reason counselors and teachers have been undercompensated for so long is the public's feeling that the educator's greatest compensation comes from his sense of satisfaction, that the job of teacher, like that of preacher, is a "calling," and that only a poorly motivated person would make an issue of wages and working conditions. This seemingly widespread cultural belief, disappearing now as public school people become more militant, has probably been a barrier to raising salaries. After all, if one is supposed to be impelled by basically altruistic motives, if one's chief aim is to "help" others, why be concerned about the things that motivate union members and others with regrettably worldly goals?

Counselors should, therefore, recognize economic motivation as a factor in their own careers and also assist students to appraise it in their lives. There appears to be little or no point for counselors or teachers who deal with vocations to ignore, play down, or disguise the meaning of economic motivation. It is something all students ought to begin to understand for it comprises an important part — whether or not consciously ignored — of one's basic value structure. Further, when students enter the adult world and discover that economic values are extremely important, the image of the teacher, principal, or counselor as a good-natured simpleton whose dream world does not allow him to comprehend what "life is all about" will be perpetuated.

The key to understanding or appraising the meaning of economic motivation does not lie in the oversimplified procedures of a half-century ago. At that time, says educational historian Raymond Callahan, the methods and values of the business world were extended to schools. Efficiency became the goal of education. Schools emulated business and applied the same yardsticks and criteria that factories used. The assumption that criteria appropriate for a profit-making institution were also appropriate for public schools was indeed a revolutionary one. Unfortunately, 50 years later this assumption is still very much alive and appears to be another factor in the underfinancing of public education in general and of salaries in particular. We know how to reward the crackerjack salesman: on the basis of how many sales he has made. But, using the same yardstick, how does one adequately compensate the teacher or counselor — on the basis of students' scores on the ITED or how many students were counseled that day? Such quantitative criteria are obviously absurd, but if not these, precisely which ones should be used?

This discussion of economic factors as they affect counselors and students may be summarized with almost the same words used to introduce the topic of the power structure: Economic motivations exist and exert much influence over the lives of all of us. For historical reasons, however, we have tended tc ignore them, and school people in particular are likely to play them down or to overlook them. The effects are regrettable in two directions: Counselors and teachers are usually under-compensated, and students mature without sufficient understanding of what economic motivation is and how it affects their lives.

Psychology and Psychiatry

IDENTIFICATION

Psychology is that branch of the social sciences which studies man's interaction with his environment. It is, in a sense, a more general discipline than other social sciences because it does not confine itself to economic or political behavior but takes *all* human behavior as its subject. Psychiatry, although sharing many of the same concerns as psychology, is a branch of medicine. The concern of psychiatry is with abnormal human behavior; to put it another way, psychiatry deals with emotional problems that are considered severe.

Psychologists may specialize in physiological psychology, a discipline that borrows heavily from biology and emphasizes such phenomena as the relationship between endocrine flow and behavior or the physiological basis of aphasia (an organic disorder characterized by loss of speech). Some psychologists are essentially mathematicians or statisticians and assist other experimenters in setting up what is called "experimental designs" and interpreting complex data. Some psychologists will study the behavior of particular groups (for example, industrial psychologists) or become specialists in aerospace medicine. Some will study a particular kind of behavior as it is observed in many groups — e.g., learning, forgetting, and remembering. Counseling psychologists are concerned with the solution of individual emotional problems and may work in institutional settings or practice privately. Social psychologists study much the same phenomena as political scientists and sociologists. Psychology — to repeat a comment made in the other sections — is therefore a rather wide-ranging discipline.

When the focus of attention is on disturbed human behavior or emotional problems, psychiatrists and psychologists may combine their skills and backgrounds in order to improve diagnosis and therapy.[41] Although psychiatry is much older than psychology,[42] specialists in the two fields have been extremely productive during the last 75 years, and from a study of their contributions emerge a number of patterns.

COMPLEXITY

Like other disciplines, psychology and psychiatry have revealed that human behavior is much more complex than was originally believed. Sigmund Freud, the Austrian neurologist and psychiatrist, suggested that the most important human motivations occur at an invisible level, the level of the unconscious or subconscious. Freud felt, and much evidence has confirmed, that what happens in a child's early life — which is almost always consciously forgotten — is crucial to his later development. The motivations Freud described, and it is to be recalled that he lived at the end of the Victorian era, involved the hitherto prohibited topic of sexuality.

In psychological laboratories all over Europe and the United States it was also demonstrated that the reasons for people's behavior were not widely recognized. The notion of "self-concept" was introduced as psychologists learned that the way an individual perceives himself strongly influences his behavior. A school of theoreticians known as Gestalt or field theory psychologists discovered that whether there is some kind of reality independent of individuals is simply not of psychological value; how a person perceives reality constitutes reality for him. Joining forces with sociologists, psychologists found that status and prestige were also important factors in motivating behavior.

These experiments and many others have revealed that human behavior is extraordinarily complex, that people act for reasons that are difficult to describe, and that any simple, unqualified generalization about behavior is probably either wrong or incomplete.

PURPOSE

At the turn of this century or slightly before, psychologists began to feel that human beings were nothing more than clever, complex machines. Just as there were laws that applied to the physical universe (gravity, centrifugal force, etc.), there were also laws that applied to human beings, laws that "governed" behavior. Once these laws were discovered, human behavior could be described and predicted completely and perfectly.[43] This somewhat simplistic notion of behavior has since given

[41] However, relationships between psychologists and psychiatrists are not always sweet. Psychiatrists, since their work is a branch of medicine, often feel that they are better trained, while psychologists often feel that they know more about human behavior. The jockeying for status between the two in institutions is a wonder to see and has supplied enough data for several dissertations — done, we might add, by social psychologists.

[42] See Franz Alexander and Sheldon T. Selesnick, *The History of Psychiatry* (New York: Harper & Row, Publishers, 1966).

[43] See "Reality as Law," in Shermis, *op. cit.* Consider also the following quotation from John Watson, the best known of American behaviorists: "Psychology as the behaviorist views it is a purely objective experimental branch of natural science. Its theoretical goal is the prediction and control of behavior." John Watson, "Psychology as the Behaviorist Views It," in Thorne Shipley (ed.), *Classics in Psychology* (New York: Philosophical Library, Inc., 1961), pp. 798–804.

way to a more complex one. That biologists and physiologists may make important contributions to the study of human behavior is undoubtedly true, but human beings are not *reducible* to machines. They have purposes and goals which are not explainable simply by reference to endocrine secretions. If we can understand these goals — and there was a clear implication that in order to do so we must study people in interaction with their physical and social environment — we have a more fruitful means of understanding behavior.

This insight was and still is not accepted by all social scientists, but it is of particular use to counselors. People exhibit behavior which at first glance appears to be bizarre or irrational. A very bright child, with a previous record of good grades and cooperative behavior, appears before the counselor, sent by a bewildered teacher who cannot understand why the child is failing all his schoolwork and has become nasty and defiant. Usually some probing by the counselor reveals that, strange as the behavior is, it is meant to realize some purpose or goal, often one that is not known to the child. Often the defiant behavior appears after the birth of a new brother or sister, and despite the fact that the child may be punished severely, it does indeed pay off: he is getting the recognition he wants, even if it is of an unpleasant and negative kind.

Another illustration of purpose appears in a classic, witty book called *Games People Play* by Eric Berne, a psychiatrist.[44] Berne describes a large number of apparently weird and self-defeating "games" wherein one person, with the active help of one or many others, repeats a pattern of destructive behavior. In the game "schlemiel"[45] the visitor unendingly spills soup on the host's rug, burns cigarette holes in furniture, or trips over the canapés. The "schlemiel" apologizes profusely and the host forgives him. Berne suggests that he has a purpose, if an unconscious one: he wishes forgiveness, and the oafishness is simply behavior designed to get it — in Berne's terms, to achieve a particular "payoff." Although Berne has drawn upon psychopathology (serious deviation from a norm of mental health), his ideas have relevance for counselors. If counselors wish to probe beyond the obvious, behind the overt behavior, they may first ask, What payoff, what purpose, does this person hope for when he does this?

[44] (New York: Grove Press, Inc., 1964).
[45] "Schlemiel" is a Yiddish word which denotes an inept and clumsy person whose lack of coordination or foresight constantly gets him in trouble.

CONFLICT

Psychologists describe two kinds of conflict, *interpersonal* and *intrapersonal*. *Inter*personal conflict is that between or among people. *Intra*personal conflict is the suffering one individual undergoes when he has two conflicting desires which he is unable to resolve. When the NAACP and the Ku Klux Klan are at odds with each other, it is a case of interpersonal conflict. When an individual is miserable because he cannot decide whether to obey his parents and go to college, which he does not wish, or go to work as a garage mechanic, which he does, he is experiencing intrapersonal conflict. This is conflict *within* an individual, and it arises out of the inability to make a satisfactory decision.

As psychologists have studied the research of anthropologists and sociologists, they have come to realize that intrapersonal conflict is very often the result of *internalizing* conflicts already existing in the culture. The boy who cannot decide whether to attend college or go to work has internalized two conflicting cultural values. It is good to obey authority, to do as one's parents wish; it is also good to do what one wants, to fulfill oneself by choosing the vocation that is most satisfying. Unhappily, one cannot always do both, and sometimes compromise is out of the question. One has to choose either/or. The inability to choose, to establish a clear preference for one value, is at the root of many different conflicts. From one standpoint, the neurotic is a person who is perpetually unable to make a choice without suffering guilt or anxiety.

LEARNING

Perhaps the most important contribution of psychologists and psychiatrists is their data and theories on learning. In a sense, learning theory is as old as Aristotle and Plato, the Athenian philosophers who addressed themselves to the question of how and why people learn.[46] Other philosophers — Locke, Kant, Rousseau, and Dewey — were concerned with learning, but not until the second half of the 19th century did psychologists attempt to study learning systematically and objectively. Unfortunately for teachers and counselors (in the second or third decade of this century), psychologists interested in learning divided into two schools. "Unfortunately" because there is considerable difference between the schools, and most textbook authors have recently tended to ignore it. Both schools, the older associationist, represented by such psychologists as Edward Lee Thorndike and more recently B. F. Skinner, and Gestalt or field theory, represented by Kurt Koffka, Max Wertheimer, Wolfgang Köhler, and Kurt Lewin, have attempted to describe learning in specific terms — specific enough so that teachers or counselors know what happens when someone learns or does not learn.

Briefly, and in a much oversimplified manner, the associationists feel that learning is essentially a mechanical matter best described in physiological terms. Thorndike, for instance, believed that learning takes place as an organism responds to a stimulus; hence the term "stimulus-response," or S-R. As the response grooves its way through the neural pathway, an individual may be said to have learned. In recent years the Harvard psychologist B. F. Skinner has considerably refined Thorndike's original position, and his work with pigeons has impressed many.[47]

However, interesting as are Skinner's experiments, some counseling theorists have objected to them on the ground that the learner is essentially a passive object who has little insight into the meaning of his acts. That is, the criticism made of Skinner is couched in philosophical terms: The person is manipulated and has lost the freedom to comprehend the significance of what is being done to him. For this reason many — but not all — counseling theorists use a variant of Gestalt theory. With its emphasis on insight, Gestalt theory seems more compatible with the belief that it is desirable to encourage independent and autonomous thought.

What Gestaltists mean by insight is, roughly, a realization or awareness of a certain relationship. At first, insight was thought to be sudden. The early experimentation with apes suggested that when an individual gets an insight he "catches on" in a rapid, almost dramatic fashion. It is now believed that insights may arrive slowly. An insight may be deep or shallow, and there is no guarantee that an insight is necessarily accurate.

When counselors wish to employ the theory of insight, they do not behave like Skinnerian "conditioners," who "reinforce" correct responses. The counselor as conditioner would probably, in a manner unknown to the counselee, encourage the latter to behave the way the counselor wanted him to.[48] The counselor who believes in the validity or importance of insight, however, attempts to get his client to utilize his own intellectual and emotional resources to become aware of certain feelings, relationships, or attitudes. There seems to be a prior assumption that the counselee has sufficient intelligence to solve his own problems and that the role of the counselor is to provide a sympathetic or assistive environment for this purpose. When a counselee develops insight — i.e., sees a certain pattern of relationships — into himself and his problem, then he may take the next step: decide what is to be done and how to do it.

Although psychiatrists have not been particularly interested in learning theory, at least one of Freud's constructs bears on this problem. Freud believed that the unconscious is able to prevent certain learning, as, for instance, when a repressed feeling "blocks" the sounding of a word, the memory of a face, or the learning of a subject.[49] For

[46] See Plato's *Republic* and *Theatatus* and Aristotle's *Politics.*

[47] A fairly complete treatment of learning theory and the differences between S-R and Gestalt is Morris L. Bigge, *Learning Theories for Teachers* (New York: Harper & Row, Publishers, 1964).

[48] For a most interesting discussion of the relationship between reinforcement and recent conditioning theory, see Jay Haley, *Strategies of Psychotherapy* (New York: Grune & Stratton, Inc., 1963).

[49] See, for instance, Freud's *New Introductory Lectures on Psycho-Analysis of 1932.*

some reason Freud's rather seminal discovery of the role of the unconscious in blocking learning has not been followed up to any considerable extent by educational psychologists. However, many teachers report instances of seemingly irrational forgetting or nonlearning, and it seems reasonable to believe that some kind of unconscious process is operative.

The educational psychologist's theories on learning, interesting as they may be to the specialized student, are not likely to have great influence on counselors, at least in the near future. At present there is no comprehensive learning theory; different theoretical positions seem to explain different phenomena. When educational psychology reaches a point where a truly systematic theory can be developed, that is, where the bits and pieces of principles and concepts are synthesized into a coherent statement, the counselors may turn to the learning theorist for assistance. As of now, he can only pick and choose and use positions whenever and however he can.

CONCLUSION

In one sense psychology is to the counselor as physiology and anatomy are to the physician. It would be possible for a physician to make a diagnosis and prescribe a pill without knowing these two subjects. But if he did so, we would call him a *technician,* one who operates in a limited way by rule-of-thumb prescriptions and without deep understanding. For the practicing counselor an understanding of the dynamics of human behavior is a *sine qua non,* an indispensable element, without which his treatment is superficial. For a counselor to deal effectively with his clientele, for a counselor to become a professional, he must understand something of how and why human beings behave as they do.

By the same token, an awareness of the social sciences, their structure and the principles and data that have arisen from this structure, is also a part of the professional education of counselors. If we assume that a distinctive characteristic of a profession is that it possess an intellectual rationale, surely the rationale includes the insights of the social sciences. To obtain the knowledge to work most effectively with his clients a counselor requires an understanding that is both broad and deep. A knowledge of human behavior is part of this understanding.

Annotated References

Alexander, Franz, and Selesnick, Sheldon F. *The History of Psychiatry.* New York: Harper & Row, Publishers, 1966.

This is a comprehensive history of psychiatry from primitive times to the present. Theories, history, case studies, and interpretation are effectively combined to paint a readable picture of psychiatry.

Beals, Ralph L., and Hoijer, Harry. *An Introduction to Anthropology.* New York: The Macmillan Company, Third Edition, 1965.

This is an introductory textbook that covers both cultural and physical anthropology.

Birket-Smith, Kaj. *The Paths of Culture.* Madison: University of Wisconsin Press, 1965.

A comprehensive introduction to cultural anthropology, this work provides a detailed interpretation of anthropology and its methods.

Cornford, Francis M. *From Religion to Philosophy.* New York: Harper & Brothers, 1957.

This scholarly essay on the transition from religion to philosophy puts particular emphasis on the difference between magico-religious and rational speculation.

Dewey, John. *Reconstruction in Philosophy.* New York: Henry Holt & Co., Inc., 1917.

One of Dewey's best-known works, this is an attempt to relate the development of philosophy to the social matrix.

Friedan, Betty. *The Feminine Mystique.* New York: W. W. Norton & Company, Inc., 1963.

This book, which has attracted much attention recently, is the author's analysis of the "problem that has no name" — the plight of the intelligent, college-trained woman who is stifling in the middle-class suburbs.

Heilbronner, Robert. *The Worldly Philosophers.* New York: Simon and Schuster, Inc., 1953.

Here is a rarity — an extremely readable work on economic theory. The author presents some of the most important economic theoreticians, describes their positions, and assesses their contributions. This is perhaps the best place to begin a study of economic theory.

Joad, C. E. M. *Philosophy.* New York: Fawcett World Library, 1962.

Designed for laymen, this is a most interesting introduction to philosophy. See especially Chapters I and II, "On Reading Philosophy" and "Subject Matter and Scope."

Kluckhohn, Clyde. *Mirror for Man.* New York: McGraw-Hill Book Co., Inc., 1944.

This readable work, an introduction to American culture for beginners, was one of the first attempts by anthropologists to study the United States as a culture.

Lieberman, Myron. *The Future of Public Education.* Chicago: University of Chicago Press, 1960.

In this controversial work on educational sociology the author analyzes the problem of teacher impotence and (in the last chapter) makes a number of specific recommendations – some of which are currently receiving attention.

Further References

Bayles, Ernest E. *Democratic Educational Theory.* New York: Harper & Brothers, 1961.

Berne, Eric. *Games People Play.* New York: Grove Press, Inc., 1964.

Bigge, Morris, and Hunt, Maurice P. *Psychological Foundations of Education.* New York: Harper & Row, Publishers, 1968.

Bronfenbrenner, Urie. "Soviet Methods of Character Education: Some Implications for Research," *American Psychologist,* Vol. 17 (August, 1962), pp. 550–564.

Drucker, Peter. *The Concept of a Corporation.* New York: Mentor Books, New American Library, 1964.

Freud, Sigmund. *New Introductory Lectures on Psycho-Analysis of 1932.* New York: W. W. Norton, & Company, 1933.

Galbraith, John Kenneth. *American Capitalism: The Concept of Countervailing Power.* Boston: Houghton Mifflin Company, 1962.

Haley, Jay. *Strategies of Psychotherapy.* New York: Grune & Stratton, Inc., 1963.

Kiev, Ari. *Magic, Faith, and Healing.* New York: Free Press of Glencoe, Inc., 1964.

Lieberman, Myron. *Education as a Profession.* Englewood Cliffs, N.J.: Prentice-Hall, Inc., 1956.

Lynd, Robert, and Lynd, Helen Merrell. *Middletown.* New York: Harcourt, Brace & Co., 1929.

Maxey, Chester C. *Political Philosophies.* New York: The Macmillan Company, 1950.

Mead, Margaret. *Coming of Age in Samoa.* New York: Mentor Books, New American Library, 1949.

Mead, Margaret. *Growing Up in New Guinea.* New York: Mentor Books, New American Library, 1953.

Milliken, Robert L., and Patterson, John. "Relationship of Dogmatism and Prejudice to Counseling," *Counselor Education and Supervision,* Vol. 6 (Winter, 1967), pp. 125–129.

Mills, C. Wright. *The Power Elite.* New York: Oxford University Press, 1957.

Nader, Ralph. *Unsafe at Any Speed.* New York: Grossman Publishers, Inc., 1965.

Packard, Vance. *The Waste Makers.* New York: David McKay Co., Inc., 1960.

Robbins, Rossell H. *Encyclopedia of Witchcraft and Demonology.* New York: Crown Publishers, Inc., 1959.

Rogers, Carl R. *Client-Centered Therapy.* Boston: Houghton Mifflin Company, 1951.

Rogers, Carl R. *On Becoming a Person. A Therapist's View of Psychotherapy.* Boston: Houghton Mifflin Company, 1961.

Shermis, S. Samuel. *Philosophic Foundations of Education.* New York: American Book Company, 1967.

Shipley, Thorne (ed.). *Classics in Psychology.* New York: Philosophical Library, Inc., 1961.

Tawney, R. H. *Religion and the Rise of Capitalism.* New York: Mentor Books, New American Library, 1942.

Warner, W. Lloyd. *Yankee City.* New Haven, Conn.: Yale University Press, 1963.

Whyte, William H. *The Organization Man.* New York: Simon and Schuster, Inc., 1956.

COGNITIVELY ORIENTED COUNSELING APPROACHES

8

The content presented in this and the next chapter is labeled in most counseling textbooks "Theories of Counseling" or "Counseling Models" or "Approaches to Counseling" or "Counseling Points of View." The latter two terms will be used here since they seem more appropriate in view of the formal meaning attached to "theory" and "model," particularly as applied to speculations about counseling. However, "theory," "model," and "approach" will often be used interchangeably in the discussion that follows for no other than stylistic reasons.

The diverse points of view discussed in this chapter and the next represent a considerable sweep of the helping relationship. Many who separate counseling from psychotherapy on any one of several dimensions would argue rather persuasively that what is presented are theories of psychotherapy rather than counseling. If this reasoning is valid, few "theories" of counseling exist. Perhaps an even more forceful argument is that the content presented may be viewed as summaries of personality theories or behavior theories. Since counseling deals with behavior, it would seem inevitable and logical that a counseling theory incorporate or be built upon a theory of behavior.

While more will be said in Chapter Ten about theory, its nature, function, and purposes, basically it is a practical means or framework for making systematic observations and explaining phenomena. Counseling theory attempts to explain and provide understandings of what happens in the counseling relationship. Some years ago, Shoben and his associates remarked that those who deal directly with clients use theoretical ideas and that "their choice is not one of theory versus no theory, but between notions of human conduct that are explicit and formalized against those that are implicit and the inarticulate product of experience."[1]

Although little or no compelling evidence exists that counseling success depends definitely upon

[1] Edward J. Shoben, Jr., *et al.*, "Behavioral Theories and a Counseling Case: A Symposium," *Journal of Counseling Psychology*, Vol. 3 (Summer, 1956), pp. 107–124.

the extent and explicitness of a counselor's theoretical orientation, or that one theory is superior to another, extensive effort within recent years has gone into theory construction. It is to be hoped that some day unification of the multiplicity of theories will take place. However, as Black has pointed out, resolution of theoretical differences may come through the critical analysis of the process rather than the promotion of a particular point of view.[2]

Examination of counseling points of view indicates great diversity. Yet each viewpoint can teach something if one evaluates the facts and opinions behind it. Basic issues cut across all approaches, and differences often appear to exist largely in emphasis and convictions.

This chapter and the next will summarize nine counseling viewpoints. We would be hard pressed to defend against the charge that we had excluded some major ones in the field. The reason for choosing these nine is that they represent clear-cut and important formulations. To date, those excluded do not seem to have attained the eminence or excited the interest of those included. The omitted ones also tend to overlap with one another and with the more polar theories presented here. It is essential for the student to realize that the clear dichotomy indicated is an exaggeration used for convenience of comparison, contrast, and discussion. Much understanding is to be found in the theories not presented. In our opinion, such understanding will come more easily if it is based on the content of this and the next chapter.

How best to organize the presentation of these viewpoints remains a difficult decision. A case could be made for ordering it chronologically, according to the following continuum:

Psychoanalytic	Trait/ Factor	Self Theory	Existential
1900	1950		2000

But this plan would give little more than some notion of the historical development of a counseling theory. Patterson has grouped existing theories into five categories ranging from cognitive to affective, as follows:[3]

Rational	Learning	Psychoanalytic	Phenomenological	Existential
COGNITIVE				AFFECTIVE

Within categories, no attempt was made to base theories upon the dimensions of the continuum. Perhaps the merit of Patterson's scheme is that it moves from the relatively simple to the more intricate, although all theories of human behavior are complex because man himself is complex. The order followed in this and the next chapter is based somewhat upon a similar continuum.

Since two excellent volumes[4] devoted entirely to counseling theory have been published recently, no attempt will be made here to present counseling theories in their entirety. The student is referred to these two sources and to other relevant books and articles throughout the discussion that follows. For each viewpoint there will be identification and discussion of (1) its proponents and relevant sources, (2) the major concepts it embodies, (3) the counselor and the counseling process, and (4) the major criticisms of it and the contributions it has made. Treatment is devoted, then, to the broad dimensions of the viewpoints rather than to the deviations, details, or refinements connected with them.

Since each individual in counselor preparation is urged to develop a personal theory of counseling, it would seem necessary to know existing viewpoints in counseling and why they exist. He is then in a better position to evolve, through practice and study, the approach most appropriate for him.

[2] J. D. Black, "Common Factors of the Patient-Therapist Relationship in Diverse Psychotherapies," *Journal of Clinical Psychology,* Vol. 8 (July, 1952), pp. 302–306.

[3] C. H. Patterson, *Theories of Counseling and Psychotherapy* (New York: Harper & Row, Publishers, 1966).

[4] C. H. Patterson, *Theories of Counseling and Psychotherapy* (New York: Harper & Row, Publishers, 1966), and Buford Stefflre and W. Harold Grant (eds.), *Theories of Counseling,* 2nd ed. (New York: McGraw-Hill Book Co., 1972).

Trait and Factor Viewpoint

PROPONENTS AND SOURCES

The best-known proponents of the trait and factor point of view have been associated with the University of Minnesota. They include Walter Bingham, John Darley, Donald G. Paterson, and E. G. Williamson. Most renowned is Williamson (1967 APGA president), who served as Dean of Students at the University of Minnesota from 1941 to 1970. While this point of view has been expounded in a number of journal articles and books, the most definitive treatments by Williamson are contained in *How to Counsel Students*,[5] *Counseling Adolescents*,[6] and *Vocational Counseling*.[7] Relevant source material also appears in two chapters written by Williamson – one in a monograph entitled *Counseling Points of View*[8] and the other in the previously cited volume edited by Stefflre and Grant.[9]

The trait and factor point of view is sometimes called "directive counseling" and "counselor-centered" theory. Like all dynamic viewpoints it has undergone change since its origin as a vocational counseling approach. It has been broadened to include a concern for total development, not solely vocational development.

MAJOR CONCEPTS

Advocates of this viewpoint explain personality as a system of interdependent traits or factors such as abilities (e.g., memory, spatial relations, verbal, etc.), interests, attitudes, and temperament. Development of the individual progresses from infancy to adulthood as these factors are energized and mature. Numerous attempts have been made to categorize people in terms of various trait dimensions. Scientific study of the individual has included (1) assessing his traits by psychological tests and other means, (2) defining or portraying him, (3) helping him to know and understand himself and his environment, and (4) predicting probable success in certain ventures. Fundamental to trait and factor counseling is the assumption that man seeks to use self-understanding and knowledge of his abilities as means of developing his potentiality. Achievement of self-discovery results in intrinsic satisfaction and reinforces efforts to become all that one is able to become.

Williamson notes that "The foundation of modern concepts of counseling rests upon the assumption of the unique individuality of each child and also upon the identification of that uniqueness through *objective* measurement as contrasted with techniques of *subjective* estimation and appraisal."[10] Psychologists have long tried to develop instruments capable of objectively assessing individuals for purposes of counseling them about educational and vocational decisions. Elaborate probability tables utilizing one or more intellective and/or nonintellective variables have been constructed to enable the counselor to help his client select courses, programs of study, a college, etc., rationally and presumably with some probability of success.

In Williamson's opinion the purpose of counseling is to facilitate the development of excellence in all aspects of human life. He further asserts that "The task of the trait-factor type of counseling is to aid the individual in successive approximations of self-understanding and self-management by means of helping him to assess his assets and liabilities in relation to the requirements of progressively changing life goals and his vocational career."[11] In his early work Williamson referred to

[5] E. G. Williamson, *How to Counsel Students* (New York: McGraw-Hill Book Co., Inc., 1939).
[6] E. G. Williamson, *Counseling Adolescents* (New York: McGraw-Hill Book Co., Inc., (1950).
[7] E. G. Williamson, *Vocational Counseling* (New York: McGraw-Hill Book Co., Inc., 1965).
[8] E. G. Williamson, "Some Issues Underlying Counseling Theory and Practice," in Willis E. Dugan (ed.), *Counseling Points of View* (Minneapolis: University of Minnesota Press, 1959), pp. 1–13.
[9] E. G. Williamson, "Vocational Counseling: Trait-Factor Theory," in Buford Stefflre and W. Harold Grant, (eds.). *Theories of Counseling, op. cit.*, pp. 136–176.

[10] Williamson, *Vocational Counseling*, p. 56.
[11] Williamson, "Vocational Counseling: Trait-Factor Theory," p. 198.

clinical counselors "who diagnose and counsel in such problem areas as mental hygiene, reading and studying difficulties, and vocational and educational orientation."[12] Counseling — by assisting the individual to modify or eliminate defects, disabilities, and limitations — facilitates personality growth and integration. It is believed that in the counseling relationship the individual is able to face, clarify, and solve immediate problems. Presumably he learns from the process and can apply what has been learned to future conflict situations.

Assumptions Underlying the Viewpoint Williamson has identified eight assumptions regarding personality, work, and society which undergird trait and factor counseling.[13] Five are summarized here:

1. Because every individual is an organized, unique pattern of capabilities and potentialities and because these qualities are relatively stable after adolescence, objective tests can be used to identify these characteristics.
2. Personality and interest patterns correlate with certain work behavior. Consequently, identification of characteristics of successful workers is information which is useful in helping individuals choose careers.
3. Different school curricula require different capacities and interests and these can be determined. Individuals will learn more easily and effectively when their potentials and aptitudes are congruent with curriculum demands.
4. Student and counselor diagnoses of student potential should precede placement in a curriculum and/or work setting. Diagnosis prior to instruction would facilitate instruction since modifications could be made based upon what is known about the individual.
5. Each person possesses the ability and the desire to identify cognitively his own capabilities. He seeks to order and maintain his life and to utilize his capabilities in achieving satisfying work and home life.

Nature of Man. Williamson has urged counselors to examine continuously their philosophic orientation and has noted that provisional answers rather than tribal dogma seem in order. He has posed and responded to such questions about the nature of man, the nature of human development, the nature of the "good life," who determines what is good, and the nature of the universe and man's relationship with it.[14] In respect to the nature of man, he believes that man is born with the potential for both good and evil. The meaning of life is to seek good and reject or control evil. He thinks that counselors should be optimistic about man and must believe that man can learn to solve his problems, particularly if he learns to utilize his abilities.

In respect to the nature of human development, Williamson believes that "Man may not be fully capable, autonomously in the Rousseauan pattern, of becoming his potentiality *without* human assistance; rather does he need other persons to aid him to achieve his full development of potentiality."[15] Responding to what is the nature of the "good life," he states,

> It is one thing to accept and advocate self-actualization or *becoming* one's full potentiality. It is another and not identical assumption that the nature or form of one's full potential and self-actualization will thus be the "best possible" or "the good" form of human nature. Indeed, man seems to be capable both of becoming his "best bestial and debasing self," as well as those forms of "the best" that are of high excellence.[16]

Williamson identifies "excellence" as one dimension of the "good" and believes that since counselors serve as role models for their clients they should strive for excellence in all things.

In respect to who determines the "good," Wil-

[12] Williamson, *How to Counsel Students,* p. 56.
[13] Williamson, "Vocational Counseling: Trait-Factor Theory," pp. 194–195.
[14] Williamson, *Vocational Counseling,* pp. 181–189.
[15] *Ibid.,* p. 183.
[16] *Ibid.,* p. 185.

liamson rejects dictating the form of determination and feels that the search for the good may well constitute the good life. He has noted that conceptions of the universe and man's relationship to it often take the form that either (1) man is alone in an unfriendly universe or (2) the universe is friendly and favorable to man and his development. Williamson urges each counselor to develop his "personal cosmology."

THE COUNSELOR AND THE COUNSELING PROCESS

The trait and factor viewpoint holds that the counselor actively influences the development of the client. Williamson contends that the individual's freedom "to become" includes self-destructive and antisocial forms of individuality as well as positive development.[17] Because of this possibility, the counselor seeks openly and frankly to influence the direction of development. Counseling help is sought because people do not possess the personal resources to determine their own individuality. Since they do not fully understand themselves, externally known diagnostic data are collected by the counselor to supplement a client's perceptions of himself. The counselor uses these data to formulate hypotheses for understanding the individual. They are tentative and have to be checked and verified.

Williamson recognizes that students who come voluntarily for counseling are easier to help, but he doubts that the completely voluntary relationship is the only possible one for counseling. He urges that the counselor not sit in his office and wait for students, but he does not advocate "forcing" or "compelling" them. "In every school surely there are many, many situations in which a little inventiveness in working out a roundabout way of persuading people to want to do what they 'ought' (or need) to do, would produce effective results and would be of great use to teachers."[18] The counseling objectives set forth by Williamson include (1) helping individuals feel better by acceptance of their perceived self and (2) helping individuals think more clearly in resolving their personal problems so that they can control their own development through rational problem-solving methods.

The counselor with a trait/factor viewpoint is active in the learning situation represented by counseling. He is involved in diagnoses, presenting information, clarifying issues, and the like. He collects and evaluates data. He sorts and appraises life history data to help the individual understand himself. Because the counselor is older or more mature and has special skills, his major role in counseling is essentially that of a teacher, with the subject matter being the counselee and his own pattern of behavior. The task of the counselor is to teach the counselee how to learn about himself and his environment while the counselee's task is to learn how to understand himself and to use this learning rationally to achieve a productive life.

The work of trait/factor counselors was divided into six steps by Williamson.[19] *Analysis* involves collecting data from a wide variety of sources to obtain an understanding of the client. *Synthesis* refers to the summarizing and organizing of the data to determine the client's strengths and liabilities. *Diagnosis* is the counselor's conclusions about the problem causes and characteristics. *Prognosis* refers to the counselor's prediction of the counselee's future development or the implications of the diagnosis. *Counseling* means the steps taken by counselor and counselee to bring about adjustment and readjustment. *Follow-up* includes whatever the counselor does to assist the counselee with new or recurring problems as well as evaluation of the effectiveness of counseling.

The counselor's techniques were placed in five general categories by Williamson[20]: (1) forcing conformity, (2) changing the environment, (3) selecting the appropriate environment, (4) learning needed

[17] Williamson, "Some Issues Underlying Counseling Theory and Practice," p. 3.
[18] *Ibid.*, p. 10.

[19] Williamson, *How to Counsel Students*, p. 57.
[20] Williamson, *Counseling Adolescents*, p. 215.

skills, and (5) changing attitudes. Five stages of counseling were conceptualized by Williamson[21]: (1) establishing rapport, (2) cultivating self-understanding, (3) advising or planning a program of action, (4) carrying out the plan, and (5) where appropriate, making referral to other personnel workers. In respect to advising, the trait and factor counselor could engage in (1) *direct advising,* which means that he states his opinion openly and frankly, (2) the *persuasive method,* wherein the evidence is marshaled in such a fashion as to lead the individual to understand the outcomes of alternative actions, or (3) an *explanatory method,* which refers to explaining the significance of diagnostic data and pointing out possible solutions.

CRITICISMS AND CONTRIBUTIONS

Common criticisms of the trait and factor viewpoint may be summarized briefly:

1. The viewpoint was developed in an educational setting and its clientele was restricted primarily to students who possessed varying degrees of maturity and self-responsibility.
2. The viewpoint overemphasizes counselor control and results in the counselee's becoming dependent upon the superior being of the counselor for direction and definition.
3. The counselee's affective concerns are at best minimized and at worst ignored or relegated to the domain of psychotherapists.
4. Too much reliance is placed upon objective data. The overuse of and overconfidence in these data are not justified because of their present limitations in reliability, validity, and completeness.
5. A dilemma exists for the counselor, who is urged to make sure that the counselee actualize his potentialities but must do this without undue exhortation or persuasion.

The contributions often cited for the trait and factor viewpoint are as follows:

1. It has sought to apply the scientific approach to assisting man with his problems. Particularly at its origin, the trait and factor viewpoint represented a protest against the prevailing shoddy practices of untrained personnel.
2. Its emphasis upon the use of objective test data led to improvements in test development, their predictive uses, and the collection and use of environmental data.
3. The emphasis given to diagnosis called attention to problems and their sources and led to the creation of techniques to deal with them.
4. The emphasis upon cognition and cognitive forces counterbalanced other viewpoints which stressed affect and emotional states.

[21] *Ibid.,* p. 224.

Rational-Emotive Viewpoint

PROPONENT AND SOURCES

Albert Ellis, a clinical psychologist specializing in the field of marriage and family counseling, has set forth the basic tenets of rational-emotive psychotherapy in his book, *Reason and Emotion in Psychotherapy.*[22] In this book he outlines the origin of the viewpoint. After becoming dissatisfied with the outcomes of his work in marriage and family counseling, Ellis completed psychoanalytic training and practiced psychoanalysis. He soon came to believe that orthodox analytical procedures with their emphasis upon insight were not sufficient to enable his clients to overcome their deep-seated fears and hostilities. Drawing upon his experiences as a private practitioner and his knowledge of behavioral learning theory, he formed rational-emotive therapy.

MAJOR CONCEPTS

Ellis has stated that he views man as both rational and irrational. People behave in certain ways because they believe that they should or must act in these ways. Man possesses a high degree of suggestibility and negative emotionalism (anxiety,

[22] Albert Ellis, *Reason and Emotion in Psychotherapy* (New York: Lyle Stuart, 1967), 442 pp. See also *Humanistic Psychotherapy: The Rational-Emotive Approach* (New York: The Julian Press, Inc., 1973), 273 pp.

guilt, and hostility). Man's emotional problems lie in his illogical thinking. By maximizing his intellectual powers man can free himself of his emotional disturbances. The rational-emotive practitioner believes that no person is to be blamed for anything he does. Blame and anger are viewed as dysfunctional and irrational feelings.

A major element in rational-emotive therapy is the assumption that thinking and emotion are not two disparate processes. Ellis believes that the two overlap and that, for all practical purposes, thinking and emotion are the same thing. Drawing upon Stanley Cobb's work, emotion is defined as:

> . . . (1) an introspectively given affect state, usually mediated by acts of interpretation; (2) the whole set of internal physiological changes, which help (ideally) the return to normal equilibrium between the organism and its environment, and (3) the various patterns of overt behavior, stimulated by the environment and implying constant interactions with it, which are expressive of the stirred up physiological state (2) and also the more or less agitated psychological state (1).[23]

Emotions, according to Ellis, can be controlled in four ways: "(a) by electrical or biochemical means (e.g., electroshock treatments, barbiturates or tranquilizing or energizing drugs); (b) by using one's sensorimotor system (e.g., doing movement exercises or using yoga breathing techniques); (c) by employing one's existing emotional states and prejudices (e.g., changing oneself out of love for a parent or a therapist); and (d) by using one's cerebral processes (e.g., reflecting, thinking or telling oneself to calm down or become excited.)"[24] While noting that these four processes are highly interrelated, Ellis stresses that emotion is caused and controlled by thinking. Emotion is biased and prejudiced thought or an intrinsically attitudinal and cognitive process. The following statement illustrates his belief that emotion does not exist in its own right:

> . . . sustained human emotions are the result of relatively reflective appraisals. Where we are quite capable of *un*reflectively or immediately noting that an apple tastes bad or that a ball is hurtling directly at us, and hence instantaneously feeling disgust or fear, we are also capable of reflectively noting that most blotchy apples taste bitter or that we may get hit by a ball if we stand too close to two boys who are having a catch. In which latter cases, we may feel disgusted by merely *thinking* about rotten apples or by *imagining* our getting hit by a ball.[25]

Ellis believes that which is usually labeled "thinking" consists of less personalized, dispassionate appraisals of a given situation, and that which is usually labeled "emoting" is composed of slanted, biased, highly personalized, passionate evaluations of some person or object. Ellis summarizes this by stating that "one's thinking often *becomes* one's emotion; and emoting, under some circumstances, *becomes* one's thought."[26] While an emotion may exist briefly without thought, Ellis has stated that " . . . it appears to be almost impossible to sustain an emotional outburst without bolstering it by repeated ideas."[27] Therefore the difference between feelings and emotions is that feelings are largely sensory appraisals (feeling good about eating ice cream) while emotions stem from cognitive sensory states (eating ice cream and thinking good things of the person who supplied it.)

Particularly important to the rational-emotive viewpoint is the concept that much of the individual's emotional behavior stems from "self talk" or internalized sentences. That which the individual tells himself *is* or *becomes* his thoughts and emotions. If an individual tells himself "That would be awful" or "That would be wonderful" in connection with a situation, his calm thinking is changed into excited emoting. Ellis states ". . . that every human being who gets disturbed really is telling himself a chain of false sentences — since that is the way that humans seem almost invariably to

[23] Stanley Cobb, *Emotions and Clinical Medicine* (New York: W. W. Norton and Company, 1950).
[24] Ellis, *op. cit.*, p. 40.

[25] *Ibid.*, p. 46.
[26] *Ibid.*, p. 49.
[27] *Ibid.*, p. 49.

think in words, phrases and sentences. And it is these sentences which really are, which constitute his neuroses."[28]

Since sustained emotion stems from self-verbalizations, a conscious effort must be made to change this internalized talk which creates negative emotions. Those people who rarely do so, according to Ellis, refrain because "(a) they are too stupid to think clearly, or (b) they are sufficiently intelligent, but just do not know how to think clearly in relation to their emotional states, or (c) they are sufficiently intelligent and informed but are too neurotic (or psychotic) to put their intelligence and knowledge to good use."[29]

Ellis has explained neurosis as consisting of stupid behavior by a non-stupid person:

> . . . a neurotic is a potentially capable person who in some way or on some level of his functioning does not realize that (or how) he is defeating his own ends. Or else he is an individual who (in rare cases) has full understanding of or insight into how he is harming himself but who, for some irrational reason, persists in self-sabotaging behavior. In any case, we may say that the neurotic is emotionally disabled because he does not know how to (or does not care to) think more clearly and behave less self-defeatingly.[30]

The major illogical ideas held and perpetuated by men and women that invariably lead to self-defeat and neurosis have been set forth by Ellis and are reproduced here.

> Irrational Idea No. 1. *The idea that it is a dire necessity for an adult human being to be loved or approved by virtually every significant other person in his community.*
>
> Irrational Idea No. 2. *The idea that one should be thoroughly competent, adequate and achieving in all possible respects if one is to consider oneself worthwhile.*
>
> Irrational Idea No. 3. *The idea that certain people are bad, wicked, or villainous and that they should be severely blamed and punished for their villainy.*
>
> Irrational Idea No. 4 *The idea that it is awful and catastrophic when things are not the way one would very much like them to be.*
>
> Irrational Idea No. 5. *The idea that human unhappiness is externally caused and that people have little or no ability to control their sorrows and disturbances.*
>
> Irrational Idea No. 6. *The idea that if something is or may be dangerous or fearsome one should be terribly concerned about it and should keep dwelling on the possibility of its occurring.*
>
> Irrational Idea No. 7. *The idea that it is easier to avoid than to face certain life difficulties and self-responsibilities.*
>
> Irrational Idea No. 8. *The idea that one should be dependent on others and needs someone stronger than oneself on whom to rely.*
>
> Irrational Idea No. 9. *The idea that one's past history is an all-important determiner of one's present behavior and that because something once strongly affected one's life, it should indefinitely have a similar effect.*
>
> Irrational Idea No. 10. *The idea that one should become quite upset over other people's problems and disturbances.*
>
> Irrational Idea No. 11. *The idea that there is invariably a right, precise, and perfect solution to human problems and that it is catastrophic if this perfect solution is not found.*[31]

Ellis contends that these ideas are taught by parents, absorbed from social agencies, and are the cause of most people's emotional disturbances. While childhood experiences strongly influence a person to think illogically, the illogical thinking can be reversed. That, of course, is the responsibility of the rational-emotive therapist: to show the client that his illogical thinking is the cause of his unhappiness and to help him change his self-sabotaging internal remarks and attitudes into rational behavior.

THE COUNSELOR AND THE COUNSELING PROCESS

The task of the counselor, according to Ellis, is to work with individuals who are unhappy and troubled and "to show them (a) that their difficul-

[28] *Ibid.,* p. 28.
[29] *Ibid.,* p. 54.
[30] *Ibid.,* p. 54–55.

[31] *Ibid.,* pp. 61–88.

ties largely result from distorted perceptions and illogical thinking and (b) that there is a relatively simple, though work-requiring, method of reordering their perceptions and reorganizing their thinking so as to remove the basic cause of their difficulties."[32] Ellis contends that all effective counselors teach or induce their clients to reperceive or rethink life events. Clients, by doing so, modify their illogical thought, emotion and behavior.

The main goal of rational-emotive therapists is to demonstrate to clients that their self-verbalizations have been and currently are the source of their emotional disturbances. The rational-emotive practitioner uncovers his clients' past and present illogical thinking by "(a) bringing them forcibly to his attention or consciousness, (b) showing him how they are causing and maintaining his disturbance and unhappiness, (c) demonstrating exactly what the illogical links in his internalized sentences are, and (d) teaching him how to rethink, challenge, contradict, and reverbalize these (and other similar sentences) so that his internalized thoughts become more logical and efficient."[33] Further, the rational-emotive therapist not only corrects the client's specific illogical thinking, but also demonstrates the main irrational ideas so that the client will not fall victim to one or more of them at a later time.

Advocates of rational-emotive therapy use relationship techniques, insight-interpretative techniques, and supportive techniques mainly as preliminary strategies designed to gain the client's trust and confidence. These techniques are useful, according to Ellis, to demonstrate that the individual is illogical and how he became that way. But relationship techniques fall short because they fail to show the client how he maintains his illogical thinking and how it can be changed. The rational-emotive therapist attacks the specific and general irrational ideas and induces the client to adopt more rational views. He does so in two main ways:

[32] *Ibid.*, p. 36.
[33] *Ibid.*, p. 58–59.

> (a) The therapist serves as a frank counter-propagandist who directly contradicts and denies the self-defeating propaganda and superstitions which the patient has originally learned and which he is now self-instilling.
> (b) The therapist encourages, persuades, cajoles, and occasionally even insists that the patient engage in some activity (such as doing something he is afraid of doing) which itself will serve as a forceful counter-propaganda agency against the nonsense he believes.[34]

Ellis has pointed out that the rational-emotive therapist must deal with the individual's *basic* irrational thinking processes that *underlie* all kinds of fears. Otherwise treatment of one specific fear will not prevent another illogical fear from cropping up at a later time. Because the therapist is supposed to be emotionally stronger and healthier than the client, he should be able to take the risk of attacking the client's defenses or resistances to changing his illogical thinking. Ellis believes that passivity on the part of the counselor encourages clients to take advantage of him and enables them to avoid facing and working on their basic problems.

Contrary to orthodox psychoanalysis, the rational-emotive therapist does not create a transference neurosis with his client, but when normal transference and countertransference relations appear, they are either directly interpreted or dealt with or simply noted but not interpreted to the client. The therapist spends considerable time in the interview, according to Ellis, analyzing and observing the philosophic basis of illogical beliefs. He then attacks the foundations of these beliefs. He uses, where appropriate, suggestion, persuasion, activity, homework assignments, and other directive methods of therapy.

Ellis has responded to charges and criticisms (1) that rational-emotive therapy is too unemotional, intellectualized, and oververbal, (2) that the use of reason is essentially limited in human affairs and psychotherapy, (3) that rational-emotive therapy is a superficial, suggestive form of psychotherapy, (4) that rational-emotive therapy is too directive, authoritarian, and brainwashing, and (5) that rational-

[34] *Ibid.*, p. 95.

emotive therapy does not work with extremely disturbed or mentally limited clients.[35]

TYPE OF CLIENTS

In his book Ellis cites cases where rational-emotive therapy was used to treat premarital and marital problems, frigidity, impotence and homosexuality, psychopathy, and borderline schizophrenia. He has repeatedly stressed its value in treating neurotics and individuals who do not believe they are emotionally disturbed but who know they are not functioning adequately in some area of their lives. Ellis has pointed out that psychotic individuals are the most difficult kind of clients and that therapeutic results with them are quite discouraging. He believes that this is due, not because they were reared to be the way they are, but because they were born with distinct psychotic tendencies exacerbated by their upbringing. However, Ellis believes they can be helped, but rarely truly cured, by intensive psychotherapy, including rational-emotive therapy.[36]

OUTCOMES

In a very forthright way, Ellis has stated that all (including himself) who present a system of counseling or psychotherapy describe clients who are treated successfully while those with whom therapy has been ineffective are rarely publicized. Some reasons for why people act self-defeatingly and resist therapy have been given by Ellis. They include (1) the human being's prolonged period of childhood, (2) difficulty in unlearning, (3) man's subjection to inertia, (4) short-sightedness, (5) the prepotency of desire over what individuals should or should not do in their own best interest, (6) oversuggestibility, (7) overvigilance and overcaution (stemming from fears), (8) grandiosity and overrebellion (the individual feels the universe revolves around him), (9) extremism rather than moderation, (10) tendencies toward change, oscillation, erraticness, and unbalance, (11) automaticity and unthinkingness, (12) forgetfulness, (13) wishful thinking, (14) ineffective focusing and organizing, (15) unsustained effort, (16) overemphasizing injustice, (17) overemphasizing guilt, (18) stress-proneness, (19) lack of self-perspective, (20) discrimination difficulties, (21) overgeneralization tendencies. These are some of the many conditions which make therapy ineffective or unsuccessful.[37]

Ellis has stated that when he practiced classical analysis he helped about 50 per cent of his total patients and 60 per cent of his neurotic ones. When he practiced analytically-oriented psychotherapy (1952–1955), he helped 63 per cent of his total patients and 70 per cent of his neurotic patients to distinctly or considerably improve. With respect to rational-emotive therapy, Ellis states that "... my own experience, as well as that of several of my associates, tend to show that whereas about 65 per cent of patients tend to improve significantly or considerably under most forms of psychotherapy, about 90 per cent of the patients treated for 10 or more sessions with RT tend to show distinct or considerable improvement. . . ." [38]

CRITICISMS AND CONTRIBUTIONS

The major criticism of rational-emotive therapy — that it relies too heavily on intellectual techniques and shortchanges emotions — have been identified and responded to by Ellis. Among the contributions attributed to the rational-emotive viewpoint is its emphasis upon extending treatment procedures outside the counselor's office and the active involvement of the counselor in the process.

Eclectic Viewpoint

PROPONENT AND SOURCES

The leading proponent of the eclectic viewpoint is Frederick C. Thorne, who in 1945 founded the *Journal of Clinical Psychology* and still edits it. Thorne earned the Ph. D. degree in psychology (Columbia

[35] *Ibid.*, p. 331–374.
[36] *Ibid.*, p. 266.
[37] *Ibid.*, pp. 375–419.
[38] *Ibid.*, p. 38.

University, 1934) and the M.D. degree (Cornell, 1938) and is a Diplomate in Clinical Psychology of the American Board of Examiners in Professional Psychology. His position has been presented in four books: *Principles of Personality Counseling,*[39] *Principles of Psychological Examining,*[40] *Clinical Judgment,*[41] and *Personality: A Clinical Eclectic Viewpoint.*[42] Recently, Brammer presented a statement advocating an "emerging eclecticism" as a view of counseling appropriate for most practitioners.[43]

MAJOR CONCEPTS

The word "eclectic" means to select, to choose appropriate doctrines or methods from various sources or systems. The eclectic believes that a single orientation is limiting and that procedures, techniques, and concepts from many sources should be utilized to best serve the needs of the person seeking help. The true eclectic maintains that he has a consistent philosophy and purpose in his work and that he employs techniques for reasons that are as well verified as possible rather than completely by trial and error. From his knowledge of perception, development, learning, and personality, the eclectic counselor develops a repertoire of methods and selects the most appropriate for the particular problem and the specific individual.

The sequence by which counselors develop an eclectic viewpoint has been described by Brammer. First, the counselor resists emphasizing theory exclusively. He observes and criticizes client and counselor behaviors. Second, the counselor studies the history of counseling and psychotherapy so that he can build upon what is known. Third, the counselor who evolves an eclectic viewpoint knows his own personality. He is aware of his interacting styles with particular kinds of clients.[44]

Thorne has attempted to analyze the contributions of all existing schools of counseling and to fit them together into an integrated system, retaining the best features of each. He refers to how the methods are combined and used as the "art of clinical practice."[45] His outline of the operational steps he envisions as necessary if an eclectic system is to be achieved follows:

1. *Compilation of all known psychotherapeutic techniques.* To a limited extent, this has already been achieved in the standard textbooks of psychology and psychiatry.
2. *Operational definitions.* There will need to be operational descriptions of exactly what goes on with each method. Verbatim transcriptions of group therapy, nondirective therapy and psychoanalytic techniques are now available; other techniques will soon be objectified by motion pictures and recordings.
3. *Evaluation of functional dynamics.* There is paramount need for the analysis of just what dynamically occurs in each therapeutic method. This will be eventually accomplished by the experimental analysis of all factors in therapy.
4. *Relating therapy to psychopathology.* A comprehensive knowledge of pathology is essential to any valid system of therapy. The hypothetical formulations of all methods of therapy must be validated experimentally in order to determine whether the actual dynamics are as postulated.
5. *Establishing indications and contraindications for each method.* It must be learned exactly what any method can be expected to do in order to establish rational indications for its use.
6. *Establishment of criteria of therapeutic effect.* Prior to any attempt to collect data concerning therapeutic efficacy, it is necessary to establish rigorous criteria concerning what constitutes a reliable index of therapeutic efficiency.
7. *Statistical analysis of large scale data.* The ultimate test of any method is its efficacy in large scale application throughout the world. Results from small scale laboratory experiments may be suggestive but not conclusive.
8. *Validation through prognosis.* If diagnostic hypotheses

[39] Frederick C. Thorne, *Principles of Personality Counseling* (Brandon, Vt.: Journal of Clinical Psychology, 1950).
[40] Frederick C. Thorne, *Principles of Psychological Examining* (Brandon, Vt.: Journal of Clinical Psychology, 1955).
[41] Frederick C. Thorne, *Clinical Judgment* (Brandon, Vt.: Journal of Clinical Psychology, 1961).
[42] Frederick C. Thorne, *Personality: A Clinical Eclectic Viewpoint* (Brandon, Vt.: Journal of Clinical Psychology, 1961).
[43] Lawrence M. Brammer, "Eclecticism Revisited," *Personnel and Guidance Journal,* Vol. 48 (November, 1969), pp. 193–197.

[44] Brammer, "Eclecticism Revisited," pp. 195–196.
[45] Thorne, *Principles of Personality Counseling,* pp. 27–28.

and therapeutic methods have been validly applied, it follows that the whole process of case handling can be predicted and directed from initial evaluation to final outcome. This is genuinely a directive process requiring the highest clinical skills.[46]

Eclecticism as perceived by Thorne would require a global evaluation of an individual in respect to his past history, present situation, and future possibilities. This evaluation would utilize methods of understanding personality development contributed by the biological and social sciences. It would require the counselor to possess direct and intimate knowledge of the individual in all his manifestations and activities.

Both affective-impulsive and rational-intellectual concerns are dealt with as they are encountered in the counselee. Eclectic counseling theory and practice are built upon the need for maximizing the individual's intellectual resources to develop problem-solving behavior. Maladjustment is believed to result from the client's failure to learn to use his intellectual resources, as he was supposed to do early in life.

Counseling is viewed as a process of reeducation and treatment and is conceptualized as training the individual. If emotions block training, they may have to be resolved but this is not an inevitable step since training may take place under unfavorable conditions. "The goal of therapy is to replace emotional-compulsive behavior with deliberate rational adaptive behavior based on the highest utilization of intellectual resources."[47]

Counseling and psychotherapy are conceived of as a learning process. The learning process, according to Thorne, involves

> . . . (a) diagnosing the etiologic psychodynamic factors in the disorder in order to formulate the problem to be learned, (b) arranging optimum conditions for learning, (c) outlining and guiding the steps of education and reeducation, (d) providing opportunities for practice, and (e) giving the subject insight into the nature of the process and its results in order to increase motivation and incentive to learn.[48]

[46] *Ibid.*
[47] *Ibid.*, p. 24.
[48] *Ibid.*, p. 28.

Counseling is defined as a "face-to-face relationship in which the counselor, a person competently trained in psychological science, consciously attempts by attitudes and verbal means to help others solve problems of life in which personality factors are the primary etiologic agents."[49] Further, it is concerned with the personality problems of normal people with intact personality resources and is regarded as a method of dealing with man's more superficial personality problems rather than defect or disorder.

Thorne believes that an individual seeks counseling assistance because he has problems with which he is unable to cope alone. The counselee expects the counselor to be more intelligent and to have more training and experience than he does. Consequently, a dominance-submission relationship is present in every counseling relationship, no matter how nondirective the counselor.

The direction of counseling lies on an active-passive continuum and is the responsibility of the counselor. Any degree or multiple degrees of this continuum may be used with a counselee according to the indications in the situation.

> Direction is an attribute of behavior indicative of specific function and variously expressed in terms of needs, drives, goals, purposes, and other concepts descriptive of integrated behavior. . . . Until such time as the person demonstrates his ability to regulate his behavior within the limits of what is socially acceptable, he is subjected to varying degrees of direction or regulation from the environment. The general rule may be stated that *the need for direction is inversely correlated with the person's potentialities for effective self-regulation,* i.e., the healthier the personality, the less the need for direction; the sicker the personality, the more the need for direction.[50]

Training and experience let the counselor know when to utilize directive or nondirective methods. And the skill with which the method is used is the critical factor, not the method per se.

Thorne believes that an individual's personality is formed and reflected as he interacts with his en-

[49] *Ibid.*, p. 85.
[50] *Ibid.*, pp. 87–88.

vironment. It is characterized as a process of changing or becoming. Personality dynamics include a series of drives: (1) the drive for higher organization (actualization, perfect functioning, integration), (2) the drive to achieve and maintain stability (self-preservation, homeostasis, control, life goals, life-style), and (3) the drive to integrate opposing functions so as to avoid imbalance. There is "a constant striving for unity manifesting itself in efforts to maintain the unity of the system of organization self-consistently." [51]

An individual's life-style is based upon his characteristic patterns of achieving unification of his strategy in satisfying needs and coping with reality. Consciousness is "considered the main organizing, integrating and unitizing mechanism determining and making possible higher level personality functioning." [52] Emotional status and disturbances in behavior result from disturbances of consciousness. Self-image is defined as what one thinks himself to be while the self-concept is defined as the evaluative core of one's self as the individual believes it appears to others. "From the eclectic viewpoint, personality development is regarded as a struggle to transcend affective-impulsive-unconscious determination of behavior by learning and perfecting rational-logical-voluntary control of behavior."[53]

Past experience may place limits upon an individual but man transcends his past by his ability to imagine and manage his future. Logic and rationality are man's best means for becoming better and healthier.

THE COUNSELOR AND THE PROCESS

The counselor's major objective is to safeguard mental health. He achieves it by either preventing or modifying causative factors producing maladjustment or mental disorder. While individuals come for help (1) to avoid future maladjustment, (2) to gain relief, (3) to avoid pressure or punishment, or (4) to gain success or avoid failure, the counselor is primarily interested in causes and secondarily in symptoms.

[51] Thorne, *Personality: A Clinical Eclectic Viewpoint,* p. 65.
[52] *Ibid.,* p. 86.
[53] *Ibid.,* p. 184.

Thorne has stated that the basic problem in counseling is to assist the individual to learn to adapt more efficiently. Learning involves

> . . . (a) the diagnosis of the causes of personality maladjustment, (b) the making of a plan for modifying etiologic factors, (c) securing proper conditions for efficient learning, (d) stimulating the client to develop his own resources and assume responsibility for practicing new modes of adjustment, and (e) the proper handling of related problems which may contribute to adjustment.[54]

Eclectic counseling is indicated, Thorne believes, for those persons

> . . . (a) who are motivated enough to seek psychological help and to enter and remain in the counseling relationship long enough to receive help, (b) with whom a satisfactory contact (rapport) can be established so that the client feels free in expressing his problems, (c) who are sufficiently articulate to deal with problems on verbal levels, (d) whose difficulties are not organic in the sense of requiring medical or psychiatric care, (e) whose personality resources are sufficient so that some solution can be worked out, and (f) who are sufficiently stable and not dangerous either to themselves or to society so that treatment outside an institution is safe.[55]

Personality counseling is contraindicated for uncooperative clients, inaccessible (dull, disturbed, confused, or disoriented) clients, dangerous (suicidal, homicidal, or felonious) clients, inarticulate clients, and those who are unavailable for prolonged periods of time, who have psychopathic personalities, or who are very young or very old.

The eclectic counselor is one who possesses superior intelligence and judgment. His training should be in the basic and applied sciences as these relate to the human organism. Ideally it is coupled with intensive training in clinical psychology, psychiatry, and psychoanalysis and augmented by clinical experience in which he is exposed to all known types of psychopathology.

[54] Thorne, *Principles of Personality Counseling,* pp. 88–89.
[55] *Ibid.,* p. 91.

Factors Determining Choice of Methods Eclectic counseling is based upon a rational plan which involves appropriate measures for (1) opening the relationship, (2) dealing with causes and symptoms, and (3) terminating therapy. Passive techniques are generally used unless definite indications exist for more active methods. Thorne has discussed the factors upon which choice of techniques depends.[56] They are paraphrased here:

1. *Specificity of action needed.* Direct curative action on the causes of disorder is preferred.
2. *Economy of action.* Briefer methods are considered before expensive, lengthy methods.
3. *Natural history of the disorder.* Behavior disorders follow definite patterns of development including prodromal stage characterized by vague, undefined symptoms, syndromal stage without client insight but apparent to others, and syndromal stage with client insight.
4. The *distributive principle.* The counselor directs treatment in a plastic, adaptive manner along directions which offer most promise of results.
5. The *total push.* Every possible influence is brought to bear upon the individual.
6. *Failure of progress.* Blind experimentation using any and all methods available.

Eclectic counseling requires the counselor to be sensitive to the developing situation so that he can evaluate the indications and contraindications for the application of any method. This does not imply that the counselor works without a plan. However, his ability to alter plans or approaches is a hallmark of eclectic counseling. As the situation changes so should the plan. Thorne has stated that the counselor formulates a plan after he becomes familiar with case details and identifies causative factors, depending upon (1) his knowledge of the various levels of functional integration as related to normal adjustment or disease, (2) his ability to evaluate the counselee's status in relation to what is possible to accomplish, and (3) his ability to estimate goals and the possibility of attaining them.[57]

[56] *Ibid.*, pp. 106–108.
[57] *Ibid.*, p. 109.

Active Versus Passive Techniques A most relevant issue for the eclectic counselor is the degree of activeness or directiveness he utilizes in his work with a counselee. After tracing the history of basic trends of thought concerning the role of the counselor, Thorne makes the following generalizations concerning the use of directive or nondirective methods:

1. In general, passive methods should be used whenever possible.
2. Active methods should be used only with specific indication. In general, only a minimum of directive interference is necessary to achieve therapeutic goals.
3. Passive techniques are usually the methods of choice in the early stages of therapy when the client is telling his story and to permit emotional release.
4. The law of parsimony should be observed at all times. Complicated methods should not be attempted (except with specific indications) until simpler methods have failed.
5. All therapy should be client-centered. This means that the client's interests are the prime consideration. It does not mean that directive methods are contra-indicated. In many cases, the client's needs indicate directive action.
6. It is desirable to give every client an opportunity to resolve his problems non-directively. Inability of the client to progress therapeutically, using passive methods alone, is an indication for utilizing more directive methods.
7. Directive methods are usually indicated in situational maladjustment where a solution cannot be achieved without the cooperation of other persons.
8. Some degree of directiveness is inevitable in all counseling even if only in reaching the decision to use passive methods.[58]

Phases of Treatment Thorne has also outlined the stages developed in the course of treating a disorder:

1. *Stage of Incipient Maladjustment.* Minimal evidences of maladjustment with no insight. Usually recognizable only by a trained psychologist or psychiatrist.
2. *Stage of Overt Maladjustment.* Here the fact of malad-

[58] *Ibid.*, pp. 112–113.

justment becomes apparent, usually to others first, but as yet its seriousness is not comprehended.
3. *Stage of Reactive Personality Disorder.* The person develops secondary emotional reactions usually in the form of defense mechanisms intended to conceal or compensate for the maladjustment.
4. *Stage of Bewilderment and Trial and Error Behavior.* The person is now dimly aware that something is wrong but does not know what. Usually rationalizes in terms of projective devices. This is the lowest level of insight that something is wrong. Here the person develops a need for help.
5. *Stage of Insight into Psychological Nature of Disorder.* With some degree of shock and embarrassment, the person learns that his problems may be "mental."
6. *Stage of Reactive Depression and Discouragement.* Following the basic insight that the disorder is psychological, or after he has made a full "confession" of painful things, there is frequently a stage of reactive depression with feelings of futility. The person is shocked with the realization of "how could this have happened to me?" and of embarrassment as he looks forward to contact with people again.
7. *Stage of Symptomatic Relief.* Some superficial improvement occurs but no alleviation of basic etiological causes has yet been accomplished.
8. *Stages of Growth and Recovery.* Following release of negative emotions and acquisition of further insights, recovery processes get under way. This stage is associated with improved feeling tone and optimism. Here the specific etiologic factors are identified and remedied through use of appropriate methods.
9. *Stage of Relapse.* In practically all cases the recovery process does not have a uniform positive acceleration but is associated with "backsliding" and relapses. These relapses may be ignored if the general trend continues in the direction of improvement. The client may even be warned to expect relapses.
10. *Stage of Cure.* The client is relieved of symptoms, understands himself better, learns more adequate solutions of problems and reestablishes his position of independence.[59]

Diagnosis and Use of Case History Eclectic counselors advocate that a comprehensive case history be taken and that objective information be obtained from many sources. Thorne has noted that marked discrepancies may exist between the history taken from the counselee and information obtained elsewhere for any one of three reasons: "(a) The nature of the client's illness, (b) conscious or unconscious withholding or falsification of facts, and (c) disordered viewpoints of the client or informants due to the difference between phenomenological viewpoints."[60] Accurate case histories are significant for their diagnostic yield. Psychological diagnosis involves determining the sequence of cause-effect relationships. This permits evaluation as to whether the behavioral disorder is environmentally stimulated or organic in nature.

[59] *Ibid.*, p. 116.

Closing Phases of Counseling Terminating counseling requires as careful attention as beginning the process. Terminal stages are characterized by problem-solving behavior on the part of the counselee. The counselor may engage in more directive activity compared to the first half of the process. Premature termination may occur because of (1) counselee relief from symptoms, (2) failure to achieve rapport, (3) crude direction by the counselor, (4) improper handling of transference by the counselor, (5) client financial problems, (6) uncontrollable environmental factors, and (7) client resistance.[61] Thorne has stated that an adequately treated client (1) expresses his affective-impulsive life more effectively, (2) has better control, (3) perceives himself and his environment more realistically, (4) thinks more logically, (5) has values, beliefs, and attitudes which are more internally consistent, (6) no longer indulges in mechanisms of repression or suppression, and (7) can be said to have grown, to have become more emotionally mature and more intellectually adequate.[62]

CRITICISMS AND CONTRIBUTIONS

Some of the more common criticisms of eclectic counseling are the following:

1. The present state of scientific progress does

[60] *Ibid.*, p. 132
[61] *Ibid.*, pp. 155–156.
[62] *Ibid.*, p. 150.

not permit detailing differential treatments for various diagnostic conditions.

2. Achieving facility in one counseling method alone is difficult, let alone achieving skill in a multiplicity of methods.

3. Counselees will be uneasy with changes in methods, and change may only be a counselor's rationalization because the selected method fails and he is uneasy or uncomfortable.

4. It is doubtful if the counselor can determine the correct or most appropriate method upon the basis of immediate client reaction.

The contributions often cited include the following:

1. An attempt at systematization of counseling in itself is valuable and worthwhile.

2. The eclectic approach deals with a wider range of etiologic factors than any single method.

3. Dogma and emotional involvement associated with a single orientation are minimized or reduced.

Psychotherapy by Reciprocal Inhibition

PROPONENT AND SOURCES

Since counseling is concerned with effecting behavioral changes, there have been attempts to interpret and explain what occurs in the process in the light of one or more of the several available learning theories. Reinforcement and conditioning theories have been applied very frequently. Ivan Pavlov's classic conditioning theory and B. F. Skinner's concepts and principles[63] have influenced many counseling theorists and practitioners.

Joseph Wolpe was educated in South Africa and received his M.D. degree from the University of Witwatersrand, Johannesburg (1948). He has served as Professor of Psychiatry at the University of Virginia (1960–1965) and Temple University (1965). The name of his conditioning therapy, "psychotherapy by reciprocal inhibition," also serves as the title for the volume he produced to describe the method.[64] In the Preface, Wolpe traces the evolution of his interest in counter-conditioning methods beginning in 1944 when as a medical officer he read enough to cause him to question the universality of Freud's Oedipal theory. His interest turned from Pavlov to Hull and from Hull to studies of experimentally-induced neuroses. The book was written during 1956–1957 while Wolpe was a fellow at the Center for Advanced Study in the Behavioral Sciences, Stanford, California.

Another source of information is *The Conditioning Therapies*, a report of the papers presented and the resulting discussion at the University of Virginia Conference,[65] and *The Practice of Behavior Therapy*.[66]

MAJOR CONCEPTS

The logic of Wolpe's approach has been briefly stated by him:

> Only three kinds of processes are known that can bring about lasting changes in an organism's habit of response to a given stimulus situation: growth, lesions, and learning. Since neurotic behavior demonstrably originates in learning, it is only to be expected that its elimination will be a matter of unlearning.[67]

Wolpe conducted experimental observations on cats in which neurotic anxiety had been induced and was later removed by having the animals eat in the presence of initially small but progressively larger doses of anxiety-evoking stimuli. When anxiety was intense, feeding was inhibited. Transient inhibition of anxiety occurred at time of feeding because the reduction of the hunger drive "stamped this in." The experiments suggested to Wolpe that human neurotic anxieties might be handled similarly, and he concluded that "fundamental psychotherapeutic effects follow reciprocal inhibition of neurotic responses."[68] Rather than ap-

[63] B. F. Skinner, *Beyond Freedom and Dignity* (New York: Alfred A. Knopf, Inc., 1970), 225 pp.

[64] Joseph Wolpe, *Psychotherapy by Reciprocal Inhibition* (Stanford: Stanford University Press, 1958).

[65] Joseph Wolpe *et al.* (eds.), *The Conditioning Therapies* (New York: Holt, Rinehart & Winston, Inc., 1964).

[66] Joseph Wolpe, *The Practice of Behavior Therapy* (New York: Pergamon Press, 1969), 314 pp.

[67] Wolpe, *Psychotherapy by Reciprocal Inhibition,* p. ix.

[68] *Ibid.*, p. ix.

plying feeding responses to overcome human neuroses, Wolpe utilizes more convenient anxiety-inhibiting responses such as assertion, relaxation, and sexual responses inside and outside the consultation room.

Learning takes place, according to Wolpe, if "a response has been evoked in temporal contiguity with a given sensory stimulus and it is subsequently found that the stimulus can evoke the response although it could not have done so before."[69] Reinforcement is defined by Wolpe as the process of learning. An individual's behavior can be judged as either *adaptive* (progress toward satisfaction of need or avoidance of possible damage or deprivation) or *unadaptive* (expenditure of energy or occurrence of damage or deprivation). Neurotic behavior was defined by Wolpe as "any persistent habit of unadaptive behavior acquired by learning in a physiologically normal organism. Anxiety is usually the central constituent of this behavior, being invariably present in the causal situations."[70] Unadaptive responses are usually extinguished; it is their persistence that is a feature of neuroses.

Anxiety Wolpe has defined anxiety as "the autonomic response pattern or patterns that are characteristically part of the organism's response to noxious stimulation."[71] He makes no differentiation between fear and anxiety, since there is no physiological difference in the response aroused by a stimulus associated with an objective threat such as a rattlesnake and unadaptive fear such as that aroused by a kitten. Neurotic behavior thus is learned. Stimuli previously incapable of provoking anxiety may acquire the power to arouse it if they happen to act on the organism when anxiety is evoked by other stimuli. Neuroses arise from the exposure of the individual either to ambivalent stimuli or to noxious stimuli (pain, discomfort), and these situations can induce high anxiety. However, not only well-defined stimuli but the ever present properties of the environment (light, shade, noise, etc.) may condition anxiety responses. If they do, the individual often suffers from pervasive anxiety.

> Since each of these enters into most, if not all, possible experience, it is to be expected that if any of them becomes connected to anxiety responses the patient will be persistently, and apparently causelessly anxious. He will be suffering from what is erroneously called "free-floating" anxiety, and for which a more suitable label would be *pervasive anxiety*.[72]

Conditions which predispose to neuroses include (1) direct evocation of anxiety (conditioned stimuli such as war experiences), (2) conflict (such as in difficult discriminations), and (3) confinement (spatial or environmental confinement).[73]

Principle of Reciprocal Inhibition Reciprocal inhibition is the inhibition, elimination, or weakening of old by new responses. The principle was stated by Wolpe: "If a response antagonistic to anxiety can be made to occur in the presence of anxiety-evoking stimuli so that it is accompanied by a complete or partial suppression of the anxiety responses, the bond between these stimuli and the anxiety responses will be weakened."[74] Wolpe points out that the bonds may be weakened by other means although when experimental extinction was sought, it was singularly ineffective. Poor extinction of anxiety responses was thought to be due to (1) the small amount of reactive inhibition generated by the autonomic response and (2) the reinforcement of anxiety responses by drive reduction when the individual is passively removed from anxiety-evoking stimuli.

THE COUNSELOR AND THE PROCESS

Individuals come for counseling because they suffer. Later they appraise therapy in terms of the relief experienced. The methods employed, according to Wolpe, should be assessed using several criteria.

[69] *Ibid.*, p. 19.
[70] *Ibid.*, p. 32.
[71] *Ibid.*, p. 34.
[72] *Ibid.*, p. 83.
[73] *Ibid.*, pp. 78–82.
[74] *Ibid.*, p. 71.

The primary criteria relate directly to the well-being of the patient. Is the suffering alleviated? If so, how quickly, how completely, and how enduringly? And how free is the accomplishment from disadvantageous sequelae? Secondary criteria are the amount of time and effort demanded of the therapist, and the cost of the treatment to the patient.[75]

Initial Interviews Wolpe has given a full account of the way interviews are conducted. The first interview lasts an hour, later ones 45 minutes. The patient faces the therapist across a desk, and notes are taken openly at every interview. Everything a patient says is accepted without question or criticism. An outline of early interviews (first 10–15) is abstracted from his remarks[76]:

1. The patient gives his name, address, age, telephone number.
2. A detailed history is taken of patient's difficulties, symptoms, precipitating events, and factors that aggravate or ameliorate symptoms.
3. Individuals who are unable to recall anything of the onset of neurotic reactions are urged to think back more carefully, but if nothing significant is produced, the point is not pressed. Wolpe tells such patients that "to overcome . . . neurotic reactions it is of greater relevance to determine what stimuli do or can evoke them at the present time."[77]
4. Attention is directed to the patient's life history, starting with the circumstances in which he grew up (attitudes and relationships with parents, siblings, and others; religious training; fears).
5. Patient gives educational experiences.
6. An occupational history is taken.
7. Patient is questioned about his sex life and marital history.
8. Bernreuter's self-sufficiency questionnaire is completed by the patient as homework.
9. Willoughby's questionnaire (a test for neuroticism) is administered in the interview situation.
10. Wolpe interprets how inhibitions or phobias or fears are learned.
11. From the patient's history, experiences which have led to present sensitivities are explained.
12. The patient is told that measures have to be taken to break down anxious habits and that some measures are applied in the consulting room while others are engaged in the life situation.
13. Methods are then introduced to inhibit anxiety and weaken neurotic habits. These include (a) assertive responses, (b) sexual responses, (c) relaxation responses, (d) respiratory responses, (e) "anxiety-relief" responses, (f) competitively conditioned motor responses, (g) "pleasant" responses in the life situation (with drug enhancement), and (h) interview-induced emotional responses and abreaction.

Methods The choice of responses depends upon the anxiety-evoking stimuli.

In general, assertive responses are used for anxieties evoked in the course of direct interpersonal dealings, sexual responses for sexual anxieties, relaxation responses for anxieties arising from any source whatever but especially from stimulus configurations that do not allow of any kind of direct action (e.g., inanimate objects), and respiratory responses for pervasive (free-floating) anxiety.[78]

These four techniques are briefly described here.

Assertive responses refer not only to more or less aggressive behavior but also to feelings of friendliness and affection. Assertive responses are used to treat anxieties arising from interpersonal relationships (e.g., inability to express one's opinion to friends lest they disagree).

The essence of the therapist's role is to encourage appropriate assertiveness, the outward expression, whenever it is reasonable and right to do so, of the feelings and action tendencies that anxiety in the past inhibited. In other words, the therapist instigates "acting out."

[75] Wolpe *et al.* (eds.), *The Conditioning Therapies,* p. 5.
[76] Wolpe, *Psychotherapy by Reciprocal Inhibition,* pp. 105–113.
[77] *Ibid.,* p. 105.

[78] *Ibid.,* p. 113.

Each act of assertion to some extent reciprocally inhibits the anxiety, and in consequence somewhat weakens the anxiety response habit.[79]

Techniques for instigating assertive behavior include (1) use of analogies, (2) behavior rehearsal in which the therapist takes the role of the persons toward whom the client has a neurotic anxiety reaction and instructs the client to express his inhibited feelings, and (3) pressure interviews, in which the individual is given a task to perform while verbal demands are simultaneously made upon him. Appropriate pressure is applied to motivate the individual to engage in the requisite behavior outside the consulting room. Wolpe has warned that assertive acts should never be instigated that have punishing consequences for the client.

Sexual responses refer to measures used to inhibit anxiety responses conditioned by various aspects of sexual situations. Sexual inhibition varies by definable properties within the situation. Wolpe indicates the essential nature of the techniques employed:

There are occasional patients of either sex in whom so high a degree of anxiety has been conditioned to individual women (or men) or classes of women (or men) that the mildest embrace or even close proximity may produce great disturbance; and if there is pervasive anxiety, as may be expected in patients so sensitive, its level is raised. Such a patient is instructed to expose himself only to sexual situations in which pleasurable feelings are felt exclusively or predominantly. The decision regarding the suitability of a situation is made *on the basis of the feelings experienced when the situation is in prospect.*[80]

Relaxation responses are methods which involve giving patients intensive training in the practice of relaxation to enable them to keep relaxing muscles not in use. Differential relaxation (tension kept to a minimum in the muscles required for an act along with relaxation of other muscles) is used. Wolpe gives training in relaxation in seven sessions to most of his patients.[81]

Respiratory responses are those used for individuals suffering from pervasive anxiety. After being shown how to empty and fill his lungs, the individual empties his lungs and then inhales a gas mixture usually consisting of 70 per cent carbon dioxide and 30 per cent oxygen. Between one and four inhalations are given at a session.

Systematic Desensitization. Most well known among Wolpe's techniques is that of systematic desensitization. Three sets of operations are involved in systematic desensitization: training in deep muscle relaxation, construction of anxiety hierarchies, and counterposing relaxation and anxiety stimuli from the hierarchies. The individual makes up a list of stimulus situations to which he reacts with graded amounts of anxiety. The most disturbing items are placed at the top and the least disturbing at the bottom. After being taught to relax, the individual (in some cases) is hypnotized and told to relax. He is then told to imagine the weakest item in the anxiety hierarchy. If relaxation is maintained, he is told to imagine the next weakest item, and so on until the strongest item can be encountered. Apparently the relaxation inhibits the anxiety and weakens the anxiety-invoking potential of the stimulus. If a stimulus is too strong and increases sensitivity, scenes are not presented for one or two interviews. The hierarchies of one patient are as follows:

A. Fear of hostility
   1. Devaluating remarks by husband
   2. Devaluating remarks by friends
   3. Sarcasm from husband or friends
   4. Nagging
   5. Addressing a group
   6. Being at social gathering of more than four people (the more the worse)
   7. Applying for a job
   8. Being excluded from a group activity
   9. Anybody with a patronizing attitude

[79] Wolpe *et al.* (eds.), *The Conditioning Therapies,* p. 11.
[80] Wolpe, *Psychotherapy by Reciprocal Inhibition,* pp. 130–131.
[81] *Ibid.,* p. 136.

B. Fear of death and its accoutrements
   1. First husband in his coffin
   2. At a burial
   3. Seeing a burial assemblage from afar
   4. Obituary notice of young person dying of heart attack
   5. Driving past a cemetery
   6. Seeing a funeral (the nearer the worse)
   7. Passing a funeral home
   8. Obituary notice of old person (worse if died of heart disease)
   9. Inside a hospital
   10. Seeing a hospital
   11. Seeing an ambulance
C. Fear of symptoms (despite *knowing* them to be non-significant)
   1. Extrasystoles
   2. Shooting pains in chest and abdomen
   3. Pains in left shoulder and back
   4. Pain on top of head
   5. Buzzing in ears
   6. Tremor of hands
   7. Numbness or pain in fingertips
   8. Dyspnea after exertion
   9. Pain in left hand (old injury)[82]

Outcomes Wolpe followed up 210 individuals he treated and reported 89 per cent recovery, which is indeed dramatic. He concludes his comparison of conditioning therapies with psychoanalysis with these words:

> The present position is clear. As far as the evidence goes, conditioning therapies appear to produce a higher proportion of lasting recoveries from the distress and disability of neurosis than does psychoanalysis. Even if a controlled study were to show an equal, or even higher, percentage of recovery for psychoanalysis, the time it requires would remain incomparably greater, and conditioning therapy would therefore deserve preference.[83]

CRITICISMS AND CONTRIBUTIONS

The more commonly cited criticisms and contributions parallel those cited for behavioral counseling (see page 202). In addition, some psychotherapists claim that recoveries represent only symptom relief rather than lasting modifications of the basic problem.

[82] *Ibid.*, pp. 142–143.
[83] Wolpe *et. al.* (eds.), *The Conditioning Therapies,* p. 15.

Behavioral Counseling Viewpoint

PROPONENTS AND SOURCES

John D. Krumboltz, Stanford University; Carl E. Thoresen, Stanford University; Jack Michael and Lee Meyerson, Arizona State University; and Ray E. Hosford, University of California, Santa Barbara, are among those who present behavioral counseling viewpoints. Primary treatment will be given here to the works of Krumboltz, Thoresen, and Hosford. The most relevant sources of information include *Revolution in Counseling,*[84] *Behavioral Counseling,*[85] five articles by Krumboltz,[86] an article by Thoresen,[87] and an article by Hosford.[88]

MAJOR CONCEPTS

Behavioral counselors define behavior as the function of the interaction of heredity and environment. Observable behavior is what counselors are concerned with and constitutes the criterion against which counseling outcomes are to be assessed. This view excludes virtually all hypothetical constructs such as those found in self-theory and in Freudian theory. "Man is not at the mercy of his

[84] John D. Krumboltz (ed.), *Revolution in Counseling.* Boston: Houghton Mifflin Company, 1966.
[85] John D. Krumboltz and Carl E. Thoresen (eds.), *Behavioral Counseling: Cases and Techniques* (New York: Holt, Rinehart, and Winston, Inc., 1969).
[86] John D. Krumboltz, "Behavioral Goals for Counseling," *Journal of Counseling Psychology,* Vol. 13 (Summer, 1966), pp. 153–159; John D. Krumboltz, "Behavioral Counseling: Rationale and Research," *Personnel and Guidance Journal,* Vol. 44 (December, 1965), pp. 383–387; John D. Krumboltz and Wade W. Schroeder, "Promoting Career Planning Through Reinforcement and Models," *Personnel and Guidance Journal,* Vol. 44 (September, 1965), pp. 19–26; John D. Krumboltz and Carl E. Thoresen, "The Effect of Behavioral Counseling in Group and Individual Settings on Information-Seeking Behavior," *Journal of Counseling Psychology,* Vol. 11 (Winter, 1964), pp. 324–333; John D. Krumboltz, "Parable of the Good Counselor," *Personnel and Guidance Journal,* Vol. 43 (October, 1964), pp. 118–124.
[87] Carl E. Thoresen, "Behavioral Counseling: An Introduction," *The School Counselor,* Vol. 14 (September, 1966), pp. 13–21.
[88] Ray E. Hosford, "Behavioral Counseling — A Contemporary Overview," *The Counseling Psychologist,* Vol. 1 (1969), pp. 1–32.

'unconscious' or his drives; for these entelechies, if they exist, can be expressed in many ways."[89]

Although there are wide divergencies in the specifics of behavioral viewpoints, fundamental agreement exists regarding the fact that most human behavior is learned. Behavior is modifiable by manipulation and the creation of learning conditions. Basically, the counseling process becomes the judicious and expert arrangement of learning or relearning experiences to help individuals change their behavior in order to solve whatever problems they manifest or select for presentation to the counselor.

Thoresen has characterized behavioral counseling with a fivefold statement:

1. Most human behavior is learned and is therefore subject to change.
2. Specific changes of the individual's environment can assist in altering relevant behaviors; counseling procedures seek to bring about relevant changes in student behavior by altering the environment.
3. Social learning principles, such as those of reinforcement and social modeling, can be used to develop counseling procedures.
4. Counseling effectiveness and the outcome of counseling are assessed by changes in specific student behaviors outside the counseling interview.
5. Counseling procedures are not static, fixed, or predetermined, but can be specifically designed to assist the student in solving a particular problem.[90]

Reinforcement Basic to behavioral counseling is the principle of reinforcement, simply defined as the creation of desirable consequences that will strengthen or facilitate certain behavior. In Ivan P. Pavlov's (1894–1936) classic conditioning studies reinforcement is defined as the presentation of the unconditioned stimulus (food) which evokes the unconditioned response (salivation) immediately following the conditioning stimulus (bell). In contrast, in B. F. Skinner's instrumental conditioning studies reinforcement is the attainment of a goal that satisfies a need. For the hungry rat in the Skinner box, reinforcement is securing food. In either view, stimuli or circumstances associated with the learning situation acquire reinforcing value, and this phenomenon is known as secondary reinforcement. In both classic and instrumental conditioning it is possible to extinguish a learned response by withholding reinforcement.

Not all human behavior can easily be fitted to the classical or Pavlovian conditioning model. The individual who learns, first of all, is motivated by some need. The need produces general exploratory activity. During the exploration, a response is made that is instrumental in achieving the appropriate goal. The response is learned.

The critical events of most human behavior are the environmental consequences of the behavior. Obviously, much of our learning is the result of secondary reinforcement. Michael and Meyerson group the stimulus events which serve as consequences of acts into three classes with respect to their effect on operant behavior.[91] Their description is paraphrased here:

1. *Positive reinforcers.* Behavior which preceded stimulus events has a good chance of occurring under similar conditions in the future. The stimulus events are called rewards and are pleasant; they include praise, affection, grades.
2. *Negative reinforcers.* Behavior which preceded the removal of stimulus events has a good chance of occurring under similar conditions in the future. Negative reinforcers or aversive stimuli are painful or unpleasant and include social disapproval, criticism, and nagging.
3. *No consequence and neutral stimuli.* Responses cease if followed by neutral stimuli. When behavior is not reinforced, operant extinction occurs.

In reality, complete extinction of behavior seldom occurs because individuals receive partial reinforcement; some responses are reinforced rather than all of them.

[89] Jack Michael and Lee Meyerson, "A Behavioral Approach to Counseling and Guidance," *Harvard Educational Review,* Vol. 32 (Fall, 1962), p. 395.
[90] Thoresen, *op. cit.,* p. 17.

[91] Michael and Meyerson, *op. cit.,* pp. 384–385.

Nature of Man The nature of man as conceived by the behavioral counselor has been outlined by Hosford[92] and described more fully by Skinner.[93] Hosford believes that man begins life, not as innately good or bad, but like a Lockean *tabula rasa* on which nothing has been written or stamped. Man reacts to stimuli he encounters in his environment. Heredity and the interaction of heredity and environment produce his behavior and form his personality. An individual's personality incorporates positive and negative habits, both of which are learned. A person's behavior is determined by the frequency and types of reinforcement provided in his life situations. Atypical behavior does not differ from normal behavior in the way it is acquired. It is atypical only because people label it as such.

Hosford points out that behaviorists do not believe it necessary to account for behavior by positing "the existence of unobservable internal states."[94] He refers, of course, to consciousness or awareness, of which Skinner has said, "Consciousness is a social product. It is not only *not* the special field of autonomous man, it is not within the range of a solitary man."[95] Further, "Rather than suppose that it is therefore autonomous man who discriminates, generalizes, forms concepts or abstractions, recalls or remembers, we can put matters in good order simply by noting that these terms do not refer to forms of behavior."[96]

Skinner defines the self as "... a repertoire of behavior appropriate to a given set of contingencies."[97] For him, the self is not a body with a person inside, but the body is itself a person "... in the sense that it displays a complex repertoire of behavior."[98] Speaking against the criticism that analyzing behavior in mechanical terms makes man into a machine, Skinner asserts that "Man is a machine in the sense that he is a complex system behaving in lawful ways, but the complexity is extraordinary."[99]

In contrast to those who believe that the individual selects the features of the world to be perceived, discriminates among them, evaluates them as good or bad, changes them and is held accountable for his actions, Skinner holds that

> ... a person is a member of a species shaped by evolutionary contingencies of survival, displaying behavioral processes which bring him under the control of the environment in which he lives, and largely under the control of a social environment which he and millions of others like him have constructed and maintained during the evolution of a culture. The direction of the controlling relation is reversed: a person does not act upon the world, the world acts upon him.[100]

THE COUNSELOR AND THE PROCESS

To Krumboltz, "Counseling consists of whatever ethical activities a counselor undertakes in an effort to help the client engage in those types of behavior which will lead to a resolution of the client's problems."[101] The behavioral counselor would agree to work on any problem presented by a client subject to three limitations: (1) counselor interest in client problem type, (2) the competences possessed by the counselor, and (3) ethical considerations.

Counseling is conceptualized in learning terms, with the counselor serving as an aid in the learning process. The counselor arranges conditions for the client to learn adaptive behavior so that he can cope with his problems.

While certain behavior problems do have organic origins, Krumboltz does not believe that the disease paradigm is appropriate for classifying behavioral problems.[102] He also rejects the notion that adaptive behavior is present in the individual and needs only to be released by a warm, accepting,

[92] Hosford, "Behavioral Counseling," pp. 1–4.
[93] Skinner, *Beyond Freedom and Dignity*, pp. 184–215.
[94] Hosford, "Behavioral Counseling," p. 3.
[95] Skinner, *Beyond Freedom and Dignity*, p. 192.
[96] *Ibid.*, p. 194.
[97] *Ibid.*, p. 199.
[98] *Ibid.*
[99] *Ibid.*, p. 202.
[100] *Ibid.*, p. 211.
[101] Krumboltz, "Behavioral Counseling: Rationale and Research," p. 384.
[102] Krumboltz (ed.), *Revolution in Counseling*, p. 7.

understanding counselor. To him, understanding is necessary but not sufficient. The client has to learn to resolve his difficulty and understanding is seen as but the first step upon which learning experiences can be built.

Krumboltz cites five advantages of conceptualizing client problems as learning problems. These are paraphrased here: (1) The theoretical and research base accumulated from current evidence and thinking about the problems of learning can generate new ideas. (2) Conceptualizing counseling as learning immediately integrates counseling with the educational enterprise. (3) Goals can be defined and reached. (4) Attention can be concentrated upon what should be done to develop more adaptive behavior. (5) Clients will feel an increased sense of responsibility for their actions because they are more aware of the consequences of their actions.

Counseling Goals Reference has been made (see Chapter Four) to the goals of counseling as stated by Krumboltz. It will be remembered that three criteria are used to assess a counseling goal: (1) It must be a goal desired by the client, (2) the counselor must be willing to help the client achieve this goal, and (3) it must be possible to assess the extent to which the client achieves this goal.[103] The three categories of goals include altering maladaptive behavior, learning the decision-making process, and preventing problems.

Counseling Methods Krumboltz has cited four general approaches from which present counseling techniques are derived.[104] From *operant learning* comes the knowledge that the timing of the counselor's reinforcements can be useful in producing client-desired behavior. The counselor's attention, interest, and approval following certain kinds of client responses determine, at least in part, the future responses the client makes. Outside the counseling interview, administrators, parents, and others can reinforce certain behavior. The timing of reinforcements both within and without the interview is most important. Hosford identifies four crucial elements necessary for implementing operant conditioning procedures. The first is that the reinforcements which the counselor employs must be potent enough to motivate the individual sufficiently to continue performing the behavior being reinforced. The second is that the reinforcement must be applied systematically. Third, the counselor must know when and how to reinforce, and fourth, the counselor must be able to elicit the behavior he plans to reinforce.[105]

Imitative learning or social modeling is applied in that the counselor can arrange for the counselee to observe models of more adaptive behavior. If clients have little idea of what constitutes appropriate behavior, models in the form of tape recordings, programmed instruction, video tapes and films, people, and autobiographies may induce imitative behavior, which can then be reinforced. Krumboltz and Thoresen point out that social models should be prestigious, competent, knowledgeable, attractive, and powerful, and that clients may be influenced more when the social model they view is similar to them in some characteristics.[106] Hosford states that social modeling techniques work with groups as well as with individuals. He believes that when clients need to learn completely new or highly complex behaviors, social modeling or combinations of social modeling and operant conditioning can best be used to promote the desired change.[107]

Cognitive learning supplies methods that include verbal instruction, contracts between counselor and counselee, and role playing. *Emotional learning* has application in that individuals with severe feelings of anxiety can be systematically relaxed when the stimuli which produce anxieties are paired with more pleasant stimuli.

The techniques employed by the behavioral

[103] Krumboltz and Thoresen, *Behavioral Counseling*, pp. 1–2.
[104] Krumboltz, *Revolution in Counseling*, pp. 13–20.

[105] Hosford, "Behavioral Counseling," pp. 9–10.
[106] Krumboltz and Thoresen, *Behavioral Counseling*, p. 164.
[107] Hosford, "Behavioral Counseling," pp. 20–21.

counselor depend on many variables. Among those cited by Hosford are (1) the client's behavioral assets and deficiencies, (2) the type of problem for which the client sought help, (3) the type and value of the various reinforcements available in the client's environment, and (4) the significant others in the client's life who might assist the counselor in promoting the desired behavior change.[108]

Evaluation of Counseling Krumboltz does not believe that counseling in its totality can be evaluated. Evaluation consists of specifying the kind of client problem, the direction of change desired by the client, the precise counseling procedure used, and the circumstances under which it is used. "What we need to know is which procedures and techniques, when used to accomplish what kinds of behavior change, are most effective with what kinds of clients when applied by what kind of counselors."[109]

CRITICISMS AND CONTRIBUTIONS

Some of the commonly cited criticisms of both behavioral counseling and Wolpe's model include:

1. Behavioral counseling is cold, impersonal, and manipulative and relegates the relationship to a secondary function.
2. Behavioral counseling has concentrated upon techniques, but the ends to which counseling is directed are equally important.
3. While behavioral counselors say they accord counselees the freedom to select counseling goals, they are often predetermined by the counselor.
4. While behavioral counselors assert that each client is unique and requires a unique, specific treatment, the problems of one client are often similar to the problems of another client and therefore do not require a unique counseling strategy.
5. The constructs of learning developed and adopted by behavioral counselors are not sufficiently comprehensive to explain learning and should be viewed only as hypotheses to be tested.

Among the contributions to the field by behavioral counselors are these:

1. They have advanced counseling as a science because they have engaged in research and applied known knowledge to the counseling process.
2. They have called attention to the fact that, if counseling outcomes are to be measured, specific behaviors will have to be made explicit.
3. They have illustrated how limitations in environments can be removed or reduced.

[108] Hosford, "Behavioral Counseling," p. 8.
[109] Krumboltz, *Revolution in Counseling,* p. 22.

Annotated References

Hosford, Ray E. "Behavioral Counseling — A Contemporary Overview," *The Counseling Psychologist,* Vol. 1 (No. 4, 1969), pp. 1–32.

Hosford identifies and explains the assumptions and major premises of behavioral counseling, the goals of counseling, and reviews the literature on such procedures as operant conditioning, social modeling, and symbolic models. The article is well-written, scholarly, and comprehensive.

Krumboltz, John D. and Thoresen, Carl E. (Eds.). *Behavioral Counseling: Cases and Techniques.* New York: Holt, Rinehart and Winston, 1969. 515 pp.

Descriptions of behavioral counseling techniques and practices are presented by various authors. The introduction by Krumboltz and Thoresen presents the essential features of behavioral counseling.

Krumboltz, John D. (ed.). *Revolution in Counseling.* Boston: Houghton Mifflin Company, 1966. 121 pp.

Chapter 1 by Krumboltz deals with counseling goals and outcomes. Chapter 2 by Sidney W. Bijou discusses the implications of behavioral science for counseling and guidance. Chapter 3 by Edward Shoben, Jr., presents the case for according worth to the individual. Chapter 4 by H. B. McDaniel attempts to put counseling in perspective, while Chapter 5 by C. Gilbert Wrenn is an attempt at rapprochement of behavioral and perceptual viewpoints.

Patterson, C. H. *Theories of Counseling and Psychotherapy.* New York: Harper & Row, Publishers, 1966. 518 pp.

Chapter 2 (pp. 16–59) presents Williamson's point of view and Chapter 3 (pp. 60–106) Thorne's personality counseling. Chapter 7 (pp. 154–178) gives Wolpe's counseling viewpoint. Patterson's coverage of these approaches is extensive and insightful.

Skinner, B. F. *Beyond Freedom and Dignity.* New York: Alfred A. Knopf, 1971, 225 pp.

Skinner presents the case for a technology of psychology based on behavioristic principles and research. He argues that freedom and dignity, features of autonomous man, are no longer relevant. Skinner presents his view of man and his ideas about designing a society that accommodates man.

Stefflre, Buford and Grant, W. Harold (eds.). *Theories of Counseling.* 2nd ed. New York: McGraw-Hill Book Co., Inc., 1972. 326 pp.

Chapter 6 (pp. 243–286) by Leonard D. Goodstein presents behavioral theoretical views and Chapter 4 (pp. 136–176) by E. G. Williamson discusses trait and factor theory. Case materials are used to illustrate each viewpoint.

Wolpe, Joseph. *The Practice of Behavior Therapy.* New York: Pergamon Press, 1969, 314 pp.

In this volume, Wolpe updates his explanations of psychotherapy by reciprocal inhibition and presents other behavioral techniques.

Further References

Andrews, W. R. "Behavioral and Client-Centered Counseling of High School Underachievers." *Journal of Counseling Psychology,* Vol. 18 (March, 1971). pp. 93–96.

Bednar, Richard L., Zelhart, Paul F., Greathouse, Larry, and Weinberg, Steve. "Operant Conditioning Principles in the Treatment of Learning and Behavior Problems with Delinquent Boys." *Journal of Counseling Psychology,* Vol. 17 (November, 1970). pp. 492–497.

Berdie, Ralph F., "The 1980 Counselor: Applied Behavioral Scientist." *Personnel and Guidance Journal,* Vol. 50 (February, 1972). pp. 451–456.

Brown, Joe H. and Brown, Carolyn. "Intervention Packages: An Approach to Self-Management." *Personnel and Guidance Journal,* Vol. 50 (June, 1972). pp. 809–816.

Bugg, Charles A. "Systematic Desensitization: A Technique Worth Trying." *Personnel and Guidance Journal,* Vol. 50 (June, 1972). pp. 823–828.

Chenault, Joann. "Counseling Theory: The Problem of Definition." *Personnel and Guidance Journal,* Vol. 47 (October, 1968). pp. 110–113.

Cook, David R. "The Change Agent Counselor: A Conceptual Context." *The School Counselor,* Vol. 20 (September, 1972). pp. 9–15.

DiCaprio, Nicholas S. "Essentials of Verbal Satiation Therapy: A Learning-Theory-Based Behavior Therapy." *Journal of Counseling Psychology,* Vol. 17 (September, 1970). pp. 419–424.

Dinkmeyer, Don. "Developmental Counseling: Rationale and Relationship." *The School Counselor,* Vol. 18 (March, 1971). pp. 246–252.

Frey, David H. "Conceptualizing Counseling Theories: A Content Analysis of Process and Goal Statements." *Counselor Education and Supervision,* Vol. 11 (June, 1972). pp. 243–250.

Gelso, Charles J. "Two Different Worlds: A Paradox in Counseling and Psychotherapy." *Journal of Counseling Psychology,* Vol. 17 (May, 1970). pp. 271–278.

Graff, Robert W., Danish, Steven, and Austin, Brian. "Reactions to Three Kinds of Vocational-Educational Counseling." *Journal of Counseling Psychology,* Vol. 19 (May, 1972). pp. 224–228.

Graff, Robert W. and Maclean, G. Donald. "Evaluating Educational-Vocational Counseling: A Model for Change." *Personnel and Guidance Journal,* Vol. 48 (March, 1970). pp. 568–574.

Hackney, Harold L., Ivey, Allen E., and Oetting, Eugene R. "Attending, Island, and Hiatus Behavior: A Process Conception of Counselor and Client Interaction." *Journal of Counseling Psychology,* Vol. 17 (July, 1970). pp. 342–346.

Jackson, Barry and Van Zoost, Brenda. "Changing Study Behaviors through Reinforcement Contingencies." *Journal of Counseling Psychology,* Vol. 19 (May, 1972). pp. 192–195.

Laxer, Robert M., Quarter, Jack, Dooman, Ann, and Walker, Keith. "Systematic Desensitization and Relaxation of High-Test-Anxious Secondary School Students." *Journal of Counseling Psychology,* Vol. 16 (September, 1969). pp. 446–451.

Laxer, R. M. and Walker, Keith. "Counterconditioning versus Relaxation in the Desensitization of Test Anxiety." *Journal of Counseling Psychology,* Vol. 17 (September, 1970). pp. 431–436.

Lytton, Hugh. "School Counseling—An Outside View." *Personnel and Guidance Journal,* Vol. 47 (September, 1968). pp. 12–17.

Matheny, Kenneth. "Counselors as Environmental Engineers." *Personnel and Guidance Journal,* Vol. 49 (February, 1971). pp. 439–444.

Mills, David H. "Counseling in the Culture Cycle: Feeling or Reason?" *Personnel and Guidance Journal,* Vol. 49 (March, 1971). pp. 515–522.

Mitchell, Kevin M. and Namenek, Therese M. "Effects of Therapist Confrontation on Subsequent Client and Therapist Behavior during the First Therapy Interview." *Journal of Counseling Psychology,* Vol. 19 (May, 1972). pp. 196–201.

Monke, Robert H. "Effect of Systematic Desensitization on the Training of Counselors." *Journal of Counseling Psychology,* Vol. 18 (July, 1971). pp. 320–323.

Osipow, Samuel H. "Cognitive Styles and Educational-Vocational Preferences and Selection." *Journal of Counseling Psychology,* Vol. 16 (November, 1969). pp. 534–546.

Osterhouse, Robert A. "Desensitization and Study-Skills Training as Treatment for Two Types of Test-Anxious Students." *Journal of Counseling Psychology,* Vol. 19 (July, 1972). pp. 300–306.

Randolph, Daniel L. "Behavioral Consultation as a Means of Improving the Quality of a Counseling Program." *The School Counselor,* Vol. 20 (September, 1972). pp. 30–36.

Staines, Graham L. "A Comparison of Approaches to Therapeutic Communications." *Journal of Counseling Psychology,* Vol. 16 (September, 1969). pp. 405–414.

Stetter, Dick. "Into the Classroom with Behavior Modification." *The School Counselor,* Vol. 19 (November, 1971). pp. 110–114.

Strong, Stanley R. "Causal Attribution in Counseling and Psychotherapy." *Journal of Counseling Psychology,* Vol. 17 (September, 1970). pp. 388–399.

Thomas, G. Patience and Ezell, Betty. "The Contract as a Counseling Technique." *Personnel and Guidance Journal,* Vol. 51 (September, 1972). pp. 27–32.

Thoresen, Carl E. "The Counselor as an Applied Behavioral Scientist." *Personnel and Guidance Journal,* Vol. 47 (May, 1969). pp. 841–848.

Thoresen, Carl E., Hosford, Ray E., and Krumboltz, John D. "Determining Effective Models for Counseling Clients of Varying Competencies." *Journal of Counseling Psychology,* Vol. 17 (July, 1970). pp. 369–375.

Toews, Jay M. "The Counselor as Contingency Manager." *Personnel and Guidance Journal,* Vol. 48 (October, 1969). pp. 127–134.

AFFECTIVELY ORIENTED COUNSELING APPROACHES

9

The previous chapter presented five counseling viewpoints: trait and factor, rational-emotive, eclectic, psychotherapy as reciprocal inhibition, and behavioral counseling. Those included in this chapter will be psychoanalytic, client-centered, existential, and gestalt therapy.

Psychoanalytic Viewpoint

ORIGINATOR AND SOURCE MATERIAL

Psychoanalysis is a method of treating individuals by psychological rather than physical means and is a branch of science. The original body of doctrine was set forth by Sigmund Freud between approximately 1890 and 1939. He won recognition as the first to map the subconscious of the human mind. Freud was born in 1856 in Freiberg, Moravia (Czechoslovakia) and died in 1939 in England. After graduating from the University of Vienna in 1881 he became interested in psychology, studied under Jean Martin Charcot, and later worked with Josef Breuer on the use of hypnosis in treating hysteria. His works, excluding those of his students and followers, require 23 volumes to reproduce and cover a time span of 40 to 50 years.[1] Freud's thinking, recognized and unrecognized, permeates many contemporary theories of personality and is the basis for many counseling practices.

Taken at its broadest meaning, psychoanalysis, according to English and English, includes not only analytic psychology, individual psychology, and other departures from orthodox Freudianism, but also the literary, political, and social ideologies which have been influenced by Freud.[2] For example, the theory of exploring the unconscious has been applied to art in surrealist painting and to literature in the "stream of consciousness" style of writing.

[1] James Strachey (ed.), *The Standard Edition of the Complete Psychological Works of Sigmund Freud* (London: Hogarth Press, 1964).
[2] Horace B. English and Ava C. English, *A Comprehensive Dictionary of Psychological and Psychoanalytical Terms* (New York: Longmans, Green & Co., Inc., 1958), p. 417.

Individuals who accepted basic Freudian principles and simultaneously sought to modernize them by attempting to incorporate the findings of contemporary psychology are usually referred to as neo-Freudians. Their ranks include the following:

Alfred Adler (1870–1937) Adler was one of the first to break from Freud (1911) because he rejected the sexual etiology of neuroses. He believed that feelings of inferiority were the cause of neuroses and that "masculine protest," common to both men and women, is a striving for power over individuals, things, objects, and territory. To cope with feelings of inferiority the person engages in (a) compensatory action (he gains power to overcome weaknesses) or (b) submission or feminine denial (retreat patterns through fantasy, projections, rationalization, denial of reality, and the like). Adler argued that sexual maladjustments were a symptom, not the basis of neuroses. Power drives are neurotic if they are directed to impractical goals. Compared to Freud, he emphasized *ego* over *id.*

Carl Jung (1875–1961) His rupture with Freud occurred in 1912 with the publication of Jung's book *The Psychology of the Unconscious.* Among his disagreements with Freud was that over the interpretation of the nature of the libido. Jung believed that libido (or life force) was primarily sexual in early human history but became desexualized as humans evolved. He accepted an individual unconscious similar to Freud's but posited also a collective unconscious containing man's "racial memories." Within this were emotional stereotypes (archetypes) common to all races of man. Examples would be the Jovian figure of the "old, wise man" and the "earth mother." Evolving a theory of character, Jung divided people into two types: introverts (interests centered on self) and extroverts (interests turned on external world). Each type was further subdivided into feeling, thinking, intuition, and sensation subtypes.

Otto Rank (1884–1939) After experimenting with short-term therapy (circa 1920), Rank broke with Freud and moved to Paris and later to New York. It seemed to him that birth trauma (shock of leaving the womb and security) rather than the Oedipal complex was responsible for emotional disturbance. He believed Oedipal feelings came too late to be decisive. Anxiety caused by birth trauma formed a sort of reservoir which should seep away gradually during maturation. If it persisted, then neurosis set in. He evolved a more active therapist role (contrasted to Freud's passive role) and established time limits for therapy. Basic to the Rankian viewpoint is the conception of the will as an expression of the positive and unifying aspects of the individual in his development of independence. Dependency strivings are often viewed as blocks to the growth of positive will.

Wilhelm Reich (1897–1957) Reich broke with Freud in 1932 in a dispute over the existence of the death instinct and its function in causing masochism. Reich utilized character analysis as a preliminary step (other analysts view it as the chief objective of therapy) prior to the main task of analysis or as education for analysis.

Karen Horney (1885–1952) Trained as a Freudian analyst in Germany, Horney came to the United States in the 1930's and soon founded a separate training institute. She repeatedly insisted that her views were corrective of Freud rather than a new approach. However, she rejected both his structural theory of the mind and his instinct theory. She sought to apply the thinking of anthropologists and sociologists to analysis. Human behavior, according to Horney, stems from the need for security. Basic anxiety results when the child is unable to manage insecurities caused by his relationships with his parents and views the world as hostile and threatening. Horney emphasized the importance of present life situations in understanding and helping an individual, for the strategies he invents to cope with his aloneness and helplessness assume the character of a drive or need and constitute irrational or neurotic behavior. She modified Adler's concept of neurotic goals because she believed that these contained their own sources of anxiety. Horney identified 10 such goals, including need for affection and approval, power, exploitation of others, personal admiration, personal achievement, perfection, and unassailability.

Theodore Reik (1888–1969) Reik never broke away from Freud, but pursued and extended Freud's explorations into love, guilt, and compulsions. His classical work, *Listening With The Third Ear,* won wide acclaim, for it portrayed the analyst's thoughts and emotions in his encounters with clients. Reik, one of the first nonmedical psychoanalysts, founded a training center for such individuals, The National Psychological Association for Psychoanalysis.

Harry Stack Sullivan (1892–1949) Sullivan held that the human individual is the product of interpersonal relationships. The pattern of the child's earliest nonsexual relationships with significant figures largely (but not rigidly) determines the pattern of later interpersonal integration. The goal of human behavior is twofold: the pursuit of satisfaction (biological) and the pursuit of security (cultural). Satisfactions include sleep, rest, sex, food, drink, and close interpersonal contacts; security refers to well-being, belonging, and acceptance. Most emotional problems, argued Sullivan, stem from the pursuit of security. Socialization is the process of becoming a human being, and the individual develops a self with three personifications: "me," "good me," and "not me." If positive experiences bring security the "good me" represents the individual's self-concept.

The theorists who accepted most of Freud's theories but whose contributions are also presented as logical extensions of Freud's ideas rather than separate systems are referred to as ego analysts. Often included in this category are Heinz Hartmann, Anna Freud (Freud's daughter), David Rapaport, and Erik Erikson, who, basically, have sought to understand and study normal human behavior. They believe that antecedents to behavior are more varied than innate psychological events (Freud's instinctual drives) and that some behavior is learned in relation to other events. They have stressed ego functions (behavior by which the individual directs his activity and deals with his environment) such as thought, language, and perceptual and sensory responses. Erikson, for example, has described the development of the normal personality by a series of eight focal problems or dilemmas.[3] These roughly parallel the Freudian stages of psychosexual development but continue into adulthood. Emphasis, however, is more clearly on the social interaction process and its outcome. The eight focal problems or dilemmas are: (1) basic trust versus basic mistrust (oral); (2) autonomy versus shame and doubt (anal); (3) initiative versus guilt (phallic); (4) industry versus inferiority (latency); (5) identity versus self-diffusion (puberty); (6) intimacy versus self-absorption (early adulthood); (7) generativity versus stagnation (later adulthood); (8) integrity versus despair (old age). For further elaboration of these problems see Chapter 3.

Among the secondary sources available for study of the psychoanalytic viewpoint are Brill,[4] Arlow and Brenner,[5] Ford and Urban,[6] Harper,[7] Beck,[8] and Alexander.[9]

[3] Erik H. Erikson, *Childhood and Society* (New York: W. W. Norton & Company, Inc., 1950).
[4] A. A. Brill (ed.), *The Basic Writings of Sigmund Freud* (New York: Modern Library, Inc., 1938).
[5] Jacob A. Arlow and Charles Brenner, *Psychoanalytic Concepts and the Structural Theory* (New York: International Universities Press, Inc., 1964).
[6] Donald H. Ford and Hugh B. Urban, *Systems of Psychotherapy.* (New York: John Wiley & Sons, Inc., 1963), chap. 5, pp. 109–178.
[7] Robert Harper, *Psychoanalysis and Psychotherapy* (Englewood Cliffs, N.J.: Prentice-Hall, Inc., 1959), chaps. 1 and 2, pp. 11–43.
[8] Carlton E. Beck, *Philosophical Foundations of Guidance* (Englewood Cliffs, N.J.: Prentice-Hall, Inc., 1963).
[9] Franz Alexander, *Fundamentals of Psychoanalysis* (New York: W. W. Norton and Company, 1963), 312 pp.

MAJOR CONCEPTS

Freud originated elaborate theories of the structure of personality and of the causes of psychological disorders. His ideas were long disregarded or attacked, partly because they were derived from clinical rather than experimental observation, partly because they often seemed rather incredible, and partly because of shock and distaste regarding what Freud stated he had discovered. Over time, however, personality research has validated parts of Freud's theories.

Objective of Psychoanalysis The major objective of psychoanalytic therapy is to help the individual achieve an enduring understanding of his own mechanisms of adjustment and thereby to help him resolve his basic problems. It is designed primarily for the treatment of neurosis but has been used with a great variety of psychological disorders.

Nature of Man A fundamental influence attributed to Freud is that of antirationalism, which stresses unconscious motivation, conflict, and symbolism as its primary concepts. Freud believed that man is essentially biological, that he is born with certain instinctual drives, and that his behavior is a function of "reacting in depth" to these drives. Man is irrational, unsocialized, and destructive of himself and others. Most notable is the drive toward self-gratification. Man's basic psychic energy, or *libido,* is equated with sexual energy by using the word "sex" broadly to stand for all pleasure. The libido (Eros or life force) drives the individual in search of pleasure. Around 1920 Freud also proposed that another drive existed in addition to Eros. This was the death wish or Thanatos and referred to the individual's aggressive drive. Harper points out that there are two hypotheses from which Freud never departed and which serve as guides to understanding his theories. The first is the concept of psychic determination (each psychic event is determined by those that precede it) and the second is the idea that consciousness is the unusual rather than the usual characteristic of mental processes.[10]

Personality Theory Freud formulated (circa 1900) a *topographic theory* of how the mind functions which has been recently discussed by Arlow and Brenner.[11] The following is based upon their presentation. Mental processes derive no more by chance or are no more arbitrary or disconnected than physical processes. Many mental processes, including some of the more important determinants of behavior and conscious thought, occur without conscious awareness. In Freud's topographic theory the mental apparatus was divided into three systems. The Unconscious (*Ucs.*) system contains mental elements accessible to consciousness only with difficulty or not at all. The Preconscious (*Pcs.*) system includes those elements readily accessible to consciousness. Finally, the Conscious (*Cs.*) system includes whatever is conscious at any given moment. Between the unconscious and preconscious systems an intersystematic censor operates to enable the preconscious to exclude objectionable elements from the conscious system. For an unconscious element to become conscious it must first become preconscious. Freud conceptualized the systems *Ucs.* and *Pcs.* in terms of energy discharge and potential. Unconscious elements function according to what he labeled the *primary process* while preconscious and conscious elements function according to *secondary processes.* The primary process, characteristic of young children, features complete discharge of mental energies without delay, and immediate gratification is uninhibited by reality factors. By contrast, in the secondary process emphasis is upon delay of wish fulfillment, recognition of reality, and cognizance of environmental factors that are favorable or unfavorable to the discharge of psychic energy.

Freud discarded the topographic theory, according to Arlow and Brenner,[12] because he found it

[10] Harper, *op. cit.,* p. 13.
[11] Arlow and Brenner, *op. cit.,* pp. 9–23.
[12] *Ibid.,* p. 28.

inadequate to explain, among other things, how the anti-instinctual forces may be accessible to consciousness if the sexual wishes they repress are not. He replaced it with the structural theory, which divided the mind into the *id*, the *ego*, and the *superego*. More precisely, the mind was divided into two parts, the id and ego, the id being the source of instinctual drives, the ego regulating or mediating between the drives and environmental demands. The moral functions in the ego separate from the other functions and constitute the superego.

These three terms simply represent convenient concepts for summarizing major aspects of personality, and no clear line exists among them. The id, as Freud conceived it, is the repository of the libido (life force) or unlearned physiological motives and unlearned primitive reactions for satisfying them. Left to itself, the id would seek immediate gratification for motives as they arose without regard to the realities of life or to morals of any kind (would in effect be governed by the pleasure principle).

The emerging human personality develops, out of intimate contacts with fellows in families and groups, the elements of a conscious "self" which is perceptive, adaptable, and self-seeking; this is the ego. The ego bridles the id. The ego includes the elaborate ways of behaving and thinking that have been learned for dealing effectively with the world. Governed by the reality principle, the ego delays satisfaction of motives or channels them into socially acceptable outlets. Seemingly, Freud's view was that man's motives are basically those of beasts overlaid and modified (but in no sense expunged) by the history of his interaction with other men, from whom he learned "you" and "yours" and the meaning of "me" and "mine." As a result, man becomes equally capable of purposeful social effort but also indulges in vanity, greed, and cruelty.

The superego corresponds to conscience and is ruled, not by the pristine seeds of passion and egotism, but by the morality principle. Into the superego component is built those socially acquired restraints, redirections, and sublimation of impulse without which men are less than human. The superego may condemn as wrong things that the ego might do in the service of satisfying the id's motives. How did this conscience come about? Concern with virtue is presumably a concomitant of awareness of vice and of a sense of guilt over acts which are "wrong." The first acts judged wrong were doubtless those which threatened the survival of the group. Perhaps primitive cannibalism initiated such sentiments as men dimly saw that the killing and eating of one another was potentially a road to death for all. Freud's thesis was that in the "primal horde," ruled by an elder male with a plurality of wives and a multiplicity of offspring, the maturing sons sought to kill the jealous and all-powerful father, to eat his flesh, and to fight to the death among themselves for the females. Patricide, incest, and fratricide spelled ruin to the group and consequently were at some point condemned, renounced, and guarded against through elaborate taboos on murder and incest, totemic myths, and rigid rules of exogamy as a means of survival. Freud thus derived conscience from these postulated relationships.

Doctrine of Infantile Sexuality Freud formulated the doctrine of infantile sexuality in which the libido, or basic psychic energy, drives the individual in search of pleasure. While the libido is primarily sexual in nature, it includes all things that stand for pleasure. Beginning in infancy the individual is pushed by the libido toward the achievement of mature development. If no serious obstacle is encountered, he progresses through certain phases. If frustrated, he persists or becomes *fixated* at a particular phase.

The infant's first search for gratification is limited to release of hunger tension. Freud considered this the beginning of the child's sexuality since the desire to suck is partly the desire for the mother's breast or the first of a long series of sexually desired objects. The *oral* phase characterizes the first year of life, and libidinal energy is centered around the mouth. In the second or *anal* phase satisfaction comes from defecation. The child's pleasures during this phase (ages 1 to 3) are concentrated upon himself (narcissistic), and satisfactions lie in achieving body control and mastery over objects.

Around the third or fourth year the genitals become a major focus of libidinal energy; this is the *phallic* phase. The penis and clitoris become a source of pleasure and a matter of pride. Any threat to their existence or functioning may result (among boys) in a fear of castration. The girl, in her exploration, discovers that she is without a penis and may deprecate all men — "penis envy." Sexual exploration and interest in the parents begin and the *Oedipal* period is initiated (ages 3 to 7). During this phase the child becomes interested in the opposite-sexed parent, desires to possess him or her sexually, and views the other parent as a hostile rival. All of this, of course, is a matter of private fantasy. Because the child soon learns that such sexual interest is forbidden, he seeks to resolve the situation. Freud believed that resolution of the situation was the crucial factor in the development of personality. Resolution could be accomplished by (1) repressing the wishes and thoughts, (2) destroying them, or (3) identifying with the same-sexed parent. If strong feelings of anxiety and guilt developed, serious personality disturbances evolved.

Following the Oedipal period is the *latency* phase (age 7 to about age 12–14), characterized by decrease in sexual interest and energy. But with the onset of puberty the intensity of biological sex energy increases again and Oedipal feelings are reactivated. If the Oedipal feelings were previously resolved satisfactorily, the healthy individual becomes interested in opposite-sexed persons outside the family and goes on to mature sexual fulfillment. The libido, therefore, reaches its original goal, the *genital* stage of development.

Harper identifies four important concepts derived by Freud from his theory of personality development.[13] They are summarized here:

1. *Concept of bisexuality of human beings.* No male is devoid of some strong wishes of a feminine nature, and no female is without some underlying masculine tendencies. At a conscious level such homosexual inclinations are very strongly repudiated, but unconsciously bisexuality (and guilt and anxiety regarding it) is of paramount importance in understanding human behavior.

2. *Concept of bipolarity of human emotions.* This process is known as ambivalence: feelings of a positive nature toward a person or group are almost invariably accompanied by negative feelings. Often negative feelings are repressed from consciousness. Examples of ambivalence include the parent who consciously loves his child but is unconscious of accompanying feelings of hostility toward the child.

3. *Concept of sublimation.* Freud believed that a certain amount of libido which is originally devoted to a sexual focus may be directed into ostensibly nonsexual channels. In other words, a substitute activity which conforms to personal and social definitions of acceptability is used to gratify a motive. Frustrated sexual urges could be partially gratified by being channeled into art, music, or some other aesthetic activity that is socially acceptable.

4. *Concept of displacement.* In his analysis of dreams, Freud discovered that the object or goal of a motive is often disguised by substituting another one in its place. That is, when one idea or image is substituted for another which is emotionally (not necessarily logically) associated with it, displacement has occurred.

Nature of Anxiety Freud first believed that anxiety resulted from undischarged, accumulated libido but later considered anxiety biologically inherited rather than culturally acquired. Anxiety arises from two sets of circumstances: traumatic situations and danger situations. Harper's description of these situations will be discussed here.[14] An example of a traumatic anxiety is the birth experience. Examples of signal or danger anxiety include (1) loss of a loved object or (2) loss of the object's love or (3) disapproval and punishment by superego. In the

[13] Harper, *op. cit.*, pp. 16–18.

[14] *Ibid.*, pp. 32–35.

danger situations the individual learns to recognize and anticipate trouble and reacts to the anticipation with anxiety.

Freud distinguished three types of anxiety. In *real* or *objective* anxiety the source of danger is external to the individual (e.g., loss of job or loss of wife). *Neurotic anxiety* results from an unsuccessful attempt to achieve harmony between id and ego (e.g., the individual is overwhelmed by an uncontrollable urge to commit some act which the ego defines as harmful). Neurotic anxiety could take three forms: free-floating, phobic, and panic. The free-floating form is exemplified in the nervous person who is apprehensive but the source of his anxiety is vague, transitory, and ill defined. The phobic form is characterized by specific irrational fear (claustrophobia). The panic form arises when the individual acts out his impulses (murder, suicide, rape). *Moral anxiety* derives from a threat from the superego or is the result of being punished by one's conscience.

Defense Mechanisms Freud noted that, to cope with frustration and its accompanying anxiety, general defenses were utilized by the individual – a change in focus of attention, fantasy, or other means of neutralizing the energy of the dangerous drive. Defense mechanisms were formulated by Freud while treating patients with conversion hysteria (individuals who have symptoms such as blindness or paralysis without organic cause) who appeared unable to remember certain traumatic experiences, yet could recall these experiences after undergoing psychotherapy. Defense mechanisms are learned and operate to some degree in normal behavioral functioning as well as in pathological ways. Although taken up singly below, they often function together or in multiple forms.

1. The most basic mechanism in reacting to anxiety is *repression,* a reaction in which a person rejects from consciousness impulses or thoughts that provoke anxiety. He refuses to recognize or admit to himself the motives or memories that make him anxious and consequently avoids or reduces anxiety.

2. A common defense mechanism, *reaction formation* covers conversion of unacceptable hostility into cloying solicitousness, seen in many do-gooders and some overprotective mothers who unconsciously reject their children. In other words, a motive is expressed in a form that is directly opposite to its original intent.

3. In employing *rationalization* an individual explains his own behavior so as to conceal the motive it expresses and assigns it to some other motive. Many examples exist in everyday affairs – the student who is motivated to have a good time rationalizes his failing grades as being due to inadequate instruction or unfair teachers, for instance.

4. By use of *projection* the individual disguises the source of conflict in himself by ascribing motives to someone else. The woman who will not leave her house because she is sure that men are waiting to attack her may be suspected of projecting her own thwarted sex desires. She projects her impulses on men as a group.

5. *Introjection* is the reverse of projection. In the example of the woman cited in the above paragraph, if through fantasy the woman identifies with a movie actress who is in the embrace of a man, she can partially achieve her wish fulfillment but successfully keeps out of consciousness the fact that she has such a sexual desire.

6. In *displacement* the object or goal of a motive is disguised by substituting another one for it. If a man who becomes angry at his employer but dares not tell him off goes home and berates his wife, he is making use of displacement.

7. *Regression* is a retreat to earlier or primitive forms of behavior. It is a relapse to habits learned earlier, or it takes the form of a more simple, less intellectual approach to problem solution.

8. Sometimes it is possible to gratify a frustrated motive, at least in part, by resorting to daydreaming. *Fantasy* is common among most people, particularly adolescents. As a form of adjustment it rarely leads to constructive action but can produce certain amounts of satisfaction. It becomes serious when it interferes with effective ways of dealing with frustrated needs.

9. *Denial of reality* is readily observable in severe

pathological cases. The brain-injured who suffers from leg paralysis, for instance, does not "see" the limb if it is brought into his area of vision. Denial of reality may be a special form of repression.

A fundamental weakness of defense mechanisms is that they are directed at anxiety, not at the motivational conflicts that give rise to it. They often conceal or disguise the real problem, leaving it ever present and operative. Their inadequacy is also bound up in the fact that they may allay anxiety from one cause but increase anxiety from another cause.

When a relatively stable balance among the id, ego, and superego is achieved, the existing state, according to Freud, constitutes the person's character structure. If the individual is relatively happy and well adapted to his environment, he is considered healthy. If his capacity for pleasure is relatively restricted and his adaptation to his environment is impaired, he is said to have a pathological character structure or a character disorder or character neurosis.

Neuroses and Psychoses A twofold classification exists to divide illnesses into psychoneuroses (more commonly called neuroses) and psychoses. Psychoneurosis, in Freud's terms, is caused by the ego's failure to control id impulses, in which case the ego works out a compromise. The neurotic uses defense mechanisms to such a degree that his functioning is impaired and he becomes too anxious or incapacitated in his work and relationships with others. Neuroses are usually classified into (1) hysterias, (2) psychasthenias, and (3) anxiety reactions. Psychoses, on the other hand, are grouped into functional (no known disease) and organic (originating from damage or disease). Three functional categories of psychoses include (1) manic-depressive, (2) paranoia, and (3) schizophrenia. Several organic types of psychoses exist, including (1) involutional melancholia, (2) senile and alcoholic psychoses, and (3) general paresis.

THE PROCESS

Classic psychoanalytic treatment required the patient to recline on a couch with the analyst seated behind the patient's head. Literally and figuratively, the analyst occupied the role of unquestioned authority. Freud's work with Breuer uncovered the fact that a hypnotized patient was helped by talking out emotional difficulties that apparently arose from early events which could not be remembered previously. While Breuer abandoned the talking out (catharsis) process because of its sexually laden content, Freud began to utilize it in a waking state (free association). After the analyst explains the general procedures, aims, and purposes of therapy, the patient is told that his behaviors and attitudes may depend upon emotional factors of which he is unaware and that these must be traced back to their unconscious motivations if they are to be understood and dealt with effectively.

Free Association An important tool of psychoanalysis is the use of free association. The individual tells all that comes to mind (free associating) especially about early trauma (or shock) regardless of how irrelevant or objectionable it may seem to him. Since infancy and much of childhood are consciously "forgotten," the patient may resist or fail to produce any words, ideas, or thoughts. *Resistance* is an inability to remember important past events or to talk about anxiety-charged subjects. It is the analyst's task to deal with resistances.

Interpretation Situations cannot be forced, but the analyst may interpret the resistance to clear the path of the associations and provide a flow for further understanding. Interpretations are tentative and are revised as free association continues.

Dream Analysis During the course of analysis the patient may report dreams, which often recapture childhood experiences. Dreams are considered important because they may provide a means of understanding the unconscious. The manifest content (reported dream product) is not as important as the latent content or motivational conflicts symbolized in the dreams. While a dream is often a wish fulfillment, there is no absolute symbolism (snakes may be phallic symbols to one dreamer but to another simply reminiscent of a trip to a zoo) and consequently no universal key to the meaning of dreams.

Transference At the core of psychoanalytic therapy is the transference that develops as analysis proceeds. Transference is the reenactment of previous relationships with people and principally of the parent-child relationship. This attachment of the patient to the analyst may actually be seen as a form of displacement since the analyst becomes the proxy for love or hatred unconsciously attached to a significant person. The therapist may become, emotionally, a father figure for the patient. When the emotions directed toward the therapist are those of affection and dependence, the transference is positive; if a hostile attitude is dominant, the transference is negative. Handling transference requires great adroitness on the part of the analyst. He normally meets the transference reaction boldly but treats it as unreal. Success in the analysis is dependent upon the utilization of the transference in understanding the patient's resistance.

Use of Paraphrases and Wit Freud often used "slips of tongue" and wit or humor as an aid in understanding unconscious motives. They were seen as individual ways of releasing pent-up energy attached to repressed wishes.

Termination of Therapy Termination is indicated when the patient gives evidence of having cleared up childhood memories that have served as resistances for important motives. Another indication is that the transference situation has been resolved and a normal relationship between analyst and patient has been established.

CRITICISMS AND CONTRIBUTIONS

Some major criticisms of psychoanalysis include the following:

1. Freud's deterministic view of man pictures him as ugly and driven too much by animalistic instincts, needs, and wants. Man is seen erroneously as being composed of two parts, the mental and physical (both derived from and dependent upon laws of cause and effect).
2. Too much stress is placed upon early childhood experiences. It tends to erode individual responsibility because it makes an individual's life seem totally determined and beyond his powers to alter.
3. It is doubtful that behavior is determined by a reservoir of psychic energy. Rather, it is probably manifested under certain situational events and not others.
4. Freud minimized man's rationality.
5. Treatment in analysis is too rational in its approach and too dependent upon reasoning as a therapeutic influence.
6. Research data do not indicate that the system results in a better percentage of recovery and improvement than occurs among groups which have had no treatment.

Among the many contributions of psychoanalysis are the following:

1. Freud made it plain that man is often motivated in thought and in behavior by impulses he does not recognize or admit.
2. Freud's bold and insightful investigations yielded the first substantial theory of personality and the first effective technique of psychotherapy.
3. Freud's identification of early influences that shape the development of personality had far-reaching implications for child rearing and stimulated research in the area.
4. Freud established a model in the use of the interview as a therapeutic vehicle. He was among the first to identify the function of anxiety in neurosis and in therapy and to emphasize the critical

nature of interpretation, resistance, and transference in the therapeutic process.

5. Freud was one of the first to stress the importance of a non-moralizing attitude on the part of the therapist.

6. Psychoanalysis represents a system in which there is a high degree of correspondence between theory and technique.

Client-Centered Counseling Viewpoint

ORIGINATOR AND SOURCE MATERIAL

Client-centered counseling is also often called self-theory counseling, nondirective counseling, and Rogerian counseling. Carl R. Rogers, its originator, labeled it "client-centered therapy." Like many others, Rogers thinks distinctions between counseling and psychotherapy are artificial and unnecessary.

In a major publication Rogers traces the development of his professional thinking and personal philosophy.[15] He was born in 1902, the fourth of six children, and reared in a close-knit home with strict and uncompromising religious and ethical views. Stress was placed upon the virtue of hard work. When Rogers was 12, his father (a prosperous businessman) purchased a farm and the family made its home there. Rogers went to the University of Wisconsin and majored in agriculture, but sometime during his first two years he decided to go into the ministry. In 1924 he entered Union Theological Seminary to prepare for religious work. Between 1924 and 1926 he took courses in the philosophy of education (under William H. Kilpatrick) and did clinical work with children (under Leta Hollingworth) at Teachers College, Columbia University. Granted an internship at the Institute for Child Guidance, Rogers was exposed to the Freudian views prevailing among the staff. Since these views conflicted with the objective, scientific, statistical ideas prevalent at Teachers College, Rogers was forced to resolve the conflict. Upon completion of the internship, he found employment as a psychologist in the Child Study Department of the Society for the Prevention of Cruelty to Children in Rochester, New York.

Rogers spent 12 years (1928–1940) in Rochester, a period in which he became disillusioned with "authority, with materials, with myself."[16] In 1940 Rogers accepted a full professorship in clinical psychology at The Ohio State University and believes that it was there, in teaching graduate students, that he realized he had developed a distinctive point of view. Moving to the University of Chicago, he spent 12 productive years there (1945–1957) as Professor of Psychology and Executive Secretary of the Counseling Center. He left Chicago in 1957 for the University of Wisconsin where he served as Professor of Psychology and Psychiatry. In 1962–1963 he was a fellow at the Center for Advanced Study in the Behavioral Sciences at Stanford, and in 1963 he joined the staff of the Western Behavioral Sciences Institute at La Jolla, California, as a Resident Fellow.

Rogers received his B.A. degree from the University of Wisconsin (1924) and his M.A. (1928) and Ph.D. (1931) from Columbia University. He is a Diplomate in Clinical Psychology of the American Board of Examiners in Professional Psychology.

Other proponents of the self-theory viewpoint include C. H. Patterson (University of Illinois), Nicholas Hobbs (Vanderbilt), and E. T. Gendlin (University of Chicago).

Rogers' theory of therapy evolved first, followed by a theory of personality. During the years 1930–1961 he presented his views in some 100 professional journal articles, contributing chapters, films, and seven books. Needless to say, all are important in attaining an understanding of his viewpoint. Particularly useful in amplifying and enriching the discussion contained in this chapter are *Counseling and Psychotherapy*,[17] *Client-Centered*

[15] Carl R. Rogers, *On Becoming a Person* (Boston: Houghton Mifflin Company, 1961), pp. 3–38.

[16] *Ibid.*, p. 10.

[17] Carl R. Rogers, *Counseling and Psychotherapy* (Boston: Houghton Mifflin Company, 1942).

Therapy,[18] *Psychotherapy and Personality Change*,[19] *Person to Person*,[20] and *On Becoming a Person*.[21] Rogers has very candidly cited three points which are especially meaningful for him: (1) learning to live in an increasingly deep therapeutic relationship with an ever widening range of clients, (2) conducting research in the helping relationship (therapy represents subjective experience while research represents an objective view of this subjective experience), (3) valuing the privilege of being alone because of the struggles generated by his views.[22]

Client-centered counseling represents a truly American approach. Many in the helping professions, eager for new concepts and tools, readily accepted it for use not only with adults and adolescents but also with children. It has also been utilized widely in group therapy.

Harper cites five reasons for the prominence achieved by Rogers' viewpoint: (1) It fitted into the American democratic tradition since the client is treated as an equal rather than as a "patient"; (2) its optimistic philosophy emphasized the individual's potentiality for constructive change and was reflective of the optimistic American culture; (3) it appealed to young, insecure therapists as an easy approach; (4) it held promise of being a swifter route to personality change than did psychoanalysis; (5) it was better understood by American psychologists because of its philosophical postulates, its respect for research, and its lack of foreign terms and methods.[23] An examination of the professional counseling journals makes abundantly clear the impact of Rogers' thinking. Many counselors and therapists have adopted the client-centered approach and others have modified their methods to incorporate features of it that appealed to them.

As is true of any idea that has immediate impact, a cultural climate of readiness existed for the introduction of Rogers' work. Over time, Rogers has (1) sharpened and modified the details and rationale of his client-centered therapy and self-theory personality system, (2) undertaken on his own investigations, and stimulated others, to research counseling process and outcomes, (3) prepared many counselors and therapists in the approach, and (4) applied it to small groups.

MAJOR CONCEPTS

This approach stresses the counselee's ability to determine the issues important to him and to solve his own problems. Counselor intervention is minimal. The most important quality of the counseling relationship is the establishment of a warm, permissive, and accepting climate which permits the client to explore his self-structure in relation to his unique experience. He is thus able to face his unacceptable characteristics without feeling threatened and anxious; he moves toward acceptance of himself and his values and is able to change those aspects of himself which he selects as needing modification.

Concept of Self Fundamental to understanding both client-centered counseling and self-theory are the concept of self and the concept of becoming or self-actualizing growth. Attention is first given to the concept of self, which will be identified and traced back to previous thinking on the topic.

Rogers states that the central construct of client-centered counseling is the self, or the self as a perceived object in a phenomenal field.

> The self-concept, or self-structure, may be thought of as an organized configuration of perceptions of the self which are admissible to awareness. It is composed of such elements as the perceptions of one's characteristics and abilities; the percepts and concepts of the self in relation to others and the environment; the value qualities

[18] Carl R. Rogers, *Client-Centered Therapy: Its Current Practice, Implications and Theory* (Boston: Houghton Mifflin Company, 1951).
[19] Carl R. Rogers and Rosalind F. Dymond (eds.), *Psychotherapy and Personality Change* (Chicago: University of Chicago Press, 1954).
[20] Carl R. Rogers and Barry Stevens, *Person to Person: the Problem of Being Human* (New York: Pocket Books, 1971).
[21] Carl R. Rogers, *On Becoming a Person* (Boston: Houghton Mifflin Company, 1961).
[22] *Ibid.*, pp. 14–15.
[23] Harper, *op. cit.*, pp. 83–84.

which are perceived as associated with experiences and objects; and goals and ideals which are perceived as having positive and negative valence.[24]

The "self" is a learned attribute constituting the individual's picture of himself. It is the "I" or "me" but is not used by Rogers as a synonym for organism. Rather it stands for "awareness" of one's being or functioning.

We have mentioned that Freud originated the concept of the developing organism whose behavior was dynamic (motivated). To this organism he attributed drives which were inborn biological needs and postulated psychic wishes (reactions in depth). Freud also conceived of the *ego*, or that construct which interacted with the real world. Jung, it may be remembered, differed from Freud in believing that behavior was determined by aims and aspirations as well as individual and racial history. He postulated the *collective unconscious* (characterized as the Shadow), which was composed of archetypes (a universal idea containing large elements of emotion), one archetype being the self. This self was life's goal, a goal that people strive for but rarely reach. Equally important in tracing the development of the concept of self is the Gestalt view of the perceptual field or psychological environment, defined by Hall and Lindzey: ". . . the way in which an object is perceived is determined by the total context or configuration in which an object is embedded. Relationships among the components of the perceptual field rather than fixed characteristics of the individual components determine perception."[25] Kurt Lewin might express this as $B = f(L)$. In this context a need is a motivational concept within the life space (L) which determines behavior in accord with its value in the environment. Stated simply, one's perception of "me," "myself," and "I" is a result of the perceptual framework of one's past, present, and future. Finally, William James and his concept of self, which included the Pure Ego or "a stream of thought which is one's sense of personal identity,"[26] led to the modern concept of self. This concept is viewed as self-as-object (attitudes, feelings, perceptions) or self-as-process (thinking, perceiving). Such dualism has contributed to a definite controversy, and various theorists adhere to one or the other notion or both. All agree, however, that the concept represents awareness: "self-theory represents a serious attempt to account for certain phenomena and to conceptualize one's observations of certain aspects of behavior."[27]

Self-Actualization Rogers has defined the actualizing tendency as "the inherent tendency of the organism to develop all its capacities in ways which serve to maintain or enhance the organism."[28] The concept of self-actualization growth goes back, at least in part, to Otto Rank and his followers Jessie Taft and Frederick Allen. Rank rejected the idea that man was pulled and pushed by impersonal forces; he spoke of "will," recognizing the positive, creative, directional nature of man's striving. In this view the neurotic was someone whose positive will conflicted with the fear of the consequences of willing. On the other hand, the healthy individual was one who could be himself without fear.

This self-actualizing characteristic, according to Patterson, means that man's behavior is motivated by this single master motive or drive — enhancement of the self and actualization of his potential — rather than multiple motives or drives. Patterson does not believe that Abraham Maslow's hierarchy of motives is needed since all are secondary to this basic tendency. Moreover, self-actualization should not be construed as self-centered or antisocial.

[24] Rogers, *Client-Centered Therapy*, p. 136.
[25] C. S. Hall and G. Lindzey, *Theories of Personality* (New York: John Wiley & Sons, Inc., 1957), p. 206.
[26] *Ibid.*, p. 468.
[27] *Ibid.*
[28] Carl R. Rogers, "A Theory of Therapy, Personality, and Interpersonal Relationships," in S. Koch (ed.), *Psychology: A Study of Science, Study I*, "Conceptual and Systemic," Vol. 3, *Formulations of the Person and the Social Context* (New York: McGraw-Hill Book Co., Inc., 1959), p. 194.

Man, a social animal, needs others to actualize himself.[29]

Theory of Personality In marked contrast to Freud's irrational and unsocialized man, Rogers' man is "basically socialized, forward-moving, rational and realistic." [30] Deep down, in the core of his being, man has no desire to strike back or to wound but rather wants to rid himself of such feelings. While negative feelings may be and often are expressed in counseling, beneath the bitterness and hate is a self that is positive, constructive, and concerned about others. The assumption is that "the subjective human being has an importance and a value which is basic: that no matter how he may be labeled or evaluated he is a human person first of all, and most deeply. He is not only a machine, not only a collection of stimulus-response bonds, not an object, not a pawn." [31]

Rogers has presented his theory of personality in the form of 19 propositions. They are given here, but the reader is urged to study Rogers' discussion and clarification of each proposition.

1. Every individual exists in a changing world of experience of which he is the center.
2. The organism reacts to the field as it is experienced and perceived. This perceptual field is, for the individual, "reality."
3. The organism reacts as an organized whole to this phenomenal field.
4. The organism has one basic tendency and striving — to actualize, maintain, and enhance the experiencing organism.
5. Behavior is basically the goal-directed attempt of the organism to satisfy its needs as experienced, in the field as perceived.
6. Emotion accompanies and in general facilitates such goal-directed behavior, the kind of emotion being related to the seeking versus the consummatory aspects of the behavior, and the intensity of the emotion being related to the perceived significance of the behavior for the maintenance and enhancement of the organism.
7. The best vantage point for understanding behavior is from the internal frame of reference of the individual himself.
8. A portion of the total perceptual field gradually becomes differentiated as the self.
9. As a result of interaction with the environment, and particularly as a result of evaluational interaction with others, the structure of self is formed — an organized, fluid, but consistent conceptual pattern of perceptions of characteristics and relationships of the "I" or the "me," together with values attached to these concepts.
10. The values attached to experiences, and values which are a part of the self-structure, in some instances are values experienced directly by the organism, and in some instances are values introjected or taken over from others, but perceived in distorted fashion, as if they had been experienced directly.
11. As experiences occur in the life of the individual, they are either (a) symbolized, perceived, and organized into some relationship to the self, (b) ignored because there is no perceived relationship to the self structure, (c) denied symbolization or given a distorted symbolization because the experience is inconsistent with the structure of the self.
12. Most of the ways of behaving which are adopted by the organism are those which are consistent with the concept of self.
13. Behavior may, in some instances, be brought about by organic experiences and needs which have not been symbolized. Such behavior may be inconsistent with the structure of the self, but in such instances the behavior is not "owned" by the individual.
14. Psychological maladjustment exists when the organism denies to awareness significant sensory and visceral experiences, which consequently are not symbolized and organized into the gestalt of the self-structure. When this situation exists, there is a basic or potential psychological tension.
15. Psychological adjustment exists when the concept of the self is such that all sensory and visceral experiences of the organism are, or may be, assimilated on a symbolic level into a consistent relationship with the concept of self.
16. Any experience which is inconsistent with the organization or structure of self may be perceived as a

[29] C. H. Patterson, "A Current View of Client-Centered or Relationship Therapy," *The Counseling Psychologist.*, Vol. 1 (Summer, 1969), pp. 3–6.
[30] Rogers, *On Becoming a Person,* p. 91.
[31] Rogers and Barry, *Person to Person,* p. x.

threat, and the more of these perceptions there are, the more rigidly the self-structure is organized to maintain itself.
17. Under certain conditions, involving primarily complete absence of any threat to the self-structure, experiences which are inconsistent with it may be perceived, and examined, and the structure of self revised to assimilate and include such experiences.
18. When the individual perceives and accepts into one consistent and integrated system all his sensory and visceral experiences, then he is necessarily more understanding of others and is more accepting of others as separate individuals.
19. As the individual perceives and accepts into his self-structure more of his organic experiences, he finds that he is replacing his present value system — based so largely upon introjections which have been distortedly symbolized — with a continuing organismic valuing process.[32]

No pretense will be made of covering adequately Rogers' theory of personality. Rather, discussion will be limited to three fundamental concepts. First, perception (translation of knowledge of one's environment into mental processes such as judgment, reasoning, and memory) is an active process. Individuals attach meaning to their experience and do not merely recognize meanings inherent in the situation. What is perceived constitutes reality for the individual, and he attends to or responds to the focus of that reality (behaves) as a total organized system. He does not want to be controlled but moves with struggle and pain toward self-government, self-regulation, and autonomy.

Second, as the individual develops, a portion of the perceptual field is differentiated and represents his awareness of his own personality. In other words, he learns to differentiate his body and behavior from other objects in his environment and becomes aware of his being. When experiences and needs appear which have not been symbolized and which are inconsistent with the self, they are, in Rogers' words, *disowned* by the individual. The unconscious mind has little place in Rogers' theory of personality. The person's self-perception is influenced by the ways others perceive him and the way he perceives self-defining references to himself. Values assigned to these experiences are based upon either introjection of others' references or direct involvement. The individual needs to be regarded positively by others. From his experiences flows the need for self-regard or worth as an individual.

The fundamental need underlying all behavior is to preserve and enhance the self. Brammer and Shostrom have pointed out that

Although the "self actualizing tendency" is postulated as being biologically determined, the direction of the growth tendencies is assumed to be culturally determined by parents, peers, teachers, and other persons significant to the child. Since the individual tends to deny perceptions which conflict with his self concept, these growth forces often become distorted in the developmental process. This condition often gives the picture of a person devoid of positive growth motives. There seems to be a strong belief on the part of the self theorists that the positive growth forces will ultimately triumph. For example, independence will supersede dependence; integration will overcome disintegration; social behavior will replace anti-social behavior.[33]

Third, the need for self-regard may lead to perceiving experiences selectively so that they are in accord with one's conditions of worth. If incongruity develops between self and experience, serious adjustment problems arise because the individual is constantly called upon to explain away evidence which is incompatible with his view of himself. This incongruity is subceived as threatening and, if symbolized into awareness, introduces inconsistency into behavior, leads to anxiety, and leads to perceptual rigidity or inaccurate views of reality.

The Fully Functioning Self The healthy person is one who can incorporate without distortion most of the data of his living, and among the most sig-

[32] Rogers, *Client-Centered Therapy*, pp. 483–524.

[33] Lawrence M. Brammer and Everett L. Shostrom, *Therapeutic Psychology*, 2nd ed. (Englewood Cliffs, N.J.: Prentice-Hall, Inc., 1968), p. 49.

nificant are his own organic reactions to experiences. Rogers has stated that the individual strives to become himself. He seeks to find the pattern or underlying order existing in the flow of his experience. The individual who becomes fully functioning (1) is open to experience, (2) lives fully each moment, and (3) trusts his own judgments and choices and depends less upon others' approval or disapproval.[34]

The Nature of Anxiety Vulnerability or anxiety occurs when there is discrepancy between the experiencing organism and the concept of self. Trouble comes when events perceived as having significance for the self are incompatible with the organization of self. In this case the events are either denied or distorted to the point of acceptability. The important point is whether they are consistent with the self. When the experiences are inconsistent, says Rogers,

> Conscious control becomes more difficult as the organism strives to satisfy needs which are not consciously admitted, and to react to experiences which are denied to the conscious self. Tension then exists, and if the individual becomes to any degree aware of this tendency or discrepancy, he feels anxious, feels that he is not united or integrated, that he is unsure of his directions.[35]

The healthy or "self-accepting" person can admit without distortion to awareness and symbolize sensory experiences arising from internal or external forces. "The emotionally maladjusted person, the 'neurotic,' is in difficulty first, because communication within himself has broken down, and second because, as a result of this, his communication with others has been damaged."[36] In effect, the neurotic acts before all the data are in. Brammer and Shostrom present a schematic diagram of adjustment and maladjustment from the self-theorist viewpoint (reproduced here as Figure 9.1).[37] These authors point out that *congruence,* the close matching of awareness and experience, is important in client-centered counseling. Incongruence between the individual's potential and his attainments, between his ideal and functioning selfs, between his actual and possible selfs bring lowered self-esteem, guilt, and anxiety. For the counselor, the implication is that he will help the client face the incongruence between his awareness and his experience so that his communication of real experiences is not defensively distorted.

Figure 9.1 Maladjustment and adjustment from the self-theorist's viewpoint

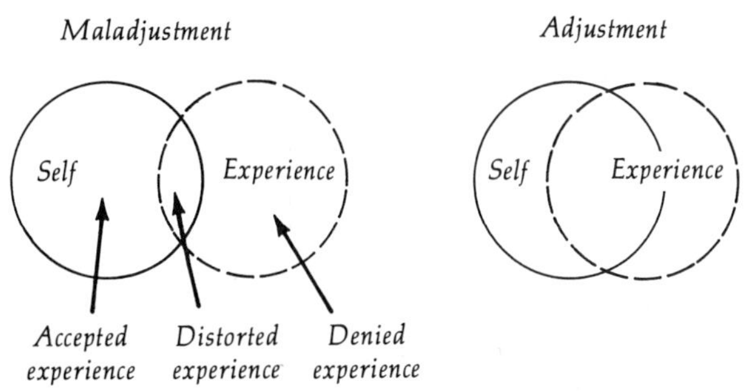

SOURCE: Lawrence M. Brammer and Everett L. Shostrom, *Therapeutic Psychology,* 2nd ed. (Englewood Cliffs, N.J.: Prentice-Hall, Inc., 1968), p. 48.

THE COUNSELOR AND THE PROCESS

Client-centered counseling focuses on the experiencing individual. In a process of disorganization and reorganization of self, it tries to reduce to a minimum perceived threat to the self and to maximize and sustain self-exploration. Change in behavior comes through releasing the client's potentiality to evaluate his experiences, permitting him to clarify and gain insight into his feelings, which presumably leads to growth. Through acceptance of the counselee, the counselor enables him to express, examine, and incorporate previously consistent and inconsistent experiences into his self-concept. By redefinition, the individual gains in self-acceptance and learns to accept others and to become a more fully functioning person.

[34] Rogers, *On Becoming a Person,* pp. 187–192.
[35] Rogers, *Client-Centered Counseling,* p. 511.
[36] Rogers, *On Becoming a Person,* p. 33.
[37] Brammer and Shostrom, *op. cit.,* p. 48.

Interviews are usually for one hour and are scheduled once or twice a week. Every effort is made to prevent the development of a dependent relationship. In general, in client-centered counseling (1) the individual, not the problem, is the focus; (2) feelings, rather than intellect, are attended to; (3) the present is given greater attention than the past; and (4) emotional growth takes place in the counseling relationship.

The Counselor The effective counselor is one "who holds a coherent and developing set of attitudes deeply imbedded in his personal organization, a system of attitudes which is implemented by techniques and methods consistent with it."[38] According to Rogers, it is the attitudes of the counselor, rather than his techniques, that facilitate therapy, and it is the counselor's basic operational philosophy that determines how long he will take to become a skillful counselor. Primary among the counselor's attitudes is his functioning behavior with others — that of according them worth, dignity, respect, right of self-direction, and the like. "We may say that the counselor chooses to act consistently upon the hypothesis that the individual has a sufficient capacity to deal constructively with all those aspects of his life which can potentially come into conscious awareness."[39] The counselor does not try to shift his role to a more directive one or undertake responsibility for the counselee's reorganization, for it is believed that in doing so he will confuse and defeat the counselee. While the counselor has his own values, insofar as possible they should be kept out of the counseling relationship to avoid their introjection by the counselee.

The counselor's role in client-centered counseling is not, as many believe, passive or laissez-faire. Passivity would probably be experienced by the counselee as lack of interest. Laissez-faire could be interpreted by the client as implying that he is not regarded as a person of worth. Rogers has also warned (in a nondirective way, of course) that formulating the counselor's role as one of clarifying and objectifying client feelings is too intellectualistic. If taken literally, objectifying such feelings would mean that only the counselor knows what the feelings are and would be interpreted by the client as disrespect for him. Rogers has formulated the role in these words: ". . . it is the counselor's function to assume, in so far as he is able, the internal frame of reference of the client, to perceive the world as the client sees it, to perceive the client himself as he is seen by himself, to lay aside all perceptions from the external frame of reference while doing so, and to communicate something of this empathic understanding to the client."[40]

Hobbs has presented the characteristics of client-centered counselors as they are involved in counseling:

1. The therapist attempts to understand what the client is saying with reference to content, feeling, and import to the client and to communicate this understanding to the client.
2. The therapist interprets what the client has said by offering a condensation or a synthesis of the expressed feelings.
3. The therapist simply accepts what the client has said with an implication that what he has said has been understood.
4. The therapist defines for the client, at moments when the issue is relevant from the client's point of view, the nature of the therapeutic relationship, the expectancies of the situation, and the limits of the therapist-client relationship.
5. The therapist attempts to convey to the client, through gestures, posture, and facial expression, as well as through words, a sense of acceptance and of confidence in the ability of the client to handle his problems.
6. The therapist answers questions and gives information when such responses are relevant to treatment, but he may refrain from giving information when the issue of dependency seems involved in the question.

[38] Rogers, *Client-Centered Therapy*, p. 19.
[39] *Ibid.*, p. 24.
[40] *Ibid.*, p. 29.

7. The therapist actively participates in the therapy situation, keeping alert, attempting to pick up nuances of feeling, interrupting the client if necessary to make certain that the therapist is understanding what the client is saying and feeling.[41]

Diagnosis is viewed as not only unnecessary but unwise. Use of test data and counselor-stated opinions about the client's problems is thought to foster dependency because the counselor will tend to be regarded as an expert. Client-centered counseling places the responsibility not upon the counselor but upon the client. While transference attitudes may appear in the process, Rogers believes they will not develop into a transference neurosis because counselor understanding and acceptance leads to client recognition that these feelings are his own, not the counselor's.

The Counselee In his first book on client-centered counseling Rogers presented eight criteria for counseling. These required that the client (1) be under tension, (2) have some capacity to cope with the circumstances of his life, (3) have an opportunity to have contact regularly with a counselor, (4) be able to express his conflicts verbally or through other media, (5) be "reasonably independent . . . of close family control," (6) be "reasonably free from excessive instabilities, particularly of an organic nature," (7) be dull-normal or above average in intelligence, and (8) be of suitable age — "roughly from ten to sixty."[42] Rogers now believes that these conditions no longer apply or are of little importance. Research and clinical experience have tended to disprove some of them, and client-centered counseling has presumably been found effective with a wide range of individuals and problems.

Steps in the Counseling Process In outlining the development of the counseling process, Rogers pointed out that these steps are not discrete. Processes mingle and shade into one another and occur only approximately in the order given. He has described and illustrated each step, but here the 12 steps will only be identified.

1. The individual comes for help.
2. The helping situation is usually defined.
3. The counselor encourages free expression of feelings in regard to the problem.
4. The counselor accepts, recognizes and clarifies these negative feelings.
5. When the individual's negative feelings have been quite fully expressed, they are followed by the faint and tentative expressions of the positive impulses which make for growth.
6. The counselor accepts and recognizes the positive feelings which are expressed, in the same manner in which he has accepted and recognized the negative feelings.
7. This insight, this understanding of the self and acceptance of the self, is the next important aspect of the whole process.
8. Intermingled with this process of insight — and it should again be emphasized that the steps outlined are not mutually exclusive, nor do they proceed in a rigid order — is a process of clarification of possible decisions, possible courses of action.
9. Then comes one of the fascinating aspects of such therapy, the initiation of minute, but highly significant, positive actions.
10. There is, first of all, a development of further insight — more complete and accurate self-understanding as the individual gains courage to see more deeply into his own actions.
11. There is increasingly integrative positive action on the part of the client. There is less fear about making choices, and more confidence in self-directed action.
12. There is a feeling of decreasing need for help, and a recognition on the part of the client that the relationship must end.[43]

Later Rogers sought to further identify the directions evident in the counseling process.[44] He conceptualized the following trends, which we paraphrase:

[41] Nicholas Hobbs, "Client-Centered Psychotherapy," in J. L. McCary, *Six Approaches to Psychotherapy* (New York: Dryden Press, 1955), p. 16.
[42] Rogers, *Counseling and Psychotherapy*, pp. 76–77.
[43] *Ibid.*, pp. 30–45.
[44] Rogers, *On Becoming a Person*, pp. 74–106.

1. The client experiences his potential self in the security of the counseling relationship.

2. The client learns to experience and accept fully and freely the positive feelings of the counselor.

3. The client not only accepts himself, he actually comes to like himself.

4. The client discovers that hate does not lie at the core of personality, but rather a self which is deeply positive and socialized.

5. The client does not continually act in terms of the form of behavior imposed upon him or he does not act in accord with the opinions and expectations of others. Rather, he comes to act on the basis of the meaning of his experiences — the realistic balancing of the satisfactions and dissatisfactions which any action will bring him. He becomes.

Necessary Conditions of Therapeutic Personality Change Rogers has addressed himself to the psychological conditions believed necessary and sufficient to bring about personality change. Change means either surface or deep changes in the personality structure, change from less conflict or immature behavior, or change in the sense of utilizing more energy for effective living. He believes that if the following conditions are maintained over a period of time, constructive personality change will take place:

1. Two persons are in psychological contact.
2. The first, whom we shall term the client, is in a state of incongruence, being vulnerable or anxious.
3. The second person, whom we shall term the therapist, is congruent or integrated in the relationship.
4. The therapist experiences unconditional positive regard for the client.
5. The therapist experiences an empathic understanding of the client's internal frame of reference and endeavors to communicate this experience to the client.
6. The communication to the client of the therapist's empathic understanding and unconditional positive regard is to a minimal degree achieved.[45]

[45] Carl R. Rogers, "The Necessary and Sufficient Conditions of Therapeutic Personality Change," *Journal of Consulting Psychology*, Vol. 21 (April, 1957), pp. 95–103.

Outcomes Since the early 1950's, Rogers and others have devoted considerable time and energy to assessing changes brought about by client-centered counseling. Among the findings were that (1) profound changes occurred in the client's perceived self, (2) the client's personality characteristics and structure changed, (3) the direction of change was toward personal integration and adjustment, and (4) the client's increased maturity was observed by his friends.[46] At a special conference on research problems in psychotherapy Rogers said he believed that "progress has been made in conceptualizing the outcomes of psychotherapy" in ways "which are specific, measurable and rooted in a context of theory."[47] However, most of the other conferees were not so optimistic. It should be noted that when Rogers uses the word "change" he does not necessarily mean "success," or "cure." He believes these latter two words are undefinable, constitute value judgments, and are not amenable to the application of scientific research.

CRITICISMS AND CONTRIBUTIONS

The following are among the major criticisms of the client-centered viewpoint:

1. It emphasizes the affective, emotional, feeling determinants of behavior but ignores or denies the intellective, cognitive, rational factors.

2. The use of information to help counselees is conspicuously absent from the theory.

3. Because it has the same goal for all clients — maximizing self — it is so broad, general, and sweeping that assessment for any one individual is impossible.

4. It specifies that the counselee sets the goal, but counseling goals are sometimes established by the setting in which the counselor and counselee are located.

5. While some evidence indicates client-centered

[46] *Ibid.*, p. 231.

[47] Carl R. Rogers, "A Tentative Scale for the Measurement of Process in Psychotherapy," in E. A. Rubinstein and M. B. Parloff (eds.), *Research in Psychotherapy* (Washington: American Psychological Association, 1958), Vol. I, p. 277.

counseling is effective with a wide range of individuals and problems, that evidence is not systematic or complete enough, particularly in respect to clients who accept little responsibility for their problems.

6. While client-centered counselors are expected to be neutral, it is impossible to be valueless in an interpersonal situation.

The most frequently cited contributions to the helping relationship are the following:

1. It has established the counselee, rather than the counselor, as the center, focus, or deciding agent of the counseling process.
2. It has identified and emphasized the counseling relationship as the primary agent in facilitating personality change.
3. It has placed in perspective the importance of the counselor's attitudes, rather than his techniques, in affecting the counseling relationship.
4. It has offered a wealth of research findings and stimulated quantitative investigations among other points of view, all of which have led to far better understanding of the process than ever before achieved.
5. It has emphasized that counseling is properly concerned with emotion, feeling, and affect.

The Existential Viewpoint

PROPONENTS AND SOURCE MATERIAL

The history of existentialism closely parallels that of psychoanalytic theory. Its origin, however, predates Freud's analytic views, lying in an extremely productive period of philosophical thought and accompanied by the rise and dominance of late 19th and contemporary 20th century science. The existentialist viewpoint — taken broadly during the last 100 years — is a meld of theology, philosophy, psychiatry, and psychology involved in a tremendous effort to understand human behavior and emotions. Among the earliest individuals associated with the existentialist concept of man and his behavior was Søren Kierkegaard, the 19th-century Danish philosopher and theologian. His works treating the relationships among man, universe, and deity are commonly considered in the forefront of existential thought.

Because of its diverse origins and the complicated contributions to it from a variety of fields, existentialism remains staggeringly difficult to understand, let alone discuss with clarity and precision. Adequate appreciation of this conceptualization of the individual requires a truly educated person, knowledgeable in all the disciplines which have contributed to its present state.

The very nature of existentialism makes it impossible to distinguish clearly and concisely among its proponents, and distinctions by contributing field are also difficult to maintain. Such theologically oriented proponents as Kierkegaard and Paul Tillich, philosophical contributors such as Martin Heidegger and Jean Paul Sartre, and psychiatric and psychological contributors like Eugene Minkowski, Ludwig Binswanger, and Rollo May have all added substantially to a highly complex theory. Indeed, this approach struggles against fractionating man in an attempt to understand him, using instead a truly holistic approach in order to grasp the reality and essence of his being. Man is thought of as being and becoming, as a dynamic process, as a complex organism in relation to the universe. While he belongs in the world of natural things, he alone can reflect, make free decisions, and set goals. Each man must learn to act as a free person rather than as a part of a crowd.

CONTRIBUTORS TO EXISTENTIAL THOUGHT

Søren A. Kierkegaard (1813–1855) Kierkegaard was a philosopher and Protestant theologian who championed religious existentialism. He believed that God could be known only through faith, not through reason. He urgently pursued the issue of becoming an individual, formulated truth as a relationship, and emphasized the necessity of commitment. Perhaps the most notable from among his over two dozen books are *Either-Or* (1834) and *The Concept of Dread* (1844), the latter a penetrating analysis of anxiety.

Paul Tillich (1886–1965) Tillich was a German-American theologian who left Germany when Hitler came to power in 1933. Most reflective of his views is *The Courage to Be* (1952), which employs existentialism as an approach to actual living crises. Both reason and religion are utilized.

Martin Heidegger (1889 –) Heidegger is often regarded as the major contributor to present-day existential thought. His main work, *Being and Time* (1927), is cited by many as source material for psychiatrists and psychologists who apply existential concepts in understanding man.

Jean Paul Sartre (1905 –) Sartre is a French philosopher, novelist, and playwright who became a leader of French intellectual life during the 1940's. His is a nihilistic, subjective existentialist point of view, stressing that the world has little or no meaning for man and that the individual must find some direction and meaning for his own personal life. The individual develops a sense of responsibility for his own decisions or actions and through this means becomes free. Sartre's existential despair has been expressed in many novels (*Nausea,* 1928), short stories (*The Wall,* 1939), plays (*The Flies,* 1943), and autobiography (*The Words,* 1964).

Eugene Minkowski (1885 –) Minkowski was born in Poland, completed secondary studies in Warsaw, and received his medical degree at the University of Munich (1909). After World War I he practiced psychiatry in Paris and conducted studies in phenomenological psychiatry. Among his contributions is a different view of the concept of time. He challenged the traditional idea that patients cannot relate to the future because of their disorder and proposed instead that the basic disorder is that of distorted attitudes toward the future which give rise to anxiety and depression.

Ludwig Binswanger (1881–1966) Binswanger studied under Jung at the University of Zurich and served as an intern under Bleuler. He was among the first to apply existential analysis to deepen basic concepts of psychoanalysis. He sought particularly to interpret man through his personal relations with fellow men and man in relation to himself. Man was conceived as one existence communicating with another. He termed his formulations *Daseinanalyse* ("being who is there").

Rollo May (1909 –) May, a well-known psychoanalytic therapist, has contributed much to interpreting existential psychotherapy to American psychology. He is the author and editor of *Existence* (1958) and other existential works.

Viktor E. Frankl (1906–) Frankl founded *logotherapy* (*logos* is usually translated as "speech" or "reason" but is defined by Frankl as "meaning"). Frankl rejects (1) Freud's view that men are driven mainly by sexual energy, (2) Adler's emphasis upon power drives, (3) Jung's archetypes, and (4) conditioning theories which define man as nothing but a machine. To Frankl, the search for meaning in life is the tap root of human striving and the search is at an intellectual rather than instinctual level. "Meaning" is the individual's own, unique to him in his situation at a given moment and contrasts to values which are shared among many people.

Some resource materials which will help the reader better understand existential thought include books by Beck[48] and May *et al.*[49] and journal articles by Dreyfus,[50] Vaughan,[51] Arbuckle,[52] Landsman,[53] and Kemp.[54]

[48] Carlton E. Beck, *Philosophical Foundations of Guidance* (Englewood Cliffs, N.J.: Prentice-Hall, Inc., 1963).
[49] Rollo May, Ernest Angel, and Henri F. Ellenberger (eds.), *Existence* (New York: Basic Books, Inc., Publishers, 1958).
[50] Edward A. Dreyfus, "The Counselor and Existentialism," *Personnel and Guidance Journal,* Vol. 43 (October, 1964), pp. 114–117.
[51] Richard P. Vaughan, "Existentialism in Counseling: The Religious View," *Personnel and Guidance Journal,* Vol. 43 (February, 1965), pp. 553–557.
[52] Dugald S. Arbuckle, "Existentialism in Counseling: The Humanist View," *Personnel and Guidance Journal,* Vol. 43 (February, 1965), pp. 558–567.
[53] Ted Landsman, "Existentialism in Counseling: The Scientific View," *Personnel and Guidance Journal,* Vol. 43 (February, 1965), pp. 568–573.
[54] C. Gratton Kemp, "Existential Counseling," *The Counseling Psychologist,* Vol. 2 (No. 3, 1971), pp. 2–30.

MAJOR CONCEPTS

The factors which led to the development of existentialism have been identified by May, who sees the fundamental basis as an attempt to understand the individual as he really is, to know him in his reality, to see his world as he sees it, to comprehend that he moves and has a being which is unique, concrete, and quite different from abstract theory.[55] May indicates that the existentialist movement sprang up spontaneously in different parts of Europe among different schools of thought and cannot be credited to any single person. Among the apparent stimuli for its application to psychotherapy were an inability to understand why cures did or did not occur, dubious theories of man, and blind spots within existing theories. In essence it was an attempt to arrive at a structure from which all therapeutic systems could be understood. It is perhaps unique among therapeutic approaches in that it has not created a new leader and does not purport to found a new "school of therapy."

May cites several factors which have tended to create resistance to the acceptance of existentialism.[56] Among these is the assumption that older therapies are sufficient to explain the nature of man and all that is needed is to sketch in the details. A second form of resistance lies in the position that existentialism represents an encroachment of philosophy upon psychiatry and psychology; it erodes disciplines viewed as sciences. Finally, other therapeutic methods tend to be preoccupied with technique and to prefer not to grapple with fundamental questions posed by an existential approach to therapy.

Beck, tracing the emergence of existential analysis, indicates that because phenomenology did not provide a framework wide enough and vital enough to meet therapy requirements, *Daseinanalyse* emerged. *Phenomenology* as a theoretical point of view advocates the study of direct experience taken at face value. It asserts that behavior is determined by experience rather than by external objective reality. It differs from the presuppositions of *Daseinanalyse,* according to Beck, in these particulars:

1. *Daseinanalyse* emphasizes the fact that, because of existential anxiety, one may live in two or more mutually exclusive worlds; phenomenology emphasizes the centrality or unity of the experiences of the organism. The *Daseinanalyse* theorist feels that the latter statement may be true of lower forms of life, but that man partakes of a different mode of existence (termed *Dasein*) and therefore faces meanings which often complicate his life meanings.
2. *Daseinanalyse* attempts to reconstruct the meaning-structure of the world of the individual, or the conflicting structures of his two or more worlds of meanings and influences; it explores how and why meanings have changed. Phenomenology stresses the present field of influences.
3. Phenomenology stresses awarenesses, consciousness, perceptions. *Daseinanalyse* is concerned with the total meaning-structure of the client: his life style, his views of life and death, his word choices, and all aspects of his relating to life.[57]

Concept of Being and Nonbeing Existentialism endeavors to understand man — most simply, to understand man as being and becoming. The grasping of another's being occurs on a different level from that of knowledge of specific things about him. "This is the classical distinction between *knowing* and *knowing about.* When we seek to know a person, the knowledge *about* him must be subordinated to the over-arching fact of his actual existence."[58] In this context, existentialism seeks to understand man at greater depth than that represented by the subject-object dichotomy which has permeated Western thought since the Renaissance. It tries to see individual man as a meaningful whole. Unless one focuses upon the fundamental fact of a person's existence and being, one cannot understand drives and behavior. All lose meaning unless viewed from the dynamic point of being and becoming.

Being is man's awareness of who he is, man's definition of himself, what he makes of himself.

[55] May *et al.* (eds.), *op. cit.,* p. 4
[56] *Ibid.,* pp. 7–9.
[57] Beck, *op. cit.,* p. 107.
[58] May *et al.* (eds.), *op. cit.,* p. 38.

The healthy individual is open to reality and creates meaning for himself. The most obvious form of *nonbeing* is death. However, the real therapeutic issue of nonbeing focuses upon live nonbeing represented by total conformity, absorption by collective society — in short, loss of uniqueness and individual identity.

Concept of Anxiety and Guilt From the existential point of view, anxiety and guilt are central in understanding existence. May states that "Anxiety is *the experience of the threat of imminent non-being.*"[59] As the individual confronts the fulfillment of his potentiality, he experiences anxiety. If he denies his potentiality or fails to fulfill it, his condition is guilt. May identified four characteristics of ontological (things that exist) guilt. First, since no one ever really fulfills his potentialities, everyone feels guilt. Second, guilt is not totally culturally determined through failure to meet the demands of society's rules; rather it stems from the realities of choice — choosing one type of behavior precludes choosing another. Third, ontological guilt differs from neurotic guilt in that it is a condition of existence. Finally, ontological guilt is to be viewed as a constructive force in human personality leading to humility, sensitivity in personal relationships, and creative utilization of one's potentialities.[60]

Concept of Time Some existentialists differ with the traditional concept of time as analogous to space and seek to understand the client's existential meaning of time. Minkowski, it may be remembered (see p. 224), proposed that distorted attitudes toward the future brought manifestations (e.g., delusions) rather than that delusion prevented the individual from relating to the future. Since man is always in the process of becoming, he can never be defined at a static point as though he were an object at a particular spot. Man can project himself backward and forward in time and thus is able to transcend the present and act and react in these dimensions. The individual may become disturbed or anxious because he comes to believe that he does not have a future.

> Repression and other processes of the blocking off of awareness are in essence methods of ensuring that the usual relation of past to present will not obtain. Since it would be too painful or in other ways too threatening for the individual to retain certain aspects of his past in his present consciousness, he must carry the past along like a foreign body *in* him but not *of* him, as it were, an encapsulated fifth column which thereupon compulsively drives to its outlets in neurotic symptoms.[61]

The future rather than the present or past is man's most dominant mode of time. Personality is best understood as a projection of man's future. His explorations into the immediate future mold and move him in distinctive ways.

Concept of Transcending the Immediate Situation Man has the ability to transcend (climb over or beyond) his immediate situation. He seeks to stand out and by his ability to think abstractly he can orient himself to project what he can be.

Concept of Freedom Some existentialists see man as becoming, as having choice and will, and, therefore, as exercising freedom. This view is diametrically contrary to that of some behaviorists who regard man as controlled by his environment and think of his behavior as governed by law. For some existentialists the self is the determiner of man's culture. Although determinism may be part of the world, it does not apply to man. "The free man lives within the laws of his culture, if he lives in a relatively 'free' culture, but he is not bound by them. They do not control him, but, rather, his self transcends them."[62] While man is not free from conditions, he is free to act upon or take a stand toward them. It is the individual who decides what his existence is to be, not his environment.

[59] *Ibid.*, p. 50.
[60] *Ibid.*, p. 55.
[61] *Ibid.*, p. 68.
[62] Arbuckle, *op. cit.*, p. 560.

Concept of Man Beck has given 13 propositions which he believes constitute a credo for counselors. In them the nature of man, as seen from the existentialist viewpoint, is evident.

1. Every man, not mentally incompetent, is responsible for his acts.
2. Man can do little to change most of the physical universe, the given, but he can predict it and make his life happier by facing reality.
3. Each man must aid others and try to understand their feelings, for mankind is left alone in an uncaring world.
4. Man creates his own nature. This is an individual choice.
5. Man should act toward others as he would want them to act toward him.
6. Decisions shall be made only by the criterion, "What is the effect on humankind?" Man must be treated with dignity; his status as a past-and-future-experiencing being, the only creature so endowed, makes this mandatory.
7. Determinism applies to physical laws; choice is a fact of human existence within the framework of the given surroundings.
8. Man counsels because no man can meet all problems alone.
9. Choices must be made by the counselee, for the counselor cannot claim omniscience.
10. The end of counseling is enabling fellow creatures better to bear the buffets of life, better to seek happiness and individual fulfillment.
11. Man must operate as if he is alone in the universe with his fellows; it is futile to argue about supernatural creation; there is no proof.
12. Man's suffering can be relieved by suggestions from those who have traveled the road before, or a road like it.
13. It would be an act of cruelty not to try to benefit others; they are involved with us in life.[63]

Prominent among some existentialists' conceptions of man is the "throwness" of life. Illustrations of this condition are the casting of dice or seeds being thrown on the ground. "Thrown" represents aspects of life beyond an individual's control. While a person does not have any choice of the ground, choice is possible, within the thrown limits, in what he becomes. Being born a male or a female is a "thrown" condition but deciding to accept or reject one's "maleness" or "femaleness" is a choice exercised by the individual. Kemp's comment about the concept is relevant here:

> Many of us also are aware of the contingency of life, its "throwness." Too many of us have wondered why we are here, not there; why it was a friend, a wife or husband [to whom something happened] and not ourselves. We would like to have a satisfying understanding but find none, and sometimes, to still our disquietude, we take refuge in some superficial explanation of time and space.[64]

THE COUNSELOR AND THE PROCESS

Individuals seek counseling for any one of several reasons. Nevertheless, Dreyfus points out, the counselor assumes that clients seek to expand their psychological world in one way or another.[65] The client's world is unique and must be understood by the counselor if he is to assist him. The premise underlying the existential viewpoint is that "The client is a figure standing out from his ground, the ground being the world of other peoples, creatures and objects. The goal of counseling is the elucidation of this client's uniqueness."[66]

The problem presented by the client may be only a socially acceptable excuse to obtain help. Consequently, the counselor encourages the client to unfold his world in their encounter so that both of them can begin to understand it and the counselee can act upon the possibilities inherent in it. Dreyfus maintains that the existential counselor "does not offer interpretations in terms of the client's past, but rather in terms of the client's present being-in-the-world."[67]

Because honesty is an essential characteristic of an encounter, the counselor must expose himself and he cannot view the client as an object to be manipulated or exploited. The counselor's ability

[63] Beck, *op. cit.*, pp. 124–125.

[64] Kemp, "Existential Counseling," p. 6.
[65] Dreyfus, *op. cit.*, p. 115.
[66] *Ibid.*, p. 114.
[67] *Ibid.*, p. 116.

to be human enables the client to become aware of similar qualities in himself. It is through this process that the individual will realize his potentialities and achieve self-growth because that becomes his responsibility.

The emphasis placed upon understanding the individual by existential counselors relegates counselor techniques to secondary importance. This is contrary to traditional views, which state that understanding follows technique. The counselor's basic task is to enter the client's world and participate with him in its realities. In the special relationship — the encounter — that comes to exist between counselor and counselee the latter is no longer an object but becomes a "thou." The intent of the encounter, according to Vaughan, is threefold: to foster freedom within the counselee, to improve his encounters with others, and to discover meaning for his existence.[68]

The existential counselor's techniques are flexible, and their application is based upon what is believed will enable the counselee to reveal his existence. Repression and resistance are seen as manifesting rejection of potentialities. The counselor's presence provides an experience for the client so that his existence becomes real to him.

In existential counseling, knowledge and insight are presumed to follow commitment. The assumption generally accepted in other counseling approaches is that decision comes after insight or knowledge. "We use the term decision as meaning a *decisive attitude toward existence,* an attitude of commitment. In this respect, *knowledge and insight follow decision rather than vice versa.*"[69] Finally, most existentialist counselors do not believe in viewing man as divided into conscious and unconscious parts. They hold that what is often called the unconscious is part of the individual's being and that the unconscious is too often used as a frivolous means of rationalizing behavior and responsibility, and as a way of avoiding the realities of one's existence. The aim of psychotherapy is to enable man to accept responsibility for himself.

[68] Vaughan, *op. cit.,* p. 555.
[69] May *et al,* (eds.), *op. cit.,* p. 88.

CRITICISMS AND CONTRIBUTIONS

Three contributions of the existentialists to the helping relationship may be cited:

1. They have moved the philosophical issues of man's goals, values, and existence to the forefront of the helping relationship and postulated them as the source of conflict. They have emphasized that a person's identity, or awareness of himself, is a basic antecedent of his behavior.
2. They have initiated behavioral study from a subjectively observable methodology (sensations and feelings) which may yield certain scientific facts that can be verified and communicated to others.
3. They have emphasized the importance of the self of the counselor rather than his techniques.

Criticisms include the following:

1. Terminology is often incomprehensible and employed in disparate ways.
2. The approach utilized is not systematic, and little attention is given to methods or techniques to implement its concepts. In short, the existential viewpoint is nonscientific.

Gestalt Therapy

ORIGINATOR AND SOURCE MATERIALS

Frederick S. Perls (1894–1970) originated and developed gestalt therapy. He has described his approach in two major publications: *Gestalt Therapy Verbatim*[70] and *In and Out of the Garbage Can.*[71] The material presented here will be drawn from these two publications and a recent article by Passons.[72] Perls was associated with the Esalen Institute, Big Sur, California at the time of his death in 1970. He views gestalt therapy as existential in nature and

[70] Frederick S. Perls, *Gestalt Therapy Verbatim* (New York: Bantam Books, 1971).
[71] Frederick S. Perls, *In and Out of the Garbage Can* (New York: Bantam Books, 1970).
[72] William R. Passons, "Gestalt Therapy Interventions for Group Counseling," *Personnel and Guidance Journal,* Vol. 5 (November, 1972), pp. 183–190.

asserts that it is in harmony with medicine, science, and the universe.

MAJOR CONCEPTS

The word "gestalt" has long been used to mean "wholes." Those who advocate gestalt theory believe that a response to a situation is a whole response to the whole situation. The whole is more than the sum of its parts. They deny that behavior consists of separate responses to a combination of separate stimuli. Gestaltists believe that specific components serve as important *figures* rather than as distinct elements. Accordingly, "parts" derive their meaning from their membership in the whole. Learning, according to gestalt theory, takes place, not by accretion, but by reorganization.

View of Man Perls believes that individual human beings always work as a whole. Each person is not merely a summation of parts (such as liver, lungs, brain, etc.), but a coordination of all parts. Health is viewed "as an appropriate balance of the coordination of all of what we are."[73]

When a person encounters another, the two seek through their communications to establish a world in which both have a common interest. The *I* and *You* changes to *We*, an ever-transforming boundary. Their encounter produces change which comes about because of dissatisfaction.

Since man is viewed as a whole, the organism cannot be separated from the environment. The boundary between the individual and the environment, according to Perls, is experienced simply as what is inside the skin and what is outside the skin. The *ego boundary* is the differentiation between self and others. *Identification* and *alienation* are two components involved in Perls' use of ego boundary. Identification means that the "I" is more prized than "others." A person identifies with his family, group, or profession. This identification results in cohesion, love, cooperation inside the ego boundary. Alienation, the other pole in the ego boundary, comes from strangeness, conflict, unlikeness. Alienation is the outcome of excluding or disowning that which is threatening to the individual. Perls has stated that "the whole idea of good and bad, right and wrong, is always a matter of boundary, of which side of the fence I am on."[74]

Personality Each individual is tortured by contrasting, conflicting, inner forces. Perls believes that Freud did not go far enough in his conception of personality. While Freud posited the superego or conscience, he never formulated its actual opposite. Perls labels the superego the "topdog" and describes its opposite as the "underdog." The former is righteous, authoritarian, perfectionistic, and knows best. The topdog manipulates the individual with its "oughts" and "shoulds" and threats of catastrophe. The underdog manipulates with good intentions and by being defensive and apologetic. Perls states that "The underdog is the Mickey Mouse. The topdog is the Super Mouse."[75]

Within each individual, topdog and underdog struggle for control. This inner conflict, never complete, is a form of persistent self-torture. Perls describes this struggle in these words:

> If the person tries to meet the topdog's demands of perfectionism, the result is a "nervous breakdown," or flight into insanity. This is one of the tools of the underdog. Once we recognize the structure of our behavior, which in the case of self improvement is the split between the topdog and the underdog, and if we understand how by listening, we can bring about a reconciliation of these two fighting clowns, then we realize that *we cannot deliberately bring about changes in ourselves or in others.*[76]

A fundamental concept in gestalt therapy is the clash between social and biological existence. Too many people try to actualize what they "should" be like rather than actualize themselves. For Perls, this difference between self-image-actualizing and *self*-actualizing is very critical. The former, the curse of the ideal, leads to the notion that one should not be what he is. Each person lives on two

[73] Perls, *Gestalt Therapy Verbatim,* p. 6.

[74] Perls, *Gestalt Therapy Verbatim,* p. 9.

[75] Perls, *Gestalt Therapy Verbatim,* p. 18.

[76] *Ibid.,* p. 20.

levels. The first is the public (or doing) level which can be observed and verified. The second is the private (or thinking) level. On the latter, the individual rehearses or prepares for future roles.

Perls suggests that the *situation* should control a person's actions or behavior. Those individuals who lack confidence in themselves, or who are not in touch with themselves or the world, react by wanting to exert control, rather than reacting spontaneously to the whole. Perls distinguishes between *end-gain* and *means-whereby* behavior. Needs of the organism determine the end-gain while means-whereby are matters of choice. Once the organism is integrated, control of the means-whereby produces satisfaction for the individual.

Frustration As he develops, the individual is confronted with two choices. He either learns to overcome frustration or is spoiled by his parents. Perls views frustration as a positive element for it forces the individual to mobilize his own resources, to discover his potential, and to manipulate the environment.

Character The child who is not sufficiently frustrated uses his potential to control adults and to create dependencies. In so doing, he acquires character. Perls does not appear to use the word "character" in its conventional sense of moral fiber. His use of the word seems to refer to rules and proscriptions which inhibit the individual from achieving his potential. He believes that the development of character leads to rigidity in responding, loss of the ability to cope freely and spontaneously, and produces predetermined behaviors. Character demands directional support from parents, teachers, and other adults. It forces the individual to play stupid and to establish dependency games. The individual expends energy in manipulating the world rather than using his energy for his own development. The outcome, according to Perls is that "The more character a person has, the less potential he has."[77]

[77] *Ibid.*, p. 35.

Pathology Pathology occurs when a person's thoughts and feelings are so unacceptable to him that he disowns them. The cost of remaining intact by disowning parts of oneself, of one's experience, or one's properties is high, for the individual's power, energy, and ability to cope with the world become less and less. He becomes more fragmented, rigid, and patterned.

Prominent among Perls' conception of pathology is the concept of self-regulation versus external regulation. Self-regulation is achieved as a result of becoming *aware* that one can trust himself. Environment control or self-manipulation which interferes with or interrupts "organismic self-control" leads to pathology.

Neurosis A neurosis, according to Perls, is a disturbance in the individual's development. He has said that a neurotic individual is one who is confused and who fails to see the obvious.

Maturing Maturation is defined by Perls as "... the transcendence from environmental support to self-support."[78] The critical point is the *impasse*, which is the point where environmental support stops but authentic self-support has yet to be generated. He illustrates the impasse with these words:

> The baby cannot breathe by itself. It doesn't get the oxygen supply through the placenta any more. We can't say that the baby has a choice, because there is no deliberate attempt of thinking out what to do, but the baby either has to die or to learn to breathe .... The "blue baby" is the prototype of the impasse which we find in every neurosis.[79]

The healthy personality is not one who adjusts to society but rather one who assimilates, understands, and relates to whatever happens. Moreover, he takes responsibility for his behavior.

Anxiety Perls defines anxiety as the gap between the now and the later. The individual experiences

[78] *Ibid.*, p. 30.
[79] *Ibid.*, p. 31.

anxiety because he leaves the surety of the now and becomes preoccupied with the future and the roles he will play. Preoccupation with future performances reflects stage fright more than existential anxiety. Stage fright comes from expecting bad things to happen in our role or patterned behavior. Realizing that this type of anxiety is only an inconvenience or unpleasantness, and not a catastrophe, is the beginning of coming into one's own.

THE COUNSELOR AND THE PROCESS

The aim of gestalt therapy is to assist the individual to discover that he need not depend upon others; rather, he can be an independent being. The process enables the individual to discover that something is possible for him. The therapist helps the client remove the blocks which keep him from being authentic.

A major focus in gestalt counseling is that of helping the individual make the transition from environmental support to self-support. The therapist does this by identifying the impasse. The gestalt therapist serves as a screen for the client who projects that which he cannot mobilize in himself. In projecting upon the therapist, the client discovers that neither he nor the therapist is complete, that everyone has holes in his personality. What is missing is a center. According to Perls:

> Without a center, everything goes on in the periphery and there is no place from which to work, from which to cope with the world. Without a center, you are not alert. . . . This achieving the center, being grounded in one's self, is about the highest state a human being can achieve.[80]

The missing parts of the personality in this conception by Perls are those that the individual has alienated or given up to the world. The therapist frustrates the client so that he is forced to find his own way or to develop his own potential. The client discovers ". . . that what he expects from the therapist, he can do just as well himself."[81] That which he disowns can be recovered. Recovery comes by understanding, playing, and becoming those parts that the individual has disowned.

A major symptom of what is disowned by the individual is *avoidance.* Some illustrations of avoidance are phobias, escapism, changing of therapists, changing of spouses. The individual who is confused, frustrated, or blocked is in an impasse. He has to discover his means of survival within himself. The surprising thing, according to Perls, is that the impasse is mostly a matter of fantasy. He is at an impasse because he prevents himself from using his resources by ". . . conjuring up a lot of catastrophic expectations."[82] Prominent in these expectations are feelings that people won't like him, of doing something foolish, of dying, etc. These catastrophic expectations stifle living, prevent the person from taking reasonable risks, and exclude *being.*

Perls points out that an individual rarely wants to get beyond an impasse. It is easier to maintain the status quo. In his words: "Very few people go into therapy to be cured, but rather to improve their neurosis."[83] It is awareness of how a person is stuck that starts recovery.

An important concept in gestalt therapy is the *here and now.* According to Perls:

> The *now* is the present, is the phenomenon, is what you are aware of, is that moment in which you carry your so-called memories and your so-called expectations with you. Whether you remember or anticipate, you do it *now.* The past is no more. The future is not yet. . . . Some people make a program out of this. They make a demand, "you should live in the here and now." And I say it's *not possible* to live in the here and now, and yet, nothing exists except the here and now.[84]

That which exists in the here and now is often an unfinished situation or an incomplete gestalt. Perls' example of a common unfinished situation is that of children who never forgive their parents. They

[80] *Ibid.,* p. 40.
[81] *Ibid.*
[82] *Ibid.,* p. 42.
[83] *Ibid.*
[84] *Ibid.,* p. 44.

blame them and make them responsible for all their problems. It is only by letting go of one's parents and forgiving them that one becomes responsible for his *being.*

Perls suggests that the gestalt counselor uses the *now* and the *how* rather than the *why* in his work with clients. The *why* only leads to rationalizations and never to understanding. *Now* includes all that exists, for the past is no more and the future is not yet. *How* is the structure or behavior and includes all that is going on. The therapist seeks to help the client to understand the "*how — how* do you behave *now, how* do you sit, *how* do you talk, all the details of what goes on *now.*"[85] Above all, the therapist tries to find out what the client avoids or is unwilling to suffer.

Perls emphasizes that the gestalt therapist does not analyze, but integrates attention and awareness. Attention is defined as a deliberate way of listening to the foreground figure or that which is unpleasant. Awareness is experiencing or being in touch with the self and the world.

Prominent among Perls' techniques is to have the client relive his dreams. He maintains that little value comes from interpreting dreams, but by having the client act his dream (viewed as a fragment of his personality) the individual can put the different fragments of his personality together. He reowns his personality and his hidden potentialities.

Passons has identified some techniques used by gestalt therapists. Some, but not all, of his techniques are summarized here:

1. *Enhancing awareness.* Clients are helped to attend to that which they are presently experiencing.
2. *Personalizing pronouns.* Clients are asked to personalize their pronouns to increase their personal awareness. Personalizing pronouns enables the individual to own his experience by projecting it.
3. *Changing questions to statements.* Encouraging the client to use statements rather than questions forces the individual to express himself unambiguously and to be responsible for his communications.
4. *Assuming responsibility.* The client is asked to substitute the use of the word "won't" for "can't". Experimentation in this substitution often uncovers the dynamics involved in the impasse and leads the individual to feel that he is in control of his fears.
5. *Asking "How" and "What."* Asking "why" leads to intellectualizations rather than experiencing and understanding. "How" and "what" enable the individual to get into the experience of his behavior.
6. *Sharing hunches.* Rather than using overt interpretation of client behaviors which too often cause defensiveness, the therapist encourages exploration by tentatively introducing his insights as "I see" or "I imagine."
7. *Bringing the past into the now.* Much of that which is dealt with in counseling is concerned with past events. Rather than rehashing the past, previous experiences or feelings can be brought to the now.
8. *Expressing resentments and appreciations.* The individual who is beset with resentments also experiences appreciations; otherwise there would be no need to retain that which was resented. The gestalt counselor helps the individual to identify and express his resentments and appreciations, for they are often part of the individual's "unfinished situations."
9. *Using body expressions.* The counselor observes the client's body expressions and focuses attention upon these to facilitate the individual's awareness.[86]

COUNSELING GOALS

Perls has stated that gestalt therapy seeks to promote the individual's growth process and to help him develop his human potentials, to take a stand. In his words "We have a very specific aim in Gestalt Therapy, and this is the same aim that exists verbally in other forms of therapy, in other

[85] *Ibid.*, p. 48.

[86] Passons, "Gestalt Therapy Interventions," pp. 184–189.

forms of discovering life. The aim is to mature, to grow up."[87]

CRITICISMS AND CONTRIBUTIONS

The contributions imputed to gestalt therapy tend to parallel those cited for existentialism. Stress is placed upon the wholeness and unity of behavior. Related to this is a tendency of this approach to recognize the importance of nonverbal behavior as an integral source of knowledge that reveals the individual.

Criticisms include:

1. The terminology tends to be idiosyncratic to the system. While not as esoterically or philosophically based as that of existentialism, it incorporates a jargon that must be thoroughly understood to be properly used. This shorthand language often uses phrases that capture complex patterns of human behavior.

2. Little or no research exists to demonstrate its effectiveness empirically.

Annotated References

Alexander, Franz. *Fundamentals of Psychoanalysis.* New York: W.W. Norton and Company, 1963, 312 pp.

Alexander's presentation of psychoanalysis is comprehensive, concise, and knowledgeable. The basic theoretical concepts of the theory and its application are treated.

Beck, Carlton E. *Philosophical Foundations of Guidance.* Englewood Cliffs, N.J.: Prentice-Hall Inc., 1963.

Chapter 4 (pp. 95–138) introduces certain basic philosophic questions which counselors must seek to answer, traces the history of existential psychology, and presents the *Daseinanalyse* point of view. Beck cites some of the implications of existential thought for the future of counseling.

Ford, Donald H., and Urban, Hugh B. *Systems of Psychotherapy.* New York: John Wiley & Sons, Inc., 1963.

Chapter 5 (pp. 109–178) presents Freud's psychoanalyses. A biographical sketch of Freud is given, the theoretical formulations of the viewpoint are stated, and Freud's conceptions of behavior and development are described comprehensively. Chapter 12 (pp. 445–480) presents a systematic discussion of existential analysis. Its major emphasis is treated and interpretation given of its central concepts. Therapy techniques and therapist's behavior are commented upon, and the viewpoint is evaluated as to its contributions and weaknesses.

Perls, Frederick S. *Gestalt Therapy Verbatim.* Moab, Utah: Real People Press, Bantam edition, 1971, 306 pp.

Perls describes his views of the nature of man, learning, anxiety, and therapeutic practices. The publication is drawn from audiotapes made at weekend seminars and gives some of the flavor of Perls at work.

Rogers, Carl R. *Client-Centered Therapy.* Boston: Houghton Mifflin Company, 1951.

This book is a fundamental source for understanding client-centered counseling. It is divided into three parts: views of client-centered therapy, application of therapy, and the self-theory of personality. The second section — application — treats play therapy, group psychotherapy, leadership and administration, student-centered teaching, and the training of counselors and therapists.

Further References

Astor, Martin H. "Transpersonal Approaches to Counseling." *Personnel and Guidance Journal,* Vol. 50 (June, 1972). pp. 801–808.

Berg, Thomas A. "Religion, Youth, and Counseling." *The School Counselor,* Vol. 19 (May, 1972). pp. 344–348.

Caldwell, Edson, "Counseling in Context." *Personnel and Guidance Journal,* Vol. 49 (December, 1970). pp. 271–278.

Chenault, Joann. "Help-Giving and Morality." *Personnel and Guidance Journal,* Vol. 48 (October, 1969). pp. 89–96.

Ciaverella, Michael. A. "The Counselor as a Mental Health Consultant." *The School Counselor,* Vol. 18 (November, 1970). pp. 121–126.

Danish, Steven J. and Kagan, N. "Measurement of Affective Sensitivity: Toward a Valid Measure of Interpersonal Perception." *Journal of Counseling Psychology,* Vol. 18 (January, 1971). pp. 51–54.

Daubner, Edward V. and Daubner, Edith S. "The Counselor as Metaphysician." *Personnel and Guidance Journal,* Vol. 50 (January, 1972). pp. 363–370.

[87] Perls, *Gestalt Therapy,* p. 28.

Dinkmeyer, Don. "Contributions of Teleoanalytic Theory and Techniques to School Counseling." *Personnel and Guidance Journal,* Vol. 46 (May, 1968). pp. 898–902.

Dinkmeyer, Don C. "Use of the Encouragement Process in Adlerian Counseling." *Personnel and Guidance Journal,* Vol. 51 (November, 1972). pp. 177–182.

Heilfron, Marilyn. "Leading Here-and-Now Groups." *Personnel and Guidance Journal,* Vol. 50 (April, 1972). pp. 673–678.

Ivey, Allen E. "Attending Behavior: The Basis of Counseling." *The School Counselor,* Vol. 18 (November, 1970). pp. 117–120.

Johnson, Ernest L. "Existentialism, Self Theory and the Existential Self." *Personnel and Guidance Journal,* Vol. 46 (September, 1967). pp. 53–58.

Kemp, C. Gratton. "Existential Counseling." *The Counseling Psychologist,* Vol. 2 (No. 3, 1971). pp. 2–30.

Mullen, John and Abeles, Norman. "Relationship of Liking, Empathy, and Therapist's Experience to Outcome of Therapy." *Journal of Counseling Psychology,* Vol. 18 (January, 1971). pp. 39–43.

Passons, William R. "Gestalt Therapy Interventions for Group Counseling." *Personnel and Guidance Journal,* Vol. 51 (November, 1972). pp. 183–190.

Patterson, C. H. "A View of Client-Centered or Relationship Therapy." *The Counseling Psychologist,* Vol. 1 (Summer, 1969). pp. 2–25.

Winborn, Bob S. and Rowe, Wayne. "Self-Actualization and the Communication of Facilitative Conditions – A Replication." *Journal of Counseling Psychology,* Vol. 19 (January, 1972). pp. 26–29.

BUILDING A PERSONAL THEORY OF COUNSELING

10

Chapter Seven presented some of the counseling contributions and insights available from disciplines related to counseling. Chapters Eight and Nine outlined nine counseling theories. This chapter seeks to discern the personal meaning of the content presented in Chapters Seven, Eight and Nine. Consideration will be given first to the characteristics and functions of theory, second to how counseling viewpoints diverge and converge, and finally to the evolution of a personal philosophy of counseling.

Characteristics and Functions of Theories

Theory is usually defined in a dictionary as a statement of general principles supported by data offered as an explanation of a phenomenon. It is generally pointed out that theory is a statement of the relations believed to prevail among a comprehensive body of facts. Theory is often contrasted to a hypothesis, the distinction being that the latter has less evidence to support it. Furthermore, in contrast to a law, theory covers a wider range of relationships.

CHARACTERISTICS OF THEORIES

Stefflre and Matheny envision theory as a human convention for keeping data in order and say that theory would be unnecessary if human memories were better than they are. Since memory is both limited and fallible, theories are needed to enable man to reduce complexities to manageable proportions. "To perform this function, a theory must consist of data plus an interrelating structure which tells us how one piece of information relates to another. . . ."[1]

The fundamental purpose of theory, then, is to describe and explain phenomena. Many visualize theory as apart from practice – as something remote, vague, impractical, and idealistic. Others

[1] Buford Stefflre and Kenneth Matheny, *The Functions of Theory in Counseling*, Houghton Mifflin's Professional Guidance Monographs (Boston: Houghton Mifflin Company, 1968), pp. 2–3.

more correctly think of it as going hand in hand with practice. Baffled by a problem, they employ theory to enlarge the range of circumstances to which attention should be paid to derive a solution. In basing practice upon theory, one must closely observe the consequences of practice in order to determine whether it corroborates the theory. If corroboration occurs, the theory is verified; if not, the theory must be rejected or modified.

The terms "paradigm" and "conceptual model" are sometimes loosely substituted for "theory" in current literature. A paradigm is a model that exhibits all the variable forms of a phenomenon; a conceptual model is a diagrammatic representation of a complex concept. A model is a schematic representation of the relationships postulated within a theory. According to Rychlak, models are useful for the generation of hypotheses but not for verification of theories.[2] Hall and Lindzey define theory as a cluster of relevant assumptions systematically related to each other and to a set of empirical definitions.[3]

Stefflre and Matheny point out that most theories have two elements in common: reality and belief.[4] Reality is the data of behavior which are observable and for which explanations are sought whereas belief involves the way individuals try to make sense out of data by relating what is observed to conceivable explanations.

Bases of Theories A theory is not generated in isolation but has personal, historical, sociological, and philosophical bases. It reflects the personality of its builder — his needs — and is a product of the time in which it appears and is used. Temporal and social forces impinge upon the theory builder, determining to some extent his interest and selection of factors in the theory. Finally, his philosophy influences the theories he constructs, either explicitly or implicitly. For these reasons, theory, especially in social science, is rarely purely scientific. Tyler describes the sources and procedures involved in generating her own personal theory of counseling: physiological and psychological laboratories, psychiatric consulting rooms, observations of people in their natural settings, the realm of formal philosophy and religion.[5]

Formal Attributes Stefflre and Matheny have cited five formal attributes which should be present in a theory.[6] A theory can be judged by how well it meets these criteria. First, a good theory is clear. It is understandable, and its general principles are not self-contradictory. Second, a good theory is comprehensive. A theory which explains the most phenomena is preferred over the one which explains a single phenomenon. Third, a good theory is explicit. Precision is evident in its terms and relationships, and its rightness or wrongness can be tested. Fourth, a good theory is parsimonious. It explains data simply and clearly without unnecessary diversions. Finally, a good theory generates useful research. Measured against these criteria, almost all counseling theories fall short and are imperfect. Those who construct them usually see them as partial and incomplete.

FUNCTIONS OF THEORY

The major functions of theory may be summarized in a fourfold statement:

1. Theory summarizes and generalizes a body of information. It is used as a sort of scientific shorthand. The principle of reinforcement — that people and animals must have some kind of reward or punishment in order to learn — is an example of a theory that may not be entirely correct but is useful because it gives the essence of literally hundreds of learning studies. Hence, to the extent

[2] Joseph F. Rychlak, *Introduction to Personality and Psychotherapy*, (Boston: Houghton Mifflin Co., 1973), p. 8.
[3] Calvin S. Hall and Gardner Lindzey, *Theories of Personality* (New York: John Wiley & Sons, Inc., 1957), p. 11.
[4] Stefflre and Matheny, *op. cit.*, p. 3.
[5] Leona E. Tyler, "Theoretical Principles Underlying the Counseling Process," *Journal of Counseling Psychology*, Vol. 5 (Spring, 1958), pp. 3–8.
[6] Stefflre and Matheny, *op. cit.*, pp. 5–6.

that it states laws or principles, a theory is a useful way of summarizing facts.

2. Theory facilitates understanding and explanation of complex phenomena. This function is somewhat related to the summarizing and generalizing function just cited. Theory points out that which may be most pertinent among a confusing array of facts and observations. It orders and relates data and thereby creates a comprehensible body of information that otherwise would tend to remain random data.

3. Theory is a predictor. It permits one to foretell what will happen under certain conditions. Prediction is an essential objective of all science. If science and/or theory were but the collection of facts and if prediction could never be made from them, little value would accrue to their collection. A well-developed theory is like a road map which depicts many, but not all, features of a geographical area. Its main purpose is to tell how the area may be traveled. In similar fashion a theory lays out in advance certain important features of an area of knowledge. A good theory presents a good approximation of the facts it encompasses. However, there need not be prediction of every detail.

4. Theory stimulates further research and fact finding. Even if inaccurate or wrong, it leads to more theorizing. It was a theory about the nature of the atom that led to experiments culminating in the atomic bomb and uses of atomic energy. Theories are guides for research and often constitute the basis for deciding next steps in fact collecting.

THEORY AND THE COUNSELOR

The functions described above apply equally well to the counselor confronted with a client. He attempts to apply, either implicitly or explicitly, the theory or theories with which he is conversant. His purpose is to give meaning and life to whatever he does in that situation.

We have said that theory summarizes and generalizes a body of information. Thus the counselor must somehow summarize the data provided to him by a particular client. These data are both complex and confusing. Whether or not he engages in diagnosis, each counselor must make comparisons between the body of unique data supplied by a client and the larger body of generalizations about human behavior.

In respect to the second function, all counselors stress understanding as fundamental to the counseling process. Understanding must go beyond merely comprehending moment-by-moment verbal interchange, although even this is often a complex task. In the helping relationship understanding involves grasping a larger part of the individual's life situation. A client presents many facets, perceptions of himself, feelings, self-descriptive statements, and the like which the counselor must comprehend and explain, at least to himself. His efforts at understanding this array of information can be usefully based upon a theory.

In respect to the third function, counselors predict at many levels. Somewhat informally, they predict as they select approaches and even as they select among alternative responses those stimuli to be presented to the client. Presumably, these are not random activities but stem from a theory about the counselee. More formally, counselors engage in prediction when they speculate, either alone or with a client, about the effects of certain courses of action available to the client. These more formal predictions derive from knowledge of the client, theories of human behavior and the environment.

Finally, theory frequently tells the counselor what facts he lacks to achieve understanding of an individual. It may also help to point out the shortcomings of his own efforts. In the latter context, if the counselor views his work in relation to a theory of counseling, he is often able to identify reasons for success and failure both with particular clients and over time with all his clientele.

Comparison of Counseling Viewpoints

Chapters Eight and Nine dealt with major aspects of nine counseling viewpoints. Table 10.1 shows the general positions of these approaches with regard to 10 important characteristics. As is true of any attempt like this, some violence may have been done to the nuances and subtleties of the theories. The intent here is to point up basic agreed-upon characteristics in which the various counseling approaches are similar and different. The information presented in the 90 cells of the table will not be recapitulated since in large part this information has been treated in Chapters Eight and Nine. Rather, attention will be drawn to the broader issue of similarities and differences among the nine counseling viewpoints.

NATURE OF MAN

The nine theories differ on the role of rationality and volition in determining human behavior. At one extreme, psychotherapy by reciprocal inhibition and the behavioral approach tend to view man as reactive and basically impotent in relation to his environment. The orthodox Freudian approach takes an equally bleak view of man's rationality and volitional capabilities but for an entirely different reason. Those who operate within the Freudian context believe that man's incapacities stem not from an overwhelming, unchangeable environment but from unconscious forces over which he exerts little if any power. At the other end of the continuum, the client-centered and existential viewpoints see man as rational and striving to determine his own destiny. Seemingly, the trait and factor viewpoint is also built on the implicit assumption that, given the necessary facts about himself and his environment, the individual is capable of independent functioning. While these views tend to use different terminology, they share the basic assumption that humankind strives for self-actualization, freedom, and self-responsibility.

The freedom-determinism issue has long been troublesome for most counselors. Gelso, in a perceptive analysis, reconceptualizes the dilemma.[7] He holds that strict determinism and free will are both valid and necessary assumptions in any complete conception of human behavior. Whether and at what times determinism or freedom is valid depend on the source of information used. On the one hand, man's actions are best understood as determined when a person *objectively* observes his own functioning or when he attempts to observe other individuals and seeks reasons for their behavior. On the other hand, belief in freedom is both necessary and possible, according to Gelso, when a person *subjectively* experiences himself or empathically experiences another person. Gelso suggests that counselors have to live with this paradox. Exclusive use of a free will model of man would not permit the counselor to gain a causal understanding of his client, and further, it would exacerbate inappropriate guilt in the client because he would view his misbehaviors as his fault alone. Gelso says that exclusive use of a deterministic model would make it difficult for counselors to empathize with their clients. Further, such a model would reinforce the client's feelings of being a pawn manipulated by external forces.

The client-centered approach stands virtually alone in considering man trustworthy, reliable, and "good." Man will move toward the good for himself and others because he has self-enhancing tendencies. The Freudian view, notes Stefflre, is less sanguine about man's basic nature: "Evil is seen as not only something done *by* man but as something natural *to* him. Counseling, then, has the function of the proper housekeeping of the part of man's nature which loves to romp."[8]

An interesting dichotomy has been presented by Ford and Urban.[9] Certain counseling theories view man, either implicitly or explicitly, as a pilot while others view him as a robot. Those (client-centered and existentialist) who take the "pilot" position see man as exercising control over his behavior and life situations and able to choose and be responsi-

[7] Charles J. Gelso, "Two Different Worlds: A Paradox in Counseling and Psychotherapy," *Journal of Counseling Psychology*, Vol. 17 (May, 1970), pp. 271–278.

[8] Buford Stefflre, "A Summing Up," in Buford Stefflre and W. Harold Grant (eds.), *Theories of Counseling*, 2nd ed. (New York: McGraw-Hill Book Co. Inc., 1972), p. 289.

[9] Donald H. Ford and Hugh B. Urban, *Systems of Psychotherapy* (New York: John Wiley and Sons, Inc., 1963), p. 595–599.

ble. Those (reciprocal inhibition, behavioral, Freudian analysis) with the "robot" image cite the automaticity of behavior. Ford and Urban point out that the data emphasized, the observational settings and procedures, and the concepts and propositions differ according to whether man is seen as pilot or robot. Neither image appears in pure form in any counseling system, but all tend to stress that behavior is characterized by automaticity and by choice making, and excessive stress upon man as pilot or man as robot leads to theoretical weaknesses.

Despite the apparently negativistic view of man in relation to his environment found in the strongly behavioristic approaches (reciprocal inhibition and behavioral) it is clear that all approaches share some optimism for man in his difficulties. Obviously all must accept to some degree the belief that man is pliable and can change his condition; otherwise there would be no reason for the existence of counseling theories or counselors! Perhaps Chenault's view is more useful:

> The question of man's nature is not clearly amenable to the goal of generalization. Were that goal achieved, the question may still remain unanswered. At least when our quest of defining man seeks commonality among men, it must take care not to define out the *commonality of idiosyncrasy.* It must not define away man's literal uniqueness, especially in a field dealing with the one-to-one relationship.[10]

MAJOR PERSONALITY CONSTRUCTS

Optimism about changing man is not independent of the various concepts of the nature of man. For each position, this philosophical base colors its conceptualizations of personality, called personality constructs in Table 10.1. They are hypothetical constructs which are in reality never actually observed.

All agree that much behavior is learned in the sense that developmental events influence any image of man at any point in time. Again the degree of emphasis placed upon prior learning varies from viewpoint to viewpoint. In some approaches (behavioristic) prior learning becomes the central focus as well as the mechanism for bringing about change. In others learning is dealt with as primarily that which has brought the individual to his current state and shapes his perceptions of his life situation.

ANXIETY

Virtually all viewpoints assign a central position to anxiety. They differ on the source of anxiety but agree that it is unpleasant or undesirable. Anxiety, fear, tension, and conflict are seen as critical in the development of disorder or as interfering with the individual's functioning. To the behaviorists, anxiety emanates from situational events of all kinds, including concrete objects, while Rogers stresses the acquisition of conflicting evaluations and the existentialists point to the conception of nonbeing. Rogers believes that anxiety is a consequence of the attention to and symbolization of certain kinds of conflict whereas Freud first thought anxiety was due to conflict and then changed to conceptualize it as the antecedent motive producing conflict.

Ford and Urban state that

> ... the diversity of viewpoints becomes quite impressive. Many of the theorists are employing the same concept-labels — anxiety, conflict, negative self-evaluative thoughts, unawareness, to cite a few. Thus, they tend to sound the same, and therefore some might conclude that they are all saying the same thing about disorder and its development. But the similarity is sometimes found to be superficial, since analysis reveals that they are employing the same terms to refer to different combinations of events.[11]

COUNSELING GOALS

Most counseling goals are expressed in abstractions rather than precise behavioral descriptions (see Chapter Four). The behavioral approach is the

[10] Joann Chenault, "Counseling Theory: The Problem of Definition," *Personnel and Guidance Journal,* Vol. 47 (October, 1968), p. 113.

[11] Ford and Urban, *op. cit.,* p. 654.

exception, and of all views it is most likely to utilize behavior as an outcome characteristic.

The approaches differ mainly in regard to range and variety of goals: from symptom removal to personality reorganization to self-actualization. There appears to be common agreement that individuality and responsibility are desirable. Behavioristically oriented approaches, while stressing symptom removal, generally posit this outcome as an intermediate step to assisting the individual to function better and achieve increasing freedom and expressiveness.

MAJOR TECHNIQUES

Variation in the use of major techniques centers around the emphasis placed upon reasoning and problem solving versus stressing the individual's affective life and experiencing. Another source of variation lies in the degree to which counseling activity is restricted to the session itself as opposed to moving beyond the relationship between counselor and client. Some approaches rely upon environmental intervention, directly urging their clientele to engage in the application and testing of themselves in anxiety-provoking situations outside the counseling room. Wolpe clearly requires this by urging patients to practice desensitizing techniques in real-life situations. Others generally work almost entirely within the relationship itself and leave the client to choose his own means of applying what he learns of himself to his life.

In those approaches which rely heavily upon the counselor-client relationship a great deal of similarity has been demonstrated among experienced therapists regardless of their theoretical orientation. Substantiation of this assertion may be found in the work of Robert Wrenn and others. Wrenn sought to determine whether theoretical orientation or situational factors affected counselor responses. His findings supported earlier findings that theoretical orientation has little influence on the manner in which experienced counselors respond.[12]

London has differentiated the approaches into insight therapies (client-centered, existential, and psychoanalysis) versus action therapies (behavioral). While noting that differences exist among the insight viewpoints, London believes that two commonalities stand out:

> 1. The single allowable instrument of the therapy is talk, and the therapeutic sessions are deliberately conducted in such a way that, from start to finish, the patient, client, analysand, or counselee does most of the talking and most of the deciding of what will be talked about.
> 2. The therapist operates with a conservative bias against communicating to the patient important or detailed information about his own life, that is to say, the therapist tends to hide his personal life from the patient.[13]

The action therapies are more concerned with symptoms, behaviors, or actions. According to London the action therapist "cares not a whit what the patient does or does not say about himself or even know about himself insofar as such *behaviors* have concrete and demonstrable value for producing change."[14] There are two major characteristics of action therapies:

> 1. The therapist assumes a much greater influence over the detailed conduct of the treatment sessions, and possibly over the outside life of the patient, than Insight therapists would.
> 2. The therapist is much more responsible for the outcome of treatment, that is, for whatever changes take place in the patient, than are Insight therapists.[15]

Despite the fact that all approaches describe and presumably employ fairly specific techniques, most theories seemingly consciously avoid clear prescriptions of what should be done in the counseling process. This curious de-emphasis of technique apparently exists because, regardless of orientation, counselors generally eschew viewing the client as an object to which something is done. Even when

[12] Robert L. Wrenn, "Counselor Orientation: Theoretical or Situational?" *Journal of Counseling Psychology*, Vol. 7 (Spring, 1960), pp. 40–45.

[13] P. London, *The Modes and Morals of Psychotherapy* (New York: Holt, Rinehart & Winston, Inc., 1964), p. 45.
[14] *Ibid.*, p. 78.
[15] *Ibid.*

objective techniques are stressed, the theorist usually insists upon maximum flexibility since he prizes the uniqueness of each client. Related to this latter point is the consensus that the client must be respected as an individual and that critical and derogatory statements by the counselor are to be avoided.

The de-emphasis upon counselor techniques led Ford and Urban to comment that

> One wonders why these theorists as a group have specified so little in the way of principles and techniques for producing behavioral change. Some have expressed concern that published techniques might come to be misused by uninformed people (Freud). Rogers started out by specifying technique but abandoned this when he realized that the same statements made by different therapists could have different effects. In his instance, we think he erred in concluding that further specification was not possible. A more appropriate conclusion would have been that since his original degree of specification was inadequate, certain other variables must be considered: tone of voice or the context of statements. More specification, rather than less, was required. Several of the theorists have discussed in very general terms what the therapist should feel toward the patient and how he should think about the patient's problems. The issue is often dropped at this point, as if appropriate actions or techniques would follow automatically. We think such an assumption is untenable and encourages one to evade the difficult task of specifying technique. It is what the therapist does, not what he thinks and feels, that directly affects the patient.[16]

APPRAISAL, HISTORY TAKING, AND DIAGNOSIS

While appraisal, history taking, and diagnosis are presented in Table 10.1 as separate entries, discussion here will apply to all three at once since they are closely related. The intent of appraisal (including life history) is to derive a diagnostic and prognostic statement permitting the counselor to form a working image of his client. Considerable variety exists among the approaches as to the kinds of data necessary to arrive at this image. A notable exception is client-centered counseling, which regards the procedures described as unnecessary and harmful to the counseling relationship. The client-centered view stresses understanding of the client's internal frame of reference while other approaches place greater emphasis upon the counselor's achieving a kind of external understanding apart from the relationship itself. Approaches which rely heavily upon external understanding of the client invariably affirm the tentative and partial nature of their understanding and also are likely to claim that the reason for formal assessment is the mutual planning of counseling activities.

CLIENTELE

The trait/factor and the eclectic approaches restrict their services to so-called "normal" individuals who exhibit adjustment problems but retain the resources necessary to cope with their difficulties. The other approaches place no limitation on their clientele except to exclude those incapable of benefiting from treatment, e.g., the extremely disturbed psychotic or those suffering from severe organic disorders. In actual practice most counselors, regardless of theoretical orientation, work with individuals having temporary situational problems, neurotic personalities, and mild neuroses. Selection criteria appear to focus upon whether the client retains the personal resources necessary to indicate hope for favorable treatment outcome. Lowe points out that:

> The criteria that therapists use in selecting clients are typically highly personal and require value judgments by the therapist.
>
> In choosing his clients the therapist first judges whether they will be able to relate and to communicate meaningfully. Counselors and therapists typically require that clients meet such objective criteria as having above-average intelligence and being between adolescence and early middle age. In addition they are likely to make more subjective judgements of client suitability, and they often insist that clients possess a working conscience, a tendency to introspection, and motivation for self-improvement.[17]

[16] Ford and Urban, *op. cit.*, p. 667.

[17] C. Marshall Lowe, *Value Orientations in Counseling and Psychotherapy* (San Francisco: Chandler Publishing Company, 1969), p. 39.

Table 10.1 Comparison of nine counseling approaches

Characteristic	*Trait/Factor*	*Rational-Emotive*	*Eclectic Counseling*	*Reciprocal Inhibition*
1. Nature of man	Man a rational being with potentialities which may be developed in either positive or negative directions; man not capable of developing autonomously but needs assistance of others to achieve full potentiality	Man, subject to powerful biological and social forces, has potential for being rational. Can rid himself of emotional difficulty by maximizing his rational thinking	Man both rational and irrational but having asocial tendencies; normal person, by conscious use of his intellectual resources, acquires self-regulatory abilities through training	Man shaped by environment; no volition, no free will, but only learned reactions; impossibility of being rational or objective; all thinking affected by conditioned feelings and needs and is thus rationalization
2. Major personality constructs	Each person an organized, unique pattern of capabilities and potentialities seeking to organize and maintain his life by utilizing his unique traits	Psychological states largely result of thinking illogically; thinking and reasoning are not two disparate processes; man rewarded or punished by his own thinking or self-talk	Personality the changing states of coping with environment; drive to achieve and maintain stability, integrate opposing functions, maximize self; life style consists of characteristic ways of unifying strategies for satisfying needs and coping with reality; development consists of perfecting rational and voluntary control	Behavior law-conforming; change a result of (a) growth, (b) lesions, (c) learning
3. Nature of anxiety	Uncertainty over utilization of one's potentialities	Overgeneralizing that an event will be catastrophic	Not explicitly described; repressed emotional conflict	Unadaptive behavior acquired by learning; unlearned anxiety characteristic response to noxious or threatening stimuli; situations requiring difficult discriminations or conflict
4. Counseling goals	To aid the individual in successive approximation of self-understanding and self-management	Elimination of anxiety, fears, etc., and the attainment of rational behavior, happiness, self-actualization	Independent self-regulation; attainment and preservation of mental health	Relief of suffering and removal of causes
5. Major techniques	Forcing conformity, changing environment, selecting appropriate environment, learning needed skills, and changing attitudes	Use of relationship techniques to establish rapport followed by teaching, suggestion, persuasion, confrontation, prescription of activities designed to rid the client of irrational ideas	Active to passive techniques employed	Assertive, respiratory, sexual, and relaxation responses including systematic desensitization
6. Use of tests and appraisal devices	Extensively used	Limited use	Limited use of standardized tests; projective techniques used as clinical data to be integrated with other data	Limited use
7. History taking	Necessary before an individual can be counseled	Relatively little use of historical clarification	Important for diagnostic reasons	Therapy begun with history taking to uncover anxiety
8. Diagnosis and prognosis	A necessary step	Used to uncover illogical ideas	Cornerstone of all clinical work; the basis for counseling approach adopted	Part of counselor activity
9. Clientele	"Normal" individuals who wish to become prepared to solve their adjustment situations before self-conflict develops	No limitation but notes that psychotics rarely completely cured	Normal people with intact personality resources who have personality problems	No limitation placed upon types of clients other than that disorders must be learned
10. Activity of counselor	Active role	Highly active	Ranges from passive to active role depending upon nature of problem and client's resources	Active role

Behavioral Counseling	*Freudian Analysis*	*Client-Centered Counseling*	*Existentialism*	*Gestalt Therapy*
Depends on theorist but man viewed primarily as mechanistic, or responding to an environment over which he has little control; living in a deterministic world, has little active role in choosing his destiny	Man both animalistic and human; shaped by biological needs, sexual drives, and aggressive instincts; behavior primarily determined by unconscious processes that are motivational and goal-directed	Man rational, good, trustworthy; moves in self-actualizing directions or toward growth, health, self-realization, independence, and autonomy	Man required to shoulder tasks set by life and hence to define meaning of life; strives for freedom from instincts and environment; individually unpredictable; man free and responsible to himself	Human beings not independent from their environment but work as a whole. Man not sum of parts but a coordination
Behavior lawful, and a function of its antecedent conditions	Personality a system composed of id, ego, and superego and a result of genetic relationship between ego functions in later life and those of infancy and childhood; outcome of a mutual interaction among tendencies of id, ego, and superego	Self-concept a regulator of behavior and perceptual field is reality for the individual; behavior a function of perceptions and organized with respect to self-concept	Behavior motivated by attempts to find meaning; man not driven but pulled by his values	Individual is considered a system in balance. He lives in a public (doing) level and a private (thinking) level. Imbalance is experienced as a corrective need. Awareness permits self-regulation and self-control
Learned reactions to cues involved in certain situations which operate as secondary or acquired drives; learned reaction to an originally neutral stimulus	Conflict between id impulses, superego demands, and ego defenses	Incongruence between self-concept and experience; conditions of worth violated; need for self-regard frustrated	Lack of meaning in life or threat of nonbeing	The gap between the *now* and the *then*; unfinished situations
Solution of whatever problems (within ethical limits) client brings to counselor	Personality reconstruction and reorientation	Self-direction and full functioning of client who is congruent, mature, and open to experience	Experiencing of existence as real so that individual can act upon his potentialities and develop a commitment	To mature, to grow up, to take responsibility for one's life, to be in touch with one's self and with the world
Reinforcement techniques, social modeling, desensitization techniques	Free association, use of dreams, transference, interpretation, etc.	Limited use of questioning, reassurance, encouragement, suggestion, but technique a way of communicating acceptance, respect, understanding	Psychoanalytic techniques often used, including free association, interpretation, transference, but emphasis on therapist's presence and patient's being	Confrontative; provide situations in which client experiences his frustrations; focus attention on body posture, gestures; enactment of dreams
May be used if needed	Projective techniques often employed	Extremely limited use; tends to be seen as inimical	Limited use	Limited use
Necessary to identify contingencies	Detailed history usually not taken	Inimical to counseling process	Most believe essential	Limited use
Necessary to assess (a) role of anxiety in symptoms and (b) client's capacity to handle anxiety and to extinguish it	Necessary for interpretation	Inimical to counseling process	Seen as necessary step by most existentialists	Limited use
Individuals who can think about and attend to the events in their environment	Therapy contraindicated for schizoid personalities, paranoid states, severe hypochondriasis; extremely guarded for marked conversion symptoms	Currently no restriction placed upon clientele	No restriction noted; most believe approach has wide applicability and utility	No limitation stated
Counselor warm and friendly but highly active	Initially passive; moves toward active, interpretive role as treatment progresses	Counselor active in providing facilitative conditions	Therapy seen as partnership, with therapist risking himself and client encouraged to be himself	Highly active

All approaches seemingly prefer the self-motivated client who voluntarily seeks help and cooperates by consenting to the rules and procedures employed with him. Almost all point out that the counselee comes for counseling because he desires change in his life situation, which is in itself a kind of self-selection. Practitioners of every approach believe that they can help those who seek their assistance, providing there is no clear indication that their professional help cannot be utilized. Few pretend to help everyone who seeks their assistance.

COUNSELOR ACTIVITY

All approaches postulate certain common conditions in a counseling relationship. These tend primarily to describe the counselor-client relationship and include warmth, acceptance, and understanding. Variations exist in the way each approach attempts to provide these conditions and the degree to which certain activities are seen as fostering or working against them. While the focus in Table 10.1 is upon active versus passive counselor behavior, a comparison of approaches on this basis should not be stretched too far. Although in general the extent of counselor activity and passivity is related to particular approaches, activity and passivity within an approach may change during a series of contacts with a given client. Another difference lies in where responsibility resides. The first six and ninth approaches assume that the counselor is responsible for the course of action; it is the professional's task to determine what is wrong and what is needed to produce change. Client-centered and existentialist counselors, on the other hand, believe that the responsibility lies chiefly with the client, who is able to determine what is wrong and what is needed because of the conditions inherent within the relationship. This distinction is a crucial one and accounts for much of the difference between these two approaches and the other approaches in a variety of characteristics descriptive of the counseling process. The philosophic assumptions concerning the nature of man cited for the nine counseling viewpoints clearly bear upon this issue.

Stefflre, commenting upon the common elements among four theories, presents 10 facets of counseling which are common to all.[18] His remarks are particularly appropriate to end this section and are paraphrased here. First is *flexibility*, and he noted that the hallmark of the experienced counselor was his ability to fit his style to the unique character of the client and the relationship. Second is *motivation*; individuals who want counseling are more likely to profit from it. Third is *relationship*, generally seen as the base on which the structure of counseling is built. Fourth is counselor *respect* for the individuality, humanness, and complexity of the individual. Fifth is *communication* between counselor and client, whether through words or non-verbal cues. Sixth is *learning*, present to some degree in all theories in that the client learns more about himself and his world and therefore performs better. Seventh is *direction* of the client by the counselor, recognized by most theories; Stefflre noted that concern has shifted from the presence or absence of direction to the extent, method, and purpose of direction. Eighth, the counselor's presence, interests, and activities are seen by all approaches as giving *support* to the client. Ninth, the counselor *rewards* the client for his presence and for some of his behavior. Finally, in respect to *purposes* of counselors, all seek a free, informed, responsible person.

Building a Personal Philosophy of Counseling

PHILOSOPHICAL ORIENTATIONS EXAMINED

Philosophy is a broad term. It is used throughout the following discussion in the narrower sense of professional philosophy. The counselor's behavior is the product of his philosophy, theoretical orientation, technique, and self-concept. At some early point in his thinking, the counselor must answer for himself: "What significance do I attach to this person?" Beck[19] has set forth the following philosophical questions which need to be discussed by counselors:

[18] Stefflre, *op. cit.*, pp. 298–302.
[19] Carlton E. Beck, *Philosophical Foundations of Guidance* (Englewood Cliffs, N.J.: Prentice-Hall, Inc., 1963), p. 96.

What is the nature of reality?
What is man's place in the universe?
What is knowledge?
How free is man?
What things (events, people) are of most worth?
Are there mandatory goals for society? For individuals?

A PHILOSOPHICAL ORIENTATION

C. Marshall Lowe[20] has described and criticized four value orientations, each of which he suggests tends to exclude the others, and each of which has been offered as an orientation for counseling. His article will serve as a basis for our discussion here.

Naturalism By "naturalism" Lowe says he means "positivism, scientism, behaviorism, and hedonism." The word positivism refers to the philosophical position of A. J. Ayer and the linguistic analysts for whom the only statements which have any meaning are those which can be empirically verified or logically induced from empirical data. "Scientism" is related to positivism and is characterized by the validation of statements by control and prediction of observed phenomena. This philosophy is eloquently expressed in B. F. Skinner's *Walden Two.* The expression of "scientism" in the field of psychology is often referred to as "behaviorism." It insists upon validation by observable and measurable "stimulus-and-response" experimental techniques. It tends, therefore, to disregard concepts like "consciousness" and "freedom" as terms to which no scientific meaning can be attached. Many criticisms of psychotherapeutic techniques have come from this source, particularly through H. J. Eysenck,[21] who quotes Raimy with relish: "Psychotherapy is an unidentified technique applied to unspecified problems with unpredictable outcomes. For this technique we recommend rigorous training." The word "hedonism" refers to the characterization of all human behavior in terms of the pursuit of pleasure, the relief of tension, or the satisfaction of needs. Joseph Samler[22] argues for the establishment of a validated system of values, the basic data of which, he maintains, will come from "man's increasing scientific knowledge." He holds that such values will be translatable, without undue difficulty, from an examination of man's needs. What man values, it seems, is to be equated with what man needs, and that is saying a great deal more than a man values what he needs.

Naturalism in counseling has been reflected in a wide range of developing trends over the last half-century. The Freudian and prescriptive schools of an earlier era rested upon deterministic foundations. More recently phenomenology has provided a framework within which deterministic views of human behavior have been set forth. Mathewson employs the phenomenological model, but strenuously rejects determinism: ". . . to discard the intuitive-artistic view of life might tend to relegate man to the position of a determinable unit in a mechanistic world . . . ."[23] Carlton Beck, who quotes Mathewson at length, rightly points out, however, that phenomenology is essentially a mechanistic psychological model. More recently still, naturalism has been reflected in the techniques advocated by such people as Wolpe, Krumboltz, and Michael and Meyerson. Thus, "observable behavior is the only variable of importance in the counseling and guidance process, and it is the only criterion against which the outcome of the process may be evaluated."[24]

Although the objectivity, replicability and predictability of behavioristic techniques are a valuable contribution to research into counseling techniques, naturalism as a philosophy for counseling is viewed as too limiting by many counselors. Carl Rogers makes the particular point that scientism is unable to answer questions about the pro-

[20] C. Marshall Lowe, "Value Orientations: An Ethical Dilemma," in John McGowan and Lyle Schmidt, *Counseling: Readings in Theory and Practice* (New York: Holt, Rinehart and Winston, 1962), pp. 119–127.
[21] H. J. Eysenck, "The Effect of Psychotherapy," in H. J. Eysenck (ed.), *Handbook of Abnormal Psychology* (New York: Basic Books, Inc., 1961), pp. 697–725.
[22] Joseph Samler, "Changes in Values: A Goal in Counseling," *Journal of Counseling Psychology,* Vol. 7 (Spring, 1960), pp. 32–39.
[23] Robert Hendry Mathewson, *Guidance Policy and Practice,* Third Edition (New York: Harper and Row, 1962), p. 141.
[24] Jack Michael and Lee Meyerson, "A Behavioral Approach to Counseling and Guidance," *Harvard Educational Review,* Vol. 32 (Fall, 1962), p. 395.

found subjectivity of human experience. Objectivity in the physical sciences is necessary and sufficient for validation; in the field of human relationships it is insufficient. What point is there, for example, in showing parents that love is a necessary condition for the healthy nurture of children, unless the parents subjectively experience love in their own existences? Paul Halmos[25] believes that the behaviorists (referred to by Halmos picturesquely as "the mechano-therapists") fail to distinguish the operational and attitudinal aspects of love. Halmos points out that Lazarus conceptualizes "handling" as "overt love." It is a truism, however, that love cannot be successfully imitated by the unloving, even in response to the most precise operational description available from behavioristic psychology.

This single criticism seems to be sufficient to show that naturalism, as a philosophical orientation to mankind, fails to "grapple with ultimate questions," or to reach "the ground of our being" in the words of Paul Tillich. There is some implication of an acknowledgment of this in Wolpe's use of terms such as "sympathetic acceptance." Such a term certainly rests upon unverifiable underlying concepts such as "consciousness" and "person," unless it is being used in a highly metaphorical sense. It is more likely, as Halmos says, that "mechanotherapeutic techniques" can only be applied against the secure background of person-to-person relationships, an element which is unacknowledged simply because it is unamenable to scientific dismemberment.

Culturalism "Culturalism" is also mentioned in Lowe's article. He quotes the American Psychological Association, whose ethical statements indicate that "the psychologist's ultimate allegiance is to society." It seems that Caiaphas and the Athenian City Fathers might have enrolled the help of the APA against Jesus and Socrates. Lowe cites Adler, Sullivan, and Horney as leading theorists who have defined neurosis in terms of social isolation and cure in terms of adjustment to society. Culturalism as a philosophical orientation is therefore the pursuit of what most people want, normally.

Among counseling professionals E. G. Williamson[26] speaks for some form of culturalism. In his article "Value Orientation in Counseling" he argues that the counseling relationship is one between client and "mentor." For the mentor, certain "outer limits" of the counselor's freedom for influencing the client are defined which will allow him to pursue on behalf of the client a variety of "loose fitting" values appropriate to a pluralistic and democratic society.

The logical fallacy in all of this is that of arguing from "what is" to "what ought to be." The possibility of "progress" is logically precluded in that "normality" is what is valued, and most people are "normal," by definition, already. Lowe rejects culturalism as a value orientation, quoting Lindner's observation that culturalism involves man in the exchange of his freedom for the doped security of accepting things as they are, and adds his own caustic remark, "Normality is nothing to brag about."

Normality is, in any event, a vague concept, and one of the reasons why it is so vague is that the concept of society is itself a highly reducible one, logically. What is valued by society will depend upon what is thought to be the origin and function of society. There is no unanimity on either of these points. In order to approach "the ground of our being" we must ask a prior question to "What is normal?" and that is "What principles of human behavior underlie social organization?" This is perhaps what C. G. Wrenn meant when he said that a counselor can never be loyal to society until he is loyal to something more than society.

Humanism The third value orientation mentioned by Lowe is "humanism." By this he means

[25] Paul Halmos, *The Faith of the Counsellors* (New York: Schocken Books, 1966), pp. 67–74.

[26] E. G. Williamson, "Value Orientation in Counseling," *Personnel and Guidance Journal*, Vol. 36 (November, 1957), pp. 175–183.

a basic commitment to the idea that man is self-sufficient. He quotes Rogers and Fromm as proponents of the view.

Carl Rogers[27] argues that the direction of therapy is towards the discovery that the core of the personality is positive. He quotes Maslow in support of the point that destructive behavior arises from the frustration of constructive behavior. Later in his book Rogers specifically identifies Søren Kierkegaard's statement, "to be that self which one truly is," with the movement of the client in the therapeutic situation. This involves movement away from facades and subjection of the self to the group and movement towards self-direction and trust of self.

Such a philosophy chooses to disregard the basic propositions of St. Paul, the Reformation, and Freud, although this need not necessarily be thought of as a criticism. Lowe, however, does make two further criticisms. One is the general observation that the most dignified self is the self least concerned with his own dignity. Certainly a re-emergent theme in philosophy is that of the ultimate futility of pursuing self-fulfillment for its own sake. "Happiness," said Aristotle, "is like the bloom on the cheek of an athlete." By this he may be taken to mean that happiness is achieved only by pursuing something more important than happiness, as such. Somewhat more recently, Bertrand Russell has condemned the "cosmic impiety" of the individualism of our romantic age. Jesus maintained that "Whoever would lose his life for my sake, he will save it!" The pursuit of self-fulfillment does not appear to have been recommended very highly by several of the world's major minds.

A further criticism made by Lowe, and one which is more readily amenable to objective validation, is that Rogers' intense individualism is closely similar to, and may be a product of, the pathology of American, middle-class, achievement-oriented society. Rogers himself says that the successful completion of therapy would mean "the establishment of an individualized value system having considerable identity with the value system of any equally well adjusted member of the human race." The question is: "Adjustment to what? To the values of American Suburbia and Mrs. Hillside?"

If we are to "grapple with ultimate questions" we must ask Rogers why he values independence and self-realization above other possible values. Naturalism and culturalism can attempt to provide some criteria for evaluating the ideals which they pursue. Rogers provides none of any substance beyond the correspondence theory of truth quoted above, which is a form of culturalism. He might be said to be concerned for a "being" for which he provides no "ground."

Rogers' identification of a philosophy for client-centered counseling with the thinking of Kierkegaard is not mentioned by Lowe, who omits any reference to existentialism from his article. The existentialist implications of his orientation are not pursued with much emphasis by Rogers himself, perhaps because Kierkegaard and his successors have been much less optimistic about mankind than Rogers. The existentialist theme is pursued at length, however, by Carlton Beck in *Philosophical Foundations of Guidance*.[28] He argues that guidance has outgrown formerly fashionable prescriptive and phenomenological models and that it now rests upon a weak philosophical framework. He recommends that the movement in the United States should follow that in Europe towards *Daseinanalyse* or existentialist therapy. Existentialism in psychology, according to Beck, is an extension of phenomenology in the direction of attributing to man a mode of experience, termed "*dasein*," which is beyond animal experience, and raises man above the deterministic conceptions attributed to him by phenomenology. "*Dasein*" means "little aware of itself," which the existentialists regard as the basic existential concept of man, inexplicable in operational terms.

At the heart of existentialism is Sartre's affirma-

[27] Carl R. Rogers, *On Becoming a Person* (Boston: Houghton Mifflin Company, 1962), pp. 73–106.

[28] *Op. cit.*

tion that man is nothing but what he makes of himself. His acts define his limits; his existence defines his essence. Concepts of "*dasein*" and freedom elaborate this basic affirmation. The writings of Buber, Maritain, and Jaspers further elaborate this theme. Jaspers in particular makes a characteristic distinction between the empirically known, predictable psychological and biological self which is the proper object of scientific study and the "authentic self" which contains the source and meaning of life. Upon such a distinction rests Buber's description of the "I-Thou" relationship. May's *Existence*[29] develops an appropriate theme for counseling and guidance, the thesis being that "the grasping of the being of another person occurs on a quite different level from our knowledge of specific things about him."

Like humanism, existentialism has a profound sense of the worth and dignity of man. "Man is free," says Carlton Beck. "This is at once a pleasant heady luxury and also the source of his discontent." [30] Certain philosophical absolutes are admitted, i.e., the belief in the freedom and dignity of the "authentic" self because people are ends, not means. Certain mandatory goals are conceived, i.e., empathy, sympathy, and genuine free action. The philosophical basis for all oughts, it is claimed, is not an *a priori* universal, but "to further the race of man and his existential amelioration." [31]

The Christian existentialist does, of course, accept certain *a priori* assumptions. While the secularists strenuously deny that they make any such assumptions, a belief in the dignity of the authentic self is not supported by the existentialists any more than it is by Rogers. Just why the "existential amelioration of man" deserves to be considered the basis of all oughts they do not say; they provide the ground of our being.

Theism Lowe deals with theism as the fourth of his value orientations. He defines theism as a commitment to the view that life has objective meaning. He argues that religion should become part of psychotherapy because it is wholly based on love, which Allport says is "incomparably the greatest therapeutic agent."

Many counselors find theistic arguments inferential. Inferential they must be since by definition they place the locus for evaluation of man outside what can be fully comprehended by human experience. Though the theistic argument may be inferential it could be maintained that the inference of theism is a necessary one. Lowe maintains that the counselor is faced with a range of orientations each of which excludes the others. Here it is argued that the various kinds of orientations attach various kinds of significance to man, i.e., as the object of scientific study, as a member and product of society, as a creative individual, as a unique member of the creature kingdom, and that each of these evaluations has its validity, none necessarily excluding any others. Each of them may therefore be regarded in some degree as a necessary part of a total evaluation of man. What is probably more accurate is that none of them, taken separately or together, is a sufficient evaluation of man since none of them reaches "the ground of our being." The further step that is necessary is a speculative extrapolation, an inference which cannot be entirely validated empirically. Such a step appears to be necessary if a complete, irreducible, and rounded attribution of the significance to man is ever to be made.

That a religious orientation appears to rest at the heart of counseling is the argument of Paul Halmos.[32] He maintains that "counsellors" (a term which he uses in a very broad sense) are committed to the "faith," a "tendermindedness" in which "spiritual solace, sanity, a state of grace, or merely adjustment" are sought for the client. He draws attention to what he calls the "ideological cramp" which has overtaken modern societies: a paralysis in the face of the seemingly insoluble complexities of modern problems. He regards scientific objectiv-

[29] Rollo May, *Existence* (New York: Basic Books, Inc., 1958), p. 38.
[30] Beck, *op. cit.*, p. 134.
[31] Beck, *op. cit.*, p. 133.

[32] Halmos, *op. cit.*

ism and individual personalism as escape routes from moral ideology. But he also regards professionalism as an escape route, or at least as a means whereby Christian *agape* can be conveniently camouflaged. Nowhere in his book does Halmos attempt a systematic philosophical analysis of what he regards as the "faith of the counsellors." However, to express this faith he frequently uses the Greek word "*agape*," translated as "love" in modern versions of the New Testament.

Formulations equating "God" with any other kind of concept are rare in biblical tradition. Indeed, Hebrew-Christian thinking is notable for its unwillingness to conceptualize God in any but metaphorical terms. The statement "God is love" does appear, however, in the First Epistle of John, and it is to be understood as a realization that the experience of interpersonal brotherly love springs from the "ground of our being" and therefore deserves to be equated with the universalized, objectified concept of "God." The first part of such a statement would receive a great deal of support from recent research into the effects of psychotherapy. The second part is an inference, but it is one which has the experiential completeness, the logical irreducibility, and the philosophical roundedness which have not been found in any of the orientations so far considered.

Lowe criticizes theistic orientations in terms of their blandness, superstition, unrealism, optimism, and prolongation of dependence. The shortcoming of this kind of criticism is that it fails to take account of the kind of distinction made above between institutionalized and existential awareness. Institutional religion is prone to all the static blandness of culturalism. Indeed, Paul Halmos appears in one place to suggest that the operation of "agape" grows in inverse proportion to the strength of the ecclesia. He points to a simultaneous increase in the number of people per clergyman and decrease in the number of people per member of the medical or paramedical professions. Such an argument is too facile, but many cannot accept that Lowe's charges may not be fairly leveled against the Jesus philosophy. For many, Jesus' teachings were not bland, unrealistic, or prolonging of dependence. They were not dependent either upon whatever superstitious thought-forms were employed to express them in the first century A.D., although the process of demythologization is not yet complete. Certainly in the mind of Tillich, the encounter with the "ground of our being" was no bland, unrealistic or dependent experience. Indeed, "the pain of looking into one's own depth is too intense for most people."

It is sometimes argued that religious counseling ought to be separately retained. This is the sense of an article by William C. Bier.[33] He maintains that "spiritual ends" require "spiritual means," and that the religious counselor ought to be retained in order to help the client to be right in the life to come. Paul Tillich makes a similar kind of distinction in saying that existential anxiety grows out of the threefold threat of death, meaninglessness, and guilt and is properly a priestly concern. Pathological anxiety he concedes as the province of the psychotherapists. In his way, Carlton Beck also argues for the separation of religious and secular counseling. "By what criterion," he asks, "could it be said that a priest or a minister is closest to such problems as the question of vocational choice in a complex industrial society?"[34]

It is a false reading of life itself to imagine that experiences can be divided between two self-contained categories. Any problem, as we have already seen, can be viewed from a number of different points of view and probed to a number of significances. "Why do I choose this profession?" may be honestly answered in a number of different ways. As Paul Tillich has it, "Look at an uneducated worker who performs a mechanical task day by day, but who suddenly asks himself, 'What does it mean for my life?' 'What is the meaning of life?' Because he asks these questions, that man is on the way into depth." At any moment in an inter-

[33] William C. Bier, "Religious Counseling: The Roman Catholic Church," in R. K. Hall and J. A. Lauwerys (eds.), *The Yearbook of Education, 1955* (Yonkers: World Book), pp. 354–362.
[34] Beck, *op. cit.*, p. 56.

view, the counselor may find himself in the presence of a client making profound observations of himself. It is the poorly equipped counselor who is unprepared to appreciate their significance and to respond to them at the level of being from which they emerge.

The comments here attempt to demonstrate that philosophic orientations to counseling are often shortsighted. Each of them eventually reaches an impasse, a point beyond which it cannot progress without, in some way, stepping outside the limits which it has defined for itself. As Halmos more colorfully puts it, "When counselors don the garb of the sceptic their moral underwear shows."[35] Where that impasse is met and ignored the orientation either fails to meet the full range of human experience (as does naturalism); or defines itself as reducible and therefore at ambiguous levels (as does culturalism); or simply omits any philosophical framework at all (as does Rogers); or provides a philosophical basis which is inadequate because it leaves certain basic questions unanswered (as do existentialism and theism). Other criticisms might have been made, but the purpose here has been to point out current failures to "grapple with ultimate issues."

THE PROCESS OF BUILDING A COUNSELING PHILOSOPHY

Counselors in training are frequently urged to develop a personalized view of themselves as counselors. In some respects this amounts basically to achieving a fairly thorough self-understanding. It is a person's own experience, personality, and view of the nature of man which influence the very choice of the theory he will operate under. He cannot accept and internalize what is foreign and repulsive to his personal makeup. He cannot operate maturely and professionally in borrowed clothes. Preferably his suit is tailor made with the cloth and style selected upon the basis of his individualistic taste.

It is unlikely that the counselor will accept all aspects of any one theory; it is essential, however, that he be able to commit himself to its fundamental tenets even while disagreeing with some of its specifics. Presumably the choice of a theory or a way of operating as a counselor begins with and is strongly influenced by his training, experience, and of course his own traits influence the impact of training. Early commitment to a counseling approach, moreover, is frequently highly tentative and subject to considerable modification as the individual moves through the common sequence of didactic course work, supervised counseling experience and actual practice. It is a fact of life that the true fit of a theory to an individual counselor cannot be determined until he attempts to practice what he claims to believe. Actual practice is what exposes discrepancies between the theory chosen and the practitioner's personality and philosophy of life.

It would be naive to assume that any theoretical approach, like any ready-made suit of clothing, could fit an individual without some minor alterations. Perhaps it would be even more naive to assume that a suit once fitted, even if it never wore out, would conform to the changing characteristics of a counselor over time. The length might, but the girth and other parts would surely begin to bind and probably appear out of date and ludicrous. What is needed is constant refitting of the suit (theory). No argument is made for totally discarding it, although this may sometimes be necessary.

Many counselor educators would argue that a counselor's attempts to choose bits and pieces from diverse theories lead only to a hodge-podge of contradictory assumptions and incompatible techniques. On the other hand, others would just as strongly assert that adoption of a single counseling viewpoint is parochial, because the theorist was bound by his time frame, clientele, personality, and society. Little doubt exists that most counselors adopt portions of various viewpoints in developing and articulating what are called counseling behaviors. The important element is that the counselor, by continuously struggling to formulate his comprehensive point of view, gives meaning to his counseling experience and slowly evolves a counseling style that fits him.

[35] Halmos, *op. cit.*

Finally, the counselor in preparation should not make the error of thinking that he can operate atheoretically. Any counselor's activities must be based on some set of assumptions, some set of organizing principles, some core of beliefs. These could well be labeled theories, and the issue would be whether they are openly and explicitly recognized as such or whether the individual chooses to deny their existence while deluding himself that theory has no place in his world.

Annotated References

Ford, Donald H., and Urban, Hugh B. *Systems of Psychotherapy.* New York: John Wiley & Sons, Inc., 1963. 712 pp.

Section III (pp. 593–690) presents a comparative analysis of 10 systems of psychotherapy — how they view the development of normal behavior and the development of disordered behavior, the goals of therapy, conditions for producing behavioral change, and evaluation of behavior change in therapy.

Lowe, C. Marshall. *Value Orientations in Counseling and Psychotherapy.* San Francisco: Chandler Publishing Company, 1969. 305 pp.

The purpose of the book, according to Lowe, is to relate the theory and practice of counseling to the broad social, philosophical, and historical issues. Particularly useful to students is his discussion of the moral overtones in counseling and psychotherapy (Chapter 2, pp. 35–51.).

Patterson, C. H. *Theories of Counseling and Psychotherapy.* New York: Harper & Row, Publishers, 1966. 518 pp.

The divergences and convergences among several counseling approaches are discussed in Chapter 21 (pp. 487–509). Treatment is centered upon philosophy and concepts, counseling process, and goals and purposes. Patterson also has a brief but sophisticated presentation on integration of theories.

Stefflre, Buford and Grant, W. Harold. (eds.). *Theories of Counseling,* 2nd ed. New York: McGraw-Hill Book Co., Inc., 1972. 326 pp.

Four counseling theories are presented, each written by a different author. In Chapter 9 (pp. 287–303) Stefflre sums up the four approaches. The nature of man, behavioral change, counseling goals, counselor role, crucial determinants of an approach, and common elements are analyzed.

Further References

Aubrey, Roger F. "And Never the Twain Shall Meet: Counselor Training and School Realities." *The School Counselor,* Vol. 20 (September, 1972). pp. 16–24.

Caldwell, Edson. "Counseling in Context." *Personnel and Guidance Journal,* Vol. 49 (December, 1970). pp. 271–278.

Carkhuff, Robert R. "Counseling Research, Theory and Practice—1965." *Journal of Counseling Psychology,* Vol. 13 (Winter, 1966). pp. 467–480.

Carkhuff, Robert R. "Toward a Comprehensive Model of Facilitative Interpersonal Processes." *Journal of Counseling Psychology,* Vol. 14 (January, 1967). pp. 67–72.

Chenault, Joann. "Counseling Theory: The Problem of Definition." *Personnel and Guidance Journal,* Vol. 47 (October, 1968). pp. 110–113.

Chenault, Joann. "Help-Giving and Morality." *Personnel and Guidance Journal,* Vol. 48 (October, 1969). pp. 89–96.

Dreyfus, Edward A. "Humanness: A Therapeutic Variable." *Personnel and Guidance Journal,* Vol. 45 (February, 1967). pp. 573–578.

Gelso, Charles J. "Two Different Worlds: A Paradox in Counseling and Psychotherapy." *Journal of Counseling Psychology,* Vol. 17 (May, 1970). pp. 271–278.

Herr, Edwin L. "Field Theory and Differential Press: Implications for Counseling." *Personnel and Guidance Journal,* Vol. 43 (February, 1965). pp. 586–590.

Rousseve, Ronald J. "Counselor, Know Thyself!" *Personnel and Guidance Journal,* Vol. 47 (March, 1969). pp. 641–649.

Schell, Edith and Daubner, Edward. "Epistemology and School Counseling." *Personnel and Guidance Journal,* Vol. 47 (February, 1969). pp. 506–513.

Stubbins, Joseph. "The Politics of Counseling." *Personnel and Guidance Journal,* Vol. 48 (April, 1970). pp. 611–618.

Tiedeman, David V. "Predicament, Problem and Psychology: The Case for Paradox in Life and Counseling Psychology." *Journal of Counseling Psychology,* Vol. 14 (January, 1967). pp. 1–8.

Wrenn, C. Gilbert. "The Three Worlds of the Counselor." *Personnel and Guidance Journal,* Vol. 49 (October, 1970). pp. 91–97.

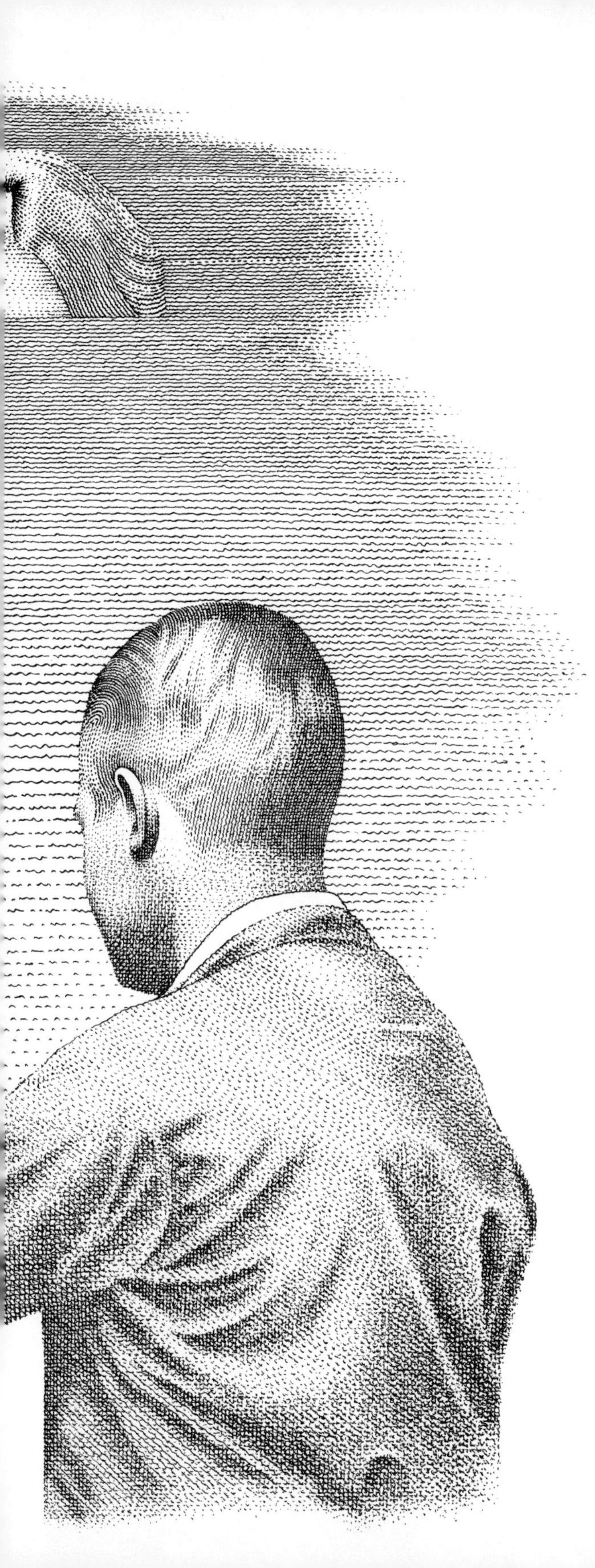

PART FOUR

COUNSELING: CONTENT, PROCESS, AND PRACTICE

Part Four explains the major content of and practices utilized in the counseling process. Practices evolve from experience and represent certain ways of behaving in particular situations which have stood the test of time.

Chapter Eleven describes the core elements — empathy, rapport, understanding, acceptance, and the like — which affect counseling. Chapter Twelve presents the basic techniques employed in the counseling relationship. Chapter Thirteen discusses diagnosis, test interpretation, referral practices, and other counseling practices, and Chapter Fourteen discusses counseling practices with some special populations. Chapter Fifteen deals with counseling in groups.

The acquisition of counseling skills and techniques can be accomplished only partially through didactic examination. Basically, they develop into personal work skills through counseling experience and eventually blend to create a personal counseling style.

CORE ELEMENTS WHICH FACILITATE COUNSELING

11

Chapter Ten indicated that establishment of a satisfactory relationship between counselor and counselee(s) was one element common to virtually all theories. The counseling relationship is a blend, a complex, and derives its distinctiveness from many factors of varying intensity. A symposium of counselors organized to draw out its "essence" would discern numerous different ideas, meanings, generalizations, rhythms, and patterns.

This chapter will take up first the significance of privacy, confidentiality, and setting to the counseling relationship. Second, the part played by the counselor's attitudes in facilitating the relationship will be considered, including how his values, understanding, and acceptance influence it. Finally, the additional factors of empathy, rapport, genuineness, attentiveness and their effect upon the relationship will be examined.

The topics discussed in this chapter are pertinent not just to the initial counseling contact but to the whole process. In many instances the initial counseling session will be the final one if these factors are not continuously present.

External Conditions Influencing Counseling

The setting in which counseling is conducted undoubtedly has some bearing upon whether the relationship will be facilitated or thwarted.

PHYSICAL SETTING

The room should be comfortable and attractive. While counseling offices may be impressive and beautiful, neither monumental character nor artistic expression is mandatory. Counseling facilities should be designed for comfort and relaxation. Pictures, draperies, carpet, plants, and the like are usually viewed as conducive to creating an unhurried climate in which the individual may express himself. Little corroborating data exist for any assertion that a sterile physical atmosphere reduces a counselee's willingness to talk, but it is axiomatic that people tend to derive a sense of well-being from a pleasant environment.

The general appearance of a counseling facility depends upon color, decor, lighting, arrangement of equipment and furnishings, and noise control. Furnishings should be harmonious and comfortable, and the decor is usually subdued but not depressing. Light, quiet colors are often used to give a feeling of friendliness. By attention to features such as these tensions are eased, feelings of warmth and comfort are engendered, and rapport and contact are encouraged. Needless to say, the same features which lead to an aesthetically pleasing environment for the counselee enable the counselor to function better.

PROXEMICS

Much speculation, but little research, has gone into the effects of the seating arrangements within the counseling office. "The manner in which man regulates the spatial features of his environment and conversely the impact of that environment on his subsequent behavior" is defined as *proxemics* by Haase and DiMattia.[1] They investigated the seating arrangement preferred by 10 counselors, 10 administrators, and 10 clients. These subjects used a Semantic Differential Scale to respond to photographs which depicted four proxemic seating arrangements common to counseling. Their findings confirmed conventional wisdom: the seating position preferred by all three subject groups was across the corner of the desk.

More recently, Widgery and Stackpole sought to determine whether desk position influenced the interviewer's "perceived credibility" among high- and low-anxiety subjects. Forty-four subjects were interviewed separately for four minutes by a professor of communication. The interviewer sat behind the desk during interviews with half the subjects; with the other 22 he sat facing each with no desk between. Highly anxious subjects recorded the interviewer's credibility as higher with no desk between while low-anxiety subjects responded inversely.[2]

That each person has a personal space within which he is comfortable in his interactions with another person is not only well known, but has been documented by considerable research. The comfortable space or distance between two persons has been ascribed to cultural background, the relationship between the two parties, the sex of the participants, the topic of their conversation, and their relative status. Haase investigated the relationship of sex and specific instructional set (academic advising or personal counseling) of counseling to students' reactions to five interpersonal interaction distances. His findings revealed that males did not differ from females in preferred distance nor did it matter whether the session was for academic advising or personal counseling. Subjects believed that distances of 30 and 39 inches represented the close and far phases of the space between counselor and client. Haase notes that this range of distance is usually reserved for interaction between closely related people (husband-wife, intimate friends).[3] Since most proxemic research has been conducted in simulated settings, the full impact of seating arrangements, physical distance between participants, and other physical features upon the counseling relationship and, even more important, its outcomes are still unknown.

PRIVACY

A most important perquisite of the physical setting is privacy. If the confidence of the counselee is to be secured, the feeling of security engendered by privacy cannot be overemphasized. Individuals desire and have a right to both *auditory* and *visual* privacy from peers, teachers, and others when they

[1] Richard F. Haase and Dominic J. DiMattia, "Proxemic Behavior: Counselor, Administrator and Client Preference for Seating Arrangements in Dyadic Interaction," *Journal of Counseling Psychology*, Vol. 17 (July, 1970), pp. 319–325.

[2] Robin Widgery and Cecil Stackpole, "Desk Position, Interviewee Anxiety and Interviewer Credibility: An Example of Cognitive Balance in a Dyad," *Journal of Counseling Psychology*, Vol. 19 (May, 1972), pp. 173–177.

[3] Richard F. Haase, "The Relationship of Sex and Instructional Set to the Regulation of Interpersonal Interaction Distance in a Counseling Analogue," *Journal of Counseling Psychology*, Vol. 17 (May, 1970), pp. 233–236.

enter into a counseling relationship. Nothing can limit the relationship more quickly than knowing that others are able to hear what is being said or watch what is taking place. The experienced counselor knows how hard it is for a counselee to state what prompted him to seek counseling if privacy is not assured.

The provision of auditory and visual privacy is basic to the ethical standard that counselors will safeguard the confidentiality of the relationship. The communication between counselor and client is privileged in that the confidence in which it is given will not be violated. According to the APGA Code of Ethics, "The counseling relationship and information resulting therefrom must be kept confidential consistent with the obligations of the member as a professional person."[4] While more extensive discussion of the matter of confidentiality will be found in Chapter Sixteen, it is sufficient to state here that confidentiality is an essential condition for counseling and that physical facilities which safeguard it also encourage the development of the counseling relationship.

TAPE RECORDING

For the past 20 years the mechanical recording of counseling interviews has been common practice. Particularly since the 1950's it has been widely used in counselor preparation because of its training value. Counselors prepared in such programs often continue to record some of their counseling sessions in order to evaluate their own work. Questions continue to be raised, however, regarding the desirability of sound-recording procedures.

In very recent years video taping has been used with increasing frequency. The same basic issues are involved. Originally much clamor centered around the ethics of mechanically reproducing the contents of counseling sessions, apparently quelled by the assurance that such material receives the same safeguards as any information acquired in the counseling setting. One proviso attached to the question of ethics is that all recordings are made with the counselee's permission and that subsequent use of recordings is made only with the counselee's written consent.

A continuing controversy is whether recording interferes with or negatively affects the counseling process. This issue is commonly raised among students in training. While the question is legitimate, raising the issue is frequently tinged with insecurity and embarrassment experienced by fledgling counselors who are forced to defend their words and deeds. In a very real sense, they often feel they must present evidence which may prove them guilty and lead to their own condemnation.

Whatever the effects of recording upon the counselor, determining its impact upon the counseling process remains difficult. The fact that relatively little research has been done in this area may in itself indicate that these procedures are generally accepted. Research by Roberts and Renzaglia clearly supports the contention that sound recording does influence certain counseling interaction variables.[5] In an experiment in which recordings were made sometimes by machines in the counseling room and at other times by hidden equipment without counselor or client knowledge, clients produced more favorable self-references when they knew they were being recorded and more unfavorable self-references when secret recordings were made. The counselors, despite exposure to what the authors describe as client-centered counseling style, tended to be less client centered when recording was open. Implementation of client-centered counseling seemed to take place when secret recording was used. The investigators suggest that this rather unusual finding may have occurred because the student counselors used in the study felt freer to use the client-centered style in sessions they believed were not being recorded.

Two serious questions may be raised about this particular study. (1) Despite the care taken by the

[4] Committee on Ethics of the American Personnel and Guidance Association, "Code of Ethics," *Personnel and Guidance Journal*, Vol. 40 (October, 1961), p. 207.

[5] Ralph R. Roberts, Jr., and Guy A. Renzaglia, "The Influence of Tape Recording on Counseling," *Journal of Counseling Psychology*, Vol. 12 (Spring, 1965), pp. 10–16.

investigators to conduct their research in a highly ethical manner, the procedures they employed were criticized on ethical grounds by Leona Tyler in a comment immediately following their article. Tyler freely admits that her objection may stem from a narrower view of the ethical practices involved. (2) The experience level of the counselor sample may have influenced the results. There would appear to be little question that the greater the counselor's experience and security, the greater the likelihood that he will behave consistently whether recorded or not.

Our experience indicates that the reaction of counselees to recordings tends to be highly individual. The vast majority raise no objection to recording when given the opportunity to (1) not have the session recorded and (2) discontinue the recording at any point in the session. On the other hand, a few counselees do object, either at the outset or when they approach highly sensitive material. Since their wishes are respected, there is no chance to determine whether refusal to stop the recording would influence the outcome.

In the authors' experience, the sigh of relief when the recorder is stopped generally comes from the counselor in training rather than from the counselee. Probably all counselor educators are accustomed to a disproportionate number of malfunctioning machines reported by a small number of highly threatened trainees. While this situation is sometimes treated jokingly with specific individuals, it can become a serious problem which must be actively coped with in supervision of the trainee.

Yenawine and Arbuckle compared and contrasted the effects of audiotape and videotape recordings on counselor trainees' practicum experiences. Each of 14 student subjects kept a log of his counseling and supervisory experiences from which data were abstracted. Their findings suggested that, of the two media, the videotape was superior for (1) it produced more complete, relevant material for review, (2) it increased the likelihood that a counselor-centered focus as opposed to a client-centered focus would be maintained in supervisory sessions, and (3) it provided a more objective basis for evaluating interviews. These investigators reported that initial anxiety and resistance were higher among those who videotaped than those who audiotaped. However, initial anxiety soon yielded to enthusiastic acceptance. Yenawine and Arbuckle state that the vividness and completeness of videotape recordings tend to make it difficult for students to become emotionally involved in the critique of a fellow counselor's work. Presumably, the completeness of the videotape may foster a situation with which peers are unable to cope fully. Therefore, they concluded that student counselors identify more easily and completely with counselor performances recorded on audiotape than videotape.[6] Feedback from either or both is not only desirable but highly necessary for developing and improving counselor skills and attitudes.

CLIENT CHARACTERISTICS INFLUENCING COUNSELING

There is no doubt that many additional factors, external to the process itself, influence counseling. Prominent among these is the characteristics of the client. The client's experiences, cultural background, and expectations for counseling are clearly brought with him and influence the process. Additionally, economic conditions, the environment of the community, and characteristics of the institution in which counseling takes place — all have an impact on the client and therefore on the process. Detailed treatment of these conditions may be found in Chapters Three, Four, Five, and Fourteen.

Counselor Attitudes Which Influence Counseling

The attitudes of the counselor, his approaches to the individual, and what he does all influence the counseling relationship to a marked degree. The counselor is the key to the initiation and development of the relationship.

[6] Gardner Yenawine and Dugald S. Arbuckle, "Study of the Use of Videotape and Audiotape as Techniques in Counselor Education," *Journal of Counseling Psychology*, Vol. 18 (January, 1971), pp. 1–6.

SOME KEY CONCEPTS

This section briefly treats two components of the philosophical orientation of the counselor: beliefs and values. Distinctions between these two terms are not easily made. Beliefs generally are seen as emotionally accepted doctrines based on unexamined, implicit grounds. Values, while closely related to beliefs, usually represent what some social scientists call "oughtnesses" or "conceptions of the desirable" which influence behavior.

Beliefs Many of the beliefs that men hold most dear may be called myths. "Every society is held together by a myth-system, a complex of dominating thought-forms that determines and sustains all its activities," says MacIver. "All social relations, the very texture of human society, are myth-born and myth-sustained. . . . Wherever he goes, whatever he encounters, man spins about him his web of myth, as the caterpillar spins his cocoon."[7] Myths can be very powerful. Men, it is said, possess thoughts, but myths possess men.

Myths vary from culture to culture and from age to age. The myths of modern man in today's "civilized" societies are perhaps more sophisticated than those of ancient Greece, but they are still myths. Myths are neither necessarily false nor evil. The word is neutral. "We include equally under the term 'myth' the most penetrating philosophies of life, the most profound intimations of religion, the most subtle renditions of experience, along with the most grotesque imaginations of the most benighted savage."[8] The great religious and political beliefs of the Western world make up a large part of our own myth system. We think our religious faiths and our democratic ideals are true. We know they are noble. Nevertheless they remain myths.

Myths are even more powerful than logic because they usually cannot be refuted. They must be taken on faith. They come in all shapes and sizes. Some are central to our whole system of beliefs; others are of lesser importance. Most basic to or central in the counselor's mythology is his belief that the counselee must be accorded dignity, equality, and individuality. The emphasis on the supreme worth of the individual has been an unbroken thread in democratic thought. It can be found in the writings of Thomas Jefferson, especially in the Declaration of Independence, where he eloquently proclaimed that all men have been endowed by their Creator with certain unalienable rights and that men create governments to secure these rights. This doctrine of individualism (not to be confused with the doctrine of laissez-faire) is the belief that there is something of supreme value in every human being.

The "rights of man" are coming increasingly under examination. "Rights" imply laws or a *law giver* to confer them, and rights which purport to transcend positive law imply the existence of a transcendent system of law. To the authors of the American Declaration of Independence this presented no difficulty: "We hold these truths to be self-evident, that all men . . . are endowed by their Creator with certain unalienable Rights, that among these are Life, Liberty and the pursuit of Happiness." A few years later the preamble to the French constitution of 1791 omitted reference to the Creator but could assume the self-evidence of natural law in which were grounded the "rights of man." Those who framed the United Nations declaration in 1948, "The Universal Declaration of Human Rights," however, could invoke a common assumption neither about a Creator nor about the reality of natural law. The status of the rights they enumerated is accordingly nebulous.

It is possible, of course, to regard all these declarations simply as specifying aspirations. In that case, their force depends upon their ability to kindle the imaginations and direct the purposes of the men of their times. If that is so, it must be confessed that the ringing brevity of the eighteenth-century documents (three rights were enough for America, four for France) is superior to the prolixity of the United Nations — 30 articles of

[7] R. M. MacIver, *The Web of Government* (New York: The MacMillan Company, 1947), pp. 4–5.
[8] *Ibid.*, p. 5.

two or three items each, descending to such banalities as "everyone has the right to participate in the cultural life of the community." And the impact is not sharpened by the proliferation of subsidiary declarations, conventions and covenants, elaborating or refining the original.

But the United Nations is not content to regard its work as a summary of aspirations. One purpose of these subsidiary instruments is to bind national governments to make their laws conform to "universal" principles formulated by the United Nations and its agencies. They also contain another development, which is perhaps more interesting. Rights depend on laws for their recognition, but on tribunals for their enforcement. And there has been some progress towards the establishment of international tribunals to vindicate rights which are internationally declared. The European Court of Human Rights furnishes one example. Another, more tentative, is found in the Convention on the Elimination of All Forms of Racial Discrimination, which has not yet come into force. In certain circumstances complainants who do not get satisfaction from a domestic tribunal may be heard by an international tribunal established for that purpose under the convention.

Perhaps the above statement that "Rights imply laws . . . ," while meant to be unexceptional, is not really so. Rights (in the sense of the word used in the various declarations) imply that others have duties to those who are said to have rights. Some duties are legal, others moral, and it is reasonable enough to distinguish similarly between legal and moral rights. Although one kind of ethical theory describes morality as "the moral law," there is no necessity to think that moral duties or moral rights "depend on laws for their existence." Discussion of moral rights often implies that they are not but ought to be a subject of law. That certain moral rights ought to be turned into legal rights is the main point of declarations of the rights of man.

Fundamental among the counselor's philosophical attitudes is a belief in the worth and value of each counselee. Men everywhere, of almost all faiths, proclaim a generalized acceptance of the brotherhood of man. Almost all men preach liberty, equality, fraternity, personal dignity, and social justice. But many of these same men are so entangled in the loves and hates stemming from particular myths, ideologies and their own self-interest that they seem quite unable to practice what they expound on an individual-to-individual basis. Recurrent experiences of frustration, fear, and misery so shape motives that many men attempt to serve the interests of all by directing their worry and rage against those they see as odious because their ways are different, disturbing, or heretical.

Another important part of the counselor's philosophic orientation is his belief in man's need for freedom. Erich Fromm says that man has freed himself from the old bonds of slavery and feudalism and become an individual, enjoying certain rights and liberties, but has not gained freedom in the positive sense of realizing his intellectual and artistic possibilities.[9] He has gained too much freedom *from* traditional controls, too little freedom to live actively and spontaneously. Fromm sees the root of this problem in the nature of modern industrial civilization — in its large-scale organization, its mobility and competitiveness, its impersonality, its sheer bigness. Gone is the old framework of custom and authority, of life in small groups and stable communities. The machine age has made man rich in material things, but in the face of today's vast problems and responsibilities he feels insecure, helpless, isolated, powerless, and lost. His individuality is an illusion.

Value conflicts exist in today's society. As cited in Chapter Seven, religion teaches the need for brotherly love while economic philosophy teaches the need for rivalry. Modern Western culture, with its stress on individual liberties and its comparative lack of religious faith, leaves people insecure, confused, and lacking in purpose. Under such conditions people seek succor from someone who can help them establish control over their environment and permit them to believe in something or somebody.

[9] Erich Fromm, *Escape from Freedom* (New York: Rinehart & Company, Inc., 1941).

A third cardinal principle of the counselor is his belief in the desirability of liberty, his conviction that freedom is good. "Liberty" and "freedom" are slippery abstractions, and the words are used here interchangeably to mean maximum opportunity to select one's own purposes in life and the means to accomplish them. The core of liberty is self-determination. Liberty means more than the absence of external restraint. It includes the power to act positively to achieve one's chosen goals. To the counselor, the freedom to make choices and to act upon them is essential to developing those characteristics that make one a human being. Denied this freedom, the individual becomes something less than human. Perhaps it is the ability to make rational choices, to distinguish the good from the bad, to decide whether to seek the good, that separates man from the other animals. In exercising his freedom he develops responsibility and self-restraint and can exploit his full capacity for growth.

Finally, most counselors are committed to the belief that the counselee possesses the ability to deal constructively with his problems. They feel that man makes his world and is capable of changing it, that his problems are soluble.

Arbuckle presented five philosophical issues in counseling.[10] The first dealt with the relationship between the counselor's self-concept, objectives, and methods. The counselor's self-concept and attitudes toward the client are reflected in what he does in the counseling session. If he believes that the client must be directed because he (the client) lacks the capacity for growth, or conversely if he believes that the client can be trusted to take action or to move in directions that are socially acceptable, his belief will be transmitted in his techniques and in turn be present in his own self-concept.

Arbuckle's second issue considers whether the counselor's religious orientation acts as a controlling agent in his relationship with the counselee. There might be, he thought, differences in attitudes but not in actions toward counselees. Hopefully, there would not be differences in attitudes because counseling goals should not be affected by religious orientation.

Arbuckle's third issue involved the counselor's concept of man. The person who is optimistic about man and his possibilities transmits these beliefs in his contacts with counselees, just as the one who regards man's nature as hostile and carnal reflects that view in his operations.

Arbuckle's fourth issue dealt with confidentiality. The counselor has to decide when his silence about confidential information is too great a price for society to pay. Arbuckle noted that few school counselors erred on the side of maintaining too much confidence.

The final issue discussed by Arbuckle was whether counselor education could in fact prepare a counselor to use certain techniques and methods. Essentially the issue is what kind of experience is needed in counselor education for the individual to become accepting of deviant behavior, sensitive to attitudes and procedures, aware of self and what one is attempting as a person and counselor.

Arbuckle's 1967 volume presents the systems of several counselors and psychotherapists and strongly stresses the philosophic orientation of each contributor.[11] The initial chapter in this valuable work sketches Arbuckle's own analysis of the philosophical bases of counseling, and his final chapter gives an overview of the fundamental philosophical issues presented by the other contributors.

Values Should a counselor convey his values to a counselee? Some counselors are of the opinion that they should have no value orientation and maintain a neutral role while counseling. They strive to appear nonmoralizing and ethically neutral in counseling. For them it is the client's values that determine counseling's direction, focus, and purposes. Patterson has written that

[10] Dugald S. Arbuckle, "Five Philosophical Issues in Counseling," *Journal of Counseling Psychology*, Vol. 5 (Fall, 1958), pp. 211–215.

[11] Dugald S. Arbuckle (ed.), *Counseling and Psychotherapy: An Overview* (New York: McGraw-Hill Book Co., Inc., 1967).

The counselor would not feel that the counseling relationship is the place to teach moral or ethical standards, or a philosophy of life. He is confident, as apparently some are not, that the client in the therapeutic relationship will be aware of and influenced by social realities. He will leave to the family, the church and school, as institutions representing the moral and ethical standards of society, the teaching of such standards.[12]

Williamson has repeatedly called for abandonment of this position in favor of an open and explicit value orientation in counseling.[13] He believes that to try to be neutral in regard to social standards leads to the danger of appearing to accept the client's unethical behavior and actually condoning if not approving it. Counselors cannot be indifferent to social and moral standards, he feels, and should not attempt to appear to be so.

It seems clear to me that we cannot and indeed should not attempt to eliminate some consideration of values from the counseling situation. It is also clear, so it seems to me, that the standards and attitudes of society and those prevailing in the counselor's educational institution, as well as those of the counselor himself, will be reflected in the counselor's behavior throughout each interview.[14]

It is Samler's opinion that change in values constitutes a counseling goal and that the counselor's values must be held in awareness. He proposes that counselor intervention in the client's values is an actuality to be accepted as a necessary part of the process and urges counselors to develop testable hypotheses relative to the values to be supported in counselor-client interactions.[15]

Patterson points out that the counselor's values influence the ethics of the counseling relationship, the goals of counseling, and the methods employed in counseling. Noting the growing opinion that it is impossible for the counselor to avoid influencing the client, Patterson cites evidence for the assertion that, no matter how passive and valueless the counselor appears, the counselee's value orientation is unconsciously influenced and comes to approach the counselor's. However, counselors are not justified, Patterson believes, in consciously and directly manipulating or influencing clients because (1) each individual's philosophy of life is different, unique, and unsuited to adoption by another; (2) all counselors cannot be expected to have a fully developed, adequate philosophy of life; (3) the appropriate places for instruction in values are the home, school, and church; (4) an individual develops a code of ethics, not from a single source or in a short period of time, but over a long time and from many influences; (5) no one ought to be prevented from developing his own unique philosophy since it will be more meaningful to him; and (6) the client must have the right to refuse to accept any ethic or philosophy of life.[16]

Dreyfus asks a penetrating question: "Does it really matter what the therapist *does* so long as he establishes a relationship with his patient?"[17] He points out that if in the therapy hour the patient learns to incorporate certain aspects of the therapist's intact ego, the patient becomes like the therapist with regard to values, mannerisms, and behavior. The counselor cannot play-act the way he feels.

Play-acting, then, gives the patient but a facade to emulate and serves to reinforce the inauthentic behavior of the patient, supplanting the patient's playing-acting-in-the-world with the therapist's. That is, the patient learns to become inauthentic . . . through the therapist who is being inauthentic. If the therapist responds in a genuine fashion to the patient, freely revealing and giving of himself, the patient then can learn to respond to the world in his own unique manner, and hence is poten-

[12] C. H. Patterson, *Counseling and Psychotherapy: Theory and Practice* (New York: Harper & Brothers, 1959), p. 74.
[13] E. G. Williamson, "Value Orientation in Counseling," *Personnel and Guidance Journal,* Vol. 36 (April, 1958), pp. 520–528.
[14] *Ibid.*, p. 525.
[15] Joseph Samler, "Change in Values: A Goal in Counseling," *Journal of Counseling Psychology,* Vol. 7 (Spring, 1960), pp. 32–39.

[16] C. H. Patterson, "The Place of Values in Counseling and Psychotherapy," *Journal of Counseling Psychology,* Vol. 5 (Fall, 1958), pp. 216–223.
[17] Edward A. Dreyfus, "Humanness: A Therapeutic Variable," *Personnel and Guidance Journal,* Vol. 45 (February, 1967), pp. 573–578.

tially capable of becoming even more human than the therapist.[18]

Dreyfus believes that humanness is the most important variable in the counseling process. In response to the question as to what it means to be human he states,

> . . . we must add that it is not only the ability to be warm, kind, supportive, etc., but also to be angry, sad, guilty. Being human does not mean loving everyone all the time, but rather recognizing that one cannot love everyone all the time and cannot be loved all the time by everyone. Being human is the capacity, willingness, and ability for self-disclosure . . . , with the acceptance and expression of all the feelings within the human emotional spectrum.[19]

There is no longer any doubt that the counselor will *expose* his values to the counselee. Since he is an individual who is present in an intimate relationship with another, his values (either consciously or unconsciously) will be brought into play. There should be no pretense that he does not possess a value system or that he is something other than he is. The real issue is whether or to what degree the counselor *imposes* his values upon the counselee. Some would argue that the counselee, by agreeing to counselor intervention, has given his consent to be influenced in any ethical way that will enable him to establish meaning in his life. Some years ago Wrenn formulated some principles of human relationships which have direct application in any consideration of values. Some pertain to the relationship between counselor and counselee and perhaps place in perspective the responsibilities one human being has for another.

1. I shall strive to see the positive in the other person and praise it at least as often as I notice that which is to be corrected.
2. If I am to correct or criticize someone's action I must be sure that this is seen by the other as a criticism of a specific behavior and not as a criticism of himself as a person.
3. I shall assume that each person can see some reasonableness in his behavior, that there is meaning in it for him if not for me.
4. When I contribute to another person's self-respect I increase his positive feelings toward me and his respect for me.
5. To at least one person, perhaps many, I am a person of significance, and he is affected vitally by my recognition of him and my good will toward him as a person.[20]

[18] *Ibid.*, p. 575.
[19] *Ibid.*, p. 576.

ACCEPTANCE

Within the language of counseling "acceptance" and "understanding" have become somewhat platitudinous. But like all platitudes they are relevant, particularly as they apply to the counseling process. Some authors classify acceptance and understanding as techniques, others as attitudes. Whether they are techniques or attitudes and whether they can be developed in training or originate in the individual's experiences in responding to people, the important point is that they are essential to any facilitating relationship.

Definition of Acceptance Acceptance of another derives from the basic attitudes held toward mankind in general and toward an individual specifically. Acceptance requires respect for the individual as a person of worth. Rogers defines acceptance in this way:

> By acceptance I mean a warm regard for him as a person of unconditional self-worth — of value no matter what his condition, his behavior or his feelings. It means a respect and liking for him as a separate person, a willingness for him to possess his own feelings in his own way. It means an acceptance of and a regard for his attitudes of the moment, no matter how negative or positive, no matter how much they may contradict other attitudes he has held in the past.[21]

[20] C. Gilbert Wrenn, "Psychology, Religion and Values for the Counselor," *Personnel and Guidance Journal*, Vol. 36 (January, 1958), pp. 331–334.
[21] Carl R. Rogers, *On Becoming a Person* (Boston: Houghton Mifflin Company, 1961), p. 34. Copyright © 1954 the Trustees of Oberlin College.

Characteristics of Acceptance Tyler identifies two components of acceptance. The first is a "willingness to allow individuals to differ from one another in all sorts of ways" and the second is "a realization that the ongoing experience of each person is a complex pattern of striving, thinking, and feeling."[22] Acceptance is a direct outgrowth of the counselor's ability to be nonjudgmental. He does not have normative or judgmental standards against which counselees are matched, balanced, and found wanting as persons. He assigns no condition to be met before he will extend his help. He does not attach "if" clauses – if you study, if you behave, if you apologize, then I will consider you a worth-while person.

Acceptance is a nurturing, lifting attitude manifested in the counselor's verbal and nonverbal behavior. It wells from the depths of his value orientation. It is a prizing of the individual that reflects a desire to help but not to control.

Robinson has noted that accepting attitudes vary and are manifested in many ways in the counseling relationship. He identifies and discusses variations in acceptance ranging from rejecting to accepting behaviors. He notes that rejecting behavior can be unintentionally demonstrated through inappropriate use of assurance and adherence to the counselor's frame of reference rather than the client's. Robinson also notes that different degrees of acceptance may exist in response to certain content presented by the client.[23] The counselor's acceptance of the client is not only indicated by his words, but also by his gestures and posture. For example, the client who perceives his counselor as relaxed and attentive rather than agitated and bored builds such a perception on cues that are both verbal and nonverbal.

The counselee experiences acceptance as a feeling of being unconditionally understood, liked, and respected. Acceptance – a positive tolerant attitude on the part of the counselor – is part of the condition that enables the counselee to change.

Finally, to be accepting of the counselee, the counselor must accept and understand himself. What he sees himself to be as a person may or may not be what he really is as a counselor. A critical factor is the client's awareness that he is accepted by the counselor. Virtually all counselors recognize its need and strive to provide this quality in the relationship. Admittedly, there are times when they fall short of the ideal communication of acceptance or are unable to transmit it as adequately to the client as they would like.

UNDERSTANDING

Everyone wants to be understood. It is through understanding that help can be given. The counselor must understand the counselee if the relationship is to be fruitful.

Understanding Defined Understanding is the ability to perceive another's relationships, meanings, content, and structure. Tyler defines understanding as "simply to grasp clearly and completely the meaning the client is trying to convey."

> Probably no human being ever fully understands another, and certainly the good counselor never feels that his client's whole personality is like an open book. Furthermore, it is neither necessary nor desirable that the counselor understand the individual better than he understands himself. In the productive interview, communication of thoughts and feelings is at a maximum; thus understanding is a sharing process. Whether the topic under discussion is the meaning of a set of objective-test scores, the facts underlying an occupational choice, or a puzzling aspect of the counselee's relationship to his wife, what the person says gives the counselor a sense of the meaning of this bit of experience, a meaning which he then attempts to put into words which will clarify it for both of them.[24]

Characteristics of Understanding The counselee's verbal behavior is only part of what the counselor seeks to understand. Equally important, if not

[22] Leona E. Tyler, *The Work of the Counselor*, 3rd ed. (New York: Appleton-Century-Crofts, Inc., 1969), p. 34.
[23] Francis P. Robinson, "The Dynamics of Communication in Counseling," *Journal of Counseling Psychology*, Vol. 2 (Fall, 1955), p. 166.

[24] Tyler, *op. cit.*, p. 36.

more so, is his ability to understand the meanings behind the words, however much disguised or hidden. The understanding counselor "feels with" or "experiences" meanings from the counselee's vantage point. Among the elements of such experiencing identified by Gendlin are the following five: (1) experiencing is felt, rather than thought, known, or verbalized; (2) experiencing occurs in the immediate present; (3) experiencing can be directly referred to by the individual; (4) experiencing guides conceptualization; and (5) experiencing is implicitly meaningful.[25]

Understanding is not a magical process. It comes through being free to attend carefully to the client. The importance of understanding as a dimension in the counseling process has been pointed up by Fiedler's description of the ideal relationship, based upon studies of therapeutic sessions:

1. The therapist is able to participate completely in the patient's communications.
2. The therapist's comments are always right in line with what the patient is trying to convey.
3. The therapist is well able to understand the patient's feelings.
4. The therapist really tries to understand the patient's feelings.
5. The therapist always follows the patient's line of thought.[26]

Levels of Understanding Understanding occurs at several levels. Davis, in a penetrating analysis, identified four levels. The first kind of understanding is knowledge *about* another individual — his behavior, his personality, his interests, etc. — but it is accompanied by evaluations or judgments. A second kind of understanding is composed of two parts, a verbal or intellectual understanding and a behavioral or operational one. Davis points out that while we are able to learn an operation intellectually we may still be unable to perform it. The third level of understanding is derived directly from the individual himself and is an attempt to step into his perceptual world, to know his internal world, his fears, loves, and anxieties. This kind of understanding is more intense, personal, and meaningful than the others. The fourth level is self-understanding, and to attain this requires much exploration within and usually in the company of another.[27]

Internal Conditions Which Influence Counseling

Four conditions — rapport, empathy, genuineness, and attentiveness — can either further or inhibit the counseling process. These components are based upon and intimately related to acceptance and understanding.

RAPPORT

Rapport is described most simply as a condition essential to a comfortable and unconditional relationship between counselor and counselee. It is established and maintained through the counselor's genuine interest in and acceptance of the client. It cannot be forced or contrived. It is a bond characterized by interest, responsiveness, and a sensitive emotional involvement.

All too often rapport is referred to as the outcome of techniques counselors use in the initial interview which put the counselee at ease and help him to express his feelings. True, some individuals have difficulty in discussing their purpose in seeing a counselor and need help in stating why they are there. But rapport means more than opening the interview smoothly and effectively. It is a quality, a mutual understanding, a respect, and a sustained interest that should be communicated from the first through the last contact.

Rapport is generated by the smoothness (lack of awkwardness, bumbling) with which the counselor

[25] Eugene T. Gendlin, "Experiencing: A Variable in the Process of Therapeutic Change," *American Journal of Psychotherapy*, Vol. 15 (April, 1961), pp. 233–245.
[26] F. E. Fiedler, "The Concept of the Ideal Therapeutic Relationship," *Journal of Consulting Psychology*, Vol. 14 (August, 1950), pp. 239–245.

[27] Donald A. Davis, "Understanding Is *Not* Enough!" APGA address, April 10, 1963, mimeographed.

opens and interacts within the relationship. Recognizing that the counselee may experience some reluctance in the beginning, the counselor usually opens the conversation by focusing upon some neutral topic or event known to both. However, artful judgment based upon cues received from the client is required since trite conversational leads may result in an increase in strained feelings.

Published suggestions for establishing rapport are abundant. Most of them emphasize the necessity of being friendly, being attentive, and demonstrating interest to reduce counselee resistance. But the beginning counselor should not make the mistake of implying that the weather, sports, or activities are what the counselee wants to discuss with him. Counseling is not a social call, and the opening conversation should be brief. Focus should be upon the reason for the counselee's being there. The counselor might say, "How may I help you?" or "Would you like to tell me what brings you here?" or "What would you like to talk about?" or "I've asked you to come in because . . . " A natural, straightforward and tactful approach which helps the counselee verbalize why he is there and enables him to begin is best used. It leads to communication and encourages commonality of interest. Versatility, flexibility, and relatability are all essential factors in establishing rapport.

But it is to be underscored that rapport is more than a pleasant greeting and putting the counselee at ease. Unfortunately, rapport is an intangible entity characterized by pleasantness, confidence, cooperation, sincerity, and interest — all qualities difficult to measure, impossible to turn on in a mechanical way, and difficult to initiate by recipe or by a bag of tricks. Patterson believes that rapport-building techniques are "neither necessary nor desirable." Techniques designed to foster rapport are usually "the result of insecurity on the part of the counselor rather than the need of the client."[28]

Basically, rapport means that an appropriate working relationship has been established and maintained between counselee and counselor. As it develops, this relationship is experienced by the counselee as being one of trust, acceptance, and understanding such as he may never before have encountered with any human being. It is rapport or the working relationship that will enable the counselee to examine himself and his concerns, rid himself of his fears and conflicts, and achieve a better understanding of himself and his connections with others. The length of time required to establish a good working relationship will depend upon the counselor's skill and upon client motivation. While no counselor is capable of establishing rapport with all individuals, he should, with adequate training and personal inclination, be able to relate to most of those who come to him for help. His competence in interviewing will foster confidence. By conveying an attentive and accepting manner through facial expressions and gestures and by asking pertinent questions, restating, summarizing, and using other techniques he demonstrates that he is interested, understanding, and observant. No doubt the reputation of the counselor partially influences the establishment and maintenance of rapport. Consequently, he should be consistent in his work with counselees in order to build a reputation of honesty, kindliness, and trust in keeping of confidences. But most of all he nurtures rapport by being sensitive to the client's needs, moods, and conflicts.

EMPATHY

Typically, empathy has been described as putting oneself in the other person's shoes. All meaningful experiences are instances of empathy. Empathy (German: *Einfühling*) means "feeling into" and plays a significant part in counseling communication. Most definitions indicate that empathy is the apprehension of the emotions of another person without feeling completely (as in sympathy) what he feels. If the counselor enters the client's internal frame of reference, perceives the client's world and how the client perceives himself, he is said to be empathic with the client. He is capable of taking the role of the client.

[28] C. H. Patterson, *Counseling and Guidance in Schools* (New York: Harper & Row, Publishers, 1962), p. 120

Evidences of empathy may be observed every day: e.g., the mother who, while nursing her baby, makes similar mouth motions; the golfer who leans one way as the ball approaches the hole; the racing crowd which swoops with the car as it moves around a curve; the football player who unthinkingly comes off the bench to make a defensive tackle. All these examples illustrate *imitative* phenomena since the observer introjects or takes on from the person acting that which he perceives and in some way identifies with and imitates it.

Dymond calls empathy "the imaginative transposing of oneself into the thinking, feeling and acting of another and so structuring the world as he does,"[29] or "the ability to feel and describe the thoughts and feelings of others."[30] Her definitions reflect that empathy is an interrelationship between two people and is dependent upon mutual agreement on the experience being shared. Empathy may be said to exist when a counselor recognizes the feeling a client presents as being the client's and not his own, and is able to communicate back to the client the same feeling so the client can recognize its similarity to the one he expressed. Rogers states that empathy is one of the necessary conditions in counseling:

> To sense the client's private world as if it were your own, but without ever losing the "as if" quality – this is empathy, and this seems essential to therapy. To sense the client's anger, fear, or confusion as if it were your own, yet without your own anger, fear, or confusion getting bound upon it, is the condition we are trying to describe.[31]

The emphasis in Rogers' remarks is upon transposition, but not imitation. One does not do exactly what the other person does, yet one makes him aware that one understands his thoughts, feelings, and actions. This is done imaginatively with one's affect and intelligence.

Other terms for empathy are "synchronicity" (H. S. Sullivan) and "recipathy" (H. S. Murray). Both convey the idea of mutuality. Buchheimer uses the word "confluence," rather than "empathy," because it reflects the quality of counselor-counselee interactions.[32] Buchheimer identified five dimensions of empathy: (1) *tone*, an expressive and nonverbal dimension reflected when two people interact in expressive harmony and unity; (2) *pace*, or appropriate timing of counselor leads; (3) *flexibility*, or the counselor's ability to discard previously thought-out tactics or goals if they do not fit the counselee's situation; (4) perception of the counselee's *frame of reference*, or the ability to abstract the core of the counselee's concern and to formulate it objectively and palatably so that he can elaborate; and (5) *repertoire of leads*, or the resourcefulness with which the counselor varies his leading in appropriate ways to apply to both manifest and dynamic content of the counselee's expression.

Empathy as a counseling variable has been the subject of considerable research. Lesser, using 11 counselors and 22 clients undergoing personal counseling at Michigan State University, reported that empathy as he assessed it was unrelated to counseling progress and he questioned the generally accepted notion of its value.[33] Nevertheless, he did find that counselor *awareness of similarity* with client was positively related to counseling progress.

O'Hern and Arbuckle use the term "sensitivity," but their definition of it embodies many of the characteristics found in definitions of empathy.[34] They developed an instrument to assess the degree

[29] Rosalind F. Dymond, "A Scale for the Measurement of Empathic Ability," *Journal of Consulting Psychology*, Vol. 13 (April, 1949), p. 127.

[30] Rosalind F. Dymond, "A Preliminary Investigation of the Relation of Insight and Empathy," *Journal of Consulting Psychology*, Vol. 12 (July–August, 1948), p. 232.

[31] Rogers, *op. cit.*, p. 284.

[32] Arnold Buchheimer, "Empathy in Counseling," APGA address, March 28, 1961, mimeographed.

[33] William Lesser, "The Relationship Between Counseling Progress and Empathic Understanding," *Journal of Counseling Psychology*, Vol. 8 (Winter, 1961), pp. 330–336.

[34] Jane S. O'Hern and Dugald S. Arbuckle, "Sensitivity: A Measurable Concept?" *Personnel and Guidance Journal*, Vol. 42 (February, 1964), pp. 572–576.

of sensitivity possessed by potential counselors. The instrument (tape-recorded counselor remarks) was administered to 212 counselors in training. Counselors judged most sensitive tended to be younger and employed for fewer years in their present position. Sex, religion, occupation, personal security, and intelligence did not differentiate between the most and the least sensitive groups.

Campbell and his associates conclude that empathy is a trait that is measurable, that individuals have this trait in varying degrees, and that empathy is subject to change by training.[35] Haase and Tepper reported that nonverbal behaviors were significant in the counselor's communication of and the client's perception of empathy. Their research indicated that nonverbal behaviors had twice the effect on perception of empathy as verbal messages of empathy.[36] Payne and his colleagues demonstrated that empathy could be taught by "modeling" procedures and by supervisors who used such didactic approaches as giving examples of responses that were empathic.[37]

To extend an empathic relationship the counselor must be able, during the interview, to free himself of his own problems so they do not interfere with his becoming congruent with the counselee. The counselor has to be able to "see" with the counselee's eyes and "hear" with his ears if his responses are to approximate the counselee's. His responses are inferences as to the counselee's thoughts and feelings, and his communication of this understanding is done in such a way that the counselee can reasonably accept it and know that he is being understood.

[35] Robert J. Campbell, Norman Kagan, and David R. Krathwohl, "The Development and Validation of a Scale to Measure Affective Sensitivity (Empathy)," *Journal of Counseling Psychology*, Vol. 18 (September, 1971), pp. 407–412.
[36] Richard F. Haase and Donald T. Tepper, Jr., "Nonverbal Components of Empathic Communication," *Journal of Counseling Psychology*, Vol. 19 (September, 1972), pp. 417–424.
[37] Paul A. Payne, Stephen D. Weiss, and Richard A. Kapp, "Didactic, Experimental, and Modeling Factors in the Learning of Empathy," *Journal of Counseling Psychology*, Vol. 19 (September, 1972), pp. 425–429.

COUNSELOR CONGRUENCE OR GENUINENESS

Experience and research demonstrate the importance of the counselor's congruence or genuineness in the counseling relationship. Rogers' description of this condition is that ". . . it means that he [the counselor] is *being* himself, not denying himself."[38] Defining congruence more fully, he states

> By this we mean that the feelings the counselor is experiencing are available to him, available to his awareness, that he is able to live these feelings, be them in the relationship, and able to communicate them if appropriate.[39]

Congruence implies honesty and candor with oneself while functioning as a counselor. The counselor does not pretend to be something he is not; he does not play a role, he is genuinely himself. Roleplaying differs from congruence in its emphasis on the attempt to be that which one is not. Indeed, "playing" a role implies acting or attempting to create a facade or an illusion that is damaging to the counseling relationship. Congruence demands authenticity and transparency of the counselor.

Patterson[40] has discussed some distortions of the genuineness concept that are relevant here. He makes two major points. First, genuineness does not mean that "anything goes," since some expressions of counselor feelings may be damaging to and nonfacilitative for the client. A notable example of these are expressions of hostility toward the client. Second, genuineness does not mean total self-disclosure by the counselor. It does mean that those aspects of himself that the counselor reveals must be honest. The counseling relationship requires sincere, spontaneous verbal interactions if it

[38] Carl R. Rogers, "The Interpersonal Relationship: The Core of Guidance," in Carl R. Rogers and Barry Stevens, *Person to Person* (Lafayette, California: Real People Press, 1967), p. 90.
[39] *Ibid.*
[40] C. H. Patterson, "A Current View of Client-Centered or Relationship Therapy," *The Counseling Psychologist*, Vol. 1 (Summer, 1969), p. 17.

is to avoid the pitfall of roleplaying by the counselor. The burden and opportunity for self-disclosure lie with the client, for the reverse raises the question of who is counseling whom.

ATTENTIVENESS

Fundamental to all counselor skills is attentiveness. As used here the term implies maximum involvement by the counselor in the client's communications. Attentiveness requires skill in listening and observing, through which the counselor comes to know and understand the core of content and feeling presented by the counselee. The information thus "collected" can then be utilized in the helping relationship, as the client realizes that he is *received* within the relationship.

Hackney, Ivey, and Oetting use the term "attending behaviors" to describe attentiveness:

> Attending implies that the counselor is emitting both verbal and nonverbal behaviors which communicate that he hears the messages emitted by the client. It implies further that the counselor is not dividing his attention between the client's messages and extraneous variables which remain unidentified to the client. Indeed, nonattending lapses by the counselor are likely to be revealed by behaviors such as frequent breaks in eye contact, intonation and vocal pitch, or characteristically, topic-jumping verbal behavior. Such inconsistencies reflect a decrease or absence of attending to the client.[41]

For many counselors, particularly those who have been teachers, listening is hard to learn since they have been accustomed to being listened to. By consciously making an effort to attend closely to what the counselee is expressing (verbally and nonverbally), the counselor is able to participate in the counselee's communication. Through this means he understands not only *what* the counselee says but *how* he says it and *why*. Moustakas has this to say about listening:

> Listening is a magnetic and strange thing, a creative force. . . . The friends that listen to us are the ones we move toward, and we want to sit in their radius as though it did us good, like ultraviolet rays. . . . When we are listened to, it creates us, makes us unfold and expand. Ideas actually begin to grow within us and come to life. . . . It makes people happy and free when they are listened to. . . . When we listen to people there is an alternating current, and this recharges us so that we never get tired of each other. We are constantly being recreated.
>
> Now there are brilliant people who cannot listen much. They have no in-going wires on their apparatus. They are entertaining but exhausting too. I think it is because these lecturers, these brilliant performers, by not giving us a chance to talk, do not let us express our thoughts and expand; and it is this expressing and expanding that makes the little creative fountain inside us begin to spring and ease up new thoughts and unexpected laughter and wisdom.
>
> I discovered all this about three years ago, and truly it made a revolutionary change in my life. Before that, when I went to a party I would think anxiously: "Now try hard. Be lively. Say bright things. Talk, don't let down." And when tired, I would have to drink a lot of coffee to keep this up. But now before going to a party, I just tell myself to listen with affection to anyone who talks to me, *to be in their shoes when they talk;* to try to know them without my mind pressing against theirs, or arguing, or changing the subject. Now my attitude is: "Tell me more. This person is showing me his soul. It is a little dry and meager and full of grinding talk now, but presently he will begin to think, not just automatically to talk. He will show his true self. Then he will be wonderfully alive. . . ."[42]

Listening is the means by which the counselor sustains, extends, and deepens his knowledge of the client. Listening in counseling is different from the partial listening one gives to a lecturing professor. In the latter instance we listen with but one ear while simultaneously thinking about something else, or we are engaged in pro and con reactions to what is being said. Superficial listening is most often observed in social interactions where the "lis-

[41] Harold L. Hackney, Allen E. Ivey, and Eugene R. Oetting, "Attending, Island and Hiatus Behavior: A Process Conception of Counselor and Client Interaction," *Journal of Counseling Psychology*, Vol. 17 (July, 1970), pp. 343–344.

[42] Clark E. Moustakas, *The Authentic Teacher* (Cambridge, Mass.: Howard A. Doyle Publishing Co., 1966), pp. 42–43.

tener" can hardly wait for the speaker to pause so that he can present his own dazzling comments.

The counselee wants the full attention of the counselor. The counselor's listening tells the client that the counselor is interested in and sensitive to the nuances of what the client seeks to convey. When the counselor is "tuned in," his inferences will be more accurate, his observations will be more acute, and his responses will contribute more to fostering a relationship. By listening he will facilitate learning as he seeks to understand the meaning an experience has for a counselee and to perceive the experience as the counselee does.

But listening is not enough. Face-to-face confrontation occurs in virtually all forms of counseling and unquestionably contributes to the quality of the relationship as well as enriching the data available to the counselor. Both participants watch as well as listen to each other. Those who have listened to sound recordings of counseling sessions can fully appreciate the fact that many subtleties of the process are lost when one is unable to observe the physical interaction between the participants.

An important element in the counselor's attentive behaviors is the accuracy and specificity of his responses to the client. Sometimes labeled "concreteness," the counseling interaction requires that the counselor's responses convey the specific feelings, experiences and behaviors emitted by the client rather than be generalities and abstractions of them. Carkhuff and Berenson indicate that this behavior accomplishes three ends. First, concreteness enables the counselor to remain close to the client's level of feelings and experiences. Second, it eliminates misunderstandings and permits the client to correct distortions of his expressions. Third, it fosters client attention to specific problem areas.[43]

Obviously many of the skills and attitudes of the counselor are transmitted to the counselee through his nonverbal behavior: facial expressions, posture, eye contact, etc. It is equally obvious that the counselor learns much of the feeling components through observations of the client. Frequently it is the counselor's recognition of the client's appearance and physical expression of a mood that lets the client know he is being attended to and understood at a level more meaningful than words alone can convey.

The counselor's nonverbal behavior is of extreme importance in establishing and maintaining a relationship. Many clients are quite able to describe counselor discomfort and, perhaps more important, perceive it as a cue to avoid certain content or perhaps even the counseling situation itself. Even the valued counselor behavior of maintaining eye contact can be carried to such an extreme that it seems to the client a hostile stare rather than friendly attentiveness. Much literature has been produced about nonverbal behavior, and this topic will be treated more extensively in the next chapter.

Counseling Relationship — The Common Denominator

All theories and approaches stress the relationship between participants as the common ground for the helping process. While viewpoints differ in the amount of emphasis and in how they treat this topic, all agree that the relationship is a necessary condition for bringing about change in the individual. The elements discussed earlier in this chapter — external conditions, attitudes, and skills — blend to foster it, and presumably these ingredients — provided or withheld, consciously or unconsciously used, or varied in quantity or quality — influence its nature.

The construct "counseling relationship" is elusive, more amenable to description than definition. Even descriptive terms vary markedly from theory to theory, each counseling practitioner knows what he means yet is often hard put to communicate verbally his personal and private meaning to others. If he attempts to approach its description

[43] Robert R. Carkhuff and Bernard G. Berenson, *Beyond Counseling and Therapy* (New York: Holt, Rinehart and Winston, 1967), p. 30.

through, for example, Freudian terminology such as "transference" and "counter-transference," he risks a negative reaction from those of a different persuasion.

The interpersonal relationship present in counseling is basically a reciprocal influence of the participants. Its characteristics were discussed in Chapter One. Chapter Four delineated the reasons for one participant's seeking help and the other's attempting to provide it. This chapter has sketched the elements which interact to produce a relationship.

It should be recognized that the counselor's attitudes and skills develop over a span of years and are a product of training and experience. Each counselor tries to provide some optimal set of conditions which facilitate the counseling relationship with most individuals. The particular mix of attitudes and skills will not always be helpful to all clients, but it is hoped that with additional experience a given counselor can work effectively and flexibly with a larger and larger variety of counselees.

Annotated References

Arbuckle, Dugald S. (ed.). *Counseling and Psychotherapy: An Overview.* New York: McGraw-Hill Book Co., Inc., 1967. 231 pp.

The editor has drawn upon various contributors to bring together their views of the helping relationship and the interaction of practice and its philosophical base. A distinguished group of contributors treat such topics as religion, existentialism, and personality theory.

Berenson, Bernard G. and Carkhuff, Robert R. (eds.). *Sources of Gain in Counseling and Psychotherapy.* New York: Holt, Rinehart and Winston, Inc., 1967. 449 pp.

The editors present several notable papers bearing on effective counseling relationships. Highlighted are the conditions that facilitate changes in clients' behaviors, regardless of the counselor's theory orientation or practice setting.

Kemp, C. G. *Intangibles in Counseling.* Boston: Houghton Mifflin Company, 1967. 208 pp.

Kemp discusses in Part Three (pp. 135–201) the "human" process. He explains motivation, behavioral changes, decision making, and counseling interactions.

Further References

Aspy, David N. "Empathy-Congruence-Caring Are Not Singular." *Personnel and Guidance Journal,* Vol. 48 (April, 1970). pp. 637–640.

Birk, Janice M. "Effects of Counseling Supervision Method and Preference on Empathic Understanding." *Journal of Counseling Psychology,* Vol. 19 (November, 1972). pp. 542–546.

Brown, Robert D. "Experienced and Inexperienced Counselors' First Impressions of Clients and Case Outcomes: Are First Impressions Lasting?" *Journal of Counseling Psychology,* Vol. 17 (November, 1970). pp. 550–558.

Campbell, Robert J., Kagan, Norman, and Krathwohl, David R. "The Development and Validation of a Scale to Measure Affective Sensitivity (Empathy)." *Journal of Counseling Psychology,* Vol. 18 (September, 1971). pp. 407–412.

Carkhuff, Robert R. and Griffin, Andrew H. "The Selection and Training of Human Relations Specialists." *Journal of Counseling Psychology,* Vol. 17 (September, 1970). pp. 443–450.

Danish, Steven J. and Kagan, N. "Measurement of Affective Sensitivity: Toward a Valid Measure of the Interpersonal Perception." *Journal of Counseling Psychology,* Vol. 18 (January, 1971). pp. 51–54.

English, R. William and Jelenevsky, Serge. "Counselor Behavior as Judged under Audio, Visual, and Audiovisual Communication Conditions." *Journal of Counseling Psychology,* Vol. 18 (November, 1971). pp. 509–513.

Haase, Richard F. and DiMattia, Dominic J. "Proxemic Behavior: Counselor, Administrator, and Client Preference for Seating Arrangement in Dyadic Interaction." *Journal of Counseling Psychology,* Vol. 17 (July, 1970). pp. 319–325.

Haase, Richard F. and Tepper, Donald T. Jr., "Nonverbal Components of Empathic Communication." *Journal of Counseling Psychology,* Vol. 19 (September, 1972). pp. 417–424.

Hackney, Harold L., Ivey, Allen E., and Oetting, Eugene R. "Attending, Island and Hiatus Behavior: A Process Conception of Counselor and Client Interaction." *Journal of Counseling Psychology*, Vol. 17 (July, 1970). pp. 342–346.

Howard, Kenneth I., Orlinsky, David E. and Hill, James A. "Content of Dialogue in Psychotherapy." *Journal of Counseling Psychology*, Vol. 16 (September, 1969). pp. 396–404.

Kaul, Theodore J. and Schmidt, Lyle D. "Dimensions of Interviewer Trustworthiness."*Journal of Counseling Psychology*, Vol. 18 (November, 1971). pp. 542–548.

Kelley, Jan, Smits, Stanley, J., Leventhal, Richard, and Rhodes, Roy. "Critique of the Designs of Process and Outcomes Research." *Journal of Counseling Psychology*, Vol. 17 (July, 1970). pp. 337–341.

Martin, Roger D. "Videotape Self-Confrontation in Human Relations Training." *Journal of Counseling Psychology*, Vol. 18 (July, 1971). pp. 341–347.

Miliken, Robert L. and Kirchner, Regis Jr., "Counselor's Understanding of Student's Communication as a Function of the Counselor's Perceptual Defense." *Journal of Counseling Psychology*, Vol. 18 (January, 1971). pp. 14–18.

Mullen, John and Abeles, Norman. "Relationship of Liking, Empathy, and Therapist's Experience to Outcome of Therapy." *Journal of Counseling Psychology*, Vol. 18 (January, 1971). pp. 39–43.

Payne, Paul A., Weiss, Stephen D. and Kapp, Richard A. "Didactic, Experiential and Modeling Factors in the Learning of Empathy." *Journal of Counseling Psychology*, Vol. 19 (September, 1972). pp. 425–429.

Schmidt, Lyle D. and Strong, Stanley R. "Attractiveness and Influence in Counseling." *Journal of Counseling Psychology*, Vol. 18 (July, 1971). pp. 349–351.

Troth, William A., Hall, Gwendolyn Lee, and Seals, James M. "Counselor-Counselee Interaction." *Journal of Counseling Psychology*, Vol. 18 (January, 1971). pp. 77–80.

Widgery, Robin and Stackpole, Cecil. "Desk Position, Interviewee Anxiety, and Interviewer Credibility: An Example of Cognitive-Balance in a Dyad." *Journal of Counseling Psychology*, Vol. 19 (May, 1972). pp. 173–177.

Yenawine, Gardner and Arbuckle, Dugald S. "Study of the Use of Videotape and Audiotape as Techniques in Counseling Psychology. *Journal of Counseling Psychology*, Vol. 18 (January, 1971). pp. 1–6.

Zimmer, Jules M. and Pepyne, Edward W. "A Descriptive and Comparative Study of Dimensions of Counselor Response." *Journal of Counseling Psychology*, Vol. 18 (September, 1971). pp. 441–447.

COUNSELING TECHNIQUES AND PRACTICES: I

12

This chapter identifies and describes the more concrete techniques and practices utilized by counselors. Some rather specialized techniques are used only occasionally, when the situation is appropriate. Some techniques are employed by some counselors and avoided by others because of personal inclination, differences of opinion as to their effectiveness, or incompatibility with their philosophy. Many practices are difficult to distinguish clearly from one another and undoubtedly represent differences in emphasis rather than in method.

In our judgment, a curious paradox exists in respect to the attention given to counseling techniques. Practitioners have been criticized for being "technique ridden" — a popular charge and one common to most professions. Those who make it believe that counselors should be more knowledgeable about the "why" of the relationship. Typically, they urge counselors to concentrate more upon attitudes of relating to individuals, the counseling process, or how the self of the counselor affects counseling. On the other hand, close examination of the counseling literature reveals that its theoreticians and practitioners have done little to specify the conditions under which techniques should or should not be used, have failed to organize techniques and practices into a meaningful system, and are unable to predict what behavioral results will be produced by certain techniques. Furthermore, those who have formulated theoretical approaches have been very imprecise about the specific procedures to be used to secure behavioral modification.

Counselors have been enjoined to think of counseling as a relationship not a "bundle of techniques or a bag of tricks,"[1] urged to avoid study of techniques since they tend to be employed without clear awareness by the counselor,[2] and told that intellectual procedures and training cannot help troubled persons.[3] Yet it is the counselor's responsi-

[1] C. H. Patterson, *Counseling and Guidance in Schools: A First Course* (New York: Harper & Brothers, 1948), p. 110.
[2] Katherine C. Cox, "Counseling: No Tricks and Only One Technique," *Clearing House*, Vol. 28 (September, 1953), p. 48.
[3] Carl R. Rogers, *On Becoming a Person* (Boston: Houghton Mifflin Company, 1961), p. 32.

bility to implement the relationship. He must do and say something, which surely constitutes technique and procedure.

It is what the therapist does, not what he thinks and feels, that directly affects the patient. . . . By accepting a patient for treatment, a therapist agrees that some outside intervention is essential, and thus implicitly accepts responsibility for performing some manipulations intended to achieve behavioral changes. If this is true, a clear specification of principles and procedures for change is essential so that verification of their effectiveness becomes possible.[4]

As one examines the wide assortment of techniques that follow, several observations should be born in mind:

1. Techniques are tied to counseling theory and philosophy. What a counselor does or says directly or indirectly reflects his theory and philosophy. However,

Many of our methods and technique courses . . . seem merely to confuse the issues, and many counselors arrive at the practicum level of their training program with some strongly held, if erroneous, views about the counseling process. They argue the differences between directive, nondirective, eclectic, and analytic counseling, for example, without realizing that many writers no longer emphasize these differences.[5]

2. Counseling techniques may be seen as a personal invention — personal in the sense that they work for a particular individual at a specific time given his attributes and training.

3. The variables dealt with in counseling are myriad, complex, and ever changing. The subject matter is the individual being — a person — possessing all the foibles of man.

4. Effective counselors adapt their repertoire of techniques to the particular problem and individual involved. Robert Wrenn reported that even though certain counselors ascribed to definite theoretical differences they chose their techniques because of individual differences and the situation at hand more than because of counseling orientation.[6]

5. Investigations seem to indicate that many counselors possess or use too few interviewing techniques. Hoffman reported that (a) they tended to use a limited repertoire of techniques, regardless of change in counselee or type of problem, (b) techniques were usually determined early in the contact, (c) some techniques were used more often than others, and (d) 5.9 was the average number of techniques used per interview.[7] Robinson explained that counselors were likely to use a limited repertoire of techniques because traditionally counselor neutrality has been seen as desirable and the emphasis has been placed upon verbal responses in preference to silence.[8]

6. Regardless of training, counselors are prone to develop a style of counseling and to adapt particular techniques to their way of responding, their experiences, current attitudes, and methods of speech. Above all, most counselors try to be themselves rather than play a role. They are conscious that their verbal delivery pattern determines, at least to some extent, the techniques they use. McGowan and Schmidt point out that if the counselor

. . . restricts his own flexibility and spontaneity by trying to force himself into a technique which does not fit him as an individual, the result is a rather sterile and flat counseling relationship. If the counselor really wants to help him the client will know it, and this is one of the basic feelings that must be communicated . . . then the counselor can use different responses and techniques, and even make certain tactical "errors" within the relationship without seriously impairing the process.[9]

7. Generally research demonstrates that (a) counselors employ rather consistent techniques

[4] Donald H. Ford and Hugh B. Urban, *Systems of Psychotherapy* (New York: John Wiley & Sons, Inc., 1963), pp. 667–668.

[5] John F. McGowan and Lyle D. Schmidt, *Counseling: Readings in Theory and Practice* (New York: Holt, Rinehart & Winston, Inc., 1962), pp. 320–321.

[6] Robert L. Wrenn, "Counselor Orientation: Theoretical or Situational?" *Journal of Counseling Psychology,* Vol. 7 (Spring, 1960), pp. 44–45.

[7] A. E. Hoffman, "Analysis of Counselor Sub-roles," *Journal of Counseling Psychology,* Vol. 6 (Spring, 1959), pp. 63–65.

[8] Francis P. Robinson, "Cubist Approach to the Art of Counseling," *Personnel and Guidance Journal,* Vol. 41 (April, 1963), p. 675.

[9] McGowan and Schmidt, *op. cit.,* p. 321.

with each counselee and (b) expertness and experience produce variability of approach.

8. The description of counseling techniques that follows is general and admittedly fragmentary in nature. As Ford and Urban point out, "The lack of clear specification of therapy techniques probably stems from the absence in many systems of a theory of behavior change or a theory of learning."[10]

Structuring the Counseling Relationship

Structuring was defined in Chapter 1 as the way the counselor defines the nature, limits, roles, and goals within the counseling relationship. It is an orientation to what counseling is about and what takes place. Its fundamental purpose is to reduce the counselee's anxiety originating from concern about the ambiguity and newness of the counseling situation. Controversy exists as to whether the counselor needs to define the relationship explicitly. Some argue that the relationship is more beneficial if the structure remains implicit and emerges naturally from the situation rather than being provided by the counselor. They believe that an implicit structure permits the client more flexibility in expressions of thought and feeling. Others urge counselors to outline the counseling process verbally during early contacts with clients. Loughary cites two purposes for doing so: (1) to let the counselee know what to expect from the counselor and (2) to give the counselee some idea of what is involved in counseling methods and purposes. Loughary expressly defends the use of structuring with high school students by stating that "the high school counselor, because of his short-term contacts with students who are unfamiliar with the counseling relationship, gains by structuring."[11]

Buchheimer and Balogh point out that the word "structure" has been absorbed in the counseling vocabulary as a transient verb but is also used and understood as a noun. Used as a noun, it "originates in and is guided by the particular self-system of the counselee – the way he constructs reality and the perceptions he has of himself." The counselee is the pacesetter, and the counselor gears the interview to him. What takes place in the relationship is a function of the self-reference clues provided by the counselee and perceived by the counselor as a result of his own self-system. The counselor's responsibility is to provide a climate so that the client's self-system may be perceived and understood. The counselor aids in this unfolding and participates in the building and rebuilding of organizations of personal constructs. Buchheimer and Balogh also point out that structuring (verb) by the counselor is necessary when counselees (1) do not have a clear image of what takes place in counseling, (2) have erroneous ideas of what is expected of them, or (3) are reticent about entering the process or fearful of its consequences. The counselor's explanations should be in broad terms.[12] The values of providing the counselee will not feel his task is formless or purposeless.

1. Common misconceptions about counseling such as "psychoanalyze me and tell me what's wrong," magical cures, advice giving, unreasonable expectations, and the like can be alleviated.
2. Anxiety can be reduced since the individual will not feel his task is formless or purposeless.

Brammer and Shostrom identify four types of structure which are paraphrased here[13]:

1. *Time limits.* Explaining how much time is available for each interview or estimating the time required for the counseling process as a whole provides some structure for the counselee.

[10] Ford and Urban, *op. cit.*, p. 668.

[11] John W. Loughary, *Counseling in Secondary Schools* (New York: Harper & Brothers, 1961), pp. 57–58.

[12] Arnold Buchheimer and Sara Carter Balogh, *The Counseling Relationship* (Chicago: Science Research Associates, Inc., 1961), pp. 4–5.

[13] Lawrence M. Brammer and Everett L. Shostrom, *Therapeutic Psychology*, 2nd ed. (Englewood Cliffs, N.J.: Prentice-Hall, Inc., 1968), pp. 207–209. Copyright © 1968. Passages on pp. 278–279 by permission of Prentice-Hall, Inc.

2. *Action limits.* While the counselor does not limit verbal expression in any way, most counselors would not permit the counselee to break windows or destroy furniture or equipment. An explanation of such limits provides structure.

3. *Role limits.* Counselors who also serve in another capacity such as teacher or administrator may find it necessary to clarify for the individual the capacity in which he is being interviewed. This clarification of authority provides structure.

4. *Procedural or process limits.* The counselee has to accept the responsibility for carrying on the major share of the interview. Certain values evolving from the process either are stated by the counselor or, because of his attitudes, come to be understood by the client. These include six suggested by Ingham and Love: (a) that it is appropriate and good to investigate ourselves, (b) that it is better to investigate than to blame, (c) that emotions are to be regarded as real and important realities, (d) that freedom of expression is complete, (e) that investigation of the past leads to an understanding of the present, and (f) that the client's present view of the world is a basis for change.[14]

Most people who come for counseling are uncertain how to begin. They will remark, "I don't know where to begin" or "I'll be glad to answer any questions you ask" or "I've never done this before and I don't really know what I'm supposed to do." At this point several options are available to the counselor. He can suggest content, explain the kind of service he offers, or respond to the feeling involved. He might respond in this fashion:

> You find it hard to know where to begin. Many find it helpful to start by telling why they wanted to see a counselor. You're free to talk about anything you like. Many discuss the things that concern or bother them. Whatever you say will be kept confidential, will be just between the two of us. Most people find that if they discuss those things that are of concern to them the counselor can help in clarifying their feelings and behavior so that they can understand themselves and others better or they can decide upon a direction or plan of action. You might begin by telling why you wanted to see me.

The definitional process is important. Conveying the essence of the relationship without engaging in a miniature lecture is most essential. When the situation calls for structuring, the counselor would do well to remember that there is no substitute for simplicity, modesty, and sensitivity in his definition.

Degree of Lead by Counselor

Previously it was mentioned that the discovery and development of a counseling style is related to the personal characteristics of the counselor. Growth as a counselor and self-development go hand in hand; change in one produces change in the other. Effective counseling requires understanding the counselee, understanding oneself, and understanding the process involved.

E. H. Porter[15] and Francis P. Robinson,[16] among others, were early interested in identifying, sorting out, and clarifying counselor technique. Robinson used the term "lead" to mean a "teamlike working together in which the counselor's remarks seem to the client to state the next point he is ready to accept."[17] In this section, "lead" is used somewhat in this fashion to refer to communications made by the counselor. It should be recognized that "lead" can also refer to the extent to which the counselor is ahead of or behind the counselee's thinking and to how much the counselor "directs" or "pushes" the client into accepting the counselor's remarks.

More recently, Norman Kagan and his associates have utilized video taping to further refine and

[14] H. V. Ingham and R. Lemore Love, *The Process of Psychotherapy* (New York: McGraw-Hill Book Co., Inc., 1954), pp. 79–81.

[15] E. H. Porter, *Therapeutic Counseling* (Boston: Houghton Mifflin Company, 1950).

[16] Francis P. Robinson, *Principles and Procedure in Student Counseling* (New York: Harper & Brothers, 1950).

[17] *Ibid.*, p. 66.

study counselor-counselee communications.[18] The exchanges between counselor and counselee represent behavioral interaction with both immediate and latent effects. The interaction, present and past, stimulates the counselee's choice of content – kind, quality, and sequence. The way the counselor leads (his statements or responses as well as his actions and feelings) the counselee affects the direction of the interview. Each counselor lead has meaning for the counselee and triggers response patterns for him. The counselee's responses, in turn, have reciprocal impact upon the counselor.

Brammer and Shostrom cite three principles to guide the counselor's leads:

1. . . . lead *only as much as the client can tolerate* at his present level of ability and understanding.
2. . . . *vary the lead.*
3. . . . *start the counseling process with little lead.*[19]

Buchheimer and Balogh have classified counselor leads into categories of techniques. These leads, the techniques they reflect, what is communicated, and the role the counselor assumes in the communication are presented in Table 12.1.

Much can be learned of techniques and practices by close study of audio and video taping of counseling sessions. The following remarks serve only to introduce the student to gross analysis of techniques. It is hoped that he will be stimulated to try analyzing his own behaviors through role playing and tape critique methods. Such activities are highly valuable learning experiences since they enable the individual to make reasonable, informed judgments about the effects of his counseling behavior.

Below is a statement made by a counselee immediately after seating himself in the counselor's office. The counselor had not met the student before. Different leads or counselor responses are given and classified.

Miss Jones told me to come down here and talk to you – I don't know why! She said I couldn't come back to class until I learned to stay awake. . . . I work at a filling station until one every night and I'm tired. Anyway, who could stay awake in there – she bores you to death.

Among the responses the counselor could make are the following:

You were bored, fell asleep, and Miss Jones asked you to leave. *(Restatement of content)*
What does she do that you find boring? *(Questioning)*
You feel put upon. *(Reflection of feeling)*
I bet that something can be worked out in this situation. *(Reassurance)*
Do you think that you might be disowning responsibility for what happened? *(Interpretation)*

These and other techniques will be briefly described.

RESTATEMENT OF CONTENT

Counselor leads which restate the content of the counselee's communications attempt to convey understanding either by simple repetition of or by rephrasing the communication. Usually little or no attempt is made to organize, clarify, or interpret it, and such a technique departs the least from the client's statement.

QUESTIONING

Questioning is a common and often overused counseling technique. It indicates the counselor's intent to seek further information and asks the counselee to elaborate upon a point. Ideally, questions used by counselors are open-ended and require more than a "yes" or "no" response; otherwise they get nowhere and only stifle discussion. However, in fact-finding interviews, questions posed by the interviewer should be straightforward, clear, and precise.

[18] Norman Kagan, David R. Krathwohl, and William W. Farquhar, *Interpersonal Process Recall: Stimulated Recall by Videotape,* Educational Research Series, No. 24 (East Lansing: Bureau of Educational Research Series, College of Education, Michigan State University, March, 1965).
[19] Brammer and Shostrom, *op. cit.,* p. 217–218.

Table 12.1 Degree of leading and kinds of leading

DESCRIPTION OF LEADS	TYPES OF COMMUNICATION	COUNSELOR ROLE
Techniques designed to elicit feeling:		
Silence	Take your time; there's no rush.	Receiving
Restatement of manifest content or feeling	This is what you said . . . *or* You say you feel . . .	Accepting
Reflection of content	In other words, it's this way . . .	Understanding
Reflection of feeling	In other words, you feel . . .	Understanding
Reflection of core	In essence, you've said this . . .	Understanding
General leads	Tell me more about it.	Searching
Techniques designed to facilitate self-understanding:		
Summarization	So far, you've said this . . .	Understanding
Tentative analysis	You seem to mean . . .	Clarifying
Interpretation	What seems to be operating is . . .	Interpreting
Direct question	What do you mean? What have you done?	Investigating
General leads	Tell me more.	Searching, understanding
Reassurance	Things could be worse. You're not alone . . .	Explaining, supporting
Assurance	You can do this; the prognosis is good.	Predicting
Information giving	The facts are . . .	Explaining
Techniques designed to facilitate action:		
Encouragement	You will get along.	Predicting
Specific suggestion	You might do this . . .	Advising
Urging	You ought to do this . . .	Advising
Cajoling	Ah, come on . . .	Directing

FROM: *The Counseling Relationship: A Casebook* by Arnold Buchheimer and Sara Carter Balogh. Copyright © 1961 by Science Research Associates, Inc. Reprinted by permission of the publisher.

The overuse of questions in personal counseling runs the risk of causing the counselee to conceptualize the situation as an inquisition in which he need only sit back and direct his thinking along the lines indicated by the questions. As Boy and Pine say,

Questions are derived from the counselor's frame of reference and are often unrelated to the client's basic feelings. The counselor decides which question to ask and when to ask it. One question usually leads to another, for this type of counselor is not likely to acquire sufficient information in his first question to evaluate the client properly. Many counselor questions come off the top of the head and have no professional content. They are merely expressions of what the *counselor* feels is relevant at a particular time.[20]

[20] Angelo V. Boy and Gerald J. Pine, *Client-Centered Counseling in the Secondary School* (Boston: Houghton Mifflin Company, 1963), pp. 65–66.

Perhaps more to the point, the counselor who puts his questions accusingly or suspiciously arouses fear and suspicion, not cooperation. Manner and tone of voice may be more important than the wording of the questions. Unnecessary probing to satisfy an interest in the esoteric is always unjustified. The counselor's safeguard in the use of questions is his true interest in understanding and aiding the individual. He then conveys that interest in his manner and tone. Questioning is best used (1) to obtain specifically needed information and (2) to direct the client's conversation to more fruitful channels. In the latter instance it encourages the counselee to talk further in relevant areas where the going may be difficult, and leading questions that cannot be answered by a "yes" or "no" are preferred. They stimulate the individual to talk freely and avoid the danger of supplying ready-made answers.

REFLECTION OF FEELING

Rogers has defined reflection as an attempt "to understand from the client's point of view and to communicate that understanding."[21] Reflection of feeling, then, indicates the counselor's intent to show that he understands correctly what the client feels or is experiencing. Reflection techniques consist of verbalizing the core of the client's attitudes. Because it is nonthreatening when properly done, reflection of feeling enables the counselee to think of his feelings as part of himself rather than external to or apart from him. It may be used immediately after a feeling has been expressed, or a summary reflection may be used. In the latter instance, the counselor attempts to tie together in one statement several feelings expressed by the client.

Reflection techniques serve not only to surface client feelings and attitudes but also to bring problems into awareness without making the individual feel that he is being pushed by the counselor. The intent is to mirror the client's attitudes so that they can be clarified and understood. Brammer and Shostrom have given counselors a note of caution about client feelings as well as an explanation:

> A common misconception arising from an emphasis on feeling is that the expression and identification of feelings have in themselves some intrinsic merit. The conclusion often drawn is that feelings are more important than intellectualizations. Expression of feelings is encouraged by the reflection technique. Its effectiveness, however, seems to reside in the idea that the expression of feeling is a means to self-confrontation and not an end in counseling.
>
> Feelings are thought by the client to be subjective and not to be trusted. They tell him of danger when there is no danger, of presence of symptoms when he is tired and discouraged. The expression of feeling, therefore, is to make possible the discovery of the idea which underlies or is attached to the feelings. The client should be taught to *trust* the expression of his feelings.[22]

Most counselors find it hard to acquire and implement techniques which reflect feelings. Too often the reflection is simply the content or intellectual component of the counselee's expression rather than underlying attitudes or feelings. Perhaps skill in the use of reflection techniques comes from a combination of intuition and experience in paying attention to the feeling tone of what is being expressed. Our experience in supervising counselors in counseling practicum and internship activities indicates that they are more adept in responding to counselees who express negative feelings toward parents, teachers, or rivals than in helping to bring to conscious expression hostile feelings toward themselves or the counselor. In the latter situations, counselors are inclined to rise to the defense of the counselee because of sympathy or react defensively because their ability as a counselor is challenged.

Brammer and Shostrom cite seven errors or dif-

[21] Carl R. Rogers, *Client-Centered Therapy* (Boston: Houghton Mifflin Company, 1951), p. 452.

[22] Brammer and Shostrom, *op. cit.*, p. 195.

ficulties in the use of reflection techniques.[23] They are paraphrased here:

1. A common error is made in reflection when the counselor uses a stereotyped introductory phrase, such as "You feel . . ."

2. If many feelings are expressed, counselors sometimes err by waiting for the client to stop talking before they reflect rather than interrupting to focus on significant feelings that might be overlooked.

3. The counselor's choice of feelings to be reflected, selected from among a variety of feelings presented by the client, may be inaccurate or not properly worked through.

4. Reflecting content in the same words rather than getting below its surface is a common error.

5. Reflecting feelings either too shallowly or too deeply causes difficulty for the client.

6. Adding to or taking away from the meaning of the client's statement is another error.

7. Finally, error occurs when the counselor uses inappropriate terminology or language that is overinterpretative or pedantic.

Brammer and Shostrom have also identified and elaborated upon the reasons why reflective techniques are effective in achieving the goals of counseling. Here the reasons are given, and the reader is urged to examine the commentary on them.

1. Reflection helps the individual to feel *deeply understood.*
2. The reflection technique helps to break the so-called neurotic cycle, often manifested in marital counseling and expressed by such phrases as, "She won't understand me and therefore I won't understand her."
3. Reflection impresses clients with the inference that *feelings are causes of behavior.*
4. Reflection causes the *locus of evaluation* to be in the client.
5. Proper reflection gives . . . the feeling that [the client] . . . has the *power of choice.*
6. Reflection *clarifies the client's thinking* so that he can see the situation more objectively.
7. . . . it helps communicate to the client the idea that *the counselor does not regard him as unique and different.* [The counselor is not shocked.]
8. Reflection helps the client to *examine his deep motives.*[24]

The point has been made that reflective techniques depend upon an alert counselor, responsive to feelings and attitudes recognized in the client's verbal expression. Recognizing and verbalizing attitudes implied but not yet expressed by the counselee can either be constructive and speed the course of counseling or create a threat for the counselee and lead to harmful resistance and resentment. Finally, it is not enough for the counselor simply and correctly to identify and understand the counselee's feelings. He must convey his understanding to the counselee so that it is received by him. It is equally important for counselors to recognize that pretending to understand when they do not is dangerous because it leads eventually to confusion and distrust. While it is probably impossible for the counselor to understand completely the attitudes and feelings contained in the counselee's statements, if he is unsure or uncertain he can ask for clarification by saying, "I'm not quite sure what you mean, but as I understand it the essence of what you say is . . ."

REASSURANCE

Reassurance goes beyond acceptance and serves as a reward or reinforcing agent. It often is used to support counselee exploration of ideas and feelings or the testing out of different behaviors. It may be helpful in reducing anxiety generated within the counseling relationship or in controlling it outside the relationship. As an example of the latter instance the counselor might reassure the counselee who has expressed anxiety about responding in class: "Since you really know the material that is being discussed tomorrow, you can surely contribute to class discussions of the westward expansion."

[23] *Ibid.*, pp. 198–200.

[24] *Ibid.*, pp. 195–196.

Reassurance may be expressed directly by the counselor. For example, the counselee enters and says, "Late again," and the counselor responds, "That's all right." It should be noted that in this instance reassurance may have been used unwisely since the counselee may have a hard time going beyond the impasse created by the counselor's remark. Reassurance may be given through predicting outcomes such as the backwash effects of discussing problems with the counselor.

Some counselors take the categorical position that reassurance techniques should never be used and are inappropriate in counseling. Rogers and others believe that reassurance techniques simply show disrespect for the counselee. Rogers views the counselee's appeals for support as subtle tests of his respect for the counselor; as such they are best met with reflective responses.[25]

Thorne, on the other hand, believes that reassurance techniques, while admittedly palliative, are warranted.[26] He has described eight types of reassurance, paraphrased here:

1. The counselor may reassure the client that his disorder is very common.
2. Reassurance may be given that the disorder has a known cause and something can presumably be done about it.
3. Reassurance may be given that symptoms are annoying but not dangerous.
4. Reassurance may be given that specific methods of treatment are available.
5. Reassurance may be given that cure is possible.
6. The counselor may need to reassure the client that his condition will not lead to insanity.
7. Reassurance may be given that relapses are sometimes inevitable but do not mean that the client is getting worse.
8. The client may need reassurance that his disorder is not a result of sinful action.

[25] Rogers, *Client-Centered Therapy*, p. 209.
[26] Frederick C. Thorne, *Principles of Personality Counseling* (Brandon, Vt.: Journal of Clinical Counseling, 1950), pp. 201–202.

Reassurance techniques can be misused. An easy error is to offer false reassurance. Such remarks as "I know you'll get a scholarship," "Everything will be all right" are far from reassuring and usually cause the counselee to doubt the counselor's understanding of the situation and his ability to help. To tell the individual who is describing how bad things are for him that others have the same problem or that his problems are not unusual gives the impression that the counselor is unsympathetic or, worse, minimizes the counselee's problems. To dismiss as unimportant a counselee's complaints which represent responses to inner conflict may be viewed as the counselor's failure to grasp what is at stake. The outcome is frustration, lack of confidence in the counselor, and termination.

Finally, the counselor's use of reassurance must be attuned to the counselee's level of development and emotional maturity. The counselee may need to know that the counselor is committed to help him through the experiences that are encountered in counseling. Understandably, he may need reassurance and encouragement to discuss his feelings and attitudes rationally to come to grips with them.

INTERPRETATION

Interpretation in counseling involves two types of data: *external* or test results and *interpersonal* data obtained through counseling communication. Test interpretation will be discussed in the next chapter. Here the concern is with interpretation of counselee remarks.

Interpretative techniques are those which identify and conceptualize patterns of relationships and explain meanings behind client statements. For some, interpretation is the *sine qua non* of achieving counseling goals; through it the individual becomes cognizant of his underlying feelings and/or attitudes and achieves integration of feeling and action. The counselor who uses interpretation infers a relationship or a meaning from what has been said or done by the counselee. Causation is generally implied or indicated in interpretative techniques.

As the counselee reveals more and more of himself, the counselor's insight deepens so that he can suggest motives, purposes, relationships, or patterns of reactions which are evident from what has been stated. In making interpretations the counselor gambles that his inference is accurate and will be accepted by the counselee. If the interpretation is unacceptable to the counselee (goes beyond what he is willing to face at the time), anxiety may be created. The counselor can gauge his use of interpretation by how well he knows the counselee and by the counselee's reactions. If the counselee is permitted to accept, modify, or reject the interpretation, the technique may speed client insight and cause little difficulty. Bordin believes, however, that the client's acceptance or rejection of an interpretative remark is a fallacious criterion.

In some cases, the too ready acceptance of an interpretation may mean that the client has succeeded in momentarily achieving an objective view of himself by divorcing this view from the affect with which it is usually associated. Momentarily, he is being rational. However, he has not learned to utilize these resources of rationality on occasions when he experiences the affect. On the contrary, when he is in the affective state he will revert to anxiety and to the associated need to defend himself against impulse expression.[27]

Bordin suggests two principles for the counselor's use of interpretation. First, whether accepted or rejected, the interpretation will be ineffectual for counselees who are conflicted and who strive to keep affect from awareness and expression. Second, the amount of emphasis on the cognitive aspects of the counselor-counselee interactions should be related to the intensity of affect expressed by the client. Further, the more intense the affect, the more cognitive the interpretation can be without causing the client to revert to cognitive processes as a means of repression.[28]

While interpretative techniques are used by many counselors, those of the client-centered persuasion do not favor them because the locus of responsibility is on the counselor. The use of interpretation, moreover, represents an attempt to change individual attitudes by the intellectual means of explaining the causes of behavior. Rogers in his early book cited some admonitions about the use of interpretation that are still germane: (1) interpretation should be avoided if the counselor feels unsure of himself; (2) it is best to use the client's terms and symbols in interpretation; (3) interpretation best deals with attitudes already expressed; (4) nothing will be gained by arguing about the correctness of an interpretation; (5) if genuine insight has been gained, the client will see spontaneously its application in new areas; and (6) after the client has achieved a new insight, temporary relapse may occur.[29]

Some time ago Colby classified interpretations, by content and technique, into three types. *Clarifications* were statements designed to crystalize the client's thoughts and feelings around a particular subject or to focus his attention on something requiring further thought. *Comparisons* were interpretations in which the counselor placed two or more sets of events, thoughts, or feelings side by side for comparison — present and past behavior, childhood and adulthood, fantasy and reality, etc. Patterns of repetitive similarities and recurring contradictions may be compared. *Wish-defense* interpretations were those pointing directly to the wish-defense components of neurotic conflict.[30]

According to Kelly, the material of interpretation is the personal construct — an anticipatory concept or predictive idea — utilized by the individual in coping with his life experiences. In interpretation, then, life events are compared and contrasted with the individual's constructs. Kelly's five steps

[27] Edward S. Bordin, *Psychological Counseling* (New York: Appleton-Century-Crofts, Inc., 1955), p. 157.
[28] *Ibid.*, pp. 83–84.

[29] Carl R. Rogers, *Counseling and Psychotherapy* (Boston: Houghton Mifflin Company, 1942), pp. 205–206.
[30] K. M. Colby, *A Primer for Psychotherapists* (New York: The Ronald Press Company, 1951), pp. 83–84.

utilized in interpretation are paraphrased here:

1. A counselee makes a generalization about himself which he utilizes as a construct to predict his behavioral events. The counselor, in turn, uses seven basic questions to obtain comprehension of the construct or complaint: (a) What is the difficulty? (b) When was it first noticed? (c) Under what conditions was it first noticed? (d) What has been done about it? (e) What changes have come with treatment or the passing of time? (f) Under what conditions is it most noticeable?

2. The counselor relates the responses to these questions to ascertain the similarities and contrasts.

3. The counselor, in *construct elaboration*, focuses upon constructs which relate to the events in the counselee's life. These constructs are likely to be dichotomous black-and-white evaluations about life since behavior expresses affirmation and denial.

4. There is *interpretative extension*, or the application of ideas or constructs to new events.

5. Finally, *validation* occurs, or constructs are tested by using them as wagers on the future.

This is an overly simplified and no doubt inadequate presentation of Kelly's system of interpretation, which he has elaborated and illustrated in a two-volume work.[31]

Interpretation may be employed early in the counseling process in respect to the counselee attitudes toward counseling. Usually it is general and tentative and serves only to open up and explain the process. A client who is afraid to talk may be encouraged by a query like "You are not quite sure that I understand?" or by an interpretative question such as "You're afraid that I will blame you as your father always does?" The latter, of course, would be appropriate only if the counselee had previously been able to express fairly freely his feeling of rejection.

Timing is most important. Interpretations should not be blindly made; rather, caution should be exercised until the counselor is sure that the client is ready to accept them. A client can profit from counselor insight only if it also becomes *his* insight. He arrives at his conclusions at his own pace. To be told that he feels anxiety or is expressing rejection or fear will not help him until he himself can recognize the existence of these feelings and voluntarily acknowledge their presence. Thus interpretations are not to be proffered until the counselor understands the counselee — possesses knowledge of his anxiety and readiness to consider and work through threatening material.

Brammer and Shostrom have discussed six criteria for judging the adequacy of interpretation. Here only the criteria, in their words, are cited:

1. There should be sufficient evidence for the interpretation.
2. The depth of the interpretation should be appropriate.
3. Whenever possible, the manifest behavior of the interpreted tendency should be specified.
4. The intensity of the interpreted trend should be estimated.
5. The interpreted tendency should be given a hierarchic position in the total personality picture.
6. The adaptive and pathological aspects of the interpreted tendency should be distinguished.[32]

Interpretations are phrased *tentatively* by the counselor rather than asserted dogmatically. Questions are a common format: "Do you think, then, that you could become an engineer when your interest patterns tend to be markedly dissimilar?" Again, it is emphasized that reactions from the counselee will enable the counselor to gauge his use of interpretations. Techniques of interpretation may be employed throughout the course of the relationship starting with mild interpretations of the counselee's attitudes toward counseling, progressively being used during the middle phases of counseling (after counselor has attained good understanding of counselee), and diminishing and becoming more general toward the closing phases of the process.

[31] G. A. Kelly, *The Psychology of Personal Constructs* (New York: W. W. Norton & Co., 1955), Vols. I and II.

[32] Brammer and Shostrom, *op. cit.*, pp. 288–289.

Facilitating Techniques

ACCEPTANCE

Acceptance is an attitude crucial to the counseling process. Most counselors strive through certain mechanisms to communicate their acceptance of the counselee. Communicating acceptance involves the verbal and nonverbal counselor behaviors which tell the counselee he is being understood and received. Such behaviors stimulate further discussion and elaboration by the counselee, enabling him to continue talking about his perceptions without threat. Verbal responses by the counselor include "Mm-hm," "Yes," "I understand," "I see," and the like. Reflection of attitudes and feelings and restatement of the counselee's remarks are frequently used.

The degree to which the counselor's techniques will effectively communicate acceptance depends upon his tone of voice and his facial expressions and movements (nodding of head, etc.) as well as his posture and distance from the counselee (such as leaning toward the client and whether he sits relatively close to him). All of these elements and others provide cues which the counselee discerns and interprets. Techniques to communicate acceptance are used extensively in the beginning phase of counseling as well as later when the individual delves deeply and painfully into his situation.

CLARIFICATION

Clarifying techniques are related somewhat to those of reflection and interpretation. Clarification is a statement by the counselor which seeks to place the counselee's feeling or attitude in a clearer or more recognizable form for the benefit of both participants. Compared to reflection, clarification goes slightly beyond what the counselee expresses verbally in such a way that the meanings can be more plainly understood and used. But there is no direct effort at interpretation of counselee feelings or implicit references to the cause of the problem. An example of clarification applied to the counselee's statement presented on page 276 might be "You feel annoyed and angry in this situation."

GENERAL LEADS

General leads are used to encourage the individual to continue talking or to elaborate upon a point he is discussing. They include such remarks as "Tell me more," "Would you explain that further?" and the like.

ENCOURAGEMENT

Techniques which encourage or give support to the counselee are sometimes used. Related to reassurance, encouragement is designed to counter feelings of inadequacy or to prompt action. It may build upon the individual's ego strength. Examples of encouragement are "That's fine," "You can do that," "You are OK," "You will get along," and so on.

Dinkmeyer points out that encouragement, a critical ingredient in the counseling process, is present either explicitly or implicitly in most major counseling approaches. As Dinkmeyer uses the term, encouragement consists of procedures that enable a client to experience and become aware of his own worth. It does not mean that bribes or undue praise or reward are lavished on the client. Rather, encouragement means that the counselor provides positive, honest feedback to the client about his attitudes, assets, goals, directions, changed behaviors, risk taking, etc.[33]

INFORMATION GIVING

School counselors are often required to give information during the counseling process. Some would argue that counseling has stopped when information is provided by the counselor. But information giving need not involve persuasion or advice. It can mean, for example, clarification of high school courses needed for admission to a particular

[33] Don C. Dinkmeyer, "Use of the Encouragement Process in Adlerian Counseling," *Personnel and Guidance Journal,* Vol. 51 (November, 1972), pp. 177–181.

college, what is assessed by certain tests, and the like.

ADVICE GIVING

School counselors serve a wide student population. Because they are there, some students come to seek advice, to obtain suggestions, or to get help in formulating rather concrete plans of action. When they ask for advice they *may* expect it to be proffered. The counselor has the problem of deciding how far direction of this type is to be carried. If, in his judgment, the individual is free enough of conflict to be able to accept advice, and the counselor has some to offer, it may be worthwhile to give it. In many instances, however, advice is futile because the client is unable either to accept or to act upon it unless it happens to confirm his own opinion.

It is also to be noted that students frequently ask advice when they don't need it. The array of advice givers — parents, teachers, neighbors, friends — available to them is great indeed. What they often seek through the socially accepted guise of asking advice is help in freeing themselves from confusion and uncertainty. They are looking for additional insight into their problem and help in utilizing their personal resources to come to a decision. Perhaps it is equally true that any rigid refusal to make suggestions may be interpreted by the counselee as unwillingness to help or be interested in him.

Without doubt, some counselees will ask, "What do you think I should do?" In most instances the counter response "What do you think?" will reveal several resourceful ideas and plans.

SILENCE

Silence is difficult to master as a technique for most counselors who have been teachers. They often believe that client silence is synonymous with counselor failure and become uncomfortable when it occurs. Because silence in social situations tends to be looked upon as rejection, defiance, or disapproval, this meaning from a different context is quite often transferred to the counseling relationship. When pauses occur, the counselor may be overcome with the desire to break the silence rather than tolerate it.

Overextended or greatly prolonged silence by the counselor sometimes appears to be almost sadistic if he refuses to speak merely because he demands the initiation of all expressions from the counselee. The client who becomes embarrassed and appears physically uncomfortable may need and appreciate assistance from the counselor to begin again. Neutral leads or expressions recognizing the client's discomfort can be very useful at such times by stimulating additional interchanges or promoting discussion of the client's embarrassment.

Pauses vary from a few seconds to several minutes. The significance of any counseling pause is dependent upon when it takes place and by whom it was initiated. Here are some of the times that silence occurs as well as possible reasons why and by whom it may be broken:

1. During initial contacts the client may become afraid of the impression he has given the counselor or what he thinks the counselor thinks of him and become silent. Appropriate rapport-building techniques may be used by the counselor in this case.
2. A pause may come because the counselee is thinking over what he has just expressed. Interruption by the counselor at this point is inadvisable.
3. Silence may come because either counselor or counselee or both have reached the end of an idea or line of thought and do not know what to say next. Often, but not always, the counselor breaks such a silence.
4. An extended contemplative pause may occur just after initial remarks and during the time in which the two individuals are settling down to the business at hand. The counselor may interrupt by saying, "It's rather hard to get under way today."
5. A pause may mean that the counselee is experiencing painful emotions which he is unable to express, yet desperately yearns to share with the counselor. Recognizing this, the counselor could appropriately say, "Feelings are sometimes difficult

to put into words, but perhaps expressing them is more important than the exact words."

6. Silence may come because the counselee is cautious about the process or has a preconceived notion that his responsibility is merely to reply to questions posed by the counselor. It may mean that the counselee is shy and that he conceptualizes silence as rejection of him. Such silence may best be interrupted by the counselor to structure or define the process or with "You don't feel much like talking," "What has brought this silence about?" "What are you thinking of?"

7. A pause sometimes occurs because the counselee wants some assurance, support, or confirmation from the counselor.

8. Finally, silence may fall just after heavily emotionally laden expression by the counselee. The counselor's quiet acceptance of this pause is, of course, appropriate.

There is no one criterion for gauging whether the counselor should remain silent or interrupt the pause. Operationally, most counselors tend to remain silent when the pause was initiated by the counselee, but sensitivity to silence and judgment about interruption come with experience. Tindall and Robinson classified *counselor* pauses into three types. The first was *deliberate* or one used for emphasis. The second was *organizational,* used to effect transitions. The third was natural *termination,* used to close counseling. They reported that organizational pauses usually helped to clarify the subject discussed and paved the way for information to be given to the counselee. Counselees, however, generally responded only after deliberate or natural terminal pauses.[34]

As a technique, silence may be productively employed to place responsibility upon the counselee to face and talk about his problems. It may also be used to slow the pace of the interview if counselee or counselor is moving too fast or pushing too hard. Following a flood of emotional expression, silence often enables the individual to gain insight or achieve integration of feeling. In this respect its value is that it leads to penetration of feelings and understanding of actions. Finally, silence may give the less articulate person a feeling of worth and help him to accept himself for what he is.

The amount of talk is occasionally used as a measure of counseling effectiveness. It is sometimes postulated that the greater the proportion of verbal exchanges engaged in by the counselee, the better the working relationship. Carnes and Robinson analyzed 353 communication units from four types of counseling interviews and concluded that "a high talk ratio is not necessary to a good relationship but it is good insurance." They reported that it was not the amount of client talk which was related to client insight; i.e., keeping silent or just getting the client to talk will not necessarily lead to insight. More important was client talk within a particular style employed by the counselor. When clients feel responsible for the interview they tend to talk more.[35]

Behavioral Modification Techniques

Techniques based on behavioral modification principles have forged to the front in the recent literature, convention presentations, and the discussions of counseling practitioners. Krumboltz and Thoresen[36] point out that behavioral counselors employ a variety of techniques; each is used for specific reasons. They urge counselors to experiment continuously and to evaluate systematically their techniques, procedures, and practices. In this way, counselors can determine what works best under what conditions with given clients.

It may be remembered (see Chapter Eight) that goal setting (a mutual undertaking by counselor

[34] R. H. Tindall and Francis P. Robinson, "The Use of Silence as a Technique in Counseling," *Journal of Clinical Psychology,* Vol. 3 (April, 1947), pp. 136–141.

[35] Earl F. Carnes and Francis P. Robinson, "The Role of Client Talk in the Counseling Interview," *Educational and Psychological Measurement,* Vol. 8 (Winter, 1948), pp. 635–644.

[36] John D. Krumboltz and Carl Thoresen (eds.), *Behavioral Counseling: Cases and Techniques* (New York: Holt, Rinehart and Winston, 1969), p. 3.

and counselee) is highly stressed by behavioral counselors. Establishing the goals of counseling depends on identifying target behaviors to be changed. This, in turn, leads to selection of techniques appropriate to changing these behaviors. Another important element in behavioral counseling is the monitoring of changes that occur as a function of the technique or techniques employed. Finally, the outcome of the monitoring procedure is either a modification of counseling techniques or the reevaluation of the goals.

The following brief description of behavioral counseling techniques draws heavily upon those identified and discussed more fully by Krumboltz and Thoresen.

REINFORCEMENT TECHNIQUES

The practices employed by behavioral counselors are based on the principle that behavior is a function of its consequences. Basically, these techniques seek to strengthen certain counselee behaviors by positive or negative reinforcement schedules. The stimuli used by counselors to reinforce behavior are many and varied but verbal expressions predominate. Additionally, tokens or trinkets or some type of a currency system are often used as reinforcers. Tokens (money, chips, tickets, etc.) are presented to subjects as they perform the desired behavior and can be exchanged for whatever reinforcers (candy, privileges, films, trips) they choose or are able to afford.

Krumboltz and Thoresen point out that *timing* is a key element in programming reinforcement consequences for desirable behaviors and in eliminating punishing or the reinforcement for undesirable behaviors. "The reinforcer must be presented immediately following the desired behavior and it must not be presented immediately following undesirable behavior."[37] Another essential factor is the *nature* of the reinforcer. Daley[38] describes a way to gain control over managing contingencies by developing a "menu" of activities based upon the Premack[39] Principle (for any pair of responses, the preferred one will reinforce the less preferred one). The menu consists of behaviors which the subject likes (eat, jump, telephone, color, etc.) Before engaging in the task to be learned, the subject is presented with the menu and allowed to select an event from it which for him at that moment is a highly preferred event. When he has completed the task to be learned, he is allowed to engage in the selected behavior.

Shaping Consequences are arranged to develop desirable behavior, such as getting to class on time. The counselor may first reinforce responses that have little resemblance to the desired behavior pattern, but then arranges consequences for responses that are progressively more like the desired behavior. Finally, only the desired behavior is reinforced until it attains suitable strength. An example of shaping techniques is the case presented by Wanda K. Castle[40] in the book by Krumboltz and Thoresen.

Fading Consequences are arranged to change the counselee's discriminations of the conditions that control his behavior. The counselee develops appropriate discriminations because those stimulus conditions in which the behavior is already highly probable are reinforced. Gradually, the desired behaviors are introduced in these stimulus conditions and come under the counselee's control. An example of fading techniques is the case described by David A. Shier[41] in Krumboltz and Thoresen.

Roleplaying and Reinforcement Roleplaying techniques are sometimes used to enable a client to practice behaviors he wants to learn. The client rehearses his new behavior, such as to speak out in

[37] *Ibid.*, p. 29.
[38] Marvin F. Daley, "The 'Reinforcement Menu': Finding Effective Reinforcer," in Krumboltz and Thoresen, *ibid.*, pp. 42–45.
[39] D. Premack, "Reinforcement Theory" in David Levine (ed.), *Nebraska Symposium on Motivation* (Lincoln, Nebraska: University of Nebraska Press, 1965), pp. 128–188.
[40] See Krumboltz and Thoresen, pp. 33–36.
[41] *Ibid*, pp. 114–123.

a classroom situation, with the counselor, who reinforces or encourages the client's attempts and suggests ways the client can improve his performances.

Behavior Contracts Counselors sometimes formulate and draft a contract or written agreement which specifies what the client and counselor or another person will do for a given period of time. The contract, in effect, makes explicit the type of behavior to be performed and its rewards and/or punishments.

SOCIAL MODELING TECHNIQUES

Techniques designed to establish new behaviors in clients with behavioral deficits are often based on imitation and observation, or social modeling. While much remains unknown about social modeling procedures (which clients does it help, with what problems, with which modes of presentation, etc.), Krumboltz and Thoresen state that the social models selected should be prestigious, competent, knowledgeable, attractive, and powerful. Moreover, clients may be more influenced when the social model is similar to them in some characteristics.[42]

Live models Live modeling techniques (often referred to as "in vivo" training) have not been extensively used in any systematic manner by counseling practitioners. Little doubt exists that counselors themselves, as well as parents and teachers, serve as models to children and adolescents. Live models have been used to illustrate certain behaviors, particularly those involving complex interpersonal situations such as interviewing for a job, engaging in a social conversation, interacting with a parent or an adult. The best live models are probably one's peers. The major limitations in using live models are (1) controlling the model's behavior so as to demonstrate the desired behavior, and (2) having them physically available precisely when needed.

[42] *Ibid*, p. 164.

Filmed models Because of the disadvantages of using live models, the behavior to be imitated has often been reproduced on films. Filmed models (examples include how to participate in class discussions, engaging in career exploration) provide the observer-learner with many important auditory and visual cues needed in learning the desired behavior. The advantages of filmed models are that they can be used again and again and have flexibility and utility.

Audiotape recorded models Clients can learn new behaviors by listening to others describe how they behave in certain situations, such as selecting a college, exploring occupations, and the like.

Self-modeling Though this technique is probably the least developed or clearly described, it holds much promise for counselors. In self-modeling, the client himself enacts the behavior that he wishes to perpetuate. It is recorded either on audio or videotape for playback. The client is then presented with a desirable form of his own behavior which can serve as a model. An example of this has been described by Ray Hosford[43] who worked with a young boy who stuttered. After audiotaping each interview, Hosford edited out all stuttering, leaving a stutter-free record of the interview. This was played back to the client and after 10 sessions, the client's stuttering within the interview had decreased to a small fraction of its original frequency.

COUNTER-CONDITIONING TECHNIQUES

Clients who cope with anxiety, fears, phobias, defense mechanisms, and other maladaptive behaviors have been helped by counter-conditioning techniques. Such techniques introduce responses which counteract, are incompatible with, or are antagonistic to fears or anxiety. The counter-conditioner, because it is stronger, suppresses and replaces the old response.

[43] Personal communication with authors, March, 1972.

Systematic desensitization In this technique, the counselor suggests situations which are potentially anxiety-producing to a relaxed client. The client is able to imagine the situations without becoming anxious. A more complete description of this technique is found in Chapter Eight, pages 197–198.

Relaxation Methods to relax clients are usually based upon Jacobson's progressive relaxation training.[44] The client is instructed by the counselor to relax by successively tensing and releasing gross muscle groups throughout the body. Other relaxation techniques include hypnoses and respiratory inhalations (client is shown how to empty his lungs and then inhales a gas mixture consisting of 70 per cent carbon dioxide and 30 per cent oxygen).

COGNITIVE TECHNIQUES

Cognition, according to Krumboltz and Thoresen, refers to the process of knowing, and cognitive techniques in counseling are those designed to help the client know himself and his environment so that he acts more appropriately in future problem situations.

Simulation These techniques are used to give clients the opportunity to practice behaviors under conditions which approach reality. Krumboltz has produced simulated materials designed to give high school students practice in solving simple but realistic problems similar to those solved by members of some 20 different occupations.

Gaming This technique places the client in a role. The *Life Career Game,* originally developed by Sarane Boocock of Johns Hopkins University, and adapted by Barbara Varenhorst as a counseling tool, is an example of a gaming technique. In such roles, the actors make plans, decide on risks, and interact to achieve objectives.

[44] E. Jacobson, *Progressive Relaxation* (Chicago: University of Chicago Press, 1938).

Confrontation Krumboltz and Thoresen describe confrontation counseling methods as those designed to give clients a point of view different from their own so that clients can see themselves and their behavior as others view them. They believe that confrontation is best used when counselees do not know their behavior is inappropriate or are unaware of its consequences. These authors point out that rude, unmannerly confrontations, especially when the client or clients have not been prepared for it, may degenerate into insults that arouse hostility, defensiveness, and resistance to change.[45]

Paradoxical intention While this technique has been reported by Frankl,[46] the existentialist, it shares many characteristics with counter-conditioning and cognitive techniques. The technique is based on the belief that anxiety or fear makes that which one fears come true, and that hyper-intention makes that which one wishes impossible. Therefore, the client is urged to "intend" precisely that which he fears.

Assertive training Assertive training includes one or more methods such as roleplaying, rehearsals, and social modeling designed to encourage the client to engage in behaviors that approximate those he desires but fears.

Analyzing Counselor Communications

Below are two excerpts of counselee-counselor interactions presented to help the learner develop insight into how attitudes influence counselor responses.[47] In each case the counselee's state-

[45] *Ibid,* Krumboltz and Thoresen, pp. 397–398.
[46] Viktor E. Frankl, *Man's Search for Meaning: An Introduction to Logotherapy* (Boston: Beacon Press, 1962), pp. 125–131.
[47] This material was abstracted from the tapes employed by Jane S. O'Hern and Dugald S. Arbuckle in their research entitled "Sensitivity: A Measurable Concept?" *Personnel and Guidance Journal,* Vol. 42 (February, 1964), pp. 572–576. Used with the authors' permission with adaptations by Robert Finley of the University of Utah.

ments are followed by the counselor's response with but little information given about the nature of the counselee. In brief, you are presented with two isolated client expressions followed in each situation by five counselor responses. You are asked to evaluate each counselor response and to select the explanation from each group of four that you believe best describes the counselor's response as it relates to what the counselee has expressed or implied. It should be remembered that rightness and wrongness of counseling techniques are concepts strictly relative to the counselor's values, training, and experience. Consequently, there is no one correct answer. You are to read the counselee statement, then each counselor's response. From the four alternatives to each counselor response select the one that you think describes the usefulness of the response.[48]

Situation 1 — This excerpt is the opening remark made by a counselee immediately after seating himself in the counselor's office. The counselor has not met the student before.

"Miss Jones told me to come down here and talk to you — I don't know why! She said I couldn't come back to class until I learned to stay awake. . . . I work at a filling station until one every night and I'm tired. Anyway, who could stay awake in there — she bores you to death."

Counselor responses:

1. "Do you have to work so much at the filling station?"
   A. A useful statement to help the counselee continue talking.
   B. Asks for information that is irrelevant at this time.
   C. Implies understanding of the counselee's problem.
   D. None of the above.
2. "What does she do that you find boring?"
   A. Asks for relevant information that the counselor needs to gain understanding.
   B. Ignores the implicit meaning in the counselee's communication.
   C. Will help the counselee focus his thought on an important aspect of the situation.
   D. Implies interest in the counselee.
3. "Going to sleep in class can get you into trouble, can't it?"
   A. Is a pertinent statement because it implies that you understand the counselee's problem.
   B. Suggests that the counselor doesn't understand the problem.
   C. Is a restatement of an obvious fact.
   D. None of the above.
4. "Teachers get angry when we don't behave the way they think we should, don't they?"
   A. Indicates that the counselor understands what the problem is.
   B. Is an irrelevant statement.
   C. Will be useful to help the counselee continue talking.
   D. None of the above.
5. "Is this the first time she has called you down for sleeping?"
   A. Ignores the implicit meaning of the counselee's statement.
   B. Asks for inappropriate information.
   C. Both A and B.
   D. None of the above.

Situation 2 — Taken from the first interview with a counselee who is on the brink of failing college:

"You know it makes me so mad, every time . . . I don't know what is wrong with this university — it seems like they are out to get me. I just keep going down in grade point and everything else — and it's not my fault. I don't know why they have these stupid required courses. It just doesn't make sense. Why do I have to take them when I am in agriculture?"

Counselor responses:

1. "If you put your mind to it and work and study, you could get something out of these courses which you might find useful to you later."
   A. Is a reality of life which the counselee must learn.
   B. Useful because it helps the counselee learn from the counselor's experience.
   C. Shows that the counselor understands what has to be done.
   D. None of the above.
2. "You feel that since you are in agriculture you don't need to know anything about literature and history?"

[48] The following were the responses most frequently selected by a group of 200 counselors in training: Situation 1 — 1B, 2B, 3C, 4C, 5C; Situation 2 — 1D, 2B, 3C, 4B, 5A.

A. Focuses on the counselee's feelings.
B. Focuses on the counselee's beliefs.
C. Asks for needed information.
D. None of the above.

3. "What are your aims in life?"
   A. Implies the counselor understands what the counselee's problem is.
   B. Asks for information that is relevant at this time.
   C. Ignores the implicit meaning in the counselee's communication.
   D. None of the above.
4. "What makes you think the university is out to get you?"
   A. Is a pertinent question if the counselor is to understand the situation.
   B. Misses a more pertinent element for exploration.
   C. Suggests the counselor is interested in the counselee's point of view.
   D. None of the above.
5. "It sounds to me like you're blaming others for your own inadequacies."
   A. Is a bad statement because it implies an insight beyond the counselee's awareness.
   B. Is a bad statement because it focuses on an irrelevant element of the counselee's communication.
   C. Is a bad statement because it makes an incorrect interpretation.
   D. Is a good statement because it states a truth the counselee should recognize and accept.

A Counselor Response Scale

Kagan and his associates have developed a counselor verbal response scale to describe the counselor's communications on four dichotomized dimensions: affect-cognitive, understanding-nonunderstanding, specific-nonspecific, exploratory-nonexploratory. A fifth dimension, effective-noneffective, provides a global rating of the adequacy of each counselor response and is made independently of the four descriptive ratings. By the replaying of video tape interview sessions, each verbal interaction between counselor and counselee represented by a counselee statement and counselor response may be judged on each of the five dimensions of the rating scale. The primary focus in judging the response is upon describing how the counselor responded to verbal and nonverbal elements of the client's communication. Figure 12.1 presents the IPR Counselor Response Rating Scale developed by Kagan and his associates.

DESCRIPTION OF RATING DIMENSIONS[49]

The description of each of the five dimensions is given by Kagan and his associates as follows:

I. Affective-cognitive dimension
The affective-cognitive dimension indicates whether a counselor's response refers to any affective component of a client's communication or concerns itself primarily with the cognitive component of that communication.
A. *Affective responses* — Affective responses generally make reference to emotions, feelings, fears, etc. The judge's rating is solely by the content and/or intent of the counselor's response, regardless of whether it be reflection, clarification, interpretation. These responses attempt to maintain the focus on the affective component of a client's communication. Thus they may:

(a) Refer directly to an explicit or implicit reference to affect (either verbal or nonverbal) on the part of the client.
    Example: "It sounds like you were really angry at him."
(b) Encourage an expression of affect on the part of the client.
    Example: "How does it make you feel when your parents argue?"
(c) Approve of an expression of affect on the part of the client.
    Example: "It doesn't hurt to let your feelings out once in a while, does it?"
(d) Present a model for the use of affect by the client.
    Example: "If somebody treated me like that I'd really be mad."

Special care must be taken in rating responses which use the word "feel." For example, in the statement "Do

[49] Norman Kagan, D. Krathwohl, and G. Griffin, *IPR — Interpersonal Process Recall: Stimulated Recall by Video-Tape in Exploratory Studies of Counseling and Teaching-Learning* (East Lansing: Michigan State University, 1966). Used by permission.

you *feel* that your student teaching experience is helping you get the idea of teaching?", the phrase "Do you feel that" really means "Do you think that." Similarly the expression "How are you feeling?" is often used in a matter-of-fact, conversational manner. Thus, although the verb "to feel" is used in both these examples, these statements do *not* represent responses which would be judged "affective."

B. *Cognitive responses* — Cognitive responses deal primarily with the cognitive element of a client's communication. Frequently such responses seek information of a factual nature. They generally maintain the interaction on the cognitive level. Such responses may:

(a) Refer directly to the cognitive component of the client's statement.
Example: "So then you're thinking about switching your major to chemistry?"

(b) Seek further information of a factual nature from the client.

Figure 12.1 IPR counselor verbal response rating scale

Judge: ________ Subject: ________ Date: ________

	DIMENSIONS							
Responses	Affective	Cognitive	Understanding	Non-understanding	Specific	Nonspecific	Exploratory	Non-Exploratory
1		√	√		√		√	
2								
3								
4								
5								
6								
7								
8								
9								
10								
11								
12								
13								
14								
15								
16								
17								
18								
19								
20								
21								
22								
23								
24								
25								
% of Responses								
TOTAL								

Counselor response evaluation			
Effective		Noneffective	
4	3	2	1
		√	

TOTAL ________

Example: "What were your grades last term?"

(c) Encourage the client to continue to respond at the cognitive level.
Example: "How did you get interested in art?"

II. Understanding-nonunderstanding dimension
The understanding-nonunderstanding dimension indicates whether a counselor's response communicates to the client that the counselor *understands* or is *seeking to understand* the client's basic communication, thereby encouraging the client to continue to gain insight into the nature of his concerns.
A. *Understanding responses* — Understanding responses communicate to the client that the counselor understands the client's communication — the counselor makes appropriate reference to what the client is expressing or trying to express both verbally and nonverbally — or the counselor is clearly seeking enough information of either a cognitive or affective nature to gain such understanding. Such responses:

(a) Directly communicate an understanding of the client's communication.
Example: "In other words, you really want to be treated like a man."

(b) Seek further information from the client in such a way as to facilitate both the counselor's and the client's understanding of the basic problems.
Example: "What does being a man mean to you?"

(c) Reinforce or give approval of client communications which exhibit understanding.
Example: CL: "I guess then when people criticize me, I'm afraid they'll leave me."
CO: "I see you're beginning to make some connection between your behavior and your feelings."

B. *Nonunderstanding responses* — Nonunderstanding responses are those in which the counselor fails to understand the client's basic communication or makes no attempt to obtain *appropriate* information from the client. In essence, nonunderstanding implies misunderstanding. Such responses:

(a) Communicate misunderstanding of the client's basic concern.
Example: CL: "When he said that, I just turned red and clenched my fists."
CO: "Some people don't say nice things."

(b) Seek information which may be irrelevant to the client's communication.
Example: CL: "I seem to have a hard time getting along with my brothers."
CO: "Do all your brothers live at home with you?"

(c) Squelch client understanding or move the focus to another, irrelevant area.
Example: CL: "I guess I'm really afraid that other people will laugh at me."
CO: "We're the butt of other people's jokes sometimes."
Example: CL: "Sometimes I really hate my aunt."
CO: "Will things be better when you go to college?"

III. Specific-nonspecific dimension
The specific-nonspecific dimension indicates whether the counselor's response delineates the client's problems and is central to the client's communication or whether the response does not specify the client's concern. In essence, it describes whether the counselor deals with the client's communication in a general, vague, or peripheral manner, or "zeros in" on the core of the client's communication. NB: A response judged to be nonunderstanding must also be nonspecific since it would, by definition, misunderstand the client's communication and not help the client to delineate his concerns. Responses judged understanding might be either specific (core) or nonspecific (peripheral), i.e., they would be peripheral if the counselor conveys only a vague idea that a problem exists or "flirts" with the idea rather than helping the client delineate some of the dimensions of his concerns.
A. *Specific responses* — Specific responses focus on the core concerns being presented either explicitly or implicitly, verbally or nonverbally, by the client. Such responses:

(a) Delineate more closely the client's basic concerns.
Example: "This vague feeling you have when you get in tense situations — is it anger or fear?"

(b) Encourage the client to discriminate among stimuli affecting him.
Example: "Do you feel ——— in all your classes or only in some classrooms?"

(c) Reward the client for being specific.
Example: CL: "I guess I feel this way most often with someone who reminds me of my father."

CO: "So as you put what others say in perspective, the whole world doesn't seem so bad, it's only when someone you value, like Father, doesn't pay any attention that you feel hurt."

B. *Nonspecific responses* — Nonspecific responses indicate that the counselor is not focusing on the basic concerns of the client or is not yet able to help the client differentiate among various stimuli. Such responses either miss the problem area completely (such responses are also nonunderstanding) or occur when the counselor is seeking to understand the client's communication and has been presented with only vague bits of information about the client's concerns. Thus such responses:

(a) Fail to delineate the client's concern and cannot bring them into sharper focus.
Example: "It seems your problem isn't very clear — can you tell me more about it?"
(b) Completely miss the basic concerns being presented by the client even though the counselor may ask for specific details.
Example: CL: "I've gotten all A's this year and I still feel lousy."
CO: "What were your grades before then?"
(c) Discourage the client from bringing his concerns into sharper focus.
Example: "You and your sister argue all the time. What do other people think of your sister?"

IV. Exploratory-nonexploratory dimension
The exploratory-nonexploratory dimension indicates whether a counselor's response permits or encourages the client to explore his cognitive or affective concerns, or whether the response limits a client's exploration of these concerns.
A. *Exploratory responses* — Exploratory responses encourage and permit the client latitude and involvement in his response. They may focus on relevant aspects of the client's affective or cognitive concerns but clearly attempt to encourage further exploration by the client. Such responses are often open-ended and/or are delivered in a manner permitting the client freedom and flexibility in response. These responses:

(a) Encourage the client to explore his own concerns.
Example: Cognitive — "You're not sure what you want to major in, is that it?"
Affective — "Maybe some of these times you're getting mad at yourself, what do you think?"
(b) Assist the client to explore by providing him with possible alternatives designed to increase his range of responses.
Example: Cognitive — "What are some of the other alternatives that you have to history as a major?"
Affective — "In these situations do you feel angry, mad, helpless, or what?"
(c) Reward the client for exploratory behavior.
Example: Cognitive — "It seems that you've considered a number of alternatives for a major, that's good."
Affective — "So you're beginning to wonder if you always want to be treated like a man."

B. *Nonexploratory responses* — Nonexploratory responses either indicate no understanding of the client's basic communication, or so structure and limit the client's responses that they inhibit the exploratory process. These responses give the client little opportunity to explore, expand, or express himself freely. Such responses:

Discourage further exploration on the part of the client.
Example: Cognitive — "You want to change your major to history."
Affective — "You *really* resent your parents treating you like a child."

V. Effective-noneffective dimension
Ratings on the effective-noneffective dimension may be made independently of ratings on the other four dimensions of the scale. This rating is based solely upon the judge's professional impression of the appropriateness of the counselor's responses, that is, how adequately does the counselor's response deal with the client's verbal and nonverbal communication? This rating is *not* dependent on whether the response has been judged affective-cognitive, etc.
A rating of 4 indicates that the judge considers this response among the most appropriate possible in the given situation while a 3 indicates that the response is appropriate but not among the best. A rating of 2 indicates a neutral response which neither measurably affects client progress nor inhibits it, while a rating of 1

indicates a response which not only lacks basic understanding of the client's concerns but which in effect may be detrimental to the specified goals of client growth.

USE OF IPR RATING SCALES

While this book cannot provide a video tape or an audio tape so that the reader may see and/or listen to counselee-counselor exchange, the foregoing materials may be employed to rate the counselor responses presented in three situations.[50] For example, if you believed that the response of Counselor 1 to Counselee I was more cognitive than affective, you would check that column in the IPR Counselor Response Scale. If you believed that the response of Counselor 1 reflected more "understanding" than "nonunderstanding," you would place a check mark in the appropriate column. The authors' evaluation of the first counselor's remark has been recorded on the form given as Figure 12.1 to serve as an example.

Counselee I: "I've been sitting here and I have been seeing you for a long time — for several months, and usually I thought, well you kind of understood me, but lately you haven't — I wonder, maybe I ought to leave."

Counselor 1: "Why do you feel that I don't understand you?"

2: "You can't tolerate it when you are not understood."

3: "Can you explain why you think I don't understand you?"

4: "It is fine if you want to leave — you're sure you know why?"

5: "What would you accomplish by leaving?"

6: "What do you expect from me?"

7: "What change has taken place which makes you think that I don't understand you?"

8: "Let's talk about what I don't understand and see if I don't understand it better."

[50] Case material used by permission of Jane S. O'Hern. Abstracted from case materials used in O'Hern and Arbuckle, *op. cit.*

9: "It's not my understanding that keeps you from making any progress."

10: "You feel as if you are not being understood — why do you need so much understanding?"

11: "My not understanding you makes you feel that you aren't worthwhile."

Counselee II: "What the hell are you asking me how it feels for? If I knew how I felt I probably wouldn't have come to see you."

Counselor 12: "You're pretty touchy today, aren't you?"

13: "I'm sorry if I intruded on your privacy, maybe we can talk about something else if you like."

14: "I am attempting to find out what your inner feelings are so that I can be of help to you in some way."

15: "If we are going to solve your problems it is important that I get to know you better."

16: "How do you think you feel at this time?"

17: "Don't you think it important to consider your feelings about yourself and your environment in order to determine why you are having trouble?"

18: "You would like for me to take the responsibility for knowing how you are."

19: "I guess we all have those days, don't we?"

20: "It makes you angry for someone to ask you how it feels — I wonder why."

21: "It is just common courtesy to ask you how you felt."

22: "Why did you come to see me?"

23: "I'm just trying to get you to express how you feel about your problem."

Counselee III: "I was thinking about it the other night and you know my father died when I was fifteen. I was just in high school and you know at the funeral I knew I was supposed to cry and act upset and everything, and I did. I put on a real good act. But you know when they first told me that he died . . . that he was dead and do you know what the first thing was that came to my mind? The first thing that I thought about was — ha, ha — all the restrictions are gone and I can be free."

Counselor 24: "Your father meant some different things to you than what the people thought. Inside you were really glad and you're wondering why these things are bothering you now."

25: "Why do you say 'at last I can be free'?"

26: "Why did you feel that you had to cry to put on a good act?"

27: "Now you think of your father as the restrictions he put on you. You really didn't have any need for him at all."

28: "Do you think this is a bad thought? Do you think people will think badly of you because you think this way? Does everyone love his father?"

29: "How do you feel about it now? How are these restrictions?"

30: "Your father's death just sorta lifted off a lot of rules and regulations and you felt that your life was your own?"

31: "You thought your father was the party who kept you from the things you really wanted to do. Without him, you're entirely free with nothing to hold you back."

32: "This bothers you because you went through all the motions socially."

33: "Do you still feel that way?"

Summary

Counseling communication is complex, myriad, and constantly changing. The techniques employed by the counselor reflect his personal growth so that each counselor tends to develop a personal style based upon his experiences. Most counselors implement a role which is performed consistently with all counselees. Some 25 years ago the use of recorded interviews was originated to study client-counselor interactions. From these early studies and from others now conducted with greater finesse, more understanding is being gained about interview dynamics. The counselee tends to approach his problems from either a cognitive or an affective framework. During segments of an interview a counselor's behavior usually reflects a certain consistency as he enacts one or another subordinate role with sensitive adjustment depending upon the topic under discussion.

Buchheimer and Balogh have conceptualized the counseling relationship in a highly useful way.[51] They believe that techniques used by the counselor are dependent upon the strategy he employs or the "set" he has toward the counselee. The set may be either *peripheral* or *central*. If it is peripheral, the counselor takes a third-person view and seemingly possesses an attitude of inquiry. Emphasis is placed upon knowing and doing, with little concern for feeling, under the assumption that the counselee does not know what he needs to know and that once he does, he will be able to act. The counselor, then, is the primary acting person while the counselee remains essentially a passive individual who is judged, evaluated, and told. The central counselor, on the other hand, takes a first-person view because he feels and thinks within the counselee's point of view. He engages in the counselee's affective life, and his leads are in "you" terms derived from the "I." Fundamentally, the counselor's aim, expressed through his techniques, is to achieve certain goals while simultaneously allowing the counselee to be responsible for himself, for his communications, and for his behavior.

Annotated References

Brammer, Lawrence M., and Shostrom, Everett L. *Therapeutic Psychology,* 2nd ed. Englewood Cliffs, N.J.: Prentice-Hall, Inc., 1968. 486 pp.

Chapters 7 through 10 (pp. 191–320) present certain relationship techniques and problems: reflection, acceptance, silence, reassurance, and the like. These authors devote a complete chapter to interpretation and special interpretative adjuncts. Their presentation is thorough and sound.

[51] Buchheimer and Balogh, *op. cit.*, p. 12.

Buchheimer, Arnold, and Balogh, Sara Carter. *The Counseling Relationship: A Casebook.* Chicago: Science Research Associates, Inc., 1961. 234 pp.

Chapter 1 (pp. 1–14) discusses beginning a relationship, counselor leads, and counseling interaction. The authors not only explain but illustrate counseling techniques. This chapter is particularly succinct, clear, and helpful to beginning counselors.

Krumboltz, John D. and Thoresen, Carl E. (eds). *Behavioral Counseling: Cases and Techniques.* New York: Holt, Rinehart and Winston, 1969. 515 pp.
The book consists of 43 articles and introductory statements by the editors which describe counseling techniques. Noteworthy among the techniques described are some that failed.

Further References

Aspy, David N. "The Helper's Tools: Chicken Soup or Rifles." *Personnel and Guidance Journal,* Vol. 49 (October, 1970). pp. 117–118.

Astor, Martin H. "Transpersonal Approaches to Counseling." *Personnel and Guidance Journal,* Vol. 50 (June, 1972). pp. 801–808.

Birdwhistell, Miriam C. and Beard, Richard L. "Intervention with Pregnant Students." *Personnel and Guidance Journal,* Vol. 49 (February, 1971). pp. 453–458.

Brown, Joe H. and Brown, Carolyn. "Intervention Packages: An Approach to Self-Management." *Personnel and Guidance Journal,* Vol. 50 (June, 1972). pp. 809–816.

Bugg, Charles A. "Systematic Desensitization: A Technique Worth Trying." *Personnel and Guidance Journal,* Vol. 50 (June, 1972). pp. 823–828.

Dilley, Josiah, Lee, James L., and Verrill, Eleanor Lynn. "Is Empathy Ear-to-Ear or Face-to-Face?" *Personnel and Guidance Journal,* Vol. 50 (November, 1971). pp. 188–191.

Dinkmeyer, Don C. "Use of the Encouragement Process in Adlerian Counseling." *Personnel and Guidance Journal,* Vol. 51 (November, 1972). pp. 177–182.

Fischer, Constance T. "Rapport as Mutual Respect." *Personnel and Guidance Journal,* Vol. 48 (November, 1969). pp. 201–204.

Garner, William Chadwick. "The Crisis Intervention Technique with Potential College Dropouts." *Personnel and Guidance Journal,* Vol. 48 (March, 1970). pp. 552–560.

Gladstein, Gerald A. "Is Empathy Important in Counseling?" *Personnel and Guidance Journal,* Vol. 48 (June, 1970). pp. 823–827.

Graff, Robert W. and MacLean, G. Donald. "Evaluating Educational-Vocational Counseling: A Model for Change." *Personnel and Guidance Journal,* Vol. 48 (March, 1970). pp. 568–574.

Hountras, Peter T. and Anderson, Derwyn L. "Counselor Conditions for Self Exploration of College Students." *Personnel and Guidance Journal,* Vol. 48 (September, 1969). pp. 45–48.

Jourard, Sidney M. and Jaffe, Peggy E. "Influence of an Interviewer's Disclosure on the Self-Disclosing Behavior of Interviewees." *Journal of Counseling Psychology,* Vol. 17 (May, 1970). pp. 252–257.

Loeffler, Dorothy. "Counseling and the Psychology of Communication." *Personnel and Guidance Journal,* Vol. 48 (April, 1970). pp. 629–636.

MacGuffie, Robert A., Jorgensen, Gary Q., and Janzen, Frederick V. "Need for Approval and Counseling Outcomes." *Personnel and Guidance Journal,* Vol. 48 (April, 1970). pp. 653–656.

Matheny, Kenneth. "Counselors as Environmental Engineers." *Personnel and Guidance Journal,* Vol. 49 (February, 1971). pp. 439–444.

May, Eugene. "Quantity or Quality in Dealing with Human Problems." *Personnel and Guidance Journal,* Vol. 49 (January, 1971). pp. 376–382.

Mazza, Paul and Garris, Donald. "Shared Student Self-Evaluation." *Personnel and Guidance Journal,* Vol. 50 (May, 1972). pp. 745–748.

Mills, David H. "Counseling in the Culture Cycle: Feeling or Reason?" *Personnel and Guidance Journal,* Vol. 49 (March, 1971). pp. 515–522.

Nighswander, James K. and Mayer, G. Roy. "Catharsis: A Means of Reducing Elementary School Students' Aggressive Behaviors?" *Personnel and Guidance Journal,* Vol. 47 (January, 1969). pp. 461–466.

O'Leary, Susan G. "Counselor Activity as a Predictor of Outcome." *Personnel and Guidance Journal,* Vol. 48 (October, 1969). pp. 135–139.

Pulvino, Charles J. and Sanborn, Marshall P. "Feedback and Accountability." *Personnel and Guidance Journal,* Vol. 51 (September, 1972). pp. 15–20.

Riordan, Richard J. and Matheny, Kenneth B. "Dear Diary: Logs in Group Counseling." *Personnel and Guidance Journal,* Vol. 50 (January, 1972). pp. 379–382.

Schmitz, Michael B. and Mickelson, Douglas J. "Hot-Line Drug Counseling and Rogerian Methods." *Personnel and Guidance Journal,* Vol. 50 (January, 1972). pp. 357–362.

Sprafkin, Robert P. "Communicator Expertness and Changes in Word Meanings in Psychological Treatment." *Journal of Counseling Psychology,* Vol. 17 (May, 1970). pp. 191–196.

Thomas, G. Patience and Ezell, Betty. "The Contract as a Counseling Technique." *Personnel and Guidance Journal,* Vol. 51 (September, 1972). pp. 27–32.

Toews, Jay M. "The Counselor as Contingency Manager." *Personnel and Guidance Journal,* Vol. 48 (October, 1969). pp. 127–134.

Warner, Richard W. Jr. and Hansen, James C. "Alienated Youth: The Counselor's Task." *Personnel and Guidance Journal,* Vol. 48 (February, 1970). pp. 443–448.

COUNSELING TECHNIQUES AND PRACTICES: II

13

This chapter is organized around the following topics: (1) things to look for in counseling, (2) nonverbal behavior, (3) diagnosis, (4) test use and interpretation, (5) nontest adjuncts to counseling, and (6) referral practices.

Things to Look for in Counseling

The majority of the material discussed here has been drawn from Annette Garrett's small booklet on interviewing.[1] This somewhat dated publication contains a great deal of meaningful material which suffers, to some degree, from lack of exposition. Perhaps it can be appreciated only after considerable counseling experience. Garrett sets forth six topics which, if put in the form of questions, can be very useful to any counselor in reviewing the conduct of a counseling session.

How do I view the association of ideas contained within the interview?

What shifts in conversation occur which might be meaningful?

What content and affect were present in the client's opening and closing statements?

What recurrent references were present?

Did inconsistencies and gaps occur which might be of particular significance?

Does a reconsideration of the session indicate an unconscious effort to conceal or hide that which is of concern to the counselee?

ASSOCIATION OF IDEAS

Careful review of any counseling session, no matter how disjointed or faltering the session may appear, commonly reveals a pattern of consistency in the ideas expressed by the counselee. Normally, the consistency is recognized more readily by the counselor after a series of contacts, for fairly obvious reasons. Initially, the counselor seeks and the client attempts to give a great deal of information, much of which may not be of importance later.

[1] Annette Garrett, *Interviewing: Its Principles and Methods* (New York: Family Service Association of America, 1942).

Especially in earlier contacts much of what takes place, as Perez indicates,[2] clearly evolves from the mutual interaction of the participants' defense mechanisms.

Presumably, a counselee seeks the helping relationship because of some concern or problem. He is looking for relief from a condition which may be relatively simple or tremendously complex. However inept and convoluted the way he approaches the situation, he is nevertheless attempting to present his problem as he perceives it. Digressions, defensiveness, and tangential references notwithstanding, in most instances the thread of the problem is embedded in the weave of the material presented. The skillful, perceptive, and experienced counselor is not only able to extract this thread but assists the client in setting it in a less tortuous pattern.

This thread is what Garrett refers to as an association of ideas; it is akin to William James's "stream of consciousness."[3] While the term "free association" is sometimes loosely applied to this phenomenon, such mental meanderings clearly contain consistency and logic if viewed from the counselee's frame of reference. The associations are there. What is missing is the grasp of the client's perceptual framework by the counselor. Even the most bizarre of human behavior can be thought of as having meaning and purpose to the individual who performs it. The point is that there are two limitations to understanding another: the client's inability to express adequately what he wishes to say and the counselor's inability to hear the essence of what is said to him. Neither should be taken as a condemnation of the participants. Both are human failings that can be overcome only by repeated contact coupled with recognition of the complexity involved in knowing and understanding communication.

Garrett points out that "association of ideas" takes place in both counselor and counselee. The counselor who uses what may be an emotionally charged word such as "divorce," "college," "mother," or "lying" may simultaneously trigger in the counselee a stream of association which has little to do with the counselor's feelings about these things. Unless the counselor recognizes his own associations, their unconscious operation may cause him to attribute feelings and emotions to the counselee that he does not have.

[2] Joseph F. Perez, *The Initial Counseling Contact*, Houghton Mifflin Professional Guidance Monograph Series (Boston: Houghton Mifflin Company, 1968).
[3] Garrett, *op. cit.*, p. 50.

SHIFTS IN CONVERSATION

To the counselor, topical shifts in the counselee's conversation may appear random and purposeless. Review of what was said previously in the interview as well as what comes after may reveal the reason for change. Topical changes may represent any of the following behaviors or others:

1. The counselee may be trying to make himself better understood by citing what he considers a relevant situation illustrating the point he is making or the feeling he seeks to convey.
2. The counselee may believe that he is revealing too much of himself. Because he is unsure of how he is being received by the counselor, he may deliberately shift the focus to what he thinks can be safely communicated and examined.
3. The counselee may be seeking relief from examination of a topic too painful or too sensitive to pursue. This is related to the second point.

OPENING AND CLOSING REMARKS

The initial remarks made by the counselee may contain much that is helpful in understanding him as well as his perspective on his situation. "The principal sent me down here" bears special study by the counselor as it probably indicates reluctance to be there. The attitudes reflected by the counselee in presenting his problem may give significant cues not only to his motivation for change but to how fully he understands himself. Similarly, concluding remarks are worth study because they often indicate the counselee's view of what has happened. They may give insight both to the meaning he attaches to what has been discussed and to his commitment to working on his problems.

RECURRENT REFERENCES

As stated earlier, a consistent theme may be visible in reviewing what has been said in a counseling session. The counselee returns to it again and again. For example, the theme may be the counselee's lack of self-acceptance, and he will repeatedly refer to his dissatisfaction with his present level of functioning in school, his unhappiness at home, his inability to establish friendships, and the like. Recurring references may indicate an inability to accept or cope with authority. During the interview or its review, then, the counselor is able to discern a pattern of behavior from the counselee's recurring descriptions of situations.

Similar to recurring references is the situation in which the individual "talks in circles." He talks and talks and talks but fails to move forward. The same ideas, the same complaints, the same explanations are presented over and over.

> Such circularity presents a stumbling block to an interviewer. When we have become aware that such an impasse has been reached, it is necessary to devise ways of inserting something new into the ritual, thus breaking up the circle and transforming it into a spiral. Here the interviewer's choice of subject to insert is often guided by clues the client has given, perhaps some topic that has been mentioned before but not explained. If we have no clue, we may even have to make an insertion blindly, by trial and error. Questions such as, "What would you like to do about it?" or "How would you like to have your husband act?" may stimulate the client to move into new and more profitable areas of discussion.[4]

INCONSISTENCIES AND GAPS

A counselee's remark may contradict one previously made, or he may present a picture that contains inconsistencies and gaps. The inconsistencies and gaps, particularly if they are repeated, may be significant to understanding the client. A counselee who describes the members of his family but omits mentioning a brother or sister leaves a gap that may contain meaning fundamental to understanding his problem. Similarly, the counselee who remarks that he "likes school" but later keeps talking of dropping out has revealed a contradiction that may well be followed up by the counselor.

CONCEALED MEANING

By listening intently the counselor is often able to discern the concealed meaning behind client statements. Some beginning counselors worry and unduly pursue every client remark in an effort to uncover hidden meaning. The senior girl who "can't tolerate boys" may be concealing her hurt that she has not been dated, and the boy who is lonely may go to great lengths to hide this by explaining that he has "too much to do to seek out and encourage friends." The presence of concealed meaning is usually far from obvious; only through careful attentiveness to the counselee's attitudes, slips of tongue, and other cues does it become apparent.

Nonverbal Behavior

The verbal exchanges between counselee and counselor are but part of the communication involved in the counseling relationship. The counselee's nonverbal behavior — gestures, body movements, blushing — supplements and indeed sometimes belies his words. Although each counselor's observation of nonverbal behavior is limited by his sensitivity and training, the meaningfulness of cues derived from expressive movements adds much to his intuitive understanding of a counselee.

Certainly the occurrence of nonverbal behavior is not random; it derives from elements within the relationship. Expressive gestures and movements are used to either accent or contradict verbal exchanges. Unfortunately for the counselor, there is as yet no codification of the meanings of nonverbal behavior. Weeping is clear and needs no explana-

[4] *Ibid.*, p. 52.

tion, but most expressive behaviors have yet to be accurately identified in respect to their stimulus situation.

It is still unknown whether gestures have common or unique meanings and under what conditions interpretations of nonverbal behavior can be generalized. Furthermore, a chasm exists between even the present level of understanding nonverbal behavior and the knowledge needed for preparing individuals to master that understanding.

GESTURES

A gesture has been defined by Hayes as "any bodily movement excepting that of vocalization made consciously or unconsciously to communicate either with one's self or with another."[5] Postural movements would be included in his definition. Gestures, while often unconscious, are assumed to be used to communicate. Hayes groups gestures into a threefold classification. *Folk gestures*, such as head nodding, shaking hands, pouting, and winking, have conscious meaning related to social activities within cultures. *Technical gestures* include umpires' signs as well as sign languages employed by the American Indian and deaf-mutes. *Austistic*, self-directed, or nervous gestures include hand wringing, doodling, twisting a necklace, shifting positions, and the like.

RESEARCH EFFORTS

Research in nonverbal communication has been carried on for decades employing a variety of procedures and settings. One mode — and the forerunner to present research — has been the use of photographs to determine whether emotions can be judged correctly. The absence of motion and the lack of information about the behavioral sequence in photographs severely limit the facets their use can uncover. Gestures have also been investigated in such settings as drama, speech, and educational administration. Nonverbal behavior within the confines of the classroom has been examined through film recordings. More recently, study has been made of nonverbal communication in interviews, particularly in respect to the relationship between emotional stress and gestures and body movements.

NONVERBAL BEHAVIOR IN THE CLASSROOM

The function of nonverbal behavior in classroom settings is receiving more and more attention. Maccoby and associates, investigating teachers' responses to student nonverbal behavior, sought to improve teacher accuracy in judging student comprehension of classroom material.[6] Nonteachers, inexperienced teachers, and experienced teachers were exposed to sound film clips of teacher-student comprehension. Student comprehension was established by test items. It was reported that verbal cues contributed significantly to accuracy of judgment while nonverbal cues (specifically visual ones) failed to improve accuracy. Further, the investigators sought to discover useful nonverbal cues and to train teachers to use them. After much study, some 22 nonverbal cues were selected that related to comprehension, and teachers were instructed as to their presence, interpretation, and meaning. Training resulted in a 7 per cent increase in accuracy of judgment, which, though modest, suggests the possibility that training can increase sensitivity to nonverbal communications.

NONVERBAL BEHAVIOR IN COUNSELING

Practicing psychiatrists have developed some literature dealing with nonverbal behavior. They have highlighted the fact that such behavior is significant and constitutes a source of information and insight. Feldman has a comprehensive listing of speech and body mannerisms and their "meaning."[7] He believes that certain bodily movements could be traced back to their original use as com-

[5] F. G. Hayes, "Gesture," *Encyclopedia Americana* (New York: Americana Corporation, 1963), Vol. 12, p. 627.

[6] N. Maccoby *et al.*, "Sound Film Recordings in Improving Classroom Communications," Report Submitted to the U.S. Office of Education, Title VII, Project 680, Institute for Communication Research, Stanford University, 1965.

[7] Sandor S. Feldman, *Mannerisms of Speech and Gesture in Everyday Life* (New York: International Universities Press, Inc., 1959).

municative tools in life struggles. In his book he presents current meanings of gestures. The reader should of course recognize that Feldman's interpretations are at best educated guesses regarding highly idiosyncratic human behavior. Below is a list of representative gestures and the "meanings" he ascribes to them:

Erect head: self esteem, self confidence, courage
Bowed head: humility, resignation, guilt, submission
Touching nose: anxiety, stage fright
Rapid eye-blinking: relief mechanism or displacement from below upwards
Artificial cough: criticism, doubt, surprise, anxiety
Whistling or humming: genuine or feigned self confidence
Fixing neckties: demonstrating masculinity
Pressing head with hands: distress, despair, helplessness
Placing head between two palms: sadness, exhaustion, meditation
Placing index finger alongside the nose: suspicion
Closing nostrils with fingers: contempt
Closing ears with hands: don't want to hear
Putting arms akimbo: firmness
Crossing arms over chest: straightjacket
Outstretched arms: call attention, surprise, alarm, blessing
Forming ring with fingers: unity, perfection
Rubbing thumb and middle finger: searching for solution
Finger or knuckle-cracking: frustration, aggression, hostility
Playing with ring or handbag: releasing tension or conflict, decision making
Embarrassed hands: repressed inclination to masturbate, suppression of bad habits

Behavioral manifestations such as facial expressions are assumed to have relationship to intrapsychic phenomena. Sainsbury observed the autistic gestures accompanying certain emotional states in psychiatric interviews.[8] He concluded that nonverbal behavior increased with stress or emotional involvement in interviews. Dittman has sought to "read" other than through words, how a subject feels at a given time.[9] He believes that nonverbal messages are often different from verbal ones and that the discrepancies as well as the congruencies between the two yield clues as to what takes place in interviews. In his opinion nonverbal information yields clues faster than words since people often react sooner than they are willing or able to speak. In one investigation Dittman counted foot movement as it related to speech disturbance but could not confirm the hypothesis that body movement and speech disturbance occur concurrently. In a second experiment he studied the association between body movement and mood as reported by the patient and confirmed by his tone of voice. While the two behaviors were significantly related, the best combination of body activity and mood made up only one-quarter of the total movement information.

Birdwhistell points out that communication has traditionally been regarded as "that process by which one individual imparted knowledge to another," rather than as "a complex and sustaining system through which various members of the society inter-relate."[10] He developed a system for categorizing body motion based upon the assumption that while body motions are unique to an individual, those of many people could be combined into groups of similar motions having the same message. Bronfenbrenner and Newcomb devised a framework within which behavior may be studied as a vehicle of emotional and dispositional expression.[11] The five formal dimensions of bodily movement in clinical situations included (1) *quality* of motion (relaxed, jerky, abortive, controlled, or immobilized), (2) *front* of body contour (closed or open), (3) *locus* of activity (peripheral, medial, central, or integrative), (4) *direction* or plane of movement (vertical, transverse, or lateral), and (5) *body*

[8] Peter Sainsbury, "Gestural Movement During Psychiatric Interviews," *Psychosomatic Medicine,* Vol. 17 (November-December, 1955), pp. 458–469.

[9] Allen T. Dittman, "Kinesic Research and Therapeutic Processes: Further Discussion," in Peter H. Knapp (ed.), *Expression of the Emotions in Man* (New York: International Universities Press, Inc., 1963), pp. 140–141.

[10] Ray L. Birdwhistell, "The Kinesic Level in the Investigation of the Emotions," in Knapp (ed.), *op. cit.,* pp. 128–129.

[11] Urie Bronfenbrenner and Theodore M. Newcomb, "Improvisations — An Application of Psychodrama in Personality Diagnosis," *Sociometry,* Vol. 1 (March, 1948), pp. 367–382.

area of activity (head, mouth, eyes, hands, trunk area, shoulder and back, legs).

Ruesch and Kees have sought to develop a theory of nonverbal communication.[12] They use the term "action language" (contrasted to sign or object language) to designate emotional expressions because of the way actions convey that which is less easily conveyed verbally. Nonverbal behavior, for Ruesch and Kees, is but one type of nonverbal communication, and their theory applies to all types of communicative behavior. They point out that the system (person, situation, society) within which communication occurs determines, at least in part, communicative behavior and that many subprocesses exist within the communication process. They compare nonverbal communication to verbal communication on such dimensions as perception, spatiotemporal characteristics, transmission of information, evaluation, codification of semantic characteristics, and the like. Ruesch discusses nonverbal communication as it applies to psychotherapy.[13] He believes that patients use nonverbal communication to augment verbal behavior and that nonverbal communication provides a meaningful basis for interaction with the patient.

Ekman reported in 1957 upon the state of nonverbal research, defining nonverbal behavior as "the body movements of the organism."[14] Such behavior consisted of motor expressions originating in various parts of the body. Ekman believes that two types of information result from nonverbal behavior: specific direct meaning and information about other behavioral variables. Reporting in 1964, Ekman used photographs of nonverbal behavior in interviews as well as short written samples to study communication.[15] Verbal-nonverbal congruence, communication about interview relationships, and differences between head and body conveyance of emotion were examined. Nonverbal behaviors, either augmenting or contradicting verbal responses, were organized into a schema according to the functions served by such behaviors. Five functions were identified: (1) emphasizing or accenting the content of the verbal message, (2) amplifying part of the content of a verbal message, (3) examining a verbal silence, (4) providing information related to the content of the verbal message, and (5) adding new information not in the content of the verbal message by (a) substituting for verbalization, (b) contradicting the verbal message, or (c) providing a context to aid in interpretation of the verbal message.

[12] Jurgen Ruesch and Weldon Kees, *Nonverbal Communication* (Berkeley: University of California Press, 1956).

[13] Jurgen Ruesch, "Nonverbal Language and Therapy," *Psychiatry*, Vol. 18 (November, 1955), pp. 323-330.

[14] Paul Ekman, "A Methodological Discussion of Nonverbal Behavior," *Journal of Psychology*, Vol. 43 (January, 1957), pp. 140-149.

[15] Paul Ekman, "Body Position, Facial Expression and Verbal Behavior During Interviews," *Journal of Abnormal and Social Psychology*, Vol. 68 (March, 1964), pp. 295-301.

A TYPOLOGY OF NONVERBAL BEHAVIOR

Kagan and his associates have developed a typology of nonverbal behavior.[16] In their study nonverbal behavior was limited to gestures, particularly arm and hand movements and postural movements limited to the client's position in a chair. They excluded lower leg or foot movements since their video tape pictures of clients were from the knees up and they also excluded facial expression and eye movement because these have been subjected to much previous research. They first established a common repertoire of client nonverbal behavior by observing numerous clients, then validated the typology by comparing the meaning of nonverbal behavior as implied by the typology with that revealed in recall interviews. Table 13.1 presents the major components of this typology. The description given below is drawn from their report to the U.S. Office of Education.

Source of nonverbal behavior Nonverbal behavior was observed as being related either to the verbal interview content or to the client's affective experience within the interview. While these components occur simultaneously, nonverbal behaviors general-

[16] Norman Kagan, David R. Krathwohl, and William W. Farquhar, *IPR — Interpersonal Process Recall. Stimulated Recall by Videotape*, Educational Research Series, No. 24 (East Lansing: Bureau of Educational Research Services, College of Education, Michigan State University, March, 1965), pp. III-1 to III-22.

Table 13.1 Nonverbal behaviors of clients in counseling interviews: degree of awareness of behavior

Source of behavior	*Unaware*	*Potentially aware*	*Aware*
Content	1. *Emphasis.* Gestures of shortest duration accompanying particular items of verbal content; function is emphasis.	2. *Facilitation.* Gestures of brief duration accompanying verbal content, serving the function of facilitating clear communication.	3. *Portrayal.* Gestures intended to portray or give example of the topic of verbal content; duration directly related to content.
Affect	4. *Revelation—unaware (unconscious).* Unconsciously motivated body motion related to feelings.	5. *Revelation–aware (conscious).* Unconsciously motivated gestures revealing some degree of tension; client is aware of body motion but neither intends nor suppresses it.	6. *Affect demonstration (conscious).* Intentional demonstration of feeling on client's part.

FROM Norman Kagan, David R. Krathwohl, and William W. Farquhar, *IPR—Interpersonal Process Recall. Stimulated Recall by Videotape,* Educational Research Series, No. 24. East Lansing: Bureau of Educational Research Services, College of Education, Michigan State University, March, 1965, p. III–10.

ly relate only to one or the other and seldom to both simultaneously.

Awareness Variation occurred in nonverbal behavior according to the client's degree of awareness of his actions. Kagan and his associates cited three categories (see Table 13.1): awareness, potential awareness, and lack of awareness. *Awareness* implies that the client not only knows of his behavior but fully intends it. *Potential awareness* occurs when the client could indicate knowledge of his action if attention were directed to it. In this state he neither overtly intends nor overtly suppresses the action. *Lack of awareness* means that the client is entirely unaware of his behavior and if his attention were directed to it he would indicate that he was oblivious to the action at the time.

Duration Nonverbal behaviors arranged themselves in regular fashion by duration (see the numbers 1 to 6 in Table 13.1), or the extent of each behavior in terms of time. The behaviors ranged from a motion occupying a fraction of a second (1) to one lasting 10 to 15 minutes almost uninterrupted (6). Kagan and his associates suggest that while an overt gesture may be only momentary, the tension state which produced it is more continuous and occurs either prior to the gesture or as a result of client anticipation of what is to come.

Source and awareness, the first two variables, interact to produce six distinct and definable categories of nonverbal behavior. The third element, duration, results from the arrangement of the six categories, each of which is described comprehensively by Kagan and his associates. The following material selected from their commentary outlines the description.

1. *Emphasis.* Gestures used for emphasis are brief and forceful, closely related to particular verbal content in respect to both time and forcefulness. Hands and arms are used primarily, followed by head and leg movements; postural movements are least used for emphasis. Because they are of brief duration (e.g., tapping of chair), the client is usually unaware of them.

2. *Facilitation.* Gestures are often used to "assist" in increasing clarity. Hand and arm gestures (most frequently quick upward and outward motions) seem to be intended to release words from within and to speed them to their purpose. Such gestures

were more often used when clients were expressing abstract ideas or were at a loss for words or believed that their verbal expression was inadequate. Clients are generally unaware of gestures for facilitation unless the motions are called to their attention.

3. *Portrayal.* Individuals wish to demonstrate what they mean and gestures can give an example or a picture of what is being communicated. Those common in ordinary conversation include listing of items on the fingers or motions accompanying "she's about this tall," etc. Clients use similar gestures to illustrate their ideas. The girl in conflict with her mother crosses and recrosses her arms before her. Portrayal and emphasis are the most direct forms of nonverbal communication in our culture; they are most easily understood and frequently used. Portrayal is generally a conscious gesture.

4. *Revelation — unaware.* Tension-motivated behavior of which the client is totally unaware is the most critical nonverbal behavior in counseling situations. In tension-packed sessions he is concerned more with verbalized content than with his own overt behavior. Such unconsciously motivated gestures or postures originate from his feelings about himself, or the topic (past, current, or potential), or the counselor, or the situation. Gestures may be continuous for an extended period of time or may recur frequently with repeated feelings of anxiety or tension. Kagan *et al.* report that only mature, perceptive clients are able to interpret such nonverbal behaviors on recall.

5. *Revelation — aware.* The client is aware of gestures in this category but attributes them to habit. While aware of the activity he is unaware of its motivation. Leg swinging, ring twisting, key jingling are examples of common tension-associated habitual behaviors adopted as "pacifiers" by many adults.

6. *Affect demonstration.* The client who wishes deliberately to demonstrate feelings uses nonverbal behaviors falling in this category. Kagan and his associates cite two reasons for such demonstration: (1) The individual "puts on an act" to deceive the counselor regarding feelings or concerns (sadness is covered by wearing a bright smile or the client appears sober and serious because he thinks a "good" client acts that way) or (2) the client has an intense desire for the counselor to know and understand his feelings (client's use of hands to tell counselor that he, the client, has nothing to say). Such nonverbal behavior is intentional and fully within awareness of the client.

SUMMARY

Nonverbal behavior is likely to be interpreted intuitively by counselors. It varies so greatly that generalizations are usually unwarranted. Presumably, the typology by Kagan and his associates gives some specificity of meaning for interpretative value and reflects some degree of universality. These researchers report that confusion in interpreting nonverbal behavior often comes from an assumption that the behavior being observed is an unconsciously motivated manifestation (this behavior would be categorized as revelation — unconscious, category 4). However, such behavior is very often the counselee's attempt to make sure that he conveys a particular role to the counselor. In essence, he is putting on an act, and the problem is to ferret out the nonverbal or verbal clues in the situation which contradict any assumed pose.

Because of the lack of commonality of nonverbal behavior among individuals, caution must be exercised in interpreting nonverbal behavior. More and more research effort is being applied to the topic. As greater understanding is gained, more and more attention will be given it in counselor education so that counselors will develop greater sensitivity to nonverbal behavior. To conclude this section, the comments of Manoil still have much meaning:

> Expressive aspects of behavior appear as dynamic, direct, and immediate communication, consequently unaltered by their crystalization into verbal symbols. What is obtained by avoiding the use of words is, however, not necessarily nearer to the truth since cultural factors and learning, operating at the nonverbal level, would

make expressive behavior also into a symbolic system. And, if expressive behavior to be intelligible and communicable has to be codified, the nature of the problem would shift only from verbal codification to nonverbal codification.
The intuitive character in nonverbal communication can be recognized, however, only as a supplementary relative clue to human interaction.[17]

Diagnosis

Diagnosis has been defined as a summary of the counselee's problems and their causes, description of the individual's personality dynamics, and understanding of the individual. As used in counseling, it generally refers to identification of abnormality by the symptoms presented and classification on the basis of observed characteristics. Williamson defined diagnosis as a "terse summary of problems, their causes and other significant and relevant characteristics of the student, together with the implications for potential adjustments and maladjustments."[18] Thorne, using a different approach, stated that "Diagnosis refers to the description of the organism and its behavior by a variety of methods whose basic purpose is to discover the personality dynamics of each individual case."[19] He cited 10 objectives of diagnosis including the demonstration of etiological factors, the nature and extent of the morbid process, the determination of prognosis and probable course, and the formulation of a dynamic hypothesis of the process as a rational basis for specific psychotherapy.

In the early days of counseling, diagnosis was accepted as an inevitable and desirable function. It included a statement of the present status or adjustment of the counselee, causal factors, suggested counseling procedures, and a prediction of future adjustment. As a process, diagnosis consisted in reducing case data by eliminating irrelevant material and arriving at a best judgment through formulating and testing hypotheses. The hypotheses were based upon generalizations from research and experience, intuition and insight. The term "best judgment" was used rather than a definite conclusion because it was made on the data then at hand and was revised as counseling progressed.

The advent of client-centered counseling cast doubt on the appropriateness of diagnosis as part of the counselor's behavior. The objections of client-centered counseling to the traditional concept of diagnosis originally formulated by Rogers were that it (1) placed the locus of evaluation in the counselor and thereby increased the client's dependent tendencies since it caused him to feel that the responsibility for understanding and improving his situation lay with the counselor and (2) resulted in certain long-range social and philosophical implications (direction of the social control of the many by the few).[20]

But even prior to the introduction of client-centered counseling, questions were being raised as to whether diagnosis could be applied to psychological problems. Medical diagnosis is the *distinguishing* of an illness or disease and its *differentiation* from other diseases. Patterson[21] and Tyler[22] have summarized the difficulties of applying diagnosis to emotional disorders. First, the classification of diseases into discrete, mutually exclusive categories (each of which has a common origin, a common course, and a common prognosis) does not fit psychosocial disturbances. While patients with the same physical disease follow rather closely the same course, those who have been diagnosed as having the same emotional disorder do not necessarily follow the same course. Second, the etiology

[17] Adolph Manoil, "Review of V.A. Film on Psychotherapeutic Interviewing," Part IV, "Nonverbal Communication," *Contemporary Psychology*, Vol. 2 (April, 1957), p. 116.
[18] E. G. Williamson, *Counseling Adolescents* (New York: McGraw-Hill Book Co., Inc., 1950), p. 178.
[19] Frederick C. Thorne, *Principles of Personality Counseling* (Brandon, Vt.: Journal of Clinical Psychology, 1950), p. 40.
[20] Carl R. Rogers, *Client-Centered Therapy* (Boston: Houghton Mifflin Company, 1951), pp. 223–224.
[21] C. H. Patterson, *Counseling and Psychotherapy: Theory and Practice* (New York: Harper & Brothers, 1959), pp. 219–230.
[22] Leona Tyler, *The Work of the Counselor*, 3rd ed. (New York: Appleton-Century-Crofts, Inc., 1969), pp. 65–72.

of physical disease is always a specifiable, and ultimately verifiable, physical or external agent (chemical, bacteriological, or viral) whereas emotional disturbances may be due to multiple factors. Third, specific remedies exist, either known or unknown, for physical disease but none has yet been devised for personality problems.

Still another reason why a medical analogy does not precisely fit diagnosis in counseling can be advanced. The degree of participation by the medical patient and the counselee varies greatly. More reliance is placed on the counselee's active participation in the process, and more weight is given his self-report statements. In the medical setting such reports are not ignored, but often actual physical tests can be used to verify them. This view could be extended to the treatment process also. Physicians are able to do things *to* patients while to a greater extent counselors must depend upon working cooperatively *with* counselees.

Another objection to the heavy emphasis placed upon diagnosis is the growing evidence that clinical predictions are insufficiently accurate to serve as a basis for life decisions. Intuitive judgments stemming from all known data have been found to be less accurate than statistical predictions derived from a regression equation based upon a few variables, especially for predicting complex behavior in variable situations.

DIAGNOSTIC CLASSIFICATION SYSTEMS IN COUNSELING

Callis suggests that "The fundamental purpose of diagnosis in counseling is to enable the counselor to make predictions about client behavior from which he in turn constructs his plans for handling the case."[23] Several diagnostic classification systems have been devised. These systems assume, perhaps questionably, that emotional disorders, like physical disorders, are separable into discrete entities and that all emotional disorders are basically similar in nature.

Williamson's Classification Since early emphasis in counseling was placed upon the area of the individual's life in which the problem arose, Williamson and Darley suggested five categories for describing problems encountered in counseling.[24] A summary of these follows:

1. *Personality problems.* Difficulties in adjusting to social groups, speech difficulties, family conflicts, and disciplinary infractions.
2. *Educational problems.* Unwise choice of courses of study, differential scholastic achievement, inadequate general scholastic aptitude, ineffective study habits, reading disabilities, lack of scholastic motivation, over- and underachievement.
3. *Vocational problems.* Uncertain vocational choice, no vocational choice, discrepancy between interests and aptitudes, unwise vocational choice.
4. *Financial problems.* Difficulties arising from need for self-support in school and college.
5. *Health problems.* The individual's acceptance of his state of health or physical disabilities or both.

Obviously the classification is an attempt to describe the individual in terms of his adjustment to the demands of his environment.

Bordin's Classification Bordin pointed to evidence of overlap among the above categories and proposed an alternate set which would be closer to the basic psychological issues involved and therefore more related to differential treatment.[25] His diagnostic categories are summarized here:

1. *Dependence.* Conflict which immobilizes the client and blocks active efforts to resolve the problem or reach a decision is fundamental to this category. Individuals with problems of this type have not learned to solve their problems and are used to playing a passive role. Such problems include how to plan use of time, how to find a part-time

[23] Robert Callis, "Diagnostic Classification as a Research Tool," *Journal of Counseling Psychology,* Vol. 12 (Fall, 1965), p. 238.

[24] E. G. Williamson and J. G. Darley, *Student Personnel Work* (New York: McGraw-Hill Book Co., Inc., 1937).

[25] Edward S. Bordin, "Diagnosis in Counseling and Psychotherapy," *Educational and Psychological Measurement,* Vol. 6 (Summer, 1946), pp. 169–184.

job, whether to take a course this semester or next. Bordin suggests that treatment includes aid in attaining insight and acceptance of the fact of feeling inadequate to cope with the problem and in obtaining experiences that will make it possible to work the problem out.

2. *Lack of information.* Sheer restriction in range or appropriateness of experience or in special opportunities to acquire necessary skills is found in this category. The client is accustomed to accepting and making decisions but faces a decision involving information or special skills out of the reach of his experience. He may lack the opportunities to compare himself with representative groups necessary to judge his abilities, or lack sufficient information about occupations to set his sights realistically, or lack knowledge of appropriate social behavior. Bordin suggests that when the ignorance is real and sufficient to account for the difficulty, treatment can be direct: the information can be given or the client referred to source materials or other individuals.

3. *Self-conflict.* Conflicts between self-concepts or between a self-concept and some other stimulus function are involved here. Individuals who fall in this category are unable to cope with problems arising from conflict between the response functions associated with two or more of their self-concepts or between a self-concept and some other stimulus function. Treatment is by nondirective techniques which enable the client to recognize and accept conflicting feelings.

4. *Choice anxiety.* The need to decide among alternative plans all of which upset present life defines this category. Individuals are usually fully informed of all alternatives open to them but come to the counselor hoping to find an alternative that will represent a way out without unpleasant social consequences. Problems of this type increase in incidence during periods of social upheaval and rapid change (e.g., military draft). Bordin suggests that treatment indicated is to let them talk it out and help them face and accept the fact that there is no escape without unpleasantness.

5. *No problem.* Some individuals will seek out the counselor in the same spirit as they visit a doctor once a year for a physical checkup. They are playing safe, or they use the contact as an occasion for making up their minds.

Bordin's categories were based more upon *source* of difficulty than on *kind* of difficulty (see Williamson's categories).

Pepinsky's Classification Pepinsky modified Bordin's categories and tested them out.[26] For "no problem" he suggested that "lack of assurance" be substituted. Individuals who have made a decision but who wish to play safe by checking with others would fall in this category. Pepinsky added a "lack of skill" category and further subdivided self-conflict into cultural, interpersonal, and intrapersonal.

Missouri Diagnostic Classification According to Callis,[27] Berezin[28] contended that neither the Williamson-Darley categories nor the Bordin-Pepinsky categories were adequate but that a two-way classification scheme utilizing both could be useful in counseling. Berezin constructed such a scheme and tested it against actual case data. Callis also reported that Apostal and Miller modified and simplified Berezin's scheme and again tested it against case data.[29] Callis describes the system and its use. The "Missouri Diagnostic Classification" is a two-dimensional scheme in which problem-goal and cause are indicated. The problem-goal dimension is (1) vocational, (2) emotional, and (3) educational and specifies not only the type of problem dealt with but also the practical goal of counseling. This dimension refers to the developed problem

[26] Harold B. Pepinsky, "The Selection and Use of Diagnostic Categories in Clinical Counseling," *Applied Psychological Monographs,* No. 15 (February, 1948).
[27] Callis, *op. cit.*
[28] Annable G. Berezin, "The Development and Use of a System of Diagnostic Categories in Counseling," unpublished doctoral dissertation, University of Missouri, 1957.
[29] R. A. Apostal and J. G. Miller, "A Manual for the Use of a Set of Diagnostic Categories" (Columbia: University of Missouri Testing and Counseling Service Report, No. 21, 1959) (mimeographed).

which the counselor and client agree to pursue; it is not necessarily the presenting problem. Callis' definitions of the three categories of this dimension follows:

Vocational (VOC) — Career choice and planning, choice of college major and similar educational planning which would ultimately implement or lead to a career plan. *Emotional* (EM) — Personal and social adjustment problems which have a primary affective component. Problems of adjustment to current situations involving emotions, attitudes and feelings. *Educational* (ED) — Lack of effective study skills and habits, poor reading ability or lack of information about institutional policies and regulations. Primarily concerned with adjustment to current academic situations rather than planning for future.[30]

Categories in the other dimension refer to the probable cause of the developed problem and attempt to answer such questions as "Why is the client unable to solve his problem within his own personal resources?" or "What is the inadequacy in the client's behavior repertoire?"

The five categories in this dimension and associated commentary are summarized as follows:

1. *Lack of information about or understanding of self* (LIS). Emphasis is upon relatively uncomplicated lack of information. The client simply does not know enough about himself in relation to certain groups.

2. *Lack of information about or understanding of the environment* (LIE). While similar to LIS, this refers to environment rather than self and includes lack of educational and occupational information. LIE may result from lack of experiences, gaps in training, or exposure to incomplete or biased propaganda. Clients who persistently distort available information about the environment would more accurately be diagnosed LIS or CS.

3. *Motivational conflict within self* (CS). Conflicting and competing motivations within self and contradictory attitudes toward self predominate. Intrapunitive attitudes, self-depreciation, anxiety, and depression are suggestive of this category. There is a gap between the client's perceived self and ideal self.

4. *Conflict with significant others* (CO). Conflict with parents, teachers, roommates, girl friends, or boy friends are common in this category. In addition, conflicts with new subcultural groups and movement from one geographic region to another or from one socioeconomic level to another may produce CO.

5. *Lack of skill* (LS). Individuals who lack skill to meet the demands imposed by their particular situation, whether educational, social, or vocational, are diagnosed LS. Poor reading ability, poor study skills, poor social skills are typical, but problems which are primarily motivational are not classified LS.

Callis indicates that since not all counseling cases can be described by one problem and one cause, his scheme makes provisions for indicating multiple problems and multiple causes. While acknowledging that the ultimate use of any diagnostic classification is in the differential choice of treatment, Callis states that the major use currently being made of his diagnostic plan is in record keeping for both training and research purposes. Some questions which the University of Missouri Testing and Counseling Center are investigating and which depend upon a diagnostic classification are: "What is the nature of our case load?" "How much time per case is devoted to different types of cases?" "Do counseling centers serving different kinds of populations (e.g., high school, college, hospital, rehabilitation agency) generate a different pattern (proportion) of diagnosis?"[31]

ESSENTIAL CHARACTERISTICS OF A DIAGNOSTIC SCHEME

Any diagnostic system must reliably classify subjects among its categories. Different judges should agree in the assignment of subjects. Most current schemes fail in this respect. Even for a gross classification, Hunt and his associates report

[30] Callis, *op. cit.*, p. 239.

[31] *Ibid.*, pp. 241–242.

only 54 per cent agreement on classifying patients as psychotic, neurotic, or personality disorder and only 32.6 per cent agreement on more specific diagnoses.[32]

Some years ago Bordin cited three characteristics which diagnostic classifications of personality problems should possess.[33] First, the classification should enable the counselor to understand more clearly the significance of the individual's behavior. In this way the counselor can be sensitized and respond more adequately to the feelings of the client.

Second, the diagnostic constructs should be mutually exclusive. Categories should not overlap but should vary independently. The more they vary independently, the closer they are assumed to be to the true causes and the farther from surface symptoms. There should be homogeneity of subjects within categories and heterogeneity of subjects among categories. In other words, a classification system should result in greater variance among categories than within categories. Few current diagnostic schemes meet this requirement because clients within the same category vary almost as much as those with different diagnoses. Thus the basis of classification, i.e., symptoms, is not a particularly relevant variable. Classification should permit significant differential predictions about individuals in different categories. This prognostic factor is not normally found in most of the present systems.

Third, the category should form the basis for treatment. This most vital characteristic indicates that significant grouping would point to differences in treatment of subjects based upon exact knowledge of the etiology and nature of the disturbance.

Because most diagnostic systems devised to date fail to meet these criteria, it has often been suggested that attempts to construct and to use psychological diagnostic systems be abandoned. But apparently this advice is not strong enough to prevail against the desire to design such a system. Classification reflects man's need to simplify and to reduce complex information. In counseling, it would provide the basis for controlling cases and permit comparison of different treatments.

DIAGNOSIS AS A COMPREHENSIVE PICTURE

Tyler believes that diagnosis should be thought of as a means of obtaining a comprehensive picture of the individual.[34] Used in this fashion, diagnosis would involve understanding the image an individual projects so that intelligent action could be taken. From the first moment of contact, the counselor begins forming a working image of the counselee. Impressions — of his development to date, of the nature of his interpersonal relationships, of his work — go into this picture and sensitize the counselor to alternate courses of action. The outcomes of tests, interviews, observations, and background data modify the image and fill in the details.

Tyler further suggests that diagnosis may be seen as the counselor's asking himself such questions as "Shall I continue working with this client?" or "What does he need most?" She points out that the diagnostic act in and of itself does not help. For example, the counselor's knowledge of a person's fears does not remove the fears. Any diagnosis must assume that somewhere, sometime the counselee is going to be able to use that diagnosis.

Patterson, however, cautions against extending the concept of diagnosis as understanding of the client because it represents a failure to distinguish *understanding of* from *knowledge about* a client.[35] Diagnostic knowledge or understanding, according to Patterson, is understanding from an external view and represents knowledge about a client rather than knowing him. Moreover, it contains an evaluative element which is detrimental to counseling.

[32] W. A. Hunt, C. L. Sittson, and Edna B. Hunt, "A Theoretical and Practical Analysis of the Diagnostic Process," in P. H. Hoch and J. Zubin (eds.), *Current Problems in Psychiatric Diagnosis* (New York: Grune & Stratton, Inc., 1953), p. 51.
[33] Bordin, *op. cit.*

[34] Tyler, *op. cit.*, pp. 65–72.
[35] Patterson, *op. cit.*, p. 229.

STRUCTURAL DIAGNOSIS

Diagnosis in counseling has been extended to mean interpreting case data. Williamson used the term to refer to the "pattern of consistency" which helps to explain or describe the client's behavior. After data analysis, the counselor selects, from the mass of case data, the relevant facts which form the basis for a prognosis and a plan for later counseling.

CAUTIONS IN USING DIAGNOSIS

Brammer and Shostrom cite and discuss five cautions in respect to diagnostic endeavor: (1) the tendency of the counselor to overextend himself when data are incomplete or inaccurate, (2) the tendency to become preoccupied with the history of the client and to neglect present attitudes and current behavior, (3) the temptation to utilize tests too quickly to facilitate diagnosis, (4) the tendency to lose sight of the counselee's individuality and to become preoccupied with morbidity rather than healthy behavior, and (5) the tendency to show a judgmental attitude toward the client.[36]

Bordin has rejected Rogers' view of diagnosis as being detrimental to counseling relationships.[37] He believes that diagnosis does not automatically mean being judgmental and nonaccepting. Bordin points out that the client's perceptual awareness is only part of his experience and that preoccupation with his own perceptions may lead the counselor to gain superficial rather than penetrating understanding.

SUMMARY

Whether to diagnose or not is a question which has produced much heated discussion during the past few years. The concept "diagnosis" can be considered from many levels and viewpoints. In its broadest sense, however, a certain amount of informal diagnosis takes place within all counseling relationships. The school counselor, for example, who gives consideration to whether he should continue working with a student or refer him for more extensive help may be said to be engaged in diagnosis. The counselor who gathers information from a counselee to help him select a particular interest or personality test in order to provide him with needed information may be engaged in diagnosis. Diagnosis, then, is not necessarily used to ascertain a basic cause or to determine the best method of treatment. It may simply be the counselor's succession of hypotheses as to what is taking place in the thinking and attitude changes of the counselee. In this sense the significance of the affective changes expressed by the counselee would be grasped and responded to by the counselor, and thus the relationship between diagnosis (understanding) and counseling seems close. The two processes generally operate concurrently, with one influencing the other. Diagnosis is a developing process, not a discrete event, and the counselor learns (about) the individual as he assists him.

[36] Lawrence M. Brammer and Everett L. Shostrom, *Therapeutic Psychology*, 2nd ed. (Englewood Cliffs, N.J.: Prentice-Hall, Inc., 1968), pp. 151–152.
[37] Edward S. Bordin, *Psychological Counseling* (New York: Appleton-Century-Crofts, Inc., 1955), pp. 134–135.

Transference and Countertransference

A fundamental process in Freudian psychoanalysis is *transference*, or the process whereby the patient displaces his feelings toward a significant person in his life onto the psychoanalyst. For example, the patient shifts the love or hatred that he had experienced for a parent to the analyst. It is essential to recognize that this process goes on in the life of an individual in his relationships with others; unresolved negative feelings toward parents may express themselves in a person's relationships with authority figures.

The resolution of transference is crucial in the classical Freudian therapeutic process. The "working through" of feelings projected onto the therapist is viewed as the key to developing or relearning appropriate and realistic reactions necessary to adequate adjustment. In treatment the patient reexamines previously held attitudes and, through the mechanism of insight, establishes more constructive attitudes and feelings.

Psychoanalysis has long recognized that positive and negative transference may develop in the therapist as well as in the patient. When this occurs, it is referred to as *countertransference.* In countertransference the therapist projects his biases, prejudices, and attitudes onto the patient. Countertransference may interfere with or be destructive to the patient's progress. Countertransference in the therapist may take a variety of forms, depending on the character structure of the analyst and the content with which he deals. In its purest sense, the term is applied only to those situations where the therapist projects feelings unresolved in his own personality onto the patient. Normal reactions of warmth, affection, or anger are excluded from this category unless they become extreme or inappropriate. Countertransference problems in therapy are commonly resolved through insight by the therapist, achieved either independently or in the supervisory process.

Since counseling is not "depth therapy" in the same sense as psychoanalysis — that is, therapy directed toward personality reconstruction — the concepts of transference and countertransference are not directly applicable. However, these concepts do have implications for what occurs in counseling, for the simple reason that the human relationship is involved in both psychoanalysis and counseling.

Counselors do not intentionally foster transference in their clients as do classically oriented psychoanalysts — the latter actively encourage its development as a necessary and integral part of treatment. Unless the counselor has a full Freudian orientation, he is far more likely to view what the Freudian sees as transference as a manifestation of dependency or positive and negative attitudes. As such, he deals with these attitudes as he would any other attitudes expressed in the relationship. The most common approach is through the use of interpretation which encourages client insight into the inappropriateness of extreme positive or negative feelings toward the counselor. The client-centered counselor views such attitudes as stemming from misperceptions of the relationship, and he believes they will correct themselves if the counselor reacts to them with understanding and acceptance. These responses lead to recognition by the client that transference attitudes exist within himself and have no basis or utility in the reality of the relationship.

Test Use and Interpretation

This book is not designed to familiarize students with basic measurement principles or to present commonly used tests in counseling. Other books and other courses exist for those functions. Here the concern is with test use and interpretation.

Some counseling viewpoints consider the use and interpretation of tests inimical, or at best of limited value, to counseling. Generally opponents of testing maintain that (1) testing encourages client dependency upon the counselor and upon an external source for solution to his problems, (2) test data prejudice the counselor's picture of an individual, and (3) test data are invalid and unreliable enough so that their value is severely limited. It is sometimes maintained that if tests are used or if a test interpretation is given, counseling as such is interrupted or terminated. But from the huge number sold in the United States it appears that most counselors must be using tests in counseling or in other ways. Not all of them, of course, were sold to or used by counselors.

Goldman views the utilization of tests in counseling as flawed. He likens it to a marriage that failed or, even more colorfully, one that was never consummated. Goldman assigns the failure to the following causes: (1) tests were designed initially for selection rather than prediction purposes, (2) the special environmental handicaps suffered by too many disadvantaged populations make the use of tests useless with them, and (3) too few counselors have the requisite knowledge and competencies to tease out and use the subtle information available from current tests.[38] Needless to say, the panel members — counselors, psychologists, test authors — who heard of Goldman's proposition argued strenuously against it by (1) stressing the validity, reliability, and utility of test data, (2) suggesting that the current deemphasis on testing represents an overreaction to test deficiencies, and (3) recommending more extensive treatment of test and measurement theory and practice in counselor education programs.[39]

CRITICISMS AND HARMFUL CONSEQUENCES

The increasing use of tests has been accompanied by a flow of critical comment, for which the present authors cited the following reasons:

> *First,* tests in and of themselves vary in quality and are far from perfect measuring instruments. . . . *Second,* tests are sometimes improperly administered. . . . *Third,* test scores are often misused. . . . *Fourth,* test data are sometimes misinterpreted. . . . *Fifth,* in many instances tests are improperly safeguarded.[40]

Ebel has summarized four harmful consequences of testing suggested by critics:

> It may place an indelible stamp of intellectual status — superior, mediocre or inferior — on a child, and thus predetermine his social status as an adult, and possibly do irreparable harm to his self esteem and his educational motivation.
> It may lead to a narrow conception of ability, encourage pursuit of a single goal, and thus tend to reduce the diversity of talent available to society.
> It may place the testers in a position to control education and determine the destinies of individual human beings, while incidentally making the testers themselves rich in the process.
> It may encourage impersonal, inflexible, mechanistic processes of evaluation and determination, so that essential human freedoms are limited or lost altogether.[41]

FUNCTIONS OF TESTS IN COUNSELING

The use of tests in counseling has been advocated for several purposes.

1. Tests may be used to help the counselor decide whether the counselee's needs are within the range of his services. Some counseling centers, as part of an intake service, routinely collect precounseling diagnostic data to help determine the locus and severity of the problem. Personality inventories and problem checklists may facilitate this rough screening. Sometimes quick estimates of the individual's intellectual functioning are made.
2. Tests may be used for informational purposes to assist the individual to gain self-understanding. Counselees may request or counselors may decide that tests will be used to help the counselee secure information about his abilities, aptitudes, interests, and personal characteristics. Lister and Ohlsen, investigating the extent to which test interpretation improved self-understanding of pupils in grades five, seven, nine, and eleven, reported that at all grade levels interpretation was associated with increased accuracy of self-estimates of achievement, intelligence, and interests.[42]
3. Tests may be used to help the counselor gain a better understanding of the individual. Estimations of the counselee's scholastic ability, school achievement, interests, and personality are often used to support data obtained through other means.
4. Tests may be used to help determine which methods, approaches, tools, and techniques will be suitable. Diagnosis is sometimes aided by the use of personality inventories. The individual's unique

[38] Leo Goldman, "Tests and Counseling: The Marriage that Failed," *Measurement and Evaluation in Guidance,* Vol. 4 (January, 1972), pp. 213–220.
[39] "Symposium: Tests and Counseling — The Marriage that Failed?" *Measurement and Evaluation in Guidance,* Vol. 5 (October, 1972), pp. 394–429.
[40] Bruce Shertzer and Shelley C. Stone, *Fundamentals of Guidance* 2nd ed. (Boston: Houghton Mifflin Company, 1971), p. 263.
[41] Robert L. Ebel, "The Social Consequences of Educational Testing," in Alexander C. Wesman (Chairman), *Proceedings of the 1963 Invitational Conferences on Testing Problems* (Princeton, N.J.: Educational Testing Service, 1964), p. 134.
[42] James L. Lister and Merle M. Ohlsen, "The Improvement of Self Understanding Through Test Interpretation," *Personnel and Guidance Journal,* Vol. 43 (April, 1965), pp. 804–810.

patterns of thinking and feeling may be uncovered by tests which indicate his basic character structure. Certainly diagnostic tests in such skill areas as reading and arithmetic give information around which to plan remedial help and counseling.

5. Tests may be used to help counselees predict future performance such as college success, work potential — as secretary or clerk, for example — performance in mechanical occupations, and the like. Tests provide an improved basis for prediction regarding the likelihood of success in those activities in which prospective performance can be measured.

6. Tests may be used to help counselees arrive at decisions in planning their educational and vocational futures. This is the major use of tests in counseling. If counseling deals with facts and with the individual's feelings about them, tests can yield information about the individual relative to the facts of an educational or vocational program. For the person who really means it when he says "I don't know what to do," test data help identify possible courses of action. They may be used to evaluate two or more alternatives or to help determine or confirm the suitability of a tentative choice, plan, or decision. Test data may reveal limitations of ability, unexpected assets, or inappropriate interests or aptitudes, all of which are relevant for counseling.

7. Tests may be used to stimulate interests not previously considered in counseling. Many high school counselors use interest inventories with students to stimulate further thinking about the work world and their interest in it. Some students learn from test interpretations about their previously unsuspected potentialities for further education or certain occupations. Or school counselors use test interpretation sessions to communicate their interest in students and to make known their availability to discuss any matter with the student.

8. Tests are sometimes used to help evaluate the outcomes of counseling. In attempting to assess the worth of their work, many counselors have turned to test data. The usual approach involves testing before and after counseling with the use of appropriate control groups. Psychological measures that have been employed include tests of achievement, social and emotional adjustment, self-concept, and social attitudes.

GUIDELINES FOR TEST USE

The individual who reads this book has no doubt been exposed innumerable times to guidelines for the use of tests. Consequently, only a few remarks will be made here. First, if tests are to be part of counseling, the counselor should know well whatever instrument is to be used — what it measures, its validity, reliability, norm group, error of measurement, administrative procedures, scoring methods, and so on. Second, the reasons why a counselee or a counselor thinks a test would be helpful should be fully explored. What are the expectations for the data once they are obtained? How will the data be used? Is a test the best, most efficacious means of obtaining the information needed? Third, the counselor should be sure that the counselee possesses at least a gross understanding of what the test measures — ability, interest, personality, or whatever. Fourth, the counselee should have some idea of the test's strengths and limitations so that his expectations are appropriate to the data elicited. The explanations of this and the preceding point to the counselee should be given in nontechnical language. Fifth, the administration and scoring should be done carefully and thoroughly. Finally, the use of tests by the counselor should be guided by ethical considerations: he provides only those services which he is qualified to render, and consideration is given to the client's well-being and welfare. Most of all, the counselor should remember that the purpose of administering tests is to help the counselee understand himself. Test data are to be used by the counselee because they provide information which he needs and wants and which is relevant to his situation.

TEST SELECTION IN COUNSELING

In by far the greater number of school situations, school-wide tests have been given prior to the initiation of a counseling relationship. But many college and agency counseling centers employ a psychometrist who administers needed testing. In such cases the counseling contact is often interrupted for a period of days or weeks. Our concern here is with test selection as part of the counseling relationship. Basically, the same principles — understanding, acceptance, and communication — that characterize the counseling relationship apply equally to test selection.

A frequent response to the counselor's query as to why the client has come to the counseling office is "I'd like to take some tests to find out what jobs I'd be good at" or "My mother said you could give me some tests which would tell me what I could do" or "Mrs. White said that since I wasn't doing too good in algebra I should come down and take some tests to see whether I should stay in it." This heavy reliance on a test orientation confronts counselors in almost every setting. Since the individual thinks tests will help him, all too often the counselor assumes the same thing and proceeds to test selection. Clearly, careful exploration of the client's request is in order to determine whether tests are really needed or will be useful. If a test is appropriate, client participation in its selection may somewhat alleviate his dependency feelings and obviate the prescriptive role fostered when counselors select tests on their own. Client participation in test selection has long been advocated, and Goldman has summarized the arguments for it. The first three of the advantages listed below were presented by Bordin, the remaining five by Goldman:

1. Clients may not return for further interviews if tests are planned without their participation. (This happens when the individual is not emotionally ready to subject himself to realistic scrutiny or is unprepared for reality testing or fails to understand the relationship between the test and his problems.)
2. Clients who feel convinced of the purpose of testing can gain insights from self-observation during testing.
3. Motivation to do his best on tests is strongest when the individual sees the relationship between them and his goals.
4. To the extent that the client has participated in the decisions to use tests, he will be more ready to accept later interpretations with a minimum of defensiveness.
5. Where dependency is a problem, complete counselor responsibility for test planning does nothing to deal with the problem of dependency except perhaps to reinforce it.
6. Where indecisiveness is a problem, with the client fearing to make a decision either because of lack of confidence in his judgment or because of lack of successful experience in decision-making, he needs the experience of making decisions.
7. . . . the client's reactions to suggestions and descriptions of various tests may provide a wealth of diagnostic data.
8. Finally, a better job of test selection is done in terms of the tests selected.[43]

Goldman has also cited the main arguments against client participation in the selection of tests:

1. All this is much ado about nothing; it makes little difference what process is used so long as the most appropriate tests are administered and skillfully interpreted.
2. Because decisions as to the use of tests require knowledge and competencies which few clients have in this area, they must be made by the counselor.
3. The client is much too emotionally involved with his problems to make objective decisions as to the testing part of planning.
4. Dependency and indecisiveness are not problems with which the counselor legitimately should deal; they more properly are the domain of psychotherapy.[44]

The effect of counselee participation in test selection in relationship to other variables has received a limited amount of investigation. Generally, the findings are contradictory and inconclusive. Seeman reported that college students who selected tests themselves (counselor described each test's values and limitations in a neutral, nonpersuasive manner) each chose a mean number of 5.71 tests (out of 25 available) while a control group took a

[43] Bordin, *Psychological Counseling,* pp. 267–268, and Leo Goldman, *Using Tests in Counseling,* 2nd ed. (New York: Appleton-Century-Crofts, Inc., 1971), pp. 41–42. Copyright © 1971 by Meredith Corporation.
[44] Goldman, *op. cit.,* p. 43.

mean number of 4.70 each.[45] The difference was not significant, but the experimental group took a significantly greater variety of tests, which suggests that they were more discriminating as to their individual needs than were counselors of the controls. Further, tests selected by the student were judged to be suitable (93.2 per cent of possible cases) for making either actuarial or clinical predictions of the client's stated objectives. In another article Seeman reports further on these same subjects.[46] Through a questionnaire, subjects were asked to give reactions to the first interview and to make judgments about the value of each test. More students who had selected their own tests than control students reported the first interview different from their expectations, but no significant difference was found in the extent to which they felt positively about the interview. Experimental subjects reported no more learning than control students nor did they rate tests as any more valuable.

Gustad and Tuma reported no significant difference among three groups of clients (ranging from client selection to counselor selection of tests) and the dependent variable, learning about self.[47]

Logic would seem to be on the side of encouraging counselee participation if only to demonstrate the counselor's belief in the counselee's ability to make decisions and judgments that affect him. But some counselors may find client selection of tests incompatible with their counseling style. The "best" way of test selection is the way in which the counselor feels comfortable and competent so that the operation is not bumbling or awkward. It should be clear that those who advocate counselee participation in test selection do not mean that the counselee decides which specific test is the better measure. This technical responsibility rightfully belongs to the counselor. As Goldman suggests,

> An approach that seems to us to have considerable merit is to ask counselees to participate in specifying alternate *courses of action* and *questions* about these alternatives. Some of these questions have nothing to do with tests, as for example, "What salaries are usual in pharmacy?" or "Which colleges offer courses in hotel management?" For those questions which may be answerable by tests, as "What are my chances of doing well in retailing?" the counselor indicates which tests can provide answers and the nature of the answers. The client can participate in deciding, first, whether this is a question he wishes answered. Second, he can participate in thinking about whether a particular kind of predictive information is already available, in his record or his memory, and if not, whether he then wants to try those tests which would be appropriate.[48]

TEST INTERPRETATION

Research studies have sought to determine the most effective means of communicating test results. Individual, group, and written interpretations have been compared. Folds and Gazda[49] replicated a prior study[50] which compared individual, group, and written interpretations on accuracy of recall of test scores and change in concepts of self and others. In both studies a control group (no test interpretation received) was used. Subjects were female college students, and standardized tests used were the Cooperative School and College Ability Test, Edwards Personal Preference Schedule, and the Bills Index of Adjustment and Values.

> The results of the "exploratory" study and the "replication" study which attempted to measure the effectiveness and efficiency of three methods of test interpre-

[45] Julius Seeman, "A Study of Client Self-Selection of Tests in Vocational Counseling," *Educational and Psychological Measurement*, Vol. 8 (Autumn, 1948), pp. 327–346.

[46] Julius Seeman, "An Investigation of Client Reactions to Vocational Counseling," *Journal of Consulting Psychology*, Vol. 13 (April, 1949), pp. 95–104.

[47] J. W. Gustad and A. H. Tuma, "The Effects of Different Methods of Test Introduction and Interpretation on Client Learning in Counseling," *Journal of Counseling Psychology*, Vol. 4 (Winter, 1957), pp. 313–317.

[48] Goldman, *op. cit.*, p. 53.

[49] Jonell H. Folds and George M. Gazda, "A Comparison of the Effectiveness and Efficiency of Three Methods of Test Interpretation," *Journal of Counseling Psychology*, Vol. 13 (Fall, 1966), pp. 318–324.

[50] George M. Gazda and Jonell H. Folds, "The Effects of Three Methods of Test Interpretation on the Recall of Test Scores and Change in Self Concept," *Journal of Student Personnel Association for Teacher Education*, Vol. 4 (December, 1964), pp. 10–21.

tation were strikingly similar: (a) for all variables which showed significant change, no significant decline in accuracy of self-estimate was noted over an eight-week follow-up period; (b) the change in the concept of self and others was not significantly different for any of the three experimental groups nor the control group; and (c) those receiving individual interpretations evaluated the "coverage" of the test interpretations as significantly more complete than those receiving group or written interpretations.

The results of the two research studies suggest that, if recall of test information is used as a criterion of test interpretation effectiveness, individual, small group and written reports are equally effective. However, if one judges effectiveness on the basis of how the student felt about the interpretation, there is a positive relationship between amount of student satisfaction and amount of individual or personal attention received by the student.[51]

Hills and Williams hypothesized that communication of educational-vocational test results would bring about substantive changes in self-perceptions of counselees engaged in brief counseling contacts. Tests include the Strong Vocational Interest Blank, the Kuder Preference Record, and the Differential Aptitude Tests, and other measures when appropriate. Experimental measures were Self-Ideal-Ordinary scores, obtained before and after counseling. The self-perceptions of 45 subjects who read written summaries of test results and who were given the Self-Ideal-Ordinary evaluation before completing counseling were compared to self-perceptions of other counselees receiving other treatments. The results indicated that communication of test results did not lead to positive changes in self-perception. Test results which differed from clients' preconceived notions of themselves appeared to have a negative effect.[52]

Some years ago Bixler and Bixler identified two crucial aspects of test interpretation: (1) presenting test results and their predictive possibilities in a manner understandable to the client and (2) selecting the methodology of dealing with the client in order to facilitate his use of this information. They recommended that counselors should

1. Give the client simple statistical predictions based upon the test data.
2. Allow the client to evaluate the prediction as it applies to himself.
3. Remain neutral toward test data and the client's reaction.
4. Facilitate the client's self-evaluation and subsequent decisions by the use of therapeutic procedures.
5. Avoid persuasive methods. Test data should provide motivation – not the counselor.[53]

What the counselor knows about a test or an inventory and how he administers and interprets it determine how effectively it will work for his counselees. Professionally competent counselors validate test data against other counselee information secured from records, interviews, observation, and other test situations.

The counselee's use of test results depends upon his understanding and acceptance of test data. Because the counselee is ill informed about test scores or profiles, the counselor must decide what he is to be told and how test data should be discussed. If the data are to be useful to the counselee, he must be able to accept and use them to change behavior or make future choices. Clearly, he can do so only if the counselor's language about the meaning of test scores minimizes threat, which is not uncommonly involved in test interpretation sessions. Basically, this means that the counselor communicates test data objectively, without introducing judgments in the meaning of the test scores.

Some counselors have found it helpful to present personality and interest inventory scores that are above or below the average part of the normative group graphically. For most personality or interest inventories this means scores below the

[51] Folds and Gazda, *op. cit.*, p. 323.

[52] David A. Hills and John E. Williams, "Effects of Test Information upon Self-Evaluation in Brief Educational-Vocational Counseling," *Journal of Counseling Psychology*, Vol. 12 (Fall, 1965), pp. 275–281.

[53] Ray H. Bixler and Virginia H. Bixler, "Test Interpretation in Vocational Counseling," *Educational and Psychological Measurement*, Vol. 6 (Spring, 1946), pp. 145–155.

16th percentile and above the 84th percentile. Such scores vary enough from the norm to reflect ways the individual differs from the middle two-thirds of the norm group. A simple expedient is to draw lines across the profile and say, "Unless scores are above or below these lines, they do not describe the individual as being different from most people on whom the inventory was standardized." Most counselees will infer that if their personality or interest inventory score is not in the "normal group" they are abnormal. It is better, therefore, to avoid use of the word "normal" in discussing personality and interest inventory scores.

In interpreting any test — personality, interest, ability, aptitude — the beginning counselor may find it helpful to experiment for a while with terms with which he feels comfortable and which are simple enough to be understood by his counselees. In brief, scores should be discussed and interpretations given in simple, lay terminology. It may be noted that when the counselor uses the same words over and over to convey the meaning of scores to different counselees he is likely to feel that his interpretations are becoming boring. But he, of course, is the only one who hears the same description repeatedly. After finding a useful way of describing a score to counselees, he should use it.

Whether a counselor discusses scores in the third person, i.e., "People with scores like these tend to . . . ,"depends upon his style and his perceptions of what the counselee can best accept and use. Through self-evaluation of his interview tapes, he can discover interpretative methods most suitable to him. In addition, his knowledge of a particular counselee will permit him to judge what the latter will be comfortable in discussing.

After interpreting the meaning of a given score it is advisable to pause to ascertain whether the counselee wants to discuss it in greater detail or understands it. While observation of the counselee's verbal and nonverbal behavior provides cues to the reception of the information, the counselor may not always be sure but can ask, "Is this clear?" or "Would you like me to run through that again?"

It should be recognized that not all counselees will accept the test results. The individual may not react in a logical, coherent manner to results that are unfavorable or different from what was expected. Test data may be threatening and reacted to as individuals respond to threat: with anger, rejection, withdrawal, disbelief, etc. Whatever emotional reaction — satisfaction, doubt, fear — is evoked by the counselor's description of test data, it is his responsibility to deal with these attitudes just as he deals with other emotional components encountered in other counseling situations. Essentially this means that the counselee is given an opportunity to verbalize his feelings and attitudes and that the counselor recognizes and responds to them. The counselee's feelings cannot be ignored or responded to by defending the validity of the instrument used. Rather the counselor accepts the feelings as feelings and responds to them in ways that are helpful to the counselee.

Organization of test data is essential if the two problems identified by Bixler and Bixler are to be met with any degree of success. Some means of coherently presenting test data are needed if they are to be incorporated into the counselee's experience, and a test profile form (see Figure 13.1) is one such means. Some counselors have the individual complete the profile as the data are communicated to him. Profiles have the advantage of keeping the test results directly in front of the counselee and encouraging integration of the data during the interpretation. They also insure that all the necessary information is discussed and thus serve as a reminder to the counselor to deal with all scores and their interrelationship as well as covering necessary points such as norm groups, type of scores used, etc. Data are not to be presented all at once. Most beginning counselors err in presenting test results too rapidly as though it were an unpleasant task which they wished to be rid of. The individual has to have time to absorb the meanings and think through the implications.

Goldman has outlined four dimensions of test interpretation and identified the types of test validity associated with each.[54] The first is *descriptive.*

[54] Goldman, *op. cit.*, pp. 146–150.

Essentially it provides an interpretation of the kind of person the individual is — how he relates to people, how he handles numerical reasoning, what he likes to do, or how he compares to others. Descriptive interpretation depends upon construct, content, and concurrent validities. The second is *genetic*. It seeks to interpret how and why the individual became the way he is. Predictive validities are used in a postdictive manner — inferences as to what happened previously are made from a present score. The third type of interpretation is *predictive*, or what is likely to happen to an individual — e.g., how he might fare at college. Predictive interpretation is directly linked to predictive validity. Finally, there is *evaluative* interpretation, which involves advice from the counselor or presentation of his judgment as to what choice — should he marry, go to this college — the counselee should make. This particular type of interpretation differs from others, not in respect to types of validities upon which it is based, but in terms of whether the counselor makes recommendations.

Figure 13.1 Purdue Guidance Clinic test record profile

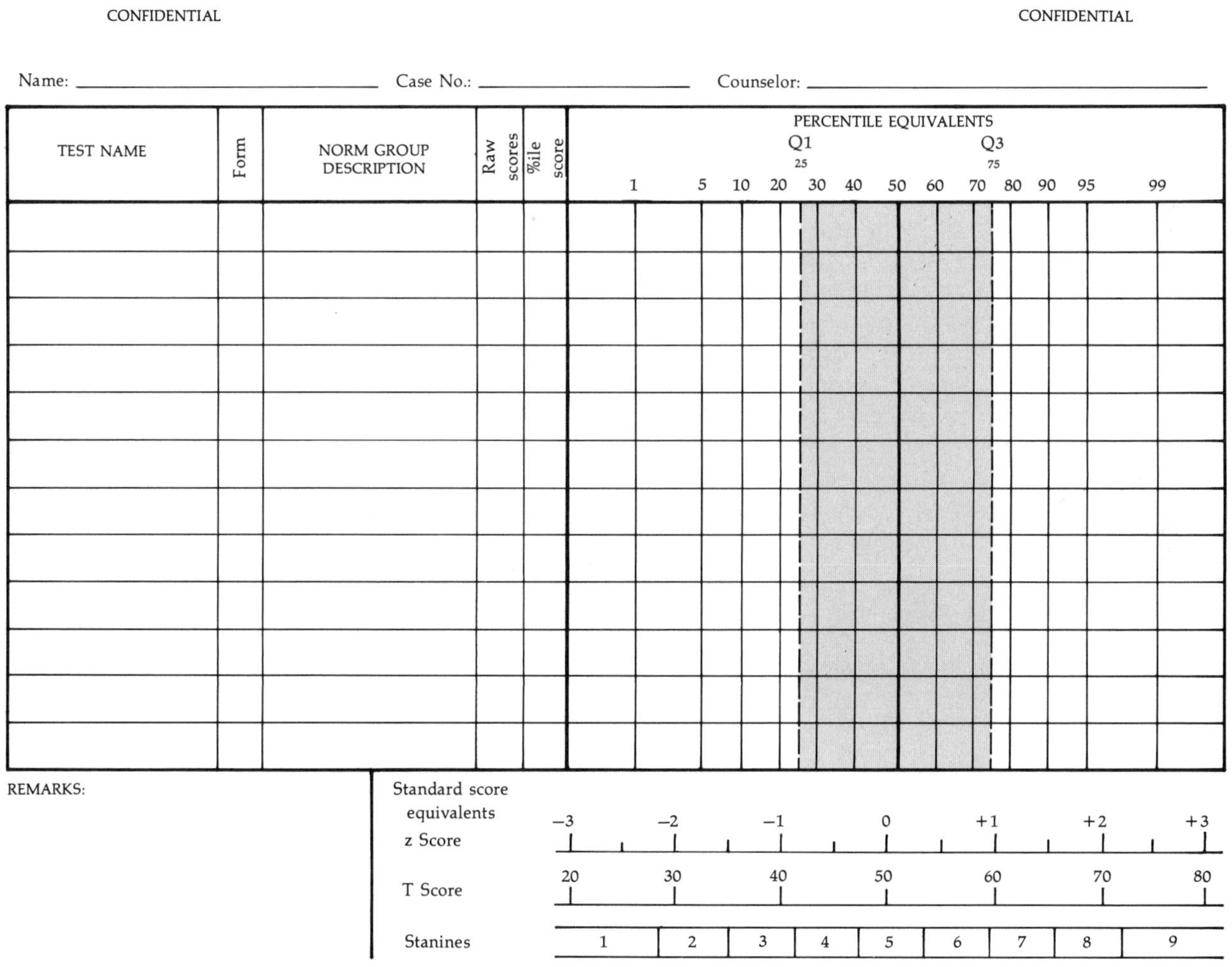

CONFIDENTIAL CONFIDENTIAL

Name: ______________ Case No.: ______________ Counselor: ______________

TEST NAME	Form	NORM GROUP DESCRIPTION	Raw scores	%ile score	PERCENTILE EQUIVALENTS Q1 (25) Q3 (75): 1 5 10 20 30 40 50 60 70 80 90 95 99

REMARKS:

Standard score equivalents

z Score: −3 −2 −1 0 +1 +2 +3

T Score: 20 30 40 50 60 70 80

Stanines: 1 2 3 4 5 6 7 8 9

Expectancy Tables Meaningful and clear interpretations of test data are the counselor's basic aim, and the use of expectancy tables is probably one of the most effective techniques available for providing them. An expectancy table can be constructed very easily by plotting scores on a specific test against scores on another criterion for a group of individuals. Expectancy tables require little mathematical or statistical sophistication for either developing or interpreting them. For example, if the raw scores on test ABC range from 1 to 60 and the grades in third-year English are available, all that is needed is a listing of the students that have taken the ABC Test and their grades in third-year English. Then an expectancy table can be drawn up showing the percentages of students receiving specific grades for the specific scores on the ABC Test (see Table 13.2). If a student receives a score of 32 on the test, other students who obtained scores in the same range (31–40) received the following marks: 15 per cent F's, 15 per cent D's, 40 per cent C's, 20 per cent B's, and 0 per cent A's. (The 0 per cent would be the least reliable because there is no score in this area, but it could be pointed out to the student that he might be the person to change the percentage.)

A score such as 32 could be interpreted in a number of ways; for example: "Students receiving scores like yours on the ABC Test have ranged from B to F; 15 per cent failed third-year English and 85 per cent passed; 60 per cent received marks of B or C." This is obviously more valuable than saying, "Your chances of passing are pretty good."

Table 13.2 Sample expectancy table

Raw scores		*Third-year English marks*			
ABC test	*F*	*D*	*C*	*B*	*A*
51–60	0%	5%	40%	40%	15%
41–50	10	15	40	25	10
31–40	15	15	50	20	0
21–30	30	30	30	10	0
11–20	80	20	0	0	0
1–10	90	10	0	0	0

Counselor Statements Byrn has developed examples of counselor statements that may be used to stimulate counselee thinking about test data and himself.[55]

The Test Interpretation – Planning Interview

1. Have confidence in the student's planning ability – even if he has shown little.
   Try: "What other information do you need about yourself before you decide?"
   Not: "Maybe we can decide what you should do by taking some tests."
2. Relate immediate plans to future plans – don't try to treat them separately.
   Try: "What can you do this year in high school to prepare for college later on?"
   Not: "Your grades aren't so good now but you have good engineering aptitude."
3. Make alternate plans sound respectable – not like second-rate crash programs.
   Try: "If that doesn't happen to work out, what else could you do?"
   Not: "If you fail in engineering you always could go back to drafting,"
4. Encourage the student to make his own plans –rather than to agree to yours.
   Try: "How do you suppose you would go about your idea of studying harder?"
   Not: "It looks to me like you've got to study a lot harder."
5. Remind girls of both career and homemaking plans – not just one or the other.
   Try: "How do you plan to work marriage and family into your future plans?"
   Not: "Your future seems all set with college and a career in journalism."
6. Open new educational and vocational doors – don't just close them to the student.
   Try: "There are 20,000 jobs besides engineering, many of which you can qualify for."
   Not: "You won't be able to get into engineering with your low grades."
7. Relate test data to other experiences – don't discuss them as abstractions.

[55] Delmont K. Byrn, "The Test Interpretation – Planning Interview," unpublished paper developed for use in training at the University of Michigan.

Try: "How does this fit in with your interests as you know them?"

Not: "That's the way your interests look. Any questions?"

8. Reflect on a student's rejection of low test scores – don't write off low performance.

Try: "You don't think this is your real ability? What other clues do you have?"

Not: "Tests aren't foolproof. There might have been a slip-up."

9. Get students involved in test interpretation – don't just recite the results.

Try: "What did you think of that test? How do you suppose you did?"

Not: "On this test you are at the 46%ile. On this one, the 23%ile."

10. Explain the purpose of the test in functional terms – not in psychological jargon.

Try: "This test allows you to compare yourself with H.S. juniors in numerical ability."

Not: "This DAT test, like the A.C.E., measures numerical perception."

11. Use test results in context with all other data – not as goals in themselves.

Try: "Add this test information to everything else you know about yourself."

Not: "According to these tests you should be in mechanical work."

12. Use test results for student planning – not for the counselor's diagnosis.

Try: "This allows you to compare yourself with other seniors in ability to learn."

Not: "This confirms my hunch that you would be able to succeed in college."

13. Refresh the student's memory on each test before discussing it – don't discuss it cold.

Try: "Remember this one on which you chose which things you liked best and least?"

Not: "On the Kuder you were high on persuasive and mechanical, low on artistic."

14. Relate scholastic aptitude to the school record – don't look only at test results.

Try: "With your ability you should be able to do A or B work with average effort."

Not: "Your grades haven't been good, but you have high aptitude for college."

15. Explain test results simply – don't use elaborate statistical devices.

Try: "This is high, this low, this average for seniors; here is about how you stand."

Not: "You fall within these fiducial limits. If you flip a coin 100 times, etc."

16. Express low test performance or unpleasant information honestly – but with perspective.

Try: "You are within the range of successful college students but well below average."

Not: "Only 20% of college students have less scholastic ability than you."

17. Turn test profile sheets so the student can read them – don't make him read upside down.

Try: (Read profile upside down yourself or follow along on a duplicate copy.)

Not: "Let's see if we can both read this profile." (both twisting)

18. Clearly establish interests as preferences – don't confuse them with ability.

Try: "You like these activities, dislike those." "Your interest patterns are –"

Not: "You are high in social service, low in mechanical."

19. Remember expressed and demonstrated interests – not just interest inventory results.

Try: "This inventory gives you another kind of picture of your interests."

Not: "This inventory shows where your interests lie."

20. Explain the Strong through occupational comparisons – not directly as with the Kuder.

Try: "You can compare your interest patterns right now (in 400 items) with those of established people in 45 different occupations."

Not: "You like accounting – probably because of math."

21. Regroup complicated profile scores – don't assume the student can assimilate them.

Try: "What are your high areas of interest? Low areas? Average ones?"

Not: "See all these red marks? What do you think of them?"

22. Have the student summarize often – don't do all the reviewing and organizing for him.

Try: "How would you summarize your interests as you see them right now?"

Not: "Your interests are highest in this, lowest in that area. Any questions?"

23. Let test interpretation be the beginning of career planning – not the end.

Try: "Now you should study occupations just as you have studied yourself."

Not: "Well, that's what the tests show. Are there any questions?"

Career Discussion Plan

Compare:

Self	with	*Occupations*
1. aptitudes		4. requirements
2. interests		5. opportunities
3. personality		6. atmosphere

Horst has described 11 things a counselor must know to predict accurately a counselee's chances for being successful in a particular activity. (1) He knows what kinds of things are to be done. (2) He knows what kinds of behaviors are regarded as desirable in what kinds of activities. That is, he knows what constitutes success in the various activities. (3) He has a way of indicating how desirable the various kinds of behaviors are even though these ways may be very crude. He has some way of making discriminations among behaviors. (4) The methods he has for discriminating among behaviors are reasonably consistent. He does not roll the dice or spin a roulette wheel in order to get numbers to characterize the performance of the client. (5) Whatever method the counselor uses, no matter how vague or crude, in evaluating behaviors in life activities, he does not arrive at evaluations with which other persons including the client will tend to agree. (6) He has some system — certain items of information — in terms of which he describes people, no matter how simple or complex. (7) He has ways of indicating to what degree these various things about people can exist. These may be very crude or they may take on any degree of refinement which he chooses. They may be all or none, more or less, yes or no, maybe yes — maybe no. (8) He has ways of knowing to what degree each of these things about people is true about a particular client. (9) He is somewhat consistent in evaluating the client with respect to each of his descriptive categories. He does not describe the same behavior as withdrawn one minute and extroverted the next. (10) He has a system for discriminating the variables, or quantifying them, such that there can be at least some measure of agreement with other observers. (11) Finally, he has a method, or system of methods, whereby he can combine or synthesize information about people in such a way that the synthesized information will indicate to what extent the client will exhibit desirable behaviors in the various activities available to him.[56] Horst explains each of these elements in detail and describes the counselor's responsibilities for knowing tests, criteria, and psychological differences well and for following up to determine his accuracy as a predictor.

Finally, it should be recognized that test interpretation in actual practice is far from being as logical or orderly as presented in this and other descriptions of it. There is considerable latitude in counselor test interpretative practices. Presumably, variability exists not only from counselor to counselor but from counselee to counselee because of the differing role each enacts during the activity. The extent of counselee participation is dependent not only upon counselor style or approach but also upon counselee personality and the interaction of his personality with that of the counselor.

Nontest Adjuncts to Counseling

Some principal adjuncts utilized in counseling are autobiography, personal data questionnaires, essays, sentence completion, and play media.

AUTOBIOGRAPHY

Production of an autobiography sometimes helps the counselee place in perspective the development of his current situation. The autobiography as a tool for understanding someone reveals not only patterns of behavior but, perhaps even more important, the personal attitudes and emotions behind the behavior. Undertaken in a cooperative manner by the counselee, it may provide insight

[56] Paul Horst, "Educational and Vocational Counseling from the Actuarial Point of View," *Personnel and Guidance Journal*, Vol. 35 (November, 1956), p. 167.

into the "inner person" — the individual's experiences and knowledge about himself. An autobiography is one's own written introspective account of his life.

The autobiography has a long history of providing source information for studying behavior. However, the rise of behaviorism in psychology relegated its use to the fringe area of scientific psychological data.

Most authorities classify autobiographies into two basic types — structured and unstructured. Naturally, it is possible to combine the two or to vary the degree of structure. Some call the two types controlled and uncontrolled; others label them systematic and unsystematic. The unstructured is perhaps the more fruitful for counseling purposes and may reveal many facets of personality not brought to the surface by other techniques. The autobiography is often difficult to interpret, particularly if the client does not present material in an organized way. Basically, the unstructured autobiography presents the individual's life without regard to specific questions. It is the individual's choice to write what he thinks has been important to him and the experiences that have had a bearing on his life. The structured autobiography is written according to an outline or in response to specific questions or topics provided by the counselor. It may be more useful for individuals who are not very verbal. Instructions or questions are given to the client to help him write about family history, personal history, major experiences, aims and aspirations, and the like.

Another way of classifying autobiographies is described by Annis.[57] The first category is *comprehensive*, and the individual covers a wide range of interrelated experiences over a relatively long period of his life. The second is *topical*, and he deals with a fairly specific theme, episode, or experience. Annis presents a graphic representation of autobiographies with respect to the degree of structure (see Fig. 13.2).

[57] Arthur P. Annis, "The Autobiography: Its Uses and Value in Professional Psychology," *Journal of Counseling Psychology*, Vol. 14 (January, 1967), pp. 9–17.

Figure 13.2 Graphic representation of an autobiographical typology

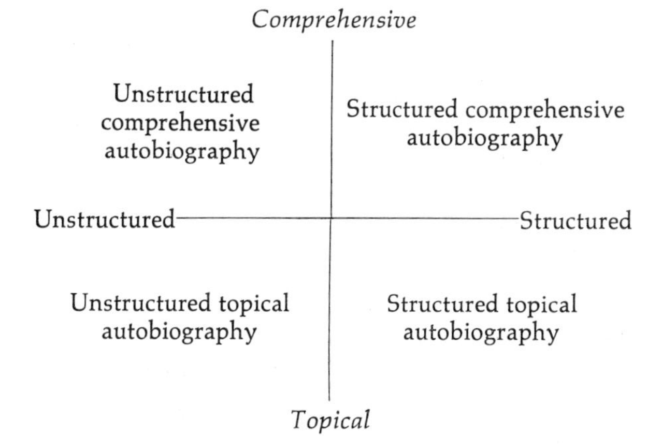

From Arthur P. Annis, "The Autobiography: Its Uses and Value in Professional Psychology," *Journal of Counseling Psychology*, Vol. 14 (January, 1967), p. 10. Copyright © 1967 by the American Psychological Association, and reproduced by permission.

Research on Autobiographies Danielson and Rothney compared structured and unstructured autobiographies written by 78 eleventh-grade students in an English class.[58] Their analysis dealt with the effectiveness of these two approaches in their ability to elicit students' problems in six areas. No significant difference was reported in four of the six problem areas. Significantly greater numbers of problems were found in "Family Relationships" in unstructured autobiographies and significantly more problems in "Education" in the structured approach. These authors concluded that selection of the autobiographical form was dependent upon the problem areas in which the counselor is interested.

Mueller, Schmieding and Schultz have also sought to determine which autobiographical form elicits the most useful responses.[59] Subjects were

[58] Paul J. Danielson and John W. M. Rothney, "The Student Autobiography: Structured or Unstructured?" *Personnel and Guidance Journal*, Vol. 33 (September, 1954), pp. 30–33.
[59] Richard J. Mueller, O. A. Schmieding, and John L. Schultz, "Four Approaches to Writing Autobiographies," *The School Counselor*, Vol. 11 (March, 1964), pp. 160–164.

203 ninth-grade students who wrote autobiographies and who were divided into groups as follows:

Group I — structured autobiography written in first person
Group II — structured autobiography written in third person
Group III — semistructured autobiography written in first person
Group IV — semistructured autobiography written in third person

Three judges, using agreed-upon criteria (references to peer problems, school problems, home problems, personal values, vocational problems, pleasurable incidents, and positive, negative, or ambivalent self-evaluations), read and rated all autobiographies. From their data the authors concluded that (1) differences exist in self-report data elicited by the four autobiographic forms; (2) semistructured, first person is the most effective form; (3) structured, third person is the least effective; (4) either form of semistructure is superior to a structured form; and (5) differences are clearly less between the first- and third-person forms than between the semistructured and structured forms.

No technique is of value unless it is put to use. Some years ago, Shaffer reported that the autobiography was used by only one-fourth of the counselors in large school systems and that only one-half of them had ever seen an autobiography.[60] Ratings obtained from 68 counselors placed the autobiography next to last in a list of 10 sources of data. The rank order was as follows: (1) interview, (2) achievement tests, (3) intelligence tests, (4) anecdotal records, (5) oral teacher reports, (6) grades, (7) written teacher reports, (8) personality tests, (9) autobiographies, and (10) questionnaires. Finally, Shaffer reported that from his study of 500 autobiographies, most appeared to be honest and accurate.

[60] E. Evan Shaffer, Jr., "The Autobiography in Secondary School Counseling," *Personnel and Guidance Journal*, Vol. 32 (March, 1954), pp. 395–398.

Interpreting Autobiographies All autobiographies, whether structured or unstructured, are limited by the individual's (1) willingness to reveal himself frankly, (2) self-insight and self-understanding, (3) ability to understand the content of the topic, and (4) ability to communicate in writing. The autobiography is a very intimate technique since it involves the direct expression of an individual. It has the weaknesses inherent in any subjective technique: individuals may overlook their limitations or magnify real or imagined strengths when judging themselves.

Baldwin's personal-structure analysis provides a quantitative analysis of autobiographies.[61] He translates content to a table of correspondence which resembles a computational scattergram for a product-moment correlation. The table is interpreted in respect to two basic assumptions. The first is the *frequency* with which an item appears. This may be used as a measure of its importance. The second is the *contiguity* of two items. The appearance of two items together more often than would occur by chance indicates a relationship to the individual's personality. In addition, Dollard and Mowrer developed a discomfort-relief quotient to assess tension change which they believed applicable to the autobiography.[62] They reported a scoring reliability of .80 for eight different scorers of a social case record.

There is no quick or easy route to foolproof analysis and interpretation of autobiographies. Interpretation takes time, careful attention to detail, and some background knowledge of the individual. The following questions can help guide the counselor's interpretation of what he is examining.

1. *What general impression is conveyed by the writer?* Note the variability in tone as the writer touches upon things that are of vital concern to him. Are

[61] A. L. Baldwin, "Personal Structure Analysis: A Statistical Method for Investigating the Single Personality," *Journal of Abnormal and Social Psychology*, Vol. 37 (April, 1942), pp. 163–183.
[62] John Dollard and O. Hobart Mowrer, "A Method of Measuring Tension in Written Documents," *Journal of Abnormal and Social Psychology*, Vol. 42 (January, 1947), pp. 3–32.

impressions of happiness, depression, good mental health present? Observe the use of emotionally charged words such as "love," "mother," "hate," and the like. The appearance of the paper, whether it is neatly or carelessly done, has little correlation with behavior patterns.

2. *From your knowledge of the client's history, has he omitted significant experiences or persons?* While autobiographies are not expected to be complete in every detail, significant omissions may be cues worthy of follow-up in counseling. If the individual has avoided mentioning family members or a known event, such omissions should be studied carefully. This does not mean the counselor should expect a blow-by-blow, day-by-day, or week-by-week account. Normally, people write briefly about peaceful, pleasant periods in their lives, concentrating on incidents of major import to them.

3. *What is the length of the autobiography?* Length is dependent upon such factors as (1) motivation to write, (2) degree of structure, (3) facility with which a person expresses himself, and (4) degree to which he believes he needs help with his problems.

4. *How is the autobiography organized?* Naturally, if the individual is given an outline, few clues for interpretation can be obtained from this guideline. However, changes in any prepared outline should be noted. The most common organization for unstructured autobiographies is chronological. Are there gaps and omissions in the material? What has the author chosen to emphasize?

5. *What is the level of expression?* If the individual believes no value will result from the autobiography, he may write in a very superficial manner. Students, particularly in upper elementary and junior high school, are likely to report fairly minor events and experiences. Extremely defensive persons may resort to shallowness in writing about their development. Lack of depth or evasiveness characterizes the papers of those who are attempting to hide, or who do not wish to disclose, their concerns or anxieties.

6. *Are there inaccuracies in the autobiography?* Inaccuracies as used here refers to attempts to deliberately falsify experiences or events or to unconscious errors in reporting. Relatively few autobiographies are distorted on purpose; the distortions occur when the writer is not convinced of the value of writing the autobiography. The ability to detect inaccuracies increases with experience in reading autobiographies as well as with previous knowledge of the individual.

Some years ago, Shaw classified the orientations with which the autobiographer responded to his task.[63] In the first category was the *chronicler,* who cites only the external events of his life. In the second was the *self-defender,* who sought to defend his activities and points of view. The *confessant* used the opportunity to communicate thoughts never before expressed, and the *self-analyst* used the autobiography as an exercise in self-analysis. Allport, in his classic monograph, specified 13 motives which usually operate several at a time in the production of any personal document: special pleading, exhibitionism, desire for order, literary delight, securing personal perspective, tension relief, monetary gain, completing an assignment, assisting in therapy, redemption and social reincorporation, scientific interest, public service, and desire for immortality.[64]

Summary The major feature of the autobiography is that it permits the person to tell his own story in his own manner. Baird points out that it is a low-cost technique which helps "the student organize and interpret his experiences in such a way as to see their personal significance and know himself better."[65] If this is the case, then surely the individual will be in a better position to work on his problems. Riccio believes that autobiography is

[63] C. R. Shaw, *The Jack-Roller: A Delinquent Boy's Own Story* (Chicago: University of Chicago Press, 1930).
[64] Gordon W. Allport, *The Use of Personal Documents in Psychological Science,* Bulletin 49 (New York: Social Science Research Council, 1942).
[65] C. R. Baird, "The Autobiography," *Education Digest,* Vol. 19 (March, 1954), pp. 39–43.

little used because counselors are more secure and comfortable with test scores.[66] Test scores can be interpreted through reference to norms while the autobiography cannot. But perhaps Bonner's criticisms of the autobiography are the most compelling reasons:

> The chief defects of the autobiographical method are, first, that it is practically impossible to determine the consistency or stability of its data short of requiring the autobiographer to write still another self-revealing document, with which to compare the first. Second, there is no criterion for evaluating the subject's internal attitudes and feelings regarding the crucial events in his life.[67]

Bonner's criticisms can be applied equally well to any self-report document.

PERSONAL DATA QUESTIONNAIRES

Personal data questionnaires have long been used to obtain vital information. Usually they contain items regarding the student's home, family, health, educational and vocational plans, current activities, present life situation, and the like.

Their purpose in counseling has been primarily that of obtaining background information. Figure 13.3 presents the Purdue Guidance Clinic form, which has been revised a number of times to obtain the specific kinds of information useful to counselors in helping high school and college students who come to the clinic.

Personal data questionnaires may provide an organized system by which individuals can begin to think about themselves; that is, they supply intake interview information. Essentially, they help the counselor better understand the client as he functions in his environment.

ESSAYS

The essay is another personal document yielding material about the counselee's self-perceptions and showing his readiness for counseling. The counselee is assigned a specific topic to write about, such as "What I Want from Life," "My Family and Me," "What I'm Like as a Person."

SENTENCE COMPLETION TECHNIQUES

Sentence completion techniques have a long history of use in studying intellectual functioning and personality. Some items are as follows: "I am . . . ," "I like people who . . . ," "What worries me is . . . ," "They . . . ." The task of the counselee is to finish the sentences in such a way as to make meaningful statements. Items such as "They . . ." and "I am . . ." are often termed *inventive* items whereas the others are referred to as *selective* items. Inventive items are viewed as being more intuitive and therefore less meaningful but they are useful in generating counselee production of projection.

Sentence completion techniques have a wide variety of purposes, chief among which are screening and diagnosis. Basically, the assumption in their use is that the individual will reflect certain of his needs or attitudes if presented with an ambiguous sentence stem. From his responses, inferences are often made as to his mode of adjustment such as withdrawal, aggression, dependence, and inaction, and the like. A recent study by Feldhusen and his associates used a sentence completion scale to differentiate "behaving" from "misbehaving" children.[68] The responses not only discriminated between these groups but yielded valuable insight into each child's personal problems.

The reader who is interested in further information about projective methods for assessing personality will find Anderson and Anderson's *Introduction to Projective Techniques* an excellent introduction to this field.[69]

PLAY MEDIA

Play media are often used by counselors who work with elementary school children. Play media include puppets, modeling clay, dolls, plastic arts,

[66] Anthony C. Riccio, "The Status of the Autobiography," *Peabody Journal of Education,* Vol. 36 (July, 1958), pp. 33-36.
[67] H. Bonner, *Psychology of Personality* (New York: The Ronald Press Company, 1961), p. 123.

[68] John F. Feldhusen, John R. Thurston, and James J. Benning, "Sentence Completion Responses and Classroom Social Behavior," *Personnel and Guidance Journal,* Vol. 42 (October, 1966), pp. 165-170.
[69] Harold H. Anderson and Gladys L. Anderson (eds.), *An Introduction to Projective Techniques* (Englewood Cliffs, N.J.: Prentice-Hall, Inc., 1951).

toy telephones, paints, crayons, pipe cleaners, building materials, rubber guns and knives, typewriters, etc., and they encourage the release of feelings without guilt. For example, the child may be able without embarrassment to do violence to a doll representing the father but in an interview situation would never allow himself to verbalize this feeling. Ginott states that "the child's play is his talk and toys are his words."[70]

The counselor, through play media, may encourage the discussion of fears and other emotional reactions. As Nelson points out, it is in play that the elementary school child (1) develops social relations, (2) tests various roles and concepts, and (3) works through his frustrations and concerns.[71] In contrast to the adolescent who can and does *verbalize* frustrations, the child *acts* his feelings of love, anger, and acceptance. Nelson believes that the use of play media is less likely to be subject to the rush and hurry of the verbal interview and is a means of facilitating communication. He recommends that elementary school counselors treat play behavior as though it were verbalized behavior and respond to the emotional content of the play behavior rather than extending play behavior into an interpretative realm.

Nelson suggests that if play moves into symbolic avenues beyond the counselor's level of training a referral is in order. Further, he recommends that the *closer the counselor's statements about play behavior relate to actual behavior expressed the more they are preferred.* He cites the following examples, with the second statement preferred in each case.

A child suddenly and violently crumbles a clay figure he has called his brother.
1. "You really hate your brother so you smashed him."
2. "You're very angry so you crushed the clay (or it)."

Ted is calm to outward appearances as he draws a picture showing a plane bombing a city.
1. "You're angry and you wanted the pilot to bomb the city."
2. "You've drawn a man in a bombing plane."

Sue starts to feed her doll, then drinks from the bottle herself.
1. "You want to be the baby now."
2. "The bottle is for you."

Mary's eyes fill with tears after the paint runs on her picture.
1. "That's all right, we'll just get another sheet of paper."
2. "It bothers you when things don't turn out well."[72]

Play media build rapport and facilitate communication with children. For children the world of play is a natural and relaxed place in which they are free to be themselves. Since these factors also characterize the counseling setting, play techniques can contribute to an optimal relationship between the child and the counselor.

Referral Techniques

Referral is the act of transferring an individual to another person or agency for specialized assistance not available from the original source. It is important to emphasize that referrals are made for the purpose of obtaining *specialized* service. They do not necessarily mean that the individual has a serious problem but may be due simply to the fact that the problem or concern is beyond the scope of the services provided. For example, high school counselors refer students to employment agencies because the latter are better equipped to assist them with job placement. Or the counselor whose client presents a problem complicated by his parents' marital difficulties may work with the parents in an effort to refer them to a marriage counseling service.

THE REFERRAL DECISION

The ability to recognize when the needs of a particular individual call for procedures beyond the scope of one's personal resources or those of the employing setting is a professional necessity. At least two misconceptions surround the nature of

[70] H. G. Ginott, *Group Psychotherapy with Children* (New York: McGraw-Hill Book Co., Inc., 1961), p. 51.

[71] Richard C. Nelson, "Elementary School Counseling with Unstructured Play Media," *Personnel and Guidance Journal,* Vol. 45 (September, 1966), pp. 24–27.

[72] *Ibid.,* pp. 25–56.

Figure 13.3 Purdue Guidance Clinic personal data inventory

Date____________________
Counselor____________________

It is often useful if your counselor can know a little about your background and present experiences. Therefore, please complete this inventory as carefully as you can. All information which you provide about yourself will be treated confidentially.

Name____
Last First Middle

Address____

School____________________Grade____________________

Age______Birthdate______________Phone__________Sex__________

School Information:

	Name of School	Grades Attended	Years Attended	Course of Study
Elementary				
Jr. High				
Sr. High				
College				
Other				

Best Liked Subjects____________________Easiest Subjects____________________

Least Liked Subjects____________________Hardest Subjects____________________

Out-of-school leisure time activities and hobbies____________________

What magazines do you read regularly?____________________

What types of books do you enjoy?____________________

Activities and Hobbies:

School Activity	Number of Years of Participation	Offices Held	Kind of Activity

Class offices held____

Figure 13.3 *(continued)*

Work Experience:

	Job Held	*When*	*What did you like best about it?*
1.			
2.			
3.			
4.			

Family and Home:

	Last name-First name	Live at Home	Age	Occupation	Years of Schooling Completed
Father					
Mother					
Bro/Sis					

Health:

Do you have normal eyesight? ________ Normal hearing? ________
Briefly summarize important factors in your health history ______________________________

Underline any of the following words which seem to describe you fairly well:

Active, ambitious, self-confident, persistent, hard working, nervous, impatient, impulsive, quick-tempered, excitable, imaginative, original, witty, calm, easily discouraged, serious, easy-going, good-natured, unemotional, shy, submissive, absent-minded, methodical, timid, lazy, frequently gloomy, hard-boiled, dependable, reliable, cheerful, sarcastic, jittery, likeable, leader, sociable, quiet, retiring, self-conscious, often feel lonely.

Plans:

What are your plans for the future? ______________________________

What occupations have you seriously considered as possible goals? Why? ______________________________

What topics would you like to discuss with your counselor? ______________________________

Comments:

____

the referral decision. First, referral is sometimes viewed as occurring only in times of emergency. Second, referral sometimes causes counselors to either unnecessarily prolong or too quickly terminate a relationship. Some counselors see nearly all contacts as being outside their personal resources or in need of others' help. Arbuckle[73] says this attitude characterizes "a referral technician rather than a professional counselor." Shertzer and Stone have also commented on the critical matter of terminating the relationship too quickly:

> Some counselors are so timid about working with emotional issues at a level appropriate to their competencies that they are completely unwilling to discuss substantive personal issues with students. In part, this timidity has been encouraged by counselor-educators and school administrators who stress that the counselor should not overextend himself or overstep the bounds of his competencies in the area of "personal problems." Forgotten and/or ignored in this situation is the fact that normal students have emotions which are not necessarily equated to serious emotional problems but do come into play materially in their daily lives. Counselors who refuse to deal with emotions frequently find it impossible to cope effectively with students who have more serious emotional disturbances when they are inevitably confronted with them. For students with disabling emotional problems, the counselor's refusal to work toward even enough understanding to permit appropriate referral, is tantamount to negligence. At a safer and less critical level, the counselor's refusal to cope with feeling components forces students to focus upon purely informational factors rather than permitting the motivations and feelings which crucially influence human decisions to come into play.[74]

Ethical and legal considerations almost invariably accompany referral decisions. APGA's ethical standard in respect to referral states that

> The member shall decline to initiate or shall terminate a counseling relationship when he cannot be of professional assistance to the counselee or client either because of lack of competence or personal limitation. In such instances, the member shall refer his counselee or client to an appropriate specialist. In the event the counselee or his client declines the suggested referral, the member is not obligated to continue the counseling relationship.[75]

The essential question is how or by what criteria the counselor decides "when he cannot be of professional assistance." It is a subjective judgment. He screens his observations of the counselee's verbal and nonverbal behavior against an image of the kind of person his experiences and beliefs have led him to believe he can help. The school counselor considers the nature of the problem, the context or life situation within which the problem exists, the amount of anxiety present, and the degree to which functioning is impaired and estimates the length of time required for counseling as well as his own competencies.

While the referral decision is ultimately the counselor's to make, he can consult with professional colleagues. He could talk the situation over with a professional counseling colleague (client's permission need not be obtained for this) or the situation could be discussed at a staff meeting.

THE REFERRAL PROCESS

When the counselor's judgment suggests referral as the appropriate course of action, discussion with the client is the next step. Making a referral does not indicate a departure from a "profound faith in the worth, dignity and great potentiality of the individual human being."[76] Patterson has called attention to the necessity for maintaining "a fundamental respect for the individual and a fundamental belief that it is best for him to work out his own problems in his own way."[77] The fact that individuals who are referred are likely to be

[73] Dugald S. Arbuckle, *Counseling: An Introduction* (Boston: Allyn and Bacon, Inc., 1961), p. 120.
[74] Bruce Shertzer and Shelley C. Stone, "Challenges Confronting Counselors," *The School Counselor*, Vol. 12 (May, 1965), p. 238.
[75] "Ethical Standards," *Personnel and Guidance Journal*, Vol. 40 (October, 1961), p. 207.
[76] "Preamble to Ethical Considerations," *Personnel and Guidance Journal*, Vol. 40 (October, 1961), p. 206.
[77] C. H. Patterson, *Counseling and Guidance in Schools* (New York: Harper & Row, Publishers, 1962), p. 331.

apprehensive, anxious, or somewhat fearful requires the counselor clearly to exhibit acceptance, understanding, and concern as communicated in his willingness to help.

An attitude of reassurance born of confidence that appropriate steps are being taken is a critical ingredient. This is a matter of realistically facing the facts and the related available alternatives. Feelings of remorse for having failed to act sooner on the basis of previous evidence can result in hasty and ill-advised referrals. Naturally, the earliest possible detection and action increase the likelihood of rational and desirable counselor functioning. The critical questions are "What kind of special service does this person require?" "Is it available and if so where?"

It is imperative that the counselor be fully familiar with referral sources before suggesting the possibility of referral to the counselee. School counselors need to include the counselee's parents in their deliberations as soon as possible without violating ethical responsibilities to the counselee. With regard to referral agencies, students, and parents, Patterson's reminders, as adapted from a Michigan State University publication, *How to Make Referrals,* remain timely:

> It is unwise and impractical to refer a student to community agencies without the knowledge, consent, and cooperation of his parents. Many child-guidance agencies will not accept students for treatment unless parents cooperate fully and are willing to present themselves for help, too. Check on the policy of your local agencies in this regard.

Further,

> When telling students or parents about available services, in the school or in the community, explain both the functions and the limitations of these services. Do not give the impression that any specialist or agency has all the answers and can work wonders.[78]

Successful referral is more likely to be accomplished by offering to arrange for the needed service rather than dwelling upon the counselor's inability to continue the relationship or the uncommon problem represented. The suggestion of referral to the individual requires a positive, helpful approach with no condition attached to it. Occasionally direct action is necessitated, but it is usually administrative action, which should not be confused with the counselor's efforts.

The actual presentation should be straightforward and tactful; labels and diagnoses should be avoided. The fact that another service is available which may provide the needed assistance should be included. The counselor should work slowly and carefully. Everything possible should be done to avoid making the referral an emergency or a crisis situation.

Whatever is required in the way of making contacts and arrangements with the referral agency should be offered by the counselor. Having provided this information, identified the referral service, and discussed what acceptance of the referral involves, he is responsible for assisting the individual (and his family) in deciding what action to take. Rejection of the referral suggestion need not be interpreted as failure on the counselor's part. The very fact that the individual is now openly facing the problem may contribute materially to a more satisfactory resolution. Resistance, doubts, fears, guilt, and defensiveness are factors with which the counselor must be prepared to cope in discussing referral. The conscientious application of his skills in these difficult situations may result ultimately in further development of both the counselor and the counselee.

LEGAL AND ETHICAL CONSIDERATIONS

Legal provisions for privileged communication and confidentiality of student records vary widely among the 50 states. Even among communities within a given state these conditions vary because of precedent or tradition. Ethical considerations almost inevitably accompany referral situations and should be carefully observed in order to minimize difficulties. It should be a matter of policy for the school counselor to obtain from the student and

[78] *Ibid.,* p. 330.

his family written permission to furnish any referral information sought by the new agency. After referral, measures to ensure the confidentiality of the fact that an individual is under the care of an outside person or agency should be taken. Such information should be available to school personnel only on a need-to-know basis. A more thorough presentation of ethical and legal matters may be found in Chapter Sixteen.

COMMUNICATIONS NECESSARY

Communication channels with other school services and community agencies must be established so that referral and outcome information can travel both ways with as little indirect handling as possible. Timing and confidentiality are basic concerns, of course, but administrative cost and efficiency are also involved. The term "reciprocity," as used in the context of the referral process, applies to the amount and kind of feedback to be expected from another agency. A given agency is usually governed by an established general policy covering this subject which may allow for either fairly comprehensive reports, on the one hand, or none at all, on the other. The central consideration always reflects the need for information rather than the satisfaction of curiosity or administrative routine. Any general policy should be identified in initial contacts with the agency, and in specific cases the request for a report should be based upon clearly defined need.

It is common practice for agencies to acknowledge acceptance of a referral. Beyond this, most agencies restrict their requests to suggestions for structuring the student's school experiences. Counselors making a referral may not be asked by the agency for a professional opinion. This omission is not a discourtesy. Such a request would be incongruent, since it is not usually necessary, and might contribute to a biased view of the individual. However, acceptance of the referral by an agency will usually be accompanied by a request for objective data about the individual's school performance and behavior.

Most referral agencies do not lack for clients. Providing for ease of counselee access to special services is the counselor's responsibility. This is fundamentally a matter of becoming acquainted with the procedures to be followed in placing the student in contact with the agency. Agency representatives are typically cooperative in explaining their organization and routine to those who take the time to inquire. Certainly, the counselor has to provide the student and his family with accurate instructions and assist in completing the referral. This may mean making telephone calls, obtaining and forwarding request or consent forms, applications, etc., and perhaps accompanying the individual and his family to the agency.

CONTINUED WORKING RELATIONSHIPS

School and community agencies from time to time share a common clientele. That is, the agency may suggest that the student continue seeing a school counselor during part or all of the time the agency is working with the student. In such cases the agency specialist will discuss with the counselor the purpose of maintaining the school counselor relationship and will usually suggest what its orientation should be. The student may require support for the periods between visits to the agency; the counselor's work with the student may be entirely different from the agency's, so that both may continue without conflict; it may be an active part of therapy or rehabilitation involving assistance in completing school tasks assigned by the agency.

Finally, in such instances two precautions are to be observed: maintaining confidentiality and staying within one's realm of responsibility. The fact that a student is working with two or more professionally qualified persons, all parties being aware of the fact, does not justify exceptions to the ordinary standards of confidentiality. Students may precipitate this breach of confidentiality, either intentionally or unintentionally, by discussing their agency experience with their school counselor or vice versa.

Annotated References

Brammer, Lawrence M., and Shostrom, Everett L. *Therapeutic Psychology*, 2nd ed. Englewood Cliffs, N.J.: Prentice-Hall, Inc., 1968. 486 pp.

Part II (pp. 133–345) includes seven chapters dealing with techniques. Chapter 5 discusses the case history and diagnosis; Chapter 8, transference, resistance, and countertransference; Chapter 9, interpretative techniques; Chapter 10, the counselor's use of advice, tests, and observation.

Goldman, Leo. *Using Tests in Counseling*, 2nd ed. New York: Appleton-Century-Crofts, Inc., 1971. 483 pp.

Goldman's book represents a most comprehensive treatment of this topic. Particularly relevant here are Chapter 3, on test selection; Chapter 7, on foundations of test interpretation; Chapter 8, on statistical bridges; Chapter 9, on clinical bridges; and Chapter 11, on interpreting test results. Several illustrative cases are presented and well used.

Patterson, C. H. *Counseling and Psychotherapy*. New York: Harper & Brothers, 1959. 322 pp.

Chapter 7, "A Systematic View of Counseling and Psychotherapy," Chapter 8, "Implementing the Point of View," Chapter 9, "Transference and Countertransference," and Chapter 10, "Diagnosis and Evaluation" are most appropriate reading. Since Patterson's views of diagnosis, testing, and the like have a client-centered orientation, examination of them is in order. His case is presented strongly, clearly, and concisely.

Further References

Barrett, Roger L. "Changes in Accuracy of Self-Estimates." *Personnel and Guidance Journal*, Vol. 47 (December, 1968). pp. 353–357.

Bogue, E. G. and Fox, Ray P. "Feedback of College Grades to High Schools." *Personnel and Guidance Journal*, Vol. 48 (November, 1969). pp. 210–217.

Doster, Joseph A. and Slaymaker, Judith, "Need Approval, Uncertainty Anxiety, and Expectancies of Interview Behavior." *Journal of Counseling Psychology*, Vol. 19 (November, 1972). pp. 522–528.

Foulds, Melvin L. "Positive Mental Health and Facilitative Genuineness During Counseling." *Personnel and Guidance Journal*, Vol. 47 (April, 1969). pp. 762–766.

Goldman, Leo. "Tests and Counseling: The Marriage that Failed." *Measurement and Evaluation in Guidance*, Vol. 4 (January, 1972). pp. 213–220.

Hershenson, David B. "Techniques for Assisting Life — Stage Vocational Development." *Personnel and Guidance Journal*, Vol. 47 (April, 1969). pp. 776–780.

Johnson, David W. and Noonan, M. Patricia, "Effects of Acceptance and Reciprocation of Self-Disclosures on the Development of Trust." *Journal of Counseling Psychology*, Vol. 19 (September, 1972). pp. 411–416.

Kelly, Gary F. "Guided Fantasy as a Counseling Technique with Youth." *Journal of Counseling Psychology*, Vol. 19 (September, 1972). pp. 355–361.

Lafleur, N. Kenneth and Johnson, Richard G. "Separate Effects of Social Modeling and Reinforcement in Counseling Adolescents." *Journal of Counseling Psychology*, Vol. 19 (July, 1972). pp. 291–294.

Mitchell, Kevin M. and Namenek, Therese M. "Effects of Therapist Confrontation on Subsequent Client and Therapist Behavior during the First Therapy Interview." *Journal of Counseling Behavior*, Vol. 19 (May, 1972). pp. 196–201.

Nighswander, James K and Mayer, G. Roy. "Catharsis: A Means of Reducing Elementary School Students' Aggressive Behaviors?" *Personnel and Guidance Journal*, Vol. 47 (January, 1969). pp. 461–466.

Older, Jules. "Interpersonal Testing and Pseudotesting in Counseling and Therapy." *Journal of Counseling Psychology*, Vol. 19 (September, 1972). pp. 374–381.

Passons, William R. and Dey, Glen R. "Counselor Candidate Personal Change and the Communication of Facilitative Dimensions." *Counselor Education and Supervision*, Vol. 12 (September, 1972). pp. 57–62.

Rickabaugh, Karl, Heapes, Richard A., and Finley, Robert. "Counselor Comfort, Counseling Climate, and Client Satisfaction: Client Ratings and Academic Improvement." *Counselor Education and Supervision*, Vol. 11 (March, 1972). pp. 219–223.

Riordan, Richard J. and Matheny, Kenneth B. "Dear Diary: Logs in Group Counseling." *Personnel and Guidance Journal,* Vol. 50 (January, 1972). pp. 279–382.

Shultz, John J. and Klein, Alice E. "Counselor Use of Multifactor Intelligence Tests, or: What Happened?" *Counselor Education and Supervision,* Vol. 12 (September, 1972). pp. 51–56.

Springer, Harry C. and Brammer, Lawrence M. "A Tentative Model to Identify Elements of the Counseling Process and Parameters of Counselor Behavior." *Counselor Education and Supervision,* Vol. 11 (September, 1971). pp. 8–16.

Strong, Stanley R. and Gray, Bonnie L. "Social Comparison, Self-Evaluation, and Influence in Counseling." *Journal of Counseling Psychology,* Vol. 19 (May, 1972). pp. 178–183.

"Symposium: Tests and Counseling – The Marriage that Failed?" *Measurement and Evaluation in Guidance,* Vol. 5, No. 3 (October, 1972).

Tsoi, Donald J. and Carlson, William A. "Client Dogmatism and Perceived Counselor Attitudes." *Personnel and Guidance Journal,* Vol. 48 (April, 1970). pp. 657–660.

Ward, G. Robert, Kagan, Norman, and Krathwohl, David R. "An Attempt to Measure and Facilitate Counselor Effectiveness." *Counselor Education and Supervision,* Vol. 11 (March, 1972). pp. 179–186.

COUNSELING SPECIAL POPULATIONS

14

The major purpose of this chapter is to call attention to some special subgroups within the general population served by many counselors. Included are blacks, Indians, Chicanos, Puerto Ricans and women. Each group has some special characteristics which may have a bearing on the counseling relationship and, even more important, its outcomes for their lives and society. However, an important concept to be borne in mind in examining the following material is that formulated by Kluckhohn and Murray: "Every man is, in certain respects, like all other men, like some other men, like no other man."[1] An individual is similar to all men because all belong to the same species and have, therefore, similar biological endowments. A person is similar to some other men because he belongs to an organized intergenerational group and so shares behavior with others in this group. He is like no other man because in some ways each person is unique.

Obviously these groups have been present in America since its beginning. It is equally obvious that the American ideal of equality within a democratic society has not held true for some groups. Recent social upheavals show that such subgroups are now committed to demanding equality. In some cases their lack of full participation in society stems from outright denial, in others, failure to recognize special problems of subgroups, and in still others, benign neglect. Recent social history clearly shows that such groups are (1) articulating more urgently than ever before their rights and privileges within a democracy and (2) banding together in more cohesive organizations to achieve their purposes. These two factors have led to a consciousness of how they differ from each other and how they differ from the dominant society. Presumably, stressing such differences focuses attention on needs which have been unmet, characteristics that require specialized consideration, and

[1] Clyde Kluckhohn and Henry A. Murray, "Personality Formation: the Determinants," in Clyde Kluckhohn, Henry A. Murray, and David Schneider (eds.), *Nature, Society and Culture*, 2nd ed. (New York: Alfred A. Knopf, 1956), p. 53.

personal and group goals not necessarily identical to those commonly held by other segments of society or expected of them by society. For the counselor who works with individuals from such subgroups, a thorough understanding of these factors and appreciation of their impact on the individual are essential.

The reader may remember that Chapter Three identifies and discusses some of the characteristics of counselees. This chapter presents additional information relevant to the counselor's understanding and work with special subgroups. It must be kept in mind that social forces far beyond the control of individuals in the helping professions have created situations in which a "minority group" in society may well be the "majority group" in a specific setting. For example, the inter city counselor may work in a school that is predominantly black.

Counseling American Indians

The American Indian suffers from much historically based stereotyped thinking. The colonial Americans' concept of the "noble red man" deteriorated across the generations as strife between western settlers and the Indians increased and finally ended toward the close of the nineteenth century. Today, millions of Americans view Indians as wild west relics, stoic and childlike. These views derive from diverse sources ranging from television images and Western movies to the paternalistic "great white father" policies practiced by the U. S. government in managing or, as many critics assert, mismanaging Indian affairs. Indian efforts to break out of this situation have been thwarted by racial prejudice, lack of opportunity, poverty, and poor education.

The writings of Spang[2] and Bryde[3] demonstrate clearly that counselors have had little contact with Indian youth and all too often they have been ineffective in the contacts that they have had. Too, many who have served as counselors to Indians have not only lacked professional counselor training but also never acquired an understanding of their clients. Both Spang and Bryde highlight the plight of the Indian who is caught between two cultural worlds, one of which lacks any appreciation and understanding of Indian cultural values and tribal diversity.

As is true in dealing with any member of a special subgroup, the counselor frequently fails because he does the only thing he knows how to do: fit, force, or mold the Indian into white middle-class ways of thinking, feeling, and acting. The counselor's failure, part of the larger failure of the educational enterprise and the society as a whole, undoubtedly contributes to the high school dropout rate, high unemployment, and massive poverty among Indians.

The counselor who seeks to establish a relationship with an Indian is faced with the obligation of understanding that his client lives in a world of colliding values, language differences, and highly transient white adult models. Not only are such models transient, particularly in reservation schools, but they often require the Indian child to reject much of his early learnings from Indian models.

A few observations about counselors and Indian clients have been given by Spang and Bryde and are summarized here. First, both of these authors have stressed the necessity of a counselor's thorough knowledge of Indian ways, including their language. Second, the client's lack of verbal responsiveness is attributed to both an English language deficiency and a value system that prizes contemplation and attentiveness to the wisdom of elders. Third, existing educational efforts that consist primarily of stressing white middle-class values and knowledge result in a gradual destruction of the mental health of the individual, culminating in feelings of rejection, depression, and anxiety. These find their expression in tendencies toward

[2] Alonzo T. Spang, Jr., "Understanding the Indian," *Personnel and Guidance Journal,* Vol. 50 (October, 1971), pp. 97–102.
[3] John F. Bryde, *Indian Students and Guidance,* Guidance Monograph Series (Boston: Houghton Mifflin Company, 1971).

withdrawal and social alienation, and are often manifested in strikingly high rates of alcoholism and suicide. Bryde cites data that indicate the emergence of these feelings as early as junior high school.[4] Given these three observations about his client, it would seem that the counselor should be able to convey the respect, understanding, and the liking necessary and basic to good counseling relationships.

Sources discussing counselor practices with Indian youth have often suggested a highly directive approach involving advice, suggestion, and persuasion. Presumably, such suggestions are based on the characteristic of Indian cultures that stresses reliance upon the wisdom of elders. It may be that such an approach is more functional while the client remains within the Indian culture than when he attempts to cope with white society. The latter situation would seemingly call for a highly sensitive and perceptive counselor, who could extend in full measure those facilitating conditions — empathy, warmth, understanding, genuineness — to his Indian client as he struggles with and examines certain value conflicts or decides on his life or career goals.

Counseling Blacks

The last two decades have been a time of increasing social change, upheaval, and searching inquiry in the realm of black-white relationships. A considerable body of literature has accumulated, some of which has only an indirect relevance to counseling but which contributes to an understanding of the existing situation. Other literature has direct relevance to the work of the counselor. It will be assumed that the reader is familiar with recent social history as well as the earlier history of black Americans. Of greater importance here is the literature and experience that applies to the work of the counselor.

Our own limited experience reveals that some black high school and college students consistently view their contacts with white counselors as discouraging and unproductive. The charges are repeatedly heard that (1) counselors have discouraged blacks' college aspirations on the grounds that there was little likelihood of admission or success in college if admitted, (2) little counselor assistance is available to black students for job placement when they leave school, and (3) black students are discouraged from taking those courses which would prepare them for entering post-high school education. Black youth are often confused about the discrepancy between the expressions of these actions and attitudes by counselors and the highly publicized improved educational and employment opportunities available to them in recent years. In particular, some college doors have inched open, not only actively recruiting black students, but also providing financial support and educational remediation for those who need it. To a lesser degree, better occupational opportunities are present, at least for those blacks who have been fortunate enough to secure advanced education or special skills.

Many variables undoubtedly interact to produce negative views of counselors by black students. It should not be overlooked that in some cases the black counselee may attribute discouragement to prejudice on the part of the counselor, when in fact that same counselor is equally discouraging to a white client, given similar personal or background data. But it should also be noted that there are very, very few situations in which a counselor can assert that an individual, either black or white, *cannot* pursue his aspirations. The counselor's approach has most often been traditionally and appropriately one of neutrality followed by questioning intended to direct the client toward examining the decision-making process and his strength of commitment to a given objective. Such an approach may be interpreted by the client as disapproving or discouraging, particularly if the counselor does not make his purposes clear to the client.

[4] Bryde, *op. cit.*, pp. 40–42.

A range of recent commentary about counseling blacks has been presented by Vontress,[5] Kincaid,[6] Smith,[7] Russell,[8] Beck[9] and many others. Their observations vary in scope, detail, and degree of optimism held about the value or even the possibility of white counselors providing assistance to blacks.

All of these sources stress the difficulty of establishing and maintaining a counseling relationship between a white counselor and a black counselee. They have suggested that these difficulties stem from (1) a lack of understanding and appreciation of black cultural values, (2) differences in life experiences, (3) prejudiced attitudes on the part of whites which preclude even the beginnings of the counseling relationship, (4) failure to see blacks as people in viewing all their problems as originating from racial attitudes and conflict, and (5) low expectancies for black performance held by whites. Vontress has identified and discussed how racial differences may influence the relationship between white counselors and black clients.[10] A prominent conclusion in his analysis is that the previous negative experiences between races adversely influence the establishment of the trusting, intimate, self-revealing relationship deemed essential in counseling. The black client may respond negatively to the white counselor because he "transfers" to him intense negative emotions stemming from previous experiences with, and feelings toward, whites in general. Similarly, the white counselor "countertransfers" preconceived ideas and attitudes about blacks in general to his black client. Also highlighted in Vontress's analysis of racial differences in counseling is a differential in self-disclosure between white and black clients. He ranks various groups in the order of their ability to self-disclose as follows: white females, white males, black females, and last, black males. The black male client, according to Vontress, is particularly reluctant to disclose his true feelings and situations to a white counselor, for to do so is to reveal his vulnerability. Without doubt, understanding, attentiveness and sensitivity on the part of the counselor are demanded in such complex situations.

Without denying the relevance of race, it should be noted that socioeconomic factors are inevitably compounded with racial characteristics. Historically, the vast majority of black Americans have occupied the lower end of the socioeconomic ladder. Further, counselors and therapists have not been noted for their successes with lower-class clients, regardless of race. Whether difficulties in establishing and maintaining a relationship occur because of race, socioeconomic variables, or a combination of both, it is the counselor's responsibility to recognize and cope effectively with his client as an individual rather than as a member of a group with whom he lacks experience.

Given these difficulties, many have argued or demanded that black counselors be employed to counsel blacks. Only by doing so, they believe, will black clients ever realize the expectations they have for counseling. Russell has outlined these expectations: (1) that black students will get a fair shake, (2) that they will be accepted rather than rejected, (3) that their dignity will be respected, (4) that their individuality will be recognized, (5) that their right of decision will be respected, (6) that their opportunity to explore, discover and learn will be upheld, and (7) that their hopes, dreams, and aspirations will be recognized and encouraged.[11] These same expectations are set forth

[5] See, for example, Clemmont E. Vontress, "Counseling Blacks," *Personnel and Guidance Journal*, Vol. 48 (May, 1970), pp. 713–720; Clemmont E. Vontress, "Racial Differences: Impediments to Rapport," *Journal of Counseling Psychology*, Vol. 18 (January, 1971), pp. 7–13; and Clemmont E. Vontress, *Counseling Negroes*, Guidance Monograph Series (Boston: Houghton Mifflin Company, 1971), 70 pp.

[6] Marylou Kincaid, "Identity and Therapy in the Black Community," *Personnel and Guidance Journal*, Vol. 47 (May, 1969), pp. 884–890.

[7] See, for example, Paul M. Smith, Jr., "Black Activists for Liberation, Not Guidance," *Personnel and Guidance Journal*, Vol. 49 (May, 1971), pp. 721–726; Paul M. Smith, Jr., "Men Who Think Black," *Personnel and Guidance Journal*, Vol. 48 (May, 1970), pp. 763–766.

[8] R. D. Russell, "Black Perceptions of Guidance," *Personnel and Guidance Journal*, Vol. 48 (May, 1970), pp. 721–728.

[9] James D. Beck, *The Counselor and Black-White Relationships*, Guidance Monograph Series (Boston: Houghton Mifflin Company, 1973).

[10] Vontress, "Racial Differences," *op. cit.*

[11] Russell, "Black Perceptions of Guidance," *op. cit.*, pp. 725–726.

in statements of the principles of counseling. Actual practice should certainly strive to provide no less.

We believe firmly that counselors should be employed because they are professionally and personally competent, regardless of race, sex, or religion. This belief is based on firm agreement with a clear, direct statement published in a recent news story about a black family who sought to retain custody of a battered Mexican-American child (Indianapolis *Star*, Dec. 17, 1972). The father observed that:

> "I have tried to teach Victor to accept people as they are," Adams said. "Victor knows he is Mexican-American, but he's never been taught 'Negro, or Mexican-American, or Anglo.' I teach him people are people."

Many black counseling practitioners are personally and professionally competent and should be employed in schools, colleges, and agencies. They and their white counterparts can serve as effective models, not only for black and white clients, but also for the community at large.

Some final comments are in order here. First, the counselor, whether black or white, must be alert as to how his own experiences are involved in his responses to his clients. If the counselor's prior experiences have left him with a residue of negative attitudes or feelings toward certain groups, he must become aware of this and attempt to resolve such attitudes and feelings. Prejudice, disrespect, complacency, or patronizing attitudes have no place in counseling.

Second, much can be done in counselor preparation programs to improve counseling with blacks by (1) exploring means of facilitating black-white relationships, (2) sensitizing counselors to black students' problems, assets, and needs, (3) familiarizing counselors with educational and vocational opportunities available to black students, (4) preparing blacks to be professional counselors, and (5) evaluating the impact of counseling practices and techniques used with black students.

Third, practicing counselors can do much that would be beneficial both to whites and blacks in schools, colleges, or agencies by conducting programs that facilitate black-white relationships. Beck has described some programs that seek, at a minimum, to prevent the conflict, indeed violence, that marks and scars many integrated schools, and beyond that, to facilitate healthy interpersonal relationships between blacks and whites which build toward shared understandings and experiences.[12]

Finally, the school and college counselor involved in career planning with black clients must be aware that encouragement and support to plan, to try, to build, and to pursue are ingredients too infrequently present in his client's life. For many blacks (and whites), encouragement and belief in them as individuals are responses that are truly facilitating.

Counseling Puerto Ricans and Mexican-Americans

Articles describing the values and needs of Puerto Ricans and Mexican-Americans have been written by Pollack and Menacker,[13] Aragon and Ulibarri,[14] and Palomares and Haro.[15] Pollack and Menacker have pointed out that these two groups share some cultural similarities, but also some major differences. They share a similar, though not identical, language and most individuals in each group share severe poverty. Because some differences exist, the two groups will be discussed separately.

PUERTO RICANS

Since Puerto Rico became a U.S. territory at the close of the Spanish-American War, most migrants to the mainland (Puerto Ricans are American citizens) have settled in New York City. During the

[12] Beck, *op cit.*

[13] Erwin Pollack and Julius Menacker, *Spanish-Speaking Students and Guidance,* Guidance Monograph Series (Boston: Houghton Mifflin Company, 1971).

[14] John A. Aragon and Sabine R. Ulibarri, "Learn, Amigo, Learn," *Personnel and Guidance Journal,* Vol. 50 (October, 1971), pp. 87–90.

[15] Uvaldo H. Palomares and Juan Haro, "Viva La Raza!" *Personnel and Guidance Journal,* Vol. 50 (October, 1971), pp. 119–129.

past two decades, they have spread to other major U.S. cities. Even today, Puerto Ricans tend to immigrate for two purposes. One segment, which usually possesses more education and skills, seeks opportunity and an improved life. This group comes to establish permanent residence on the mainland. The other group seeks seasonal employment as farm labor and returns to Puerto Rico.

The Puerto Rican value structure differs in important respects from that of the American middle class. Ties to, and a love for, their homeland seem stronger than that of the highly mobile American population. The Puerto Rican family tends to be more patriarchal and quite protective of female members. Puerto Ricans exhibit a more relaxed attitude toward time schedules and demands. Authorities, especially officials, tend to be approached with much more formality. These and other values influence the behavior and personal relationships of those who migrate to this country.

Puerto Rican students often do not complete high school. Many boys leave school to supplement the family income while girls drop out in order to care for younger children while the mother works. Pollack and Menacker describe the recently migrated student as polite, respectful toward teachers who are viewed as high-status individuals, and well behaved in school.[16] In their new culture, Puerto Rican migrant students are confronted with problems of language differences, conflicts with parents over the adoption of new customs and behaviors that clash with their parents' traditions, and a high probability that they will not complete their education because of family economic problems.

MEXICAN-AMERICANS

As an ethnic group, Mexican-Americans are concentrated in the southwestern portion of the United States. Many Chicanos trace their origins to the early California territory. They automatically became U.S. citizens when that section of the country was ceded to the United States in 1848. Many others have emigrated from Mexico over the years.

Many generalizations are made about Chicano culture. Pollack and Menacker cite several authorities in their monograph who support the contention that such generalizations stem from poverty rather than ethnicity.[17] Specific attributes which most accurately characterize many Chicanos include coming from Mexico, speaking Spanish, being of Catholic faith, and being dark-skinned. Additionally, most are reputed to lack education and adequate income. Stereotypically, the Mexican-American is pictured as emphasizing manliness in males, submissiveness and responsibility in females, enjoyment of the present, work only when necessary, and resignation to fate.

Chicano students and their parents commonly place a high value on education as an ideal. However, the reality of the situation is that Mexican-American students leave school early at a fantastically high rate (approaching 90 per cent in many localities). Undoubtedly, impoverished family situations which demand early employment contribute heavily to this contradiction between aspiration and reality. A serious language deficiency is another factor since the Chicano child is often described as knowing neither Spanish nor English well. Another factor which smothers aspirations is pervasive discouragement and pessimism about the chances of breaking the cycle of poverty and prejudice.

To be effective with any group of Spanish-speaking Americans, the counselor must know their language and their cultural background. His attention should focus on the conflict between the culture of the majority and that of his Spanish-speaking client. This is extremely important for it is here that conflict develops and misunderstanding and failure occur. Counselors may find that extensive counseling and/or consulting with parents of Spanish-speaking youth pays dividends in expediting their children's acculturation.

[16] Pollack and Menacker, *op. cit.*, pp. 27–33.

[17] *Ibid.*, pp. 14–17.

Counseling Women

The literature[18] on women's rights, discrimination, and sexism has proliferated the past five years, and more will undoubtedly be forthcoming. Much of this literature portrays the historic and contemporary stereotyping of women, its causes, and in particular, its negative results on both women and men.

The many fictions about women are undoubtedly well known to counselors and need only be mentioned here. Among them are that women: are weak and need to be sheltered; are intellectually inferior to men; rightfully belong only in the home; should only work in teaching, nursing, or secretarial work; are not good bosses; are absent from work more frequently than men; become emotional in a crisis situation. These and other fictions persist and are used to restrict and limit women's choices and life styles.

Women have engaged in a long, hard struggle to gain equal rights. Many individuals, groups, and organizations have been involved in this pursuit. Even before 1800, efforts were launched to expose the inequities suffered by women. These efforts were followed in the mid-1800's by a series of conventions directed toward achieving such rights as the right to vote, to hold property, and other important civil rights. Following the Civil War, the drive to secure suffrage for women became a dominant theme among advocates of women's rights. This struggle, begun with the introduction of voting rights legislation in the late 1870's, achieved success in 1920 with the adoption of the Nineteenth Amendment. This amendment was followed by a forty-year period of relative quiet until the recent resurgence of interest in a broad range of women's rights and life styles came to the forefront and culminated in the passage by Congress of the Equal Rights Amendment. This amendment explicitly forbids discrimination on account of sex in civil rights, employment, and the holding of property. As with any legislation, acceptance by the public, enforcement, and implementation are essential if the amendment is to achieve its promise.

Recent literature clearly points out that sexist attitudes and practices are embedded in the very fabric of society. They pervade virtually all institutions including the home, church, school, and employment setting. Until recently, the effects of many traditional practices upon women remained unexamined. The chain of events in restrictive practices begins early in the life of females. The family traditionally influences female children toward "acceptable" female roles. The school perpetuates this beginning by encouraging girls to follow certain educational paths viewed as desirable and possible, and employment practices fulfill the prophecy by hiring women only for stereotyped "feminine" positions. Added to this pattern is the tendency of both males and females to view the woman who resists or breaks this cycle as atypical, deviant, and threatening to the social system.

The many women's rights and liberation groups have stressed not only the inequities faced by women in a society that operates in the above manner, but also have clearly pointed out the effects such inequities have on the lives of women. Figure 14.1 depicts key events at various age points during an average woman's life span.

The purpose of presenting this average life span is to call attention to the decisions which confront women at various critical stages. Crucial to each stage are the developments of the preceding and subsequent stages. The typical pattern is completion of school, short-term employment, marriage, and the rearing of children, followed either by reentry into the labor market or 30 years of domestic, volunteer, and/or social activities.

The education years are critical, both to initial employment and labor market reentry after children leave home. It is during those years that skills are developed and knowledge obtained that

[18] See, for example, Judy Lewis (Guest Editor), "Woman and Counselors," *Personnel and Guidance Journal*, Vol. 51 (October, 1972), pp. 85–160 and Beverly Stone and Barbara Cook, *Women and Guidance*, Guidance Monograph Series (Boston: Houghton Mifflin Company, 1973).

Figure 14.1 An average American woman's lifeline

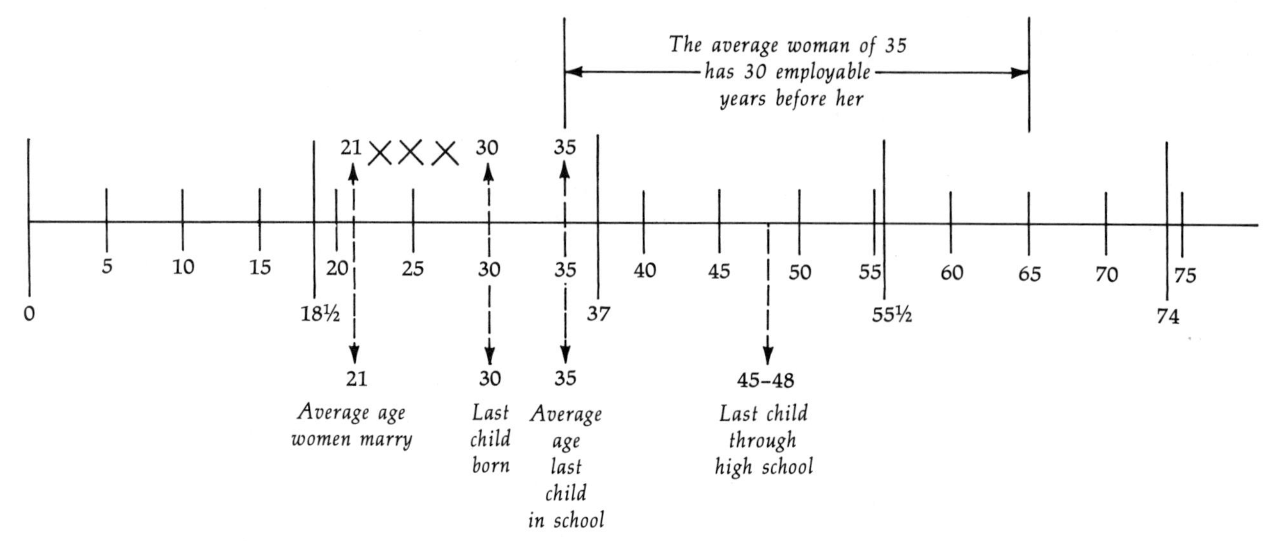

SOURCE: Span Plan, Office of Dean of Women, Purdue University, Lafayette, Indiana. Adapted from U.S. Department of Labor, Women's Bureau, 1969.

permit meaningful employment initially and later in life.

The difficulty facing many counselors lies in accommodating the counseling process to the realities of this life pattern when their female clients struggle with choice, decision making and long term life plans. Those in the forefront of women's rights emphasize strongly the necessity for a woman to make informed choices between the following: marriage, a career, a career in combination with a marriage, marriage with a career later in life. At present, they believe that an enlightened choice for many women is extremely difficult, if not impossible, to attain because of pervasive sexist attitudes.

The counseling relationship is often criticized as being vulnerable to unexamined sexist attitudes and beliefs. It should be noted that such attitudes and beliefs affect both client and counselor. The female client who attempts to redefine her situation as a woman often experiences conflict in her struggle against prevailing stereotypes. Too, the male counselor in particular (and the female counselor to some degree) is often caught responding and thinking about a client as female rather than as a person. These and other factors have led many feminists to take a position analogous to that of the black who asserts that no white can effectively work with a black client because he cannot fully understand the meaning of blackness. The extreme feminist position is that no male counselor can ever effectively work with a female client because he can never know what it means to be female.

Counselors, male or female, must be sensitive to and aware of their beliefs about women and their role in contemporary society. Without doubt, these beliefs have an impact upon a female client, may well influence the counseling relationship, and may have an effect on the client's future life. The female client must be treated as an individual rather than simply as a member of the female sex. Both participants must consider the future difficulties faced by the liberated female in a society which modifies its expectancies very slowly and grudgingly.

Counseling the Exceptional

The term "exceptional child" as used in education refers to many kinds of students who differ from the "normal." Any and all physical, mental, and emotional characteristics may contribute to applying the label "exceptional." The physically handicapped, the mentally retarded, the emotionally disturbed, and the academically superior student are traditional categories of exceptionality. Depending upon one's interest, any one of several new subgroupings may be observed within these larger categories. Here, attention will be given to the mentally retarded, the emotionally disturbed, and the superior student.

THE MENTALLY RETARDED

Historically, the majority of counselors have not been involved to any great extent with retarded children in schools. Many factors have contributed to this condition and will continue to do so. Not the least is the hard fact that relatively few mentally retarded individuals receive much schooling, even in special education programs. The shortage of school-based programs for the mentally retarded is complicated by the fact that most special education programs exist at the elementary school level while counseling services have been concentrated in secondary schools. For these and other reasons, school counselors rarely come into contact with retarded youth, and consequently have little opportunity to acquire knowledge of or provide services to them.

Traditionally, approximately 3 per cent of the population could be classified as retarded by conventional individual intelligence measures. Several categories, based on intelligence quotient ranges, are used to identify this population. Schools commonly use the following categories: educable (50–75 I.Q.), trainable (30–50 I.Q.), custodial (below 30 I.Q.). Where special school programs exist, they usually serve only the educable retarded. The American Association on Mental Deficiency recommends use of a five-category classification system: borderline (70 to 84 I.Q.), mild (55 to 69 I.Q.), moderate (40 to 55 I.Q.), severe (25 to 39 I.Q.), and profound (below 25 I.Q.)

During the sixties, increasing attention at national, state, and local levels has been devoted to the mentally retarded. Perhaps more important, material and monetary support has been provided and still more is being actively sought by a number of organizations interested in the retarded. All this promises improved identification, treatment, and education of this segment of the population.

It has been known for many years that conventional educational procedures are inappropriate and unproductive particularly with the more severely retarded child. Current efforts are being made to conceptualize and actualize programs that more realistically prepare the retarded for as normal a life as possible given the degree of disability. The thrust of these contemporary programs includes the incorporation of multiple services such as physical therapy, work adjustment training, and vocational education, and deemphasizes but does not exclude repetitive efforts to remedy educational deficiencies. Specialized community agencies have joined public schools in extending services to children well below the conventional age for entering school.

THE EMOTIONALLY DISTURBED

A definition of the emotionally disturbed has been presented in Chapter Three. Briefly, the emotionally disturbed individual exhibits an inability to learn which can not be attributed to intellectual, sensory, or health factors; has difficulty in his interpersonal relationships; exhibits inappropriate behavior or feelings; is generally unhappy or depressed and develops physical symptoms connected with personal or school problems. Estimates of the proportion of emotionally disturbed school age children vary widely from 4 to 20 per cent.

Emotional disturbance in students is often expressed in disruptive behaviors, defiance of authority, truancy, stealing, lying. Withdrawal, pervasive unhappiness, alienation, and marked decline in academic performance are also signs of disturbance. The severely disturbed usually do not remain in the normal classroom but are either institutionalized or attend special schools or programs.

THE SUPERIOR STUDENT

Classification of students in this category varies widely based on the use of I.Q. scores as cutoff points. Some are called "superior" who score above an I.Q. of 115. Other classification systems use a much higher I.Q. score of 140. Using the lower figure, approximately 16 per cent of the population would qualify; with the higher figure, less than 1 per cent would be included.

The superior student has been characterized as exhibiting a high level of intellectual development at an early age, possessing a wide range of interests, and perhaps exhibiting greater intellectual maturity than social or emotional maturity. Many researchers have cited ways in which superior students differ that have implications for counselors. Among them are that they have greater educational and vocational opportunities open to them; that they are able to conceptualize early and at high levels; that they are constantly exposed to parent, teacher, and peer pressures to excel; and that, in general, they frequently lack adult models who are also intellectually superior.

The counselor's work with the exceptional individual involves several activities. Among these are identification, specialized efforts to design individualized programs for them, consulting with teachers, administrators, and parents about the exceptionality and, not least of all, providing counseling that sensitively applies knowledge and understanding of their problems and concerns. Especially in the case of the mentally retarded and emotionally disturbed, reliance upon and work with nonschool community services that provide specialized help and programs are essential. There are probably no other students for whom highly individualized attention is more essential if they are to capitalize on their strengths and realize their potential, whether limited or promising.

Summary

This chapter has discussed several special subgroups among the counselor's clientele. Some of the specialized problems of each group result from complex social forces beyond the control of an individual counselor. Some individuals have special problems caused by society's attitudes and beliefs. To paraphrase the statement by Kluckhohn and Murray cited at the beginning of this chapter, each client is like all other clients, like some other clients, and like no other client. This chapter urges the counselor to work with individuals while recognizing the tremendous impact on an individual that membership in a cultural, social, ethnic, racial, sexual, or exceptional subgroup can have.

The recent upsurge of interest in specialized subgroups should sensitize the counselor by expanding his knowledge and increasing his effectiveness with individual members of such groups. Simultaneously, it complicates his work for there are no easy answers to complex situations. Despite the many implied shortcomings in counselors' practice and effectiveness with special groups, probably no other personal interaction setting holds greater promise for providing individualized attention to, and appreciation for, the differences between these special individuals. As always a deep social and personal commitment, a broad experience, and continuous updating of knowledge are essential to effective work with any special subgroup among the counselor's clientele.

Annotated References

Lewis, Judy (Guest Editor), "Women and Counselors," *Personnel and Guidance Journal,* Vol. 51 (October, 1972). pp. 84–160.

This special issue is devoted exclusively to the problems and opportunities inherent in counseling women. The articles by many prominent women in the counseling profession treat a variety of forces and factors that impinge upon counselors and women clients.

Smith, Paul (Guest Editor), "What Guidance for Blacks?" *Personnel and Guidance Journal,* Vol. 48 (May, 1970). pp. 699–791

This issue highlights viewpoints about the inequities confronting blacks and the attitudes toward them. Special attention is given to what school and college counselors do that either hinder or help blacks.

Stone, Beverly and Cook, Barbara. *Women and Guidance.* Guidance Monograph Series. Boston: Houghton Mifflin Company, 1973.

These two authors describe the salient historic and contemporary factors and forces that influence women's roles and rights. They identify the major groups involved in the struggle for equality between the sexes and set forth their objectives. Their monograph provides recommendations for, and program descriptions of, what is being done and what needs to be done to alter current counseling practices with women.

Stone, Shelley C. and Shertzer, Bruce (eds.). *Guidance and the Exceptional Student.* Guidance Monograph Series V. Boston: Houghton Mifflin Company, 1970.

Ten monographs, each of which presents an area of exceptionality, have been written by authors prominent in each field. Some areas of exceptionality include speech and hearing disorders, mental retardation, learning disabilities, reading deficiencies, underachievement, academic talent, etc.

Stone, Shelley C. and Shertzer, Bruce (eds.). *Minority Groups and Guidance.* Guidance Monograph Series VI. Boston: Houghton Mifflin Company, 1971.

These eight monographs, each of which treats a separate subgroup, provide much information and many suggestions for counselors who work with minority group clients.

Further References

Adkins, Winthrop R. "Life Skills: Structured Counseling for the Disadvantaged." *Personnel and Guidance Journal,* Vol. 49 (October, 1970). pp. 108–116.

Aragon, John A. and Ulibarri, Sabine R. "Learn, Amigo, Learn." *Personnel and Guidance Journal,* Vol. 50 (October, 1971). pp. 87–90.

Birdwhistell, Miriam C. and Beard, Richard L. "Intervention with Pregnant Students." *Personnel and Guidance Journal,* Vol. 49 (February, 1971). pp. 453–458.

Buckley, Mary. "Counseling the Aging." *Personnel and Guidance Journal,* Vol. 50 (May, 1972). pp. 745–748.

Callao, Maximo Jose. "Culture Shock – West, East, and West Again." *Personnel and Guidance Journal,* Vol. 51 (February, 1973). pp. 413–416.

Farber, Harris and Mayer, G. Roy. "Behavior Consultation in a Barrio High School." *Personnel and Guidance Journal,* Vol. 51 (December, 1972). pp. 273–279.

Farmer, Helen S. "Helping Women to Resolve the Home-Career Conflict." *Personnel and Guidance Journal,* Vol. 49 (June, 1971). pp. 795–801.

Fredrickson, Ronald H. and Fonda, Thomas. "College Admissions Assistance by Secondary School Counselors." *Personnel and Guidance Journal,* Vol. 49 (January, 1971). pp. 383–389.

Kiehl, Robert. "Opportunities for Blacks in Engineering – A Third Report." *Personnel and Guidance Journal,* Vol. 50 (November, 1971). pp. 204–208.

Kincaid, John and Kincaid, Marylou. "The Draft and Counseling." *Personnel and Guidance Journal,* Vol. 49 (December, 1970). pp. 284–291.

Kincaid, Marylou. "Identity and Therapy in the Black Community." *Personnel and Guidance Journal,* Vol. 47 (May, 1969). pp. 884.

McCarthy, Barry W. and Berman, Alan L. "A Student-Operated Crisis Center." *Personnel and Guidance Journal,* Vol. 49 (March, 1971). pp. 523–528.

"Puerto Rican Youth Speaks Out: Some Quotations." *Personnel and Guidance Journal,* Vol. 50 (October, 1971). pp. 91–96.

Smith, Paul M., Jr. "Black Activists for Liberation." *Personnel and Guidance Journal,* Vol. 49 (May, 1971). pp. 721–726.

Spang, Alonzo T., Sr. "Understanding the Indian." *Personnel and Guidance Journal,* Vol. 50 (October, 1971). pp. 97–102.

Sue, Derald Wing and Sue, Stanley. "Counseling Chinese-Americans." *Personnel and Guidance Journal,* Vol. 50 (April, 1972). pp. 637–644.

Vontress, Clemmont E. "Racial Differences: Impediments to Rapport." *Journal of Counseling Psychology,* Vol. 18 (January, 1971). pp. 7–13.

Vontress, Clemmont E. "The Black Militant as a Counselor." *Personnel and Guidance Journal,* Vol. 50 (March, 1972). pp. 574, 576–580.

Warner, Richard W., Jr. and Hansen, James C. "Alienated Youth: The Counselor's Task." *Personnel and Guidance Journal,* Vol. 48 (February, 1970). pp. 443–448.

Wyne, Marvin D. and Skjei, Priscilla. "The Counselor and Exceptional Pupils: A Critical Review." *Personnel and Guidance Journal,* Vol. 48 (June, 1970). pp. 828–835.

GROUP COUNSELING

15

Enthusiasm for group counseling has been clearly evident during the past few years. Group processes are being utilized in many forms in diverse settings by many individuals. Attention in this chapter is given to (1) why group counseling appeals to counseling practitioners, (2) definition, terminology, and classification employed in group helping relationships, (3) recent research findings, (4) operational practices involved in group counseling, (5) the values and limitations of group counseling, and (6) the similarities and differences between group and individual counseling.

The Appeal of Group Counseling

Much is expected of group counseling. Several factors account for its persistent and increasing popularity. Examination of these factors in no way implies that the authors view group counseling as a fad or a gimmick. Rather, the attempt is to help the reader place group counseling in perspective.

ECONOMIC APPEAL

One reason why group counseling has gained in popularity among practitioners is its economy. A frequently cited advantage is that group work is efficient use of counselor time. The counselor is able to have contact during a given time period with five or six individuals rather than one. In schools, where the counselor-pupil ratio is often unrealistically high – 400 or more students to one counselor – group counseling may be a means of establishing counselor contact with more students. Further, group counseling sometimes stimulates people to enter individual counseling.

PSYCHOLOGICAL APPEAL

The psychological appeal of group counseling derives from the knowledge that often it is through interaction with others that self-concepts are formed or altered. In addition, the individual's relationships with others constitute both a major source of problems for him and a major source of information about himself. Personality change and personal adjustment can occur in any group relationship in which there is an interplay of feelings, emotions, attitudes, and needs. Because the individual acts with and reacts to others, social learning and relearning are always possible outcomes.

PROFESSIONAL SOPHISTICATION APPEAL

It is at present fashionable to conduct group counseling. The practitioner who is able to assert that he has *x* number of groups functioning often raises his professional stature in the eyes of his peers by a cubit. Less facetiously, only during the past ten years have most counselor education institutions provided didactic and practicum experiences in group counseling. Consequently, it is the recent graduates of counselor education programs who have led the movement to utilize group counseling in educational settings. Today's counselor is viewed as incompletely prepared if he cannot counsel with groups.

Terminology and Classification

Considerable confusion exists over the precise meaning of such words as "groups," "group dynamics," "group guidance," and "group counseling." This lack of precision is evident in the literature produced by those in the field and contributes markedly to the faulty impressions generated by communications about group work. Some of the terminology and primary concepts that are basic to group work will be presented briefly in this section.

GROUP DEFINED

In the dictionary the word "group" has many meanings. The least important definition of group for the counselor is the aggregation or collection of objects in close proximity but without any interplay among them. Presumably, an adequate definition would include at least the size, the quality of interaction, and the potential for change within the group. In counseling, a group consists of two or more persons who voluntarily have contact, proximity, and interaction which produce changes in each individual. As a result of participation, members interact with and influence each other. Modification occurs in each member because of participation and experiences shared with other members.

A primary criterion is that there is psychological contact among the members. This means that, for each member, the others exist in a meaningful way, and their behavior toward other members and the outside world has an influence upon the member. Loeser states that groups have (1) dynamic interaction among members, (2) a common goal, (3) a relationship between size and function, (4) volition and consent, and (5) a capacity for self-direction.[1]

CLASSIFICATION OF GROUPS

Groups have been classified in numerous ways. Size, nature of interaction, goals or purposes, and organization have been used as variables in categorizing. A common basis of differentiation has been the main function served by the group: educational, religious, recreational, political, and so on. Degree of permanence is another basis for cataloguing; groups range all the way from the very temporary to the highly stable. But such classifications, while frequently encountered in the literature on groups, are of limited usefulness. Reference here will be to three types of groups.

Primary Versus Secondary Groups Primary groups are those in which the members meet "face to face" for companionship, mutual aid, and the resolution of questions that confront them. Examples of primary groups include the family, the play group, the partnership, and the study group. Such groups are called primary because they are first in time and importance. They are characterized by (1) small size, (2) similarity of members' background, (3) limited self-interest, and (4) intensity of shared

[1] Lewis Loeser, "Some Aspects of Group Dynamics," *International Journal of Group Psychotherapy*, Vol. 7 (January, 1957), pp. 5–19.

interest. Secondary groups are those in which the members are not as intimate and contact is more casual. Examples include large lecture classes and committees.

Ingroup Versus Outgroup Groups with which the individual identifies, by virtue of his awareness or "consciousness of kind," are his ingroups — his family, his sex, his club, his occupation, his religion. An individual's expression of subjective attitudes frequently reveals his ingroup memberships, which in turn, are often related to particular social circumstances.

It follows that the outgroup is defined by the individual with relation to the ingroup, usually by the expression of contrast between "we" and "they," or "other." Outgroup attitudes are characterized by expressions of difference and sometimes by varied degrees of antagonism, prejudice, hatred, or apathy.

Socio Versus Psyche Groups Coffey differentiates socio (school dropout committee) from psyche (boys' gang) groups in a number of respects.[2] There is no visualized goal in the psyche group, but goals are an essential characteristic of the socio group. Informal structure, few rules or regulations, voluntary and homogeneous membership characterize the psyche group. Membership in the socio group is often voluntary, but there may be those for whom membership is not by personal inclination but derives from serving as a representative of some organization.

Socio groups are usually more heterogeneous in respect to age, status, and vocation than psyche groups. The purpose of socio groups is to reach some defined goal expressed by the group. The psyche group's purpose — rarely made explicit — is to satisfy the emotional needs of its members. Neither socio nor psyche groups exist in pure form, most groups being a mixture. However, Coffey warns against any deliberate attempt to place simultaneous emphasis upon psyche group and socio group processes because the strain frequently leads to dissolution of the group. A therapeutically oriented counseling group would be most like a psyche group.

Goldman differentiates among several types and levels of groups.[3] He has represented the interaction of content and process in group guidance, group counseling and group therapy and his representation is reproduced here as Table 15.1. Three levels (I, II, and III) of process are presented across the top of the table. Three examples (A, B, C) of content are presented down the left side of the table. Process moves from traditional teacher-directed methods to more group-centered methods. Content moves from traditional academic subject matter to more personal, typically nonschool topics. Cell 1 represents typical interaction between content and process while cell 9 typifies a group therapy situation. Cell 5 represents group guidance activities. Goldman points out that group guidance and group counseling have, in many instances, been ineffective because they have been in cell 2 and 3 kind of operations, rather than cells 5 or 6. In such situations, the content of group guidance differs from that of traditional school subjects, while the process has not. In Goldman's opinion, this has produced ineffective group guidance in the schools.

GROUP PROCESS

Process has been described (see Chapter One) as continuous, dynamic, and directional movement. Group process refers to the actions and interactions used by a group to develop and maintain its identity as a group and its effects upon individuals who compose the group. Process (why and how) is often contrasted to content (what). Process incorporates the sequence by which certain experiences

[2] Hubert S. Coffey, "Socio and Psyche Group Process: Integrative Concepts," in C. Gratton Kemp (ed.), *Perspectives on the Group Process*, 2nd ed. (Boston: Houghton Mifflin Company, 1970), p. 50.

[3] Leo Goldman, "Group Guidance: Content and Process," *Personnel and Guidance Journal*, Vol. 40 (February, 1962), pp. 518–522.

Table 15.1 Interaction of content and process in group guidance, group counseling, and group therapy

		PROCESS	
	Level I	*Level II*	*Level III*
	Leader plans topics; lecture and recitation; facts and skills emphasized; units in regular classes	Leader and group members collaborate in planning topics; discussions, projects, panels, visits; attitudes and opinions emphasized; separate guidance groups meet on schedule	Topics originate with group members; free discussion, role-playing; feelings and needs emphasized; groups organized as needed, meet as needed
Type A Usual school subject-matter (mathematics, English, etc.)	1	4	7
CONTENT *Type B* School-related topics (the world of work, choosing a college, how to study, etc.)	2	5	8
Type C Non-school topics (dating behavior, parent-child-relations, handling frustrations, etc.)	3	6	9

FROM Leo Goldman, "Group Guidance: Content and Process," *Personnel and Guidance Journal*, Vol. 40 (February, 1962), p. 519. Copyright © 1962 American Personnel and Guidance Association. Reprinted with permission.

and activities occur, the methods used to provide the experiences, and the approaches to others utilized by group members.

In social behavior the movement is largely from individual to individual, whereas in group behavior there is a tangible qualitative interdependence of each upon others which operates in three ways: individual to individual, individual to whole, and whole to individual. . . . This quality in the relationship of individuals is the group and the way they work together to produce it is the process. . . . Group process is the way people work together to release an emergent quality, called psychological climate, group morale, esprit de corps, or cooperative unity, through which each discovers and develops his inner capacities, experiences, and learns how to create this emergent quality in all life situations.[4]

GROUP DYNAMICS

"Group dynamics" is a term used to convey many different aspects of group work. Fundamentally, it refers to the interacting forces within groups as they organize and operate to achieve their objectives. Herrold, some time ago, suggested that the term be reserved for processes used by

[4] L. Thomas Hopkins, "What Is Group Process?" in Kemp (ed.), *op. cit.*, p. 93.

groups with problem-solving or action purposes.[5] In such groups the needs of individuals become subservient to the goals of the group. To Jenkins the term "group dynamics" includes group process and group roles.[6] Several techniques have been developed for facilitating group control and group problem-solving. One such technique employed by specialists in group dynamics is the utilization of an observer whose task is to keep a running account of the group meeting to discover why things go well or why they bog down. These observations are presented to the group at appropriate intervals. For some types of groups, particularly counseling and therapy groups, the presence of a nonparticipating, judgmental person may limit the security individuals need before they can afford to face the threat within them.

What, then, is group dynamics? The phrase has gained popular familiarity since World War II but, unfortunately, with its increasing circulation its meaning has become imprecise. According to one rather frequent usage, group dynamics refers to a sort of political ideology concerning the ways in which groups should be organized and managed. This ideology emphasizes the importance of democratic leadership, the participation of members in decisions, and the gains both to society and to individuals to be obtained through cooperative activities in groups. The critics of this view have sometimes caricatured it as making "togetherness" the supreme virtue, advocating that everything be done jointly in groups which have and need no leader because everyone participates fully and equally. A second popular usage of the term, group dynamics, has it refer to a set of techniques, such as role playing, buzz-sessions, observation and feedback of group process, and group decision, which have been employed widely during the past decade or two in training programs designed to improve skill in human relations and in the management of conferences and committees. These techniques have been identified most closely with the National Training Laboratories whose annual training programs at Bethel, Maine, have become widely known. According to the third usage of the term, group dynamics, it refers to a field of inquiry dedicated to achieving knowledge about the nature of groups, the laws of their development, and their interrelations with individuals, other groups, and larger institutions.[7]

GUIDANCE GROUPS

"Group guidance" usually refers to any part of a guidance program that is conducted with groups of students rather than one individual. Lifton places the emphasis in group guidance on the imparting of information[8] whereas Caldwell states that "It should also be said at the outset that the common idea of 'group guidance' as an information-giving device is inappropriate to the concept presented here."[9]

Kirby has defined group guidance as follows:

> Incremental group guidance refers to a group process whereby the participants (group members) approach the topics or problems presented for group consideration on the here-and-now level, without necessarily having full knowledge nor even seeking full information about the individual or his ultimate goal.[10]

Bennett has cited seven common misconceptions about group guidance:

1. That group guidance, group process, and group dynamics are identical.
2. That the major purpose of group guidance is personal development.
3. That group guidance is primarily an information service.
4. That group guidance or counseling may be substituted for individual counseling.
5. That group counseling is group therapy.

[5] Kenneth F. Herrold, "Evaluation and Research in Group Dynamics," *Educational and Psychological Measurement,* Vol. 10 (Autumn, 1950), Part II, pp. 492–504.
[6] David H. Jenkins, "What Is Group Dynamics?" *Adult Education Journal,* Vol. 9 (April, 1950), pp. 54–60.

[7] Dorwin Cartwright and Alvin Zander (eds.), *Group Dynamics,* 3rd ed. (New York: Harper & Row, Publishers, 1968), p. 4.
[8] Walter M. Lifton, *Working with Groups,* 2nd ed. (New York: John Wiley & Sons, Inc., 1966), p. 14.
[9] Edson Caldwell, *Group Techniques for the Classroom Teacher* (Chicago: Science Research Associates, Inc., 1960), p. 10.
[10] Jonell H. Kirby, "Group Guidance," *Personnel and Guidance Journal,* Vol. 49 (April, 1971), pp. 596–597.

6. That any member of the school staff can carry on the group guidance function.
7. That group guidance may stifle individuality and creativity.[11]

Major reasons for conducting group guidance include (1) providing educational-vocational and personal-social information to students, (2) enabling students to discuss and engage in personal and career planning activities, and (3) giving students opportunities to investigate and discuss common problems, goals, and solutions.

The difference between group guidance and group instruction is not always clear cut, nor are the terms used with precision. The thread of distinction appears to be related to leadership roles. When the major responsibility for group activities is focused upon the adult leader (teacher), the term "group instruction" seems appropriate. When the focus shifts to the members of the group, the term "group guidance" is applicable.

GROUP COUNSELING

In group counseling one counselor is involved in a relationship with a number of counselees at the same time. Most authorities cite six as the optimum number, with a range from four to twelve. Group counseling is usually concerned with developmental problems and situational concerns of members. Focus is upon the attitudes and emotions, the choices and values involved in interpersonal relationships. Bonney has stated that the primary goal is the "creation of an interpersonal helping climate (counseling atmosphere) which will allow each individual to develop insight into himself and to achieve healthier personal adjustment. The vehicle for accomplishing this goal is the discussion of personal concerns at an affective level."[12] Group counseling is essentially preventive in nature, hoping to prevent problems from growing to the point where the individual needs special help to cope with them.

Group counseling has been defined by Gazda as follows:

> Group counseling is a dynamic interpersonal process focusing on conscious thought and behavior and involving the therapy functions of permissiveness, orientation to reality, catharsis, and mutual trust, caring, understanding, and support. The therapy functions are created and nurtured in a small group through the sharing of personal concerns with one's peers and the counselor(s). The group counselees are basically normal individuals with various concerns which are not debilitating to the extent requiring extensive personality change. The group counselees may utilize the group interaction to increase understanding and acceptance of values and goals and to learn and/or unlearn certain attitudes and behaviors.[13]

Gazda emphasizes that group counseling is problem centered and feeling oriented. Reflection and clarification of feelings and modification of attitudes are its focal points. The major concern is with helping members deal with their problems and experiences, and the emphasis is upon growth and adjustment rather than upon cure or deficit behavior. Characteristic problems among adolescent groups include conflicts or emotional upheavals such as sibling rivalry, independence-dependence, and the like. Educational-vocational concerns would be dealt with on a feeling level rather than an information-giving or instructional level.

Some have used the term "multiple counseling" rather than "group counseling," referring apparently to the fact that participants have a therapeutic effect upon one another. However, "multiple counseling" is increasingly being used to mean the presence of two or more counselors with counselees.

T-GROUPS

T-groups were formulated in 1947 by the Basic Skills Training Group of the National Training Laboratory for developing interpersonal skills and

[11] Margaret E. Bennett, *Guidance and Counseling in Groups* (New York: McGraw-Hill Book Co. Inc., 1963), pp. 20–25.
[12] Warren C. Bonney, "Pressures Toward Conformity in Group Counseling," *Personnel and Guidance Journal*, Vol. 43 (June, 1965), p. 970.

[13] George M. Gazda, *Group Counseling: A Developmental Approach* (Boston: Allyn and Bacon, Inc., 1971), p. 8.

sensitivity to communications. The participant in a T-group is involved in an experience in which he learns from his behavior, the T-group being an unstructured group of 10 to 12 people in which interpersonal relationships and behavior patterns are stressed. Group members learn to recognize the effect they have on others and how others see them. Usually they probe the strengths and weaknesses of each other's personalities in an unstructured atmosphere.

The current concept of the T-group and its relationship to therapy are as follows:

> Each individual may learn also about groups in the processes of helping to build one. He may develop skills of membership and skills for changing and improving his social environment as well as himself. The staff who work with T-groups do not see any necessary opposition between participation in groups and autonomous individual functioning, though they are well aware that opposition does occur in many associations of our lives and that group forces may be used to inhibit personal development. In the T-Group, on the contrary, the objective is to mobilize group forces to support the growth of members as unique individuals simultaneously with their growth as collaborators. Influences among peers are paramount in this learning process. In the T-Group, members develop their own skills in giving and receiving help. They learn to help the trainer (or teacher) as he assists in the development of individual and group learnings.
>
> While there are many obvious similarities between the T-Group and the therapy group — in part because any effective education has therapeutic overtones — the T-Group differs in a number of important ways. It tends to utilize data about present behavior and its consequences rather than delving into genetic causes. It tends to deal with conscious and preconscious behavior rather than with unconscious motivation. The T-Group makes the important assumption that persons participating are well rather than ill.[14]

Three factors that characterize the T-group have been cited by Golembiewski and Blumberg: (1) it is a learning laboratory, (2) it focuses on learning how to learn, and (3) it places emphasis on immediate ideas, feelings, and reactions.[15]

PERSONAL GROWTH GROUPS

Several names have been used for groups designed to facilitate personal growth: encounter, sensitivity, human awareness, human potential. Such groups are usually composed of eight to twelve members and their focus is upon the members' interactions within the group with attention to its implications for behavior outside the group. Goals of such groups include facilitating personal growth, increased sensitivity to the feelings of the individual and others, and greater awareness of self and others. Personal growth groups are often led by "facilitators" who are sometimes trained psychotherapists (some of whom have become highly dissatisfied with dyadic therapy) while others are led by individuals who lack professional counseling or clinical preparation. Many groups have two or more leaders or facilitators. An overview of encounter groups and descriptions of their theory and practice appear in a volume edited by Arthur Burton.[16]

FAMILY GROUP CONSULTATION

A form of group counseling called family group consultation has been developed by the staff of the Division of Continuing Education of the Oregon State System of Higher Education with the assistance and encouragement of the Department of Psychiatry. The term "consultation" was used rather than "counseling" because the staff believed it described more adequately the interfamily communication involved.

In family group consultation three or four families (consisting of up to 20 individuals) meet together weekly with three or four counselors. Zwetschke and Grenfell have described the typical

[14] Leland P. Bradford, Jack R. Gibb, and Kenneth D. Benne (eds.), *Two Educational Innovations. T-Group Theory and Laboratory Method* (New York: John Wiley & Sons, Inc., 1964), p. 2.

[15] Robert T. Golembiewski and Arthur Blumberg (eds.), *Sensitivity Training and the Laboratory Approach* (Itasca, Illinois: F. E. Peacock Publishers, Inc., 1970), p. 5.

[16] Arthur Burton (ed.), *Encounter* (San Francisco: Jossey-Bass, Inc., 1969), 207 pp.

procedure.[17] During the first hour, all family members are together with all counselors in one large group. During the second hour, adult family members and children meet with one or more counselors assigned to each of the two groups.

The process, reports Grenfell, was initiated to help overcome "the poverty of understanding" which appears in families having some degree of disorganization. Grenfell reports five considerations with which family group consultation is occupied:

1. . . . to improve communication and interaction within the family organization.
2. . . . to reduce the individual's distortion within situational events.
3. . . . to help individuals develop a sense of awareness of their personal impact upon others and the reactions created.
4. . . . to clarify for each individual whether the role(s) he plays meets family expectations.
5. . . . to determine the effect of individual role expectations upon family interaction.[18]

Conjoint Family Therapy Virginia Satir has formulated and practiced a theory and technique of working with families entitled "conjoint family therapy."[19] The theory and technique are based on the premise that successful intervention with an individual is contingent on understanding his role and position within a family. The individual who seeks help is referred to by Satir as the "identified patient," because he is the one most obviously affected by a troubled family unit. His behavior occurs within a family context consisting of interacting roles, rules, and values. According to Satir, communication between family members occurs at both a "denotative" level, conveying the literal message, and a "metacommunicative" level. Feelings and emotions are conveyed at the latter level.[20] Communication patterns have been classified by Satir into five categories or targets:

1. Where the literal message is one of *agreement*
   Where the affective message is *pleasing and placating*
2. Where the literal message is *disagreement*
   Where the affective message is *blaming and attacking*
3. Where the literal message is *changing the subject*
   Where the affective message is *being irrelevant* or *withdrawing*
4. Where the literal message is *being reasonable*
   Where the affective message is *conniving*
5. Where the literal message is *reporting oneself*
   Where the affective message is *making a place for others* [21]

Conjoint therapy theorizes that communications within the family are efforts to influence or ask something of a person to whom they are directed. In short, messages are requests. In this approach, the focus is on developing family members' ability to send and receive clear, functional communications.

GROUP THERAPY

Group therapy is usually defined as the application of therapeutic principles to two or more individuals simultaneously to clarify their psychological conflicts so that they may live normally. It is likely to be reserved for the more seriously disturbed and treats deeper personality problems. Slavson is reputed to have introduced the term "group therapy" to meet criticisms regarding the use of the term "group psychotherapy" by persons other than psychiatrists or clinical psychologists.[22] "Therapy," however, has become practically synonymous with psychotherapy in professional literature.

[17] Earl T. Zwetschke and John E. Grenfell, "Family Group Consultation: A Description and a Rationale," *Personnel and Guidance Journal*, Vol. 43 (June, 1965), pp. 974–980.
[18] John E. Grenfell, "Family Group Consultation: A Description," paper delivered to the American Personnel and Guidance Association Convention, San Francisco, March 24, 1964.
[19] Virginia Satir, *Conjoint Family Therapy*, Rev. ed. (Palo Alto, California: Science and Behavior Books, Inc., 1967), 208 pp.
[20] *Ibid.*, pp. 75–90.
[21] As reported in Lawrence M. Brammer and Everett L. Shostrom, *Therapeutic Psychology*, 2nd ed. (Englewood Cliffs, N.J.: Prentice-Hall, Inc., 1968), pp 323–324.
[22] As reported in Bennett, *op. cit.*, p. 21.

Hinckley and Hermann describe group therapy through the use of four characteristics: (1) the therapeutic aim of the group; (2) the alleviation of emotional tensions by sharing experiences and increasing self-awareness; (3) the permissive and supportive role of the therapist; and (4) the direct interest in and attack upon personal problems in order to foster attitudinal modifications.[23]

Group therapy for young married couples, delinquents, executives, and troubled families is increasing rapidly in clinics all over the country. More and more therapists are using video tape playback as a technique to let members see what, how, and why certain behaviors occurred in the interaction. Group psychotherapy has increasingly made use of certain techniques such as videotape playback, saturation sessions, physical movement and contact among members during sessions, and the like.

SPECIAL THERAPY GROUPS

In his book Mowrer refers to special groups and associations which are inspired and operated largely by laymen, and designed mainly to provide restorative experiences for their members.[24]

Previously, Mowrer had stated that in private practice

> . . . the patient, in now revealing his long-hidden sins, does so only to one person who, in turn, promises to be as secretive about them as he himself has been. It's as if the patient were suffocating in a closet and the therapist, instead of helping him get out into the fresh air, said to him: "Move over, and I'll get in there with you. This way I can treat you privately, without the necessity of anyone else's knowing what your trouble is." [25]

[23] Robert C. Hinckley and Lydia Hermann, *Group Treatment in Psychotherapy* (Minneapolis: University of Minnesota Press, 1952), pp. 19–20.
[24] O. Hobart Mowrer, *The New Group Therapy* (Princeton, N.J.: D. Van Nostrand Co., Inc., 1964).
[25] O. Hobart Mowrer, "Payment or Repayment? The Problem of Private Practice," *American Psychologist,* Vol. 18 (September, 1963), pp. 577–580.

Alcoholics Anonymous is an example of the approximately 265 such groups in the United States. Mowrer tells why he believes the groups came into existence:

> In short, these groups reflect, first of all, a general loss of confidence in professional "treatment," regardless of whether in an individual or group context. Also they reflect the pervasive failure of existing "natural" groups to perform the ideological and therapeutic functions which they should have been performing. Thus, in "inventing" group therapy for themselves, laymen seem to be creating a new social institution — one might also say a *new culture* — in which a kind of redemptive concern and competence exist which is not otherwise to be found in our time.[26]

MARATHON GROUPS

Groups which meet in continuous session longer than the usual one to two hours are often referred to as marathon groups. During such saturation sessions — often lasting 15–20 hours or more — members explore thoroughly their views about themselves and others, their relationships with others, their aspirations and goals, and typical ways of reacting to threat, disagreement, and prejudice. By confronting and challenging, yet accepting each other, members strive to develop open, authentic, self-responsible behavior.

SUMMARY

Table 15.2 presents a classification of several kinds of groups that attempts to differentiate between them in 10 dimensions. It should be noted that the clear-cut distinctions implied in the classification are difficult to maintain or defend. In reality, a better perspective would be to view the categories as lying on a continuum with overlap occurring to some degree as one moves along the continuum. It should also be noted that little, if any, overlap would occur between categories that are at great distance from each other. Additional

[26] Mowrer, *The New Group Therapy,* p. v.

Table 15.2 A classification of groups

DIMENSIONS/CATEGORIES	TASK GROUPS	GUIDANCE GROUPS	TRAINING GROUPS	COUNSELING GROUPS
1. *Common names*	T-group; planning committee; task force; discussion group	Discussion group; reaction group; planning group; information group; career group	T-group; interpersonal and intra-personal laboratories	Group counseling
2. *Kind of members*	Self- and other-selected according to potential contribution	Self- or other-selected by need for knowledge in area treated	Self-selection to learn group skills	Self- or other-selected because of perceived need for change
3. *Usual size*	5 - 15	12 - 25	8 - 12	6 - 12
4. *Focus*	Assigned task independent of member needs	Educational, vocational and personal information and planning	Self-disclosure and feedback; here-and-now interaction patterns; behavioral styles of members	Observable behavior; interaction patterns of members; here-and-now behavior
5. *Typical goals or objectives*	Completion of assigned task	Increased knowledge of environmental and personal influences in planning to aid decision making	Improving the quality of the individual's relationships and skills of interacting with others, primarily in group settings	Provide environment that facilitates self-exploration and allows for alternative behaviors
6. *Usual leadership*	Single elected or appointed chairman	Single counselor or teacher	Often co-led by trainers (educator, psychologist, social worker)	Either singly or co-led by counselors
7. *Usual leadership style*	Ranges from authoritarian or directive to democratic	Leader determines the direction of group and plans content	Leader determines direction of group according to perceived member needs	Ranging from directive to group centered
8. *Duration of group*	Length determined by time necessary to complete task	Length usually predetermined by nature of material to be transmitted	Length predetermined but usually ranges from one to 10 days	Length often determined by nature of setting but usually ranges from five to 25 meetings
9. *Length of session*	One to three hours	From 10 to 15 minutes	Usually eight to 12 hours per day	Usually one to two hours
10. *Setting*	Varies by nature of task, e.g., community, education, industry. Sometimes held in retreat or workshop	Educational (school, college)	Industrial, religious, educational, medical, and other organizations; sometimes held in retreat or workshop	Educational, religious, and community

PERSONAL GROWTH GROUPS	THERAPY GROUPS
Sensitivity; encounter; human awareness	Group therapy; group psychotherapy
Self-selection on basis of awareness of personal growth possibilities	Self- or other-selected because of perceived disordered behaviors
8 - 12	4 - 10
Quantity and quality of members' interactions within the group and implications for behavior outside the group	Members' behavior in and outside the group; psychological history of members
Personal growth; increased sensitivity to the feelings of others and self; more awareness of others and self	Personal change; modifying disordered behaviors
Often co-led by facilitators (lay and professional)	Therapist (clinical psychologist, psychiatrist, psychiatric social worker); often co-led
Leadership style individualistic depending on facilitators' experience, training, and personal orientation	Leadership style individualistic depending on therapist's experience, training, and personal orientation
Length varies from one to 14 days	Length varies from few weeks to several years
Usually eight to 12 hours per day	Usually one to two hours
Setting varies but usually removed from member's normal environment; sometimes held in retreat or workshop	Institution, clinic, or private practice

commentary on some of the dimensions cited in Table 15.2, as well as other dimensions, is presented later in this chapter.

Recent Research

Mounting interest in group counseling has led to a sizable crop of research studies. We shall confine ourselves to examining the extent to which current research is seeking solutions to perennial problems that remain unsolved and to discussing efforts to study uncharted ground.

CONTENT AND STAGES

Content Bates's analysis of tapes of group counseling sessions conducted with adolescents revealed that seven themes were discussed, but no particular sequence as to the emergence of each theme was noted.[27] The themes were given somewhat facetious titles. The topic "My Vices" — smoking, drinking, etc. — tended to appear early but, once worked over, was given little further attention. Bates explains that "My Vices" at times consisted of members' efforts to top each other's tales but usually involved a serious discussion of values.

The second theme was entitled "Outwitting the Adults" and seemed to crop up in one form or another in almost every session. Even though teenagers spend considerable time and energy in this activity, the "game" as such was not taken particularly seriously by them. Adults include teachers, parents, juvenile authorities. Bates suggests that this theme places the greatest pressures on any "teacher trace" remaining in the counselor but that if the counselor were able to resist giving evaluative comments group members themselves would present society's views of right and wrong.

"Parent Problem," the third theme, was seen as reflecting adolescents' struggle for independence and identity. It recurred throughout the course of

[27] Marilyn Bates, "Themes in Group Counseling With Adolescents," *Personnel and Guidance Journal,* Vol. 44 (February, 1966), pp. 568–575.

group counseling sessions. Bates divided the theme into two subcategories: irritation over being told what to do and resentment over not being able to make plans with friends because parents reserve the right to make last-minute changes.

The fourth theme, "My Brother, the Brat," usually involved discussions and/or reenactments of sibling rivalry. Discussion of "My Public Image," the fifth theme, tended to reflect the adolescent's struggle to clarify his value system. Discovering "Who am I?" was an ever present thread in the sessions and points up teenagers' intense preoccupation with self. A sixth theme, "Nobody Loves Me," involved discussion of school attitudes and elaboration of student feelings of helplessness and loneliness. The seventh theme was "Let's Change the Rules" and originated from group members who devised "better" ways of doing things around school. Usually groups engaged in this game as an academic exercise, but at times a press for action arose. In such situations, the unwary counselor may be trapped into defending and justifying school rules or into being the group's "front man" with the administration.

Bates's final words ring true:

> The world of the adolescent is a very real world and the rules are for keeps. Your entree of trusted counselor that permits you to enter this world carries with it the responsibility to understand and to accept. If you dare judge or moralize, the masks will be assumed and politely but firmly the doors to this world will be closed. If you can enter into this world, reflecting, clarifying, summarizing, in the group but not *of* the group, functioning as a counselor and not a member, then through the group process the counselees can clarify their value system as they struggle with their search for identity. You, as a counselor, may even do a little of the same.[28]

Stages and Topics Foley and Bonney analyzed tape-recorded group counseling sessions as an adjunct to a graduate course in the topic.[29] Certain stages of development were noted, and an "affect-topic" classification system was used to sort the verbal output. During the first stage, *establishment*, members revealed individual characteristics through verbal and nonverbal expression and received feedback from others. This stage usually occupied from one to four meetings. Then came a *transition* stage, climaxed by members' acceptance that the group's goal was to develop a situation that would permit therapeutic experiences. Movement into the transition stage often brought a reluctance to discuss personal problems. A period might ensue when there was lack of involvement of group members. This was eventually resolved through acceptance of a new group norm: members must discuss personal problems.

Topics dealt with during the development of the group were classified as "self," "group," "significant others," and "things and ideas." The latter category contained superficial discussions at an intellectual rather than at an affective level. The topic "group" involved discussion of group goals, processes, and norms or rules necessary for the development of the group. Personal feelings, attitudes, and concerns were classified under "self," and relationships with "significant others" had that heading. A frequency count of each member's verbal output was made from the tape recording of each session and an affect-topic rating of each verbalization was obtained and classified as follows: positive affect, negative affect, and no affect.

Group members, reported Foley and Bonney, spent about 50 per cent of their verbalization on "self," approximately 30 per cent on "group," 19 per cent on "significant others," and 4 per cent on "things and ideas." In respect to "affect," group members' self-references tended to be positive at the beginning of the sessions, negative during the middle sessions, and positive during the termination sessions. "Self" was discussed with positive affect 61 per cent of the time and negatively 30 per cent of the time.

Expression of Feelings Zimpfer classified counseling interactions according to underlying feelings expressed early and late in a series of 12 sessions involving 70 high school students divided into nine

[28] *Ibid.*, p. 575.

[29] Walter J. Foley and Warren C. Bonney, "A Developmental Model for Counseling Groups," *Personnel and Guidance Journal*, Vol. 44 (February, 1966), pp. 576–580.

counseling groups.[30] Categories included warmth (movement toward others), hostility (movement against others), and flight (movement away from others). Findings revealed that warmth was not related to increase in reported self-ideal congruence, but as counselees showed more warmth they were seen as more acceptable by their peers. Reduction in expressions of hostility did not accompany increased self-acceptance. However, Zimpfer reports that as the frequency of counselee refusals to become involved with the group diminished, he became more acceptable to group members.

ACTIVITY OF PARTICIPANTS

Salzberg compared the spontaneity and content of verbal behavior in group psychotherapy with and without a therapist.[31] When the therapist was absent, there was greater spontaneity among group members but their responses were less relevant to the problem. In leaderless groups, individual patients placed less emphasis on personal problems but became increasingly concerned over problems of other group members. Members often discussed the therapist's personal habits and their displeasure over his absence. When a member assumed the therapist's typical role, the session seemed to run smoothly and elicited favorable comments afterwards. If this failed to occur, the session floundered, and communication broke down into several separate conversations.

Seligman and Sterne[32] compared the verbal behavior of two groups of male patients in a VA hospital. One group participated in a sequence of five daily therapist-led sessions followed by a five-session sequence in which every other meeting was leaderless. The second group was treated with the sequences reversed. Finally, therapist-led, alternating sequence sessions, and leaderless sessions were compared. Both leaderless and alternating sessions produced more conventional or socially-oriented behavior than the therapist-led meetings. However, the therapist-led meetings were considered more pertinent, task-oriented, and confrontive than the leaderless sessions. These outcomes were supported in a replicated study by the two investigators.[33]

Conyne compared three facilitator-directed (FD) groups with three self-directed (SD) groups. Each group had eight college students and met for 25 hours. Statistical significance between the two treatment models was demonstrated. The FD group members, compared to SD group members, perceived more positive understanding in their respective group climate and viewed their groups as being more open, less superficial, and less phony.[34]

A generally accepted principle is that successful counseling depends upon the counselee's motivation: he must recognize his need for counseling and be willing to invest himself in the process. Mezzano questioned whether a group member's investment in group counseling was related to change in his academic achievement.[35] "Investment" was defined as participation in group discussion and actions and attitudes that indicated a willingness to explore and communicate feelings. The investigator asked school counselors to identify the two most and two least "invested" students in their groups. He reported a significant relationship between degree of investment in group counseling and change in academic achievement. He suggests that counselees in groups who are spectators be removed from the group and be given individual counseling.

[30] David G. Zimpfer, "Expression of Feeling in Group Counseling," *Personnel and Guidance Journal*, Vol. 45 (March, 1967), pp. 703–708.

[31] Herman C. Salzberg, "Verbal Behavior in Group Psychotherapy With and Without a Therapist," *Journal of Counseling Psychology*, Vol. 14 (January, 1967), pp. 24–27.

[32] Milton Seligman and David M. Sterne, "Verbal Behavior In Therapist-Led, Leaderless, and Alternating Group Psychotherapy Sessions," *Journal of Counseling Psychology*, Vol. 16 (July, 1969), pp. 325–328.

[33] David M. Sterne and Milton Seligman, "Further Comparisons of Verbal Behavior in Therapist-Led, Leaderless and Alternating Group Psychotherapy Sessions," *Journal of Counseling Psychology*, Vol. 18 (September, 1971), pp. 472–477.

[34] Robert K. Conyne, "Facilitator-Directed and Self-Directed Sensitivity Models: Their Effect on Self-Perceived Change," Unpublished Doctoral Dissertation, Purdue University, 1970.

[35] Joseph Mezzano, "A Consideration for Group Counselors: Degree of Counselee Investment," *The School Counselor*, Vol. 12 (January, 1967), pp. 167–169.

Group counseling is often applied as remediation for school underachievement. Presumably, the attempt is made to resolve problems that interfere with educational performance. Broedel's comparison of the effects of group counseling with those of no counseling for underachieving gifted adolescents showed a significant difference between the two groups only with respect to "increase in self acceptance."[36] In a later study Broedel and his associates counseled four groups of underachieving ninth graders.[37] Three of the groups showed significant growth in achievement test scores, increased acceptance of self and others, and an improved ability to relate to peers, siblings, and parents.

Baymur and Patterson reported that underachieving high school students who had a series of individual or group counseling sessions or a single motivational counseling session showed an increase in Q-sort adjustment score and grade average significantly greater than that of controls.[38] Jensen held small group counseling sessions for primary school underachievers with the result that participants improved in achievement and ability to do independent schoolwork.[39]

Benson and Blocher sought to determine whether group counseling would help tenth graders cope more effectively with their role as students.[40] Statistically significant changes (.02 level of confidence) in academic grades occurred; while not statistically significant, fewer disciplinary referrals were made; significant changes (.01 level of confidence) occurred in feelings of adequacy in coping with problems (SRA Youth Inventory); and more counselees compared to controls remained in school.

Woal wanted to find out whether group counseling could help selected students (1) reduce subject matter failures, (2) improve work habits, or (3) improve behavior.[41] The group consisted of six students educationally retarded up to three years, were generally in a poor environment, had negative experiences with teachers, and came from unstable homes. The words "counseling" and "guidance" were avoided, and the group was called a club, which met once weekly for 45 minutes for 28 weeks. Subject failures were reduced from 13 to 3 and failing marks from 16 to 4. There was some reduction in behavior difficulties.

Orsburn, studying whether group procedures were related to improved classroom behavior, compared eight weeks of sensitivity training to eight weeks of lecture sessions. High school student behavior was judged by classroom teachers, and/or by changed "real-self" and "ideal-self" congruence, as rated by students. He reported that (1) sensitivity training was more effective than either the lecture sessions or no treatment (as judged by classroom behavior), (2) both sensitivity training and lecture sessions were more effective than no treatment, (3) sensitivity training was more effective than either lecture sessions or no treatment for influencing the real-self, ideal-self congruence, (4) lectures had a temporary influence on the real-self, ideal-self congruence, (5) lecture sessions resulted in greater immediate change in behavior, but sensitivity groups continued to improve after treatment had ended, and (6) improved real-self, ideal-self congruence did not necessarily precede or accompany improved behavior.[42]

[36] J. W. Broedel, "A Study of the Effects of Group Counseling on the Academic Performance and Mental Health of Underachieving Gifted Adolescents," *Dissertation Abstracts,* Vol. 19 (May, 1959), p. 3019.
[37] J. Broedel, M. Ohlsen, F. Proff, and C. Southard, "The Effects of Group Counseling on Gifted Underachieving Adolescents," *Journal of Counseling Psychology,* Vol. 7 (Fall, 1960), pp. 163–170.
[38] F. B. Baymur and C. H. Patterson, "A Comparison of Three Methods of Assisting Underachieving High School Students," *Journal of Counseling Psychology,* Vol. 7 (Summer, 1960), pp. 83–90.
[39] George E. Jensen, "Small-Group Counseling for Underachieving Primary School Children," in H. I. Driver (ed.), *Counseling and Learning Through Small-Group Discussion* (Madison, Wisconsin: Monona Publications, 1958), pp. 286–290.
[40] Ronald L. Benson and Donald L. Blocher, "Evaluation of Developmental Counseling with Groups of Low Achievers in a High School Setting," *The School Counselor,* Vol. 14 (March, 1967), pp. 215–220.
[41] S. Theodore Woal, "A Project in Group Counseling in a Junior High School," *Personnel and Guidance Journal,* Vol. 43 (February, 1964), pp. 611–613.
[42] J. D. Orsburn, "Sensitivity Training vs. Group Lectures with High School Problem Students," *Dissertation Abstracts,* Vol. 28, 503A, 1967.

Mitchell and Ng investigated the effects of group counseling and behavior therapy on the academic achievement of 30 Australian university students. The students, rated high on test anxiety and low on study-skill competence, were randomly assigned to five experimental conditions and given treatment that involved either single-model procedures (either desensitization or counseling) or multi-model procedures (combinations of both). Significant reductions of test anxiety occurred in groups given desensitization, but both decreased test anxiety and improved study skills occurred in those groups given combinations of desensitization and counseling. Multi-model treatment group members, but not single-model treatment group members, improved their academic achievement as measured by course average, passing grades, and change in achievement scores.[43]

Dickenson and Truax reported that 24 neurotic underachieving college freshmen showed greater improvement in grade-point average than 24-matched noncounseled control subjects.[44] Further, the counseled students who received the highest level of therapeutic conditions — accurate empathy, nonpossessive warmth, and genuineness — improved the most.

The effects of two different methods of group counseling — leader structured and group structured — on personality characteristics typical of the male college underachiever and grade-point average were studied by Gilbreath.[45] Men in the leader-structured groups increased in ego strength (Diffidence-Egoism scale, Stern Activities Index) compared with those in the control group and had a significantly higher rate of positive change in grade-point averages than men in either the group-structured or the control groups. After counseling, group-structured subjects' rate of change in grade-point index was also greater than the controls'. Counseled men were more likely to express hostile feelings overtly than controls. Three months after counseling the leader-structured group's rate of positive change in grade-point average was significantly greater than the controls' but no greater than group-structured members'.

Lodata and his associates sought to determine whether group counseling could provide changes in attitudes toward school, the learning situation, self-concepts, and the like in individuals classified as "slow-learning" students.[46] Groups met from three to five times a week and engaged in activities such as pantomime, role playing, psychodrama. The results for the participants included (1) positive changes in attitudes toward learning and authority figures (teacher judgments), (2) increase in positive self-concepts (indicated by figure-drawing projectives), (3) improved school attendance, (4) greater integration of students into regular classrooms, and (5) increased tolerance, insight, and understanding of such students by teachers.

ON-THE-JOB AND VOCATIONAL STUDENTS

Hoffnung and Mills[47] reported that 28 male adolescents in a job training program for culturally disadvantaged young people were provided with 14 weeks of on-the-job "situational group counseling." The purpose of the group counseling was to supplement more conventional casework approaches. Interdisciplinary teams of group leaders (psychologist, caseworker, work trainer) met with work-training crews for discussions of issues relevant to the present life situation of the trainees. The adolescents who met twice weekly showed greater improvement in job performance and in overall adjustment than did those meeting once per week. Control subjects who did not receive counseling

[43] Kenneth R. Mitchell and Kim T. Ng, "Effects of Group Counseling and Behavior Therapy on The Academic Achievement of Test-Anxious Students," *Journal of Counseling Psychology,* Vol. 19 (November, 1972), pp. 491–497.

[44] Walter A. Dickenson and Charles B. Truax, "Group Counseling with College Underachievers," *Personnel and Guidance Journal,* Vol. 45 (November, 1966), pp. 243–247.

[45] Stuart H. Gilbreath, "Group Counseling with Male Underachieving College Volunteers," *Personnel and Guidance Journal,* Vol. 45 (January, 1967), pp. 469–476.

[46] Francis J. Lodata, Martin A. Sokoloff, and Lester J. Schwartz, "Group Counseling as a Method of Modifying Attitudes in Slow Learners," *The School Counselor,* Vol. 12 (October, 1964), pp. 27–29.

[47] Robert J. Hoffnung and Robert B. Mills, "Situational Group Counseling with Disadvantaged Youth," *Personnel and Guidance Journal,* Vol. 48 (February, 1970), pp. 458–464.

showed less gain than either of the counseled groups.

Prediger and Baumann reported on the outcomes of "developmental group counseling" conducted with 30 groups of randomly selected vocational high school students for a minimum of one academic year. Each group was composed of six to eight members and met 40 minutes each week. Two types of control groups, inactive and placebo, were used for comparative purposes. Outcome was assessed on each of 30 measures, many of which were described as socially-valued, external, and objective. No experimental-control group difference of practical significance was observed on these measures despite substantial differences between counseling group and placebo control group members in their perceptions of personal benefits.[48]

SUMMARY

Most studies of group counseling report successful outcomes. However, Shaw and Wursten note in their review of the literature that it is difficult to accept outcomes at face value owing to inadequate controls, inadequate statistical procedures, and inadequate outcome criteria.[49] Noteworthy also is the fact that relatively little attention has been paid to such questions as the kinds of problems best dealt with through group counseling, how groups may best be composed for greatest effectiveness, and the most appropriate size for dealing with certain problems.

Operational Practices

Some of the practices of initiating and working with counseling groups are identified and discussed here. Generally, group counseling principles are similar to those underlying individual counseling.

[48] Dale J. Prediger and Reemt R. Baumann, "Developmental Group Counseling: An Outcome Study," *Journal of Counseling Psychology*, Vol. 17 (November, 1970), pp. 527–533.
[49] Merville C. Shaw and Rosemary Wursten, "Research on Group Procedures in Schools: A Review of the Literature," *Personnel and Guidance Journal*, Vol. 44 (September, 1965), pp. 27–34.

SELECTING GROUP MEMBERS

Who should be in group counseling? Frequently the answer given is that members should have similar interests or problems, but this is not a necessity as long as the members can develop and function as a group. A variety of problems often enriches the group's experience. Homogeneous grouping in relation to age and social maturity is usually viewed as desirable, and it is often advantageous to have both sexes in a group.

There are some guidelines useful in selecting individuals who can benefit from group counseling. The counselee must want help, be willing to talk about his concerns, and appear to fit into a group. It is recommended that the counselor interview each potential member to determine whether he would fit into a group or the kind of group most appropriate for him. If the counselor believes the person could benefit from group counseling, he then explains how the group functions and what is expected of its members. Whether to become a group member is left up to the counselee. "The individual who knows what the group expects from him, and what he can expect from others, if allowed to decide without pressure, will usually be able to determine whether he should join a counseling group."[50] Some enter the group only to find it too threatening and withdraw. Individual counseling should be made available to the person who withdraws.

Not all individuals fit well into certain counseling groups. The very aggressive, the extremely shy, and the seriously maladjusted make poor members of a "normal" group. Previous relationships of members should be considered; close friends or relatives should not be in the same group, so that sharing will be more honest and threat from self-disclosure reduced. Hobbs feels that it is desirable not to have interaction of members outside the group session.[51] Undoubtedly this restriction would not be possible in a small school.

[50] Nicholas Hobbs, "Group-Centered Psychotherapy," in Carl R. Rogers, *Client-Centered Therapy* (Boston: Houghton Mifflin Company, 1951), p. 312.
[51] Hobbs, *op. cit.*, p. 313.

SIZE OF GROUP

The usual school practice is to select six to eight members, but there may be as many as 10 or 12. Most counselors feel more comfortable with five to eight members. As groups increase in size, collateral relationships are often weakened. The tendency is to depend upon the counselor rather than to become involved with other members. The counselor, in turn, is inclined to speak increasingly to the group as a whole rather than to members as individuals.

LENGTH AND FREQUENCY OF SESSIONS

The appropriate length of sessions for group counseling is generally given as an hour to an hour and a half for adolescents and 30–45 minutes for elementary school children. The first hour is usually very active and productive, but accomplishments dwindle rapidly during the second hour. In the school setting the length of session can be regulated by class periods. Many counselors report that the time between sessions should not exceed one week, and two sessions per week are often preferred. Some time lapse between sessions is valuable in that it gives the individual a chance to think over the experience. If counseling groups meet more than two or three hours weekly, productivity of the group may decline.

CLOSED AND CONTINUOUS GROUPS

The groups may operate as "closed" or "continuous." The closed group is made up of only those who were present when the group started. No one else joins. This is the most common practice in schools. The continuous group allows others to join at almost any stage. This open policy often creates problems of communication, acceptance, support, and the like among group members.

DEVELOPING THE RELATIONSHIP

The counselor is responsible for getting the group organized — quite often, by discussing the role of the counselor and explaining how the group should function if maximum results are to be obtained. The counselor states that each member has a responsibility for understanding and helping each other member as well as striving to solve his own problems. Members are encouraged to share freely and try out new ideas.

Attention is usually given, early in the process, to time of meeting, place, and confidentiality. Counselors often have members draw up mutually devised rules and guidelines; this participation can be helpful in establishing a working climate. By words and actions the counselor must help group members accept responsibility for developing and maintaining a therapeutic climate. Nelson suggests that the counselor explain at the beginning of group counseling that during each session each member is expected to spend time in (1) deep listening (hearing what is being said), (2) helping another to talk, (3) discussing problems and concerns, (4) discussing feelings, (5) confronting (pointing out when what is said doesn't seem right), and (6) planning (proposing to do something). Moreover, time at the end of each group session, Nelson proposes, should be saved to evaluate whether, and to what extent, these six activities were engaged in by group members.[52]

Nature of Relationship Opinions differ about the nature of the group counseling relationship. Essentially, the point of contention is whether group members have therapeutic potential by interacting with one another or whether only the counselor is the therapeutic agent. Those who believe that through their interactions members act as counselors conceptualize the relationship as presented in Figure 15.1 on page 364.

Others believe that gains by members are made primarily through members' interaction with the counselor. In other words, as the counselor is involved with one member, his involvement with another is less than meaningful. Basically, group counseling in this situation is viewed as individual counseling conducted in a group setting. Such a relationship is represented by Figure 15.2 (see p. 364), in which the essential focus of the rela-

[52] Richard C. Nelson, "Organizing for Group Counseling," *Personnel and Guidance Journal,* Vol. 50 (September, 1971), pp. 25–28.

Figure 15.1 Member-based group counseling

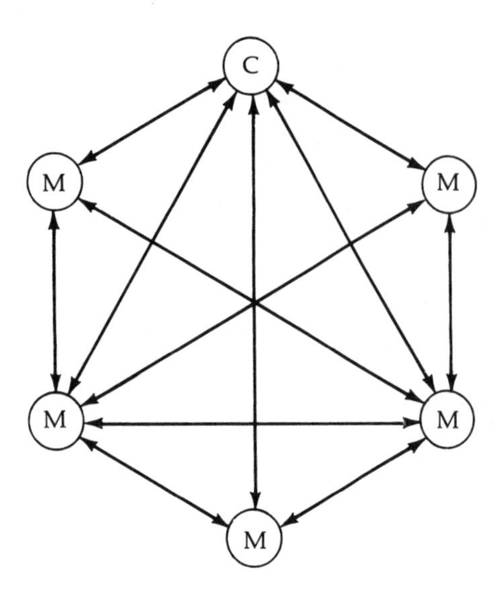

Figure 15.2 Counselor-based group counseling

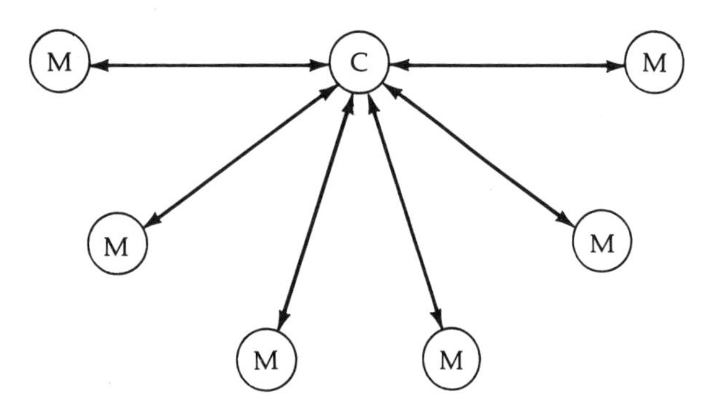

tionship is the counselor and his interactions with each member. Interactions between and among members tend not to be considered meaningful or helpful.

Getting Discussion Started Many counselors successfully employ the technique of "going around" the group and encouraging each member to tell why he is in it, what he hopes to accomplish in the sessions, or how he reacts to a particular matter. The counselor tries to help members learn to interact dynamically with one another. Given below are some leads — arranged from least to most structured — typically employed, following introduction of self and group members, by counselors for initiating discussion in the group.

1. Remain silent. Wait for a group member to begin.
2. Shall we get started? Who would like to begin? What would you like to talk about?
3. Perhaps someone will get us started.
4. You can discuss anything that you wish. This time is yours to use as you see fit.
5. What is the reason for our being here? Perhaps each of us can discuss what he wants to achieve from being here.
6. Each of you has been selected with the thought that you might gain something from a group experience and that you could help others gain from the experience. Perhaps someone is willing to share some of his feelings or concerns.
7. Some groups have found it helpful by having each member tell a little about himself and what he is doing. Would one of you take a few minutes to tell us something about his background and life history?

If the group does not respond, or if later silence develops, the following leads may be employed:

1. Everyone is very quiet. It is difficult to talk, to get started. It's sometimes hard to speak up, to be the first to talk.
2. I wonder why the group is silent? What do you think is keeping us from talking?
3. Can anyone guess why the group is so silent now? There must be reasons for remaining silent — does someone have an idea?
4. Are we trying to figure out what to say? Are we all waiting for the leader to begin? Do we feel that we can't say anything until the leader does? Are you waiting for me? Are we willing to share feelings?
5. Let's start talking about. . . . I'd like to raise a question. . . .

MAINTAINING THE RELATIONSHIP

The pace and topics are determined by group members. A general theme may evolve as a focal point for discussion and be used for some time or abandoned early in the counseling session. Group members usually venture into personal problems and return to a central theme. Sharing of personal concerns often builds like a symphony: the theme is the base and as the members recapitulate the whole problem begins to take form and make sense to the individual. "Formal structure is absent, but there is a clear pattern of development, an unmistakable direction and intent."[53] Members learn to be themselves, to discuss their concerns, and to identify their real feelings. By trusting, accepting, and trying to understand each other, they provide the mutual encouragement needed to struggle with problems and to try to change. As this becomes evident, members become more ego-involved and participate more meaningfully.

Increasingly, group members learn to play the counselor's role and, if encouraged, develop interpersonal skills and create feelings of mutuality and respect. Brammer and Shostrom suggest that communication within the group will be promoted if the following guidelines are agreed to and observed by the group:

1. One should not withhold feelings about another member in the group. These should be communicated directly to the person involved. The person should be addressed by his name or pronoun (you) and one should look at the person while talking.
2. Whenever a question is asked, one should state why he is asking the question. Example: "What is your reaction when someone bawls you out? I wonder if you don't feel like I do?"
3. When giving advice one should speculate on how he would react to this particular advice. Example: "I think you should reconsider before dropping out of school. I'm sure thankful Dad helped me to weigh things before I decided."[54]

[53] *Ibid.*, p. 296.
[54] Lawrence M. Brammer and Everett L. Shostrom, *Therapeutic Psychology*, 2nd ed., (Englewood Cliffs, N.J.: Prentice-Hall, Inc., 1968). pp. 339–340.

THE COUNSELOR'S RESPONSIBILITY

The counselor's skills and confidence are the keys to successful group counseling. Experience in individual counseling often provides a foundation for working with groups. The counselor's responsibilities in group counseling parallel those in the individual situation. He must convey feelings of acceptance, warmth, and understanding. He must be aware of his own needs and limitations and try not to let them interfere with the counseling situation. As the group proceeds, he must give full attention to the members and their interaction, allowing each to express himself as he wishes. He seeks to communicate confidence in each member's ability to solve his problems. As the counselor works, he helps define the working relationship, displays consistency, and sets an example in accepting and helping others. Unique to group counseling are the crosscurrents which develop among members. The counselor must handle these objectively, being sensitive as to their purpose and usefulness.

The way the counselor demonstrates his skills has considerable effect on how the group functions. Research by Powdermaker and Franks supports some of the following counselor behaviors in working with adolescents in group counseling:

> . . . (1) generalize from one client's remarks in the hope that other clients will see the relevance of the discussion for them; (2) emphasize the similarity between two or more clients' problems and emotions; (3) paraphrase a client's statements to clarify them for other members of the group; (4) encourage mutual respect by referring questions to another client or to the rest of the group; (5) emphasize the continuity of the meetings by reviewing important events at the beginning of the next; (6) apply general statements to immediate situations; and (7) help clients discuss relationships being developed among them.[55]

As in individual counseling, the counselor must capture and reflect the counselee's feeling, help him tell his story, and set the stage for desirable

[55] Florence B. Powdermaker and J. D. Franks, *Group Psychotherapy* (Cambridge, Mass.: Harvard University Press, 1953), p. 391.

learning experiences. His task is more complicated because he must be aware of group interaction and convey feelings of acceptance and understanding to members.

Ohlsen has suggested that the counselor can help maintain the counseling relationship if he

1. communicates to clients that he is trying to understand them;
2. invests in clients without becoming unwholesomely involved in their private lives;
3. detects and responds to clients' feelings;
4. conveys to clients how to detect and respond to client's feelings; and
5. develops in clients the feeling of responsibility for developing and maintaining a climate conducive to client growth.[56]

Bach has presented some do's and don'ts for the counselor:

1. Do try on the deepest emotional level to be an accurate reflector of the experiences of the patients.
2. Do remember that you are a service-rendering member of the group.
3. Do think of a group of patients as a basically constructive force, a manifestation of the capacity for mutual aid in man, which can and will grow.
4. Do recognize your responsibility for expert clinical leadership, for the therapist is both promise and threat to the group.
5. Do contribute to the group, through your clinical helpfulness and democratic leadership, rather than through lecturing about all that you understand.
6. Do share what you can of your knowledge and also of your personal feelings, experiences, and values with the group, when such sharing can serve as a useful stimulus.
7. Do help patients in the group to increase their tolerance for individual differences, which has impressed you so much in your training.
8. Do always attempt to gauge correctly and reflect the majority group consensus concerning any topic.
9. Do learn to distinguish among the group pressures on individuals.
10. Do acknowledge being puzzled.
11. Do always keep in mind that the goal of psychotherapy is the well-being of each individual patient.
12. Do at all times reflect and reinforce the group's own natural, but usually latent interest in becoming aware of all the elements involved.
13. Do learn to see and respect the constructive wisdom of the unconscious which manifests itself in the patients.
14. Do accept your role as a guardian of a therapeutically beneficial milieu in which the suppressed and unconscious creative as well as non-creative aspects of the patients can find explicit shared communications.
15. Do clearly formulate the therapeutic objectives you wish to attain and the means by which they may be accomplished.
16. Do, even though personality structure information is frequently unreliable, continue to try for better pre-therapeutic screening, diagnosis, and prognosis of every patient in apparent need of intensive psychotherapy.
17. Do recognize the principles of the social interdependence of human personalities.
18. Do engage in research. Keep records. Exchange ideas with colleagues.

1. Do not underestimate your own unconscious drives and motives.
2. Do not behave spontaneously in a therapy group as you would in an ordinary social discussion group.
3. Do not encourage or reinforce the patients' natural tendency to cure themselves by and through authority.
4. Do not get discouraged by the complexity of the life of the psychotherapy group, and the variety and intensity of emotions.
5. Do not lend your hand to a new group's attempts to reject pathology and to demand conformity in terms of normality.
6. Do not let your concern with helping to create and maintain a level of cohesiveness in the group trick you into overzealous tendencies to suppress realities.
7. Do not allow yourself to be pushed into the role of guardian of the communication-suppressing forces of the macrocommunity.
8. Do not forget the patients after completion of psychotherapy.
9. Do not think you are or that you have to be a father to your adult groups.

[56] Merle M. Ohlsen, *Guidance Services in the Modern School* (New York: Harcourt, Brace & World, Inc., 1964), p. 171.

10. Do not forget that, inevitably, you help your own psychological growth, that in a sense, you are a patient in your groups.[57]

THE CLIENT'S RESPONSIBILITY

The client has certain responsibilities in group counseling. By choosing to be in a group he agrees to share the challenge of helping to build a relationship. Through interaction, each member helps create and maintain a psychological climate which is conducive to sharing experiences and problem solving. This takes time to develop, but it can be done if the counselor's actions and attitudes set a good example. Each member has a responsibility to listen and help others express themselves. Members usually learn quickly to encourage others to define their thoughts and goals and to think and help others express themselves. Many authorities have recognized the therapeutic potential of the group which evolves from interaction among members. The primary process is not between member and counselor but evolves into member-to-member interactions. Emphasis is upon the assistance which is potentially forthcoming from each group member. Commitment to change is enhanced by helping members discover affiliation with other members who work to make similar changes. The counselor acts as a facilitator in this process and plays an ambiguous role, with structure and content evolving from the group itself.

Members of any group enact several roles at different times during group sessions. Benne and Sheets present some of these roles and their work adapted by Lifton appears here.[58]

A. Group Task Roles. Facilitation and coordination of group problem-solving activities.
   1. *Initiator contributor.* Offers new ideas or changed ways of regarding group problem or goal. Suggests solutions. How to handle group difficulty. New procedure for group. New organization for group.
   2. *Information seeker.* Seeks clarification of suggestions in terms of factual adequacy and/or authoritative information and pertinent facts.
   3. *Opinion seeker.* Seeks clarification of values pertinent to what group is undertaking or values involved in suggestions made.
   4. *Information giver.* Offers facts or generalizations which are "authoritative" or relates own experience *pertinently* to group problem.
   5. *Opinion giver.* States belief or opinion pertinently to suggestions. Emphasis on his proposal of what should become group's views of pertinent values.
   6. *Elaborator.* Gives examples or develops meanings, offers rationale for suggestions made before, and tries to deduce how ideas might work out.
   7. *Coordinator.* Clarifies relationships among ideas and suggestions, pulls ideas and suggestions together, or tries to coordinate activities of members of subgroups.
   8. *Orienter.* Defines position of group with respect to goals. Summarizes. Shows departures from agreed directions or goals. Questions direction of discussion.
   9. *Evaluator.* Subjects accomplishment of group to "standards" of group functioning. May evaluate or question "practicability," "logic," "facts," or "procedure" of a suggestion or of some unit of group discussion.
   10. *Energizer.* Prods group to action or decision. Tries to stimulate group to "greater" or "higher quality" activity.
   11. *Procedural technician.* Performs routine tasks (distributes materials, etc.) or manipulates objects for group (rearranging chairs, etc.).
   12. *Recorder.* Writes down suggestions, group decision, or products of discussion. "Group memory."

B. Group Growing and Vitalizing Roles. Building group-centered attitudes and orientation.

[57] George R. Bach, *Intensive Group Therapy,* pp. 204–209. Copyright 1954 The Ronald Press Company, New York.
[58] Kenneth Benne and P. Sheets, "Functional Roles of Group Members," in Lifton, *op. cit.,* pp. 20–21.

13. *Encourager.* Praises, agrees with, and accepts others' ideas. Indicates warmth and solidarity in his attitude toward members.
14. *Harmonizer.* Mediates intragroup scraps. Relieves tensions.
15. *Compromiser.* Operates from within a conflict in which his idea or position is involved. May yield status, admit error, discipline himself, "come halfway."
16. *Gatekeeper and expediter.* Encourages and facilitates participation of others. Let's hear about . . . Why not limit length of contributions so all can react to problem?
17. *Standard setter or ego ideal.* Expresses standards for group to attempt to achieve in its functioning or applies standards in evaluating the quality of group processes.
18. *Group observer and commentator.* Keeps records of group processes and contributes these data with proposed interpretations into group's evaluation of its own procedures.
19. *Follower.* Goes along somewhat passively. Is friendly audience.

C. Antigroup Roles. Tries to meet felt individual needs at expense of group health rather than through cooperation with group.

20. *Aggressor.* Deflates status of others. Expresses disapproval of values, acts, or feelings of others. Attacks group or problem. Jokes aggressively, shows envy by trying to take credit for other's idea.
21. *Blocker.* Negativistic. Stubbornly and unreasoningly resistant. Tries to bring back issue group intentionally rejected or bypassed.
22. *Recognition seeker.* Tries to call attention to himself. May boast, report on personal achievements, and in unusual ways struggle to prevent being placed in "inferior" position, etc.
23. *Self-confessor.* Uses group to express personal, nongroup oriented, "feeling," "insight," "ideology," etc.
24. *Playboy.* Displays lack of involvement in group's work. Actions may take form of cynicism, nonchalance, horseplay, or other more or less studied out of "field behavior."
25. *Dominator.* Tries to assert authority in manipulating group or some individuals in group. May be flattery, assertion of superior status or right to attention, giving of directions authoritatively, interrupting contributions of others, etc.
26. *Help seeker.* Tries to get "sympathy" response from others through expressions of insecurity, personal confusion, or depreciation of himself beyond "reason."
27. *Special interest pleader.* Verbally for "small business man," "grass roots" community, "housewife," "labor," etc. Actually cloaking own prejudices or biases on stereotype which best fits his individual need.

ROLE PLAYING IN GROUP COUNSELING

Role playing is sometimes useful in group counseling with adolescents since it provides an opportunity for acting as well as talking out problems. It enables each group member to gain a better perspective of himself and others. The utility of role-playing techniques lies in their spontaneity. Because role playing is novel, it may require some preparation of group members before it can be used effectively and without resistance. The counselor who introduces it should know group members well if certain pitfalls are to be avoided. The part of the unpopular character should be played by someone who is well liked or by the counselor himself. As the group becomes more familiar with role playing, the characters may shift parts, volunteer, and the like.

Unless role playing is used judiciously, it may have some damaging effects. Bach states that misuse may cause trauma if threatening materials are externalized prematurely.[59] When can role playing be used effectively? Ohlsen suggests that it is applicable in the following situations:

[59] Bach, *op. cit.*, p. 161.

When a client is having difficulty describing a situation or communicating his feelings about it to others.
When a client wants to know how others perceive him and his situation.
When a client wants to know how others react to his proposed actions.
When a client feels that he needs practice with social skills or that he needs to develop the confidence to act.[60]

Role playing is no different from other counseling techniques in that basic principles governing human behavior should be observed. Before it is used, the counselor should explain how it works and perhaps give a short demonstration. Its purpose should be understood by the group members. The person who is most closely related to the scene to be acted out should describe the setting and the roles of each of the participants. Each individual who volunteers or is assigned to a particular role should play it as he perceives it; his responses should be spontaneous. As role playing proceeds, any actor should feel free to stop the skit whenever he pleases. Members of the group may see the roles differently and want to change roles and replay the situation. This can often be profitable for it can convey how others feel in the same situation.

TERMINATION AND EVALUATION

Groups should be terminated when the majority decide to stop or when the situations and concerns which the group wishes to examine are exhausted.

Figure 15.3 presents a process group evaluation scale used in informally studying graduate student process groups at Purdue University. Part I is composed of five behavioral characteristics commonly encountered in group situations. Each member ranks the members of his group, including himself, on the basis of behavior observed in the just completed session. Position 1 (under "Ranking") on each scale represents the greatest frequency or intensity for each of the dimensions. Four continua are represented in Part II. Each describes an important aspect of a group situation and can be of value to the counselor or the group as a whole in assessing group progress.

[60] Ohlsen, *op. cit.*, p. 175.

Values and Limitations

The life of man is many sided. Aesthetic, economic, and religious facets are discernible, but blending into them all is the social facet. In everything he does, man relates to man. He incorporates a marvelously intricate and ever changing behavior pattern in his relationships with his fellow man. Other individuals play a vital part in his life, shaping his disposition and character. It is this factor, more than any other, that has led to the use of the group as a means of extending help to individuals. This section attempts to put into perspective other values and the limitations of group counseling.

VALUES

Group counseling builds upon fundamental ways in which people respond to one another and modify one another's behavior. With his predilection for life in groups, man is, as Aristotle said, "a political [social] animal." No evidence exists that any internal drive impels him to seek the company of his fellows; sociability is best explained on the basis of need and habit. "People are born into a group, grow as part of a group, develop through a group, create as a member of a group and in death leave the group."[61]

Group counseling appears to develop members' insights into their problems and feelings and helps them to arrive at some understanding of the causes of their concerns. Members talk about themselves, the things that disturb them, and what they can do to improve themselves. Each one learns to express himself in actions, feelings, and attitudes. Members learn that they can interact and discuss with one

[61] Cornelius Beukenkamp, *Fortunate Stranger* (New York: Rinehart & Company, Inc., 1958), p. 197.

Figure 15.3 Process group evaluation scale

Staff Leader____

Date____

In completing the Scale, please consider only the session just ended. In Part I you are asked to rank the members of your group by name, including yourself, with regard to each of the five behavioral characteristics described below. Position 1 represents greatest frequency or intensity and Position 6 refers to least frequency or intensity.

Part I

Ranking	*Behavioral Characteristics*
______________ 1.	*Contributing* — Relates experiences pertinently to group discussion, gives information and/or opinions related to the topic, and, in general, contributes to the discussion.
______________ 2.	
______________ 3.	
______________ 4.	
______________ 5.	
______________ 6.	
______________ 1.	*Stimulating* — Encourages the participation of others by introducing topics of mutual interest; stimulates discussion by soliciting comments from members of the group.
______________ 2.	
______________ 3.	
______________ 4.	
______________ 5.	
______________ 6.	
______________ 1.	*Adapting* — Appears willing to adjust attitudes as a result of logical arguments; remains flexible; open to new ideas and insights.
______________ 2.	
______________ 3.	
______________ 4.	
______________ 5.	
______________ 6.	
______________ 1.	*Identifying* — Seems to believe the topics are important; identifies with the group and appears to be affected by the discussion.
______________ 2.	
______________ 3.	
______________ 4.	
______________ 5.	
______________ 6.	
______________ 1.	*Facilitating* — Demonstrates an awareness of process by interpreting and integrating the reactions of participants; wants the group as a whole to show progress toward a goal.
______________ 2.	
______________ 3.	
______________ 4.	
______________ 5.	
______________ 6.	

Part II

Please indicate your reactions to the session just completed by placing an "X" at what you believe is *the most descriptive* point on each of the following continua:

1. Content (the topics and issues discussed)

_______________ The topics discussed were clearly appropriate for the group's consideration.
_______________ Most of the conversation seemed relevant and productive.
_______________ In spite of much superficial discussion, many topics were worthwhile.
_______________ A few of the topics seemed to be vital but most were unrelated to the group's objectives.
_______________ The topics in this session seemed entirely irrelevant.

2. Process and Climate (interaction among the members; the characteristics and atmosphere in the session)

_______________ The members seemed to be involved and concerned; they reacted to each other.
_______________ Some topics were followed up by the group in a productive way.
_______________ The members used each other for try-out, clarification, interpretation.
_______________ The group indicated more positive than negative feelings, but it wasn't a vital meeting.
_______________ The session lacked cohesiveness; it seemed like we needn't have met today.

3. Leadership (quantitative) — the amount of leader behavior.

_______________ He/she was quite active and spoke very often.
_______________ He/she participated verbally on several occasions.
_______________ There were a few times where he/she had something to say.
_______________ He/she said almost nothing.
_______________ He/she did not speak during this session.

4. Leadership (qualitative) — the nature and effect of leader behavior.

_______________ The leader's comments seemed to elicit insight, to facilitate interaction and mutual understanding.
_______________ The leader functioned primarily as a discussion leader and stimulator.
_______________ His/her comments were received as statements of fact upon which the group could center its discussion.
_______________ He/she participated as a member with no particular leadership influence.
_______________ He/she tended to dominate the discussion with little apparent concern for either group or individual progress.

---

another and that the group will help each person draw out his feelings. Alternate ways of behaving may be elicited from and tried out in the group.

Many counselors have reported that individuals respond better in a group of peers than in individual counseling relationships. Adolescent needs for conformity and acceptance by their peer group and for the opportunity to share reactions and ideas, to define meaningful life situations, and to gain independence are all met in part through group counseling. Ohlsen suggests that an adolescent benefits particularly from group counseling in that he learns (1) that his peers have problems too; (2) that, despite his faults, which his peers want to help him correct, they accept him; (3) that at least one adult, the counselor, can understand and accept him; (4) that the adolescent is capable of understanding, accepting, and helping his peers; (5) that he can trust others; and (6) that expressing his own real feelings about himself and others as well as about what he believes helps him to understand and accept himself.[62]

[62] Ohlsen, *op. cit.*, p. 148.

Combs and his associates cite five advantages of group counseling:

1. In dealing with several students simultaneously, it [group counseling] spreads the effect of the counselor and at the same time preserves his effectiveness.
2. It seems to be more readily accepted by students in that, since it occurs within a peer group, it is not as "different" or as threatening to them as individual counseling.
3. It makes effective use of the social setting and peer identification.
4. The adult experienced by students in group counseling is unique in that he is accepting of them and facilitates their experiences, rather than imposing an external judgment. He is a resource, a catalyst, and perhaps a new kind of adult.
5. Often, the establishment of counseling groups within the school may facilitate individual counseling and other new opportunities to meet the needs of the students.[63]

In his interviews with group members to determine what they thought were the beneficial effects of group counseling experience Harris reported (1) that they had looked forward to coming to school on the day of their group counseling session, (2) that they did not believe the experience had "straightened them out" or solved any problems, (3) that it had given them an opportunity to ventilate feelings.[64] One boy said he felt more relaxed around school and attributed this feeling to his group participation. Another reported that he had gained in understanding. One boy stated that he had changed for the group. Another said he was surprised to find that others had the same things bothering them as he had.

Pearson believes that the unique characteristics of groups are threefold: (1) The group is able to elicit commitment and involvement from members; (2) since group members share in determining goals and direction, the group, as an agent of assistance, can be sensitive to the particular needs of members; and (3) the group is able to exert powerful influence upon the attitudes of group members.[65]

Three other values may be briefly cited:

1. Participation in group counseling facilitates the development of mutual interaction in realistic and lifelike situations. Members can learn new, more flexible, satisfying ways of relating to each other.

2. Members of counseling groups may accept ideas and suggestions proposed by their peers which they might reject if proposed by adults. Reinforcement provided by members often makes decisions more likely to be viewed as commitments rather than acquiescence to an authority figure.

3. Reference is frequently made about the efficiency of group counseling in terms of time and money. However, a more meaningful criterion would be a measure of the extent to which group counseling achieves its goals.

LIMITATIONS

All methods have limitations, and group counseling is no exception. Occasionally, individuals are unable to function as a member of a group. They need to experience a relationship with one individual before they can relate and interact with a group. There are other major limitations:

1. The counselor's work becomes more diffused and difficult. Within the group, his contacts with individuals are diluted and his attempts at being one who is interested, accepting, and understanding are difficult to maintain.

2. The personal problems of certain participants may become secondary to the more general problems of the group.

3. While the presence of peers undoubtedly has value in many situations, it is sometimes a barrier. For some individuals, revelation of negative feel-

[63] Charles F. Combs, Benjamin Cohn, Edward J. Gibian, and A. Mead Sniffen, "Group Counseling: Applying the Technique," *The School Counselor,* Vol. 11 (October, 1963), p. 18.
[64] Wallace K. Harris, "A Beginning Counselor's Experience with Group Counseling," *The School Counselor,* Vol. 13 (October, 1965), pp. 47–50.

[65] Richard E. Pearson, "Group vs. 'Mass' Procedures — For What?" *The School Counselor,* Vol. 14 (November, 1966), pp. 97–100.

ings or attitudes or unacceptable acts may be too threatening if peers are present.

4. Still an unknown factor is knowledge of what concerns can best be dealt with in groups and what concerns require individual counseling.

The potential for harm exists in group counseling just as it does in individual counseling. Many in the counseling field are deeply concerned about the rush to group activities among those who are ill-prepared and inexperienced for such activities. Many ethical issues are unique to groups and others are compounded within the group setting. Currently, professional organizations are heavily involved in formulating ethical standards for group work.

Individual and Group Counseling

SIMILARITIES

1. The overall objectives in group and individual counseling are frequently similar. Both seek to help the counselee achieve self-direction, integration, and self-responsibility. In both approaches, counselees are helped toward self-acceptance and understanding of their motivations.

2. In both individual and group counseling an accepting, permissive climate must be provided if the participants' need to maintain their defenses is to be reduced. In both, individuals feel free to examine their feelings and experiences because respect has been accorded them. Both approaches strive to engender confidence in the counselee's ability to be responsible for his own choices.

3. In both individual and group counseling the counselor's techniques are important: clarification of feeling, reflection of feeling, restatement of content, structuring, acceptance, and the like. The counselor's skills are used to draw out counselees so that they are aware of their feelings and attitudes and can examine and clarify them.

4. The recipients of individual and group counseling are individuals who experience normal developmental problems. Both approaches deal with the common needs, interests, concerns, and experiences of the generality of individuals.

5. For both approaches, individuals need privacy and a confidential relationship in order to develop and to make use of their personal resources.

DIFFERENCES

1. The group situation provides immediate opportunities to try out ways of relating to individuals and is an excellent way of providing the experience of intimacy with others. The physical proximity of the members to one another brings emotional satisfactions. A counselee may get his peers' reactions and suggestions concerning alternate ways of behaving with others. An immediate firsthand opportunity is present to test others' perceptions of oneself in relation to others.

2. In group counseling, the counselees not only receive help but also help others. The more stable and cohesive the group, the more the mutual assistance. The cooperative sharing relationship helps the members feel closer to others, to understand and accept them. The interaction nurtures members, facilitates mutual expression of feelings and interpretation of meanings, and influences behavior.

3. The counselor's task is more complicated in group counseling. He not only has to understand the speaker's feelings and help him become aware of them but also must observe how the speaker's comments influence other group members. The counselor must be aware not only of the discussion but of the interplay of relationships among the members.

Our discussion has focused upon the values and limitations of group counseling and the similarities and differences between individual and group counseling. It should be noted that documentation rests primarily upon opinion and belief rather than upon experimental findings. Group counseling is not totally new but it is relatively recent. Therefore its merits and demerits, its use and contraindications, its appropriateness and inappropriateness await the test of time. The obvious need is to determine which individuals in what situations are best helped solely by a group approach or in combination with an individual approach. The answer to this question will not be easy to come by, nor, as has been the case of individual counseling, will the evidence satisfy everyone.

Annotated References

Berg, Robert C. and Johnson, James A. (eds.). *Group Counseling: A Sourcebook of Theory and Practice.* Fort Worth, Texas: American Continental Publishing Company, Inc., 1971. 342 pp.

This book of readings presents 36 articles and brief commentaries on each section by the editors. Articles have been selected which discuss group dynamics and communication, group counseling with children, and organizing and using group procedures in schools and colleges.

Diedrich, Richard C. and Dye, H. Allan. (eds.). *Group Procedures.* Boston: Houghton Mifflin Company, 1972. 256 pp.

Diedrich and Dye have brought together some 46 noted articles from a wide variety of sources that identify and discuss many fundamental group work practices and principles. These editors have laced the articles together in a way that gives unity to their topics.

Dinkmeyer, Don C. and Munro, James J. *Group Counseling: Theory and Practice.* Itasca, Illinois: F. E. Peacock Publishers, Inc., 1971. 355 pp.

Presents material on group dynamics, group counseling approaches, and change processes in group procedures. Identifies and discusses organizational procedures, starting and leading groups, and group counseling skills. Chapter 9 discusses group counseling with children and attention is given in Chapters 11 and 12 to consulting with teachers and parents.

Gazda, George M. *Group Counseling.* Boston: Allyn and Bacon, Inc., 1971. 273 pp.

The author presents procedures, principles, and practices useful in group counseling at all age levels. He views group counseling as developmental in nature and stresses that it is a preventive-remedial process. Treatment is given in Chapter 7 to summarizing group counseling research and, in the final chapter, to identifying some of the ethical and professional issues involved in group counseling.

Kemp, C. Gratton (ed.). *Perspectives on the Group Process,* 2nd ed. Boston: Houghton Mifflin Company, 1970. 351 pp.

This book consists of 57 selections chosen from scholarly works in education, psychology, sociology, and philosophy. Some classic analyses and researches on group processes are presented along with an introduction and summary by the editor.

Lieberman, Mortan A., Yalom, Irvin D. and Miles, Matthew B. *Encounter Groups: First Facts.* New York: Basic Books, Inc., 1973. 495 pp.

Describes encounter group process and outcomes, leader styles and influence, and practical applications.

Ohlsen, Merle M. *Group Counseling.* New York: Holt, Rinehart and Winston, Inc., 1970. 303 pp.

The author, recognized nationally for his work in group counseling, provides both theoretical ideas and practical suggestions for engaging in group counseling. He draws on the research and literature in the field to highlight the conditions useful in helping individuals in groups.

Further References

Beymer, Lawrence. "Confrontation Groups: Hula Hoops?" *Counselor Education and Supervision,* Vol. 9 (Winter, 1970). pp. 75–86.

Dreyfus, Edward A. and Kremenliev, Elva. "Innovative Group Techniques: Handle With Care." *Personnel and Guidance Journal,* Vol. 49 (December, 1970). pp. 279–283.

Gazda, George (Guest Editor). "Groups in Guidance." *Personnel and Guidance Journal,* Vol. 49 (April, 1971). pp. 591–684.

Guinan, James F. and Foulds, Melvin L. "Marathon Groups: Facilitator of Personal Growth?" *Journal of Counseling Psychology,* Vol. 17 (March, 1970). pp. 145–149.

Heilfron, Marilyn. "Leading Here-and-Now Groups." *Personnel and Guidance Journal,* Vol. 50 (April, 1972). pp. 673–678.

Hinds, William C. and Roehlke, Helen J. "A Learning Theory Approach to Group Counseling with Elementary School Children." *Journal of Counseling Psychology,* Vol. 17 (January, 1970). pp. 49–55.

Hoffnung, Robert J. and Mills, Robert B. "Situational Group Counseling with Disadvantaged Youth." *Personnel and Guidance Journal,* Vol. 48 (February, 1970). pp. 458-464.

Johnson, Robert L. "Game Theory and Short-Term Group Counseling." *Personnel and Guidance Journal,* Vol. 47 (April, 1969). pp. 758-761.

Mitchell, Kenneth R. and Ng, Kim T. "Effects of Group Counseling and Behavior Therapy on the Academic Achievement of Test-Anxious Students." *Journal of Counseling Psychology,* Vol. 19 (November, 1972). pp. 491-497.

Nelson, Richard C. "Organizing for Group Counseling." *Personnel and Guidance Journal,* Vol. 50 (September, 1971). pp. 25-28.

Passons, William R. "Gestalt Therapy Interventions for Group Counseling." *Personnel and Guidance Journal,* Vol. 51 (November, 1972). pp. 183-190.

Prediger, Dale J. and Baumann, Reemt R. "Developmental Group Counseling: An Outcome Study." *Journal of Counseling Psychology,* Vol. 17 (November, 1970). pp. 527-533.

Riordan, Richard J. and Matheny, Kenneth B. "Dear Diary: Logs in Group Counseling." *Personnel and Guidance Journal,* Vol. 50 (January, 1972). pp. 379-382.

Sauber, S. Richard. "Multiple-Family Group Counseling." *Personnel and Guidance Journal,* Vol. 49 (February, 1971). pp. 459-465.

Seligman, Milton and Sterne, David M. "Verbal Behavior in Therapist-Led, Leaderless and Alternating Group Psychotherapy Sessions." *Journal of Counseling Psychology,* Vol. 16 (July, 1969). pp. 325-328.

Sterne, David M. and Seligman, Milton. "Further Comparisons of Verbal Behavior in Therapist-Led, Leaderless and Alternating Group Psychotherapy Sessions." *Journal of Counseling Psychology,* Vol. 18 (September, 1971). pp. 472-477.

Tosi, Donald J., Upshaw, Kenneth, Lande, Angela, and Waldron, Mary Ann. "Group Counseling with Nonverbalizing Elementary School Students: Differential Effects of Premack and Social Reinforcement Techniques." *Journal of Counseling Psychology,* Vol. 18 (September, 1971). pp. 437-440.

Warner, Richard W., Jr. and Hansen, James C. "Verbal-Reinforcement and Model-Reinforcement Group Counseling With Alienated Students." *Journal of Counseling Psychology,* Vol. 17 (March, 1970). pp. 168-172.

Wiegel, Richard G., Dinges, Norman, Dyer, Robert, and Straumfjord, A.A. "Perceived Self-Disclosure, Mental Health and Who Is Liked in Group Treatment." *Journal of Counseling Psychology,* Vol. 19 (January, 1972). pp. 47-52.

Winder, Alvin E. and Savenko, Nicholai. "Group Counseling With Neighborhood Youth Corps Trainees." *Personnel and Guidance Journal,* Vol. 48 (March, 1970). pp. 561-567.

PART FIVE

COUNSELING: AN EMERGING PROFESSION

Part Five brings together material directly and indirectly pertaining to the rapidly evolving professionalization of counseling. This part closes with an effort to identify some persistent topics of concern to the profession.

Chapter Sixteen treats counseling considerations of a legal and ethical nature. Chapter Seventeen focuses upon problems and means involved in the crucial area of evaluating the service provided by counselors. Chapter Eighteen examines the process of preparing counselors. Finally, current issues and trends which, in the authors' judgment, are of importance are identified, examined and discussed.

COUNSELING: LEGAL AND ETHICAL CONSIDERATIONS

16

This chapter treats some of the complex problems of the law and ethics as they bear upon the field of counseling. Little direct case material is available, and few legal precedents exist which are specifically applicable to the counseling situation. Comparatively more material related to professional ethics is available.

Legal Considerations

There are many disparate meanings attached to the terms "law" and "legality." Diversity in definitions occurs because writers are generally concerned about different aspects. "Law" is frequently applied to a body of rules recognized by a state or community as binding upon its members. It also refers to the condition of society brought about by observance of these rules. "Legal" refers to law or the state of being lawful. Legal considerations that bear upon counselors are those which society requires of them in the performance of their profession or erects to limit their professional activities.

Basic legal provisions having implications for education are found in the federal constitution and in each state constitution. Laws as well as constitutional provisions relating to education should be of concern to all employed in educational settings. Laws express policies of the people and may be as significant in certain respects as constitutional provisions in determining the scope and adequacy of the educational program.

Any law may be constitutional or unconstitutional. Laws are assumed to be constitutional unless or until they are declared unconstitutional. Courts do not, on their own initiative or volition, rule on the constitutionality of a law. Rulings come only when there has been a proper legal action based upon a question or a challenge regarding the constitutionality of a particular law or some aspect of it. Some of the aspects of the law as it relates most directly to counselors are described here.

CONFIDENTIALITY AND PRIVILEGED COMMUNICATION

Those who seek counseling usually reveal intimate, personal, sometimes painful details and experiences. They turn to the professional so that they can disclose their feelings of anxiety, hostility, guilt, indecision, and so on without being hurt or punished. Because such highly personal and private revelations may bring embarrassment or ridicule, they do not wish them to be disclosed and usually assume that others will not have access to their disclosures without their express consent. When someone enters counseling under this assumption, a confidential relationship exists, and the professional person is obligated to protect the best interests of his client by maintaining it. Confidentiality has both an ethical (see next section) and a legal aspect.

Legal dimensions of a confidential relationship are as follows: (1) There is no disclosure of information, even though it is accurate, to individuals not entitled to it, and (2) material about the relationship entered in written records is accurate, reliable, and safeguarded. In some confidential relationships communications between the client and the professional are privileged and *need not be disclosed at judicial proceedings.* In this sense the professional is immune or exempted from testifying to personal and confidential information received in the relationship.

The term " privileged communication" means that a professional, under certain prescribed conditions, is not subject to arrest or prosecution for withholding information needed by the court in its determination of truth. Privileged communications are defined by Black as "any communications made to a counselor, solicitor, or attorney, in professional confidence, and which he is not permitted to divulge; otherwise called a 'confidential communication.' "[1] As used here, "counselor" refers to legal adviser.

Generally, the disclosure of all facts relevant to a litigated issue takes precedence over any consideration of the inviolability of a communication made in reliance on personal confidence. Consequently, even though a communication is made in confidence, either expressed or implied, it is not privileged per se unless the persons concerned bear to each other a relationship which the law specifically recognizes or construes as one that must be retained.

The sanctity of the attorney-client relationship was apparently the first professional one to be widely accepted legally and goes far back in English common law. It evolved from court decisions rather than legislation. Similarly, the clergy-parishioner relationship found protection without legislation. While privileged communication for the clients of both lawyers and ministers was established through court action, it was attained for the patients of doctors through both court action and legislation.

The rationale for granting the privilege is now and has always been the same: Confidentiality promotes full disclosure by the client and better enables the practitioner to help him. The privilege belongs to the client and extends only to the practitioner he has engaged. It does not apply to a client's relationship with an expert of the court or to the professional person of an opposing side in court to whom he may voluntarily submit for examination. It should be noted that the relationship between patient and physician is not completely protected because gunshot wounds, tuberculosis, and venereal disease must be reported to the proper authorities in many, if not most, states. Privileged communication does not accord any direct benefit or immunity to the professional person.

Statutory law grants no privilege to withhold relevant but confidential communications from a court except in a few defined instances. The common law recognizes only one absolute privilege — for communications made for the purpose of avoiding or settling litigation, which means chiefly communications between a client and his legal advisers, unless they be for the furtherance of crime or fraud. The privilege is granted not primarily out of respect for the confidentiality of information, but to secure the efficient administration of justice. It is not difficult to see that this aim would be seriously frustrated if the privilege were not available. The privilege has been extended beyond litigious matters to cover all professional com-

[1] C. Henry Black, *Law Dictionary* (St. Paul, Minn.: West Publishing Co., 1953), p. 29.

munications between a client and his lawyers, the extension being justified on the ground that anything which calls for legal advice carries some risk, however remote, of future litigation. The extension is capable of abuse. A company, to be on the safe side, might send through its legal department all documents which it would prefer not to be disclosed, and then improperly claim privilege for them. The remedy is for the courts to make better use of their power to inspect documents for which privilege is claimed, and to require more particularity in their description.

A conflict of public interest arises in some cases between the establishment of the truth in the determination of justice and the preservation of confidential relationships, whether personal or professional. General rules are of little assistance in resolving conflicts of this kind which must be settled in the light of the particular circumstances. The presumption is that the interests of the administration of justice should prevail. But that does not mean that they should invariably prevail.

The common law grants no other absolute privilege to confidential communications. It offers them various degrees of protection, all within the discretion of the judge. Communications between priest and penitent and between doctor and patient are the favorites. The first remains in practice inviolate, not in the least because instances very seldom come up for decision. Concerning doctors, laymen may be surprised to learn how ready the courts are to disregard the Hippocratic oath. Hospital notes do not apparently attract privilege. About other confidential relationships, involving such people as bankers, accountants, journalists, and counselors, there is little to say except that a duty not to divulge is recognized by the courts and implemented by judges so far as is consistent with the overriding claims of the interests of justice.

Wigmore sets forth four conditions which he believes should be met for granting privileged communication.

1. The communications must arise in a confidence that they will not be disclosed.
2. Confidentiality must be essential to the full and satisfactory maintenance of the relation between parties.
3. The relation must be one which in the opinion of the community ought to be sedulously fostered.
4. The injury which would inure to the relation by the disclosure of the communications must be greater than the benefit thereby gained for the correct disposal of the litigation.[2]

As previously stated, the major reason for privileged communication is that it supposedly promotes the full disclosure by the client that is necessary for the professional to be of help. Geiser and Rheingold believe that the privilege is needed by psychologists only if they function as psychodiagnosticians and/or as psychotherapists.[3]

One can certainly raise the question of whether or not the clients of psychologists need the privilege at all. A recent survey by the *Yale Law Journal* asked lawyers and judges their opinions on the need for a privilege for various professional groups. (*Yale Law Journal*, 1962). Of 125 lawyers surveyed on the question of privilege for psychologists' clients, 42 favored it, 50 opposed it, and 33 had no opinion. By contrast, 83 favored a privilege for psychiatrists, 49 for marriage counselors, and 24 for social workers.[4]

Further, according to Geiser and Rheingold, the Yale article reports no substantial evidence suggesting that the treatment of clients is hindered more in states without privilege for confidential communications with psychiatrists and psychologists than in states which extend the privilege. Explanations for this situation, they suggest, are that (1) patients mistakenly assume they have the privilege, and (2) since many clients never heard of the privilege, they tell professionals what they think is necessary regardless of the law.

Finally, Geiser and Rheingold believe that privileged communication should be granted to the client seeking services, regardless of what professional person he consults, for the purpose of obtaining a diagnosis of a mental, emotional, or ad-

[2] Wigmore, *Evidence*, 3rd ed., 1940, Sec. 2285.
[3] Robert L. Geiser and Paul D. Rheingold, "Psychology and Legal Process: Testimonial Privileged Communications," *American Psychologist*, Vol. 19 (November, 1964), pp. 831–837.
[4] *Ibid.*, p. 835.

justment difficulty, or for treatment by psychotherapy, counseling, or casework.

1. The community has a vested interest in the mental health of its members, and as such, diagnostic or therapeutic relationships with mental health professionals should be fostered as a desirable social policy.
2. Diagnostic and therapy relations are typically of the most personal, private, and intimate nature and a person's right to privacy in these vital human relations should be protected.
3. In order to effectively carry on diagnosis and/or therapy, and only these functions, an attitude of privacy and confidentiality is essential.
4. To violate these relationships in legal proceedings would be tantamount to asking the individual to testify against himself.
5. It is seldom that the only proof of events which transpired outside of the confidential relation, but revealed therein, is to be obtained by violating these relationships. The litigant should be forced to look elsewhere for his evidence.
6. As judicial distrust of social scientists decreases, we may look forward to the increasing appearance of professionals in court as witnesses. Hence, it is imperative that the clients' rights be protected and the privilege retained or granted for the functions of diagnosis and treatment.[5]

While both lawyers and ministers established privileged communications by withstanding court pressure, physicians, psychologists, counselors, and social workers have sought to do so through both legislation and court procedure. If a school counselor were called as a witness and claimed privileged communication immunity — refused to testify — the court might (but probably would not) accede and a common law precedent of considerable value to counselors would be established. Counselors need not feel obligated to give information obtained in counseling to any official unless they are in court under oath. Instances of this nature sometimes occur in connection with suits for divorce and child custody. A counselor may be called by the court because of his knowledge of the children involved, particularly in determination of the fitness or parental competence of the father and mother.

[5] *Ibid.*, p. 836.

Counselors in many states are working to establish statutes to safeguard the right to confidentiality of the personal information received in counseling. Because of the differences in state laws, it is difficult to determine exactly which states do or do not provide confidentiality and to what degree. The Michigan statute appears to furnish confidentiality:

No teacher, guidance officer, school executive or other professional person engaged in character building in the public school or any other educational institution, including any clinical worker of such schools and institutions, who maintains records of students' behavior or has such records in his custody, or who receives in confidence communications from students or juveniles, shall be allowed in any proceedings, civil or criminal, in any court of this state, to disclose any information obtained by him from such records or such communications nor to produce such records or transcripts thereof. . . .[6]

Oklahoma's code merely states that "It shall be unlawful and a misdemeanor for any teacher to reveal any information concerning any child obtained by him in his capacity as teacher except as may be required in the performance of his contractual duties."[7] A recent Indiana statute states,

Section 2. Any counselor duly appointed or designated a counselor for the school system by its proper officers and for the purpose of counseling pupils in such school shall be immune from disclosing any privileged or confidential communication made to such counselor by such pupil herein referred to. Such matters so communicated shall be privileged and protected against disclosure.[8]

Gade reports that North Dakota passed a privileged communication law in 1969 for school counselors.[9] It reads that

[6] *Michigan Compiled Laws*, 1948, Sec. 617.85.
[7] *Oklahoma Statutes*, 1951, Title 70, Article 6–16.
[8] Sec. 2, House Enrolled Act No. 1309, 1965.
[9] Eldon M. Gade, "Implications of Privileged Communication Laws for Counselors," *The School Counselor*, Vol. 19 (January, 1972), pp. 150–152.

For the purpose of counseling in a school system, any elementary or secondary school counselor possessing a valid North Dakota Guidance credential from the Department of Public Instruction, and who has been duly appointed a counselor for a school system by its proper authority, shall be legally immune from disclosing any privileged or confidential communication made to such counselor in a counseling interview. Such communication shall be disclosed when requested by the counselee.

Huckins summarizes the nationwide status of privilege as it applies to the counselor-counselee relationship:

. . . (1) six states have recognized the confidentiality of the relationship specifically, though in varying degrees, (2) approximately seven have given state boards of education the power to establish confidentiality for counseling information, (3) eleven more have made confidential communications possible for counselors through licensure as psychologists, and (4) three others have made their protection contingent upon such varied criteria as being regarded as a practitioner of the healing arts, status as a public officer or as an employee of a public officer.[10]

Communications to a public officer (see Huckins' statement) considered privileged must meet three conditions: First, the information or communication must have been made to a public officer; second, it must have been made to him in official confidence; and third, the presiding judge must determine that the public interest would suffer by disclosure. School board members and superintendents have been held to qualify as public officers — individuals whose positions have been created by constitution or legislation. Teachers, counselors, and principals may be classified as employees and not officers.

While Huckins reports that in 1968 six states had recognized, at least to some degree, privileged communication for counselors, Gade reports that only four states (Michigan, Wisconsin, Indiana, and North Dakota) had specifically done so by 1972. More recently, the APGA *Guidepost* (August 31, 1973) reported that confidentiality laws for counselors had been enacted in 15 states: Hawaii, Delaware, Colorado, Idaho, Indiana, Maryland, Michigan, Montana, Nevada, North Carolina, North Dakota, Oregon, Pennsylvania, Washington, and Maine.

Counseling Interview Information as Hearsay Some authorities have speculated that a great deal of information which a school counselor would be called upon to reveal in court would be considered "hearsay" and therefore not admissible as evidence. But there are many exceptions to the hearsay rule. Basically, hearsay law prohibits testimony or other proof of statements made out of court by persons not under oath and not presented as witnesses and thus not available for direct and cross examination. Wrenn, in a widely quoted article, described most of what a counselee tells a counselor as "almost always hearsay evidence and therefore not admissible in court."[11] Counselor recordings of counselee comments might also be considered inadmissible as evidence in the same manner as counselor testimony concerning a happening or situation described to him by a counselee. However, two considerations should be noted. First, although the counselor's testimony regarding something he hears his counselee say might be termed "hearsay," the fact that he heard him say it would not be. Second, while a witness is not expected to testify to knowledge derived from the statements of others, he can testify to knowledge which he himself has acquired in line of duty or employment.

Records Generally, most authorities believe that counselor-made notes or summaries of the events and/or experiences which occur in counseling can be withheld from subpoena and public inspection because (1) they are not kept by public officers

[10] Wesley C. Huckins, *Ethical and Legal Considerations in Guidance,* Houghton Mifflin Professional Guidance Monographs (Boston: Houghton Mifflin Company, 1968, p. 37.

[11] C. Gilbert Wrenn, "The Ethics of Counseling," *Educational and Psychological Measurement,* Vol. 12 (Summer, 1952), pp. 161–177.

and are not "school records," and (2) they are made for the counselor's own convenience. Under common law public records are open to public inspection although in some jurisdictions the right of inspection is limited to those who can demonstrate special interest. School records do, however, meet many of the tests established for public records (one test being that they are required by the law).

A few states provide by statute that the cumulative records of students may be open to parent inspection. Some include the notation that the inspection may take place in consultation with an employee of the school. A 1961 New York case has received much publicity in this respect. Burt has described this case, in which certain members of a school faculty advised a parent to secure psychological treatment for his son.[12] The parent retained a physician, who requested in written form that the school board direct the superintendent to make the student's school records available for the parent's inspection. Since the school board's policy was that parents were to be kept informed about their children through report cards, conferences with teachers, and interpretations during conferences with school personnel, the board offered the parent full cooperation under this policy but refused to allow direct access to the records. The parent sought to compel production of the records through an action in mandamus. The court granted the petition for mandamus.

Essentially, then, parents, who inherently possess an interest in the school records of their children, probably have a right at common law to inspect these records. Communications to parents by counselors, if made in good faith and without malice, about recorded information would not have liability. Rezny, discussing inspection and release of records to professional school staff, asks, "Who shall see the pupil records?"[13] His answer is that they should be seen only by those staff members who have an interest in the general welfare of the pupil. "Interest" is suggested as being determined by whether it is for the good of the pupil.

To move to a somewhat different area: School counselors often are asked to submit evaluations of pupils who are applying for admission to college. In many cases the counselor's opinion as to the student's probable success or failure is requested. Most college admission officers would not reveal the counselor's comments or ratings to the parents or students, but because of the pressure in many families to gain college admission, counselors often express concern and distress lest their remarks, observations, and ratings be revealed. As previously noted, such statements would probably be judged to have qualified privilege, and no liability would be attached where such recommendations were made in good faith and without malice.

EXPERT WITNESS

School counselors have not, to any appreciable degree, sought recognition as expert witnesses. Psychologists have engaged actively in gaining recognition that their testimony is expert and in establishing a definition of psychology acceptable to legal authorities. At present whether a psychologist receives professional recognition in a court depends largely upon the discretion of the court, except where states have statutes defining a psychologist.

An expert witness is one qualified to give testimony requiring special knowledge, skill, experience, or training. The presiding judge makes the decision as to whether the expert's testimony is admissible. Testimony may be taken in any one of four different ways: by affidavit, by deposition, by interrogatory, and orally from the witness stand. The fundamental qualification governing the competence of a witness to express a professional expert opinion is that he have sufficient experience with the subject of his testimony to enable him to testify with reliability. The expert witness must demonstrate that he possesses some special and peculiar experience before he is permitted to pro-

[12] Loren A. Burt, "Inspection and Release of Records to Parents," in Martha L. Ware (ed.), *Law of Guidance and Counseling* (Cincinnati: The W. H. Anderson Co., 1964), pp. 43–45.
[13] Arthur A. Rezny, "Inspection and Release of Records to Professional School Staff," in Ware (ed.), *op. cit.*, p. 53.

ceed to the substance of his testimony. But there is nothing arcane about this special and peculiar experience. As stated by Wigmore,

> This special and peculiar experience may have been attained, so far as legal rules go, in any way whatever; all the law requires is that it has been attained. Yet it is possible here to group roughly two classes of experience which are usually, though not necessarily, found separately:
> (a) There is, first, an *occupational* experience. . . .
> (b) There is, secondly, a *systematic training*. . . .
> Now, the line, if any can be drawn, between these two had no general legal significance. In truth, no accurate line can be drawn. Each shades into the other imperceptibly. In some instances, the witness will need both; in some instances he may have both, though he does not need both. Neither is generally favored above the other by the Courts. The question in each instance is whether the particular witness is fitted to the matter at hand.[14]

Psychiatrists and clinical psychologists are sometimes called upon as expert witnesses to testify as to criminal responsibility. The primary tests of criminal responsibility in the United States are based upon two rules, the McNaughten Rule and the Durham Decision. The McNaughten Rule, formulated in England in 1843, essentially states that every man is presumed to be sane and to possess reason so as to be responsible for his crimes and that to establish defense on the grounds of insanity it must be clearly proved that at the time of committing the act, the individual did not know that what he was doing was wrong. The essence of the Durham Decision (1954) is that an accused criminal will not be held responsible if his criminal act was the product of a mental disease or defect, and this is made a matter of fact for the jury to decide.

Liefer provides a penetrating analysis of these two rules and the nature of expert witness by psychiatrists in cases of challenged responsibility.[15] The McNaughten Rule, he points out, asserts that responsibility is a function of the intellect, that reason is aligned with responsibility and defect of reason with nonresponsibility. The key to determination of responsibility is whether the accused *knows* the nature and quality of his act and *knows* that what he was doing was wrong. Liefer suggests that the applicability of the verb "to know" is based upon the evaluation of the behavior of the person in question, but contrary to popular belief, psychiatrists do not infer from behavior what is going on in that private sphere of events, the mind. Rather, evaluation of another person's knowledge is a commentary about his behavior. Whether a man "knows" can be told only by applying conventional standards which link behavior and language. Essentially, if the accused replied to questions with irrelevant and disconnected phrases, he would be considered not to know the nature and quality of the act in question. On the other hand, if he could give a detailed, coherent account of his actions, he would be considered, by convention, to know the nature and quality of his acts.

Liefer further points out that the ambiguous terms employed by the McNaughten Rule — right and wrong, nature and quality, and knowing — led to the use of psychiatric experts to aid the court. This has resulted in the impression that determination rests on scientifically determined fact rather than ambiguous semantics. The Durham Decision changes the legal definition of responsibility from imputing it to a competent intellect to imputing it to a well-integrated personality. It acknowledges that the intentionality of human actions is not a function of the intellect alone but results from a complex of cognitive, emotional, and unconscious factors. However, Liefer states that even under the Durham Decision the ascription of responsibility was not made any more scientific because

> In psychiatry, the characteristic of behavior which negates its intentional nature and qualifies it for the designation "illness" is precisely that it is unconventional; that is to say, no acceptable conventional explanations can be offered by the actor. It is therefore a history of unconventional behavior of a socially disruptive nature

[14] Wigmore, *Evidence*, 3rd ed., 1940, Sec. 556.
[15] Ronald Leifer, "The Psychiatrist and Tests of *Criminal* Responsibility," *American Psychologist*, Vol. 19 (November, 1964), pp. 825–830.

which defeats the ascription of both mental health and intention.[16]

Essentially, Liefer's conclusion is that the primary effect of the Durham Decision was to make the psychiatrist more comfortable with his testimony.

Vocational counselors are employed as expert witnesses in processing claims for disability insurance under Section 216 (I) and Section 223 of the Social Security Act. In this capacity, expertness must be demonstrated in the assessment of skills and abilities and in knowledge of jobs and the labor market. Wiener states that "The prime difference posed by this experience is that the vocational counselor has no contact with the claimant (client) prior to the hearing and must make his assessment on the basis of official exhibits and the testimony elicited during the hearing."[17]

The counselor in this capacity appears at the request of the government, but he is not to testify on behalf of the government. Rather his reason for being there is to give expert testimony and he should not go beyond the recognized boundaries of his expertness.

Schofield cites some principles which govern expert testimony. These are summarized here:

1. The expert witness should state the facts as clearly as possible.
2. In addition to a clear statement of his procedures and findings, the expert should state his interpretation of those findings, i.e., his opinion, in a clear form.
3. The expert should adapt his terminology and his grammar to the level of the average lay person.[18]

LIBEL AND SLANDER

Libel and slander are a form of defamation. While state statutes vary somewhat in defining defamation, Shrewsbury states that defamation (1) involves exposure to hatred, ridicule, contempt, or pecuniary loss; (2) must affect a living person by blackening the memory of one dead or the reputation of one alive; and (3) must, for purposes of recovery, be revealed to a third party.[19] Defamation is the invasion of an individual's interest in his reputation and good name, causing others to shun him or to have unpleasant or derogatory feelings about him. If defamation is in written or printed form, it is libel; if in spoken form, slander.

Seitz points out that distinctions between slander and libel have significance and that in civil actions for slander at common law there can be no recovery of damages unless the comment fell within one of four categories or unless special or actual money damages could be demonstrated. The four categories that justify recovery of money for slander are (1) imputation of serious crime, (2) imputation of certain loathsome diseases, (3) imputation of unchastity in a woman, and (4) imputation affecting the plaintiff in his business, trade, or profession.[20] The plaintiff must prove the factors that made the charge defamatory and must prove specific application of the defamation to him. Damages can be recovered to the extent that mental suffering and loss of reputation can be proved.

Laws of slander and libel have implications for the school counselor. First, care must be taken in the preparation, handling, and storage of counseling records and notes. If records containing certain statements about a counselee could be interpreted as damaging or as untrue as revealed to a third person, actions for libel could be initiated. Second, a counselor should consider carefully what he says about individuals who have entered into a counseling relationship with him and the situations in which his remarks are made. Truthful and sincere consultations about clients with professional col-

[16] *Ibid.*, p. 830.

[17] Frederick Wiener, "The Role of the Vocational Counselor as an Expert Witness," *Personnel and Guidance Journal*, Vol. 43 (December, 1964), p. 348.

[18] William Schofield, "Psychology, Law and Expert Witness," *American Psychologist*, Vol. 11 (January, 1956), p. 3.

[19] Thomas B. Shrewsbury, "Legal Implications for Student Personnel Workers," in Esther Lloyd-Jones and Margaret R. Smith (eds.), *Student Personnel Work as Deeper Teaching* (New York: Harper & Brothers, 1954), p. 306.

[20] Reynolds C. Seitz, "Law of Slander and Libel," in Ware (ed.), *op. cit.*, p. 22.

leagues or administrators would normally not be considered slanderous.

Truth is an absolute defense for charges of slander or libel. The defendant has the burden of convincing the jury that his statements were true. However, some statutes have removed truth as a full defense and require that utterances must be published with good intentions and justifiable ends. At times the law excuses and sanctions dissemination of defamatory material in oral or written form if such statements are of social importance. Seitz states that the law does this under what is known as absolute or qualified privilege.[21] *Absolute privilege* refers to occasions when it is to the public's interest for the utterer to speak his mind fully and fearlessly. The privilege is so firmly entrenched that the courts do not permit inquiries into the intentions of the person who makes the statement. Absolute privilege is limited to comments by judges in judicial proceedings, comments by legislators in session, and communications of certain executive officers of the government in the discharge of their duties. *Qualified privilege* recognizes that information must be given whenever it is reasonably necessary for (1) the protection of one's own interest, (2) the interest of third parties, or (3) certain interests of the public. Most jurisdictions afford protection against liability even if, unknowingly, misinformation is given so long as there is an honest and reasonable effort to protect the interest in question.

Qualified privilege differs from privileged communication. While both terms deal with communication of knowledge about clients, Krauskopf points up the differences:

> The former [qualified privilege] is a principle (developed by the courts without the aid of statutes) which protects a defendant from liability if he made a defamatory statement in good faith under justifiable circumstances. The law recognizes that it is sometimes socially desirable for information concerning people to be communicated to others. For example, it is socially desirable for a student's professors to furnish information to prospective employers. A defamatory statement made in good faith and under these circumstances is said to be qualifiedly privileged. In other words qualified privilege is an expression which connotes only a substantive defense to tort action. . . .
> Privileged communication, as used in the law of evidence, is a right of clients of professional persons to prevent the professional person from revealing communications of the client in legal proceedings.[22]

[21] *Ibid.*, pp. 23–24.

RIGHT OF PRIVACY

The right of privacy is a fairly recent rule of law since historically privacy was not respected or physically possible in the home, place of work, or public accommodation. Although protection has long been given to private property and against defamation of reputation and bodily injury, the law was slow to recognize the primacy of the individual and his claim to freedom, dignity, and privacy. The recent use and misuse of electronic eavesdropping devices have stimulated legal attention to this situation. New guidelines were recently established (1967) by the federal government to curtail electronic eavesdropping by federal agents. Under the rules, the attorney general is now the sole official who can authorize such procedures, and federal investigators must obtain advance approval from him in order to use them. In emergencies, federal agency heads are permitted to authorize eavesdropping gear but they must explain to the attorney general within 24 hours why it was an emergency. Criteria that were established require that agencies seeking approval to eavesdrop specify (1) the reason for the action, (2) the type of equipment to be used, (3) the name of the person involved, (4) the proposed location of the equipment, (5) the duration of its planned use, and (6) the manner in which it is to be used.

In June, 1967, the Supreme Court seemed to impose so many restrictions on electronic eavesdropping that it was impossible to bug constitutionally. But in December, 1967, the Court ruled that eaves-

[22] Charles J. Krauskopf, "Schmidt Is Wrong on Privileged Communications," *Journal of Counseling Psychology*, Vol. 9 (May, 1966), p. 425.

dropping was constitutional after all — within certain narrowly defined limits — and set out new guidelines for permissible bugging. It makes no difference whether the bugging is in a private home or a public phone booth since the Fourth Amendment's ban against unreasonable search and seizure "protects people, not places." The court noted that today's electronic devices have completely eliminated any need to trespass, therefore, the reach of the Fourth Amendment could not turn upon the presence or absence of a physical intrusion.

The Court's decision almost certainly reopened the way to carefully controlled eavesdropping. What will now become known as the Katz rule holds that eavesdropping is constitutionally acceptable if the eavesdropper obtains a warrant by showing probable cause to a proper judicial authority. Then, during the bugging, he must observe the precise limits outlined by the court when the warrant was obtained, and finally, he must report back to the court on just what was overheard as a result of the surveillance. But the Court did not say anything that would keep an eavesdropper from using any of the dozens of new, sophisticated devices.

Ruebhausen and Brim state that, in respect to right of privacy, "More than 30 states have now recognized some form of a common law right of privacy; four have created at least a limited right by statute. Yet another four states have rejected the existence of a right of privacy at common law, although the rejection may be more verbal than substantive."[23]

Privacy, in the sense that it indicates the absence of undue interference in the affairs of an individual, is comparable to freedom. The right of privacy is the right to be left alone, to be exempt from the inspection and scrutiny of others. Invasion of privacy is the intrusion into or compulsory exposure of one's private affairs and/or papers. When it causes him "emotional disturbance" or damages his feelings, it is actionable.

[23] Oscar M. Ruebhausen and Orville G. Brim, Jr., "Privacy and Behavior Research," *American Psychologist*, Vol. 21 (May, 1966), p. 425.

> Psychologically, then, privacy is a two way street consisting not only of what we need to exclude from or admit into our own thoughts or behavior, but also of what we need to communicate to, or keep from, others. Both of these conflicting needs, in mutually supportive interaction, are essential to the well-being of individuals and institutions, and any definition of privacy, or of private personality must reflect this plastic duality: sharing and concealment. . . . The essence of privacy is no more, and certainly no less, than the freedom of the individual to pick and choose for himself the time and circumstances under which and most importantly, the extent to which his attitudes, beliefs, behavior, and opinions are to be shared with or withheld from others.[24]

Schmidt points out that invasion of privacy differs from libel and slander in that damage under the latter is to the individual's memory or reputation. While libel and slander involve false or malicious statements, invasion of privacy may result from truthful but damaging publications.

> Normally, the counseling or clinical psychologist is commonly in possession of information concerning his clients, the revelation of which could amount to an invasion of privacy.
>
> Such a claim can be made only by the person whose privacy was thought to be invaded, and a suit for recovery of damages may be brought by him only. The damages claimed need not be proved special damages and perhaps might be sought on the basis of "mental anguish" resulting from the failure of a counseling or clinical psychologist to protect a client's privacy.[25]

While mental anguish suffered by a plaintiff in a suit of this nature is not easy to assess in terms of actuality or degree, damages can be recovered. The possibility of feigned injury, analogous to false "whiplash" claims paid by insurance companies, is

[24] *Ibid.*, p. 426.

[25] Lyle D. Schmidt, "Some Legal Considerations for Counseling and Clinical Psychologists," *Journal of Counseling Psychology*, Vol. 9 (Spring, 1962), p. 40.

always present and does little to increase the emotional serenity of counselors.

Within the past five years, threat to and abrogation of privacy has been charged in three matters of especial concern to counselors: use of personality tests, use of human beings as research subjects, and use of large-scale data processing systems. Any test is an invasion of privacy for the individual who does not wish to reveal himself, but personality tests are more often regarded as a surreptitious invasion of an individual's rights. A special House of Representatives subcommittee held hearings on the use of personality tests and questionnaires in federally financed research and on their use in selecting personnel for placement in civil service and other government positions. On the grounds that such tests ask the examinee intimate questions about family life, religious views, sexual experiences, and personal values the committee proposed that four statements be included as guidelines in federally contracted research: (1) that tests were strictly voluntary, (2) that parental consent was obtained for students below college age, (3) that a copy of the test was available for inspection by parents, and (4) that parents were given an explanation of test items before their consent was sought.[26] Brayfield, then Executive Officer of the American Psychological Association, presented the Association's view of such restrictions: "In our view, legislators may define the roles and functions of psychologists in the Federal Government; it should not dictate the methods and procedures for carrying out these roles and functions. These methods and procedures are more properly reserved for professional judgments."[27] Brayfield and others have pointed out that the misuse and abuse of personality tests result from those not competent to administer or interpret them and have contributed significantly to the problem. Consent of the individual to take such tests is the usual procedure in counselor practice. Cronbach observes that

> The personality test obtains the most significant information by probing deeply into feelings and attitudes which the individual normally conceals. One test purports to assess whether an adolescent boy resents authority. Another tries to determine whether a mother really loves her child. A third has a score indicating the strength of sexual needs. These and virtually all measures of personality seek information in areas which the subject has every reason to regard as private, in normal social intercourse. He is willing to admit the psychologist into these private areas only if he sees the relevance of the questions to the attainment of his goals in working with the psychologist. The psychologist is not "invading privacy" when he is freely admitted and when he has a genuine need of the information obtained.[28]

As previously stated, the force of law in most cases protects the confidential nature of communications between lawyer and client, psychiatrist and patient, pastor and penitent. Yet scientists studying antisocial or abnormal human behavior have no such protection, and are open to arrest for participating in illegal activities or concealing information about them. The result, many of these scientists claim, is that little meaningful research is being done in the field of deviant behavior. The perils of this work were recently exemplified by the dilemma that faced California sociologist Lewis Yablonsky, whose books on teen-age gang life in New York (*The Violent Gang*) and the Synanon cure for drug addiction (*Synanon: The Tunnel Back*) have been widely praised for their realism. *Time* (December 22, 1967, p. 34) reports that Yablonsky lived with the people he studied and was subpoenaed to testify at the marijuana trial of a flower child. On the stand, Yablonsky pleaded possible self-incrimination and refused to answer nine questions aimed at discovering whether he had observed anyone smoking pot. Yablonsky reported that the possibility of arrest or being forced to reveal sources was a constant state of concern and anxiety to him throughout his research. He argued that to free the social scientist, states should either

[26] "Testimony Before House Special Subcommittee on Invasion of Privacy of the Committee on Government Operations," *American Psychologist*, Vol. 21 (May, 1966), p. 405.
[27] *Ibid.*, p. 413.

[28] Lee J. Cronbach, *Essentials of Psychological Testing*, 3rd ed. (New York: Appleton-Century Crofts, Inc., 1970), p. 510.

pass laws granting immunity against prosecution to qualified researchers or allow attorney generals to grant immunity for specific projects. Some sociologists, on the other hand, fear that such laws would bring closer supervision by courts and police and might provide protection for unethical, nonacademic researchers seeking thrills.

Ruebhausen and Brim state that the three traditional research methods (self-descriptions by interviews, questionnaires, and personality tests; direct observations and recording of individual behavior; descriptions of a person by another serving as an informant) may, on occasion, violate privacy. Each method engages the researcher in one or both of two central issues: the degree of individual consent that exists and the degree of confidentiality that is maintained. These two authors observe that sensitivity on the part of the researcher to maintaining confidentiality of data, provision of civil or criminal remedies for breach of privacy, definition of contexts in which the cost in privacy is marginal or permissible because of positive gains, and preclusion of public officials from disclosure of confidential information acquired during employment would help to secure an accommodation for our society on this issue. They suggest seven principles that should be included in a general code of ethics to guide behavioral research.[29]

Large-scale data collecting and processing systems raise the specter of a massive invasion of the individual's right to privacy. Lister points out that credit records for more than 100 million people are currently kept in several thousand data bank locations across the United States. Moreover, proposals have been made repeatedly to establish a national data bank that would include several categories of sensitive public records available from schools, colleges, health, welfare, credit, state and federal internal revenue agencies. Lister identifies some of the advances in computerized record keeping that pose dangers to individual privacy. The first is that improved storage and retrieval systems enlarge the sheer quantity of data collected and it becomes less restricted. The second is that data that once might have been immediatedly discarded because of inconvenience and expense of storage are now more easily retained. The third is that new data systems permit greater use of information collected (correlational analyses can reveal patterns of attitudes and beliefs that previously escaped attention). The fourth is that remote terminals have now made it possible to disseminate information and materials quickly to widely scattered groups of interested but not necessarily authorized recipients. The fifth advance, according to Lister, is that information received through computerized record keeping is usually assumed to have great value or reliability because it comes from a computer.[30]

While many individuals and groups have advocated the abolition of large-scale personal data systems, few believe that such a measure is wise or realistic. Lister suggests some remedies which, if applied, would do much to reduce many flagrant inequities associated with present data bank systems. Among these are that (1) information about an individual could be collected only when he gives prior, informed consent, (2) data could be released or disseminated only when a compelling valid social advantage exists and subjects have given their consent, (3) a subject could have the right to examine his files and challenge the accuracy or completeness of its content, and (4) a legal recourse could be established for those who are injured by neglect or wilful misconduct by those responsible for the data system.

MALPRACTICE

Malpractice has been defined as "any professional misconduct or any unreasonable lack of skill or fidelity in the performance of professional or judiciary duties."[31] Review of relevant statutes and court decisions points up the fact that although schools and colleges, or government agencies, are

[29] Ruebhausen and Brim, *op. cit.*, pp. 436–437.

[30] Charles Lister, "Privacy and Large-Scale Personal Data Systems," *Personnel and Guidance Journal*, Vol. 49 (November, 1970), pp. 207–211.

[31] *Corpus Juris Secundum*, 54:1111.

generally shielded by the state's sovereign immunity, the counselor has always been and continues to be liable for negligent acts. Good defines liability in these words: "Liability is the legal responsibility of the teacher, school board, or any officer or agent of the school in case of accidents occurring in the school, on school property or in activities under school supervision conducted away from school property."[32] Liability may be of two types: criminal and civil. Criminal liability is the failure to exercise certain responsibilities explicitly demanded by law. Civil liability derives from negligence in carrying out responsibilities. Negligence arises (1) when the school employee fails to exercise the duties, care, or responsibilities expected of reasonably prudent persons in the situation and (2) when injuries are sustained by students to whom the employee owes a duty he has not performed. The principle of foreseeability is employed in determining negligence. That is, would a reasonably prudent person have been able to foresee that a certain act would lead to injury or harm?

Krauskopf and Krauskopf state that malpractice actions differ from other negligence actions in that the defendant purports to be a skilled person.[33] The skill is one which is specially acquired and is not possessed by a lay person. The jury decides the level of this skill and how a reasonable person having the skill would have acted. Juries usually make the decision upon the basis of testimony of expert witnesses. According to these two authors, the standard employed is not that of the highly skilled or even the average skill but rather that of persons recognized as competently qualified by the profession. The standard, therefore, is one of minimum competence.

Some years ago (1958), a question of negligence in counseling was raised.[34] The parents of a female student who had committed suicide because of alleged emotional maladjustment brought suit against the college director of student personnel services who had counseled with the girl for some five months. The complaint alleged that the defendant negligently and carelessly failed to perform his duties. Specifically, it was alleged that (1) he failed to secure or attempt to secure emergency psychiatric treatment after he was aware or should have been aware of her inability to care for her own safety; (2) he failed to advise the parents or contact them concerning the true mental and emotional state of their daughter, thus preventing them from securing proper medical care for her; (3) he failed to provide proper student guidance.

Realization of the dangerous precedent which a decision against the defendant would have established for counselors was indicated by the fact that the American Personnel and Guidance Association requested and received permission from the Wisconsin Supreme Court to submit a brief as *amicus curiae* (friend of court) concerning how it believed the case should be decided. The defense was that the director of student personnel was not trained in medicine or psychiatry and therefore had no legal duty to be aware of the client's suicidal tendencies. The trial court had reasoned that "To hold that a teacher who has had no training, education or experience in medical fields is required to recognize in a student a condition the diagnosis of which is in a specialized and technical field, would require a duty beyond reason." The court ruled in favor of the defendant and the state supreme court upheld the verdict, saying,

> Plaintiffs allege defendant was charged with the maintenance of a counseling and testing center for various educational, vocational and personal problems which students of the college might have, but that fact does not qualify him as an expert in the field of medicine or psychiatry. Granting that he had some knowledge of the student's emotional and other difficulties as the result of his meetings with her during a period of five months, as a teacher he cannot be charged with the same degree of care based on such knowledge as a person trained in medicine or psychiatry could exercise.

[32] Carter V. Good, *Dictionary of Education* (New York: McGraw-Hill Book Co., Inc., 1945).
[33] Joan M. Krauskopf and Charles J. Krauskopf, "Torts and Psychologists," *Journal of Counseling Psychology*, Vol. 12 (Fall, 1965), pp. 227–237.
[34] *Bogust vs. Iverson, supra,* n. 4.

Also no causation was shown, for even had the director done the three things the allegations stated that he should have done, the girl might still have committed suicide. It should be noted, however, that the court's opinion cannot be construed as being helpful in determining what standards of competence should be applied to school counselors or in determining negligence in this and other situations. Future litigation may well decide such standards, and its possibility adds to the necessity for circumspection on the part of counselors.

Beymer predicts that

> Within this decade we are likely to see a charge of malpractice made against a counselor. The lawsuit will not charge that the client was not helped by the treatment, or was worse off after the treatment, or that the counselor made an error in judgment. It will be charged that the counselor behaved in a careless, negligent, or stupid manner; that he could have and should have known better. The client's suit may allege that the procedure followed is not within the realm of presently accepted professional practice, or that a technique was used that the counselor was not trained to use, or that the counselor failed to follow some procedure which might have been more helpful. Or it may charge that the possible consequences of the treatment were not satisfactorily explained to the client and/or his parents.[35]

Ethical Considerations

Schmidt has defined ethical conduct as the standards of right and wrong. He relates it to "what the counselor, morally, philosophically, and otherwise, expects from himself as a counselor or limits himself to in his work with clients."[36]

Ethical standards are codified or systematized outlooks which have grown out of man's experiences. Therefore, ethical codes define certain ways of behaving which have stood the test of time for a given social group. Both the American Psychological Association[37] and the American Personnel and Guidance Association[38] have developed ethical codes which apply to their membership. Members who were directly involved in writing the codes reviewed and examined a wide range of ethical behavior and problems of professional practice which were of concern to a broadly based membership. Both codes stress adherence to rigorous professional standards and to exemplary behavior, integrity, and objectivity toward clients. The necessity for review and modification of the codes to maintain their salience to evolving professional practice is noted. The setting down in 1953 of a list of ethical standards for psychologists and the approval by the APGA in 1961 of a code of ethics for its membership were major achievements by both organizations in providing ethical standards for all counselors, whether members of these organizations or not.

PURPOSES OF ETHICAL CODES

McGowan and Schmidt believe that the major purposes of an ethical code are that it:

> 1. . . . provides a position on standards of practice to assist each member of the profession in deciding what he should do when situations of conflict arise in his work.
> 2. . . . helps clarify the counselor's responsibilities to the client and protects the client from the counselor's violation of, or his failure to fulfill, these responsibilities.
> 3. . . . gives the profession some assurance that the practices of members will not be detrimental to its general functions and purposes.
> 4. . . . gives society some guarantee that the services of the counselor will demonstrate a sensible regard for the social codes and moral expectations of the community in which he works.

[35] Lawrence Beymer, "Who Killed George Washington?" *Personnel and Guidance Journal,* Vol. 50 (December, 1971), pp. 249–254.
[36] Lyle D. Schmidt, "Some Ethical, Professional and Legal Considerations for School Counselors," *Personnel and Guidance Journal,* Vol. 44 (December, 1965), p. 377.

[37] American Psychological Association, "Ethical Standards of Psychologists," *American Psychologist,* Vol. 18 (January, 1963), pp. 56–60.
[38] American Personnel and Guidance Association, "Ethical Standards," *Personnel and Guidance Journal,* Vol. 40 (October, 1961), pp. 206–209.

5. . . . offers the counselor himself some grounds for safeguarding his own privacy and integrity.[39]

Prior to the development of either the APA or the APGA code of ethics, Wrenn, among others, called attention to the need of an ethical code for the counseling profession.[40] He stated that there were two major reasons for the mounting interest in the ethics of counseling. First, counseling was becoming a profession and consequently was concerned with its dual obligations to society and to the client. A generally accepted characteristic of a profession is that it adopt a code of ethics. Second, the emphasis in counseling was changing. Disclosures of self-information, attitudes, emotions, and self-concepts were increasingly common to counseling, and a greater emphasis was being placed upon interview elements outside the client which related to his environment. Even back in 1947 Wrenn had suggested a credo for counselors. It still has salience:

I will respect the integrity of each individual with whom I deal. I will accord to him the same right to self-determination that I want for myself. I will respect as something sacred the personality rights of each person and will not attempt to manipulate him or meddle in his life.
I will define my personal and ethical responsibility to my client as well as my legal and vocational responsibility to my organization and to society. I work for both the group to which I am responsible and for each individual that I serve as a client. This dual responsibility must be defined and understood by my employer and by myself.[41]

Wrenn applied the APA ethical code, then being formulated by the Hobbs committee, to the counselor's work and analyzed the counselor's loyalties to his client, society, employing institution, profession, and himself. He identified and discussed some of the conflicts that develop because of overlapping loyalties and responsibilities to these groups. Even then, Wrenn was of the opinion that the counselor "is primarily responsible to his client and ultimately to society."[42] Essentially, as Wrenn points out, in the ethical judgments that must be made by a counselor, some system of values is employed. Further, the ethical principles in any profession are based upon the value system of that field of endeavor. Adoption and knowledge of a code of ethics do not, in themselves, solve the ethical problems for the counselor because the code reflects that the counselor has overarching responsibilities.

THE APGA ETHICAL STANDARDS

The code does not contain any classification of misbehavior nor is there any set of penalties attached to misconduct. Rather, preoccupation is with guidelines of professional conduct. The statement of ethics reflects the experiences and judgments of the members; it is not a formulation of arbitrary standards or edicts. The fundamental consideration is that respect and protection must be given to the counselee, something that can be done only by counselors who manifest honesty, integrity, and objectivity in their behavior toward the recipients of their service. These characteristics apply to both oral and written verbalizations. They apply to every human being with whom the school counselor comes in contact professionally and are observed with extreme care in the case of those who are emotionally disturbed, who are in trouble, who are young and immature.

The APGA ethical standards are primarily directed to its membership rather than being addressed to the public served by them. The actions of its members have as their object the human being, the code holds up the dignity and integrity of the individual — his rights, interests, and privacy — as the main guide to practitioners.

While the standards state that a member is obligated to attempt to rectify situations in which he

[39] John F. McGowan and Lyle D. Schmidt, *Counseling: Readings in Theory and Practice* (New York: Holt, Rinehart & Winston, Inc., 1962), pp. 584–586.
[40] Wrenn, *op. cit.*
[41] C. Gilbert Wrenn, "Trends and Predictions in Vocational Guidance," *Occupations*, Vol. 25 (May, 1947), pp. 503–515.

[42] Wrenn, "Ethics of Counseling," p. 173.

observes or possesses information concerning unethical behavior of members, little machinery has been established by the professional organization for dealing with such behavior. The procedures to do this should be formulated by the APGA so that investigations could be made and penalties assessed which would correspond to the various degrees of misconduct by members.

The APGA "Ethical Standards" contains a preamble and seven sections: general, counseling, testing, research and publication, consulting and private practice, personnel administration, and preparation for personnel work. Shertzer and Morris used a critical incident questionnaire to investigate APGA members' ethical discriminatory abilities. Some 729 members were able to discriminate ethically appropriate responses from plausible distractors in 12 critical incidents at a level significantly better than chance. Members tended to be more discriminating in the "testing" and "counseling" areas than in "general" ethical situations.[43]

Conflicts in Responsibilities Considered independently, each statement of an ethical standard seems abundantly clear and simple, yet it often masks ethical conflict. For example, statements in the counseling section stress the counselor's responsibility to the client: "The member's *primary* obligation is to respect the integrity and promote the welfare of the counselee or client with whom he is working." It is further stated that information is to be kept confidential. But the general section maintains that "The member has a responsibility to the institution within which he serves. His acceptance of employment by the institution implies that he is in substantial agreement with the general policies and principles of the institution." The question is often asked, "Where is the counselor's first or primary obligation?" when conflicts develop. And conflicts, while not existing in every activity, are numerous enough to pose dilemmas for the school counselor. We present some examples:

[43] Bruce Shertzer and Kenneth Morris, "APGA Members' Ethical Discriminatory Ability," *Counselor Education and Supervision,* Vol. 11 (March, 1972), pp. 200–206.

The unmarried pregnant girl who voluntarily seeks the help of the counselor but is afraid or refuses to inform her parents and/or school administrators of her situation.

The counselee who reveals to the counselor that he has engaged in shoplifting or has committed robbery.

The teacher who refers a student to the counselor and later inquires about the nature of the counselor's interviews with the student so that she can be of help to the individual in the classroom.

The girl who informs the counselor that she is going to elope.

The individual who, during counseling, reveals that he plans to commit suicide.

The police who request information from the counselor about a counselee who has revealed in counseling his guilt in destroying private property.

The counselee who tells the counselor that he cheated on a test. The counselor keeps it confidential but the student is later caught and tells the principal that he told the counselor all about it.

As previously noted, Wrenn has suggested that the counselor's values will enter into his decision as to which ethical standard he will uphold. This, of course, means that each counselor should be aware of his personal values and his reasons for adhering to them. *Ethical Standards of Psychologists* places these conflicts in bold relief:

> Very often the resolution of ethical problems requires that the psychologist choose between two or more interests that are in conflict. Are the psychologist's obligations primarily to the social group, or to his individual client, or to his profession, or to himself? There is, of course, no simple answer to this question. Most situations where ethical decisions are necessary involve an implicit hierarchy of values, and this hierarchy has to be redefined for each situation. The equation of ethical responsibility is a complex one: weights for the variables must be computed anew as each new ethical problem is solved.[44]

[44] Committee on Ethical Standards for Psychologists, *Ethical Standards of Psychologists* (Washington: American Psychological Association, 1953).

Confidentiality It seems clear that maintaining confidentiality of the information received in a counseling interview is one of the most complex and pervasive problems confronting the counselor. As indicated above, confidentiality brings into sharp focus the issue of the counselor's responsibilities to the profession, the school system which employs him, and, most of all, the individual who seeks his help. These conflicts have been commented upon and positions taken by several individuals in the profession.

Carol E. Smith in 1956 surveyed professional members of the National Vocational Guidance Association in respect to the degree to which they favored revealing confidential information to some authorized agencies or persons. The respondents most closely associated with secondary schools showed the greatest preference for loyalty to society rather than to the counselee. Those who had more years of public school teaching indicated a higher loyalty to society. Those who had more graduate course units in guidance, psychology, or related areas indicated more loyalty to the counselee. Neither years of counseling experience nor amount of time devoted to counseling proved to be statistically significant in comparing responses to the questionnaire.[45]

Schneiders calls the information imparted in counseling an *"entrusted secret"* — information revealed with the condition that it be kept secret.[46] He believes the condition need not be explicitly defined since it is understood from the nature of the relationship. In his opinion the counselor's obligation to maintain confidentiality varies with (1) the nature of information imparted and (2) the effect its revelation would have upon the client. Confidential material may be used in research programs and publications, is often requested by various people interested in the client, can help parents who are interested in their children, is valuable in training purposes, and so on. Schneiders notes that it is common practice to communicate certain kinds of data to teachers and administrators and just as common to withhold other data.

Schneiders' seven general principles which govern confidentiality and communication have to be interpreted for each situation. He says:

(1) The obligation of confidentiality is relative rather than absolute since there are conditions which can alter it.
(2) Confidentiality depends on the nature of the material so that material which is already public or can easily become so is not bound by confidentiality in the same way as is the entrusted secret.
(3) Material that is harmless does not bind the counselor to confidentiality.
(4) The material that is necessary for a counselor or an agency to function effectively is often released from the bonds of confidentiality.
(5) Confidentiality is always conditioned by the intrinsic right of the counselee to his integrity and reputation, to the secret, and to resist aggression. Such rights can be protected by the counselor even against the law.
(6) Confidentiality is limited also by the rights of the counselor to preserve his own reputation and integrity, to resist harm or aggression, and to preserve privileged communication.
(7) Confidentiality is determined and limited by the rights of an innocent third party and by the rights of the community.[47]

Finally, Schneiders states that the obligation of secrecy lapses when (1) the common welfare demands revelation, (2) the secret is invalid, (3) there is unjust aggression, (4) the client gives consent, or (5) there is publication of the secret.

Warman recommends that the school or agency establish a written policy about confidentiality.[48]

[45] Carol E. Smith, "Development of Ethical Standards in the Secondary School Counseling Relationship for the Use of Counseling Information," unpublished doctoral dissertation, University of Southern California, 1956.
[46] Alexander A. Schneiders, "The Limits of Confidentiality," *Personnel and Guidance Journal*, Vol. 42 (November, 1963), pp. 252–253.

[47] *Ibid.*, p. 253.
[48] Roy E. Warman, "Confidentiality Interpreted by Established Agency Policy," *Personnel and Guidance Journal*, Vol. 42 (November, 1963), pp. 257–259.

He believes that it helps the counselor by (1) presenting him with a ready course of action, (2) providing him with the security that this course of action represents the considered thought of his colleagues and himself, (3) supporting him at those times when he is pressed to do something he feels is not right, and (4) providing him with the knowledge that there is consistency within the agency.

Clark outlined four positions which have been taken by individuals and organizations regarding the confidentiality of information received by a school counselor in a counseling interview with a minor.[49] The positions are summarized here:

1. The counselor must decide for himself the nature and direction of his loyalties and responsibilities.
2. The counselor must operate within the limitations imposed by the institution which employs him and by the amount of freedom it is willing to give him.
3. Information obtained in a counseling interview (and interview records) must be kept confidential in accordance with the obligations of the counselor as a professional person (if counselor learns of conditions which are likely to harm the counselee or others, he is expected to report *the condition*).
4. The counselor should maintain complete confidentiality of information received in a counseling interview.

Clark reports surveying 12 school administrators and 80 school counselors to determine their attitudes about the confidentiality of information received by the school counselor. Some 68 per cent of the administrators *agreed* and 92 per cent of the counselors *disagreed* with the position that a counselor should furnish any information obtained in a counseling situation to parents or the principal upon legitimate request. Finally, 52 per cent of the administrators *agreed* and 93 per cent of the school counselors *disagreed* with the position that a counselor should report to the principal infractions of school rules or civil laws discussed by a client.

The school administrators' position lacks internal consistency, Clark notes, and he interprets the position as one in which the counselor should guard the client's privacy but not to the point of complete confidentiality. He infers that when a client is a minor, counseling information must be shared with parents and school officials in some form or manner. Consequently, the school counselor would give only limited confidentiality to his clients. He suggests that the degree of professional authority granted the counselor by the school official determines the amount of confidentiality delegated to the counselor. Further, guidelines in respect to the nature of confidentiality, the form in which pertinent information is to be transmitted, method of transmission, and appropriate receivers should be arrived at by mutual consent of the administrator and the counselor before counseling is undertaken. The counselor, in turn, communicates these conditions or limits to pupils before a counseling relationship is established. In such a situation, information obtained in a counseling situation will not usually be shared without the previous knowledge and consent of the client.

Phillips and Margoshes disagree with Clark's contention that when a pupil is a minor information obtained in counseling must be shared with parents in some manner or form.[50] They also disagree that the amount of confidentiality given to the counselor should be determined by the school or its principal, and that where there is conflict between the school's interests and the pupil's interests the counselor should give preference to the school. They point out that in counseling, as in other areas, the minor requires more protection than the adult and ought to be able to rely upon

[49] Charles M. Clark, "Confidentiality and the School Counselor," *Personnel and Guidance Journal*, Vol. 43 (January, 1965), pp. 482–484.

[50] John L. Phillips, Jr., and Adam Margoshes, "Confidence and Confidentiality," *The School Counselor*, Vol. 13 (May, 1966), pp. 235–238.

it from the counselor. They urge that counselors not wait until they start counseling before discussing these matters with the principal but do so before accepting employment at a school.

Finally, it is the counselor himself who must exercise judgment in these stressful ethical situations. He must be prepared to take personal risks in his protection of confidence for those who make use of his services. Such is the lot of those who claim counseling as their life endeavor. No one can fulfill all these obligations perfectly, but the counselor is expected to come closer to the ideal than others. He alone will make the decisions when conflicts arise for it is his obligation and his professional trust.

CAUSES OF UNETHICAL PRACTICES AND BEHAVIOR

Schwebel sought to identify the causes of unethical behavior and practice.[51] He calls "practice" an act but not the motivation of the practitioner while "behavior" refers to the motivation and the underlying values of the person. Thus, unethical practices are acts not in accord with accepted standards. Unethical behavior occurs when conflicting personal interests lead to unethical practice, and unethical practices result from ignorance and inadequate training and/or supervision. Schwebel cites three hypotheses. In respect to the first — that self-interest causes unethical behavior and unethical practice — he believes that the personal profit motive, need for self-enhancement, and need to maintain security and status are causes. His second hypothesis is that unsound judgment due to inadequate training and/or inadequately supervised experiences leads to unethical behavior. He cites confidences obtained in relationships with staff members and confidences obtained from counselees about antisocial behavior as two examples of where unethical conduct may arise due to lack of training. For his third hypothesis, that ignorance causes unethical practices, Schwebel cites (1) ignorance of technical information and (2) ignorance of the counselor's values.

[51] Milton Schwebel, "Why Unethical Practice?" *Journal of Counseling Psychology,* Vol. 2 (Summer, 1955), pp. 122–128.

Summary

The ethical and legal considerations discussed here were presented in the hope that the counselor might attain greater objectivity in confronting professional problems. An important lesson to be learned from studying the legal and ethical conditions of counselors is the difficult, yet vital, necessity of maintaining a proper balance between professional privileges and responsibilities. Counselors must beware of using ethical and legal considerations to protect their associates under the guise of safeguarding the interests of their counselees. The traditional reluctance to criticize a professional colleague does not protect the counselee but rather encourages sharp practice and protects the colleague. A related problem which often contributes to shoddy practice stems from situations where counselors who meet state certification requirements receive an unearned increment of status when they are really marginal counselors who barely manage to have the required certificate but are nevertheless protected from justifiable criticism. It is the obligation of these individuals to seek adequate training and the responsibility of the more adequately prepared to encourage those only partially prepared to pursue complete training rather than remain only minimally qualified. Fully prepared counselors are aware of and live within the proper legal and ethical restrictions of their profession.

While codes of ethics may imply the limits within which a counselor can "get away with anything," their intent is to establish positive boundaries of responsible behavior. They also provide a valuable introspective stimulus for the practitioner. Thoughtful deliberations lead to a perspective on how to (1) maintain competence over the years, (2) place the counselee's interests ahead of his own,

(3) show concern for his colleagues, and (4) reflect standards of good practice. Maturity in one's professional field and being able to work creatively in it come slowly and painfully — and often with anxiety, discouragement, guilt feelings, and despairing inner struggles. Despite this price, maturity can be gained by discussion and reasoning about the challenges faced by the professional.

Annotated References

Bakken, Clarence J. *The Legal Basis for College Student Personnel Work.* Student Personnel Series No. 2. Washington: American College Personnel Association, 1961. 55 pp.

The basic purpose of this monograph is to provide legal information for those employed in college personnel services. Selected laws and court decisions are cited to illustrate topics discussed. The author suggests some operational procedures for certain situations based upon his judgment and interpretation of laws in effect at the time the monograph was prepared. The author was a member of the Minnesota bar.

Christiansen, Harley D. *Ethics in Counseling.* Tucson, Arizona: The University of Arizona Press, 1972. 260 pp.

The author presents specific case history examples of ethical conflict situations and then discusses, using a simulated conversational format, the possible applications of an ethical code. The problem situations and the commentary about them were collected from more than 60 counselors and 100 journal articles.

Committee on Scientific and Professional Ethics and Conduct. *Casebook on Ethical Standards for Psychologists.* Washington: American Psychological Association, 1967.

The 19 principles in the code of ethics for psychologists are presented, each illustrated by actual cases involving alleged violations and actions taken by the APA's Ethics Committee. Applications of the code to industrial psychology, test scoring and interpretation, directory listings of private practice, and the care and use of animals are given.

Ethical Practices Committee. *Ethical Standards Casebook.* Washington: American Personnel and Guidance Association, 1965. 55 pp.

Specific situations are presented, appropriate to statements in the *Ethical Standards.* Four incidents involving ethical behavior are drawn from each of the 56 statements in the standards. These incidents help clarify the meaning and intent of the ethical standards and should stimulate discussion and consideration of ethical practices.

Huckins, Wesley C. *Ethical and Legal Considerations in Guidance.* Guidance Monograph Series. Boston: Houghton Mifflin Company, 1968. 70 pp.

Huckins presents a valuable extended discussion of the ethical and legal considerations that bear on the counselor's work. Attention is given to right of privacy, malpractice, liability, expert witness, and unethical practices.

Nygaard, Joseph M. *The Counselor and Student Rights.* Guidance Monograph Series. Boston: Houghton Mifflin Company, 1973. 86 pp.

The monograph presents the complex issues and problems involved in protecting the rights of students. Nygaard's treatment of this highly changing area is thorough, comprehensive and highly readable. His work focuses on informing the counselor of students' legal rights.

Ware, Martha (ed.). *Law of Guidance and Counseling.* Cincinnati, Ohio: The W. H. Anderson Co., 1964. 178 pp.

The law of confidentiality, slander and libel, student records, search of students and premises, and duties and liabilities of counselors are explored independently by different authors. Suggestions, in the form of guides, are given to the practitioner for the fulfillment of his responsibilities.

Further References

Beck, Carlton E. "Ethical Aspects of Change in Counselor Education." *Counselor Education and Supervision,* Vol. 6 (Spring, 1967). pp. 216–221.

Daubner, Edward V. and Daubner, Edith Schell. "Ethics and Counseling Decisions." *Personnel and Guidance Journal,* Vol. 48 (February, 1970). pp. 433–442.

"Ethical Standards of Psychologists." *American Psychologist,* Vol. 18 (January, 1963). pp. 56–60.

Gade, Eldon M. "Implications of Privileged Communication Laws for Counselors." *The School Counselor,* Vol. 19 (January, 1972). pp. 150–152.

Geiser, Robert L., and Rheingold, Paul D. "Psychology and the Legal Process: Testimonial Privileged Communications." *American Psychologist,* Vol. 19 (November, 1964). pp. 831–837.

Heayn, Maurice H. and Jacobs, Howard L. "Safeguarding Student Records." *Personnel and Guidance Journal,* Vol. 46 (September, 1967). pp. 63–67.

Jeffrey, Ray. "The Psychologist as an Expert Witness on the Issue of Insanity." *American Psychologist,* Vol. 19 (November, 1964). pp. 838–843.

Killian, John D. "The Law, the Counselor, and Student Records." *Personnel and Guidance Journal,* Vol. 48 (February, 1970). pp. 423–432.

King, Arnold J., and Spector, Aaron J. "Ethical and Legal Aspects of Survey Research." *American Psychologist,* Vol. 18 (April, 1963). pp. 204–208.

Kinsey, Susan. "Student Rights: A Program for Counselors." *Personnel and Guidance Journal,* Vol. 50 (September, 1971). pp. 52–57.

Krauskopf, Charles J. "Schmidt Is Wrong on Privileged Communications." *Journal of Counseling Psychology,* Vol. 9 (Fall, 1962). pp. 279–280.

Krauskopf, Joan M., and Krauskopf, Charles J. "Torts and Psychologists." *Journal of Counseling Psychology,* Vol. 12 (Fall, 1965). pp. 227–237.

Lammers, Claude C. "The Right to Attend School." *Personnel and Guidance Journal,* Vol. 43 (January, 1965). pp. 475–481.

Leifer, Ronald. "The Psychiatrist and Tests of *Criminal* Responsibility." *American Psychologist,* Vol. 19 (November, 1964). pp. 825–830.

Lewis, Michael D. and Lewis, Judith A. "The Counselor and Civil Liberties." *Personnel and Guidance Journal,* Vol. 49 (September, 1970). pp. 9–13.

Lister, Charles. "Privacy and Large-Scale Personal Data Systems." *Personnel and Guidance Journal,* Vol. 49 (November, 1970). pp. 207–211.

Long, Thomas, (Guest Editor). "Ethical Practice: Preserving Human Dignity." *Personnel and Guidance Journal,* Vol. 50 (December, 1971). pp. 247–340.

Miller, Theodore K. and Pilkey, George P. "College Student Personnel and Academic Freedom for Students." *Personnel and Guidance Journal,* Vol. 46 (June, 1968). pp. 954–960.

Noland, Robert L. "Damaging Information and the College Application." *Personnel and Guidance Journal,* Vol. 49 (March, 1971). pp. 544–553.

Nugent, Frank A. "Confidentiality in College Counseling Centers." *Personnel and Guidance Journal,* Vol. 47 (May, 1969). pp. 872–877.

Panther, Edward E. "Counselors and Legislators: A Case History." *Personnel and Guidance Journal,* Vol. 50 (April, 1970). pp. 667–672.

Pardue, Jerry, Whichard, Willis, and Johnson, Elizabeth. "Limiting Confidential Information in Counseling." *Personnel and Guidance Journal,* Vol. 49 (September, 1970). pp. 14–20.

Phillips, John L., Jr., and Margoshes, Adam. "Confidence and Confidentiality." *The School Counselor,* Vol. 13 (May, 1966). pp. 235–238.

Ruebhausen, Oscar M., and Brim, Orville G., Jr. "Privacy and Behavioral Research." *American Psychologist,* Vol. 21 (May, 1966). pp. 423–437.

Russell Sage Foundation, "Proposed Principles for the Management of School Records." *Personnel and Guidance Journal,* Vol. 49 (September, 1970). pp. 21–23.

Schmidt, Lyle D. "Some Legal Considerations for Counseling and Clinical Psychologists." *Journal of Counseling Psychology,* Vol. 9 (Spring, 1962). pp. 35–44.

Schmidt, Lyle D. "Some Ethical, Professional and Legal Considerations for School Counselors." *Personnel and Guidance Journal,* Vol. 44 (December, 1965). pp. 376–382.

Shertzer, Bruce and Morris, Kenneth. "APGA Members' Ethical Discriminatory Ability." *Counselor Education and Supervision,* Vol. 11 (March, 1972). pp. 200–206.

EVALUATION OF COUNSELING

17

Does counseling do any good? How does one know it is effective? How is success determined? These and other questions about the efficacy of counseling are raised with increasing frequency. The present chapter discusses (1) the need for evaluation, (2) outcome research, (3) problems of research, (4) some representative studies of the effectiveness of counseling in educational settings, and (5) the counselor and research.

The Need for Evaluating Counseling

Evaluation is not intended to be a threatening process; its purpose is to provide new insights that will help counselors perform at higher and more professional levels. Whether in a school or a clinic, counseling services are expensive to those who support them. From both a financial and a psychological viewpoint, providing such services demands much support from staff members and the community. Consequently, it is necessary to determine their value by applying standards, and this process is referred to as evaluation. Briefly, then, the major aim of evaluation is to ascertain the current status of the counseling service within some frame of reference and on the basis of this knowledge to improve its quality and efficacy. Evaluation is the vehicle through which one learns whether counseling is doing what is expected of it.

During the past decade or so disconcerting results of numerous investigations have seriously challenged the efficacy of counseling and psychotherapeutic endeavors. One possible alternative to the negative results obtained would be to junk the entire enterprise, i.e., counseling, but it is doubtful that this course of action will be chosen by most in the field.

While the value of counseling has long been disputed, a publication on the topic by H. J. Eysenck, of the Institute of Psychiatry, University of London, touched off a frenzy of reactions. Eysenck concluded from his investigation that "roughly two-thirds of a group of neurotic patients will recover or improve to a marked extent within about two years of the onset of their illness, whether they are treated by means of psychotherapy or not."[1] Further, "This figure appears to be remarkably stable from one investigation to another, regardless of type of patient treated, standard of recovery employed, or method of therapy used." These conclusions were derived from studying the results of 19 studies reported in the literature, covering 7,293 cases treated by either psychoanalytic or eclectic therapy. Treatment results from these 19 studies were classified under four headings: "Cured or much improved"; "Improved"; "Slightly improved"; "Not improved" — died, discontinued treatment, etc. Eysenck was able to place only 4,661 of the 7,293, or 64 per cent, in the first two categories. Because approximately one-third of the psychoanalytic patients broke off treatment, the percentage of successful treatment of patients who finished their course was placed at 66 per cent. Eysenck stated that:

> Patients treated by means of psychoanalysis improve to the extent of 44 per cent; patients treated eclectically improve to the extent of 64 per cent; patients treated only custodially or by general practitioners to the extent of 72 per cent. Thus there appears to be an inverse correlation between recovery and psychotherapy; the more psychotherapy, the smaller the recovery rate.[2]

A similar investigation, conducted by Eugene Levitt of the Psychiatric Institute at the Indiana University Medical Center, obtained findings comparable to Eysenck's with respect to results of psychotherapy with children.[3] Of 3,399 cases (age range from preschool to 21 years with the median age estimated at 10 years) surveyed from 18 reports of evaluation at close of therapy and 17 at follow-up, two-thirds of the evaluations at close and three-quarters at follow-up showed improvement. Levitt indicated that time is a factor in improvement in the follow-up studies and that the rate of improvement with time is negatively accelerating.

Rosenzweig has criticized the validity of Eysenck's investigation and conclusion.[4] Because the criteria of success varied widely in the studies used by Eysenck, Rosenzweig believes that no valid comparison of rates or percentages of success is possible.

> Needless to say, degree of improvement is extremely difficult to assess and the difficulty is increased when one is dealing at second hand with cases treated by diverse methods and by various therapists. The most significant obstacle to the evaluation of degree of recovery lies, however, in the differences in improvement standards. In the present instance, it is this particular difficulty which looms large.[5]

Bixler has also called into question the efficacy of counseling and psychotherapy and believes that they are no more effective than routine care or no treatment at all.[6] He stated that "there is ample evidence that the status value of counseling and psychotherapy as we know them is on the decline, and this trend will be intensified as the knowledge regarding their ineffectiveness is increasingly disseminated." [7] Bixler raised the question of spontaneous remission and the placebo effect and urged that evaluation of counseling and psychotherapy take into account the rate of recovery which would occur without treatment.

> Note should be taken of the fact that some counselors and therapists defend the efficiency of their treatment methods by claiming that they are too subtle to be subjected to objective research and analysis. They may

[1] H. J. Eysenck, "The Effects of Psychotherapy: An Evaluation," *Journal of Consulting Psychology,* Vol. 16 (October, 1952), p. 322.

[2] *Ibid.*

[3] Eugene E. Levitt, "The Results of Psychotherapy with Children: An Evaluation," *Journal of Consulting Psychology,* Vol. 21 (June, 1957), pp. 189–196.

[4] Saul Rosenzweig, "A Transvaluation of Psychotherapy: A Reply to Hans Eysenck," *Journal of Abnormal and Social Psychology,* Vol. 49 (April, 1954), pp. 298–304.

[5] *Ibid.,* p. 301.

[6] Ray H. Bixler, "The Changing World of the Counselor: I — New Approaches Needed," *Counselor Education and Supervision,* Vol. 2 (Spring, 1963), pp. 100–105.

[7] Ray H. Bixler, "The Changing World of the Counselor: II — Training for the Unknown," *Counselor Education and Supervision,* Vol. 2 (Summer, 1963), p. 169.

even hold that the evidence of cure, remission of symptoms, and evidence of relapse, hospitalization, are not pertinent to the question of efficiency. . . . Until these workers can offer evidence that their techniques are more effective than placebos, we must look upon their contributions as no more than that. Faith and *ad hominem* arguments about the "worth and dignity and integrity" of man may be temporarily persuasive but they are very poor substitutes for evidence.[8]

Gonyea found a negative relationship between the extent to which counselors developed the ideal therapeutic relationship and the degree to which their clients reported themselves to be improved.[9] The correlation was -.14, not significantly different from zero, but indicating that those counselors who were most ideal produced the least improvement in clients.

Strupp acknowledges the many difficulties in measuring "success and/or outcomes" in general, regardless of the type of therapy employed.[10] He says that

. . . the outcome problem in psychotherapy has been receiving relatively scant attention in recent years — not because the problem has lost its importance but rather because of a realization on the part of researchers that a new approach to the issue must be found, and that more pressing matters must be dealt with first before we can address ourselves meaningfully to the question of the effectiveness of psychotherapy. This rationale partly accounts for the great interest in so-called process studies which have swept the scene during the last decade.[11]

In addition to outcome studies in their narrowest sense, such opinions have led to investigations of other variables in the patient (client), the therapist, the patient-therapist interaction, comparisons of methods of therapy used, and the life situation of both therapist and patient.

In 1964 Eysenck, in response to the article by Strupp, reasserted his earlier views. He quoted opinions given by E. Glover (a British psychoanalyst), O. H. Mowrer (University of Illinois), and D. H. Malan (Senior Hospital Medical Officer at the Tavistock Clinic of London) as supporters of his contention that there is no conclusive evidence at present to substantiate the worth of psychotherapy. Eysenck reports Malan as saying, "There is not the slightest indication from the published figures that psychotherapy has any value at all." Eysenck sums up his argument thus:

Psychoanalysts and psychotherapists generally assert that their methods cure psychoneurotic disorders, and are in fact the only methods which can achieve this end. Clearly, therefore, it is on them that the onus of proof must rest. They must define clearly and unambiguously what is meant by cure; they must put forward methods of testing the effects of treatment which are not dependent on the subjective evaluation of the therapist, and they must demonstrate that their methods give results which are clearly superior to any alternative methods, such as those of behavior therapy, or of spontaneous remission. It is indisputable, I suggest, that psychotherapists and psychoanalysts have failed to do any of these things, and until they have all been done I find it very difficult to see how any doubt can be thrown on my conclusion that published research has failed to support the claims made.[12]

A somewhat different view of the difficulty in measuring outcomes, and indeed of the meaning of outcome in the counseling or therapeutic context, is held by Silverman.[13] Psychotherapy is seen as an attempt to *teach* the individual to develop more constructive concepts of himself. Silverman uses the word "cure" and says that it comes about when the client finds relief from his current diffi-

[8] *Ibid.*, pp. 169–170.
[9] G. Gonyea, "The Ideal Therapeutic Relationship and Counseling Outcome," *Journal of Clinical Psychology*, Vol. 19 (October, 1963), pp. 481–487.
[10] Hans H. Strupp, "The Outcome Problem in Psychotherapy Revisited," *Psychotherapy: Theory, Research and Practice*, Vol. 1 (August, 1963), pp. 1–13.
[11] *Ibid.*, p. 1.

[12] H. J. Eysenck. "The Outcome Problem in Psychotherapy: A Reply," *Psychotherapy: Theory, Research and Practice*, Vol. 1 (May, 1964), pp. 97–100.
[13] H. L. Silverman, "Psychotherapy: A Survey and Evaluation," *Psychiatric Quarterly Supplement*, Vol. 36 (Winter, 1962), pp. 116–135.

culties. "Cure" need not be lifelong freedom from emotional conflict and problems. Thus, Silverman would hold that any change which occurred in the person in counseling or therapy, regardless of its duration, is an outcome, and it may even be a "cure" if it helps him to deal more effectively with his present life situation.

At a special conference on research problems in psychotherapy held in Washington, Rogers stated that he believed "progress has been made in conceptualizing the outcomes of psychotherapy" in ways "which are specific, measurable, and rooted in a context of theory." Parloff and Rubinstein indicated that most of the participants at that conference were not as optimistic as Rogers:

> Although great care was taken repeatedly to express the right of the investigator to conduct his research in any area and in any fashion that he deemed appropriate, the conferees implied that at the present time research in the area of outcomes enjoys a status lower than that of either process or personality investigation. The tenor of the discussion strongly suggested that "outcome" research was generally scorned as being "applied" in contrast to the other two aims, which had the more lofty designation of "basic" research.[14]

Researchers who met for a second such conference three years later expressed a more positive view regarding the future of this "applied" area.

What good is counseling? It is as good as man's faith in his humanity. Men have always believed in their ability to change for the better and to help each other to change through mutual assistance, love, religion, and the like. People can and do change through counseling, and the changes are not illusory. Presumably the question is not, then, whether counseling is any good. One could as well ask, "Is life worth living?" The basic question is how counseling accomplishes its objectives where it manages to succeed.

Rogers has stated that

> The careful evaluation of the research findings enables us to draw certain conclusions such as these: That profound changes occur in the perceived self of the client during and after therapy; that there is constructive change in the client's personality characteristics and personality structure, changes which bring him closer to the personality characteristics of the well-functioning person; that there is a change in directions defined as personal integration and adjustment; that there are changes in the maturity of the client's behavior as observed by friends.[15]

The preceding is perhaps the most provocative statement Rogers has made about the effectiveness of client-centered counseling. He is referring to "the research findings" of his work of the late 1940's and early 1950's, which was performed at the Counseling Center of the University of Chicago. As will become evident as the reader reviews this body of research and more recent studies on the subject of "outcomes," there are still many unanswered questions about the measurement of the effectiveness of therapy, client centered or otherwise. These questions will be reviewed in some detail later.

Outcome Research

Edgar has described the assumptions underlying counseling research: (1) Counseling is lawful and orderly; (2) a cause-and-effect relationship exists within counseling; (3) the counseling relationship is a part of the whole context of the client's life; and (4) predicted outcomes of counseling can be verified by conceivable operations.[16]

Most research in counseling can be classified as either process research or outcome research. *Process research* focuses upon what occurs as counseling proceeds; it generally investigates such factors as

[14] M. B. Parloff and E. A. Rubinstein, "Research Problems in Psychotherapy," in *Research in Psychotherapy* (Washington: American Psychological Association, 1958), Vol. 1, p. 277.

[15] Carl R. Rogers, *On Becoming a Person* (Boston: Houghton Mifflin Company, 1961), p. 231.

[16] Thomas E. Edgar, "Wishful Wish: Evaluation Without Values," *Personnel and Guidance Journal*, Vol. 44 (June, 1966), pp. 1025–1029.

shifts in content from session to session by the counselee, the relationship of content to the counselor's remarks, counselee attention on himself versus others, and the like. *Outcome research* is directed toward assessing the final product of counseling and usually focuses upon such issues as which techniques work best with which counselees, whether counseling was successful, and whether counseling effects were lasting.

CLIENT-CENTERED OUTCOMES

Amidst the intermittent barrages of fire from the "for outcome" and "against outcome" camps, a steady flow of research has continued over the past 15 to 20 years, not the least of which has been the contribution made by client-centered practitioners. Rogers and his associates have added to the growing body of research in this field, generally buttressing his theories. Rogers describes the changes that take place in the individual during counseling: "It is my hypothesis that in such a relationship the individual will reorganize himself at both the conscious and deeper levels of his personality in such a manner as to cope with life more constructively, more intelligently, and in a more socialized as well as more satisfying way."[17]

He continues by revealing what he believes to be the characteristics of the ideal product of a successful client-centered counseling relationship, stating that research on measured behavior change is now available:

> Here I can depart from speculation and bring in the steadily increasing body of solid research knowledge which is accumulating. We know now that individuals who live in such a relationship even for a relatively limited number of hours show profound and significant changes in personality, attitudes, and behavior, changes that do not occur in control groups. In such a relationship the individual becomes more integrated, more effective. He shows fewer of the characteristics which are usually termed neurotic and psychotic, and more of the characteristics of the healthy, well-functioning person. He changes his perception of himself, becoming more realistic in his views of self. He becomes more like the person he wishes to be. He values himself more highly. He is more self-confident and self-directing. He has a better understanding of himself, becomes more open to his experience, denies and represses less of his experience. He becomes more accepting in his attitudes toward others, seeing others as more similar to himself.
>
> In his behavior he shows similar changes. He is less frustrated by stress, and recovers from stress more quickly. He becomes more mature in his everyday behavior as this is observed by friends. He is less defensive, more adaptive, more able to meet situations creatively.
>
> These are some of the changes which we now know come about in individuals who have completed a series of counseling interviews in which the psychological atmosphere approximates the relationship I described. Each of the statements made is based on objective evidence. Much more research needs to be done, but there can no longer be any doubt as to the effectiveness of such a relationship in producing personality change.[18]

Rogers has not limited his claims regarding the changes which can accrue, and be measured, to the client-centered approach. He has emphasized that "change" comes about through other types of therapy as well, and that results are measurable by such methods as the Q-sort. He has also described various dimensions of the client's "experiencing" of himself, which he says can be scored by impartial judges from recorded segments of interviews. These postulated dimensions of change can then be related to "improvement."

It should be emphasized that when Rogers talks about "change" and "outcome" he does not necessarily mean what might be termed "success." He addresses himself to these semantics as follows:

> There is widespread acceptance of the idea that the purpose of research in this field is to measure the degree of "success" in psychotherapy, or the degree of "cure" achieved. While we have not been uninfluenced by such thinking, we have, after careful consideration, given up these concepts because they are undefinable, are essentially value judgments, and hence cannot be a part of

[17] Rogers, *op. cit.*, p. 36.

[18] *Ibid.* Copyright © 1954 the Trustees of Oberlin College

the science of this field. There is no general agreement as to what constitutes "success" – whether it is removal of symptoms, resolution of conflicts, improvement in social behavior, or some other type of change. The concept of "cure" is entirely inappropriate, since in most of these disorders we are dealing with learned behavior, not with disease.[19]

Rogers has expounded further on the problem of defining "success" in terms of measured outcomes by pointing out that what the more fully functioning person (after completing therapy) may come to view as acceptable and desirable behavior will quite possibly be viewed as deviant behavior by society in general. Rogers believes that even the more conventional therapist may question this existential person.

It seems possible then that the openness, adaptability, and existential living which are characteristic of the person who has received maximal aid from therapy, may be seen by a diagnostician, operating in terms of population norms, as signs that the person is "falling apart." What to the client are deeply enriching qualities of his life, may in terms of population norms be seen as deviant pathology.[20]

Thus, though Rogers asserts that changes do take place during therapy and can be measured with available instruments as specific outcomes of it, he does not claim to have all the answers and is concerned over the reaction of a typical community toward a "fully functioning person" who has received "maximal aid from therapy."

Rogers' major research effort, a "classic evaluation of client-centered therapy,"[21] was conducted at the Counseling Center at the University of Chicago. With a corps of therapists, all trained in the client-centered approach, he directed the research program, and its results were published in book form (Rogers and Dymond, eds., *Psychotherapy and Personality Change*, 1954). Findings of three portions of that program which seem to be related to the topic at hand will be given some attention here.

Some comments should first be made about the overall research design. Several measuring instruments were employed using a "pre-wait," "pre-therapy," and "post-therapy" administering scheme. The pre-wait method provided an "own-control" procedure, which was also cross-validated with an outside control group matched with the experimental subjects, when possible, by sex, age, and socioeconomic status. In one part of the study, follow-up data were also obtained.

Subjects in the experimental group numbered 29 (18 males and 11 females) and ranged in age from 21 to 40 years with a mean of 27. Sixteen of the 29 participants were students at the University of Chicago and 13 were from the surrounding community. The number of interviews ranged from as few as 6 to as many as 108 in one instance. The control group was composed of 23 persons (12 males and 11 females) who were nontherapy "normals." The nature of the illnesses of those in the control group ranged from "neurotic" to "borderline psychotic."

A total of 12 different therapists worked with one or more of the 29 patients. Although the therapists were schooled in client-centered methods, some were still in training at the time of the study, pursuing advanced degrees, while others were more experienced and had been practicing for a number of years.

One portion of the study seems to pertain more directly to the question of ultimate outcomes than the other parts. In this portion Rogers states that his purpose was to examine the hypothesis that following the completion of client-centered therapy the individual's behavior would indicate greater emotional or behavioral maturity, a change evident both to the client himself and to observers. The basic question asked was, "Does the client's everyday behavior change in such a way that the

[19] *Ibid.*, p. 227.
[20] Carl R. Rogers, "The Concept of the Fully Functioning Person," *Psychotherapy: Theory, Research and Practice*, Vol. 1 (August, 1963), p. 23.
[21] Herbert J. Cross, "The Outcome of Psychotherapy: A Selected Analysis of Research Findings," *Journal of Consulting Psychology*, Vol. 28 (October, 1964), pp. 413–417.

changes can be observed, and is the nature of the changes positive?"[22]

The Willoughby Emotional-Maturity Scale (E-M Scale) was used to measure observable change. It was completed by the client himself, the therapist, and two friends designated by the subject as persons who knew him well. They were asked by the researchers not to discuss their involvement in the study with the subject on whom they completed the E-M Scale. The instrument was administered four times: (1) pre-wait (six months before therapy began), (2) pre-therapy, (3) following therapy (which varied in duration of time for each client), and (4) at a follow-up point at least six months after the conclusion of therapy.

From this part of the research project Rogers concludes that, as measured by the E-M Scale,

> There were significant changes in clients' behavior whose therapy was rated by the counselor as being at least moderately successful. In these instances there was a significant increase in the maturity of the daily behavior of the client, whether the behavior was judged by the client himself or by his observer-friends who knew him well. In those instances where the counselor rated the therapy as unsuccessful, the observer-friends noted a deterioration in the maturity of behavior, but the clients (defensively?) rated themselves as much more mature.
>
> The overall conclusion appears justified that, where client-centered therapy is judged to be successful, an observable change in the direction of maturity of behavior takes place in the client. Where therapy is judged not to have occurred in significant degree, some deterioration of behavior is observed.[23]

Dymond reports other findings from the project.[24] As far as could be determined from the report, the same research design was used, but not all of the experimental and control subjects completed the measuring instrument, which was designed to indicate some sort of global self-understanding and adjustment changes. There were 25 (15 males and 10 females) in the experimental group and 23 (14 males and 9 females) in the control group. Dymond describes the results obtained with an adjustment criterion derived from the self-descriptive Q-sort. The self-descriptions of those presenting themselves for therapy were significantly less well adjusted than those produced by the no-therapy control group. After therapy had been completed, the adjustment scores of the experimental subjects were significantly higher than their scores before therapy and not significantly different from those of the control group. The control group's adjustment scores showed no change over a period of time matched in length to that taken in therapy by the experimentals.

Using another instrument, the Thematic Apperception Test (TAT), Dymond reports findings from 25 persons (15 males and 10 females) in the experimental group and 10 subjects (sex not indicated) as controls.

> In this study the no-therapy control group was again discovered to be significantly better adjusted than the client group before their therapy and not significantly different from them after their therapy had been completed. The TAT ratings agreed with the counselor's estimation of the success of the therapy, with the adjustment scoring of their self-descriptive Q-sorts in terms both of score and of degree of change in adjustment, and with the change in the correlation of their self and ideal sortings.[25]

Frank is one experimentalist who has criticized the "own-control" and experimental group-control group approaches such as were used by Rogers and his associates.[26] Since both methods necessi-

[22] Carl R. Rogers, "Changes in the Maturity of Behavior as Related to Therapy," in C. R. Rogers and R. F. Dymond (eds.), *Psychotherapy and Personality Change* (Chicago: University of Chicago Press, 1954).
[23] *Ibid.*, p. 236.
[24] R. F. Dymond, "Adjustment Changes over Therapy from Self-sorts," in Rogers and Dymond (eds.), *op. cit.*, pp. 76–84.

[25] *Ibid.*, p. 120.
[26] D. Frank, "Problems of Controls in Psychotherapy as Exemplified by the Psychotherapy Research Project of the Phipps Psychiatric Clinic," in Parloff and Rubinstein (eds.), *op. cit.*, pp. 10–26.

tate some contact with the subjects in the control groups, he believes bias may enter into the designs. This does seem to be a legitimate point; however, since no two persons live in exactly the same environment, the small amount of bias evoked by experimenter contact would not seem to present any more serious a problem than other situational environmental factors, such as having read an article about mental health (or not having read one), watching a television program or film featuring a therapist, and/or having heard comments about psychotherapy — good or bad. Others have criticized the "own-control" method because the wait and therapy periods in many cases were not the same length but were based on need for counseling instead.

One of the more comprehensive research projects completed in recent years dealing with the topic under consideration is that of Cartwright, Kirtner, and Fiske.[27] Their study investigated the factorial structure of changes which take place under client-centered therapy. Data were collected from 93 subjects who sought psychotherapy at the University of Chicago Counseling Center between November, 1956, and March, 1958. The group was made up of 54 students and 39 persons from the surrounding community. Ages ranged from 17 to 52 years; males totaled 52, females 41. Length of time in therapy during the study ranged from 3 interviews to 181. The subjects are described as being predominantly middle class, with the larger proportion occupying white-collar and professional positions.

Eight female and 22 male therapists treated the subjects. Counseling experience ranged from 1 year of clinical practice to 24 years. A total of 79 different measures were taken using various instruments at pre-therapy and again at post-therapy intervals. A follow-up questionnaire collected biographical data, information about the subject's experience in therapy, and reasons for terminating therapy. Evaluative tools included the MMPI, TAT, Q-sort (Butler and Haigh, 1954), Social Attitude Scales (Ethnocentrism, Traditional Family Ideology, etc.), the follow-up questionnaire, etc.

After subjecting their data to sensitive statistical methods, such as analysis of variance, prediction equations, and factor analysis, the researchers concluded that "No single test score, no one rater's rating can be considered adequately representative of the diversity of measured changes accompanying psychotherapy."[28] A measurable change was found in how subjects evaluated themselves. They seemed to be generally less critical and more acceptant of themselves after therapy; also, according to the TAT, they tended to consider themselves more "adequate" as persons. However, attempts to differentiate personality variables which changed during therapy proved fruitless. The "global" change factor, as observed by the therapist and reported by the client, seemed to be supported, as reported in earlier studies.

The question of amount of change or outcome associated with client-centered therapy has been explored by Cartwright and Vogel.[29] Using the TAT and the Q-sort, they collected data on 22 subjects — 11 students and 11 nonstudents — ranging in age from 27 to 41 years. Total length of therapy ranged from 6 hours for one client to 97 hours for another, with a mean of 33.4 hours.

A total of 19 therapists, both experienced and inexperienced, participated in the experiment. The 10 experienced therapists had each treated an average of 25.8 cases prior to this study. The nine inexperienced counselors had each treated less than five cases, and some had never engaged in therapy before the study participation. (An average of one case had been treated by the nine inexperienced therapists prior to the experiment.)

[27] Desmond S. Cartwright, W. L. Kirtner, and D. W. Fiske, "Method Factors in Changes Associated with Psychotherapy," *Journal of Abnormal and Social Psychology*, Vol. 66 (February, 1963), pp. 164–175.

[28] *Ibid.*, p. 175.

[29] Rosalind D. Cartwright and John S. Vogel, "A Comparison of Changes in Psychoneurotic Patients During Matched Periods of Therapy and No Therapy," *Journal of Consulting Psychology*, Vol. 24 (April, 1960), pp. 121–127.

The fascinating part of this study is that Cartwright and Vogel used the "own-control" cross-validation procedure employing equal times with each individual client for pre-wait and in-therapy retesting. In other words, if a subject was in pre-wait for five months, the evaluative instrument was readministered exactly five months after therapy began. This procedure corrected the situation for which several individuals had criticized Rogers. The authors describe their method in the following manner:

> Twenty-two self-referred psychoneurotic patients were tested at four points in time: (a) Pre-wait — on first being accepted as therapy cases and placed on the waiting list; (b) Pre-therapy — after a waiting time which varied in length; (c) In-therapy — after therapy had begun at a point equal to the waiting interval; and (d) Post-therapy.[30]

Four related hypotheses were explored. These, and the conclusions drawn from the findings, are summarized in our words:

1. There will be more change during a period of therapy than during an equal period of no therapy. This was confirmed for the Q adjustment score but not for the TAT.
2. Longer periods of therapy will be associated with more improvement than shorter periods. This hypothesis was not confirmed for either test.
3. Longer waiting periods will not be associated with more improvement than shorter periods. This was confirmed for the Q adjustment but not for the TAT. Those who waited longer did in fact improve on the TAT, and those with shorter waits did not. Those in the long waiting period who improved appear to be a spontaneous remission group with respect to the TAT.
4. Patients in therapy with experienced therapists will improve more in the in-therapy period than those in therapy with inexperienced therapists. The hypothesis was confirmed for the TAT but not for the Q-sort.

[30] *Ibid.*, p. 126.

As Cartwright and Vogel point out, the post-therapy tests revealed that those in therapy with experienced therapists improved significantly on both the Q-sort and the TAT, and that those in therapy with inexperienced therapists (the reader will recall that some of these therapists were students who had attempted little therapy before) did not improve significantly on either test but, in fact, even bordered on a significant decrease in overall scores on the TAT. The authors' conclusions are as follows: (1) Therapy affects adjustment based on self-description, whereas equal waiting time does not. (2) A long waiting period for this type of patient improves the mental health picture as revealed by the TAT. (3) Equally long therapy does not necessarily improve the mental health picture. (4) An experienced therapist is effective in improving mental health both as revealed by the TAT and as self-described. (5) An inexperienced therapist is ineffective in improving the self-picture and may actually cause a decrease in health as revealed by the TAT. (6) From the last two conclusions, it appears that therapists have special effects, depending on the level of their experience.

BEHAVIORAL COUNSELING OUTCOMES

Conditioning or behavioral therapists have been inclined more than other practitioners to report success rates of their treatment approaches. Not only have data on outcomes been reported but these data indicate a very high rate of recovery, as high as 80 or 90 per cent! Wolpe presents a number of evaluative reports in his recent book.[31] The studies he cites include those relying on clinical experience as well as controlled experimental studies. A few major highlights of his report will be given here.

Wolpe cites recovery rates (patients classified as "apparently cured" or "much improved"), derived from uncontrolled statistical studies, ranging from 78 to 89 per cent. He gives comparable rates for psychoanalytic and general hospital therapies as 60

[31] Joseph L. Wolpe, *The Practice of Behavior Therapy* (New York: Pergamon Press, 1969), pp. 266–278.

and 53 per cent, respectively. Wolpe reports several well-controlled outcome studies in which systematic desensitization techniques were compared with nonbehavioral therapy approaches. Rate of recovery for the desensitization techniques applied in group treatment versus another group in conventional dynamic group treatment favored desensitization by 72 versus 12 per cent. Similarly, a study of individual treatment improvement rates using three approaches — insight therapy, suggestion and supportive therapy, and systematic desensitization and a control group — yielded differential success proportions markedly favoring desensitization procedures.

Dua reported that behaviorally oriented group procedures were more effective than psychotherapy re-education group procedures in producing changes in constructs, attitudes, and self-evaluative statements of belief relating to emotionality, extraversion, and externality.[32] Andrews compared behavioral (combination of desensitization and reinforcement) and client-centered counseling to evaluate their effectiveness in reducing anxiety and raising high school students' achievement (grades). Significant anxiety reduction occurred in the behavioral group but not in the client-centered group. However, neither group showed improvement in achievement.[33]

Much attention has been given in the literature to the success of achieving "behavioral" counseling outcomes compared to that obtained by "dynamic" approaches. Determining the accuracy of claims for various treatment approaches, assuming an adequate research design is used, is complex and difficult. Certainly, the behavioral approaches have the advantage of being able to clearly specify treatment goals (e.g., elimination of a tic, alleviation of sexual impotence) and also to specify more precise treatment procedure. Judgment of "cure" or "much improvement" rests on the disappearance of the symptom for which the client seeks treatment. The dynamic therapists are clearly at a disadvantage in any such comparisons because their goals are often vaguely and broadly stated and because their treatment procedures are usually not clearly specified.

Cure, recovery, improvement — regardless of approach — all call for a judgment of some type by the researcher. Here again, the behavioral counselors are at a great advantage because of their use of observable behaviors as outcomes. Many of the doubts about success rates reported by behavioral counselors focus on the narrowness and superficiality of their criteria. It may be noted that many individuals who see themselves as practicing nonbehavioral counseling also report the disappearance of symptom-like, habitual maladaptive behavior when asked about improvement in their clients.

Problems Involved in Conducting Counseling Research

Many reasons have been advanced for why school counselors fail to concern themselves with evaluating their services. Previously these reasons were summarized by the authors as follows:

1. Many school counseling practitioners state that they do not have time for evaluation. They claim that the great amount of time and energy demanded for the conduct of programs does not permit them to evaluate, except informally. . . .
2. Many school counselors legitimately insist that they do not have the training to conduct either research or evaluative studies. . . .
3. . . . The modification of human behavior is not easily assessed through observation or other tools of measurement. . . .
4. From a pure research point of view, available school data tend to be incomplete and fragmentary. . . .
5. Evaluation costs time and money. . . .

[32] P. S. Dua, "Comparison of the Effects of Behaviorally Oriented Action and Psychotherapy Reeducation on Introversion-Extraversion, Emotionality and Internal-External Control," *Journal of Counseling Psychology*, Vol. 17 (November, 1970), pp. 567–572.

[33] W. R. Andrews, "Behavioral and Client-Centered Counseling of High School Underachievers," *Journal of Counseling Psychology*, Vol. 18 (March, 1971), pp. 93–96.

6. Employing a suitable control group . . . is a difficult problem. . . .
7. Obtaining appropriate, assessable criteria is a difficult problem in evaluation and research in guidance.[34]

To Herr these reasons, while plausible and contributory, are not sufficient to explain the lack of evaluative studies:

> More important, and perhaps basic, is the need to develop a comprehensive, conceptual theory of guidance based upon a series of postulates derived from (a) observation and study of developmental needs of children variously classified, (b) the continuous examination of the contribution of particular guidance services to the broad or specific socialization of children, (c) an awareness that those concerns and services appropriate to the college-bound, middle-class student may have scant relevance to the larger student group which Hoyt has labeled specialty-oriented students.[35]

This lack of a comprehensive framework within which to judge counseling outcomes is a fundamental problem. Some years ago, Pepinsky cited several limitations of research designed to evaluate the effects of counseling, such as

> . . . (a) uncontrollable stimuli which impinge upon the client outside the counseling situation, (b) difficulty in establishing controls for the many possible factors in the counseling situation which may be related to changes in client behavior, and which may or may not be responsible for changes attributed to counseling, (c) lack of adequately tested, systematized knowledge requisite to setting up meaningful criteria of change, and (d) lack of adequate criterion measures.[36]

Complicating the problem of defining counselor effectiveness, identifying criteria, and constructing instruments are a host of conflicting observations, hunches, assumptions, and theories. For example, counselors work on different levels with different problems and perform different tasks. Their behavior is viewed by individuals (administrators, counselees, parents, supervisors) with different expectancies. Instruments usually embody limited aspects of counselee change, counselor activity, or segments of existing counseling theory. Finally, there is a growing realization that counseling acts are not good or bad but can be judged only in relation to specific conditions, purposes, counselees, and the particular counseling process dynamics. Clearly, the conceptualization of counseling outcomes and the methods employed to bring counseling under scrutiny must be adequate to handle the complex, many-faceted, dynamic phenomena under study.

Many have identified and discussed the myriad problems that plague those who attempt to assess the outcomes of counseling. Here the major problems will be briefly discussed.

THE CRITERION PROBLEM

The major difficulty besetting any evaluator of counseling is often referred to as the criterion problem, and it is crucial, for on it depends the degree of confidence that can be placed in the results. The problem has many subissues. According to Jensen, Coles, and Nestor, a criterion is "a behavior or condition which is or can be described in terms of an ideal and which is a goal."[37] These authors discuss the necessary characteristics of a criterion and include such attributes as that it be definable, stable, and relevant. Essentially, then, a criterion is some demonstrable characteristic which serves as a standard for making a qualitative or quantitative judgment.

Traditional Criteria In the case of the research on counseling, the judgment usually concerns counseling outcomes or processes considered more

[34] Bruce Shertzer and Shelley C. Stone, *Fundamentals of Guidance*, 2nd ed. (Boston: Houghton Mifflin Company, 1971), pp. 452–453.
[35] Edwin L. Herr, "Basic Issues in Research and Evaluation of Guidance Services," *Counselor Education and Supervision*, Vol. 4 (Fall, 1964), pp. 9–16.
[36] Harold B. Pepinsky, "Counseling Methods: Therapy," *Annual Review of Psychology* (Stanford, Calif.: Annual Reviews, Inc., 1951), Vol. 2, p. 329.
[37] Barry T. Jensen, George Coles, and Beatrice Nestor, "The Criterion Problem in Guidance Research," *Journal of Counseling Psychology*, Vol. 2 (Spring, 1955), pp. 58–61.

efficient or desirable. For example, client self-reports, counselor judgment of improvement, improved grades, change in test scores, and indices of behavioral change, as well as others, have been traditionally used as criteria.

Virtually no criterion is entirely acceptable to all researchers. Too often studies depend upon a single criterion when multiple criteria are needed. Rothney and Farwell reported that investigators used some 12 diverse criteria of counseling effectiveness including such things as persistence in school or job performance, grade-point average, satisfaction with job, client self-knowledge, level of affect, etc.[38] These writers concluded that the use of varied criteria was a result of the wide assortment of assignments that counselors undertook or were delegated.

Many workers have indicated that far too many of the criteria employed in counseling research are not appropriate. The criticism is made, for example, that reduction of the problems checked by students on a problem checklist or an inventory immediately after counseling has led to the conclusion that counseling was very effective whereas later information has indicated that changes were of short duration.

One of the frequently used but weakest criterion employed in counseling research is the counselee's self-report. Self-reports are highly biased at best since it would be unusual for anyone to request help and invest considerable time and effort in counseling without tending to report that the process was of value to him. Without other supporting evidence these reports are usually viewed with skepticism. Another commonly used criterion is the counselor's rating of improvement, which needless to say is not independent of the counseling process and has the same shortcomings as the counselee self-report.

Criteria of life adjustment and postcounseling behavioral improvement are difficult to quantify, and sometimes obtaining the information upon which to base such judgments presents a difficult problem. Furthermore, each counselee's life situation varies from that of others, and data collected are seldom comparable. Test data used as a criterion are frequently questioned on the grounds that there may be no logical reason for counseling to have impact upon traits measured by tests.

Performance Criteria The weaknesses of traditional criteria and increasingly urgent demands for accountability both without and within the counseling profession sparked efforts to conceptualize and apply "behavioral" or "performance" criteria. These latter two terms have become highly fashionable watchwords in recent years. However, it should be remembered that they are a direct outgrowth of efforts beginning as early as the late 1940's to improve the assessment of educational objectives by specifying clearly the actual behaviors that demonstrate the attainment of the objective.

Behind what are currently called performance criteria lie more than 20 years of formulating and classifying educational objectives. Earlier, these efforts focused on the absolute necessity of defining objectives in terms of observable behavior. A description of these efforts may be found in the handbooks of *The Taxonomy of Educational Objectives*. These handbooks reflect years of monumental effort by such individuals as Benjamin S. Bloom, David R. Krathwohl and many others who contributed through their individual work and a series of conferences which culminated in the publication of the taxonomy.[39]

Mager is frequently cited as one who popularized the specification of criteria in a small book about instructional objectives.[40] Three basic ele-

[38] John W. M. Rothney and Gail F. Farwell, "The Evaluation of Guidance and Personnel Services," *Review of Educational Research*, Vol. 30 (April, 1960), pp. 168–175.

[39] See Benjamin S. Bloom (ed.), *Taxonomy of Educational Objectives*, Handbook I: Cognitive Domain (New York: David McKay, Inc., 1956), and David Krathwohl, Benjamin S. Bloom, and Bertram S. Masia, *Taxonomy of Educational Objectives*, Handbook II: Affective Domain (New York: David McKay, Inc., 1964).

[40] Robert F. Mager, *Preparing Educational Objectives* (Palo Alto, California: Fearon Publications, Inc., 1962).

ments considered by Mager as essential to a performance objective are that (1) the terminal behavior expected of the learner or client must be specified, (2) the conditions under which the behavior will be enacted must be stated, and (3) the means used to judge attainment of the criteria must be set forth.[41]

In recent years the rationale involved in the early work in educational objectives has been applied to the field of counseling. While the terminology varies slightly, the relevance to counseling of its fundamental principles is clearly evident. Those counselors subscribing to learning theory approaches or behavioral counseling models have particularly relied on these principles in their practice and research. This way of thinking about counseling has broader application than modifying client behaviors as is seen in counseling outcome research. It also can be applied as a systematic means of designing and evaluating counselor preparation especially in the skill acquisition area.

The application of performance criteria to counseling, as described by Mager, is considered incomplete by many behavioral counselors. They have added the element of specifying the intermediate or enabling behaviors that lead to the terminal behavior. Perhaps an example of the use of performance criteria in counseling is in order. An eleventh-grade girl presents her fear that she is failing English to the school counselor. Clarification of the problem and the client's goals led to the following sequence of events and activities:

Terminal behavior: Present a suitable, required oral report on Bret Harte (necessary for passing subject).

Conditions: Report will be 10 minutes long and will be presented in the presence of 29 other students and the teacher of an 11th grade English class.

Techniques or Strategies Used: (1) Role play with counselor and/or teacher, (2) Self-modeling via audiotape, and (3) self-monitoring of activities.

First Set of Intermediate Behaviors: (1) Talk to counselor about giving the report, (2) talk to teacher about giving the report, (3) prepare a report and tape record in counselee's room, (4) play back report to counselor, (5) play back recorded report to teacher, (6) present an oral report on Bret Harte to counselor, (7) present an oral report to teacher alone.

Second Set of Related Intermediate Behaviors: (1) Respond to a teacher's question in class discussion, (2) ask a question in class discussion, (3) serve as a recorder for a committee discussion, (4) read the committee's report to class, (5) serve as a panel member and present a three-minute statement of her views on a topic.

Criteria for Judging Attainment of Intermediate Behaviors: Checklist of behaviors formulated by counselee and counselor. Counselee checks off behaviors she achieves. Counselor, teacher, and parents check off behaviors that counselee demonstrates in their presence.

Performs Terminal Behavior: Presents oral report on Bret Harte.

Criteria Used to Judge Attainment of Terminal Behavior: Timed presentation of 10 minutes duration established by teacher and evaluated by teacher and fellow students.

Numerous examples of performance criteria applied to counseling outcomes have been set forth by Krumboltz and Thoresen. Their volume contains case descriptions that illustrate specification of (1) counseling goals, (2) techniques to be utilized to effect modification in behavior, (3) criterion behaviors of the client, (4) the conditions under which these behaviors will be produced, and (5) the means to assess the attainment of goals.[42] The publication by Hackney and Nye provides an excellent example of the application of behavioral methods and performance criteria to the teaching of specific counseling skills.[43]

[41] *Ibid.*, p. 12.

[42] John D. Krumboltz and Carl E. Thoresen (eds.), *Behavioral Counseling: Cases and Techniques* (New York: Holt, Rinehart and Winston, 1969), 515 pp.

[43] Harold L. Hackney and Sherilyn Nye, *Counseling Strategies and Objectives* (Englewood Cliffs, New Jersey: Prentice-Hall, Inc., 1973), 167 pp.

Accountability Performance criteria may be viewed as a means of specifying more clearly the activities engaged in and the outcomes sought in counseling. Viewed in this manner, they bear a direct relationship to the current emphasis on accountability. However, the concept of accountability implies a wider-ranging responsibility than intraprofessional evaluation.

The demand for accountability contains a strong emphasis on justifying a professional's activities to those he serves and those who finance his work. True professionals have always tried to evaluate their work with an eye toward improvement. They have always needed to know what was productive. Now, more than ever, counseling practitioners are being called on to demonstrate and articulate the outcomes of their work to their employers and the public.

THE CONTROL PROBLEM

The use of control groups is mandatory in all sound research. The control group is established in order to judge whether the treatment provided the counseled group is the variable that produced the change observed. Presumably, if change occurs in the group receiving treatment and not in the control group, it is brought about by what was done to the counseled group. Generally, control and experimental groups are selected to be as similar as possible on a large number of variables. Most of the variables do not present major problems — e.g., age, sex, social class — but in counseling research the most relevant characteristics are the hardest to match between counseled and control group subjects. The most obvious of these relevant characteristics is motivation to enter counseling. It is not difficult to come up with two groups in a school setting which are similar in age, sex, and IQ; however, matching on only these attributes is meaningless if the counseled group actively sought assistance and the control group showed no interest in or need for it. Obviously, the control group must contain individuals who also want and need the counselor's services.

It is at this point in counseling research that a serious ethical issue comes into play. How can an individual who expresses a need for counseling be relegated to a control group without seriously affecting and possibly harming him? Two compromises are frequently used to cope with this issue: delay of counseling and minimal attention. In the case of limited delay, control group subjects are held on a waiting list while experimental subjects receive counseling. Both groups are then assessed for change, following which the withheld control subjects receive counseling. The minimal attention approach to establishing a control group involves very limited noncounseling contact to assure the waiting individual that he will receive help. It is also used to permit counselor judgment of the counselee's status while waiting.

The commonly accepted procedure of selecting control group subjects on the basis of their current comparability with experimental subjects has been questioned by Rothney and Lewis. The fact that control subjects are similar to experimental subjects at the time the groups are established does not guarantee that their development up to that time has been similar or that it would continue to be so if there had been no special intervention. The point made by Rothney and Lewis is that differences between groups of subjects are all too often attributed to experimental treatment, when in fact the differences may be related to patterns of development not observed in the original data. These authors note that the cost of procuring longitudinal developmental data on control subjects is high but they urge that it be done or that researchers exercise caution in attributing outcomes to treatment rather than to developmental effects.[44]

Another important factor involves the counselor rather than the research subject. In meaningful research, control of, or at least information concerning, the counselor himself is included. Numerous

[44] John W. M. Rothney and Charles W. Lewis, "Use of Control Groups in Studies of Guidance," *Personnel and Guidance Journal*, Vol. 49 (January, 1969), pp. 446–449.

studies have described the importance of the counselor's personal characteristics and the necessary and sufficient conditions which must be created if the counseling relationship is to develop and be effective. Of particular relevance is the extent of the counselor's training and experience so that judgment can be made as to whether the outcome was a function of the counselor rather than the counseling process.

PLACEBO EFFECT

A critical issue often raised with respect to adequate research designs is the placebo effect. In medicine a placebo is a substitute for a specific medication which is known to be of no value in the treatment of the disease. For example, some patients are given distilled water injections in lieu of injections of medications or they are administered harmless sugar pills as a substitute for the actual medicine.

Bixler states that

> A placebo sets up an expectation of relief. So usually do religious healers, surgeons, charlatans, and counselors. That the beneficial effects of some surgery can be attributed purely to the patient's expectation of help has been clearly demonstrated. The placebo effect is omnipresent. If we are to establish the efficacy of any healing medium we must prove it to be more successful than a placebo-like treatment of the same problem. . . .
> I want to be certain that I am understood. If the placebo effect is omnipresent it obviously follows that the therapist must demonstrate that his treatment is better than doing nothing at all.[45]

Patterson points out that there are four aspects of the placebo effect which have apparently been overlooked:

> The first concerns the nature of the effect being studied, or the criteria. In any comparison we must specify the criteria, which must be appropriate or pertinent, and the same criteria must be applied in all situations. That is, we cannot accept the removal of symptoms as an adequate or appropriate criterion for the comparison of psychotherapy and the placebo effect, faith healing, or chiropractic. If the latter are as good as therapy in this respect, it does not follow that they are as good in all respects, or that they achieve other results or effects which may occur in psychotherapy. . . .
> Second, an adequate comparison must involve more than a comparison limited to one point in time, such as immediately following psychotherapy and the administration of the placebo. It is quite possible that the effects of the placebo, even when symptom removal is used as a criterion, dissipate quickly, while the effects of psychotherapy continue or persist.
> Third, . . . there is no such thing as spontaneous remission. This term only covers our ignorance as to the reasons for the recovery. It is suggested that spontaneous recovery may, in some instances at least, be the result of the inadvertent application of the necessary and sufficient conditions of therapeutic change.
> Finally, the nature of the placebo in counseling or psychotherapy must be considered. The placebo effect in medicine is the result of psychological factors. These are usually considered to be suggestion or prestige, but they also include interest, attention and related factors.[46]

Patterson suggests that what is considered a placebo in counseling may actually be the specific remedy. Finally, personal interest and attention, rather than being considered extraneous factors to be excluded or controlled in comparing treatment methods, should be recognized as a powerful, specific remedy, the essence of counseling or psychotherapy.

ASSESSMENT DEVICES

Adequate assessment of changes in the dependent variable as well as assessment of status used for classification purposes is essential if counseling is to be evaluated. Analyses are based upon pre- and post-measures. If the assessment devices are

[45] Bixler, "The Changing World of the Counselor: I — New Approaches Needed," p. 102.

[46] C. H. Patterson, "A Note on the Effectiveness of Counseling and Psychotherapy," *Counselor Education and Supervision*, Vol. 3 (Spring, 1964), p. 130.

insensitive, unreliable, or subject to distortions or contaminating influences, interpretations become difficult if not impossible.

Volsky and his associates have pointed out that certain data usually will be more important than others in evaluating the construct validity of a measure to be used in a treatment evaluation study.

> First, in order for a device to be useful for assessing changes that take place over time, it must reflect a high degree of stability between two administrations in the absence of intervening treatment. Second, an estimate of the internal consistency or homogeneity of the test may be important.[47]

These authors also say that the most casual approaches to the evaluation of treatment outcomes have made use of assessment devices which do not do what they are supposed to do: provide reliable and valid assessments of the outcome variable. Much time, effort, and resources are necessary to assure that assessments, particularly novel ones, mean what they are supposed to mean. Many individuals have observed that an inverse relationship exists between the significance of the variables used in counseling research and their accessibility to measurement.

Studies of Counseling Effectiveness in Educational Settings

Three studies of the effectiveness of counseling in educational settings are reviewed here. Each describes counseling at a particular educational level – elementary, secondary, or college. The latter two studies were selected because of the longitudinal quality of their work and the size of the samples involved. Comparable elementary school counseling studies have yet to be published.

COUNSELING WITH ELEMENTARY SCHOOL CHILDREN

Kranzler and his associates sought to assess the results of counseling with fourth-grade students.[48] The criterion, change in sociometric status, was selected because sociometric status has been shown to be related to many other personal and social characteristics such as achievement, personality traits, social skills, and physical skills. The authors believed that the combination of special attention and close personal relationships provided children assigned to counseling would result in significantly greater gain in sociometric status when compared with a control group.

Procedures A sociometric instrument was administered by teachers to four fourth-grade classes (size not specified) at Indiana University Elementary School during early December, 1963. Each teacher was asked to stress the confidentiality of the instrument, to inform the pupils that they could choose a boy or girl who was absent if they desired, and to tell the children that groups would be arranged so that members would be able to sit near one or more of the pupils they had chosen. The sociometric instrument asked each pupil to list three individuals with whom he would most like to sit, work on committees, and play. Students were told that those chosen might be the same for all three tasks or they could be different. After tabulation of choices, the teacher was given a seating chart or suggested committee work groupings in which each student was placed with at least one of his choices. The five pupils of lowest sociometric status were placed with their first choices.

Subjects in the investigation were five pupils in each of the four fourth-grade classrooms with the lowest number of choices. The 20 subjects were randomly assigned to one of three conditions: counseling (eight subjects), teacher guidance (four subjects), or control (eight subjects).

[47] Theodore Volsky, Jr., Thomas M. Magoon, Warren T. Norman, and Donald P. Hoyt, *The Outcomes of Counseling and Psychotherapy* (Minneapolis: University of Minnesota Press, 1965), p. 60.

[48] Gerald D. Kranzler, G. M. Mayer, C. O. Dyer, and P. F. Munger, "Counseling with Elementary School Children: An Experimental Study," *Personnel and Guidance Journal*, Vol. 44 (May, 1966), pp. 944–949.

The eight pupils assigned to counseling met as a counseling group twice a week for six weeks, after which the group was divided in two, each meeting once a week for another 12 weeks. In addition, each subject was counseled individually for 12 weeks. In counseling, subjects were informed that they could discuss any concerns or difficulties that they or their friends might have and told that their communications would be held in confidence. They were informed of the limitations — no destruction of school property and no physical harm to any group member. A client-centered counseling approach was employed. The excerpts of individual counseling presented by the authors reflect counselee concerns over relationships with teachers and parents.

Children assigned to teacher guidance were identified and described to the teachers as being of low sociometric status. Teachers were given a list of procedures to use including praise of students' work, assigning them important tasks, and allowing them to work in self-preferred groups. Neither the eight pupils assigned to the control condition nor their teachers were informed that they were subjects, and no unusual attention was paid them.

At the end of five months (April, 1964) the sociometric instrument was readministered, and in November, 1964, seven months after termination of counseling and teacher guidance, it was administered a third time. At the time of the third administration all subjects had been promoted to fifth grade and had been placed in various classrooms.

Results Change in sociometric status was assessed by comparing total number of choices received by the subject on a post-test with the number received on the pre-test. At the first post-testing (soon after treatment conditions terminated) none of the subjects assigned to the counseling or teacher guidance conditions had decreased in sociometric status whereas 57 per cent of control subjects (four of seven, since one had left the school district) had decreased. Indeed, 75 per cent of the counseled and 100 per cent of the teacher guidance subjects had increased in sociometric status compared to 29 per cent of control subjects. Statistical treatment of the pre- and post-data revealed that the counseled group differed (.05 level) from the control group but the teacher guidance group did not differ significantly from either the counseled or the control group. Results of the second post-testing (seven months after termination of treatment) showed that the differences between counseled and control groups were still statistically significant and that the relative percentages of subjects in the counseled and control groups who had increased or decreased in sociometric status remained the same. However, sociometric status of pupils assigned to the teacher guidance condition decreased between the two test administrations.

In their discussion of the findings, Kranzler and his associates recognized the limitations imposed upon their data by the small numbers involved. Nevertheless, they believe the study shows that certain kinds of behavior modification can be brought about in classroom situations by teachers if they are aware of students' low sociometric status and are given suggestions for coping with it. The data suggest that behavioral modifications brought about by teacher guidance do not carry over into a new situation but gains from counseling do.

WISCONSIN SECONDARY SCHOOL COUNSELING STUDY

John W. M. Rothney, of the University of Wisconsin, has long been engaged in studying the value of counseling.[49] His subjects were selected in 1948 when they were sophomores in four representative Wisconsin high schools. Some 870 students were distributed randomly into control and experimental groups. The latter received counseling throughout Grades 10, 11, and 12 from qualified counselors who were members of the University of Wisconsin staff. Evaluative criteria were (1) measures of satisfaction with and adjustment to post-high school status, (2) measures of optimism in outlook, (3) measures of reflection on post-high

[49] John W. M. Rothney, *Guidance Practices and Results* (New York: Harper & Brothers, 1958).

school education, and (4) measures of persistence in post-high school endeavors. Follow-up studies of the 690 who graduated were conducted 6 months, 2½ years, 5 years, and 10 years after high school graduation.

During the first year all control group subjects were interviewed once and experimental subjects were interviewed twice. Guide sheets were used in the initial interviews and an assortment of information — parents' education and occupations, number of siblings and subjects' relationship with them, parents' vocational expectations for subjects, subjects' vocational and educational aspirations and plans — was discussed with the subjects and collected.

During the second year (subjects' junior year) selected parts of the Differential Aptitude Test were administered to all subjects. Rapport was maintained with control group subjects, and individual counseling was extended to experimental subjects. Again, general guide sheets were used in interviewing unless the counselee preferred to discuss other topics. Changes in family situation, present educational and vocational plans, part-time work, school activities, health concerns, and relationships with other pupils, teachers, and parents were topics. In addition, behavioral descriptions, autobiographies, and samples of students' classwork were collected.

Interviewing (again, general interview guides were used) was also the major activity of the third year, the last year the subjects were in school. The focus of the interviews was upon students' strengths, weaknesses, personal problems, and present and future educational and vocational problems and plans. One month before graduation all subjects indicated their post-high school plans in one of six categories: education, employment, armed forces, work on parents' farm, uncertain, or married within a year (for girls only). Different forms of a senior report questionnaire were then given to each student according to his indicated post-high school plan category. Students were asked about their long-term plans, their retrospective feelings about school, and their attitudes toward the future.

Six-Month Follow-Up Six months after high school graduation all 690 subjects who had remained in school to complete their educational programs were contacted by a postcard questionnaire inquiring about their present individual status and degree of satisfaction with this status. The return of questionnaires received in this follow-up, as well as in 1953 (two and one-half years after high school graduation), was 100 per cent.

Five-Year Follow-Up During 1956–1957, after the subjects had been out of high school for five years, a comprehensive three-page questionnaire was sent to the 658 students still alive. Intensive taped interview studies of 50 selected subjects, their employers, and anyone else who had information about their activities were carried out. The four criterion measures of counseling effectiveness (satisfaction and adjustment to school, optimism, reflections on success or failure of high school training, and persistence in post-high school endeavors) were derived from questionnaire data.

Rothney stated that after five years the counseled students, compared with noncounseled students,

1. Achieved slightly higher academic records in high and post-high school education;
2. Indicated more realism about their own strengths and weaknesses at the time they were graduated from high school;
3. Were less dissatisfied with their high school experiences;
4. Had differing vocational aspirations;
5. Were more consistent in expression of, entering into, and remaining in their vocational choices, classified by areas;
6. Made more progress in employment during the five-year period following high school graduation;
7. Were more likely to go on to higher education, to remain to graduate, and to plan for continuation of higher education;

8. Were more satisfied with their post-high school education;
9. Expressed greater satisfaction with their status five years after high school and were more satisfied in retrospect with their high school experiences;
10. Participated in more self-improvement activities after completing high school;
11. Looked back more favorably on the counseling they had obtained.[50]

Merenda and Rothney, in a further report on the results of the five-year study, concluded that desirable outcomes may be enhanced by providing intensive counseling services to high school students.[51] The differences, they noted, were not large between counseled and uncounseled students on criterion variables obtained five years after high school graduation, but they speculated that the "more subtle and lasting effects of counseling require a longer period of time in order to become more clearly apparent." This speculation was based upon the likelihood that the early years after high school graduation are given over to exploratory and continued training experiences.

Ten-Year Follow-Up In 1961, 10 years after high school graduation, all subjects responded to a four-page questionnaire. While the complete results[52] of this 10-year study have not yet been published in the professional journals, Rothney reported a study of trained and nontrained males 10 years after high school graduation.[53] The 179 males who constituted the *training* group continued their education after high school either by enrollment in a school or college or by entering a formal apprenticeship. The 142 members of the *no-training* group did not enroll in any educational institution or apprenticeship during the decade after high school graduation. Some members of both groups had attended service schools while in the armed forces.

The most significant differences between the counseled and comparison groups in the follow-up studies were in the number of counseled subjects who went to and completed post-high school training. Rothney reports that the training group contained a much higher proportion of counseled students but did not specify the proportion.

Ten years after high school the trained group (and significantly more of them were counseled students) had left their own hometowns, married later, earned more money, were more optimistic, looked back more favorably on their high school experience, reported more educational and vocational plans for the future, and belonged to more organizations and held a few more offices in them. No significant difference existed between the trained and nontrained groups in respect to satisfaction with current status, job satisfaction, satisfaction with what they had done during the past 10 years, appraisal of their personal assets, persons to whom they went for advice, confidence in making decisions, numbers of self-improvement activities, and satisfaction with counseling they had received.

In his discussion of the results Rothney asked, "Who can say that the boy who stayed in or near his home town, enjoyed marriage and a family earlier, belonged to fewer organizations (perhaps because fewer were available) and did not burden himself with too many offices was less well off than the boy who went into training?"[54]

[50] *Ibid.*, pp. 479–480.
[51] Peter F. Merenda and John W. M. Rothney, "Evaluating the Effects of Counseling – Eight Years After," *Journal of Counseling Psychology*, Vol. 5 (Fall, 1958), pp. 163–168.
[52] John W. M. Rothney, "Educational, Vocational and Social Performances of Counseled and Uncounseled Youth Ten Years After High School," report submitted to Cooperative Research Program, Department of Health, Education, and Welfare, 1963, Project No. SAE 9231.
[53] John W. M. Rothney, "Trained and Non-trained Males Ten Years After High School Graduation," *Vocational Guidance Quarterly*, Vol. 14 (Winter, 1966), pp. 247–250.

MINNESOTA COLLEGE STUDENT COUNSELING STUDY

Williamson and Bordin sought to determine the effectiveness of counseling provided at the Univer-

[54] *Ibid.*, p. 249.

sity of Minnesota Student Counseling Bureau.[55] Their subjects were 384 students who, during 1933–1936, had come to the Counseling Bureau before November of their freshman year for counseling help with educational, vocational, or personal problems.

The 384 counseled students were designated as the experimental group and selected solely on the basis that complete counseling folders were available. One year later these students were individually paired and matched with other, noncounseled students on college entrance test scores, English proficiency test score, high school rank, age, sex, size and type of high school and college class. The second group was the control group and could have received counseling from other students, administrators, or other staff members. All 768 students were registered in the College of Science, Literature and the Arts (SLA). Half were men; half were women.

Both groups were interviewed roughly one year after counseling (range = 1–4 years; mode = 1 year) and rated on a scale called "Adjustment," which centered mainly upon educational-vocational progress. Without benefit of counseling, 68 per cent of the control group achieved what was considered by themselves and the evaluating judges to be satisfactory adjustment with respect to their vocational choices and progress in classes. In contrast, 81 per cent of the counseled students achieved what was judged to be a correspondingly satisfactory adjustment. Conversely, 27 per cent of the noncounseled cases and 15 per cent of the counseled students failed to achieve satisfactory adjustment. The two groups were also compared on first-quarter grade-point average (GPA). The results showed that

1. The counseled students rated significantly higher on the Adjustment scale.

2. The counseled students earned significantly better grades than noncounseled students – 2.18 to 1.97 respectively (on a four-point scale).

Because criticism was directed at the Williamson-Bordin study on the ground that the two groups were not equated for motivation to seek counseling, Campbell, in a 25-year follow-up study, identified a third group (N = 62) of former control students who sought counseling after the original study.[56] Both precounseling and postcounseling measures were available for these students. The results showed that before counseling this "better" control group resembled the control students; after counseling, the counseled students.

Twenty-five-Year Follow-Up In 1961–1962 Campbell followed up the individuals in the Williamson-Bordin counseled and noncounseled groups to assess the effects of counseling over a 25-year period.[57] Virtually all "students" – then roughly 45 years old – were located, 761 of the 768. Thirty had died, about 10 per cent would not cooperate, and 62 had sought help from the Counseling Bureau during the interval and therefore could no longer be used as controls. Information was collected on their achievements and job and life satisfaction.

Campbell reports that, compared to noncounseled students, counseled students had earned significantly better grades (2.20 versus 2.06 on a 4.00 scale), been graduated in roughly one-fourth greater numbers (59 versus 48 per cent), been elected to Phi Beta Kappa (6 versus 2 per cent), earned more M.A. degrees (6 versus 2 per cent) and more Ph.D. degrees (2 versus 0.3 per cent), reported more participation in campus activities, and been elected more often to offices in these activities.

[55] E. G. Williamson and E. S. Bordin, "Evaluating Counseling by Means of a Control-Group Experiment," *School & Society*, Vol. 52 (November, 1940), pp. 434–440.

[56] David P. Campbell, "A Counseling Evaluation with a 'Better' Control Group," *Journal of Counseling Psychology*, Vol. 10 (Winter, 1963), pp. 334–339.

[57] David P. Campbell, "Achievements of Counseled and Non-Counseled Students Twenty-five Years After Counseling," *Journal of Counseling Psychology*, Vol. 12 (Fall, 1965), pp. 287–293.

While more of the counseled group than the noncounseled reported they had published, won athletic awards, been awarded patents, and given invitational addresses, the differences (some statistically significant) were small and discounted by Campbell. The annual family income of counseled males ranged from $1,600 to $150,000 with a median of $14,670 compared to the $4,000 to $70,000 range reported for noncounseled males (their median was $13,500, and the $1,200 difference in median income was not statistically significant). The difference in annual family income between counseled and noncounseled females ($13,300 median versus $13,000) was not statistically significant.

Campbell drew together all achievement data and had each subject rated on a "Contribution to Society" scale by three psychologists working independently (16 raters participated). There was perfect agreement among the raters in 299 of the 724 cases, or 41 per cent. In the remaining 59 per cent, two of the raters agreed, and the third deviated by only one point. The differences between the counseled and noncounseled groups were all in favor of the counseled students but were not statistically significant. However, when the counseled male was compared to his matched noncounseled control (123 pairs of males), differences were significant at the .05 level. This procedure failed to hold for the female matched pairs.

Two conclusions from the follow-up about the effect of counseling on students were drawn by Campbell. First, a very mild difference in achievement existed between counseled and noncounseled students 25 years later, especially among men. Second, counseling did exert a beneficial effect on the students' achievement. While the effect was most visible on immediate criteria such as grades and graduation, and although it declined somewhat, it did not completely disappear over 25 years. These conclusions are not too surprising, Campbell points out, since counselors are more effective in dealing with immediate problems and these frequently concern grades and graduation. It is his judgment that counseling is best justified as immediate help to the student bewildered by an increasingly complex range of educational and occupational opportunities.

The School Counselor and Research

According to Krumboltz, much counseling research seems designed to determine whether a vaguely defined process (counseling) is a possible panacea for all the problems brought to counselors.[58] All too often, hypotheses state "that juvenile delinquents will become pro-social, that underachievers will become achievers, that vocationally unhappy persons will become satisfied, that complacent persons will become concerned, that shaky marriages will become stable, that fearful persons will become confident — all as the result of the same kind of contact with another person called a counselor." Krumboltz believes that, since most evaluations of counseling produce negative findings, the profession ought to abandon the search for some criterion measure which is affected by one process (counseling). Varieties of processes, procedures, and techniques are possible, but they need careful experimental testing. In his words, the agenda for counseling must provide answers to this question:

> For clients desiring help on each type of problem of
> concern to the counselor
> What techniques and procedures,
> When used by what kind of counselor,
> With which type of clients,
> For how long,
> and in what sequence,
> Will produce which types of behavior change?

Any sophisticated review of the literature on counseling effectiveness will demonstrate that the results have been modest and contradictory. Few if any facts are now deemed established, and many

[58] John D. Krumboltz, "The Agenda for Counseling," *Journal of Counseling Psychology*, Vol. 12 (Fall, 1965), p. 226.

findings have been repudiated. Considering the present state of research on counseling effectiveness, the temptation is great to become a prophet of doom crying out for suspension of further fruitless efforts to determine the outcomes of counseling. However, an alternative action is available to the counselor. That is to ask what it is in his *modus operandi* which consistently leads to conclusions intuitively sensed by every counselor as incomplete. Most practitioners believe that any counselor who chooses to make a difference will do so. Possibly by retracing some of the work in counseling effectiveness and listening with sharpened hearing to the comments of the investigators, often offered parenthetically, fresh approaches may be formulated to investigate unexplored research avenues.

Careful attention needs to be given to the area of counseling theory and how its corresponding implementation in the counseling process produces results. Generally, researchers work with fragmented elements of counseling behavior rather than with a process model. Instruments have often tended to be collections of *post hoc* memories by counselees and counselors, rather than time samples of behavior in context.

It is impossible at this stage to speak of trends, but there is certainly within the current *Zeitgeist* a growing concern for formulating models of the counseling process and a shift to systematic recordings, by either trained recorders or video tape, of total counselor-counselee interactions. Evaluation, in this case, becomes a matter of the degree of correspondence between the behavior observed and that required by the model.

Counseling researchers have been hesitant to formulate counseling models which may be prematurely prescriptive. Yet, even in those situations defined strictly in terms of observables, the observables are themselves abstractions representing judgments to describe some behaviors while ignoring others. Questions of value judgments underlying counseling objectives are inescapable, and perhaps the initial task is to hammer them out anew in public and professional discourse. Given agreement on objectives, systematic study can then be initiated on the conditions and behaviors which maximize the likelihood of their attainment. Certainly, a wider range of psychological and counseling theory is available to draw on than was formerly the case. Technology now permits us to capture and hold for repeated study samples of counseling transactions. Can we use these new tools of theoretical and empirical analysis to replace the search for correlations between counselor traits and observer ratings which have characterized past studies? Can we view counseling behavior as one component in a counseling system performing first one function, then another, as a particular kind of learning sequence unfolds? Can present-day counseling theory eventually culminate in conceptual models useful in evaluating counseling behavior? What institutions, groups, or individuals are committed to these tasks?

No one doubts that conducting counseling research is an extremely complex endeavor. The results of counseling vary from setting to setting, from counselor to counselor, and from counselee to counselee. The counseling process involves many kinds of counselors attempting to apply many varieties of techniques to a wide range of psychological problems exhibited by many kinds of counselees. While all these factors are present in questions concerning whether counseling is of value, progress will depend upon breaking down the general question into a series of less complicated and more precise questions which lend themselves to systematic investigation.

The aura of desirability surrounding research frequently leaves the nonresearcher feeling like a second-class citizen because he is not engaged in high-level evaluation of his activities. About counselors in particular, one frequently hears the criticism that they are little inclined to do research because they are service oriented. Counselors themselves are likely to reverse this statement and use it as an apology for not doing research. It is extremely difficult to carry on an active counseling program and conduct research at the same time. Often it is undesirable for the researcher to be an active participant in his own study lest he bias the results.

A counseling staff should not undertake research because it is the "thing to do" or because someone expects it of them. As can be seen in the foregoing discussion, research into meaningful questions using appropriate criteria and incorporating adequate controls requires a great deal of time and effort and can be disruptive to the counseling service. It should be entered into only when one has a question sufficiently important to justify paying the price attendant upon such disruption. Obviously, good research cannot be conducted without sufficient skills and resources. Many school staffs would be well advised to have it done for them rather than attempting to do it themselves. While bringing in outsiders may be threatening because it involves exposure of what is done, the school which is seriously inclined toward evaluating its counseling services rarely loses in the process, if the long view is taken.

Annotated References

Allen, Thomas W. and Whiteley, John M. *Dimensions of Effective Counseling.* Columbus, Ohio: Charles E. Merrill Publishing Company, 1968. 192 pp.

The book defines and describes cognitive flexibility and psychological openness in operational terms. These two constructs are viewed as dimensions that must be present for effective counseling to take place. Both are viewed as sources of important counseling skills.

Cramer, Stanley H., Herr, Edwin L., Morris, Charles N., and Frentz, Thomas T. *Research and the School Counselor.* Boston: Houghton Mifflin Company, 1970. 202 pp.

The authors present practical suggestions to counselors which may be helpful to them in conducting research that will facilitate their work with clients, administrators, teachers, and parents. They present several types of studies of value to counselors and then indicate *why* the investigation should be done, *how* it can be accomplished, and *what* can be done with the results. The authors clearly explain such topics as descriptive statistics, correlation, data processing, and programmatic research. They show how local norms and expectancy tables may be developed and used, how to assess the school environment, how to conduct follow-up studies, and many other "research" activities highly useful to counselors.

Volsky, Theodore, Jr., Magoon, Thomas M., Norman, Warren T., and Hoyt, Donald P. *The Outcomes of Counseling and Psychotherapy.* Minneapolis: University of Minnesota Press, 1965. 209 pp.

This is a report of the findings of a 10-year project conducted at the University of Minnesota Student Counseling Bureau based upon assessments of counseling. The authors have sought to apply current statistical methods to results of contemporary counseling theory and practices. The problems of counseling research are identified and discussed, methodological considerations are explained, and a conceptual framework that incorporates variables relevant to the goals of counseling is formulated.

Whiteley, John M. (ed.). *Research in Counseling.* Columbus, Ohio: Charles E. Merrill Books, Inc., 1968. 320 pp.

Presents summaries of research efforts on the relationship of selection of clients and counselors to counseling outcomes. The book presents recommendations for future research on client and counselor selection and assessment of counseling process and outcomes.

Further References

Andrews, W. R. "Behavioral and Client-Centered Counseling of High School Underachievers." *Journal of Counseling Psychology,* Vol. 18 (March, 1971). pp. 93–96.

Bates, Marilyn. "A Test of Group Counseling." *Personnel and Guidance Journal,* Vol. 46 (April, 1968). pp. 749–753.

Bishop, John B. "Another Look at Counselor, Client, and Supervisor Ratings of Counselor Effectiveness." *Counselor Education and Supervision,* Vol. 10 (Summer, 1971). pp. 319–323.

Bradley, Richard W. and Smith, R. Douglas. "Studies and Projects To Improve Vocational Guidance Services." *Vocational Guidance Quarterly,* Vol. 19 (June, 1971). pp. 281–288.

Crowder, James E., "Relationship Between Therapist and Client Interpersonal Behaviors and Psychotherapy Outcome." *Journal of Counseling Psychology,* Vol. 19 (January, 1972). pp. 68–75.

Dua, P. S. "Comparison of the Effects of Behaviorally Oriented Action and Psychotherapy Reeducation on Introversion-Extroversion, Emotionality and Internal-External Control." *Journal of Counseling Psychology,* Vol. 17 (November, 1970). pp. 567–572.

Ehrle, Raymond A. "Performance Contracting for Human Service." *Personnel and Guidance Journal,* Vol. 49 (October, 1970). pp. 119–122.

Graff, Robert W., Danish, Steven, and Austin, Brian. "Reactions to Three Kinds of Vocational-Educational Counseling." *Journal of Counseling Psychology,* Vol. 19 (May, 1972). pp. 224–225.

Hansen, James C. "Job Satisfaction and Effective Performance of School Counselors." *Personnel and Guidance Journal,* Vol. 46 (May, 1968). pp. 864–869.

Hoeltzel, Kenneth E. "Evaluating Short-term Vocational Guidance Programs Through Site Visits." *Vocational Guidance Quarterly,* Vol. 20 (September, 1971). pp. 15–20.

Kelley, Jan, Smits, Stanley, J., Leventhal, Richard, and Rhodes, Roy. "Critique of the Designs of Process and Outcome Research." *Journal of Counseling Psychology,* Vol. 17 (July, 1970). pp. 337–341.

Lytton, Hugh. "School Counseling – An Outside View." *Personnel and Guidance Journal,* Vol. 47 (September, 1968). pp. 12–17.

MacGuffie, Robert A., Jorgensen, Gary Q., and Janzen, Frederick V. "Need for Approval and Counseling Outcomes." *Personnel and Guidance Journal,* Vol. 48 (April, 1970). pp. 653–656.

Mitchell, Kenneth R. "Repeated Measures and the Evaluation of Change in the Individual Client During Counseling." *Journal of Counseling Psychology,* Vol. 16 (November, 1969). pp. 522–527.

O'Leary, Susan G. "Counselor Activity as a Predictor of Outcome." *Personnel and Guidance Journal,* Vol. 48 (October, 1969). pp. 135–139.

Pulvino, Charles J. and Sanborn, Marshall P. "Feedback and Accountability." *Personnel and Guidance Journal,* Vol. 51 (September, 1972). pp. 15–20.

Rickabaugh, Karl, Heaps, Richard A., and Finley, Robert. "Counselor Comfort, Counseling Climate and Client Satisfaction: Client Ratings and Academic Improvement." *Counselor Education and Supervision,* Vol. 11 (March, 1972). pp. 219–223.

Rothney, John W. M. "Some Not-So-Sacred Cows." *Personnel and Guidance Journal,* Vol. 48 (June, 1970). pp. 803–808.

Rothney, John W. M. and Lewis, Charles W. "Use of Control Groups in Studies of Guidance." *Personnel and Guidance Journal,* Vol. 47 (January, 1969). pp. 446–449.

Schwartz, Richard K. and Ohlsen, Merle M. "A Content Analysis Technique for Evaluating Outcomes in Counseling." *Personnel and Guidance Journal,* Vol. 47 (December, 1968). pp. 346–352.

Sieka, F., Taylor, D., Thomason, B., and Muthard, J. "A Critique of Effectiveness of Counselors and Counselor Aides." *Journal of Counseling Psychology,* Vol. 18 (July, 1971). pp. 362–364.

Thoresen, Carl E., Hosford, Ray E., and Krumboltz, John D. "Determining Effective Models for Counseling Clients of Varying Competencies." *Journal of Counseling Psychology,* Vol. 17 (July, 1970). pp. 369–375.

Truax, Charles B. and Lister, James L. "Effectiveness of Counselors and Counselor Aides." *Journal of Counseling Psychology,* Vol. 17 (July, 1970). pp. 331–334.

Ward, G. Robert, Kagan, Norman, and Krathwohl, David R. "An Attempt to Measure and Facilitate Counselor Effectiveness." *Counselor Education and Supervision,* Vol. 11 (March, 1972). pp. 179–186.

Warner, Richard W., Jr. "Alienated Students: Six Months After Receiving Behavioral Group Counseling." *Journal of Counseling Psychology,* Vol. 18 (September, 1971). pp. 426–430.

THE EDUCATION OF THE COUNSELOR

18

This chapter will analyze (1) the criticisms of and modifications made in counselor education, (2) standards for preparing counselors, (3) the character of counselor education programs, (4) selection of counselors, (5) content in counselor education, and (6) characteristics of counselor educators. Attaining competence in counselor skills and attitudes is presumably a lifetime commitment. Certainly, four years of college and one or two years of graduate study do not guarantee complete mastery or understanding of all that is involved in becoming a counselor.

Since about 1958, nearly all established programs of counselor education have expanded greatly in numbers of students and staff. In addition, many new programs have emerged in colleges and universities which had not previously engaged in such work.

Criticisms of and Modifications in Counselor Education

In recent years many counselors have engaged in the pastime of criticizing or expressing dissatisfaction with counselor education. For example, Aubrey has consistently criticized the incongruity that exists between counseling as it is visualized by counselor educators and counseling as it is practiced in schools. He believes that counselors are not being prepared to think or act as strategists or tacticians in school and community settings; that present-day counselors are not being prepared to function in a rapidly changing society; that counselors are not being prepared to work closely with teachers and administrators; and that counselors are not being prepared to act as change agents or as advocates for students.[1] Counselor educators have joined in the complaints and have been quick with critical comments about the influences which, if not detrimental, are at least noncontributory to

[1] Roger F. Aubrey, "And Never the Twain Shall Meet: Counselor Training and School Realities," *The School Counselor*, Vol. 20 (September, 1972), pp. 16–24.

the education of counselors. Such criticism, particularly when thoughtfully and constructively given, is healthy and challenging to those engaged in counselor preparation. But the criticisms are not always consistent because the critics hold different values or are not familiar with the object of their concern.

CRITICISMS OF COUNSELOR EDUCATION

Lack of Substantive Subject Matter A long-standing criticism of counselor preparation programs is that they lack substantive content and are superficial if not artificial. It is often said or implied that teachers who do not want to be school administrators or fear to pursue graduate work in their subject matter specialties enter counselor training because the academic demands are minimal, the challenges are negligible, and the intellectual involvement is superficial. Nationwide, counselor education undoubtedly still remains a mixture of the good and the bad, the worthwhile and the pointless, the genuine and the shoddy. Nevertheless, the most thoughtful and systematic of counselor education faculties have striven to keep their programs genuine, their objectives clearly stated, and their educational experiences valuable.

Lack of Practicality and Utilitarianism Those who pursue counselor education often deplore its emphasis upon theory devoid of the reality which practicing counselors face in the work setting. Students study theories of counseling, theories of child or adolescent development, theories of vocational development, they say, but never have an opportunity to apply them or test them out ("When will we get to something practical in this course?"). It is true that up to 1960 the proportion of counselor education programs which did not provide their students with supervised laboratory, practicum, and/or internship experiences was greater than the number which did. Not unusually, the charge of impracticality was directed at counselor educators: they were isolated from what went on in schools and would not be able to understand a real, live adolescent counselee if they came into contact with one.

Many have commented that in America learning is not encouraged for its own sake but because it leads to vocational ends and can satisfy immediate and expressed utilitarian demands. While to some degree utilitarianism is expected in specialized fields of graduate study, it should be noted that usefulness can be defined in various ways and that what is needed is the distinction between kinds of usefulness and clear designation of program goals. There is no doubt that counselor education should always be assessed in relation to its relevance for the practitioner. In this respect, the trend in textbooks used in counselor education courses plainly exhibits conflict among authors and within the writings of authors. There is an effort to provide materials meeting the student's particular demands for utility while simultaneously attempting to apply a rigorous scientific and theoretical approach to content.

Fundamentally, the assumption is that what counselors do, as well as what is expected of them, ought to determine the content of graduate preparation. But all too often the actual job functions of school counselors are determined by expediency and emotionality, frequently leading to routine office duties, clerical and quasi-administrative chores, or functions which are no different from those of classroom teachers or administrators. Some who completed counselor education programs based directly upon perceptions of what counselors were actually doing have in times of stress realized that this kind of utility was not the kind most instrumental in helping persons bewildered by complex personal situations.

Lack of Coherence Counselor education in many institutions is measured by accounting methods. That is, the definition of counselor competence is that a certain number of courses (10, 11, 12, etc.) have been taken. The rules do not require that anything learned must be remembered long or that it be related to other learnings. With the view that knowledge comes ready-made in course-sized packages, students concentrate on passing term examinations and securing grades. Little chance or stimulus exists for discovering relationships which are not purely intradisciplinary. Part-time study by part-time students contributes to the lack of coherence and continuity.

In such situations counselor education is organized around nothing in particular. The ideas encountered cannot be placed in any framework. Conflicting ideas tend to be accepted with little attention to their incompatibility. Contributions of related disciplines and experiences leading to a set of interrelated ideas and attitudes to help the individual meet new situations and integrate ambiguities are lacking.

Counselor education institutions which admit anyone who applies and which stress mass production of counselors thwart the development of a coherent, integrated program. Programs designed for large numbers of students obviously run the risk of becoming impersonal, and impersonality makes it especially difficult for even the most able student to shape his education into a meaningful and connected pattern. Contact with faculty members surely must be important in the student's attempts to see for himself an orderly world in counseling.

The introductory course, if it follows leading textbooks, teaches a little of everything but fails to base it upon any clear theoretical, comprehensive framework. There is usually no organizing principle or dimension cutting across more than two or three courses. Perhaps the most common instance of lack of coherence is found where the instructor believes it is necessary to introduce the student to everything the instructor knows, and he covers so many topics regardless of whether they have been or can be understood as conceptually independent.

Overlap, Repetition, and Boredom The lack of coherence often leads to the charge that counselor education represents wasted motion on the part of the student and results in overlap, repetition, and boredom. Although different levels of motivation are present in any class, when students encounter concepts and materials previously studied they will become bored. Close scrutiny, not only of repetition within a series of "counselor education courses" but also of that in "related fields," is essential to avoiding overlap and redundancy. Carefully planned repetition and review do provide opportunity for attaining mastery of subject matter, but unwitting repetition and duplication are likely to prevent the core learning experiences from becoming conceptualized or organized into a coherent whole by the student. Indeed, if nothing different happens after the introductory course, false feelings of mastery of the field may be engendered.

Lack of Responsibility by Counselor Educators A criticism increasingly being aired is that some counselor educators fail to exercise any professional judgments about the competences of those who enter and graduate from counselor education programs. Principals, superintendents, and school counselors either openly state or subtly imply that certain graduates do not possess the personal characteristics or professional skills suitable for school counseling positions. Presumably, their evaluations are based upon direct, on-the-job observation of graduates' personal traits and analysis of their professional adequacy. This charge is particularly serious. One criterion of a profession is that it imposes and enforces standards of admission to the field and performance following entry.

Such irresponsibility apparently stems from sheer lack of experience in making administrative decisions, from failure to formulate clear-cut attitudes, opinions, and values, and perhaps most of all from a lack of motivation to exercise mature judgment about the competence and behavior of those who graduate from counselor education programs. A laissez-faire approach will not contribute anything to the profession or provide a satisfactory basis for quality control in admitting individuals to the profession. Clearly, adopting the position "Let the school employing official beware!" does a disservice to the profession, the school, and the students the counselors are employed to serve. This does not mean that decisions about the capabilities, attitudes, and behavioral characteristics are easy, uncomplicated, or error free. But, in any worthy program counselor educators must and do render their best judgment about the fitness of the graduate to take a position in counseling.

Lack of Innovation Reform and updating of instructional practices are needed in many counselor education programs. The charge is made from outside the profession that it is exceptionally difficult to introduce educational innovations in counselor education and that those responsible for it resist change directed toward improving ways of learning. Further, while standards of preparation must be upheld, stereotypical approaches and provincialism mark many programs. Numerous exceptions exist, but inertia has all too often been the response to the use of new media and new ideas.

The curriculum in counselor education typically grows and becomes more specialized by a process of accretion rather than by careful planning and reduction of unnecessary course work. As new courses are added, rarely are old ones dropped. Elimination of courses is often threatening to the staffs because it is viewed as meaning reduction of personnel.

Clearly counselor education programs should abandon their rigidity and break away from the notion that didactic education is necessarily the best or the only way to develop skills in the helping relationship. Those who hope to provide the quality education needed by today's counselors will be stimulated to try out innovative curricular plans, will engage their students in supervised and independent helping relationship experiences in a multiplicity of settings, and will seek to establish new or modified program objectives.

Summary In discussing the criticisms of counselor education we have tried to include some of the compensating arguments and extenuating circumstances. The validity of the evidence on which certain criticisms are based and the total strength of the evidence cannot be readily determined. Hopefully, constructive comment and factually based, sincere criticism facilitate thorough examination of counselor education programs and lead to the reformulation of their objectives and content.

MODIFICATIONS IN COUNSELOR EDUCATION

An analysis of counselor education since its inception at Harvard in 1911 reveals modification of many kinds, interrelated or interdependent, and to a great extent reflects changes in concepts of counseling as well as change in our society.

More Specific and Definitive Image of the Counselor In many respects the model of the counselor exhibited in counselor education in this country until 1958 was general in character — general in the sense that it was of a guidance person whose role and functions were diverse and often conflicting. A large number of those who entered counselor education became deans, assistant principals, directors of student activities, or curriculum coordinators. Little attention, time, or effort was devoted to the counseling relationship.

Thus a good deal of latitude was allowed as to what courses were to be taken. Candidates were permitted progressively more electives and often chose courses which corresponded closely with immediate vocational demands. As the candidate exhibited a special interest, e.g., in testing, further course work in that area was pursued. He then developed some identification with and competence in the area. Counselor education programs had few required courses — an introductory survey, occupational information, counseling practices, and measurement — and the individual usually rounded out his program by other courses in student activities, curriculum, educational psychology, administration, and the like.

Current counselor education is more restricted in scope in the sense that the model upon which it is based is that of establishing and maintaining the counseling relationship. With the emergence of counseling as the primary function of those employed in school guidance programs, modifications have been incorporated in counselor education which in effect limit preparation to that considered appropriate to the school counselor, i.e., to the demands of counseling. Standards of training and practice have been stepped up and correspondingly, in many programs, fewer electives permitted. Individual and group counseling are emphasized. Appropriate consideration of various theories is included. Study based on case conferences, recordings, role playing, and laboratory experiences receives greater attention than ever before.

More Content and Emphasis Drawn from the Behavioral and Social Sciences Because it is essential that the counselor understand the dynamics of human behavior and of the individual in his culture, programs now require more study in psychology, sociology, and the humanities. Certainly, more programs require candidates to develop greater understanding in child and adolescent psychology, personality theory, and learning theory. The fields of sociology, anthropology, and economics — becoming more evident in counselor education — are viewed as vehicles for providing candidates with a heightened awareness of social forces and cultural changes which impinge upon individuals.

Move Away from Traditional Emphasis upon Methods, Materials, and Techniques Integration of theory and practice is sought through a planned sequence of educational experiences which spiral toward more advanced concepts. The counselor is no longer regarded as a technician but is considered a professional able to utilize relevant techniques because he understands human behavior, the community, and complex social forces.

More emphasis is being given to the philosophy and principles of counseling, the nature and range of human characteristics, professional relationships, and ethics governing the counselor's behavior. The "why" of certain factors influencing man is examined to enhance the counselor's skill in analysis and to increase his capacity for dispassionate judgment, which typifies the professional rather than the technician. Counselor education seeks to make it possible for candidates to pursue knowledge and to master information and attitudes of many kinds so that the professional's grasp of reality is broadened and the deadening hand of traditionalism is reduced.

Opportunities to Achieve Self-Awareness and Self-Understanding It is essential for the counselor to examine his own values and those of society, the sources of his motivation, and his relationships with others. Opportunities are now provided through workshops and T-groups, through individual and group counseling for trainees, and through seminars for thorough examination of the self. The candidate in counselor education extends his personal philosophy and becomes sensitive to his own outlook and style of dealing with the world. Self-understanding contributes to personal and professional maturity as well as to the capacity for good judgment.

Expansion of Staff and Utilization of Staff Members from Related Disciplines The number of counselor educators is increasing (since 1960, from 500 to approximately 2,500), the one-man counselor education department slowly becoming a thing of the past. A research committee of the Association for Counselor Education and Supervision, under the chairmanship of Don Blocher of the University of Minnesota, reported that the average counselor educator spent about one-half of his time in teaching or supervision, one-sixth of his time in administration, one-eighth of his time in individual or group counseling, and the remainder in research, service, and writing.[2]

While most counselor education programs are located within departments of education, the staff is becoming increasingly interdisciplinary in background. Individuals from the behavioral and social sciences are staff members and instruct in their content areas. Because they are qualified through

[2] Donald Blocher (Chairman), "A Survey of the Membership, 1966–1967," ACES Research Committee, March, 1967 (mimeographed).

academic preparation and appropriate experience to teach content in their particular disciplines, perspective and depth within these fields are greatly enhanced for counselor candidates.

Extended Core of Supervised Counseling Experiences
Experiences are provided those in counselor education through laboratories, counseling practicums, and internship. Laboratory experiences are either self-contained or integrated with classroom instruction. They deal with testing, study and development of case records, observation of actual counseling, role playing, and the like. Counseling practicum provides experiences in actual individual and group counseling either on or off campus. Internship supplies on-the-job counselor activities under the joint supervision of the local school counselor and a university supervisor. The purpose of these supervised experiences is to transform the student counselor into an independently functioning counselor. Supervised experience is seen as the most critical and necessary component of a counselor education program. It receives further attention later in this chapter.

Standards for Preparing Counselors

The need to improve the quality of counselor education led to the development of standards for preparing secondary school counselors. Many organizations and professionals have, over a period of time, called for a change in counselor education. In 1963 the American Psychological Association defined the contributions of psychology in the preparation of school counselors.[3] In March, 1964, the American Personnel and Guidance Association issued a statement of policy which applied to the professional preparation and role of the counselor in any setting in our society.[4]

A cooperative national study of counselor education was launched officially by the present Association for Counselor Education and Supervision (ACES) in April, 1960, under the joint chairmanship of Robert Stripling and Willis Dugan. Five regional chairmen were appointed and more than 70 local study groups were organized to examine the essential elements in counselor education programs. From the efforts of the local study groups, position papers were prepared which delineated issues and guidelines for counselor education. These papers were delivered and discussed at national conventions of the Association in 1962 and 1963. The activities of the study groups, the presentation of position papers, and discussions at professional meetings led to the development of standards for the preparation of secondary school counselors. The standards were accepted on a provisional three-year basis at the 1964 San Francisco national convention and were applied on an experimental basis for institutional self-study and evaluation.

A new committee under the chairmanship of George E. Hill was appointed to examine and revise the 1964 statement during 1964–1967. From 1964 through 1967 some 105 counselor education programs across the country applied the standards, either through self-study or by self-study followed by use of a visiting team. In 1967 the standards,[5] revised according to the experiences of institutions which applied them and the thoughtful opinions of others, were adopted by the Association for Counselor Education and Supervision through a mailed ballot. The adoption marked a most significant turning point in the preparation of secondary school counselors.

EXTENSION OF STANDARDS TO OTHER EDUCATION LEVELS

Since the standards were developed for the preparation of secondary school counselors, efforts by professional associations have been directed to formulating standards for preparing elementary

[3] Division of Counseling Psychology, *The Scope and Standards of Preparation in Psychology for School Counselors* (Washington: American Psychological Association, 1963).
[4] American Personnel and Guidance Association, *The Counselor: Professional Preparation and Role* (Washington: The Association, 1964).

[5] "Standards for the Preparation of Secondary School Counselors — 1967," *Personnel and Guidance Journal,* Vol. 46 (September, 1967), pp. 97–106.

school counselors and college student personnel workers. In November, 1964, the Commission on Professional Development of the Council of Student Personnel Associations published *A Proposal for Professional Preparation in College Student Personnel Work.* In 1967 an interdivisional committee of the American Personnel and Guidance Association, composed of members from the Association for Counselor Education and Supervision and the Student Personnel Association for Teacher Education, formulated a statement concerning the role and preparation of the college counselor and other student personnel specialists in junior colleges, colleges, and universities. The statement,[6] published in 1968, is deliberately similar in content, style, and format to the secondary school counselor education standards.

A joint committee of the American School Counselor Association and ACES was assigned the duty of providing a statement of standards[7] for the preparation of elementary school counselors. The committee, chaired by Merle Ohlsen, completed its work and submitted its statement to the American Personnel and Guidance Association. Again, the standards for preparing elementary school counselors follow closely those set forth in the other two standards statements.

CRITICISM OF THE STANDARDS

Many counselor educators expressed their belief that the standards would be a deterrent to introducing innovative and creative practices in counselor education. To them, the standards tend to have a freezing effect upon experimentation because they may put the stamp of finality on existing program content.

Some counselor educators were critical of the statement that two years of graduate preparation were needed before the individual is accorded "professional counselor status." Other counselor educators struck out at quantifying such matters as the minimum number of counselor educators needed (three) in a program to prepare counselors. Still others were critical because full time, rather than part time or summer, study was advocated by the standards.

CURRENT DEVELOPMENTS

In a 1970–1971 survey, ACES members indicated that the three sets of standards should be combined into one document. There were two reasons for doing so. First, considerable overlap existed among the three sets and second, there was difficulty in applying three different sets. During 1971–1972, an ACES commission was formed that revised and combined the three sets into one. The proposed standards are to be submitted to a mail ballot of ACES members in November, 1973. At this writing, the outcome of that ballot is unknown.

Four major sections compose the composite standards statement. The first section requires that the institution develop a stated philosophy of education and a set of objectives for counselor education which is consistent with that philosophy. No one particular philosophy is expressed or implied in the standards. Rather, it is recommended that the philosophy and counselor education objectives be developed cooperatively by staff members and state and local guidance personnel and representatives from related disciplines.

The second section outlines the program of studies and supervised experiences in counselor education. Full-time study is recommended. A planned sequence of educational experiences is to be defined and prerequisites must be identified.

The third section sets forth standards for selection, retention, endorsement, and placement of students.

The fourth section outlines the support, administrative relations, and institutional resources required for a program of counselor education. Three full-time qualified staff members are viewed as the minimum in a program. Budgets, physical facilities, library resources, and student financial aid are established as essential.

[6] "Standards for the Preparation of Guidance and Personnel Workers — In Colleges and Universities," *Personnel and Guidance Journal,* Vol. 47 (January, 1969), pp. 493–498.
[7] Merle M. Ohlson, "Standards for the Preparation of Elementary School Counselors," *Counselor Education and Supervision,* Vol. 47 (Spring, 1968), pp. 172–178.

At least two issues remain to be settled before the future of standards in counselor education can be ascertained. The first issue is whether a set of standards is necessary. We believe that the profession should at least establish minimum characteristics of any program that prepares counselors. The second issue is how and by whom the standards will be used to accredit counselor education programs. The ACES Commission on Standards and Accreditation has worked with the executive officer of the National Council for the Accreditation of Teacher Education (NCATE) to establish that (1) the team of educators that visits institutions which are applicants or renewal applicants for NCATE membership will contain at least one counselor educator (counselor educator team members are recommended to NCATE by the APGA Commission) and (2) those counselor education programs that meet NCATE approval will be publicized by both NCATE and APGA.

Proposals have been advanced that APGA (or Division 2, The Association for Counselor Education and Supervision) use the standards to approve counselor education programs. However, the tremendous expense incurred in conducting such an operation almost precludes that possibility. Additionally, university or college presidents have long sought to reduce the number of accrediting bodies that visit their institutions. Others have proposed that a voluntary association be formed of institutions that have applied, through self-study, the counselor education standards and then been visited by an external evaluation committee. To date, little progress has been made on either of these proposals.

The Character of Preparation Programs

Institutions which offer programs in counselor education are multiplying rapidly — so rapidly as to arouse concern over the quality of training programs and to contribute directly to the development and adoption of preparation standards. Much diversity exists in the content and character of these institutions, and change in most of them is being actively sought.

There are many who have set down the characteristics of an effective counselor education program. Krumboltz, for example, proposes four criteria for desired behavior on the part of those who participate in such a program:

1. The counselor should learn for each individual client to specify the objectives of counseling in terms of changes in the client's behavior mutually desired by client and counselor.
2. The counselor should learn to apply facts about the learning process to the modification of client behavior.
3. The counselor should learn that the responses of his client, not the judgment of his practicum supervision, provide the criterion for judging the success of his counseling.
4. The counselor should learn to examine the research literature and to participate in research studies in order to find improved ways of helping client.[8]

A few counselor preparation programs have designed and implemented a systems approach. Primary features of such programs include (1) the identification of training goals, (2) flow charts that depict the relationship of the components to each other and to the system as a whole, and (3) feedback mechanisms that facilitate goal attainment and efficiency of those in the system. Some systematic programs have sought to reduce competitive grading and to provide ways for students to progress (or recycle) at their own rate of learning. Figure 18.1 presents a flow chart that depicts the systematic counselor education program at Michigan State University.

Brammer and Springer describe the key characteristics of counselor education and certification (State of Washington) based on behavioral criteria and objective performance standards. Individuals to be certified as counselors are assessed against be-

[8] John D. Krumboltz, "Changing the Behavior of Behavior Changers," *Counselor Education and Supervision,* Vol. 6 (Spring, 1967, Special Issue), pp. 222–229.

Figure 18.1 Systematic counseling

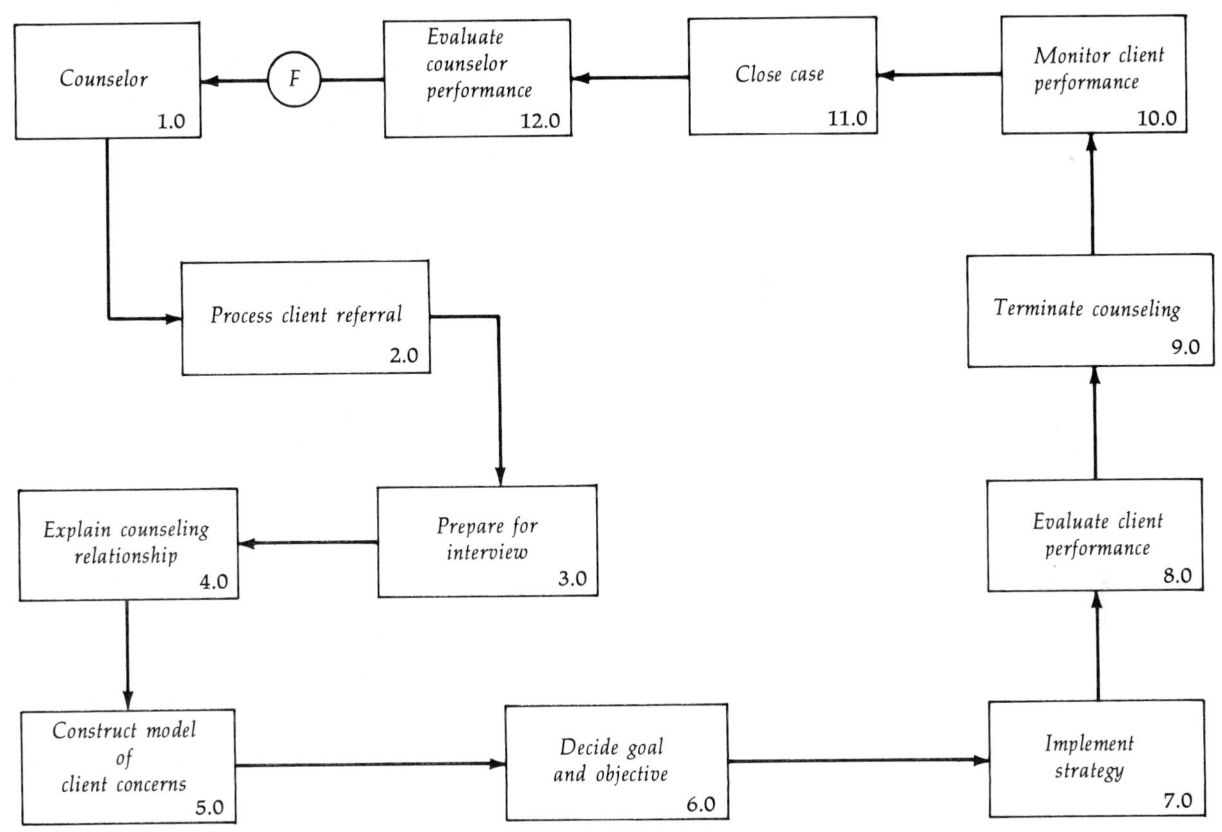

Reproduced by permission of Norman R. Stewart, Bob B. Winborn, Richard G. Johnson, Herbert M. Burks, Jr., and James R. Engelness, Michigan State University, 1971.

havioral objectives. The first category of such objectives includes counselor traits (flexibility, spontaneity, etc.) judged to be significant by practicing school counselors. The second category to be assessed is counselor performance with clients, and the third is the counselor's knowledge of measurement principles, sources of information, and referral agencies. Figure 18.2 depicts the Washington State system for counselor development and certification.

Brammer and Springer state that the Washington preparation programs are individualized in the sense of moving counselors to higher levels of professional development. Formal preparation is assumed to be a continuous lifelong process and a training partnership with school districts, university counselor education programs, and professional associations is responsible for developing programs and recommending candidates for counselor certification.[9]

Pierson, on the other hand, believes that APGA official statements tend to view the counselor and student personnel worker as applied scientists.

[9] Lawrence M. Brammer and Harry C. Springer, "A Radical Change in Counselor Education and Certification," *Personnel and Guidance Journal*, Vol. 49 (June, 1971), pp. 803–808.

Figure 18.2 A system for counselor development and certification

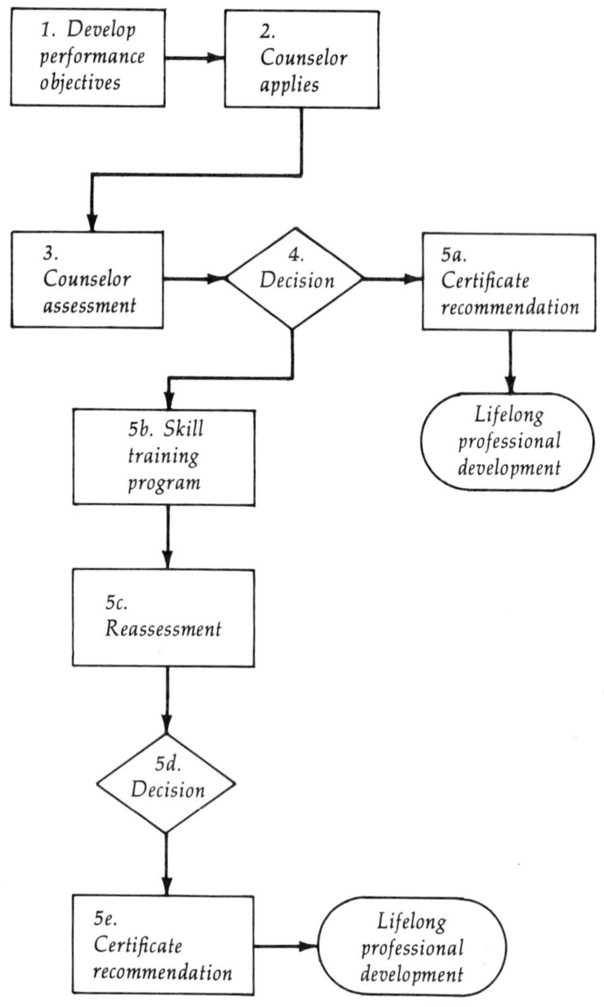

SOURCE: Lawrence M. Brammer and Harry C. Springer, "A Radical Change in Counselor Education and Certification," *Personnel and Guidance Journal*, Vol. 49 (June, 1971), p. 806. Copyright 1971 American Personnel and Guidance Association. Reprinted with permission.

Many counselor educators "have joined the ranks of those behavioral and social scientists who believe that the scientific way of thinking applies to the problems of human nature just as it applies to the problems of non-human nature."[10] Because counselors deal with problems of human nature, it is Pierson's contention that the scientific perspective is not always appropriate. The cause-and-effect concept, basic to scientific thought and developed to study the behavior of nonhumans, is not necessarily applicable to humans, who are self-aware and can choose alternate courses of action. In his view, counselor education programs overlook the fact that counseling and student personnel work is an art as well as a science. Pierson believes that (1) the practice of counseling and student personnel work should be regarded as a human relations art, (2) counselor education institutions should exercise freedom and imagination in developing and administering their programs, (3) a broad outline of a core of basic training has emerged, (4) the major emphasis in preparation programs should be upon supervised practice and supervised work experience, (5) few universities are now equipped to provide counselor education and the number of institutions engaged in such training should be kept relatively small, (6) counselor educators must be active in developing programs for training counseling subprofessionals and support personnel, and (7) the advantages of keeping counseling and student personnel work together as specialties within a single profession outweigh the disadvantages.

Landsman, too, saw a social order moving toward mechanization and suggested that present psychotherapists received their training at a time when psychology fostered the idea of man's being like a machine. However, underneath the mechanistic appearance of society is a basic hunger for individual fulfillment. In Landsman's view, most counselor educators attempt to have their classes approximate a group therapy situation. He saw both information and personality as being involved in the work of the counselor. If personality growth is a major purpose of counselor education,

[10] George A. Pierson, "The Art and Science of Counseling and Student Personnel Work," *Counselor Education and Supervision*, Vol. 6 (Spring, 1967), pp. 251–254.

. . . then our best hope to achieve such a program would be in the organization of an entire program rather than one course, toward personality growth. This would mean the maintenance of a growth-producing atmosphere in our graduate schools rather than the traditional, threatening, "make it tough so they'll know it's worth it" characteristic of most doctoral programs in all areas of modern university life.[11]

To recommend providing experiences through which self-awareness as well as external knowledge may be attained is not to advocate soft or easy programs. Indeed, many programs would have to acquire new staff members in order to provide such experiences. Landsman predicted that a more conservative direction would probably be taken by American counselor preparation programs, with emphasis on improved practicum training and toward didactic psychotherapy.

The characteristics of a two-year program have been set forth by Malcolm. The thrust of the first semester is toward experiences that enable the counselor to understand the dynamics of human behavior, including his own. All courses emphasize personal implications and the chief subject matter is the student himself. Attention during the second semester of the first year shifts from self-study to the forces at work in the environment. Independent and individual study begins to replace cooperative group activities as the student assumes increasing responsibility for his personal and professional development. Practicum experiences during the first semester focus on counselor behavior but shift during the second semester to understanding the client's problems.

The thrust of the second year is toward advanced study of human behavior. Malcolm urges that didactic instruction during this second year be interdisciplinary in nature and individually designed, based on the student's needs. Practicum experiences during the second year are heavily supervised and intensive so that integration of technical competence and theory takes place.[12]

Parker[13] has identified and discussed five issues in counselor education that illustrate much of the present character of such programs. The first is whether counselor preparation should be viewed as "training" or "education." The second is whether the program should focus on personal development of the counselor or on mastering a body of knowledge and skills. The third issue is whether students in such programs should be evaluated. The fourth issue is whether prospective counselors should be taught one systematic approach or exposed to many with encouragement to select and construct an approach that fits them. The fifth issue is whether clients or supervisors are the best source of feedback regarding counseling effectiveness. Parker concludes that:

The five issues have a seemingly common polarity. Theorists who emphasize empirical approaches to the accumulation of knowledge and its dissemination tend to see counselor education as rational rather than experiential, as education rather than training, as requiring carefully evaluated controlled growth rather than allowing self-development, as containing a body of knowledge and techniques universally applicable in counseling rather than depending on individual counselor approaches, and as relying on supervisor knowledge rather than client feedback. Theorists at the other pole emphasize the experiential, self-development, and the importance of individualized approaches or theories of counseling.[14]

The major purpose of any counselor education program is to facilitate an individual's personal and professional development. Most programs are designed to encourage students to develop (a) human relationship skills, (b) technical skills (understand-

[11] Ted Landsman, "Humanistic Training for a Mechanistic Society," *Counselor Education and Supervision*, Vol. 2 (Spring, 1963), p. 118.

[12] David Donald Malcolm, "A Two-Year Program of Counselor Education," *Counselor Education and Supervision*, Vol. 10 (Winter, 1971), pp. 171–179.

[13] Clyde A. Parker, "Issues, Evidence, and A Beginning," in Clyde A. Parker (ed.), *Counseling Theories and Counselor Education* (Boston: Houghton Mifflin Company, 1968), pp. 4–7.

[14] *Ibid.*, p. 7.

ing tests, etc.), and (c) conceptual skills (theorizing and explaining) so they can function as counseling professionals. Blocher[15] reasons that the counselor in preparation draws on program resources involving certain response modes. He identifies three such response modes. The first is the *immediate-intuitive,* or that doing what feels right is the basis for behavior. The experiential process is emphasized through sensitivity training or variants of small-group work. Such programs stress supportive functions, communication and feedback, and awareness of interpersonal behavior. Personal experience, paramount in such programs, constitutes what Hallberg labels the "silent curriculum" in many programs.[16]

The second response mode available to the counselor in preparation, according to Blocher, is the *cognitive-theoretical,* in which some set of cognitive structures is used to assign meanings to the individual's perceptions of the interpersonal situations. Programs characterized by this response mode stress didactic activities such as reading, lectures, discussions, and laboratories.

The third response mode is the *empirical-pragmatic,* or determination of one's behavior by what gives predictable results. Preparation programs characterized by this response mode stress practicum, field work, and internship activities so that the counselor can test his skills and knowledge. Feedback to the counselor from clients, not just supervisors, is highly important and differentiates this mode from the first two modes. Without doubt, the counselor in a preparation program which supplies all three response modes integrated into a cohesive, consistent pattern of behavior would be truly effective.

Lister notes an aversion to theory among most counselors in preparation.[17] The student dislikes content emphasizing counseling principles, assumptions, objectives, philosophy, or ethics because it appears irrelevant in the real world of the schools. Contributing to a distaste for theory are the following: (1) Staff positions in personnel work are filled by individuals disinclined to ask basic questions; (2) students resist theories inconsistent with their value systems, motivation patterns, or life styles; (3) dissonance occurs between the student's actual practices and theoretical content, and therefore the student resolves the conflict by (a) distorting or misinterpreting the theory to justify his practices, (b) redefining his practices to fit the theory, or (c) introducing reasons why his behavior is justified under the circumstances; (4) the student does not see the theory translated into practice or expressed in operational, behavioral terms; and (5) theory and techniques are too often presented as separate packages. Lister suggests that counselor candidates be given opportunities to relate their personal theory to the formal theory encountered. If such opportunities are not given, presentation of theory often "drives underground" the values and attitudes the candidate brings to the program, where they remain dormant for a while but become active and operational in counseling experiences.

Hunt has provided a penetrating descriptive analysis of the developmental phases of counselor change during a preparation program. Five different types of attitudes were recognized among enrollees in NDEA Counseling and Guidance Institutes. Hunt's formulation, while based upon an Institute program, still seems to characterize the experience of many students and is therefore presented here. While given as distinct categories, the phases blend gradually and sometimes imperceptibly. Regressions and progressions take place, but the categories represent a hierarchy of

[15] Donald H. Blocher, "Counselor Education: Facilitating the Development of a Helping Person," in Clyde A. Parker (ed.), *Counseling Theories and Counselor Education* (Boston: Houghton Mifflin Company, 1968), pp. 133–144.
[16] Edmond C. Hallberg, "The Silent Curriculum in Counselor Education," *Personnel and Guidance Journal,* Vol. 50 (November, 1971), pp. 198–201.

[17] James L. Lister, "Theory Aversion in Counselor Education," *Counselor Education and Supervision,* Vol. 6 (Winter, 1967), pp. 91–96.

development. A summary of the five categories, described more comprehensively by Hunt, follows:

1. *Initial period.* The individual with some previous counseling experience often has a naive faith in and is comfortable with his ability to handle the interpersonal relations existing in counseling. Such individuals believe they know the answer to the counselee's problem. A facade of knowledge is sometimes presented as a mask for feelings of inadequacy. Some are openly fearful and freely admit their lack of knowledge and anxiety.
2. *Mechanical period.* Since measurements, tests and test interpretations are often stressed during the early portion of preparation, they influence counseling conduct. Acceptance of this phase offers a safe transition into further work. The individual sees himself as an object for giving tests and questioning the individual. Little effort is made to determine what test data mean to a client and the client is viewed as an object to give and receive data. There is a mechanical manipulation of data in the interviews and the subject of informal talk between and among counselors is that of cases, case procedures and what can be done for the counselee.
3. *Discovery period.* The impact of different views and different methods, academic coursework, more counseling, wider reading and critical analysis brings the counselor to a point where he begins to be confused as to what he is doing. Feelings of inadequacy arise, self-doubt is generated and critical questioning as to the worth of counseling follow. Some students stop here, some move out of the program, some revert to a mechanical stage.
4. *Fuller realization of self.* Recognition comes that they doubt themselves and reflection is engendered regarding self and how it interacts in the work they are doing. Students explore patterns they have established for viewing life and much soul searching takes place of prejudices, fears and opinions, and inadequacies are exposed and examined.
5. *Transcending the former view of self.* New views are incorporated into a broader view of self and the counselor gains confidence that he can counsel and can be honest in the counseling relationship.[18]

[18] Clifford M. Hunt, "Developmental Phases of Counselor Growth," *Counselor Education and Supervision*, Vol. 2 (Fall, 1962), pp. 45–48.

SUMMARY

Thus the character of counselor preparation is changing. More and more attention is being devoted to the learning processes used. Admittedly, these processes are often merged and sometimes confused. The emphasis is away from authoritarian, instructor-dominated, information-oriented classrooms and toward the use of group dynamics to encourage interpersonal processes and student involvement and self-direction. The hope is that students will achieve self-direction, become critical learners able to evaluate their own and others' work, and acquire relevant knowledge which can be adapted flexibly and intelligently to new situations. Fundamentally, the procedures used in any particular program of counselor education reflect the views of the staff, their personalities, the content included, and the numbers of candidates involved. Little doubt exists that processes encouraging humanness, sensitivity, and maturity provide a climate which facilitates learning and increases morale.

Selection of Counselors

An urgent problem in counselor education is selecting those who are to become counselors. Practicing counselors should be concerned because professional groups are judged by their members. Physicians and lawyers are universally held in high esteem, and the public generally regards them as being highly trained, competent, and conscientious. On the other hand, a common criticism is that counseling has attracted individuals of rather mediocre ability and inferior personality attributes. Little documentary evidence is presented by people who make such charges, but a considerable number of professionals seem to believe that students preparing for counseling do not rank as high as candidates for medicine, law, and engineering.

Obviously, counselors interested in advancing their profession should actively promote its desirability as a lifework. However, there is no intention here to imply that practicing counselors are responsible for screening out unlikely candidates for admission to counselor education. That duty rightfully belongs to the college or university where preparation is sought.

Few individuals involved in counseling in any capacity disagree with the proposition that selection of prospective counselors is important and should be done rigorously. But no exact criteria for evaluating candidates for admission have yet been established. While relatively little research has focused on predictions of counselor effectiveness in schools or colleges, there appears to be no one yardstick for measuring probable success or failure. Generally, the individual's initial decision to seek admission to counselor education involves self-selection and is purely voluntary. If serious weaknesses become evident, however, somewhere along the line a decision to reject him as a counselor candidate must be made by the preparing institution.

Hill, who has written more about counselor selection than anyone else, concluded, first, that the literature on counselor selection is meager compared with the general guidance literature; second, that only a limited amount of research has dealt with identification, selection, screening, placement, and follow-up of counselors; and third, that the profession has arrived at a point where concerted attention to these problems is needed.[19] Selecting individuals to prepare for and engage in the work of the school counselor, he points out, is complicated by such conditions as the variety of roles and relationships involved in the counselor's work, the diversity of skills expected of the counselor from school to school, and the fact that studies of counselor characteristics have failed to produce a standard personality pattern. Hill also presented some "facts of life" germane to any consideration of counselor selection. Among these is that a necessary component of effective counselor selection is some model or conception of the professional for whom a preparation program is designed and that research is needed on counselor effectiveness to cope with selection.

The fact that counselor selection is viewed as an urgent problem has stimulated some research. A number of personality variables important to counseling effectiveness have been hypothesized (see Chapter Five), and identification of the most promising and relevant to predicting success in a counselor preparation program has been attempted. Demos and Zuwaylif administered the Allport-Vernon-Lindzey Study of Values, Kuder Preference Record – Personal, and Edwards Personal Preference Schedule to a 30-member summer NDEA Counseling and Guidance Institute.[20] Statistical tests (t tests) were used to ascertain significant differences between the 15 most successful and the 15 least successful candidates (based upon supervisors' ratings). Only the Edwards Personal Preference Schedule differentiated the above-average from the below-average. The most effective counselors exhibited significantly more nurturance and affiliation; the least effective, more autonomy, abasement, and aggression. Blocher used a multiple regression approach to predicting success in counselor education.[21] Again, the subjects were 30 enrollees in an NDEA Counseling and Guidance Institute. The criterion was staff members' rankings of predicted performance as a school counselor. Predictor variables included peer rankings, NDEA Counseling and Guidance Comprehensive Examination data, Kuder Personal Preference (Form D) scores, and fall quarter grades, which were combined in a multiple regression equation for predicting final staff rating. A total multiple correlation coefficient of .77 with the criterion was obtained. Elimination of grades detracted little from the final prediction coefficient. Because the high school counselor score of the Kuder provided a factor

[19] George E. Hill, "The Selection of School Counselors," *Personnel and Guidance Journal,* Vol. 39 (January, 1961), pp. 355–360.

[20] George D. Demos and Ladil H. Zuwaylif, "Characteristics of Effective Counselors," *Counselor Education and Supervision,* Vol. 5 (Spring, 1966), pp. 163–165.

[21] Donald H. Blocher, "A Multiple Regression Approach to Predicting Success in a Counselor Education Program," *Counselor Education and Supervision,* Vol. 3 (Fall, 1963), pp. 19–22.

negatively related to other predictors but having substantial positive correlation with the criterion, Blocher believed that the measure was uniquely valuable in a multiple correlation approach.

Tests of scholastic ability have frequently been used to screen for prospective counselors, but their validity has not been well established. Callis and Prediger sought to identify the relative effectiveness of the Ohio State University Psychological Examination (OSUPE), Miller Analogy Test, Cooperative English Test: C2 Reading Comprehension, and grade-point average in predicting the academic achievement of graduate students in counseling and guidance.[22] Subjects were NDEA Counseling and Guidance Institute enrollees during the 1959, 1960, and 1961 summers. Some combination of OSUPE and the Reading Comprehension (subtest of the Cooperative English Test) generally produced the highest multiple correlation, but the increments in correlation achieved by using two predictors instead of one were slight from a practical standpoint. Major conclusions were that (1) measures of reading comprehension were the most effective predictor of those studied, and (2) using criteria in combination rather than singly had little practical significance.

Thweatt undertook to test the hypothesis that the inadequate student would tend to transfer or drop from the counseling curriculum if he were provided the opportunity to develop self-insight and were given the choice.[23] Effectiveness or readiness to perform as a counselor was defined as giving more affective than cognitive responses to 30 recorded client statements. Of the 15 students classified as having inadequate counseling potential, 12 decided to discontinue their training, while all 40 of those classified as adequate made self-derived decisions to continue. Thweatt concludes that self-selection can be a highly successful screening technique if the training program stresses self-insight.

Cheney reports the use of nondirective interviewing techniques in selecting enrollees for counseling institutes.[24] A team of four staff members interviewed applicants. After establishing rapport, they elicited information about the applicant's home, family relationships, educational experiences, why teaching and counseling were selected as occupations, and the applicant's attitudes and feelings. Enrollees believed the interview was helpful to them because they gained an understanding of the program and became acquainted with staff members.

Rogers' postulates that congruence, empathic understanding, unconditional positive regard, and the ability to communicate these conditions were necessary and sufficient for positive change led Steph to design an instrument for predicting the relationship orientation of applicants in a 1962–1963 NDEA Counseling and Guidance Institute.[25] His Wisconsin Relationship Orientation Scale (WROS) measures the degree of psychological closeness the respondent would allow. Three independent judges used the WROS to evaluate institute members' responses to eight hypothetical counseling situations taped prior to selection for training. As criteria, Steph employed staff ratings, peer ratings, and ratings of randomly drawn segments from taped practicum interviews conducted by the subjects. He was able to demonstrate both the reliability and the predictive validity of his scale. Following Steph's study, Wasson sought to determine whether the WROS was contributing unique information not obtained from such instruments as the Minnesota Multiphasic Personality Inventory (MMPI), the EPPS, and the Miller Analogies Test.[26] The

[22] Robert Callis and Dale J. Prediger, "Predictors of Achievement in Counseling and Guidance Graduate Study," *Counselor Education and Supervision,* Vol. 3 (Winter, 1964), pp. 63–69.
[23] Roger C. Thweatt, "Development of Counselor Trainee Self-Insight: Evaluation of Effectiveness of Self-Selection," *Counselor Education and Supervision,* Vol. 2 (Winter, 1963), pp. 78–81.

[24] Truman M. Cheney, "Using Non-Directive Techniques in Selecting Enrollees for Counseling Institutes," *Counselor Education and Supervision,* Vol. 2 (Spring, 1963), pp. 149–151.
[25] J. A. Steph, "Responses to Hypothetical Counseling Situations as a Predictor of Relationship Orientation in School Counselors," unpublished Ph.D. dissertation, University of Wisconsin, 1963.
[26] Robert M. Wasson, "The Wisconsin Relationship Orientation Scale as a Unique Variable in the Assessment of Applicants for Counselor Education," *Counselor Education and Supervision,* Vol. 4 (Winter, 1965), pp. 89–92.

WROS, he concluded, was essentially uncorrelated with intellectual, personality, and interest measures. Steph's and Wasson's results appear to be quite challenging for counselor selection. If further study demonstrates continued superiority of the WROS over most predictive studies, an impressive methodological breakthrough will have been made.

A task force, drawn from an invitational conference on research problems in counseling, formulated some 200 specific recommendations in the area of research on counselor selection. Prominent recommendations were that an assessment of the effects of a training program be made; that the presence and extent of a "g-factor" in counselor characteristics be investigated; that definitions of "effectiveness" be further clarified; that the warmth/coldness continuum is a fruitful area for study and that the use of socially valued, external, objective criteria as outcome measures be related to counselor selection in research studies.[27]

TYPICAL SELECTION CRITERIA AND PROCESSES

Typical criteria for admission to counselor education programs include the candidate's undergraduate grade-point average, a measure of academic ability such as the Miller Analogies Test or the Graduate Record Examination (ability section), results of personality inventories such as the Edwards Personal Preference Schedule or the Guilford-Zimmerman Temperament Survey, and results of interest inventories such as the Strong Vocational Interest Blank or the Kuder Preference Record — Personal. An increasing number of institutions request that individuals who express interest in entering counselor education be personally interviewed by staff members before action is taken on their applications.

Currently, most counselor education institutions place substantial reliance upon intellective measures in selecting candidates. These estimate whether the individual can succeed in graduate study and usually work best to eliminate those who could not cope intellectually with course work. But study after study suggests that nonintellective variables rather than intellect are of crucial significance to effective counseling. Because of this dilemma, the search for an objective approach to assess nonintellective variables goes on. Brams notes that available objective personality instruments are not adequate for evaluating test-sophisticated graduate students.[28] Others have suggested that present devices are most useful in screening out misfits rather than making fine discriminations regarding degrees of potential effectiveness.

Given well-defined selection criteria that are applied stringently, some students are admitted to counselor education programs who do not successfully complete graduate degrees. In some cases they withdraw of their own volition; in others, they are asked to leave as soon as the evidence becomes known. Still another kind of error in selection procedures is the rejection of applications from students who can and do succeed elsewhere, sometimes brilliantly. Errors of this kind are a result of many factors. First, an honest mistake may have been made in estimating the rejected applicant's potential because undue weight was given to one or more of the selection criteria (e.g., a recommendation, a test score, marginal grades). Secondly, the student's application papers may have had such omissions as a missing transcript or a late letter of recommendation. Thirdly, the error may have been made because the application was compared with a set of far superior applications. (This "context effect" can, of course, work in the opposite way; an ordinary application may look very good compared with a set of poor papers.)

Hill has indicated that counselor education programs must formulate well-defined procedures for (1) identifying promising candidates, (2) selectively

[27] "Refocus of Research in Counselor Selection: Task Group Recommendations," in John M. Whiteley (ed.), *Research in Counseling* (Columbus: Ohio: Charles E. Merrill Books, Inc., 1968), pp. 244–251.

[28] Jerome Brams, "Counselor Characteristics and Effective Communication in Counseling," *Journal of Counseling Psychology,* Vol. 8 (Spring, 1961), pp. 25–31.

admitting candidates, (3) endorsing the candidates to state certifying agencies, and (4) helping to place candidates.[29] Thus, selection for counselor training is viewed as a continuous process which takes place not only at the point of admission to the program but throughout as well as at completion of preparation. Selection as a concept, therefore, has continuous applicability to admission, didactic course enrollment, practicum and field practice enrollments, and job placement. After entry, screening should be undertaken in respect to how well the individual performs in course work, how well he is able to meet the demands of supervised experiences, and how ready he is for an entry-level counseling position in a school or college. However, dismissal of a student who has gained entry into a program is painful to all concerned. While it is sometimes done, it is not desirable for those in counselor education to allow "borderline" students to pass through and be granted degrees. Presumably, no university program of any kind is free of this kind of problem. In truth, both the discipline and the student suffer from it.

The "Standards for the Preparation of Counselor and other Pupil Personnel Specialists" contains six statements pertaining to selection, retention, endorsement, and placement:

1. Applicants accepted meet the institution's standards for admission to graduate study.
2. A continuing evaluation through systematic review is made of students as they progress through the program.
3. In situations where evaluations of a student indicate an inappropriateness for the counseling field, staff members assist in facilitating change to an area more appropriate for the student.
4. A statement of policy relating to the institution's procedure for formal endorsement has been adopted and approved by the faculty and administrative authorities.
5. Endorsement is given by the counseling staff only for the particular job setting for which the student has been prepared by his course work and supervised experiences.
6. The institution has a placement service with policies and procedures consistent with recognized placement practices.[30]

[29] George E. Hill, "Student Selection and Placement," in *Counselor Education: A Progress Report on Standards* (Washington: American Personnel and Guidance Association, 1962), pp. 39–40.

Content in Counselor Education

Counselor education content varies from state to state and from institution to institution both in quantity of offerings and in quality. Prior to the adoption of the standards for counselor education, even casual observation revealed that common elements among programs could be traced most directly to state certification for school counselors. Usual offerings included courses in (1) introduction to guidance, (2) occupational information, (3) tests and measurements, (4) counseling techniques, and (5) organization and administration of guidance programs.

Major influences on the selection of content for counselor education programs include (1) Wrenn's *The Counselor in a Changing World*, (2) the NDEA Counseling and Guidance Institute programs, and (3) the process of developing and adopting counselor preparation standards. Wrenn recommended that a two-year counselor preparation program incorporate a core in psychology, a core in the social sciences (sociology, economics, etc.), a core in counseling and supervised experiences, and a core in educational philosophy, curriculum, and research.[31] The NDEA Counseling and Guidance Institutes demonstrated the need and desirability for full-time study and supervised counseling experiences. Development and adoption of the standards dramatized the need for a minimum floor of preparation.

[30] Commission on Standards and Accreditation, "Standards for the Preparation of Counselors and Other Personnel Service Specialists," Washington, D.C.: Association for Counselor Education and Supervision (Fall, 1973), pp. 11–13. Mimeographed.
[31] C. Gilbert Wrenn, *The Counselor in a Changing World* (Washington: American Personnel and Guidance Association, 1962), pp. 161–168.

According to the program of studies outlined by the standards, (1) information about the educational setting (purposes, organization, curriculum, and philosophy) was to be presented; (2) content was to be drawn from the behavioral sciences (growth and development, personality dynamics and theories, learning theories, and the like); (3) professional studies in counseling (counseling theory, techniques, group procedures and processes, individual appraisal, vocational development theory, professional identification, and ethics) were necessary; and (4) supervised experiences in counseling were to be provided.[32]

Some counselor educators have discussed their views on the content or preparation programs. Tolbert has suggested that the introductory guidance course is largely shaped by textbooks utilized in the course.[33] The major emphasis given in a first course, he feels, should be on a comprehensive survey of the elements of guidance and personnel services, then the relationships of each service to others and to the educational program should be explored, and finally attention should be given to competence development, self-analysis, and career planning. Such a course should be designed to accommodate a wide range of individuals — teachers, administrators, and beginning counselors — and their interchange of ideas and attitudes would constitute a valuable by-product of the course.

Brammer raises the question as to when and how theory should be taught.[34] He believes that theory should pervade the entire counselor education program. But early in the program, a thorough exposure should be given to various theories of personality with implications for counseling. Following this introduction, both didactic and practicum experiences are needed if the counselor is to make his theory explicit. Finally, Brammer recommends a seminar in counseling theory where the student can reflect on his practical experiences and personal values and, in effect, engage in personal theory building (see Chapter Eleven).

Much recent research has gone into the nature of supervised counseling experiences. Johnston and Gysbers, for example, sought to identify the kind of relationship, strategy, and structure employed in supervisory situations.[35] They devised nine situations considered illustrative of typical supervisory contacts with counselor candidates in practicum, and 100 supervisors indicated their degree of agreement or disagreement with the 15 alternatives following each situation. Three types of relationships may be identified, Johnston and Gysbers suggest: (1) *paternalistic*, in which counselor candidates are not encouraged to participate in planning supervisory activities, (2) *democratic*, in which candidates participate in supervisory activities, and (3) *laissez-faire*, in which supervisors avoid involvement or provide assistance only on request. The practicum supervisors expressed preference for democratic relationships. In respect to the strategies employed by supervisors in handling situations, the respondents chose alternatives in which they remained personally involved (demonstration, intervention, evaluation, or discussion). As far as structure went, the respondents expressed preference for alternatives classified as minimal. Johnston and Gysbers note that their findings differ from those of Walz and Roeber, who suggested that "the relationship between supervisor and counselor [is] more like that of the subject matter teacher and pupil."[36] Rather, the former authors report a learner-centered type of supervisory relationship advocated by Patterson, who urged that supervision should be more like counseling and psychotherapy than didactic teaching.[37] Delaney and

[32] Commission on Standards and Accreditation, *op. cit.*
[33] E. L. Tolbert, "Basic Guidance Course: Forgotten But Not Gone," *Counselor Education and Supervision*, Vol. 5 (Spring, 1966), pp. 148–153.
[34] Lawrence M. Brammer, "Teaching Counseling Theory: Some Issues and Points of View," *Counselor Education and Supervision*, Vol. 5 (Spring, 1966), pp. 120–130.

[35] Joseph A. Johnston and Norman C. Gysbers, "Practicum Supervisory Relationships: A Majority Report," *Counselor Education and Supervision*, Vol. 6 (Fall, 1966), pp. 3–10.
[36] Garry R. Walz and Edward C. Roeber, "Supervisor Reactions to a Counseling Interview," *Counselor Education and Supervision*, Vol. 2 (Fall, 1962), pp. 2–7.
[37] C. H. Patterson, "Supervising Students in the Counseling Practicum," *Journal of Counseling Psychology*, Vol. 11 (Spring, 1964), pp. 47–53.

Moore administered a scale designed to gather information about the supervisor's role to 123 prepracticum students and reported that their subjects entered practicum with a conceptual picture of the supervisor's role as primarily instructional.[38]

CURRICULUM CHANGE

Counselor educators who seek to change the curriculum are confronted with a number of issues which must be resolved. One is selecting content from the many disciplines related to counseling. While it is generally insisted that contributions from related disciplines are essential, the problem lies in deciding just what content truly enhances counselor functioning and understanding.

A second major tactical decision is where and how counseling theory is to be presented to students: in a separate course or combined with techniques and practices? Many have expressed dissatisfaction with current modes of exposing students to counseling theories. Presentation of theory is generally characterized as consisting of a motley set of views, some current and some outdated, taught without connecting ties to information obtained in other prior content areas. A middle-ground approach may be the only realistic or practical resolution.

A third issue is whether counseling practicum is to be offered at the beginning and continue throughout preparation or only during the terminal portion. Those who advocate that it be introduced early view it as an opportunity for testing out theory. Those who advocate that it constitutes a terminal experience argue that a foundation of theory, understandings, and skills must be developed before counselors can help counselees professionally and ethically.

Finally, a persisting issue is how much content should be devoted to statistics, testing, and research. Many have been critical of school counselors' lack of test and research sophistication. How can counselor education programs provide carefully selected experiences so that the student acquires more competent skills and understanding of what psychological data and research procedures mean?

Policy decisions in these matters do not come easily. They require continuing reasoning to search out and deal forthrightly with persisting problems. Implementation of change depends upon program objectives, local circumstances, staff available, and, not least, the degree of compromise that can be struck.

Counselor Educators: Problems and Characteristics

The emotional well-being of counselor candidates and the level and quality of the competences they develop can be traced in large measure to their relationships with counselor educators. The effect of what a counselor educator does is due not exclusively to his intentions but to the perceptions of his students. Every counselor educator assumes many roles, the obligations of which he is expected to discharge in his position. In each situation the role is a mixture of the expectancies projected by students, the expectancies of the profession, the personal intent of the counselor educator, and the demands of the university and the wider community. Some counselor educators are more comfortable in these roles than others. Some never quite meet the demands of the roles. Some form superb relationships with students.

Like everyone else, counselor educators aspire to enhanced status as their careers develop. Those possessing certain status signs tend to protect them. Status quite often is associated with rank, salary, size of teaching load, hour of day courses are given, amount of research time and space and equipment, number of graduate assistants, and so on. An institutional pecking order tends to be established and defended. While such status signs are in general influential in career progress, varying weights may be attached to certain ones in particular institutions.

A major expectation of counselor educators is that they must be both scholar and teacher. Con-

[38] Daniel J. Delaney and James C. Moore, "Student Expectations of the Role of Practicum Supervisor," *Counselor Education and Supervision*, Vol. 6 (Fall, 1966), pp. 11–17.

flict often develops over the balance maintained between these two functions, and it may be experienced directly — one is appointed because a teaching position is open, but promotions come primarily upon research or scholarly output. How to live with this state of affairs or whether to seek a change in it is a focus of much concern. Today's counselor education department tries to reduce status strivings among its staff members, since much wasted effort goes into them.

A counselor educator may have some responsibilities not shared by other faculty members. For example, he often discusses matters which are sensitive in nature, which are personal and private. He must give thought to the fact that such topics are likely to arouse anxiety among students over their own personal adjustment problems and that many will need help to resolve the conflicts engendered by this anxiety. Reference has been made to the fact that counselor educators have to make judgments that their graduates are personally and professionally ready for entry-level counseling positions. The judgments cannot be based upon whim, personal appeal, expediency, or emotion. They must honestly answer the question "Is this the kind of person whom the public can trust in a counseling position?" Competence, independence, courage, and understanding are fundamental characteristics of counselor educators. Sensitivity to the demands placed upon them by virtue of their position, the ability to take a stand on matters of principle, and personal integrity are attributes which not only stimulate students but advance counselor education and those engaged in it.

The choice of teaching procedures is determined in part by program objectives, class enrollments, personal characteristics, and the like. Many have pointed out that the teaching methodology is itself a communication about counseling and what it means to be a counselor. Clark believes that conflict often exists because counselor educators seek to communicate a self-actualization model of counseling but utilize a behavioristic approach.[39] Sorenson describes how he has conducted courses in school counseling as laboratory experience.[40] Each student counselor, he believes, must be taught a conceptual framework of ethical and psychological propositions as well as a parallel set of rules which he can keep in mind and consciously use as a guide until the rules become automatic. The student counselor provides himself with one or more out-of-class counselees with whom he works during the semester, and class sessions take the form of counseling interviews between pairs of student counselors. The objective is to examine the counselor's goals, alternative actions, and obstacles in working with his client. Perrone and Sanborn have described how beginning graduate students were assigned to observe counseling over a series of interviews, made critiques of tapes, and discussed cases with counselors in informal groups immediately following counseling interviews.[41] These authors believe that such experiences led to concentration upon the "why" and reduced the tendency to ask for the "how" of counseling.

TRAINING AND INTEREST OF COUNSELOR EDUCATORS

Surveys have been taken of the training, attitudes, and interests of those engaged in counselor education and supervision by Riccio in 1961,[42] 1965,[43] and 1966[44]; by Johnston,[45] by Knowles,[46]

[39] Donald L. Clark, "The Counselor Educator and His Own Teaching Approach," *Counselor Education and Supervision*, Vol. 6 (Spring, 1967), pp. 166–169.

[40] Garth Sorenson, "Laboratory Experiences: Counseling Courses," *Counselor Education and Supervision*, Vol. 5 (Spring, 1966), pp. 148–153.

[41] Philip A. Perrone and Marshall P. Sanborn, "Early Observation: An Apprenticeship Approach to Counselor Education," *Counselor Education and Supervision*, Vol. 6 (Fall, 1966), pp. 63–68.

[42] Anthony C. Riccio, "The Counselor Educator and the Guidance Supervisor: Graduate Training and Occupational Mobility," *Counselor Education and Supervision*, Vol. 1 (Fall, 1961), pp. 10–17.

[43] Anthony C. Riccio, "The Expressed Interests of ACES," *Counselor Education and Supervision*, Vol. 4 (Winter, 1965), pp. 61–63.

[44] Anthony C. Riccio, "Counselor Educator and Guidance Supervisor: A Second Look at Graduate Training," *Counselor Education and Supervision*, Vol. 5 (Winter, 1966), pp. 73–79.

[45] Joseph A. Johnston, "Membership in ACES," *Counselor Education and Supervision*, Vol. 7 (Winter, 1968), pp. 137–142.

[46] Richard T. Knowles, "The Attitudes of ACES Members," *Counselor Education and Supervision*, Vol. 7 (Spring, 1968), pp. 305–314.

and by Scott.[47] These and other reports show that some 85 to 90 per cent of counselor educators and 35 to 50 per cent of state supervisors possess the doctorate, earned at a variety of universities. Columbia, Indiana, Minnesota, Michigan State, Missouri, Ohio State, and Stanford predominate. Some four-fifths belong to either or both the American Personnel and Guidance Association or the American Psychological Association. From one-half to three-fourths of the counselor educators have had counseling experience in public schools. Most expressions of interest were of two kinds: general (e.g., education of counselors) and specific (e.g., school dropouts).

Summary

Counselor education in America is in a process of profound change. A balance is being struck between theory, practice, self-exploration, and the like, which seems almost inevitable, because method cannot be taught in the abstract. Content is being ordered more into sequential arrangements. The educational process is coming under scrutiny, expectations are that genuinely independent study by individuals or by groups of students will be utilized to a greater extent in the future. Certainly, more opportunities are being given for personal contacts with students and informal discussions. Counselor educators are making themselves available to students and evidence accepting attitudes that are believed to be conducive to high student morale.

Essentially, present-day counselor education stresses mastery of the counseling relationship. Consequently, the assembly of materials for particular courses tends to be eclectic, there is more insistence upon small classes, firsthand experience, free discussion as a technique of teaching; more systematic thought by the student. Future efforts to achieve rigor will probably include combining courses to give them fuller meaning, organizing courses around a particular theoretical system, and affording opportunities for the student to counsel in a variety of settings.

[47] C. Winfield Scott, "Characteristics of Counselor Educators," *Counselor Education and Supervision,* Vol. 10 (Winter, 1971), pp. 99–111.

Annotated References

Hill, George E. and Munger, Paul F. (eds.). "Up-Grading Guidance Practice through Improved Preparation of Guidance Workers," *Counselor Education and Supervision,* Vol. 7 (Spring, 1968), pp. 162–236.

This special issue is devoted to a discussion of the standards movement in counselor education, accreditation of counselor education and specific areas of counselor preparation needful of the profession's attention.

Parker, Clyde A. (ed.). *Counseling Theories and Counselor Education.* Boston: Houghton Mifflin Company, 1968. 166 pp.

Papers are presented that were prepared for an invited seminar on counselor education. Authors include Clyde A. Parker, Jack R. Gibb, Harold B. Pepinsky, C. H. Patterson, Forrest L. Vance, Edward S. Bordin, Donald H. Blocher, and Charles B. Truax. Excerpts from the discussions are also given.

Riccio, Anthony C., and Walz, Garry R. (eds.) "Forces for Change in Counselor Education and Supervision," *Counselor Education and Supervision,* Vol. 6 (Spring, 1967), pp. 213–284.

Some of the forces for change now influencing counselor education and supervision are set forth. Stripling's article "The Role of Professional Associations in Counselor Education" is particularly thoughtfully done. Walz and Rich's treatment of the impact of information systems upon preparation and practice is a much needed examination of the topic.

Wrenn, C. Gilbert. *The World of the Contemporary Counselor.* Boston: Houghton Mifflin Company, 1973. 294 pp.

Chapter 10 enumerates and discusses some of the trends in contemporary education and psychology. Chapter 12 presents material directly related to counselor selection and education.

Further References

Arbuckle, Dugald S. "Educating Who for What?" *Counselor Education and Supervision,* Vol. 11 (September, 1971). pp. 41–48.

Aubrey, Roger F. "And Never the Twain Shall Meet: Counselor Training and School Realities." *The School Counselor,* Vol. 20 (September, 1972). pp. 16–24.

Bartlett, Willis E. and Thompson, Charles L. "Counselor Preparation: A Semantic Differential Evaluation." *Counselor Education and Supervision,* Vol. 11 (December, 1971). pp. 129–136.

Bauman, William F. "Games Counselor Trainees Play: Dealing with Trainee Resistance." *Counselor Education and Supervision,* Vol. 11 (June, 1972). pp. 251–256.

Befus, Ray, and Miller, Lyle L. "Paid Clients in Counselor Education — An Investigation." *Counselor Education and Supervision,* Vol. 10 (Fall, 1970). pp. 80–86.

Boller, Jon D. "Counselor Certification: Who Still Needs Teaching Experience?" *Personnel and Guidance Journal,* Vol. 50 (January, 1972). pp. 388–391.

Brammer, Lawrence M. and Springer, Harry C. "A Radical Change in Counselor Education and Certification." *Personnel and Guidance Journal,* Vol. 49 (June, 1971). pp. 803–808.

Danish, Steven J., "Film-Simulated Counselor Training." *Counselor Education and Supervision,* Vol. 11 (September, 1971). pp. 29–35.

Engel, Annette and Maes, Wayne R. "Teaching Personality Theory: A Games Approach." *Counselor Education and Supervision,* Vol. 11 (September, 1971). pp. 24–28.

Felker, Donald W. and Brown, Darine F. "Counselor Candidates and Graduate Students in Education: A Comparison of Characteristics." *Counselor Education and Supervision,* Vol. 9 (Summer, 1970). pp. 286–291.

Foley, Walter J. and Adams, Harold J. "Counselor Education Program Development: A Communication-Information Model." *Counselor Education and Supervision,* Vol. 9 (Spring, 1970). pp. 148–156.

Gust, Tim. "Extending Counselor Supervision." *Counselor Education and Supervision,* Vol. 9 (Spring, 1970). pp. 157–161.

Gysbers, Norman C. and Moore, Earl J. "Using Simulation Techniques in Counseling Practicum." *Counselor Education and Supervision,* Vol. 9 (Summer, 1970). pp. 277–285.

Haase, Richard F. and DiMattia, Dominic J. "The Application of the Microcounseling Paradigm to the Training of Support Personnel in Counseling." *Counselor Education and Supervision,* Vol. 10 (Fall, 1970). pp. 16–22.

Hackney, Harold L. "Development of a Pre-practicum Counseling Skills Model." *Counselor Education and Supervision,* Vol. 11 (December, 1971). pp. 102–109.

Hallberg, Edmond C. "The Silent Curriculum in Counselor Education." *Personnel and Guidance Journal,* Vol. 50 (November, 1971). pp. 198–203.

Hansen, James C. and Warner, Richard W., Jr. "Review of Research on Practicum Supervision." *Counselor Education and Supervision,* Vol. 10 (Spring, 1971). pp. 261–272.

Horan, John J. "Behavioral Goals in Systematic Counselor Education." *Counselor Education and Supervision,* Vol. 11 (March, 1972). pp. 162–170.

Hylbert, Kenneth W. "Undergraduate Education for Counselors." *Counselor Education and Supervision,* Vol. 11 (June, 1972). pp. 284–292.

Island, David. "An Alternative for Counselor Education." *Personnel and Guidance Journal,* Vol. 50 (May, 1972). pp. 762–766.

Jakubowski-Spector, Patricia, Dustin, Richard, and George, Rickey L. "Toward Developing a Behavioral Counselor Education Model." *Counselor Education and Supervision,* Vol. 10 (Spring, 1971). pp. 242–250.

Jansen, David G., Robb, George P., and Bonk, Edward C. "Characteristics of High-Rated and Low-Rated Master's Degree Candidates in Counseling and Guidance." *Counselor Education and Supervision,* Vol. 9 (Spring, 1970). pp. 162–170.

Jones, Lawrence K. and Cox, Wray K. "Support Personnel: Attitudes Toward Functions and Training Responsibility." *Counselor Education and Supervision,* Vol. 10 (Fall, 1970). pp. 51–55.

Kehas, Chris D. "Invited Comment on 'And Never the Twain Shall Meet: Counselor Training and School Realities,'" *The School Counselor,* Vol. 20 (September, 1972). pp. 25–29.

Kennedy, C. E., Danskin, D. G., Edelman, S. K., and Steffen, J. D. "The Practicum in Study of Student Development: Its Relation to Counselor Preparation." *Counselor Education and Supervision,* Vol. 9 (Summer, 1970). pp. 272–276.

Lewis, Michael D. and Lewis, Judith A. "Counselor Education: Training for a New Alternative." *Personnel and Guidance Journal,* Vol. 49 (May, 1971). pp. 754–758.

Long, Thomas J. "Sources for Short-Term Group Training Experiences." *Personnel and Guidance Journal,* Vol. 49 (April, 1971). pp. 645–648.

Malcolm, David Donald. "A Two-Year Program of Counselor Education." *Counselor Education and Supervision,* Vol. 10 (Winter, 1971). pp. 171–179.

Mallars, Patricia B. "Team Counseling in Counselor Education." *Personnel and Guidance Journal,* Vol. 46 (June, 1968). pp. 981–983.

Masih, Lalit K. and Kushel, Gerald. "A Comparison of the Job Values of Prospective Teachers and Counselors." *Counselor Education and Supervision,* Vol. 10 (Fall, 1970). pp. 75–79.

Mazer, Gilbert E. and Engle, Kenneth B. "Personality and Attitude Change in Counselor Trainees: An Evaluation." *Counselor Education and Supervision,* Vol. 10 (Spring, 1971). pp. 273–282.

Panther, Edward E. "Simulated Consulting Experiences in Counselor Preparation." *Counselor Education and Supervision,* Vol. 11 (September, 1971). pp. 17–23.

Salim, Mitchell, Leonard, Natalie J., and Heinrich, L. William. "Counselor Selection: A Critical Event in Program Management and Development." *Counselor Education and Supervision,* Vol. 10 (Summer, 1971). pp. 337–342.

Scott, C. Winfield. "Changes in Follow-Up Data Following Marked Changes in a Counselor Education Program." *Counselor Education and Supervision,* Vol. 9 (Spring, 1970). pp. 195–204.

Scott C. Winfield. "Characteristics of Counselor Educators." *Counselor Education and Supervision,* Vol. 10 (Winter, 1971). pp. 99–111.

Spivack, James D. "Laboratory to Classroom: The Practical Application of IPR in a Master's Level Prepracticum Counselor Education Program." *Counselor Education and Supervision,* Vol. 12 (September, 1972). pp. 3–16.

Springer, Harry C. and Brammer, Lawrence M. "A Tentative Model To Identify Elements of the Counseling Process and Parameters of Counselor Behavior." *Counselor Education and Supervision,* Vol. 11 (September, 1971). pp. 8–16.

Trotzer, James P. "Do Counselors Do What They Are Taught?" *The School Counselor,* Vol. 18 (May, 1971). pp. 335–341.

Truax, Charles B. "An Approach to Counselor Education." *Counselor Education and Supervision,* Vol. 10 (Fall, 1970). pp. 4–15.

Truax, Charles B. and Lister, James L. "Effects of Short-Term Training Upon Accurate Empathy and Non-Possessive Warmth." *Counselor Education and Supervision,* Vol. 10 (Winter, 1971). pp. 120–125.

Van Hoose, William H. "Conflicts in Counselor Preparation and Professional Practice: An Analysis." *Counselor Education and Supervision,* Vol. 9 (Summer, 1970). pp. 241–247.

Wehrly, Beatrice L. "Differentiation in Elementary School Counselor Preparation Programs Among ACES Regions." *Counselor Education and Supervision,* Vol. 10 (Summer, 1971). pp. 343–350.

Winborn, Bob B., Hinds, William C., and Stewart, Norman R. "Instructional Objectives for the Professional Preparation of Counselors." *Counselor Education and Supervision,* Vol. 10 (Winter, 1971). pp. 133–137.

ISSUES AND TRENDS IN COUNSELING

19

The first part of this chapter identifies and discusses some of the current issues in counseling. They were implicit in the content of earlier chapters but are presented separately for clarity. The second part presents several major trends and forecasts. Both sections are subdivided into a general category, a counselor education and supervision category, and a counselor role and function category. Overlap among categories cannot, of course, be totally avoided.

General Issues

Issue 1: The term "guidance" should be abandoned.

No, because:

1. The term accurately describes certain noninstructional activities which must be performed in any school.
2. The term conveys appropriately the notion that many individuals are involved in helping students.
3. The term has historic worth, and its use places in perspective the role of the counselor within the educational setting.
4. A better, more acceptable, term cannot be found to replace it.

Yes, because:

1. The term is meaningless, vague, and ambiguous especially when applied directly to the work of the counselor.
2. The concepts most called to mind by the term are those of direction, authoritarianism, and paternalism, which are in direct opposition to what counselors attempt to do.

Discussion As Wrenn and others have suggested, "guidance" is an outmoded term meaning various things to different people and possibly never accurately describing what is done. Laymen tend to think of guidance as "steering" and "directing" students while practitioners view it broadly as an entire complex of services designed to help students become what they are capable of becoming. Perhaps the very fact that we can never reconcile the two divergent views calls for abandonment of the term.

Social psychologists, in an effort to highlight the interdependence of language and environment, point out that the Eskimo vocabulary contains numerous words for snow, in all its forms, and very few words for earth. In contrast, our vocabulary has many highly descriptive words for earth in all its forms and relatively few for snow. Clearly, both in their diversity and in their specificity, vocabularies incorporate that which is important to people. As it now stands, "guidance" is most commonly used to refer to a set of services; its practitioners, by hook or crook, bear a title, "counselor," which derives from only one of these services. We face a curious semantic dilemma in using the term "guidance." It no longer has any logical relationship to what its practitioners do, if indeed it ever did. It is devoid of the specificity required for what counselors mean when they use it now. If its usage were restricted to the actual meaning of the word, those practicing guidance should be called guides, not counselors. They then properly could perform guidance. However, no self-respecting counselor would agree to the title "guide" because it implies activities inimical to counseling.

While educators *usually* are aware of what they mean by guidance, they have never quite been able to explain the term adequately to the public. The school's boiler fireman may refer to himself as an "engineer," but any parent who asks him what he actually does immediately knows that he is not a professional engineer but tends the furnace. The parent who is told by a member of the school staff that he is a "school counselor" and asks what this means receives an answer which can only confuse him. Frequently this answer includes little, if any, reference to actual counseling with students. It is usually a listing of many activities which better describe the several services comprising the entire guidance program. Perhaps concern with this issue will dissipate when school counselors counsel and supporting guidance services are assigned to subprofessionals. But one thing is evident: we need to eliminate vague language and move to a term more clearly descriptive of what counselors do which is understandable and acceptable to laymen and professionals alike.

Issue 2: Should the ranks of teachers constitute the sole source of counselor supply?

Yes, because:

1. Teacher preparation and experience rightfully constitute the basic training for those employed in schools.
2. Classroom experience contributes meaningfully to counseling performance by providing knowledge of learning processes.
3. Individuals recruited from other disciplines would tend to be the marginal, and less competent than those who remain in their respective fields.
4. Prior teaching experience facilitates counselor acceptance by other educational personnel.
5. Teacher preparation and experience demonstrate professional commitment to education.
6. Previous teaching experience permits wiser selection of an area of specialization within education.

No, because:

1. Counseling and teaching are fundamentally different activities.
2. Experienced counselor educators frequently cite the difficulties encountered in altering teaching-oriented attitudes which are detrimental to counseling.
3. Present-day counseling practitioners drawn from teacher ranks have not been successful in establishing ideal relationships with teachers.
4. Use of personnel from other disciplines would provide a means for attracting stronger candidates than are usually available from the ranks of teacher education.
5. Carefully directed and supervised practicum and internship experiences are more effective ways of providing an understanding of schools, students, teachers, and the learning processes.
6. Requiring teacher education and experience

unrealistically lengthens the time before entry into the counseling profession and undoubtedly discourages potential candidates.

Discussion This issue is a long-standing one. It has been the source of many heated discussions within professional groups and among those responsible for certification regulations.

Counseling services have expanded into many nonschool agencies, which frequently compete for counselor personnel trained for the public schools. At the same time the schools, because of their rigid adherence to the teaching profession as a source of supply for counselors, deny themselves any alternate recruiting source and, in fact, discourage entry of experienced counselors from other fields. This factor, coupled with the many barriers to entry into school counseling from other nonteaching fields, tends to perpetuate a closed system.

Little evidence exists to indicate that schools and/or state certification regulations permit entry to the field except by the traditional route. Consequently, this issue will continue to be debated on the basis of tradition colored with emotion rather than logic or evidence. It is unfortunate that the schools go on denying themselves a potentially valuable source of counseling personnel. It is especially unfortunate that they do not take a flexible, experimental approach which would permit the trial and evaluation of nontraditionally trained school counselors.

Issue 3: Should professional journals stress theory and research or application and practice?

Application should be stressed, because:

1. Counseling practitioners do not possess the research skills to assimilate much of the technical research material that is published in professional journals.
2. Most working school counselors tend to take a practical "how and what to do" approach to their work.

Theory and research should be stressed, because:

1. The problem of consumer inability to assimilate published material stems from inadequate preparation and does not reflect upon the appropriateness of journal content, since advances in the field depend upon competent research.
2. Application depends on soundly conceived theory and research. It is common sense that "how and what to do" must stem from a thorough understanding of why things are done.
3. Journals can publish only what is contributed. Editorial boards have relatively little power except that inherent in the obligation to select the best from among the contributions submitted for publication.

Discussion Many practicing school counselors have long claimed that the professional journals do not reflect their interests or contain what they need to improve their functioning. They complain that journals exist to serve professors who must publish or perish. Seemingly, they want articles that will provide them with specific direction in particular situations. These same people tend to overlook the lack of realism involved in prescribing general solutions for specific settings. Indeed, they appear to overlook their own obligation to draw conclusions and implications for their own setting from that which does appear in the literature. All journals clearly state their publication policy, which provides the consumer with information concerning the kind of content available. He must then translate it to his own situation and needs.

Issue 4: Should school counselors be paid higher salaries than teachers with comparable preparation and experience?

Yes, because:

1. Compared to teachers, the counselor's responsibility is greater and his task more complex and more difficult since he is concerned with individual personal development.
2. The counselor's day is longer because his evenings are spent in counseling with students, parent conferences, research, and the like.
3. The counselor has to deal with a wide-ranging public and is more exposed to public pressures.

No, because:

1. The degree of difference in responsibility is not demonstrable.

2. The teacher's day is similarly extended through grading homework and tests, the supervision of student activities, and so on.

3. There is no function in the school more important than teaching.

Discussion Some counselors are currently paid salary increments above those received by classroom teachers with equivalent training and experience in their field of specialization. However, the additional pay often results from an extension of contract time with some pre- and post-school year responsibilities. Payment of increments without extended employment is frequently due to supply and demand considerations rather than the weight of the arguments cited above.

Given equivalent preparation, e.g., currently a master's degree, there seems little to support a pay difference for counselors unless an extended work period is involved. Undoubtedly, the practice of rewarding experience and extensive training will continue to prevail, as will the necessity to entice specialized personnel financially.

Counselor Education and Supervision

Issue 5: Are two years of full-time graduate study needed to prepare school counselors?

Two years are needed, because:

1. The complexity of the counselor's job demands better preparation for effective discharge of his obligations.

2. Counselors themselves report that they are inadequately prepared after only a single year of training.

3. Extended periods of practicum and internship experience are needed if counselors are to be adequately prepared. The didactic background courses plus practicum and internship cannot be completed properly in a single year or by part-time study.

4. Part-time study leads to partial and fractionated knowledge and fails to produce an occupational identity as a school counselor.

Only one year is needed, because:

1. Existing counselor-pupil ratios demand that counselor supply be increased. The addition of a second year of preparation will curtail the number of counselors available.

2. Requiring two years merely represents empire building by counselor educators, who strive to hold on to students and secure physical facilities simply to increase their own stature in universities.

3. The nature of the school counselor's present assignment does not require an additional year of preparation. A second year will isolate him from other school personnel, who will view him with suspicion because he has more education.

4. Part-time study is a practical necessity for most since sufficient financial support is unavailable for counselor trainees.

Discussion Basically, this issue turns on the matter of quality versus quantity. There seems to be little to counter the argument that more extensive training, well organized and purposefully directed, will produce a better counselor. Few counselor educators would dispute the fact that continuous full-time study is far superior to disjointed, piecemeal preparation over several years.

Many factors could be cited which inhibit the quick acceptance of two years of full-time study. Not the least is the discontinuance of counselor education programs which lack the staff and resources necessary to provide more than occasional courses on a part-time basis.

Issue 6: How can existing professional standards for preparing counselors be implemented?

Implementation should be left to the judgment of each educational institution, because:

1. Application of standards fosters inflexibility and tends to stifle innovation.

2. Not enough counselors are produced under existing conditions, and the application of demand-

ing standards would further reduce the number of candidates completing training.

3. Application of externally derived standards impinges upon institutional and academic freedom.

Implementation should be administered through an agency independent from counselor education institutions, because:

1. Professionalization will be attained only when members of the profession assume responsibility for the quality preparation of those who enter its ranks.

2. Institutional self-evaluation would be ineffective because vested interests have to be protected and many programs would constantly be "moving toward" meeting standards.

3. Implementation of standards is a pressing responsibility since its ultimate aim is to protect the consumer of counseling service by assuring at least minimal quality of practitioners.

Discussion This is a salient issue in contemporary counselor education. Beginning in 1960 and up to the present time professional groups such as ACES and ASCA have made a tremendous effort to formulate standards for counselor education. During the past decade the standards have been developed, published, tried, and refined. The profession is now confronted with taking the extremely difficult step of implementing them.

The issue resolves itself into the fundamental question: How should the standards be enforced? One alternative is independent, voluntary institutional application through self-study followed by responsible action to improve in areas which the institution finds itself lacking. Presumably, subtle forces such as program reputation, the persuasive efforts of professional groups, public opinion, and awareness of shortcomings would gradually bring compliance with the standards. A second alternative would be a step short of formal accreditation but would involve fairly formalized procedures designating approved preparation programs by a committee of a professional association. The committee would study, evaluate, and publish listings of approved programs after making judgments based upon the standards. The most rigorous form of application would be the enforcement of the standards by a formal accrediting association. Without doubt the latter step would accomplish the quickest compliance. Undoubtedly it would also reduce the number of institutions which purport to prepare counselors.

Issue 7: Should counselor preparation be conducted at the undergraduate level?

Yes, because:

1. Existing graduate level education requires too much time in preparation and contributes to shortages of counseling personnel.

2. The vagueness and level of generality that characterizes the content of counselor preparation does not warrant graduate status.

3. Considerable financial savings could accrue to both the individual and the employing institution if counselors could enter the profession on completion of undergraduate degrees.

No, because:

1. The counselor's work requires a mature and widely experienced individual.

2. Counselor preparation consists of specialized graduate level content built on broad undergraduate preparation in the social and behavioral sciences.

3. Within the traditional status hierarchy of schools and other institutions, undergraduate-trained counselors would be at a disadvantage in comparison with professionals with advanced degrees.

Discussion This issue surfaced during the early 1970's and has become the focal point of much heated discussion at professional meetings, particularly when training standards and certification requirements are under discussion. To many, adoption of undergraduate preparation represents a step backwards and undercuts efforts invested in developing standards and upgrading the profession. Others view it as an innovation long needed to infuse life into a field weighed down by the past.

At least two states, Texas and South Carolina, have recently adopted certification regulations that permit "counselors" with only undergraduate training to be employed in public secondary schools. However, it should be noted that in Texas certification as a professional school counselor requires a year of graduate preparation. This underscores the fact that some who advocate undergraduate preparation of counselors view it as a subprofessional entry point or as incomplete education for the professional counselor.

We believe that preparation of professional counselors should remain in graduate programs. The effectiveness of the counselor depends on a broad understanding of the individuals with whom he works and the complex, varied factors that influence individuals. This understanding requires extensive, in-depth study in those fields that can contribute necessary understanding and knowledge. To eliminate the breadth obtained in undergraduate work and substitute premature specialization would only serve to substantiate the claims of many critics that counselors are ill-prepared to deal with the concerns of their clients. Moreover, premature specialization at the undergraduate level requires a vocational commitment which few are prepared to make.

Issue 8: At what point should supervised experiences be introduced in the preparation of counselors?

At entry, because:

1. Such experiences facilitate the early development of an occupational identity.
2. These experiences represent an ideal example of "learning by doing" and enable the enrollee to test out theory.

After familiarization with basic skills, because:

1. A minimal professional competence is required to maximize counselor learning as well as to insure gainful client experience.
2. Ethics demand that some minimal screening of counselors in the areas of skills and personal characteristics precede contact with live clients.

Discussion Supervised experience is viewed as the focal point for the integration and synthesis of prior didactic and laboratory work in counselor training. Didactic preparation and laboratory experience lead directly to application in actual counseling activity in practicum and internship under supervision. Sequential programs result in preparation which progresses logically toward increased responsibility for live counseling activities. It is the consensus of most counselor educators that preparatory work, particularly in the areas of educational and occupational information, testing and appraisal techniques, and counseling theory and technique, is requisite to adequate performance when the candidate assumes individual responsibility for clients. Besides, synthesis of prior learnings and new learning increments appear to occur best when adequate preparation in these content areas precedes application in the actual counseling setting.

Usually laboratory experiences are integrated with course work. Courses taken during the first year of the two-year program have laboratory sessions devoted to application of statistical procedures, familiarization with tests, observation of interviews, familiarization and analysis of occupational materials, role playing, use of case records, and the like. These are a continuing part of counselor education.

Usually, practicum activities consist of direct counseling experience with elementary, high school, college students, and/or other clients drawn from the community. Close supervision is given to candidates engaged in individual counseling of clients. Ideally, supervision employs direct observation, tape recordings, and video tapes.

Most counselor educators believe that the nature of the supervisory process determines in large measure the success with which counselors begin to function independently. Careful attention is given at all times to observing the trainee as he works with the client; the supervisor normally evaluates the counselor's progress in such aspects as rapport, structure, empathy, content variables and process variables. Practicum supervisors are available for immediate consultations with counselors as well as for scheduled case conference discussions. In all supervised contacts precautions are taken to protect counselees in accordance with the ethical principles of the profession.

After the student counselor has completed contact with the counselee, conferences between the counselor and the supervisor clarify counselor-counselee interaction or deal with specifics needing attention. Counselor and supervisor review the many aspects of the interview. They tend to move from an instructor-student relationship to a more process-oriented relationship. The chief focus of these conferences is the counselor's progress and professional development. He discusses his actions, feelings, and attitudes, his perceptions of the client, and the client's needs and resources. In case conferences conducted with small groups of student counselors other trainees attending the conference relate their perceptions of the case, question the counselor and supervisor about any variable, and make suggestions for the participant.

Counselor Role and Functions

Issue 9: Who and what should determine counselor functions?

The counselor and his work setting, because:

1. The professional counselor is prepared to exercise judgment in determining how best to utilize his skills and qualifications.
2. Settings vary both subtly and dramatically. Specific functions, therefore, should match the existing situation if they are to be effective.

His administration and public, because:

1. The employer hires someone to perform a specific set of well-defined tasks.
2. The consumers of a service are in the best position to determine what they want from the employee.

Discussion An important point to be noted here is that functions differ from role. A role is legitimately viewed as a set of expected behaviors. The consumer, therefore, has a stake in defining the role through his expectancies. Functions are seen as the activities in which a professional engages in performing his role. Therefore, judgment of the functions to be performed remains the prerogative of the professional as long as they fulfill the normative expectations of the role.

Functions differ from setting to setting and within a given setting from individual to individual. For example, a counselor in a setting characterized by stable, goal-directed student behavior may perform quite different functions from those he would undertake in a school with a high delinquency rate. Even within the latter setting, the counselor may be confronted with two delinquent boys, one of them emotionally disturbed, the other merely conforming to that part of society in which he must live. The approach and procedures employed would differ to best serve the individuals involved and the settings.

Issue 10: Is the school counselor essentially a psychologist or an educator?

Educator, because:

1. He is employed in an educational institution which has certain expectations of all employees.
2. The clientele he serves is not universally restricted to a defined population.
3. The major thrust of his work is directed not toward the repair of long-term disability but toward facilitating learning.
4. His undergraduate and graduate preparation does not entitle him to be called a psychologist.

Psychologist, because:

1. The success of his contact work with students depends upon how well he understands human behavior.
2. His preparation in counseling consists of instruction in interpersonal relationships, use of tests in counseling, personality and counseling theory, group processes, etc., all of which fall within the domain of psychology.

Discussion The issue as just stated has been cast in the form most commonly presented among practicing counselors and educational personnel. At the outset it should be made clear that, so stated, it represents a meaningless and phony beacon in the field which generates more heat than light. The pros and cons confuse setting and function, as well as place of work and activity. At least implicitly involved are overtones of an extremely parochial and outdated view of the training and background of practitioners of both psychology and counseling. Moreover, if a work setting is structured in a particular direction, status and success follow conformity to the demands of the work situation. Perhaps even more importantly, such mistaken and overly simplified concepts needlessly encourage divisionists and establish hostile camps.

There would seem to be little argument that school counselors function in an educational setting, are recruited almost exclusively from the ranks of education, and are charged with facilitating the learning experiences of children. It is equally obvious that the means they use to meet their obligations, the training they receive during counselor preparation, and their personal inclinations require them to function very much like psychologists. These two views are not, and should not be, incompatible. Extremists of either camp frequently drag forth this issue as a defensive smoke screen for their inability to understand and perform those tasks which are commonly accepted as appropriate for counselors. Extremists at the educational pole expect the counselor to function as a teacher without a classroom or in a tutorial manner with a highly restricted population. His activities, they think, should consist of presenting occupational information, encouraging conformity to the institutional milieu through manipulative disciplinary procedures, evaluating students so that decisions can be made about and for them (rather than with them), and, in general, not letting the student off the end of that famous Mark Hopkins log until all is orderly, precise, and decided. Extremists at the other pole expect the counselor to confine his contacts to a select group of deviant students, avoid the thought of even dealing with anything that is not highly emotionally charged, completely forgo the use of any kind of information, educational, vocational, or whatever, and totally ignore the educational pond in which the log of learning floats. Not even Sigmund Freud would last in Admiral Rickover's school! The humanistically oriented counselor would stand little chance in a school operated by the traditional advocates of "basic education." By the same token, little reward would await the "educationalist" counselor who attempted to work in a permissive, child-centered setting emphasizing individual development.

Issue 11: Should counseling activities or guidance activities constitute the major focus for the school counselor?

Counseling activities, because:

1. The counselor spends the bulk of his time in individual or small group student contacts.
2. It is only through counseling that the goals of guidance are achieved.
3. Other personnel can be utilized in performing most guidance activities.

Guidance activities, because:

1. Particular kinds of information are needed by large numbers of pupils.
2. Training limitations do not permit him to function effectively as a counselor.

Discussion Involved in this issue is whether the counselor is a generalist or a specialist. Historically, he has been a generalist and frequently even occupied multiple roles by simultaneously teaching and counseling. Increasingly, the contemporary counselor holds a full-time position and concentrates on the counseling function from among the usual services falling under the umbrella of "guidance." A sound argument could be made that guidance services such as the informational service and student appraisal service should exist and be emphasized only to the degree that they contribute to improving the counseling service. This is not to be misinterpreted to mean that the mere giving of these kinds of information should be called counseling. Rather, concern here is for effective and sophisticated use of these valuable types of information as part of true counseling.

Also involved is whether counselors should be called "school counselors" or "guidance specialists." Title can influence expectancies. To the consumer, the title often conveys the deed. Many who would balk at being guided might readily accept the services of a counselor. It is to be hoped that the title "school counselor" will be fully accepted and come to reflect the kind of service it implies. Those who practice under this title will truly perform the function of counseling and not employ it as a mask for information giving and individualized instruction.

Issue 12: Can the counselor serve the school both as an agent of change and as a counselor?

Yes, because:

1. The factors responsible for success in both functions are essentially the same: understanding people and understanding institutions.
2. The counselor is most likely to have a unique kind of access to students which provides him with intimate knowledge of concerns and difficulties arising directly from the institution.
3. Many students cannot solve their problems through counseling alone because the problems are rarely entirely internal to but stem also from the individual's interaction with the environment. Consequently, counselors are sometimes required to effect modification in the environment.

No, because:

1. Few counselors possess the needed knowledge of or have the authority to influence the power structure of the school and community to effect change.
2. Counselors are usually temperamentally unfit to undertake the struggle to instigate and complete a change cycle in a setting.
3. Leadership for effecting institutional change lies in the sphere of administration.

Discussion Within the past few years many have urged the counselor to be the school's agent of change. Seemingly, their case is built upon the assumption that administrators are increasingly alienated from their traditional role of educational leadership and more and more isolated from students and staff. Administrators are viewed as devoting the majority of their time to budgets, buildings, and public relations. Unquestionably their activities create a leadership vacuum into which some seem eager to thrust the school counselor by making him responsible for change.

This effort is not without merit, nor would such an assignment be unattractive to one who seeks power and influence. However, in view of the usual administrative hierarchy found in education, assumption of this role is presumptuous. Further, counselors who are now being urged to become agents of institutional change frequently lack certain essential personal characteristics for doing so: aggressiveness, persuasiveness, persistence in the face of disinterest and lethargy, belief in the art of compromise, and political acumen. Needless to say, this list of attributes hardly characterizes the school counselor, who has other, equally positive traits necessary for working intimately with individuals.

It should be noted that some see the counselor's background and training as eminent qualifications. This view, however, often derives from the distorted idea of the counselor in the thoroughly distasteful image of a "hidden persuader," maneuvering and manipulating to accomplish devious ends.

Perhaps the more legitimate view would be that of a counselor as a catalyst of change rather than the agent of change. In this case the counselor serves a consultative function and brings to bear his unique, intimate knowledge of the school setting derived from knowledge of the students and teachers who populate it, and his contacts with parents, employers and the community. Essentially the difference here lies in regarding the counselor as one whose role is identifying and conceptualizing areas of change, providing justification for legitimately needed modifications, and transmitting his ideas to leaders who are responsible for effecting change.

Issue 13: The school counselor who is truly a counselor never advises students.

True, because:

1. Students can get advice from teachers, parents, and peers. The counselor should be seen as different from them.
2. If counselors present advice which students follow, responsibility for success or failure for their action rests with the counselor.
3. Students don't seek advice from counselors; they seek to establish a relationship which facilitates self-understanding.

False, because:

1. Advice giving is a time-honored function of any relationship in which trust and understanding are present.
2. Advice – predicting the probability of success in a future venture – can be given to students who exhibit no undue anxiety and possess good self-understanding.

Discussion If advice is defined as providing a ready-made solution, most counselors would tend to avoid this kind of activity. One reason is that providing solutions is likely to defeat achievement of the goals of counseling, which strives for responsible self-sufficiency. Advice giving, on the other hand, fosters dependency and blocks the individual's progress toward mastery of decision-making processes.

Most counselors undoubtedly give advice on occasion. In many instances individuals ask advice because they lack the necessary information to make complex decisions. It is essential that the counselor determine whether a request for advice arises from lack of information or from other, more complicated personal reasons. If the latter is the case, such requests could more properly be labeled a symptom of a problem which may in itself call for longer-term attention.

In essence, each request must be weighed against the incontrovertible fact that advice giving generally frustrates and sometimes totally prevents the achievement of most commonly accepted counseling goals. In other helping professions, such as law and medicine, practitioners rely heavily upon advice giving primarily because these fields encompass a highly complex body of knowledge which is unavailable to their clientele. The equally complex and technical body of knowledge of the counselor is applicable only when combined with a thorough knowledge of the individual counselee. The point is that, for law and medicine, solutions arise from the knowledge upon which they are based while in counseling the individual's solution stems from self-understanding and awareness.

Issue 14: School counselors should be exempt from supervision of student activities, corridors, lunchroom, study halls, and the like.

Yes, because:

1. These activities drain time away from counseling.
2. Participation in such activities represents waste of professional skills and competences.
3. These activities are administrative and should be performed by administrators.
4. The evaluative, disciplinary, or corrective function demanded of the counselor in these situations causes conflict in establishing an appropriate role definition among students.

No, because:

1. Inherent in every institution, particularly the public school with its broad scope of activities, are certain peripheral tasks not directly related to the basic purpose of the institution. Almost all employees must be involved to some degree in these.
2. Teachers will more readily identify, accept, and respect the counselor who shares in supervising such activities.
3. The counselor can "learn" about students and learn to know more students by performing these tasks.

Discussion This is a perennial issue among school personnel. One reasonable objection is that supervision in these situations is generally donated by the employee. Even more cogent is the fact that supervision of corridors, study halls, and so on contributes little to the education process.

Perhaps the most telling objection, which may be unique to counselor involvement with this kind of burden, is that the counselor is placed in a position incompatible with his role as it is usually conceived. By their very nature the activities cited are difficult to supervise and constantly present discipline problems. The chief aim is to maintain order and discipline, and nothing will more surely compromise the image the counselor wishes to convey to students. Since he is acting as a disciplinarian, he is immediately and constantly confronted with the problems discussed in Issue 15. (See below.)

The rationalization is frequently used by administrators, and readily accepted by some counselors who must justify their involvement, that supervision of these activities represents "a golden opportunity" to learn to know the student body in its natural habitat. Unfortunately, like most rationalizations, there is some truth in this one. On the other hand, such supervision can represent a tender trap which produces questionable knowledge about the student body better and more systematically arrived at by other, less damaging means. In addition, once the counselor is ensnared, his reputation among the student body, especially if he must serve as an informer, may be severely tarnished.

Issue 15: The school counselor should be exempt from the student discipline process.

No, because:

1. Those who misbehave are most in need of counseling to clarify their emotions and actions.
2. If counselors are not involved in disciplinary cases, their usefulness is limited to the well-behaved, conforming pupil.
3. Since the causes of misbehavior must be diagnosed and treated, it is logical that the counselor, as the knowledgeable person in school in this field, be involved.
4. Disciplinary work at its best is preventive, and the counselor's skills and attitudes are attuned to preventive work.
5. The goals of discipline — self-control, self-direction, self-growth, and self-development — match those of counseling.

Yes, because:

1. Supervision and enforcement of regulations are a responsibility of the administration.
2. Counselors involved in discipline become identified as authority figures; in consequence, the accepting, nonjudgmental role required for effective counseling is threatened.
3. Adequate handling of discipline cases requires exhaustive investigation, which would allow counselors little time to use their skills with other students.
4. Counseling calls for a permissive, self-initiated relationship rather than the compelled relationship which characterizes discipline.
5. Discipline — enforcing conformity — is a public process; counseling is private and confidential.

Discussion This is the oldest unresolved issue in the field, although the contemporary tendency seems to be toward little or no *direct* involvement of counselors in the disciplining of students. The more appropriate view appears to be that, while counselors retain some responsibility in the disciplinary process, they do not serve as disciplinarians. Most regard the counselor's role in the discipline process as working with students who have done something requiring disciplinary action in an effort to help them modify the kind of behavior which brought about punishment or as working with students to help them understand the disciplinary action taken against them and their reactions to it.

There are still large numbers of people who equate discipline and counseling. They overestimate the effect of their "counsel" and, perhaps even more detrimentally, view the counselor's task as persuading, cajoling, and subtly maneuvering students into conforming to institutional rules and requirements.

No one expects the counselor to abrogate his adult responsibilities when confronted with a serious breach of school rules. Like any adult, he cannot ignore or walk away from serious behavior infractions. However, this is a different order of events from being deliberately placed in a position which constantly requires the exercise of disciplinary authority.

Issue 16: Is vocational counseling a distinct specialty within the field of counseling?

Yes, because:

1. The increasing complexity of vocational decisions demands expert specialized assistance.
2. Despite its seeming narrow specificity, this type of helping relationship is highly complex.
3. Choice of a vocation is the fundamental factor in achieving happiness and satisfaction in life and therefore merits special treatment.

No, because:

1. Choice of a vocation cannot be separated meaningfully from the totality of the individual's life choices.
2. Decision making based upon self-examination and awareness is a basic outcome of all counseling and should be applied to all areas of life, not just the vocational.
3. Vocational pursuits are no more fundamental to a happy and successful life than many others.

Discussion In the history of counseling an early and almost exclusive preoccupation with vocational choice was followed by a swing toward viewing vocational decisions as only a part of the broader problem of existence. The current literature on career education indicates a resurgence of interest in vocational counseling, stemming in part from an increasing concern for the relatively large proportion of young people who enter the labor market directly after completion of high school. Critics claim that this group — conservatively estimated at over half the school population nationally — receive little assistance in career choice. Counselors give preference to students who continue their education and consequently are not immediately pressed to make binding vocational choices.

One of the original reasons for abandoning a narrow vocational emphasis in counseling was a growing awareness of the complexity of vocational choices. What appears on the surface to be a simple decision involves such factors as the assessment of job requirements and worker characteristics, a highly fluid labor market, and the entire complex of the individual's psychological makeup. Many would argue that despite the tremendous advancements of the past 50 years counselors are not much better able to cope with vocational choice than they were decades ago. Additional knowledge has served to contribute to the intricacy of the problem rather than to its solution.

The only reasonable solution seems to be to provide assistance to individuals which will permit them to make the best available decision in all life situations, whether vocational, educational, social, or personal.

General Trends

Trend 1: Increasing numbers of counselors will be employed in a great variety of settings.

This projection is easily documented by reference to the numbers of counselors employed from year to year and by the amounts of money spent for salaries and on preparation programs. During the past decade the annual growth rate for counselor employment was approximately 6 per cent. Projections for the 1970's indicate that the annual growth rate will be approximately 3 per cent. Counseling services have been extended downward into elementary schools and upward into higher education. Nonschool demands for counselors have increased in community action programs, the Job Corps, and the like. There is every indication that such demands will continue at a reduced rate.

Obviously, the well-trained counselor has the advantage in competing for employment. This enables him not only to choose his work setting discriminatingly but to be influential in determining its work demands and defining the services offered.

Trend 2: Professionalization in school counseling will intensify.

Professional organizations will become more and more influential in interpreting school counselor role and functions. A greater proportion of school counselors will participate actively in professional organizations which work to determine the direction, influence, and growth of the work of the counselor. Increased professionalization among school counselors parallels longer and better training programs. It will continue to facilitate the development of the image the counselor desires and make it easier for him to extend the kind of helping relationship to clients which he deems appropriate to the work setting.

Trend 3: Accountability in counselor education and counseling practice will continue to exert influence.

Recent emphasis on accountability applies to all aspects of the educational enterprise, including the preparation of counselors and the services they provide after they are employed. Undoubtedly, advances in greater specification of objectives, more clearly defined functions, and improved evaluation procedures will benefit both the profession and the public it serves.

Trends in Counselor Education and Supervision

Trend 4: Modifications in counselor education programs will continue but at a slower rate than in the past decade.

Massive changes have occurred, particularly if one compares counselor education of the 1950's with that of the 1970's. Improvement in quality stemmed from intensification of two areas present in high quality programs: an interdisciplinary core of course work and extended supervised counseling experiences (practicum, field practice, and/or internship).

Much study has been devoted to the contributions that related disciplines can make to the preparation of counselors. Without doubt, the most directly contributory will be the disciplines of psychology and sociology. They are most closely related to, and indeed frequently undergird, the work of the counselor. It is highly probable that extended core programs will continue to rely more heavily upon knowledge from these fields than in the past.

Laboratory work and direct experience with live clients currently enjoy a favored position in quality preparation programs. Probably they will be emphasized to a greater degree both by spreading them throughout the training period and by intensifying the amount and diversifying the kind of experiences provided, particularly in the later stage of training. As the demand for counselors for nonschool agencies increases, supervised practicum and internship experiences in a wider variety of settings will become available. In all probability counselor education programs will attempt to integrate the advantages of nonschool settings with school-related experiences. The focus will be on breadth and variety of experience rather than preparation for work within a specific setting.

Supervisory practices will be refined and will make better use of the mechanical paraphernalia facilitating the supervision process. Most notable so far is video taping of interview sessions, which is far superior to sound recordings and frequently has the advantage of being less disruptive than direct observation. A benefit not to be overlooked in the use of television is the flexibility provided in scheduling supervisory activities. Most high quality counselor education programs are attentive to student input and will continue to incorporate their contributions. Undoubtedly caution will be exercised in this area as it is in the inclusion of all new modifications.

Trend 5: Supervision and education will continue after initial entry into the counseling field.

Improved and extended training as well as the movement toward professionalization will combine to force continued study and upgrading among counseling practitioners. The arrival of better qualified personnel will result in extended on-the-job supervision of novice counselors. As the number of schools employing several counselors increases, it will be essential that their activities be coordinated and supervised. This activity will go beyond the mere administrative overseeing of guidance services and be similar to the supervision received in counseling practicum and internship experiences.

If counselors are to become true professionals, they obligate themselves to upgrade their skills continuously, both by formal education and by additional in-service training. Used in this context, in-service education involves professional upgrading of counseling skills and personal development rather than the sort of training other school personnel undergo.

Trends in Counselor Role and Functions

Trend 6: Increasingly school counseling will become a lifetime career commitment.

Several factors are instrumental in making counseling attractive as a lifetime career commitment. Nationwide, the salaries of educational personnel have advanced, and consequently educational institutions have more holding power than ever before. With less discrepancy between administrative salaries and those of personnel in other echelons, the lure of administrative positions is lessened. Furthermore, specialized preparation programs in administration and counseling mitigate against shifting fields of professional endeavor. Paralleling distinctions between training programs is the increasing emphasis upon an extended educational experience so that the individual's original choice of one field and his investment in securing specialized training operate to produce greater loyalty and commitment to that field.

In addition, the efforts toward professionalization presumably will create a climate in which the counselor can strongly identify with a professional group. He will no longer have to go outside the "profession" to secure the status and recognition for which he strives.

Trend 7: Specialization in school counseling will continue and intensify.

As public receptivity of counseling services expands, utilization of and expectations for the counselor will become increasingly sophisticated. Knowledge that certain kinds of people can best provide assistance with specific kinds of problems will facilitate choice among the various services. Many schools now employing several counselors already make work assignments in accordance with the strengths, interests, and skills of their personnel as well as the particular needs of the student body. Thus, for example, heavy reliance is placed upon one counselor who is an expert in vocational training and placement.

Contributing to this trend as well as those already discussed is the factor of extended training, which will permit the counselor to implement preferences and competences for certain kinds of counseling activities. Thoroughly trained individuals are more likely to be aware of the fact that they enjoy and do their best work with, for example, clients with educational and vocational problems while others realistically see their strengths in working with clients with personal-social problems.

Trend 8: Increasingly the school counselor will become a consultant to teachers, administrators, parents and others.

Counselors' skills will be utilized to serve the student population indirectly by working directly with those who interact daily with the student body, i.e., teachers, parents, and administrators. Increasing focus in the recent literature is upon the counselor's consultant role and upon viewing the counselor as an agent of environmental change.

The key to how much of a consultant the counselor becomes lies with the counselor education institutions, which are emphasizing the need for such activities and providing experiences in conducting them. Presumably, preparation stimulates practice, and unless the experiences are provided in training there seems little likelihood that more than an occasional counselor will make consultative efforts, which often require particular skills, knowledge, and temperament. During the past five years many high school counselors have reported rewarding contacts with more and more parents and teachers. Undoubtedly these contacts will continue and increase since they result in valuable gains for students.

Trend 9: Small group counseling will receive more emphasis in schools.

The advantages cited for small group counseling in Chapter 15 will become increasingly attractive. Moreover, a greater number of preparation programs will incorporate training in group procedures. As group procedures are employed more frequently, more will be learned of their utility and appropriateness for certain clients and problem situations.

Trend 10: Subprofessionals or support personnel will be utilized by counseling professionals.

The advent of preparation for subprofessionals in 1964, e.g., the CAUSE program, stimulated much controversy over the use and qualifications of such personnel. For many, the threat stemmed from the fact that little was known about their proposed role and function. The initial statements were ambiguous, and misunderstandings arose. This controversy led to a policy statement formulated by a subcommittee on support personnel of the Professional Preparation and Standards Committee.[1] Adopted by the APGA Executive Council in November, 1966, the statement provides guidelines for the development of job descriptions for support personnel. Support personnel will be involved in both direct and indirect helping relationships, and appropriate use of them will facilitate and extend the work of the counselor and make his total endeavor more effective.

Trend 11: Conflict, dissension, and professional differences will continue to characterize the field of school counseling.

While some consensus exists and will persist, no truly vital field should be devoid of controversy, discussion, and debate, from which emerge change and improvement. For the individual who is committed to the field this factor represents stimulation rather than discouragement.

Trend 12: The work of the counselor will no longer be confined to that which takes place in his office.

The concept of the counselor as one who sits in his office and waits for self-referred clients is gradually being replaced by one involving more active outreach activities. Such activities range from teaching minicourses to being available in informal settings where students are during their nonclass time. Several advantages accrue from abandonment of the more traditional role. One is that a much wider segment of the school population will come in contact with counselors. That is, the counselor's clientele will no longer consist strictly of those who are college bound and those who have committed disciplinary infractions. Another advantage is that the counselor is directly exposed to the realities in which his clients live and struggle. He no longer hears secondhand descriptions or has to react out of an assumed set of beliefs based on what the school hopes to do rather than on what is actually going on. An additional advantage is that his scope of contacts is broadened to include parents, personnel in community agencies, and a wider range of school staff. It is important to note that the fundamental purpose of this type of activity is to increase the counselor's effectiveness and availability. There is no doubt, however, that the bulk of his time will be spent privately with individuals because of the very nature of counseling.

[1] "Support Personnel for the Counselor: Their Technical and Non Technical Roles and Preparation," *Personnel and Guidance Journal*, Vol. 45 (April, 1967), pp. 857–861.

And so we close this volume (after far too many words) with the belief that those who fully commit themselves to providing the helping relationship will welcome the challenge found in a fluid and evolving field of human endeavor. Because of their commitment, the challenge gives their activities meaning and purpose. Both the commitment and the challenge become a trust.

Annotated References

Johnson, Dorothy E. and Vestermark, Mary J. *Barriers and Hazards in Counseling.* Boston: Houghton Mifflin Company, 1970. 244 pp.

The authors identify and describe many personal and professional issues that confront the counselor. Some of these originate with the counselor, others from his interactions with clients, and still others from the institutional setting. These authors present these issues and other matters knowledgeably and with clarity, insight, and understanding.

Wrenn, C. Gilbert. *The World of the Contemporary Counselor.* Boston: Houghton Mifflin Company, 1973. 294 pp.

Change — its form, meaning, and implications — is the focus of Wrenn's work. His grasp of that which is taking place in many sectors of life is comprehensive and sure. Recommendations, based on his analysis of change, are made that will be helpful not only to counselors but those whom they serve.

Further References

Aubrey, Roger F. "School-Community Drug Prevention Programs." *Personnel and Guidance Journal,* Vol. 50 (September, 1971). pp. 17–24.

Austin, Brian and Altekruse, Michael K. "The Effects of Group Supervisor Roles on Practicum Students' Interview Behavior." *Counselor Education and Supervision,* Vol. 12 (September, 1972). pp. 63–67.

Bellucci, JoAnn Elizabeth. "Microcounseling and Imitation Learning: A Behavioral Approach to Counselor Education." *Counselor Education and Supervision,* Vol. 12 (December, 1972). pp. 88–97.

Berdie, Ralph F. "The 1980 Counselor: Applied Behavioral Scientist." *Personnel and Guidance Journal,* Vol. 50 (February, 1972). pp. 451–456.

Bernstein, Paul M. and Barcikowski, Robert S. "A Comparison of Counselor Ratings by Male Volunteers and Referred Clients." *Measurement and Evaluation in Guidance,* Vol. 5 (October, 1972). pp. 443–445.

Biehn, Jennifer. "Community as Counselor." *Personnel and Guidance Journal,* Vol. 50 (May, 1972). pp. 730–734.

Biggers, Julian L. and Mangusso, David J. "The Work of the Guidance Administrator." *Counselor Education and Supervision,* Vol. 12 (December, 1972). pp. 130–136.

Brammer, Lawrence M. and Springer, Harry C. "A Radical Change in Counselor Education and Certification." *Personnel and Guidance Journal,* Vol. 49 (June, 1971). pp. 803–808.

Callis, Robert. "APGA: Love It? or Leave It?" *Journal of College Student Personnel,* Vol. 13 (November, 1972). pp. 484–486.

Delaney, Daniel J. "A Behavioral Model for the Practicum Supervision of Counselor Candidates." *Counselor Education and Supervision,* Vol. 12 (September, 1972). pp. 46–50.

Friend, Byron L. "Apprenticeships in the '70's." *Vocational Guidance Quarterly,* Vol. 20 (June, 1972). pp. 291–293.

Gazda, G. M., Duncan, J. A., and Sisson, P. J. "Professional Issues in Group Work." *Personnel and Guidance Journal,* Vol. 49 (April, 1971). pp. 637–644.

Healy, Charles C. "A Political Action Role for APGA." *Personnel and Guidance Journal,* Vol. 51 (September, 1972). pp. 45–47.

Healy, Charles C. "Manpower Trends: Counseling or Political Solutions?" *Personnel and Guidance Journal,* Vol. 51 (September, 1972). pp. 39–44.

Hoffman, Doretta S. and Hoeflin, Ruth. "Freshman and Sophomore Women: What Do They Want Most in the Future?" *Journal of College Student Personnel,* Vol. 13 (November, 1972). pp. 490–493.

Humes, Charles W., II. "Accountability: A Boon to Guidance." *Personnel and Guidance Journal,* Vol. 51 (September, 1972). pp. 21–26.

Hutchinson, Roger L. "The Itinerant Counselor." *Personnel and Guidance Journal,* Vol. 50 (November, 1971). pp. 213.

Hylbert, Kenneth W. "Undergraduate Education for Counselors." *Counselor Education and Supervision,* Vol. 11 (June, 1972). pp. 284–292.

Jacobson, Thomas J. "Career Guidance Centers." *Personnel and Guidance Journal,* Vol. 50 (March, 1972). pp. 599–604.

Lawton, Ronald. "Counselors Need a Green Light Organization." *Personnel and Guidance Journal,* Vol. 49 (May, 1971). pp. 759–763.

Lipsman, Claire K. "Revolution and Prophecy: Community Involvement for Counselors." *Personnel and Guidance Journal,* Vol. 48 (October, 1969). pp. 97–100.

Marple, Betty Lou N. "Guidance in 1995: The Possible Dream." *Personnel and Guidance Journal,* Vol. 51 (November, 1972). pp. 191–194.

Miller, Thomas V. "Simulation and Instructional Objectives in Counselor Education." *Counselor Education and Supervision,* Vol. 12 (December, 1972). pp. 83–87.

Navin, Sally. "Future Planning of College Women: Counseling Implications." *Vocational Guidance Quarterly,* Vol. 21 (September, 1972). pp. 12–17.

Panther, Edward E. "Simulated Consulting Experiences in Counselor Preparation." *Counselor Education and Supervision,* Vol. 11 (September, 1971). pp. 17–23.

Pearson, Richard. "Education and Testing in a Period of Qualitative Change." *Measurement and Evaluation in Guidance,* Vol. 2 (Summer, 1969). pp. 82–87.

Pierce, Richard M. and Schauble, Paul G. "Toward the Development of Facilitative Counselors: The Effects of Practicum Instruction and Individual Supervision." *Counselor Education and Supervision,* Vol. 11 (December, 1971). pp. 83–89.

Pressey, Sidney L. and Pressey, Alice D. "Major Neglected Need Opportunity: Old-Age Counseling." *Journal of Counseling Psychology,* Vol. 19 (September, 1972). pp. 362–366.

Pulvino, Charles J. and Sanborn, Marshall P. "Feedback and Accountability." *Personnel and Guidance Journal,* Vol. 51 (September, 1972). pp. 15–20.

Sinick, Daniel, Gorman, William E., and Hoppock, Robert. "Research on the Teaching of Occupations, 1965–1970." *Vocational Guidance Quarterly,* Vol. 20 (December, 1971). pp. 129–137.

Sprinthall, Norman A. "Humanism: A New Bag of Virtues for Guidance?" *Personnel and Guidance Journal,* Vol. 50 (January, 1972). pp. 349–356.

Stubbins, Joseph. "The Politics of Counseling." *Personnel and Guidance Journal,* Vol. 48 (April, 1970). pp. 611–618.

Tripp, Philip A. "We Can't Go Home Again." *The Journal of College Student Personnel,* Vol. 13 (November, 1972). pp. 487–489.

Walton, Francis X. and Sweeney, Thomas J. "Useful Predictors of Counseling Effectiveness." *Personnel and Guidance Journal,* Vol. 48 (September, 1969). pp. 32–38.

Walz, Garry R. "Technology in Guidance: A Conceptual Overview." *Personnel and Guidance Journal,* Vol. 49 (November, 1970). pp. 175–182.

Wrenn, C. Gilbert. "The Three Worlds of the Counselor." *Personnel and Guidance Journal,* Vol. 49 (October, 1970). pp. 91–97.

INDEX OF NAMES

INDEX OF SUBJECTS